MONOCACY CEMETERY

BEALLSVILLE
MONTGOMERY COUNTY
MARYLAND

Elizabeth R. Frain

HERITAGE BOOKS
2012

HERITAGE BOOKS
AN IMPRINT OF HERITAGE BOOKS, INC.

Books, CDs, and more—Worldwide

For our listing of thousands of titles see our website
at
www.HeritageBooks.com

Published 2012 by
HERITAGE BOOKS, INC.
Publishing Division
100 Railroad Ave. #104
Westminster, Maryland 21157

Copyright © 1997 Elizabeth R. Frain

Other Heritag Books by the author:

Fairfax County, Virginia Death Register, 1853–1896

Loudoun County, Virginia Death Register, 1853–1896
Elizabeth R. Frain and Marty Hiatt

Loudoun County, Virginia Marriages after 1850, Volume 1: 1851–1880
Patricia B. Duncan and Elizabeth R. Frain

Monocacy Cemetery, Beallsville, Maryland

Union Cemetery, Leesburg, Loudoun County, Virginia: Plats A & B, 1784–1995

Union Cemetery, Leesburg, Loudoun County, Virginia: The Later Plats, 1880–1995

All rights reserved. No part of this book may be reproduced or transmitted in any form or by any means, electronic or mechanical, including photocopying, recording or by any information storage and retrieval system without written permission from the author, except for the inclusion of brief quotations in a review.

International Standard Book Numbers
Paperbound: 978-1-888265-22-4
Clothbound: 978-0-7884-9123-8

This book is dedicated to
Charles William Elgin
1915-1997
and his wife
Dorothy "Dots" Jones Elgin

This couple
has been unbelievably important to Poolesville for the last
sixty years or more,
caring for the town and the cemetery.
They are the reason the records are so complete.

Charles and Dots
have been equally important to me
for the last seven years or so as I searched for family. They
are the reason this book has been written.

Table of Contents

Introduction	vii
Old Ground	1
Angle	4
Boundary Avenue South	7
Central Avenue North	13
Central Avenue South	19
Row A	26
Addition to A	44
Row B	47
Addition to B	66
Row C	68
Row E	105
Row F	120
Row F North	136
Row G	139
Row H	163
Row I	190
Row K	218
Row L	245
Row M	259
Potters Field or Free Ground	270
Index	273

Introduction

Monocacy Cemetery at Beallsville, Maryland dates back to pre-Revolutionary times. It was one of two Anglican chapels between Rock Creek Parish and Frederick, Maryland until about 1800. The original chapel was built sometime between 1734 and 1747. Around 1760 the chapel was replaced. The parish was known as St. John's, then Prince Georges (1726), All Saints (1742), Eden (1770) and St. Peter's (post-Revolution).

The grounds of the chapel and cemetery were originally one acre. In 1794 5/8 of an acre was added by Walter White. In June, 1830, John Adlum conveyed 10 3/4 acres to the grounds. In 1847 a church was built at Poolesville, Maryland and designated as the parish church. Some services were still held in the old chapel until the Civil War, when Federal troops used the chapel, then destroyed it beyond repair. The present chapel was erected about 1915 by the E.V. White Chapter, United Daughters of the Confederacy.

After the war, the cemetery became a public cemetery and in 1872 was turned over to the Monocacy Cemetery Society of Montgomery County, Maryland.

In preparing this book, I have combined information from the original interment books, burial permits, the card files kept by the cemetery, both of individuals and lots, and finally the tombstones themselves. To save space, I have used the following abbreviations:

> s/o, d/o, f/o, m/o, i/o, c/o, w/o, h/o denotes son of, daughter of, father of, mother of, infant of, child of, wife of, husband of, etc.

> TS: denotes items on the tombstone. Items within brackets, [ ] indicate information which comes from the card files and is not on the tombstone. Any information not designated as from the tombstone is from the card files.

> Ages are given as year-month-day. 72-1-0 means 72 years, 1 month, 0 days.

I must thank the Elgins and Tom Bodmer for giving me access to the records, and Jane Sween for saving me much time in the researching the history of the Monocacy Cemetery.

At the top of the cemetery, near the Chapel, stands a large stone listing the Confederate soldiers buried in the cemetery. This is a replacement of the original stone marker. The marble for the original stone was brought from England by Benjamin White and used in a tan yard on his farm near Buck Lodge, Montgomery Co., Maryland. It was later moved to his homestead and used as a garden seat. In 1911 permission was granted to use the marble for the following tablet. The present tablet rests on a part of the original stone for support.

The stone reads as follows:

In Loving memory of the valor and self sacrifice of the Maryland soldiers in the Confederate Army whose names are inscribed hereon.

War of 1861-1865

J. Collison White	Richard P. Hays
Thomas H. White	James W. Reed
Alonzo Sellman	George W. Butler
Frances T. Williams	Wallace Sellman
Lieut. Edward J. Chiswell	B. Franklin Pyles
Samuel C. White	Wm. F. Dade
M. Thomas Pyles	W. Seneca Veirs
Dr. Edward Wootten	Elijah Veirs
Benjamin J. Jones	John W. Holland
Capt. Geo. W. Chiswell	Wm. H. Dickerson
Henry B. Veirs	Chas M. Butler
Elias Price	Elias Moulden
John P. Sellman	Richard S. Stallings
John P. Bouic	Wm. H. Waesche
Francis E. Burch	John B. Munger
Maj. B.S. White	

This tablet was erected by the Ladies of Old Medley's District, Montgomery Co., MD 1911
Replaced by Ladies Auxiliary of Monocacy 1975

Elizabeth R. Frain
North Potomac, MD

Monocacy Cemetery, Beallsville, Montgomery County, Maryland

Old Ground

Old Ground is the area immediately around the Chapel, the original cemetery area for St. Peter's Church.

Lot &Owner Unknown

Site	Miss Catharine Austin	No marker	Burial: 23 Apr 1890
Site	Child of Ashby Belt	No marker	Burial: 2 Aug 1889
Site	Grover C. Carlisle	No marker	Burial: 26 Jan 1889
Site	John Douglas	Death: 2 Nov 1832	
	TS: of Castle Stewart Wigto Scotland, age 36 yrs.		
Site	Mrs. Phebe Dugan	No marker	Burial: 18 Dec 1881
Site	Alfred Fawcett	No marker	Burial: 22 Dec 1898
Site	Mrs. Louisa V. Hall	No marker	Burial: 22 Aug 1883
Site	Child of George Johnson	No marker	Burial: 30 Nov 1877
Site	Daughter of George Johnson	No marker	Burial: 5 Mar 1895
Site	Mr. J. Thomas Johnson	No marker	Burial: 20 Jun 1910
Site	Miss Lule Johnson	No marker	Burial: 3 Feb 1895
Site	John Jones	No marker	Burial: 3 Dec 1883
Site	Mrs. Lanon	No marker	Burial: 5 Apr 1874
Site	Gracie E. Lee	No marker	Burial: 13 Apr 1908
Site	Mrs. Margaret Macabee	No marker	Burial: 13 Apr 1882
Site	Amy Orms	No marker	Burial: 11 Jan 1892
Site	Mr. John Robertson	No marker	Burial: 23 Oct 1879
Site	William Whalen	No marker	Burial: 19 Jul 1908

Lot Owner: Cross

Site 2　John Cross　　　　　　　Death: 13 Sep 1838
　　　　TS: s/o John & Mary Cross, age 25-7-23
Site 3　Sarah Elener Cross　　　Death: 27 Feb 1841
　　　　TS: d/o John & Mary Cross , age 17- 6-0
Site 4　Joseph Thomas Cross　　Death: 4 Sep 1842
　　　　TS: s/o John & Mary Cross, age 25- 4-0
Site 5　Mary Cross　　　　　　Death: 6 Feb 1845
　　　　TS: w/o John Cross, age 52 yrs.
Site 6　John Cross　　　　　　　　　　　　　　　　　　TS: Age 72 yr-1-19
　　　　Birth: 25 Aug 1782　　Death: 14 Oct 1854　　　h/o Mary Cross
Site 6　Anastatia Cross　　　　　　　　　　　　　　　TS: d/o John & Mary Cross
　　　　Birth: 29 Mar 1831　　Death: 8 Aug 1855
Site 6　Mary Cross　　　　　　　　　　　　　　　　　TS: d/o John & Mary Cross
　　　　Birth: 22 Jan 1815　　Death: 8 Aug 1855

Monocacy Cemetery, Beallsville, Montgomery County, Maryland

Lot Owner: Dade

Site	Rev. Townsend Dade	Death: 6 Nov 1822	TS: Age 80 yrs.
	Revolutionary Patriot Plaque		
Site	Mr. James Andrew Dobson		Burial: 15 Apr 1904
Site 1	Catherine H. Dade		w/o Robert T. Dade
	Birth: 20 Dec 1818	Death: 22 Oct 1859	
Site 2	Infant Dade	No marker	i/o Mrs. Robert T. Dade
			Burial: 15 Dec 1881
Site 2	Robert T. Dade		h/o Catherine H. Dade
	Birth: 27 Nov 1817	Death: 3 May 1881	Burial: 5 May 1881
Site 3	Col. Robert T. Dade	illegible	h/o Ruth Dade
	Birth: 11 Oct 1786	Death: 17 Feb 1873	Burial: 19 Feb 1873
Site 4	Ruth Dade	Death: 11 Mar 1864	illegible
	w/o Col. Robert T. Dade, age 64 years		
Site 5	Anna Laura Dade	Mort: Hilton & Hall	Place: Poolesville
	Birth: 1861	Death: 21 Aug 1939	Burial: 22 Aug 1939
Site 6	John H. Dade		h/o Sarah E. Dade
	Birth: 9 May 1819	Death: 13 Sep 1905	Burial: 15 Sep 1905
Site 7	Sarah E. Dade		TS: w/o John H. Dade
	Birth: 9 Jan 1828	Death: 28 Jul 1903	Burial: 30 Jul 1903
Site 8	Edwin Franklin Dade		TS: s/o John H. & Elizabeth Dade
	Birth: 31 Mar 1852	Death: 20 Jul 1863	

Lot Owner: Davis

Site	Solomon Davis	Death: 10 Jul 1822	Age 48 yrs.

Lot Owner: Ernest Talbott

Site 2	Mary J. Talbott		On stone with Roy Linwood Talbott
	Birth: 16 Oct 1904	Death: 14 May 1980	Burial: 17 May 1980
Site 3	Roy Linwood Talbott	Mort: M.W. Etchison	Place: Frederick, MD
	Birth: 10 Jun 1892	Death: 5 Jun 1966	Burial: 8 Jun 1966
Site 5	Ernest Linwood Talbott		Place: Gaithersburg
	Birth: 22 Nov 1865	Death: 1 May 1944	Burial: 3 May 1944
	Mort: Wm. R. Pumphrey		h/o Rose E. Talbott
Site 6	Rosie Elizabeth Talbott		Place: Gaithersburg
	Birth: 26 Jul 1869	Death: 15 Oct 1959	Burial: 17 Oct 1959
	Mort: E.C. Gartner		TS: w/o Ernest L. Talbott

Lot Owner: F.S. Poole

Site 1	Frederick S. Poole		h/o Mary T.D. Poole
	Birth: 19 Jun 1809	Death: 8 Jun 1888	Burial: 23 Jun 1886
Site 2	Mary T.D. Poole	Death: 22 Jan 1883	Burial: 24 Jan 1883
	TS: w/o Frederick S. Poole, age 70- 5-18		
Site 3	Frederick S. Poole	Birth: 21 Aug 1842	Death: 29 Oct 1843
	TS: s/o Mary T.D. & Frederick S. Poole, age 1-2-0		
Site 4	Robert Willson Poole	Birth: 15 Mar 1838	Death: 13 Dec 1838
	TS: s/o Frederick S. & Mary T.D. Poole, 0-8-0		

Monocacy Cemetery, Beallsville, Montgomery County, Maryland   3

Site 5 John Frederick Sprigg Poole
       Birth: 3 May 1836   Death: 28 Nov 1838
       TS: s/o Frederick S. & Mary T.D. Poole, age 2 yrs
Site 6 Wilson Poole   Birth: 1 Dec 1849   Death: 20 Jan 1850
Site 7 Blanche Poole   d/o Frederick S. & Mary T.D. Poole
       Birth: 30 Apr 1848   Death: 25 Jan 1850
Site 8 Robert Willson Poole   h/o Eleanor Poole
       Birth: 13 Sep 1762   Death: 4 Nov 1835
Site 9 Eleanor Poole   TS: w/o Robert Willson Poole
       Birth: 21 Jul 1773   Death: 21 Aug 1851
Site 10 Mary Gertrude Poole   TS: d/o Frederick S. & Mary T.D. Poole, age 6-2-10
       Birth: 10 Mar 1847   Death: 20 May 1853   Burial: 20 May 1853
Site 11 Fannie E. Poole   Birth: 31 Mar 1840   Death: 11 Mar 1860
Site 12 Cumberland Willson Poole   Birth: 27 May 1834   Death: 22 Nov 1836
       TS: s/o Frederick S. & Mary T.D. Poole, age 2-5-0
Site 12 Robert Willson Poole   Birth: 3 Mar 1838   Death: 13 Dec 1838

Lot Owner: Mrs. Nora B. Stephens
Site 4 Joseph Elwood Bouis   Mort: Warner E. Pumphrey   Place: Olney
       Birth: 11 Mar 1919   Death: 6 Jun 1950   Burial: 8 Jun 1950
Site 5 Nora Blake Talbott Stephens   Place: Gaithersburg
       Birth: 1 Jun 1871   Death: 17 Feb 1942   Burial: 19 Feb 1942
       Mort: R.W. Pumphrey   TS: w/o Charles E. Stephens
Site 6 Charles E. Stephens   Place: Olney
       Birth: 22 Mar 1867   Death: 18 Nov 1947   Burial: 21 Nov 1947
       Mort: W.R. Pumphrey   h/o Nora Blake Stephens

Lot Owner: Jonathan Talbott
Site   Charles H. Bowlus   Birth: 11 Aug 1844   Death: 10 Aug 1863
Site   Emma Gertrude Talbott Mort: M.R. Etchison   Place: Hagerstown
       Birth: 8 Jun 1869   Death: 29 Apr 1960   Burial: 3 May 1960
Site   Fannie B. Talbott   No marker   d/o Jonathan Talbott, age 0-10- 6
                                                                        Burial: Jun 1865
Site   Hattie M. Talbott   Death: 25 Feb 1902   Burial: 27 Feb 1902
       TS: w/o Joseph N. Talbott, age 25- 7- 24
Site   Henry W. Talbott   h/o Sarah Talbott
       Birth: 12 Nov 1789   Death: 7 Feb 1859   TS: Age 69-4-0
Site   Hilda Virginia Talbott   TS: w/o Joseph Nathan Talbott, Jr.
       Birth: 5 Jan 1902   Death: 7 Dec 1979   Burial: 10 Dec 1979
Site   Child of Jonathan Talbott   Death: 12 Jan 1872   Burial: 13 Jan 1872
Site   Jonathan Talbott   Place: Adamstown
       Birth: 10 Jan 1832   Death: 31 Dec 1914   Burial: 3 Jan 1915
       Mort: W.T. Hilton & Sons   h/o Sarah F. Talbott
Site   Joseph Nathan Talbott   Place: Olney
       Birth: 1 Jun 1871   Death: 13 Jul 1932   Burial: 16 Jul 1932
       Mort: W.R. Pumphrey   h/o Hattie M. Talbott
Site   Joseph Nathan Talbott Jr.   Place: Daubs
       Birth: 8 Jun 1901   Death: 3 Oct 1956   Burial: 6 Oct 1956
       Mort: M.R. Etchison   h/o Hilda V. Talbott

Monocacy Cemetery, Beallsville, Montgomery County, Maryland

Site	Marion Talbott	Child No marker	Burial: 7 Jul 1896
Site	Nathan J. Talbott	No marker	Burial: 15 Oct 1902
Site	Miss Sarah Talbott	No marker	Burial: 21 Mar 1902
Site	Sarah Talbott	Death: 25 Jan 1883	Burial: 27 Jan 1883
	TS: w/o Henry Talbott, age 88-7-11		illegible
Site	Sarah F. Talbott	Birth: 1 Feb 1839	Death: 13 May 1893
	w/o Jonathan Talbott		
Site	Ann M. Williams	illegible	w/o John T. Williams
	Birth: 3 Jun 1817	Death: 23 Mar 1889	Burial: 29 Mar 1889
Site	Child of Jonathan Talbott	No marker	Burial: 12 Feb 1873

Lot Owner: Trail

Site 7 Hannah Lawrence Trail   TS: w/o Nathan L. Trail, age 80-2-0
       Birth: 25 Dec 1784   Death: 25 Feb 1865
Site 7 Richard F. Trail   illegible   h/o Elizabeth E. Trail
       Birth: 10 Apr 1820   Death: 4 Jul 1876   Burial: 5 Jul 1876
Site 8 Nathan L. Trail   illegible   Burial: 1882
       h/o Hannah Lawrence Trail, age 63 yrs
Site 8 Elizabeth E. Trail   illegible   w/o Richard Trail
       Birth: 12 Sep 1821   Burial: 14 Feb 1837
Site 9 Sarah E. Trail   Burial: 8 Sep 1873   Age 47 yrs
       illegible

Angle

Lot: 1 Owner: Mrs. Mary Sellman

Site 1 Isabel E. Sellman   Death: 22 Mar 1892   Burial: 28 Mar 1892
       TS: d/o R.E. & M.I. Sellman, age 0-9-8
Site 1 Ellis T. Sellman   Death: 29 Jun 1893   Burial: 3 Jul 1893
       TS: s/o R.E. & M.I. Sellman, age 0-8-10
Site 2 Marion L. Sellman   d/o Mary I. Sellman
       Birth: 1890   Death: 2 Feb 1976   Burial: 4 Feb 1976
       On stone with Richard E. & Mary I. Sellman
Site 3 Mary I. Sellman   Place: Washington, DC
       Birth: 1861   Death: 9 Jun 1954   Burial: 14 Jun 1954
       Mort: J. Wm. Lee Sons   On stone with Richard E. Sellman
Site 4 Richard E. Sellman   Moved: 14 Jan 1914
       Birth: 1865   Death: 1895   Burial: 15 Jul 1895
Site 5 Edward J. Sellman   Mort: Clagett Hilton   Place: Boyds
       Birth: 1 Aug 1894   Death: 11 Jan 1914   Burial: 14 Jan 1914
Site 9 Maggie J. Buckey   Place: Washington, DC
       Birth: 1864   Death: 24 Jun 1955   Burial: 27 Jun 1955
       Mort: Francis J. Collins   On stone with Charles Wesley Buckey

Monocacy Cemetery, Beallsville, Montgomery County, Maryland 5

Site 10 Charles Wesley Buckey   Place: Washington, DC
         Birth: 1860   Death: 9 Mar 1940   Burial: 11 Mar 1940
         Mort: S.H. Hines Co.   h/o Maggie J. Buckey

Lot: 2 Lower   Owner: Clarence Price
Site   Ida M. Price   Mort: Hilton & Hall
         Place: Washington, DC   Death: 17 Apr 1927   Burial: 19 Apr 1927
Site   Thomas Price   Burial: 17 Jun 1902   No marker
Site 1   Wilford Price   Death: 21 Mar 1899   c/o Clarnece & Ida M. Price
Site 2   Clarence Price   Burial: 26 Sep 1912   No marker
Site 3   Mrs. Mary E.H. Price   Burial: 14 Oct 1910   No marker

Lot: 2 Upper   Owner: James W. Hillard
Site 1   Erma White Hillard   Death: 16 Aug 1898
         d/o James W. & Gertrude Hillard, age 1 day
Site 2   Child Hillard   Burial: 18 Aug 1901   No marker
Site 2   Child of James H. Hubbard Burial: 8 Aug 1901
Site 3   Gertrude E.V. Hillard   No marker   Mort: Deal Funeral Home
         Place: Washington, DC   Death: 28 Mar 1953   Burial: 31 Mar 1953
Site 4   James W. Hillard   No marker   Mort: W.W. Deal
         Place: Washington, DC   Death: 23 Jan 1954   Burial: 26 Jan 1954

Lot: 3   Owner: Trundle Bros.
Site 1   Perry Lewis Trundle   Burial: 19 Oct 1900
         s/o John Trundle   No marker
Site 2   Norman Trundle   Burial: 15 Jun 1905   No marker
Site 3   John R. Trundle   No marker   Mort: Hilton & Hall
         Place: Staunton, VA   Death: 1 Oct 1919   Burial: 3 Oct 1919
Site 4   Clara Brunner Trundle   Mort: Hilton & Hall   Place: Washington, DC
         Birth: 30 Sep 1871   Death: 19 Feb 1918   Burial: 22 Feb 1918
Site 5   John Horatio Trundle   Mort: Hilton & Hall
         Place: Martinsburg   Death: 6 Mar 1926   Burial: 8 Mar 1926
         h/o Lulu Spates Trundle   No marker
Site 6   Lulu Spates Trundle   Burial: 8 Jun 1901
         1st w/o John Trundle   No marker
Site 7   David Trundle   Place: Washington, DC   Mort: Hilton
         Birth: 13 Jan 1910   Death: 24 Jun 1965   Burial: 26 Jun 1965
         s/o John Horatio & Clara Jennings Trundle   No marker
Site 8   Della Brunner Trundle   Death: 16 Feb 1924
         w/o William Beauregard Trundle   No marker
Site 9   William B. Trundle   No marker   Mort: Hilton & Hall
         Place: Poolesville   Death: 16 Dec 1924   Burial: 18 Dec 1924
Site 10 Barbara Jennings Trundle Place: Richmond, VA   Mort: Wm. Hilton
         Birth: 10 Oct 1898   Death: 8 Nov 1970   Burial: 12 Nov 1970

Lot: 4   Owner: Mrs. Carson Hyatt & sister
Site 3   Alvin L. Hyatt   Death: 15 May 1905   Burial: 18 May 1905
         TS: s/o Carson & Ann W. Hyatt, age 31-1-6

Monocacy Cemetery, Beallsville, Montgomery County, Maryland

Site 4 Miss Mary E. Hyatt   Death: 7 Apr 1897   Burial: 9 Apr 1897
        TS: d/o Carson & Ann W. Hyatt, age 18-1-1
Site 8 Florence May Williams White   Mort: E.C. Gartner
                                      Death: 30 Mar 1949   Burial: 2 Apr 1949
        Place: Cascade, Washington Co.   2nd w/o Nathan Smith White V
Site 9 Nathan Smith White   Mort: W.R. Pumphrey   Place: Boyds
        Birth: 13 Jan 1852   Death: 11 Aug 1934   Burial: 14 Aug 1934
        h/o Sarah Aldah White &   TS: h/o Florence May White
Site 10 Sarah Aldah White   TS: w/o Nathan Smith White
        Birth: 2 Aug 1854   Death: 9 Nov 1911   Burial: 11 Nov 1911
Site 11 Elizabeth Ann Jarboe   TS: w/o R.T. Jarboe   Reinterment
        Birth: 6 Jun 1822   Death: 16 Oct 1892   Burial: 20 Sep 1909

Lot: 5   Owner: B.R. White
Site 1 Benjamin Rush White   h/o Mary F. Matthews White
        Birth: 1828   Death: 1913   Burial: 12 Feb 1913
Site 2 Ella F. White   Place: Washington, DC
        Birth: 1842   Death: 4 Jun 1918   Burial: 6 Jun 1918
        Mort: W.R. Pumphrey   On stone with Benjamin Rush White

Lot: 6   Owner: Frank Reed
Site 1 John R. Gray   Death: 26 Jun 1898   Burial: 28 Jun 1898
        TS: s/o John R. & Sallie E. Gray, brother/o G. Robert Gray, age 28 days
Site 2 Ruth N. Reed   On stone with Frank Levin & Lula Lucretia Reed
        Birth: 20 Jan 1906   Death: 21 Aug 1906   Burial: 3 Sep 1907
Site 3 Lulu Lucretia Reed   On stone with Frank Levin Reed
        Birth: 18 Dec 1884   Death: 28 Sep 1979   Burial: 1 Oct 1979
Site 4 Frank Levin Reed   Place: Gaithersburg
        Birth: 18 Nov 1865   Death: 27 Mar 1947   Burial: 30 Mar 1947
        Mort: E.C. Gartner   h/o Lulu L. Reed
Site 5 Helen DeAtley
        Birth: 20 Dec 1903   Death: 17 Jan 1994   Burial: 6 Apr 1994

Lot: 7   Owner: Miscellaneous
Site 2 Rev. John Edwin Williams   h/o Pauline Williams
        Birth: 8 Jan 1921   Death: 18 Sep 1968   Burial: 23 Sep 1968
        TS: Rector-St. Peter's Episcopal Church 1960-1968
Site 3 Emily D. Mercier   Place: Landen
        Birth: 13 May 1852   Death: 8 Jul 1918   Burial: 10 Jul 1918
        Mort: M.R. Etchison   TS: w/o Richard G. Mercier
Site 4 Richard G. Mercier   Mort: M.R. Etcherson   Place: Gandey
        Birth: 17 Oct 1842   Death: 1 Feb 1920   Burial: 3 Feb 1920
Site 5 Sallie E. Betson   w/o Harry C. Betson   No marker
        Birth: 1895   Death: 16 Apr 1974   Burial: 20 Apr 1974
Site 6 Donna Marie Betson   grand d/o Harry C. Betson   No marker
        Infant   Death: 8 Mar 1950   Burial: 8 Mar 1950
Site 6 Harry C. Betson   Place: Frederick Hospital
        h/o Sallie E. Betson   Death: 23 Feb 1945   Burial: 26 Feb 1945
        Mort: W.B. Hilton   No marker

Monocacy Cemetery, Beallsville, Montgomery County, Maryland

Lot: 8 Owner: Frank Money

Site 1 Frank J. Money Mort: W.T. Hilton & Sons Place: Frederick
Birth: 14 Jan 1860 Death: 23 Jul 1930 Burial: 25 Jul 1930

Site 2 James E. Money Mort: Hilton & Hall Place: Poolesville
Birth: 2 Oct 1863 Death: 21 Mar 1918 Burial: 23 Mar 1918

Site 3 Rose Anna Money TS: Mother w/o James H. Money
Birth: 15 Oct 1833 Death: 3 Mar 1908 Burial: 5 Mar 1908

Site 4 James H. Money Sr. illegible h/o Rose Anna Money
Birth: 16 Jul 1836 Death: 14 Aug 1901 Burial: 16 Aug 1901

Boundary Avenue South

Lot: 0 Owner: W.T. Griffith

Site Child of J. Howard Griffith No marker Burial: 13 Nov 1908

Site Dorcas Hammontree Death: 21 Feb 1836
TS: Consort of William W. Hammontree, age 37-11-12

Site 2 William Griffith Pyles Mort: Robert A. Pumphrey Place: Baltimore
Birth: 4 Mar 1913 Death: 8 Oct 1959 Burial: 12 Oct 1959
h/o Nellie Jenkins Pyles, s/o Dr. Charles T. & Mary Griffith Pyles

Site 3 Dr. Charles Thomas Pyles Place: Berkley Springs, WV
Birth: 4 Aug 1885 Death: 20 Dec 1948 Burial: 23 Dec 1948
Mort: Charles R. Bast h/o Mary Griffith Pyles

Site 4 Mary Elizabeth Griffith Pyles Place: Berkley Springs, WV
Birth: 16 Jun 1886 Death: 31 Dec 1951 Burial: 3 Jan 1952
Mort: Howard J. Grane w/o Dr. Charles Thomas Pyles, age 65

Site 5 Elizabeth Dade Pyles illegible Place: Hancock, MD
Birth: 1 Feb 1916 Death: 25 May 1916 Burial: 26 May 1916
Mort: M. Jenkins & Sons d/o Charles Thomas & Mary Griffith Pyles

Site 7 C. Dade Griffith Mort: Wm. R. Pumphrey Place: Washington, DC
Birth: 22 Dec 1888 Death: 25 Nov 1943 Burial: 28 Nov 1943

Site 8 William Thomas Griffith Place: Hancock
Birth: 1 Mar 1856 Death: 17 Apr 1931 Burial: 18 Apr 1931
Mort: T.P. Jenkins h/o Elizabeth Griffith

Site 9 Elizabeth Dade Griffith Place: Hancock
Birth: 1858 Death: 31 Mar 1941 Burial: 2 Apr 1941
Mort: L.P. Jenkins On stone with William Thomas Griffith

Site 10 William Howard Griffith TS: s/o William T. & Lizzie D. Griffith
Birth: 11 Jul 1887 Death: 22 Nov 1890 Burial: 23 Nov 1890

Site 11 Infant Griffith Death: 8 Sep 1890 Burial: 15 Sep 1890
TS: s/o William T. & Lizzie Griffith, age 6 days illegible

Monocacy Cemetery, Beallsville, Montgomery County, Maryland

Lot: 0   Owner: (No markers)
- Site   Solomon Hall   No marker   Burial: 2 Apr 1909
- Site   Susie Elizabeth Hall   Mort: Hilton & Hall   Place: Poolesville
  Birth: 1843   Death: 25 May 1933   Burial: 27 May 1933
- Site   William T. Hall   Burial: 30 ? 1878   Month is illegible in records
- Site 2   John William Hall   Mort: Hilton & Hall   Place: Poolesville
  Birth: 1847   Death: 8 Apr 1924   Burial: 10 Apr 1924
- Site 5   E. T. Hall   No marker   Burial: 9 Aug 1898

Lot: 00   Owner: Cady
- Site 3   Mary Cady   c/o William A. & Sarah Cady
  Birth: 4 Mar 1857   Death: 8 Dec 1857
- Site 4   Josephine Cady   Death: 13 Apr 1864
  TS: only d/o William A. & Sarah Cady, age 4-11-2
- Site 5   Sarah Ellen Poole Cady   illegible   w/o William Appleton Cady
  Birth: 1 May 1830   Death: 23 Oct 1904   Burial: 28 Oct 1904
- Site 6   William Appleton Cady   Birth: 24 Apr 1819   Death: 28 Apr 1861
  TS: h/o Sarah E. Cady, age 42-0-4
- Site 9   John S. Manly   Death: 8 Mar 1817
  TS: s/o John S. & Mary Manly, in his 48th year

Lot: 000
- Site 1   Benjamin Poole   Age 71 yrs
  Birth: 28 Sep 1773   Death: 18 Dec 1813   Burial: Feb 1844
- Site 2   Ann W. Poole   Age 84 yrs
  Death: 14 Oct 1832   Burial: 14 Oct 1852

Lot: 1   Owner: John P. Sellman
- Site 2   Elizabeth L. Sellman   Place: Daviess, IN
  Birth: 1872   Death: 11 Feb 1960   Burial: 28 May 1960
  Mort: W.Hayes Gill   On stone with John P. Sellman, MD
- Site 3   John P. Sellman MD   h/o Elizabeth L. Sellman   Place: Olney, IL
  Birth: 16 Jun 1874   Death: 19 Aug 1943   Mort: James C. Gill
- Site 4   Miss Ann Estelle Sellman
  Birth: 28 Jul 1880   Death: 1894   Burial: 9 Apr 1894
- Site 5   Miss Ida Lee Sellman
  Birth: 1870   Death: 1893   Burial: 21 Aug 1893
- Site 7   Marie Sellman Pearre   Mort: C.E. Cline & Son   Place: Takoma Park
  Birth: 29 Mar 1877   Death: 30 Jan 1943   Burial: 3 Feb 1943
- Site 8   John Poole Sellman   h/o Ann Hempstone Sellman
  Birth: 11 Dec 1840   Death: 22 Jul 1908
- Site 9   Ann Hempstone Sellman   Place: Frederick
  Birth: 17 Feb 1844   Death: 23 Apr 1928   Burial: 25 Apr 1928
  Mort: Thos. P. Rice   On stone with John Poole Sellman
- Site 10   Florence May Sellman   Mort: W.B. Hilton   Place: Takoma Park
  Birth: 1 May 1867   Death: 9 Oct 1945   Burial: 13 Oct 1945
- Site   Hunton Dade Sellman   Birth: 1900   Death: 1992

Monocacy Cemetery, Beallsville, Montgomery County, Maryland   9

Lot: 2   Owner: W.W. Metzger
Site 1 Nathan Hazel Metzger   Mort: Hilton & Hall   Place: Poolesville
        Birth: 1877   Death: 11 Oct 1918   Burial: 13 Oct 1918
Site 2 Amanda E. Cashell Metzger Place: Poolesville
        Birth: 1837   Death: 25 Oct 1915   Burial: 27 Oct 1915
        Mort: Hilton & Hall   TS: w/o William W. Metzger
Site 3 William W. Metzger   h/o Amanda E. Cashell Metzger
        Birth: 10 Sep 1840   Death: 9 Nov 1906

Lot: 3   Owner: Lucinda Pyles (No stones in lot)
Site   Edward Heffner   No marker   Mort: Hilton & Burdette
        Place: Olney   Death: 3 May 1936   Burial: 3 May 1936
Site 3 Isaac Jones Pyles   No marker   Age 57-6-24
                                 Death: 5 Jul 1895   Burial: 7 Jul 1895
Site 4 Mrs. Lucinda R. Pyles   Mort: Webster J. Burdette   Place: Hyattstown
        Birth: 22 Dec 1851   Death: 8 Dec 1913   Burial: 10 Dec 1913

Lot: 4   Owner: Algernon Poole
Site 1 Infant of H. D. Brown   Mort: H.D. Brown   Place: Takoma Park
        Birth: 12 Feb 1920   Death: 12 Feb 1920   Burial: 13 Feb 1920
Site 1 Eric Turley Mace   s/o William H. Mace
        Birth: 19 May 1972   Death: 21 May 1972   Burial: 23 May 1972
Site 2 Mary Waters Poole   Age 87   Place: Atlantic City
        Birth: 1864   Death: 18 Dec 1951   Burial: 21 Dec 1951
        Mort: Jeffreis & Keates   TS: w/o Algernon Poole
Site 3 Algernon Poole   h/o Mary Waters Poole
        Birth: 1856   Death: 1906   Burial: 3 Feb 1906
Site 4 Mildred Poole   d/o Algernon & Mary W. Poole
        Birth: 23 Dec 1902   illegible   Burial: 4 Dec 1904
Site 4 Edward Poole   illegible   TS: s/o Algernon & Mary W. Poole
        Birth: 21 May 1893   Death: 21 May 1893   Burial: 22 May 1893
Site 5 William T. Poole   illegible   TS: s/o Algernon & Mary W. Poole
        Birth: 4 Apr 1867   Death: 15 Nov 1893   Burial: 16 Nov 1893
Site 7 Paul P. English
        Birth: 9 May 1901   Death: 16 Aug 1982   Burial: 18 Aug 1982
Site 11 Sarah Dickerson Poole
        Birth: 23 Nov 1899   Death: 19 May 1985   Burial: 21 May 1986

Lot: 5 Lower   Owner: Miscellaneous
Site 1 Laura Louise Rhoton   Place: Baltimore
        Birth: 1884   Death: 19 Apr 1966   Burial: 22 Apr 1966
        Mort: Harry W. Haight   On stone with Isaac T. Rhoton
Site 2 Isaac T. Rhoton   Place: Glenwood, Howard Co.
        Birth: 1879   Death: 11 Oct 1944   Burial: 14 Oct 1944
        Mort: Roy Barber   h/o Laura Louise Rhoton
Site 3 Martin Slemp Carter   Mort: W.B. Hilton   Place: Poolesville
        Birth: 10 Sep 1911   Death: 18 Jan 1945   Burial: 21 Jan 1945
Site 4 Ada May Sellman   Death: 8 Aug 1904   Burial: 10 Aug 1904
        d/o John & Amanda Sellman, age 66-1   illegible

Site 5 William Thomas Kohlenburg Mort: W.B. Hilton
        Birth: 1872   Death: 17 Jun 1946   Burial: 20 Jun 1946
        Age 74 yrs   Place: Riverdale   TS: h/o Georgia Kohlenberg
Site 6 Alvin Gassaway Sellman   TS: Age 13-6-19
                                 Death: 21 Aug 1901   Burial: 23 Aug 1901

Lot: 5 Upper   Owner: Lemuel Beall
Site 2 Mary Elizabeth Beall   illegible   w/o Lemuel Larkin Beall
        Birth: 26 Mar 1840   Burial: 1 Oct 1900
Site 3 Lemuel Larkin Beall   h/o Mary Elizabeth Beall
        Birth: 1 Jul 1814   Death: 30 Aug 1881   Burial: 31 Aug 1881

Lot: 6 Lower   Owner: Miscellaneous
Site 1 Clarke Morningstar   Death: 8 Apr 1942   Burial: 10 Apr 1942
        Place: Washington, DC   Mort: W.B. Hilton
Site 2 Maude M. Lester   w/o Charles E. Lester   Mort: W.B. Hilton
        Place: Beallsville   Death: 29 Jan 1940   Burial: 1 Feb 1940
Site 3 Charles E. Lester   h/o Maude M. Lester, age 70   Mort: J. A. Walters
        Place: Colesville   Death: 16 Jul 1950   Burial: 19 Jul 1950
Site 4 Amy Robertson   Death: 9 Mar 1865   Age 70-0-5
Site 6 Ida L. Kegley Smith   Place: Olney
        Birth: 2 Mar 1884   Death: 24 Aug 1935   Burial: 26 Aug 1935
        Mort: Hilton & Hall   TS: w/o William F. Smith
Site   John M. Hall   Birth: 1847   Death: 1924

Lot: 6 Upper   Owner: John W. Hillard
Site   Child of Thomas Hillard Burial: 11 Sep 1897   No marker
Site   Child of Thomas Hillard Burial: 12 Oct 1901   No marker
Site 3 Helen E. Hillard   Birth: 1836   Death: 1878
        TS: w/o John W. Hillard
Site 4 John W. Hillard   h/o Helen E. Hillard
        Birth: 1825   Death: 1895   Burial: 16 Dec 1895
Site 5 Hattie Hillard   Place: near Boyds
        Birth: 14 Jun 1876   Death: 26 Sep 1939   Burial: 28 Sep 1939
        Mort: W.B. Hilton   TS: w/o Thomas Bolden Hillard
Site 6 Thomas Bolden Hillard   Place: Sandy Spring
        Birth: 3 Oct 1869   Death: 4 Jul 1958   Burial: 7 Jul 1958
        Mort: Hilton   h/o Hattie Hillard

Lot: 7 Lower   Owner: Miscellaneous
Site 1 Mary Alice Veatch Gutherie   Place: Poolesville
        Birth: 6 Jun 1856   Death: 20 Feb 1940   Burial: 20 Feb 1940
        Mort: Hilton & Hall   TS: w/o George W. Gutherie
Site 1 George W. Louden (Doc)   Mort: W.B. Hilton   Place: Cedar Grove
        Birth: 1865   Death: 2 Jul 1944   Burial: 4 Jul 1944
Site 2 James M. Soper   Place: Suburban Hospital, Bethesda, MD
                                 Death: 3 Apr 1945   Burial: 5 Apr 1945
        Mort: W.B. Hilton   h/o Georgia K. Soper

Monocacy Cemetery, Beallsville, Montgomery County, Maryland 11

Site 3 Georgia K. Soper w/o James M. Soper Mort: W.B. Hilton
 Place: near Boyds Death: 30 Oct 1940 Burial: 2 Nov 1940
Site 4 Francis E. Davis Place: Barnesville
 Birth: 23 Sep 1870 Death: 14 Feb 1940 Burial: 16 Feb 1940
 Mort: W.B. Hilton h/o Lulu H. Davis
Site 5 Lula H. Davis Place: Arlington
 Birth: 14 Sep 1873 Death: 4 May 1947 Burial: 6 May 1947
 Mort: C.J. Ives On stone with Francis E. Davis
Site 6 Francis E. Davis Mort: W.B. Hilton Place: Washington, DC
 Birth: 14 Apr 1900 Death: 22 Jan 1941 Burial: 25 Jan 1941

Lot: 7 Upper Owner: Mrs. James Reed
Site 3 James W. Reed h/o Jennie L. Reed
 Birth: 17 Nov 1836 Death: 31 Mar 1905 Burial: 3 Apr 1905
Site 4 Jennie L. Reed On stone with James W. Reed
 Birth: 17 Oct 1848 Death: 27 Feb 1912 Burial: 1 Mar 1912
Site 5 Charles H. Reed Death: 6 Jul 1871
 TS: Only c/o James W. & Jeannie Reed, age 0-9-25

Lot: 8 Owner: W.W. Metzger (No stones in lot)
Site 3 Bernard Metzger
 Birth: 2 Mar 1810 Death: 2 Mar 1810 Burial: 5 Sep 1841
Site 4 Gerhart & Elizabeth Ann Metzer Burial: 20 Jun 1881
 c/o Gerhart & Elizabeth Ann Metzger in grave w/ mother Reinterment
Site 4 Elizabeth Ann Metzger w/o Gerhart Metzger Reinterment
 Birth: 7 Feb 1813 Death: 12 Jun 1881 Burial: 20 Jun 1881
Site 5 Sarah Ellen Metzger Buried with mother Reinterment
 Birth: 21 Sep 1841 Death: 11 Oct 1841 Burial: 20 Jun 1881
Site 6 John H. Metzger Buried with mother Reinterment
 Birth: 26 Mar 1843 Death: 8 Aug 1843 Burial: 20 Jun 1881

Lot: 9 Lower Owner: Miscellaneous
Site 1 William Waters Birth: 12 May 1864 Burial: 22 Jul 1865
 illegible
Site 1 James Franklin Martin Mort: W.B. Hilton Place: Dickerson
 Birth: 1885 Death: 22 Mar 1956 Burial: 24 Mar 1956
Site 2 Bertha Higgins Burial: 12 May 1863 Age 4-1-23
 illegible
Site 3 George T. Higgins Death: 7 Jul 1861 illegible
Site 4 Louis B. Scholl Mort: W.B. Hilton Place: Washington, DC
 Birth: 1856 Death: 11 Nov 1934 Burial: 13 Nov 1934
Site 5 Ada Belle Cornwell Mort: W.B. Hilton Place: Lisbon
 Birth: 1871 Death: 22 Mar 1949 Burial: 25 Mar 1949
 On stone with Lafayette A. Cornwell
Site 6 Lafayette A. Cornwell Birth: 1849 Death: 1931

Lot: 9 Upper Owner: Mrs. John Grimes
Site Bertie Estelle Grimes No marker Burial: 8 Jun 1884
Site Mrs. John R. Grimes No marker Burial: 12 Mar 1898

Monocacy Cemetery, Beallsville, Montgomery County, Maryland

Site	Samuel D. Grimes	No marker	Mort: M.R. Etchison & Sons
	Place: Brunswick	Death: 6 Feb 1945	Burial: 9 Feb 1945
Site	William W. Grimes	No marker	Mort: Clyde Nichols
	Place: Washington, DC	Death: 20 Jun 1927	Burial: 22 Jun 1927
Site	Mary E. Moulden	Burial: 30 Oct 1893	No marker
Site 5	John R. Grimes	Death: 5 Feb 1876	Burial: 7 Feb 1876
	TS: Age 37-8-3		
Site 5	Elias Moulden	Death: 22 Feb 1893	Burial: 23 Feb 1893

Lot: 10 Lower   Owner: Barney Norris

Site 1	James Lawson Norris	Mort: W.T. Hilton & Sons	Place: Frederick
	Birth: 3 May 1836	Death: 8 Jan 1918	Burial: 9 Jan 1918
Site 2	Charles William Norris		
	Birth: 1833	Death: 1888	Burial: 17 May 1888
Site 3	Bernard T. Norris		h/o Ann R. Norris
	Birth: 1803	Death: 1888	Burial: 18 Jun 1888
Site 4	Ann R. Fyffe Norris		w/o Barnett T. Norris
	Birth: 9 Sep 1801	Death: 19 Feb 1860	TS: Age 58-4-29

Lot: 10 Upper   Owner: Miscellaneous

Site 1	Annie Ruth Davis		Place: Parkville, MD
	Birth: 1874	Death: 2 Jan 1969	Burial: 4 Jan 1969
	Mort: Robt. E. Dailey		On stone with John J. Davis
Site 2	John J. Davis		Place: Greenfield
	Birth: 1863	Death: 15 Jan 1949	Burial: 18 Jan 1949
	Mort: C.E. Clive & Son		h/o Annie R. Davis
Site 3	Frances Lucille Davis		Place: Washington, DC
	Birth: 13 Jun 1936	Death: 4 May 1941	Burial: 6 May 1941
	Mort: W.R. Pumphrey		TS: d/o C.H. & M.L. Davis
Site 4	Mildred Lucille Briggs Davis		Place: Greenfield
	Birth: 15 Oct 1911	Death: 13 May 1937	Burial: 16 May 1937
	Mort: C.E. Cline & Son		On stone with Chester H. Davis
Site 5	Chester H. Davis		h/o Mildred Briggs Davis
	Birth: 17 Feb 1906	Death: 16 Dec 1993	Burial: 20 Dec 1993

Lot: 11   Owner: Richard T. White

Site 2	Richard T. White Jr.		Place: Buck Lodge
	Birth: 1866	Death: 5 Oct 1943	Burial: 7 Oct 1943
	Mort: Wm. B. Hilton		s/o Richard T. & Mary E. White
Site 3	Mary E. White	Death: 23 Oct 1890	Burial: 25 Oct 1890
	TS: w/o Richard T. White Sr., age 60-3-2		
Site 4	Richard T. White Sr.		Place: Buck Lodge
	Birth: 18 Nov 1829	Death: 10 May 1917	Burial: 12 May 1917
	Mort: W.T. Hilton & Sons		h/o Mary E. White
Site 7	Harriet A. Derr	Place: Boyds	Mort: W.B. Hilton
	Birth: 1858	Death: 5 Apr 1938	Burial: 7 Apr 1938
Site 8	Hannah R. Derr	Mort: W.B. Hilton	Place: Boyds
	Birth: 1859	Death: 24 Dec 1942	Burial: 26 Dec 1942

Monocacy Cemetery, Beallsville, Montgomery County, Maryland   13

Lot: 12 Owner: Mrs. Ella C. White
Site 3 Ella Clarke Bouic White   Place: Rockville
        Birth: 16 Dec 1849   Death: 20 Sep 1931   Burial: 22 Sep 1931
        Mort: W.R. Pumphrey   TS: w/o Dr. N. Smith White
Site 4 Dr. N. Smith White   h/o Ella Clark Bouic White
        Birth: 28 Mar 1840   Burial: 21 Jul 1885
Site 5 Maj. Benjamin Stephen White   Mort: C.E. Roberts
        Birth: 11 Mar 1828   Death: 21 Mar 1891   Burial: 10 Oct 1921
        h/o Sarah Ellen Nichols White   Removed from Barnsville
Site 6 Sarah Ellen Nichols White   Mort: C.E. Roberts
        Removed from Barnsville Death: 15 May 1856   Burial: 10 Oct 1921
        TS: w/o Major Benjamin Stephen White, d/o Jacob & Sarah Nichols,
        age 26-1-19
Site 6 Sarah Ellen Nichols White   Mort: C.E. Roberts
        Removed from Barnsville Death: 11 Aug 1856   Burial: 10 Oct 1921
        TS: d/o Benjamin & S.E. White, age 0-3-21

Lot: 13 Owner: Mrs. Claudia Ward
Site 1 Gertrude Emma Thom   Mort: Robert A. Pumphrey   Place: Sykesville
        Birth: 1893   Death: 17 Feb 1965   Burial: 20 Feb 1965
Site 2 William Thomas Mockbee   On Warren King Lot
        Birth: 1838   Death: 30 Sep 1909
Site 3 Mary Ann King   TS: w/o Warren King
        Birth: 13 May 1805   Death: 9 Jul 1885
Site 4 Warren King   h/o Mary Ann King
        Birth: 31 Jan 1794   Death: 12 Jan 1871

Central Avenue North

Lot: Unknown
Site   Mrs. Sarah E. Baker   No marker   Burial: 27 Apr 1897
Site   Mrs. Annie Virginia Hagan   No marker   Burial: 24 Feb 1894
Site   Mrs. Fannie Thierles   No marker   Burial: 8 Mar 1898
Site   Child of Algernon Poole   No marker   Burial: 6 Apr 1904

Lot: 0 Owner: Unknown
Site 1 John Manly   Death: 25 Nov 1816 h/o Mary Manly, age 64 yrs
Site 2 Mary Manly   Death: 18 Jun 1823
        TS: w/o John Manly, age 52 yrs

Monocacy Cemetery, Beallsville, Montgomery County, Maryland

Lot: 1 Owner: John L. Young
Site 2 Jane Hunton Young   Place: Washington Grove
        Birth: 14 Oct 1868   Death: 7 Jun 1952   Burial: 10 Jun 1952
        Mort: James A. Gill & Son Age 83
Site 3 Miss Irene Mary Young   TS: d/o John & Minnie Young
        Birth: 4 Nov 1876   Death: 24 Apr 1895   Burial: 24 Apr 1895
Site 4 Victoria Hampton Young   illegible   c/o John L. & Minnie H. Young
        Birth: 14 Sep 1881   Death: 11 May 1894   Burial: 13 May 1894
Site 5 Minnie Hunton Young   TS: w/o John L. Young, age 50-3-27
        Birth: 29 Jul 1842   Death: 26 Nov 1892   Burial: 28 Nov 1892
Site 6 John L. Young   illegible   Place: Charles Town
        Birth: 27 Jun 1836   Death: 7 Dec 1919   Burial: 10 Dec 1919
        Mort: W.T. Hilton & Sons   h/o Minnie Hunton Young

Lot: 2 Owner: Joseph White
Site 1 Jenny Katherine Westesson White   w/o Roger White
        Birth: 12 Jul 1893   Death: 13 Mar 1972   Burial: 16 Mar 1972
Site 2 Joseph Roger White   Mort: John H. Rohde   Place: Cincinatti, OH
        Birth: 16 Nov 1889   Death: 18 Mar 1951   Burial: 21 Mar 1951
        h/o Jenny Katherine White, s/o J. Furr White
Site 3 Maria Louise Hillary White TS:w/o J. Furr White
        Birth: 7 Nov 1857   Death: 27 Sep 1900   Burial: 30 Sep 1900
Site 4 J. Furr White   Place: Frederick Hospital
        Birth: 26 Sep 1860   Death: 15 Apr 1949   Burial: 18 Apr 1949
        Mort: W.B. Hilton   Reinterment   h/o Maria Louise White
Site 7 Stephen N. White   Death: 16 Oct 1865   Burial: 8 Jun 1901
        h/o Mary Elizabeth Veirs White   TS: age 72 yrs,
Site 8 Mary White   Death: 6 Jun 1855   Burial: 8 Jun 1901
        TS: w/o of Stephen White, age 61 yrs   Reinterment
Site 9 Stephen N. White Jr.   Death: 10 Dec 1852   Burial: 8 Jun 1901
        s/o Joseph & Ann White   Reinterment   No marker
Site 10 Rachel Ann White   No marker   Burial: 8 Jun 1901
        d/o Joseph & Ann White, infant
Site 11 Elijah White   s/o Joseph & Ann White, blind
        Birth: 8 May 1863   Death: 28 Feb 1913   Burial: 2 Mar 1913
Site 12 Ann Veirs White   TS: w/o Joseph White
        Birth: 4 Mar 1827   Death: 5 Mar 1903   Burial: 8 Mar 1903
        d/o Stephen N. & Mary Elizabeth Veirs White
Site 12 Joseph White   h/o Ann White
        Birth: 11 Jan 1825   Death: 26 Feb 1903   Burial: 1 Mar 1903
Site   Ingrid Ann White   Birth: 18 Jun 1923   Death: 20 Sep 1993

Lot: 3 Owner: Mrs. C.R. Hershey
Site 2 Christian R. Hershey
        Birth: 17 May 1820   Death: 8 Oct 1905   Burial: 10 Oct 1905
Site 3 Victoria Amelia Hershey   Place: Comus
        Birth: 10 Dec 1838   Death: 7 Dec 1922   Burial: 9 Dec 1922
        Mort: W.T. Hilton & Sons   TS: w/o Christian R. Hershey

Monocacy Cemetery, Beallsville, Montgomery County, Maryland 15

Site 6 Margaret E. Hershey   Mort: E.C. Gartner   Place: Gaithersburg
        Birth: 4 Sep 1925   Death: 14 Sep 1925   Burial: 16 Sep 1925
Site 6 James Edward Hershey   Mort: W.T. Hilton & Sons   Place: Comus
        Birth: 29 Sep 1920   Death: 16 Jun 1921   Burial: 16 Jun 1921
Site 7 Miss Annie Mary Young   c/o John & Mary Catherine Schaeffer Young
        Birth: 1833   Death: 13 Feb 1896   Burial: 15 Feb 1896
Site 8 John Young Sr.   h/o Mary C. Young   Reinterment
        Birth: 1790   Death: 1862   Burial: 10 Jul 1896
Site 8 Mary Catherine Schaefer Young   w/o John Young, Sr   Reinterment
        Birth: 1802   Death: 1876   Burial: 10 Jul 1896
Site 10 Amos S. Young   Mort: W.T. Hilton & Sons   Place: Comus
        Birth: 1842   Death: 3 Jan 1915   Burial: 5 Jan 1915
        s/o John & Margaret Catherine Schaeffer Young

Lot: 4 Owner: Frederick Jones
Site 1 Frederick Jones   illegible   Place: Barnesville
        Birth: 18 Nov 1846   Death: 20 Oct 1917   Burial: 22 Oct 1917
        Mort: W.T. Hilton & Sons   h/o Nettie L. Jones
Site 2 Nettie L. Jones   illegible   TS: w/o Frederick Jones
        Birth: 9 Nov 1848   Death: 26 Dec 1899   Burial: 28 Dec 1899
Site 3 Fannie Jones Elgin   Place: Paeonian Springs, VA
        Birth: 24 Oct 1876   Death: 29 Jun 1951   Burial: 1 Jul 1951
        Mort: Lloyd Slack   TS: w/o Charles William Elgin
Site 4 Charles William Elgin   Place: Poolesville
        Birth: 30 Sep 1867   Death: 28 Oct 1934   Burial: 30 Oct 1934
        Mort: Hilton & Hall   h/o Fannie Jones Elgin
Site 7 Arthur L. Jones   Place: Poolesville
        Birth: 24 Feb 1873   Death: 26 Jul 1930   Burial: 28 Jul 1930
        Mort: Hilton & Hall   h/o Bettie L. Jones
Site 8 Bettie L. Jones   Place: Barnesville
        Birth: 3 Mar 1880   Death: 22 Jan 1920   Burial: 24 Jan 1920
        Mort: W.T. Hilton & Sons   TS: w/o Arthur L. Jones
Site 8 Infant Jones   No marker   Mort: W.T. Hilton & Sons
        Place: Barnesville   Death: 22 Jan 1920   Burial: 22 Jan 1920
        i/o Arthur L. & Bettie L. Jones
Site 9 Nettie Lee Jones Burroughs Place: Baltimore   Mort: W.B. Hilton
        Birth: 17 Jun 1907   Death: 27 Nov 1940   Burial: 30 Nov 1940
        d/o Arthur & Bettie L. Jones   TS: w/o Leonard Burroughs

Lot: 5 Owner: W.W. Darby
Site 3 William W. Darby   Place: Sellman
        Birth: 9 Oct 1853   Death: 10 Dec 1932   Burial: 12 Dec 1932
        Mort: W.T. Hilton & Sons   h/o Laura Darby
Site 4 Laura Darby   Place: Sellman
        Birth: 12 Mar 1842   Death: 25 Feb 1923   Burial: 27 Feb 1923
        Mort: W.T. Hilton & Sons   w/o William W. Darby
Site 8 William Darby Pyles   h/o Elsie Wood Pyles
        Birth: 29 Jul 1916   Death: 31 Jan 1989   Burial: 3 Feb 1989

16 Monocacy Cemetery, Beallsville, Montgomery County, Maryland

Site 9 John O. Pyles
    Birth: 13 Nov 1882   Death: 27 Apr 1952   Place: Sellman
    Mort: W.B. Hilton   Burial: 30 Apr 1952
                                                       h/o Anna L. Pyles, age 69
Site 10 Anna Laura Pyles   Place: Poolesville
    Birth: 29 Sep 1884   Death: 25 Oct 1964   Burial: 27 Oct 1964
    Mort: Hilton   w/o John O. Pyles

Lot: 6 Owner: J.F. Byrne
Site 1 Sarah Frances Gochenour   d/o Gertrude B. Moler
    Birth: 2 Jul 1922   Death: 20 Jun 1977   Burial: 23 Jun 1977
Site 2 Gertrude B. Moler   Place: Washington, DC
    Birth: 1893   Death: 7 Aug 1945   Burial: 10 Aug 1945
    Mort: S.H. Hines Co.   d/o James F. & Sarah E. Byrne
Site 3 James F. Byrne   Place: Washington, DC
    Birth: 19 Aug 1858   Death: 25 Apr 1923   Burial: 28 Apr 1923
    Mort: J.W. Lee & Sons   h/o Sarah E. Byrne
Site 4 Sarah E. Byrne   Mort: S.H. Hines Co.   Place: Silver Spring
    Birth: 19 Jul 1868   Death: 15 Jun 1960   Burial: 18 Jun 1960
    On stone with James F. Byrne   d/o Leonidas Jones
Site 5 Audrey Lee Moler Milne   d/o Gertrude Byrnes Moler
    Birth: 22 Feb 1918   Death: 23 Jan 1992   Burial: 3 Feb 1992

Lot: 7 Owner: Leonidas Jones
Site 2 Joseph W. Jones   Mort: W.T. Hilton & Sons   Place: Dickerson
    Birth: 18 Dec 1853   Death: 23 Apr 1921   Burial: 26 Apr 1921
Site 3 Leonidas Jones   TS: Age 75-0-2   h/o Elizabeth Jones
    Birth: 27 Jan 1827   Death: 26 Apr 1902   Burial: 28 Apr 1902
Site 4 Elizabeth J. Jones   Place: Dickerson
    Birth: 14 Oct 1830   Death: 7 Nov 1916   Burial: 9 Nov 1916
    Mort: W.T. Hilton & Sons   TS: w/o Leonidas Jones
Site 5 William Edward Jones   No marker   Burial: 13 May 1884
    s/o Leonidas & Elizabeth Jones, age 6-7-19
Site 6 Edgar Hartley Jones   Death: 3 Apr 1862   ·   No marker
    s/o Leonidas & Elizabeth Jones, age 2-6-3
Site 9 Helen N. Jones   Place: Washington, DC
    Birth: 1855   Death: 20 Jul 1955   Burial: 23 Jul 1955
    Mort: S.H. Hines Co.   d/o Leonidas & Elizabeth Jones
Site 10 Susie E. Veihmeyer   Place: Washington, DC
    Birth: 1873   Death: 27 Dec 1946   Burial: 30 Dec 1946
    Mort: J. Wm. Lee & Son   d/o Leonidas & Elizabeth Jones
Site 11 Annie M. Henry   Mort: S.H. Hines Co.   Place: Washington, DC
    Birth: 2 Apr 1866   Death: 19 Jan 1944   Burial: 22 Jan 1944
    w/o Edwin D. Henry, d/o Leonidas & Elizabeth Jones
Site 12 Edwin D. Henry   Place: Washington, DC
    Birth: 1875   Death: 23 Oct 1927   Burial: 26 Oct 1927
    Mort: J.W. Lees Sons   h/o Annie M. Henry

Monocacy Cemetery, Beallsville, Montgomery County, Maryland   17

Lot: 8 Owner: L.A. White
Site 2 Joseph Alexander Gray   Mort: DeVal   Place: Washington, DC
         Birth: 7 Sep 1897   Death: 19 Nov 1968   Burial: 22 Nov 1968
         h/o Evelyn White Gray, s/o Joseph & Augusta Gray
Site 3 Evelyn White Gray   TS: w/o Joseph Alexander Gray
         Birth: 1 Aug 1897   Death: 19 Dec 1984   Burial: 21 Dec 1984
         d/o Lawrence A. & Annie Belt White
Site 4 Lawrence Allnutt White   Place: Dickerson
         Birth: 23 Jul 1854   Death: 16 Apr 1933   Burial: 18 Sep 1933
         Mort: Hilton & Price   h/o Annie Oliver Belt White
Site 5 Annie Oliver Belt White   Place: Dickerson
         Birth: 19 Apr 1853   Death: 6 Nov 1940   Burial: 8 Nov 1940
         Mort: W.B. Hilton   TS: w/o Laurence Allnutt White
Site 7 Rev. William B. Everett III   Place: Washington, DC
         Birth: 28 Jun 1870   Death: 14 Nov 1944   Burial: 17 Nov 1944
         Mort: C.J. Jones   h/o Annie White Everett
Site 8 Annie Duvall White Everett   TS: w/o William B. Everett
         Birth: 27 Jul 1895   Death: 3 Mar 1978   Burial: 6 Mar 1978
         d/o Laurence A. & Annie B. White
Site 9 Julia Nannette White Williams   Mort: W.E. Pumphrey   Place: Potomac
         Birth: 5 Dec 1892   Death: 1 May 1940   Burial: 4 May 1940
         d/o Laurence A. & Annie B. White   TS: w/o Arthur Williams
Site 11 Lottie E. White Jones   TS: w/o Frederick Jones   Place: Monroe, LA
         Birth: 16 Mar 1884   Death: 25 Dec 1967   Burial: 28 Dec 1967
         Mort: Speare Funeral Home   d/o Laurence A. & Annie B. White
Site 12 Frederick A. Jones   h/o Lottie White Jones   Place: Monroe, LA
         Birth: 17 Apr 1881   Death: 28 Jul 1950   Burial: 30 Jul 1950
         Mort: Hal Q. Laymon   TS: s/o Frederick & Nettie Hempstone Jones

Lot: 9 Owner: Frederick P. Hays
Site 1 Robert T. Hays   Place: Washington, DC
         Birth: 1887   Death: 18 Aug 1939   Burial: 21 Aug 1939
         Mort: S.H. Hines Co.   s/o Ida Lee & Frederick Poole Hays
Site 2 Lawrence Dade Hays   s/o Ida Lee & Frederick Poole Hays   Place: FL
         Birth: 30 Sep 1890   Death: 30 Sep 1966   Burial: 15 Oct 1966
Site 3 Kathryn White Hays   w/o Frederick Poole Hays
         Birth: 23 Oct 1896   Death: 2 Oct 1985   Burial: 7 Oct 1985
Site 4 Frederick Poole Hays   h/o Kathryn White Hays
         Birth: 31 Oct 1892   Death: 27 Apr 1983   Burial: 3 May 1983
Site 5 Mary Hays Darby   Mort: John Burns & Sons   Place: Towson
         Birth: 12 Aug 1882   Death: 27 May 1956   Burial: 29 May 1956
         w/o Reginald J. Darby, d/o Frederick P. & Ida Lee Hays
Site 6 Reginald J. Darby   Place: Washington, DC
         Birth: 1882   Death: 28 May 1941   Burial: 30 May 1941
         Mort: W.B. Hilton   h/o Mary Hays Darby
Site 7 William Reginald Hays   Place: Barnesville
         Birth: 1884   Death: 27 May 1913   Burial: 29 May 1913
         Mort: W.T. Hilton & Sons   s/o Ida Lee & Frederick Poole Hays

Monocacy Cemetery, Beallsville, Montgomery County, Maryland

Site 8 Ida Lee Hays TS: DAR Place: Barnesville
Birth: 21 Oct 1854 Death: 2 May 1946 Burial: 4 May 1946
Mort: W.B. Hilton w/o Frederick Poole Hays
Site 9 Frederick Poole Hays Place: Barnesville
Birth: 18 Mar 1846 Death: 20 Mar 1921 Burial: 23 Mar 1921
Mort: W.T. Hilton & Sons h/o Ida Lee Hays
Site 11 Frederick Leonard Hays Place: Barnesville
Birth: 1885 Death: 26 Jul 1942 Burial: 28 Jul 1942
Mort: W.B. Hilton s/o Ida Lee & Frederick Poole Hays

Lot: 10 Owner: William T. Aud
Site 1 Carrie Virginia Aud Place: Poolesville
Birth: 11 Oct 1885 Death: 14 Feb 1944 Burial: 17 Feb 1944
Mort: W.B. Hilton w/o William Lee Aud
Site 2 William Lee Aud Place: Poolesville
Birth: 25 Dec 1863 Death: 15 Oct 1957 Burial: 17 Oct 1957
Mort: Hilton h/o Carrie V. Aud
Site 4 Susan Ann Veirs Aud w/o William T. Aud
Birth: 5 Aug 1830 Death: 21 Feb 1898 Burial: 23 Feb 1898
Site 5 William Thomas Aud h/o Susan A.V. Aud
Birth: 22 May 1822 Death: 18 May 1895 Burial: 23 Feb 1898
Site 6 Annie L. Aud Turner Mort: W.R. Pumphrey Place: Rockville
Birth: 11 Mar 1868 Death: 30 Dec 1931 Burial: 3 Jan 1932
Site 10 Edgar T. Aud Place: Linganore
Birth: 8 Jan 1902 Death: 30 Jan 1939 Burial: 2 Feb 1939
Mort: W.B. Hilton h/o Ena M. Aud
Site 11 Laura T. Pugh Aud Place: Silver Spring, MD
Birth: 12 Sep 1833 Death: 15 Dec 1970 Burial: 24 Dec 1970
Mort: Warner Pumphrey w/o Seneca V. Aud
Site 12 Seneca Veirs Aud Place: Olney
Birth: 23 Dec 1866 Death: 9 Mar 1943 Burial: 12 Mar 1943
Mort: W.B. Hilton h/o Laura T. Aud

Lot: 11 Owner: D.P. Griffith
Site 5 William Thomas Griffith Place: Westmore
Birth: 1864 Death: 31 Aug 1934 Burial: 2 Sep 1934
Mort: W.R. Pumphrey s/o David Porter Griffith
Site 6 David Porter Griffith Father/o William T. Griffith
Birth: 22 Jan 1835 Death: 9 Jan 1903 Burial: 11 Jan 1903

Lot: 12 Owner: Leonard Hays
Site Frederick Sprigg Hays Jr. TS: Killed in action Place: Korea
Birth: 27 Sep 1928 Death: 22 Aug 1952 not buried in Monocacy
s/o Frederick Sprigg & Eleanor Hays, LT US Army
Site 1 Richard Shirley Hays s/o Leonard I. & Mary White Hays
no dates on stone Death: 3 Aug 1973 Burial: 6 Aug 1973
Site 2 Leonard I. Hays h/o Mary White Hays
Birth: 8 Sep 1838 Death: 20 Aug 1901 Burial: 22 Aug 1901

Site 3 Mary E. White Hays   Place: Barnesville
        Birth: 2 Oct 1867   Death: 15 Jan 1960   Burial: 18 Jan 1960
        Mort: Hilton   w/o Leonard I. Hays
Site 4 Dr. Leonard Hays   no dateson stone
        Birth: 28 Aug 1898   Death: 10 May 1982   Burial: 12 May 1982
Site 9 Frederick Sprigg Hays   No dates on stone   h/o Eleanor Hays
        Birth: 23 Jul 1893   Death: 17 Oct 1973   Burial: 20 Oct 1973
Site 10 Eleanor Ray Hays   No dates on stone   w/o J. Sprigg Hays
        Birth: 24 Nov 1899   Death: 26 Aug 1994   Burial: 29 Aug 1994

Central Avenue South

Lot: 1 Owner: J.H. Spurrier
Site 2 John H. Spurrier   Place: Walkersville
        Birth: 12 Jul 1846   Death: 8 Apr 1915   Burial: 10 Apr 1915
        Mort: Putnam & Barton   h/o Martha J. Spurrier
Site 3 Guy H. Spurrier   TS: s/o John H. & Martha J. Spurrier
        Birth: 7 Jun 1877   Death: 11 Aug 1896   Burial: 12 Aug 1896
Site 4 Martha J. Spurrier   TS: w/o John H. Spurrier
        Birth: 9 Nov 1841   Burial: 12 Jun 1896
Site 5 Willie Brunner Spurrier   TS: s/o John H. & Martha J. Spurrier
        Birth: 6 Dec 1871   Death: 14 Mar 1895   Burial: 17 Mar 1895
Site 6 Emily Hartley Rogers   Mort: W.H. Hunteman   Place: Washington, DC
        Birth: 1870   Death: 23 Nov 1945   Burial: 25 Nov 1945
Site 9 Ethel Grubb Spurrier   Place: Frederick
        Birth: 18 Jan 1874   Death: 17 Feb 1963   Burial: 20 Feb 1963
        Mort: Hilton   On stone with Howard Wilson Spurrier
Site 10 Howard Wilson Spurrier   Place: Frederick
        Birth: 3 Jul 1874   Death: 22 May 1956   Burial: 24 May 1956
        Mort: W.B. Hilton   h/o Ethel Grubb Spurrier
Site 11 Addie May Spurrier Reddick   Place: Poolesville
        Birth: 29 May 1869   Death: 28 Mar 1961   Burial: 31 Mar 1961
        Mort: Hilton   w/o George W. Reddick
Site 12 George W. Reddick   h/o Addie Spurrier Reddick
        Birth: 22 Feb 1855   Death: 16 Feb 1912   Burial: 18 Feb 1912

Lot: 2 Owner: I.A. Devilbiss
Site   Donald E. Hubble   Mort: W.B. Hilton
        Place: Dickerson   Death: 27 May 1943   Burial: 30 May 1943
        s/o Herman & Clara Hubble   Moved to Mt. Olivet, Frederick
Site 1 Mrs. Tracy Bussard   Birth: 22 Jul 1834   Burial: 12 Jul 1910
Site 4 Caroline Devilbiss   TS: w/o I..A. Devilbiss
        Birth: 5 Jul 1826   Death: 24 May 1896

Monocacy Cemetery, Beallsville, Montgomery County, Maryland

Site 5 I. A. Devilbiss
   Birth: 22 Dec 1831   Death: 4 Sep 1910   Burial: 6 Sep 1910
   h/o Caroline Devilbiss   2nd Supt. of Monocacy Cemetery

Lot: 3 Lower Owner: Marion Bassford
Site   Gladie Bassford   Burial: 12 Jun 1907   No marker
Site   Child of Marion Bassford   No marker   Burial: 14 Jun 1900
Site 3 Bessie May Wire Bassford   Place: Baltimore Co.
   Birth: 23 Mar 1873   Death: 25 Sep 1965   Burial: 28 Sep 1965
   Mort: Takoma Funeral Home   On stone with Marion Isaac Bassford
Site 4 Marion Isaac Bassford   Place: Takoma Park
   Birth: 15 Apr 1868   Death: 8 Apr 1957   Burial: 10 Apr 1957
   Mort: J.Arthur Walters   h/o Bessie Wire Bassford

Lot: 3 Upper Owner: William H. Rollison
Site   Twin of Ambrey Lewis Ball   No marker   Mort: Hilton & Hall
   Place: Poolesville   Death: 14 Jul 1923   Burial: 16 Jul 1923
Site   Twin of Ambrey Lewis Ball   No marker   Mort: Hilton & Hall
   Place: Leesburg, VA   Death: 28 Jul 1923   Burial: 30 Jul 1923
Site 1 John Carter Rollison   No marker   Mort: Hilton & Hall
   Place: Poolesville   Death: 25 Mar 1930   Burial: 27 Mar 1930
Site 2 Audrey Marie Rollison   No marker   Mort: Hilton & Hall
   Place: Ashburn, VA   Death: 12 Jan 1929   Burial: 13 Jan 1929
Site 3 Laura Bell Rollison   Place: Charlottsville, VA
   Birth: 1894   Death: 6 Jul 1943   Burial: 8 Jul 1943
   Mort: Slack Funeral Home   On stone with Charles Edward Rollison
Site 4 Charles Edward Rollison   Place: Leesburg, VA
   Birth: 1885   Death: 27 Jun 1936   Burial: 29 Jun 1936
   Mort: W.B. Hilton   h/o Laura Bell Rollison
Site 5 Harriet Rollison   On stone with William H. Rollison
   Birth: 1838   Death: 1911   Burial: 15 Mar 1911
Site 6 William H. Rollison   h/o Harriet Rollison
   Birth: 6 Jun 1836   Death: 23 Dec 1900   Burial: 25 Dec 1900

Lot: 3A Owner: Miscellaneous
Site 1   James Buchanan Hickman   Birth: 16 Jan 1857   Death: 9 Feb 1912
Site 3   Ethel Gray   Mort: Hilton & Hall   Place: Frederick Hospital
   Birth: 1890   Death: 5 Mar 1924   Burial: 8 Mar 1924
Site 5   James A. Cornwell   Mort: Hilton & Hall   Place: Edwards Ferry
   Birth: 1835   Death: 13 Sep 1915   Burial: 15 Sep 1915
Site 6   Alfred T. Lucas   TS: Age 1-3-0   Mort: Hilton & Hall
   Place: Poolesville   Death: 4 Apr 1915   Burial: 5 Apr 1915
   TS: s/o Charles & Mary Lucas   No marker
Site 6   Infant of Charles & Mary Lucas   Mort: Hilton & Hall
   Place: Poolesville   Death: 28 Feb 1916   Burial: 29 Feb 1916
Site 6   John Scrimeger   Burial: 7 Nov 1830   Age 23 yrs
Site 10 Jesse McRoberts   Mort: Hunteman   Place: Washington, DC
   Birth: 1893   Death: 30 May 1947   Burial: 2 Jun 1947

Monocacy Cemetery, Beallsville, Montgomery County, Maryland   21

Lot: 4   Owner: Thomas C. Darby
Site 1   Infant Darby   TS: s/o T.C. & Estelle Darby   No dates on stone
                                                                  Burial: 17 Jun 1900
Site 2   Mary Elizabeth Darby   d/o Thomas C. & Estelle Allnutt Darby
         Birth: 25 Aug 1902   Death: 21 Jan 1992   Burial: 24 Jan 1992
Site 3   Estelle Allnutt Darby   Place: Dawsonville
         Birth: 4 Nov 1868   Death: 13 Jul 1941   Burial: 15 Jul 1941
         Mort: W.B. Hilton   w/o Thomas Chiswell Darby
Site 4   Thomas Chiswell Darby   Place: Germantown
         Birth: 8 Jul 1866   Death: 15 Oct 1952   Burial: 18 Oct 1952
         Mort: W.B. Hilton   h/o Estelle A. Darby, age 86
Site 5   Valeria W. Darby   d/o Thomas C. & Estelle A. Darby
         Birth: 9 Jan 1898   Death: 25 Oct 1976   Burial: 27 Oct 1976
Site 6   Margaret Eleanor Darby   d/o Thomas C. & Estelle A. Darby
         Birth: 19 Nov 1904   Death: 3 Jul 1991   Burial: 5 Jul 1991
Site 7   Estelle Allnutt Darby   d/o Thomas C. Darby
         Birth: 3 Apr 1908   Death: 28 Jun 1992   Burial: 2 Jul 1992
Site 9   Garnett Cawood Ball   h/o Sarah Darby
         Birth: 3 Nov 1912   Death: 2 Sep 1981   Burial: 5 Sep 1981

Lot: 5   Owner: Richard Bowman
Site   Ruth Gue Bowman   TS: w/o Rezin Bowman   Reinterment 1901
         Birth: 15 Aug 1780   Death: 16 Sep 1873   Burial: 11 Jan 1901
Site 1   John H. Bowman   TS: Age 61 yrs   brother/o Martha Ellen Bowman
         Birth: 17 Dec 1837   Death: 16 Sep 1896   Burial: 8 Sep 1897
Site 2   Martha Ellen Bowman   No marker   sister/o John H. Bowman
         Birth: 19 Oct 1850   Death: 29 Apr 1896   Burial: 1 May 1896
Site 7   Ruth R. Darby Bowman   w/o Frederick Bowman   Reinterment
         Birth: 10 Aug 1810   Death: 1 Jun 1860   Burial: 11 Jan 1901
Site 8   Frederick Bowman   h/o Ruth R. Darby Bowman
         Birth: 7 Jan 1810   Death: 4 Dec 1900   Burial: 6 Dec 1900
Site 9   Benjamin Franklin Bowman   Place: Gaithersburg
         Birth: 1 Apr 1839   Death: 9 Feb 1923   Burial: 11 Feb 1923
         Mort: Geo M. Gartner   TS: Age 84 yrs
Site 10 Mary Elizabeth Bowman   No marker   Mort: Hilton & Hall
         Place: Poolesville   Death: 29 Jan 1924   Burial: 31 Jan 1924

Lot: 5A Owner: Unknown
Site 4   Edgar Ernest Gregg
         Birth: 23 Nov 1898   Death: 6 Jun 1988   Burial: 8 Jun 1988
Site   Evaline Duvall Gregg   Place: Bethesda, MD   Mort: Francis Barber
         Birth: 10 Apr 1890   Death: 26 Jun 1971   Burial: 29 Jun 1971

Lot: 5A Lower   Owner: Miscellaneous
Site 1   William D. Duvall   TS: Age 49-6-12
         Birth: 7 Feb 1852   Death: 10 Aug 1901   Burial: 14 Apr 1906
         h/o Malinda E. Duvall   Removed to Monocacy from Old Ground

Monocacy Cemetery, Beallsville, Montgomery County, Maryland

Site 2 Malinda Eliza Duvall Place: Dickerson
 Birth: 21 Mar 1853 Death: 28 Apr 1932 Burial: 30 Apr 1932
 Mort: W.T. Hilton & Sons TS: w/o William D. Duvall
Site 3 Richard H. Gray Mort: W.T. Hilton & Sons Place: Beallsville
 Birth: 1848 Death: 14 Mar 1918 Burial: 17 Mar 1918
Site 4 Mary C. Gray Place: Darnestown
 Birth: 1844 Death: 12 Jan 1936 Burial: 14 Jan 1936
 Mort: Warner E. Pumphrey TS: w/o Richard H. Gray
Site 5 Thomas Peyton Collier Mort: W.T. Hilton & Sons Place: Harpers Ferry
 Birth: 23 Feb 1858 Death: 19 Feb 1922 Burial: 21 Feb 1922
Site 6 Martha Virginia Collier No marker Mort: W.R. Pumphrey
 Place: Washington, DC Death: 23 Sep 1930 Burial: 25 Sep 1930

Lot: 5A Upper Owner: Carter
Site 1 Elsbey Carter Burial: 6 Sep 1907 TS: Age 27-11-10
Site 2 Jane E. Carter Place: Darnestown
 Birth: 3 Jun 1859 Death: 23 Jun 1926 Burial: 26 Jun 1926
 Mort: W.T. Hilton & Sons TS: w/o James A. Carter
Site 3 James A. Carter Place: Darnestown
 Birth: 25 Jan 1859 Death: 29 Mar 1933 Burial: 1 Apr 1933
 Mort: R.W. Pumphrey h/o Jane E. Carter
Site 4 Rebecca M. Hall Mrs. Cine Hall On stone with L.C. Hall
 Birth: 1841 Death: 1908 Burial: 16 Jan 1908
Site 5 L. C. (Quintis) Hall h/o Rebecca M. Hall
 Birth: 1841 Death: 1910 Burial: 2 Oct 1910
Site 6 Mrs. Harriet Vinson Death: 10 Sep 1850 TS: w/o John T. Vinson
 TS: Age 38 yrs, died at her residence, Montgomery Co., MD
Site 6 Henry Clay Mason TS: 49th Inf. VA CSA
 Birth: 1840 Death: 1911 Burial: 13 Aug 1911

Lot: 5B Lower Owner: Miscellaneous
Site 1 Dorothy J. Belcher Place: Dickerson
 Birth: 3 Apr 1928 Death: 18 Jul 1928 Burial: 18 Jul 1928
 Mort: W.T. Hilton & Sons TS: d/o H.F. & D.L. Belcher
Site 6 Donald Lee Belcher Place: Dickerson
 Birth: 21 Feb 1933 Death: 29 Apr 1935 Burial: 30 Apr 1935
 Mort: Hilton & Price TS: s/o J.W. & M.B. Belcher

Lot: 5B Upper Owner: Miscellaneous
Site 1 John W. Anderson Mort: W.B. Hilton Place: Washington, DC
 Birth: 16 Dec 1939 Death: 7 Aug 1940 Burial: 8 Aug 1940
Site 2 Infant Daughter Belcher TS: d/o H.F. & D.L. Belcher Mort: Hilton & Hall
 Place: Poolesville Birth: 26 Aug 1924 Death: 27 Aug 1924
Site 3 Infant Shry Place: Barnesville
 Birth: 9 Nov 1915 Death: 9 Nov 1915 Burial: 10 Nov 1915
 Mort: W.T. Hilton & Sons TS: d/o Sydney W. & Laura I. Shry

Monocacy Cemetery, Beallsville, Montgomery County, Maryland   23

Lot: 6   Owner: Mrs. George W. Leapley
Site   George Edward Leapley   No marker   Mort: M.R. Etchison &
          Place: Frederick   Death: 14 Jan 1945   Burial: 16 Jan 1945
Site   2 daughters of George W. Leapley   No marker Burial: 13 Jun 1898
Site   Margaret Leapley   No marker   Mort: Hilton & Hall
          Place: Washington, DC   Death: 9 May 1914   Burial: 13 May 1914
Site 9   George W. Leapley   TS: Age 57 yrs
                                   Death: 28 Nov 1894   Burial: 1 Dec 1894

Lot: 6A   Owner: Miscellaneous
Site   Infant of W.S. & M.S. Swank   No marker   Mort: Hilton & Hall
          Place: Poolesville   Death: 1 Feb 1916   Burial: 1 Feb 1916
Site 1   Ruth Gue   Death: 15 Aug 1780   Age 93-1-1
          No marker
Site 1   Rufus W. Stevens   Place: Gaithersburg
          Birth: 10 May 1849   Death: 17 Nov 1928   Burial: 19 Nov 1928
          Mort: E.C. Gartner   h/o Mary E. Stevens
Site 2   Mary E. Stevens   Place: Gaithersburg
          Birth: 8 Mar 1846   Death: 28 Apr 1922   Burial: 30 May 1922
          Mort: W.T. Hilton & Sons   On stone with Rufus W. Stevens
Site 5   Infant Gilliam   TS: s/o L.C. & L.G. Gilliam Mort: Hilton & Hall
          Place: Poolesville   Death: 27 Jan 1921   Burial: 28 Jan 1921
Site 6   Robert Davis   TS: Age 1-6-12   Mort: W.T. Hilton & Sons
          Place: Sellman   Death: 25 Feb 1918   Burial: 26 Feb 1918
Site 7   Agnus T. Manuel   Death: 3 Jul 1909   Burial: 5 Jul 1909
          TS: d/o Harry & Carrie T. Manuel, age 2 weeks
Site 8   Jane Plater Williams
          Birth: 17 Mar 1799   Death: 9 May 1881   Burial: 9 May 1881
          w/o Snowden Pleasants, formerly Mrs. Elisha Williams
Site 9   James S. Pleasants   Burial: 6 Oct 1863   TS: In his 46th yr
Site 10   Elisha Williams   h/o Jane Plater Williams, age 76 yrs
          illegible   Burial: 1 Sep 1851
Site 11   Sarah Ann Gumaer   w/o Elias Gumaer, age 25 yrs
          No marker   Burial: 14 Oct 1842
Site 12   Mrs. Ann Vinson   Death: 4 May 1862   Age 73 yrs
Site 12   Mrs. Mary Vinson   Death: 11 Nov 1861   Age 75 yrs
Site 12   Florence Ray Williams   Death: 9 Jul 1867
          d/o Elisha & Jane Plater Williams, age 14 yrs No marker

Lot: 7   Owner: Mrs. J.E. Pyles
Site   Miss Catherine Beall   Burial: 24 Aug 1897   No marker
Site 1   Benjamin T. Poole   Place: Poolesville
          Birth: 8 Jan 1850   Death: 4 Mar 1926   Burial: 10 Mar 1927
          Mort: Hilton & Hall   h/o Mary Cooley Poole
Site 1   Mary Cooley Poole   w/o Benjamin T. Poole No marker
Site 3   Ruth E. Pyles   TS: w/o William F. Pyles, age 80-5-10
          Birth: 12 Dec 1825   Death: 12 May 1906   Burial: 14 May 1906

Site 4 William Francis Pyles   TS: age 82-11-29   h/o Ruth E. Pyles
       Birth: 17 Feb 1818   Death: 16 Feb 1901   Burial: 18 Feb 1901
Site 5 Miss Catherine Beall Pyles   d/o W.F. & R.E. Pyles
       Birth: 11 Oct 1866   Death: 5 Jul 1902   Burial: 8 Jul 1902
Site 6 George Willard Hobbs   Place: Washington, DC
       Birth: 1856   Death: 5 May 1921   Burial: 8 May 1921
       Mort: Hilton & Hall   h/o Margaret Emma Hobbs
Site 6 Margaret Emma Hobbs   Place: Washington, DC
       Birth: 1851   Death: 18 May 1914   Burial: 22 May 1914
       Mort: Hilton & Hall   TS: w/o George Willard Hobbs
Site 7 Annie E. Pyles   Cause: Stillborn   d/o J.E. & Ruth O. Pyles
       illegible   Burial: 7 Jul 1896
Site 7 Enon Kenneth Pyles   s/o J. E. & R.O. Pyles, age 5 yrs 6 mo
       illegible   Death: 10 Sep 1895   Burial: 12 Sep 1895
Site 9 Ruth Olive Roberts Pyles   Place: Hyattsville
       Birth: 6 Jul 1869   Death: 30 Jun 1963   Burial: 3 Jul 1963
       Mort: Lee Funeral Home   w/o James E. Pyles
Site 10 James E. Pyles   Place: Washington, DC
       Birth: 24 Aug 1849   Death: 3 Mar 1923   Burial: 5 Mar 1923
       Mort: Hilton & Hall   h/o Ruth Olive Pyles

Lot: 7A Lower   Owner: Miscellaneous
Site 1 Infant of Arthur Michael   No marker   Mort: W.T. Hilton & Sons
       Place: Washington, DC   Death: 29 Jun 1925   Burial: 1 Jul 1925
Site 1 Dorothy How Michael   No marker   Mort: W.T. Hilton & Sons
       Place: Washington, DC   Death: 12 Aug 1925   Burial: 13 Aug 1925
Site 2 Mrs. Mary Hilleary   Death: 20 Jun 1816
       w/o Capt. Clement T. Hilleary, age 32 yrs
Site 3 Robert H. Blevins   Mort: W.B. Hilton   Place: Germantown
       Birth: 1890   Death: 7 Jun 1946   Burial: 10 Jun 1946
Site 4 Sofronia E. Waddle   Place: Poolesville
       Birth: 1856   Death: 20 Feb 1929   Burial: 21 Feb 1929
       Mort: Hilton & Hall   On stone with Robert H. Blevins
Site 5 Carrie Shumaker
       Birth: 20 Feb 1889   Death: 23 Apr 1909   Burial: 3 Sep 1926
       TS: w/o W.S. Shoemaker   Removed from Mt. Pleasant
Site 6 Soper Hines   Mort: Hilton & Hall   Place: Poolesville
       Birth: 1860   Death: 7 Jul 1926   Burial: 9 Jul 1926

Lot: 7A Upper   Owner: Miscellaneous
Site 6 Bettie Lou Kitts   Mort: W.B. Hilton
       Place: Poolesville   Death: 9 Dec 1940   Burial: 10 Dec 1940
       i/o Vaden & Lulu Whisman Kitts   No marker
Site 6 Doris Elizabeth Kitts   Mort: W.B. Hilton
       Place: Poolesville   Death: 6 Feb 1944   Burial: 7 Feb 1944
       i/o Vaden & Lulu Whisman Kitts   No marker

Monocacy Cemetery, Beallsville, Montgomery County, Maryland

Lot: 8 Lower Owner: Dr. S.N.C. White
Site 1 Martin T. Fisher   Reinterment
        Birth: 6 May 1833   Death: 30 Mar 1890   Burial: 1 Apr 1903
Site 2 Arthur White   TS: s/o Dr. S.N.C. & Elizabeth White
        Birth: 18 Nov 1811   Death: 6 Feb 1847
Site 3 Elizabeth C. White   2nd w/o Dr. Stephen N.C. White Reinterment
        Birth: 21 Mar 1816   Death: 28 Dec 1884   Burial: 3 May 1905
Site 4 Dr. Stephen Newton Chiswell White   h/o Elizabeth C. White
        Birth: 29 Oct 1800   Death: 11 Mar 1860   Burial: 3 May 1905
Site 5 Annie Belt Trundle White
        Birth: 3 Feb 1805   Death: 10 Jun 1835   Burial: 31 Jan 1906
        1st w/o Stephen Newton Chiswell White   Reinterment

Lot: 8 Upper Owner: Dr. S.N.C. White
Site 1 Child of Mary E. Belt   Burial: 26 Mar 1877
        d/o J.R. & Mary B. Belt   illegible
Site 2 Virginia Lee Belt   Mort: W.T. Hilton   Place: Washington, DC
        Birth: 21 Jun 1866   Death: 16 Jan 1914   Burial: 19 Jan 1914
Site 3 Mary Barbara Belt   Place: Washington, DC
        Birth: 2 Aug 1832   Death: 8 Mar 1917   Burial: 11 Mar 1917
        Mort: W.T. Hilton & Sons   w/o John R. Belt
Site 4 John Richard Belt   h/o Mary Barbara Belt
        Birth: 14 Feb 1816   Death: 16 Jun 1884   Burial: 18 Jun 1884

Lot: 8A Owner: Johnson
Site 1 Sarah Ann Johnson   Death: 31 Aug 1856
        w/o William I. Johnson, age 62-8-11
Site 2 William I. Johnson   h/o Sarah Ann Johnson
        Birth: 17 Feb 1848   Death: 18 Jul 1861

Row A

Lot: 1 Owner: Arthur Fletchall

Site 1 Judge Charles W. Woodward
Birth: 21 Feb 1895   Death: 16 May 1969
Mort: Tyson Wheeler
Place: Bethesda, MD
Burial: 19 May 1969
h/o Clarine Fletchall Woodward

Site 2 Clarine Fletchall Woodward
Birth: 13 Mar 1891   Death: 22 Dec 1978
TS: w/o Judge Charles W. Woodward
Burial: 26 Dec 1978

Site 3 Annette Rose Fletchall
Birth: 18 Jul 1900   Death: 26 Aug 1966
w/o John Fletchal
Burial: 29 Aug 1966

Site 4 John T. Fletchall   Birth: 1896   Death: 12 Jan 1981

Site 8 Bertha Estelle Fletchall
Birth: 1893   Death: 3 Jan 1963
Mort: Hilton
Place: Rockville
Burial: 5 Jan 1963
d/o Arthur P. & Lulu Fletchall

Site 9 Lulu Hall Fletchall
Birth: 1862   Death: 21 Dec 1941
Mort: W.B. Hilton
Place: Rockville
Burial: 23 Dec 1941
w/o Arthur Poole Fletchal

Site 10 Arthur Poole Fletchall
Birth: 13 May 1857   Death: 18 Jan 1936
Mort: Hilton & Hall
Place: Poolesville
Burial: 20 Jan 1936
h/o Lulu Hall Fletchall

Site 11 Genevieve Fletchall
Death: 1890
id/o Lulu & Arthur Fletchall
Burial: 7 Mar 1890

Site 11 Lulu Fletchall   Death: 1886
id/o Lulu Hall & Arthur Poole Fletchall

Lot: 2 Owner: Hugh Anderson

Site   Jessie I. Anderson   No marker   Mort: S.H. Hines Co.
Place: Washington, DC   Death: 31 Dec 1932   Burial: 3 Jan 1933

Site 1   Elizabeth E. Anderson   Death: 11 Mar 1896   Burial: 13 Mar 1896
TS: w/o Hugh Anderson, age 45-10-10

Site 2   Daisy Irene Anderson   Death: 28 Mar 1898   Burial: 30 Mar 1898
TS: d/o Elizabeth E. & Hugh Anderson, age 19-2-8

Site 3   Hugh Anderson   illegible   Place: College Park
Birth: 22 Jun 1848   Death: 15 Feb 1933   Burial: 18 Feb 1933
Mort: F. Gasch Sons   h/o Elizabeth E. Anderson

Site 5   Claude Anderson   No marker   Mort: Gasch
Place: Cheverly, MD   Death: 30 Mar 1957   Burial: 2 Apr 1957

Lot: 2 1/2 Owner: Mrs. Mollie Mobley

Site 1 Nina R. Davis   No marker   Mort: W.W. Chambers
Place: Baltimore   Death: 23 May 1935   Burial: 25 May 1935
d/o Howard S. & Mollie E. Mobley

Site 2 Howard S. Mobley
Death: 6 Dec 1896
h/o Mollie E. Mobley
TS: age 40-5-16

Site 3 Mollie E. Mobley
Place: Washington, DC   Death: 6 Oct 1920
Mort: W.W. Chambers
Burial: 8 Oct 1920
TS: w/o Howard S. Mobley, age 58-10-0

Monocacy Cemetery, Beallsville, Montgomery County, Maryland 27

Site 4 Howard Victor Mobley Place: Washington, DC
  Birth: 22 Nov 1894 Death: 29 Jun 1956 Burial: 3 Jul 1956
  Mort: W.W. Chambers TS: Dist. of Col. S2 USNRF WWI

Lot: 3 Owner: Mrs. B.A. Allnutt
Site Barbara Ann Allnutt Death: 27 Feb 1876 Burial: 9 Feb 1876
  TS: Wife of James N. Allnutt, age 64
Site James N. Allnutt Death: 1 Jun 1854 TS: age 63 yrs
  h/o Barbara Ann Allnutt
Site 3 Henrietta Dawson Death: 31 Mar 1855 TS: In her 76th yr.
Site 4 Rebecca Dawson Birth: 15 Jan 1820 Death: 14 Apr 1824
  TS: d/o Robert Doyne & Henrietta Dawson, age 4-2-20
Site 5 Henrietta Dawson Birth: 24 Mar 1818 Death: 17 Mar 1837
  TS: d/o Robert Doyne & Henrietta Dawson, age 18-11-24
Site 7 Elizabeth Allnutt Burial: 16 Aug 1872 TS: Age 84-0-9

Lot: 4 Owner: Mrs. B.A. Allnutt
Site 3 Minerva Henrietta Allnutt Death: 21 Dec 1836 Burial: 24 Dec 1836
  TS: d/o James N. & Bettie Ann Allnutt, age 0-9-15
Site 4 Elizabeth Virginia Allnutt   Burial: 18 Mar 1841
  d/o James N. & Bettie Ann Allnutt, age 0-1-5 No marker
Site 4 James Robert Allnutt Death: 27 Mar 1841
  TS: s/o James N. & Bettie Ann Allnutt, aged 2-8-8
Site 5 Juliana Virlinder Allnutt   Died: 12 Jun 1844
  TS: d/o James N. & Bettie Ann Allnutt, age 1-3-19
Site 11 Robert Henry Clay Allnutt Place: Dawsonville Mort: Hilton & Hall
  Birth: 10 Feb 1848 Death: 23 Nov 1922 Burial: 24 Nov 1922
Site 12 James N. Allnutt Mort: Hilton & Hall Place: Poolesville
  Birth: 12 Jun 1846 Death: 23 Jul 1920 Burial: 25 Jul 1920

Lot: 5 Owner: Phillip Mossburg
Site 1 Lela Marie Mossburg   2nd w/o Claude Mossburg
  Birth: 29 Jun 1895 Death: 7 Feb 1974 Burial: 11 Feb 1974
Site 1 Lois Reynolds No marker Burial: 18 Feb 1988
  Sister/o Lela M. Mossburg
Site 2 Jesse K. Mossburg Mort: Hilton Place: Washington, DC
  Birth: 1886 Death: 30 Dec 1959 Burial: 31 Dec 1959
Site 3 Raymond H. Mossburg   illegible
  Birth: 14 Mar 1894 Death: 21 Aug 1894 Burial: 22 Aug 1894
  TS: s/o Phillip F. & Annie M. Mossburg, age 0-5-7
Site 4 Phillip F. Mossburg   Place: Poolesville
  Birth: 1852 Death: 24 Feb 1922 Burial: 26 Feb 1922
  Mort: Hilton & Hall   h/o Annie M. Mossburg
Site 5 Annie Mary Mossburg   Place: Poolesville
  Birth: 28 Mar 1852 Death: 22 Nov 1939 Burial: 24 Nov 1939
  Mort: Hilton & Hall   TS: w/o Phillip F. Mossburg
Site 7 Claude Eugene Mossburg No marker Place: Bethesda
  Birth: 6 Nov 1875 Death: 22 Nov 1964 Burial: 24 Nov 1964
  Mort: Robert A. Pumphrey   h/o Agnes & Lelia M. Mossburg

Site 8 Agnes B. Mossburg   Place: Washington, DC
        Birth: 1891   Death: 2 May 1923   Burial: 4 May 1923
        Mort: S.H. Hines Co.   TS: [1ˢᵗ] w/o Claude M. Mossburg
Site 9 Martin Irenius Wise   Place: Gaithersburg   Mort: Hilton
        Birth: 11 May 1890   Death: 28 Oct 1962   Burial: 30 Oct 1962
Site 10 Anna Genevieve Wise   On stone with Martin I. Wise
        Birth: 31 Dec 1895   Death: 15 Sep 1980   Burial: 17 Sep 1980

Lot: 6 Owner: Isaac N. Staub
Site 1 Newton Staub   Death: 19 Dec 1894   Burial: 20 Dec 1894
        s/o Isaac & Mary A. Staub
Site 3 Mary Ann Staub   Place: Beallsville
        Birth: 24 Dec 1860   Death: 27 Aug 1940   Burial: 29 Aug 1940
        Mort: W.B. Hilton   w/o Isaac Newton Staub
Site 4 Isaac Newton Staub   Place: Sykesville
        Birth: 27 Sep 1855   Death: 23 Jun 1924   Burial: 26 Jun 1924
        Mort: W.T. Hilton & Sons   h/o Mary Ann Staub
Site 5 William E. Staub   Place: Washington, DC
        Birth: 30 Nov 1882   Death: 6 Dec 1955   Burial: 9 Dec 1955
        Mort: W.B. Hilton   w/o Mary Ann & Isaac Staub
Site 10 George A. Staub   Place: Frederick Hospital
        Birth: 5 Aug 1880   Death: 7 Sep 1944   Burial: 9 Sep 1944
        Mort: W.B. Hilton   h/o Jennie Butler Staub
Site 11 Jennie C. Staub Kimberling   w/o George A. Staub & John Kimmerling
        Birth: 30 Aug 1899   Death: 7 Feb 1977   Burial: 14 Feb 1977

Lot: 7 Owner: John R. Hall
Site   Child of Mr. John R. Hall No marker   Burial: 17 Oct 1877
Site 1 Annie Hall   illegible   d/o John R. & Sarah C. Hall
        Birth: 28 Oct 1872   Death: 5 Apr 1873   Burial: 6 Apr 1873
Site 2 Luther Hall   illegible   s/o John R. & Sarah C. Hall
        Birth: 6 Apr 1871   Burial: 23 Jul 1871
Site 3 Sallie Hall   illegible
Site 4 Minnie Hall   illegible
Site 5 Sarah C. Hall   w/o John R. Hall
        Birth: 21 May 1840   Death: 13 Mar 1886
Site 6 John R. Hall   TS: Age 18-2-10   h/o Sarah C. Hall
        Birth: 29 Mar 1832   Death: 9 Jun 1880   Burial: 17 Jun 1880
Site 7 Margaret Rebecca Hall   illegible   d/o Julius & Margaret Dutrow Hall
        Birth: 24 Apr 1909   Death: 6 Jun 1912   Burial: 8 Jun 1912
Site 8 John R. Hall   s/o Julius & Margaret D. Hall, age 74 yrs
        Birth: 1911   Death: 30 Sep 1985   Burial: 2 Oct 1985
Site 8 Margaret M. Dutrow Hall   Place: Germantown
        Birth: 1876   Death: 1 Jan 1957   Burial: 4 Jan 1957
        Mort: Hilton   On stone with Julius R. Hall
Site 9 Julius Hall   Place: Poolesville
        Birth: 1870   Death: 16 Feb 1947   Burial: 18 Feb 1947
        Mort: W.B. Hilton   h/o Margaret Dutrow Hall

Monocacy Cemetery, Beallsville, Montgomery County, Maryland

Site 10	Catherine A. Hall Winder		
	Birth: 1906	Death: 28 Feb 1973	Burial: 12 Mar 1973
	d/o Julius & Margaret Hall		TS: w/o Edward R. Winder
Site 10	Edward R. Winder	Birth: 1901	Death: 1994
	h/o Catherine A. Hall Winder		
Site 11	Dora C. Hall	Mort: W.B. Hilton	Place: Poolesville
	Birth: 1871	Death: 10 Jun 1949	Burial: 12 Jun 1949
	On stone with Rebecca Hall		sister/o Julius Hall
Site 12	Rebecca Hall	Mort: W.B. Hilton	Place: Poolesville
	Birth: 1869	Death: 30 Sep 1945	Burial: 2 Oct 1945
	On stone with Dora C. Hall		sister/o Julius Hall

Lot: 8 Owner: Thomas R. Hall

Site	Stephen Williams	Burial: 14 Dec 1889	Child No marker
Site 1	Minnie E. Hall	Death: 10 Oct 1863	
	d/o Thomas R. & Clarinda Beecher Hall		TS: Age 2-8-0
Site 2	Abigail Hall	Death: 12 Sep 1869	
	d/o Thomas R. & Clarinda Beecher Hall		TS: Age 2-1-0
Site 3	Clarinda Beecher Hall		Place: Poolesville
	Birth: 11 Dec 1842	Death: 21 Apr 1914	Burial: 23 Apr 1914
	Mort: Hilton & Hall		TS: w/o Thomas Randolph Hall
Site 4	Thomas Randolph Hall	Death: 18 Oct 1884	Burial: 19 Oct 1884
	h/o Clarinda Beecher Hall		TS: Age 55-11-12
Site 5	Sarah R. Hall Hardcastle		Place: Pitts Co., VA
	Birth: 1866	Death: 9 Aug 1932	Burial: 11 Aug 1932
	Mort: Hilton & Hall		w/o Edmund L. Hardcastle
Site 6	Edmund L. Hardcastle		Place: Richmond, VA
	Birth: 1867	Death: 2 Mar 1936	Burial: 4 Mar 1936
	Mort: A.W. Bennett & Co.		h/o Sarah R. Hardcastle
Site 8	Richard Owens	Death: 8 Dec 1907	
	c/o Preacher Owens		s/o Richard S. & E.H. Owens
Site 9	Annie Owens	Death: 8 Dec 1907	
	c/o Preacher Owens		TS: s[sic]/o Richard S. & E.H. Owens

Lot: 9 Owner: Benjamin White (Son of Stephen)

Site	Infant of G.M. & Sarah Louise		Burial: 5 Nov 1908
	Cause: Stillborn		No marker
Site	Child White	No marker	Burial: 8 Mar 1906
	Cause: Stillborn		c/o Harvey J. & Ida D. White
Site 1	Flora Darnell White		illegible
	Birth: 18 Feb 1872	Death: 19 Aug 1872	Burial: 1876
	d/o Benjamin & Sarah E. White		Reinterment
Site 2	Lutie White		d/o Benjamin & Sarah E. White
	Birth: 19 Aug 1874	Death: 2 Jul 1876	illegible
Site 3	Marshall White		TS: s/o Benjamin & Sarah E. White
	Birth: 8 Mar 1877	Death: 29 Jan 1879	
Site 4	Anna Dade White		d/o Benjamin (of Stephen) & Sarah E. White
	Birth: 10 May 1873	Death: 28 Jan 1879	Burial: 30 Jan 1879

30   Monocacy Cemetery, Beallsville, Montgomery County, Maryland

Site 5 Infant White i/o Benjamin & Sarah Elizabeth Jones White
 illegible Death: 8 Dec 1879
Site 6 John Russell White TS: s/o Benjamin & Sarah E. White
 Birth: 12 Mar 1883 Death: 30 Mar 1884 Burial: 1 Apr 1884
Site 7 Sarah Elizabeth Jones White TS: w/o Benjamin White
 Birth: 16 Feb 1841 Death: 24 Jun 1894 Burial: 26 Jun 1894
Site 8 Benjamin White h/o Sarah Elizabeth Jones White
 Birth: 3 Oct 1825 Death: 16 Feb 1907 Burial: 19 Feb 1907
Site 11 Miss Mary E. White TS: d/o Stephen & Mary White
 Reinterment Death: 22 Feb 1839 Burial: 7 Jun 1901
Site 12 William Turner Veirs
 Birth: 6 Feb 1796 Death: 1886 Burial: 7 Jun 1901

Lot: 10   Owner: Emily W. Hall
Site 1 Infant of William J. Williams Death: 28 Nov 1902
Site 2 Mary V. Williams d/o W.J. & Elizabeth Williams
 Birth: 7 Dec 1889 Death: 1891 Burial: 17 Mar 1891
Site 3 Elizabeth Adell Schaeffer Williams w/o William J. Williams
 Birth: 1861 Death: 1892 Burial: 26 Oct 1892
Site 4 William J. Williams Place: Poolesville
 Birth: 30 Dec 1854 Death: 21 Jul 1924 Burial: 23 Jul 1924
 Mort: Hilton & Hall h/o Elizabeth A. Williams
Site 5 Mary Virginia Schaeffer Williams Place: Littletown, PA
 Birth: 17 Oct 1863 Death: 6 Apr 1939 Burial: 8 Apr 1939
 1st w/o Daniel Getzendanner & William Jeremiah Williams   Mort: J.W. Little
Site 6 Samuel Joseph Blair h/o Adelle Lydanne Blair
 Birth: 1921 Death: 19 Feb 1977 Burial: 2 Feb 1977
Site 7 Albert N. Gallion
 Birth: 17 Jan 1831 Death: 5 Oct 1906 Burial: 6 Oct 1906
Site 8 Richard Walter Williams Place: Olney
 Birth: 9 Sep 1886 Death: 3 Nov 1925 Burial: 5 Nov 1925
 Mort: Hilton & Hall h/o Archibelle Arnette Williams
Site 9 Thomas Lyddane Mort: Hilton & Hall Place: Washington, DC
 Birth: 1882 Death: 31 Jul 1926 Burial: 2 Aug 1926
Site 10 Emily Wiliiams Lyddane Hall Place: Gaithersburg
 Birth: 21 Sep 1884 Death: 7 May 1956 Burial: 10 May 1956
 Mort: E.C. Gartner w/o Thomas Lyddane & Ira Hall
Site 12 Francis Foster Mort: E.C. Gartner Place: Bethesda
 Birth: 18 Dec 1909 Death: 9 Aug 1965 Burial: 11 Aug 1965
 h/o Virginia Lyddane Darby Foster TS: Maryland CY US Navy WWII

Lot: 11   Lower   Owner: Ernest Wood
Site Infant of Worth Wood No marker Mort: Hilton & Hall
 Place: Dickerson Death: 7 Oct 1924 Burial: 8 Oct 1924
Site 1 Columbia Wood TS: w/o Charles W. Wood, age 69 yrs
 Death: 10 May 1909 Burial: 12 May 1909
Site 2 Charles W. Wood TS: age 71 yrs
 h/o Columbia Wood Death: 19 Jun 1907 Burial: 21 Jun 1907

Monocacy Cemetery, Beallsville, Montgomery County, Maryland

Site 6 Mary L.G. Wood   Death: 27 Sep 1900   Burial: 29 Sep 1900
        TS: w/o Ernest Wood, age 29-11-8

Lot: 11 Upper Owner: William T. Jones
Site 2 James W. Jones   Mort: Norval H. Walker Place: Washington, DC
        Birth: 24 Oct 1861   Death: 15 May 1929   Burial: 17 May 1929
Site 3 Julia Ada Jones   Mort: M.R. Etchison & Son   Place: Frederick
        Birth: 19 Jan 1867   Death: 13 Aug 1936   Burial: 16 Aug 1936
Site 4 Harvey T. Jones
        Birth: 4 Jan 1879   Death: 6 Jun 1907   Burial: 8 Jun 1907
Site 5 Alethea A. Jones   w/o William T. Jones
        Birth: 25 Mar 1833   Death: 13 Jan 1909   Burial: 15 Jan 1909
Site 6 William T. Jones   of W.C.
        Birth: 15 Aug 1838   Death: 6 Mar 1898   Burial: 7 Mar 1898

Lot: 12 Owner: William B. & Thomas W. Vinson
Site   Eliza W. Vinson   No marker   Mort: Thomas F. Murray
        Place: Washington, DC   Death: 22 May 1932   Burial: 24 May 1932
Site   John Vinson   Burial: 9 Oct 1890   No marker
Site   William Vinson   Burial: 17 Jan 1880   No marker
Site 2 Thomas W. Vinson   h/o Annie E. Vinson
        Birth: 1836   Death: 1900   Burial: 24 Jan 1900
Site 3 Annie E. Vinson   TS: w/o Thomas W. Vinson
        Birth: 1845   Death: 1874   Burial: 1874
Site 4 B. Frank Vinson   On stone with Thomas W. & Annie E. Vinson
        Birth: 1856   Death: 1906   Burial: 28 Mar 1906
Site 7 William B. Vinson   h/o Louisa M. Vinson
        Birth: 12 Jan 1812   Death: 13 Sep 1901   Burial: 16 Sep 1901
Site 8 Louisa M. Vinson   TS: w/o William B. Vinson
        Birth: 23 Jul 1819   Death: 3 Sep 1880
Site 9 William R. Vinson   TS: s/o William B. & Louisa M. Vinson
        Birth: 10 Nov 1846   Death: 15 Jan 1880
Site 11 Elmer P. Vinson   Death: 26 May 1886
        TS: s/o Frank & Annie Elizabeth Vinson, age 0-5-12

Lot: 13 Owner: James Phillips
Site   Child of James E. Phillips No marker   Burial: 28 Sep 1885
Site   John L. Phillips   No marker   Burial: 28 Dec 1900
Site   William Phillips   No marker   Burial: 14 Nov 1895
Site 5 Matilda Phillips   Death: 21 Apr 1885
        TS: w/o Phillip L. Phillips, age 82 yrs
Site 7 Lena L. May Reed   Death: 12 Dec 1876   Burial: 13 Dec 1876
        TS: d/o Thomas J. & Julia E. Reed, age 2-9-8
Site 8 Julia Etta Phillips Reed   Burial: 22 Dec 1876
        TS: w/o Thomas J. Reed, age 58-8-0   Stone broken
Site 11 Miss Mary E. Phillips   Death: 13 Feb 1885   Burial: 14 Feb 1885
        TS: d/o Phillip & Matilda Phillips, age 65-0-27

Monocacy Cemetery, Beallsville, Montgomery County, Maryland

Lot: 14 Owner: James Phillips

- Site Edgar Phillips No marker Mort: Fred A. Krause Sons
  Place: Baltimore Death: 31 Jan 1931 Burial: 4 Feb 1931
- Site Ethel C. Phillips No marker Mort: A.J. Schippert
  Place: Washington, DC Death: 15 Mar 1925 Burial: 17 Mar 1925
- Site Child of James E. Phillips No marker Burial: 8 Aug 1891
- Site Lucille Phillips No marker Burial: 30 Jul 1910
- Site 4 Susie Phillips TS: w/o James E. Phillips, age 36 yrs
  TS: Mother Death: 5 Apr 1893 Burial: 7 Apr 1893
- Site 5 James E. Phillips TS: Age 54 yrs
  TS: Father Death: 13 Feb 1904 Burial: 16 Feb 1904
- Site 7 Algye Poole Phillips Place: Clinton, MD
  Birth: 1877 Death: 1 Aug 1950 Burial: 4 Aug 1950
  Mort: Robert A. Pumphrey On stone with Milton W. Phillips
- Site 8 Milton W. Phillips Mort: Hilton & Price Place: Barnesville
  Birth: 1879 Death: 26 Mar 1934 Burial: 28 Mar 1934
- Site 10 James E. Phillips Place: Washington, DC
  Birth: 14 Sep 1904 Death: 18 Feb 1960 Burial: 22 Feb 1960
  Mort: Robert A. Pumphrey w/o Hazel H. Phillips
- Site 11 Hazel H. Phillips On stone with James E. Phillips
  Birth: 6 Dec 1901

Lot: 15 Owner: Daniel Howard

- Site Frances M. Howard No marker Mort: W.R. Pumphrey
  Place: Quince Orchard Death: 25 Sep 1929 Burial: 29 Sep 1929
- Site 1 Daniel F. Howard
  Birth: 13 Oct 1870 Death: 13 Sep 1895 Burial: 14 Sep 1895
- Site 2 Brooklin Howard TS: s/o D.M. & Fanny M. Howard
  Birth: 24 Jan 1880 Death: 21 Dec 1899 Burial: 23 Dec 1899
- Site 10 Helen Violette Ferris Place: Winter Park, FL
  Birth: 14 Jul 1911 Death: 27 Nov 1961 Burial: 2 Dec 1961
  Mort: Cox & Parker w/o Clarence Alfred Ferris
- Site 11 Katie Howard Violette Place: Berkley Springs, WV
  Birth: 25 Jun 1876 Death: 19 Nov 1964 Burial: 21 Nov 1964
  w/o Arthur Violette, m/o Helen Violette Ferris Mort: W.W. Helsley
- Site 12 Arthur Violette Place: Berkley Springs, WV
  Birth: 6 Mar 1869 Death: 4 Feb 1962 Burial: 7 Feb 1962
  Mort: Helsey Funeral Home h/o Katie Howard Violette

Lot: 16 Lower Owner: H.J. Norris

- Site Carol L. Dickinson Place: Washington, DC
  Birth: 1900 Death: 22 Jun 1941 Burial: 25 Jun 1941
  Mort: W.W. Chambers On Norris stone
- Site Henry Low Burial: 15 Feb 1895 No marker, 70 years old
- Site Mrs. Henry J. Norris Jr. Burial: 18 Dec 1899 No marker
- Site Miss Ida M. Norris Burial: 29 Apr 1898 No marker
- Site James C. Norris No marker Mort: W.W. Chambers
  Place: Washington, DC Death: 30 Oct 1934 Burial: 2 Nov 1934

Monocacy Cemetery, Beallsville, Montgomery County, Maryland   33

Site   Sarah C. Lowe Norris   No marker   Mort: John R. Wright Co.
        Place: Washington, DC   Death: 12 Apr 1926   Burial: 14 Apr 1926

Lot: 16 Upper   Owner: H.J. Norris
Site   Henry J. Norris   No marker   Mort: W.W. Chambers
        Place: Washington, DC   Death: 16 Jan 1944   Burial: 19 Jan 1944
Site 1 C. Larue Norris   No marker   Burial: 3 Dec 1886
Site 1 Thomas A. Norris   Birth/Death: 1886   Burial: 3 Dec 1886
Site 2 Mary Magdeline Norris   Mort: M.R. Etchison Son Place: Frederick
        Birth: 1861   Death: 11 Sep 1932   Burial: 14 Sep 1932
Site 3 Josiah Norris   s/o Mr. H. J. Norris
        Birth: 1865   Death: 24 May 1882   Burial: 26 May 1882
Site 4 Margaret A. Norris   w/o H.S. Norris
        Birth: 1843   Death: 9 Jul 1881   Burial: 10 Jul 1881
Site 5 Henry J. Norris   h/o Laura B. Norris
        Birth: 1838   Death: 17 Dec 1909   Burial: 19 Dec 1909
Site 6 Infant Norris   Death: 31 Jan 1884   Burial: 1 Feb 1884
        Cause: Stillborn   No marker   i/o H.J. & Laura B. Norris
Site 6 Laura B. Norris   w/o H.J. Norris
        Birth: 1858   Death: 31 Jan 1884   Burial: 7 Feb 1884

Lot: 17   Owner: John E. Padgett
Site   Arthur Padgett   No marker   Burial: 16 Dec 1903
Site   Child of Arthur Padgett   No marker   Burial: 4 Oct 1889
Site   Daughter of Arthur Padgett   No marker   Burial: 19 Aug 1900
Site   Fannie Padgett   No marker   Burial: 19 Feb 1908
Site   Mrs. John Padgett   No marker   Burial: 13 May 1884
Site   Robert T. Stevens   No marker   Mort: Warner Pumphrey
        Place: near Purdum   Death: 11 Jun 1934   Burial: 14 Jun 1934
Site 2 Isabel Padgett   d/o John E. & Elizabeth Padgett
        Birth: 11 Apr 1861   Burial: 17 Dec 1886
Site 3 Elizabeth Padgett   Death: 1 Apr 1879
        w/o John E. Padgett,   TS: In her 60th yr
Site 4 John Padgett
        Birth: 17 Apr 1822   Death: 20 Nov 1902   Burial: 22 Nov 1902
Site 6 James Padgett   illegible
        Birth: 18 Jun 1818   Burial: 4 Mar 1887
Site 7 Clara J. Padgett   Place: Germantown
        Birth: 26 Aug 1853   Death: 21 Apr 1921   Burial: 23 Apr 1921
        Mort: Hilton & Hall   TS: w/o Thomas E. Padgett
Site 8 Thomas E. Padgett   Mort: Hilton & Hall   Place: Seneca
        Birth: 8 Dec 1849   Death: 31 Aug 1915   Burial: 2 Sep 1915

Lot: 18 Lower   Owner: John Henderson
Site   Daughter of John B. Henderson No marker   Burial: 23 Apr 1894
Site 3 John B. Henderson   Mort: J.W. Lees, Sons   Place: Washington, DC
        Birth: 1857   Death: 2 Dec 1930   Burial: 5 Dec 1930

Site 4 Mollie E. Henderson   w/o John B. Henderson   Mort: Geo. W. Wise Co
        Place: Washington, DC   Death: 21 Aug 1943   Burial: 25 Aug 1943
        No marker
Site 5 Miss Carrie Henderson
        Birth: 1886   Death: 1896   Burial: 29 Apr 1896
Site 5 Miss Maggie Henderson
        Birth: 1880   Death: 1896   Burial: 12 Aug 1896
Site 6 Chester Henderson   Birth: 1893   Death: 1894

Lot: 18 Upper   Owner: John C. Whalen
Site   Child of John C. Whalen   No marker   Burial: 22 Sep 1894
Site 1 Richard H. Collier   Birth: 17 Apr 1823   Burial: 3 Jun 1894
Site 2 Mrs. Mary F. Collier   TS: Age 80-6-13
        Birth: 1 Jan 1824   Death: 12 Jun 1904   Burial: 15 Jun 1904
Site 3 John C. Whalen   No marker   Mort: W.T. Hilton & Sons
        Place: Dickerson   Death: 26 Dec 1926   Burial: 28 Dec 1926
Site 4 Mrs. Fannie F. Whalen   Death: 2 Nov 1911
        TS: w/o John C. Whalen, age 52-7-0
Site 5 John A. Whalen   s/o Fannie F. & John C. Whalen
        Birth: 13 Mar 1886   illegible   Burial: 26 Apr 1887
Site 6 Mary C. Whalen   d/o John & Fannie Whalen
        Birth: 21 May 1880   illegible   Burial: 18 Jul 1881
Site 6 Henry L. Collier   No marker   Mort: W.T. Hilton & Sons
        Place: Dickerson   Death: 27 Dec 1929   Burial: 29 Dec 1929

Lot: 19   Owner: J.W. Collier
Site 1 William F. Collier   Mort: J.W. Lees Sons   Place: Washington, DC
        Birth: 9 Oct 1886   Death: 5 Apr 1929   Burial: 8 Apr 1929
Site 3 Harry C. Houser Jr.
        Birth: 15 Aug 1910   Death: 28 Nov 1993   Burial: 2 Dec 1993
Site 5 Annie C. Martin   Mort: Joseph Gawlers
        Place: Washington, DC   Death: 7 Feb 1960   Burial: 10 Feb 1960
        On stone with Maitland Rex Martin
Site 5 Maitland Rex Martin   Mort: S.H. Hines Co.
        Place: Washington   Death: 23 Oct 1956   Burial: 26 Oct 1956
Site 6 Harry C. Houser   Mort: S.H. Hines Co.
        Place: Washington, DC   Death: 1 Oct 1936   Burial: 3 Oct 1936
Site 6 Mary E. Houser   TS: w/o Harry C. Houser Mort: S.H. Hines Co.
        Place: Gaithersburg   Death: 30 Nov 1941   Burial: 3 Dec 1941
Site 6 Infant Olga Lou Bussard   Mort: Jos. F. Birch & Sons
        Place: Washington, DC   Death: 2 Aug 1946   Burial: 4 Aug 1946
        TS: i/o L.T. & Thelma C. Bussard
Site 6 Olga Hume Collier   Death: 28 Oct 1910   Burial: 30 Oct 1910
        TS: d/o W.F. & J.T. Collier, age 0-11-28
Site 7 Beulah L. Collier   Mort: J.W. Lee   Place: Washington DC
        Birth: 11 Apr 1892   Death: 30 Dec 1918   Burial: 1 Jan 1919
Site 8 John W. Collier   TS: Age 58-5-12   h/o Annie C. Collier
        Birth: 30 Nov 1849   Death: 12 May 1908   Burial: 14 May 1908

Site 9 Annie C. Collier   TS: Age 45-3-26   w/o John W. Collier
        Birth: 20 Apr 1855   Death: 26 Jul 1900   Burial: 28 Jul 1900
Site 10 Miss Ruth L. Collier   TS: Age 7-2-11   d/o William Collier
        Birth: 24 Jan 1894   Death: 4 Apr 1901   Burial: 5 Apr 1901
Site 11 Child of William Collier No marker   Burial: 1 Mar 1898
Site 12 John R. Collier   TS: Age 15-4-19   s/o J.W. Collier
        Birth: 7 Mar 1880   Death: 26 Jul 1895   Burial: 28 Jul 1895

Lot: 20 Owner: James W. Darby
Site   Grayson Dade   Burial: 5 Nov 1894   Child No marker
Site   Child of J.W. Darby   No marker   Burial: 30 Apr 1879
Site 1 Gertrude E. Darby   Mort: Hilton & Hall   Place: Lee, VA
        Birth: 1863   Death: 8 Jul 1929   Burial: 10 Jul 1929
Site 6 James W. Darby   Mort: Hilton & Hall   Place: Poolesville
        Birth: 26 Oct 1851   Death: 10 Jan 1925   Burial: 12 Jan 1925
Site 7 Mollie J. Darby   Birth: 4 Jun 1853   Burial: 12 Sep 1885
Site 8 Nellie Darby   Child
        Birth: 1876   Death: 1877   Burial: 1877
Site 9 Harry Darby (Child)
        Birth: 1879   Death: 1879   Burial: 29 Jul 1879
Site 10 Baby Darby   Birth: 1885   Burial: 1885
Site 11 Lee W. Darby   c/o James W. Darby
        Birth: 1889   Death: 1890   Burial: 10 Sep 1890
Site 12 Thomas P. Darby   c/o James W. Darby
        Birth: 1901   Death: 1901   Burial: 1 Mar 1901

Lot: 21 Owner: R.P. Hays
Site 1 Child Hays   No marker   Burial: 15 Feb 1879
        c/o Richard P. & Bettie B. Hays
Site 1 Child Hays   No marker   Burial: 2 Dec 1878
        c/o Richard P. & Bettie B. Hays
Site 2 Robert Lee Hays   Mort: W.T. Hilton & Sons Place: Dickerson
        Birth: 8 Sep 1895   Death: 25 Jun 1920   Burial: 27 Jun 1920
        TS: s/o Richard Poole & Bettie Batson Hays
Site 3 Richard Poole Hays   TS: s/o Leonard & Eliza Hays
        Birth: 18 Dec 1840   Death: 8 Apr 1912   Burial: 10 Apr 1912
Site 4 Bettie Batson Hays   Place: Dickerson
        Birth: 25 Mar 1855   Death: 23 Feb 1923   Burial: 25 Feb 1923
        Mort: W.T. Hilton & Sons   TS: w/o Richard Poole Hays
Site 5 Nana P. Hays   Place: State Sanatorium
        Birth: 16 Jan 1880   Death: 19 Jul 1926   Burial: 21 Jul 1926
        Mort: W.T. Hilton & Sons   TS: d/o Richard P. & Bettie B. Hays

Lot: 22 Owner: R.P. Hays
Site 2 Miss Elizabeth Z. Hays   TS: d/o Richard Poole & Bettie Batson Hays
        Birth: 13 Feb 1882   Death: 1 Sep 1926   Burial: 4 Sep 1926
        Mort: W.T. Hilton & Sons   Place: State Sanatorium

Monocacy Cemetery, Beallsville, Montgomery County, Maryland

Site 3 Leonard Batson Hays
      Birth: 26 Mar 1884   Death: 27 Dec 1947
      s/o Richard Poole & Bettie Batson Hays, age 63
      Place: Washington, DC
      Burial: 30 Dec 1947
      Mort: W.K. Hunteman

Site 4 Richard Kenton Hays
      Birth: 5 Jan 1886   Death: 5 Jul 1952
      Mort: Etchison & Son
      Place: Dickerson
      Burial: 8 Jul 1952
      s/o Richard P. & Bettie B. Hays, age 66

Lot: 23 Owner: Peter K. Mossburg

Site George Mossburg
      Birth: 1857   No marker
      h/o Sara (Sallie) Elizabeth Hoyle
      Burial: 25 May 1910

Site George LeRoy Mossburg
      Birth: 1892   Death: 25 Feb 1925
      Mort: W.R. Pumphrey
      Place: Sykesville
      Burial: 27 Feb 1925
      No marker

Site 1 George Edwin Matthews   Death 9 May 1888
      TS: s/o J. Edwin & Annie S. Matthews, age 5-9-22

Site 5 Miss Alice L. Mossburg
      Birth: 7 Mar 1891   Death: 28 Sep 1903
      d/o George & Sarah E. Mossburg
      Burial: 30 Sep 1903
      TS: Age 12-6-21

Site 6 Sarah E. Mossburg
      Birth: 2 Mar 1861   Death: 5 Apr 1896
      w/o George P. Mossburg
      Burial: 10 Apr 1896

Site 6 Miss Mary Mossburg   Sister/o Peter K. Mossburg
      Birth: 1815   Death: 23 Feb 1896
      TS: Age 81-5-29
      Burial: 25 Feb 1896

Site 9 Peter K. Mossburg
      Birth: 3 May 1825   Death: 1 Jun 1904
      TS: Age 79-0-28
      Burial: 3 Jun 1904

Site 10 Margaret L. Mossburg   Death: 8 May 1885
      TS: w/o Peter K. Mossburg, age 57-10-4

Lot: 24 Owner: Annie Matthews

Site Child of Thomas Hillcary No marker Burial: 24 Jul 1883

Site Edward Matthews   Burial: 11 Jun 1886
      s/o J. Edwin & Annie S. Matthews No marker

Site Margaret T. Miles No marker Mort: W.T. Hilton & Sons
      Place: State Sanatorium Death: 2 Apr 1923 Burial: 5 Apr 1923

Site 1 J. Edwin Matthews   h/o Annie S. Matthews
      Birth: 29 Mar 1859   Death: 11 Jun 1886   Burial: 3 Jun 1891

Site 2 Linda Mae Claggett   Place: Silver Spring
      Birth: Jan 1965   Death: 11 Jan 1965   Burial: 13 Jan 1965
      Mort: Hilton   d/o Minnie Flood & Richard Claggett

Site 2 Annie S. Matthews   TS: w/o J. Edwin Matthews
      Birth: 11 Sep 1859   Death: 3 Jun 1912   Burial: 5 Jun 1912

Site 3 Laura LaVonne Claggett   Place: Silver Spring
      Birth: Jan 1965   Death: 8 Jan 1965   Burial: 9 Jan 1965
      Mort: Hilton   TS: d/o Mae Flood & Richard G. Claggett

Lot: 24 1/2 Owner: Mrs. Carrie Mossburg

Site 2 Edward Clinton Mossburg   Place: Washington, DC
      Birth: 10 Jan 1872   Death: 25 Sep 1926   Burial: 27 Sep 1926
      Mort: W.R. Pumphrey   h/o Carrie May Mossburg

Monocacy Cemetery, Beallsville, Montgomery County, Maryland

Site 3 Carrie May Mossburg   Mort: W.B. Hilton
        Place: Poolesville   Death: 22 Jun 1948   Burial: 25 Jun 1948
        w/o E. Clinton Mossburg   No marker
Site 4 Carolyn Irene Mossburg Seymour   Place: Takoma Park
        Birth: 8 Jan 1901   Death: 6 Apr 1925   Burial: 8 Apr 1925
        Mort: W.R. Pumphrey
Site 5 Reubie G. Mossburg   c/o Clinton & Carrie May Mossburg
        Birth: 24 Aug 1905   Death: 3 Oct 1905   Burial: 5 Oct 1905
Site 6 Irving E. Mossburg   c/o Clinton & Carrie May Mossburg
        Birth: 11 Apr 1899   Death: 9 Aug 1899   Burial: 10 Aug 1899
Site 6 William E. Mossburg   s/o E. Clinton & Carrie May Mossburg
        Birth: 21 Jul 1904   Death: 24 Aug 1904

Lot: 25 Owner: Richard B. Astlin
Site   Mr. Richard B. Astlin   No marker   Burial: 15 Apr 1884
Site   Mrs. Richard B. Astlin   No marker
                                    Death: 10 Mar 1884   Burial: 10 Mar 1884
Site   Walter W. Astlin   Place: Seneca
        Birth: 10 Jun 1845   Death: 5 Jul 1918   Burial: 6 Jul 1918
        Mort: Hilton & Hall   h/o Indiana Astlin
Site   Mrs. Washington Geiger   Burial: 14 Jan 1895   No marker
Site   Mr. Lowe   Burial: 1 Feb 1892   No marker
Site   Richard H. Lowe   Burial: 20 May 1886   No marker
Site   Mrs. Gertrude Matthews   Burial: 19 Aug 1901   No marker
Site 3 Mrs. Indiana Astlin   TS: w/o Walter W. Astlin
        Birth: 22 Feb 1846   Death: 17 May 1905   Burial: 18 May 1905

Lot: 26 Owner: James Stephens
Site   James A. Stephens   Mort: W.R. Pumphrey
        Place: Germantown   Death: 28 May 1943   Burial: 31 May 1943
        h/o Catharine T. Stephens   No marker
Site 1 Lola Lee Stephens   No marker   d/o James & Catharine T. Stephens
        Birth: 19 Apr 1899   Death: 16 Jul 1899   Burial: 17 Jul 1899
Site 2 Catharine T. Stephens   TS: w/o James A. Stephens, age 53 yrs
                                    Death: 10 Apr 1909   Burial: 12 Apr 1909
Site 3 Mary E. (Mollie) Stephens   No marker   Mort: W.R. Pumphrey
        Place: Old Germantown   Death: 22 Jun 1945   Burial: 25 Jun 1945
Site 7 Mabel C. Stephens   Place: Washington, DC
        Birth: 16 Jul 1885   Death: 17 Jun 1961   Burial: 20 Jun 1961
        Mort: S.H. Hines   w/o Cabble Carr Stephens
Site 8 Cabble Carr Stephens   Place: Washington, DC
        Birth: 8 Dec 1883   Death: 26 Nov 1948   Burial: 28 Nov 1948
        Mort: S.H. Hines Co.   h/o Mabel C. Stephens
Site 10 Edith Virginia Stephens   No marker   Mort: R.A. Pumphrey
        Place: Bethesda   Death: 17 Aug 1957   Burial: 19 Aug 1957

Lot: 27 Owner: J.H. Reid
Site John A. Reid   Monument states he is buried in Barnesville
Site John W. Reid
      Birth: 1890   Death: 1891   Burial: 1891
      s/o J.H. & Rhoda Stewart Reid   buried in Barnesville
Site 1 Clifton S. Reid   s/o John H. & Rhoda Stewart Reid
      Birth: 1904   Death: 1904   Burial: 2 Nov 1904
Site 2 Henry Lee Reid
      Birth: 1898   Death: 1905   Burial: 20 Nov 1905
Site 3 Rhoda C. Stewart Reid   Place: Washington, DC
      Birth: 16 Dec 1869   Death: 15 Feb 1943   Burial: 18 Feb 1943
      Mort: S.H. Hines   w/o John H. Reid
Site 4 John Henry Reid   Place: Washington, DC
      Birth: 1865   Death: 1 Jan 1956   Burial: 4 Jan 1956
      Mort: Nalley Funeral Home   h/o Rhoda Stewart Reid
Site 5 Roy O'Dell Reid   Place: Bethesda, MD
      Birth: 1891   Death: 14 Oct 1969   Burial: 18 Oct 1969
      Mort: Tyson Wheeler   s/o John H. & Rhoda Stewart Reid
Site 12 Eliza A. White Reid No dates on stone   Mort: W.T. Hilton & Sons
      Place: Boyds   Death: 29 Jul 1913   Burial: 31 Jul 1913

Lot: 28 Owner: Rufus Davis
Site 1 Victorine Smith Davis   Mort: Wm. R. Pumphrey   Place: Gaithersburg
       Birth: 1849   Death: 3 Dec 1934   Burial: 5 Dec 1934
Site 2 Rufus Hamilton Davis   Mort: W.R. Pumphrey   Place: Gaithersburg
       Birth: 1846   Death: 18 Jan 1933   Burial: 20 Jan 1933
Site 3 Catherine S. Davis   w/o Isaac Davis
       Birth: 2 Oct 1822   Death: 5 Jul 1897   Burial: 30 Apr 1901
                                TS: Age 82-8-21   h/o Catherine S. Davis
Site 4 Isaac Davis
       Birth: 12 Jun 1818   Death: 5 Mar 1901   Burial: 30 Apr 1901
Site 5 George Vernon Davis   Mort: M.R. Etchison & Sons   Place: Frederick
       Birth: 1857   Death: 19 Apr 1924   Burial: 21 Apr 1924
Site 6 Clara P. Davis   Mort: M.R. Etchison & Sons   Place: Hyattstown
       Birth: 1859   Death: 13 Feb 1927   Burial: 17 Feb 1927
Site 7 Mary Harrison Davis   Place: Baltimore
       Birth: 1864   Death: 24 Jan 1937   Burial: 26 Jan 1937
       Mort: George J. Smith   w/o Wilson Davis DDS
Site 8 Dr. L. Wilson Davis DDS   Place: Baltimore Co.
       Birth: 1862   Death: 18 May 1947   Burial: 21 May 1947
       Mort: John A. Moran   h/o Mary Harrison Davis, DDS
Site 12 Gilbert Dean Wilkinson Place: Gaithersburg   Mort: W.R. Pumphrey
       Birth: 1899   Death: 21 Nov 1936   Burial: 23 Nov 1936
       h/o Eileen Davis Wilkinson

Lot: 29 Owner: Mrs. George Webster
Site Mrs. E. Webster   No marker   Burial: 31 Dec 1903
Site Alice W. Whipp   No marker   Mort: W.T. Hilton & Sons
      Place: Boyds   Death: 17 Apr 1917   Burial: 19 Apr 1917

Monocacy Cemetery, Beallsville, Montgomery County, Maryland   39

Site 2 Amos Whipp   TS: MD Private   Mort: W.T. Hilton & Sons
        Place: Boyds   Death: 13 May 1919   Burial: 15 May 1919
Site 4 M. W. Webster   No marker
Site 5 George Webster   TS: Age 72-10-8
        Birth: 21 Jun 1829   Death: 29 Nov 1901   Burial: 2 Dec 1901
Site 7 Raymond E. Webster   illegible   Place: Baltimore
        Birth: 16 Jun 1897   Death: 28 Sep 1917   Burial: 1 Oct 1917
        Mort: W.T. Hilton & Sons   s/o Harvey & Annie M. Webster
Site 8 Miss Maggie L. Webster   d/o Harvey & Maggie M. Webster
        Birth: 1 Sep 1888   illegible   Burial: 30 Jul 1911

Lot: 30 Lower   Owner: William Stottlemeyer
Site   Walter Behers   Burial: 12 Apr 1905   No marker-child
Site 1 Roy Thomas Beacht   TS: s/o Edward & Nellie Beacht
        Birth: 8 Aug 1906   Death: 29 Mar 1907   Burial: 30 Mar 1907
Site 3 Viola A. Stottlemyer   Place: near Comus
        Birth: 1871   Death: 1 Jun 1938   Burial: 3 Jun 1938
        Mort: W.B. Hilton   TS: w/o William L. Stottlemyer
Site 4 William L. Stottlemyer   Place: Frederick Hospital
        Birth: 1874   Death: 13 Mar 1948   Burial: 15 Mar 1948
        Mort: W.B. Hilton   h/o Viola A. Stottlemyer

Lot: 30 Upper   Owner: William Stottlemyer
Site 1 Harry F. Stottlemyer Death: 5 Sep 1907   Burial: 7 Sep 1907
Site 2 Mahala C. Stottlemyer Mort: Lloyd Kaiserl   Place: Laurel
        Birth: 15 Feb 1846   Death: 4 Aug 1932   Burial: 5 Aug 1932
Site 5 Alice Murphy Stottlemyer   Place: Washington, DC
        Birth: 16 Sep 1869   Death: 16 Feb 1926   Burial: 19 Feb 1926
        Mort: W.T. Hilton & Sons   TS: Mother
Site 6 Rosalie Marie Stottlemyer   Place: Montgomery County Hospital
        Birth: 12 Jun 1906   Death: 12 Mar 1925   Burial: 14 Mar 1925
        Mort: W.T. Hilton & Sons   TS: d/o Martin L. & Alice C. Stottlemyer

Lot: 31 Lower   Owner: T.F. Darne
Site 1 Isabel E. Darne   Place: Catonsville
        Birth: 17 Sep 1868   Death: 25 Feb 1949   Burial: 28 Feb 1949
        Mort: W.B. Hilton   w/o Thomas F. Darne
Site 2 Thomas F. Darne   Place: Sellman   Mort: W.B. Hilton
        Birth: 17 Aug 1867   Death: 22 Mar 1945   Burial: 24 Mar 1945
        h/o Isabel E. Darne
Site 3 Cora Arnelia Darne   w/o Dorian Darne
        Birth: 1 Sep 1895   Death: 31 Aug 1976   Burial: 3 Sep 1976
Site 4 Dorian P. Darne   h/o Cora Arnelia Darne
        Birth: 10 Jul 1897   Death: 3 Jun 1988   Burial: 6 Jun 1988
Site 6 James E. Stevens   h/o Kathryn Darne Stevens
        Birth: 15 Feb 1916   Death: 9 Jul 1996   Burial: 12 Jul 1996

Lot: 31 Upper   Owner: M.M. Mossburg

Site 1 Ella Mossburg Cooley
    Birth: 22 Aug 1910   Death: 5 Jan 1982
    On stone with Mitchell W. Cooley
    Burial: 26 Jun 1983

Site 1 Mitchell W. Cooley
    Birth: 27 Nov 1911   Death: 11 Sep 1981
    h/o Ella Mossburg Cooley
    Burial: 26 Jun 1983

Site 2 Carol Jean Cooley
    Birth: 8 Mar 1942   Death: 9 May 1945
    Mort: W.B. Hilton
    Place: Riverdale
    Burial: 10 May 1945
    TS: d/o M.W. & E.M. Cooley

Site 3 Esther Compher Mossburg
    Birth: 6 Jul 1879   Death: 4 Apr 1962
    Mort: Hilton
    Place: Poolesville
    Burial: 6 Apr 1962
    w/o Maurice M. Mossburg

Site 4 Maurice Milton Mossburg
    Birth: 7 Sep 1869   Death: 17 Sep 1954
    Mort: W.B. Hilton
    Place: Poolesville
    Burial: 20 Sep 1954
    h/o Esther C. Mossburg

Site 5 Clara Beall Hillard Mossburg
    Birth: 1864   Death: 23 Jul 1941
    Mort: W.B. Hilton
    Place: Barnesville
    Burial: 26 Jul 1941
    w/o Thomas Gilbert Mossburg

Site 6 Thomas Gilbert Mossburg
    Birth: 1861   Death: 28 Jul 1933
    Mort: Hilton & Price
    Place: Sellman
    Burial: 30 Jul 1933
    h/o Clara Bell Hillard

Lot: 32   Owner: Baker & Compher

Site 1 Miriam E. Compher
    Birth: 1896   Death: 22 Feb 1971
    Mort: Harding-Jamison Inc.
    Place: East Bruns. NJ
    Burial: 25 Feb 1971
    TS: w/o W. Clinton Compher

Site 1 Wilfred Clinton Compher
    Birth: 1896   Death: 1984
    h/o Miriam E. Compher
    Burial: 15 Jun 1984

Site 2 William J. Compher
    TS: Place: France   Death: 26 Sep 1918
    TS: Corp. Co. C 312th MGBN WWI, age 31-11-8
    Mort: Hilton & Hall
    Burial: 11 Sep 1921

Site 3 Henrietta Compher
    Birth: 20 Jan 1850   Death: 29 Dec 1918
    Mort: Hilton & Hall
    Place: Poolesville
    Burial: 31 Dec 1918
    TS: w/o Jonas C. Compher

Site 4 Jonas C. Compher
    Birth: 24 Mar 1849   Death: 23 Jul 1907
    h/o Henrietta Compher
    Burial: 25 Jul 1907

Site 6 Maurice C. Mossburg
    Birth: 6 Jan 1909   Death: 3 Feb 1910
    TS: s/o M.M. & E.M. Mossburg
    Burial: 5 Feb 1910
    Mort: W.B. Hilton

Site 7 Infant Baker
    Place: Dickerson   Death: 4 Oct 1948
    Cause: Stillborn
    i/o William & Viola W. Baker
    Mort: W.B. Hilton
    Burial: 5 Oct 1948
    No marker

Site 8 Charles Russell Baker
    Place: Dickerson   No marker
    Death: 5 Jan 1919
    Mort: W.T. Hilton & Sons
    Burial: 7 Jan 1919

Site 9 Katherine Virginia Baker
    Place: Dickerson   No marker
    Death: 10 Aug 1947
    Mort: W.B. Hilton
    Burial: 12 Aug 1947

Site 10 Walter Baker
    Place: Spring State Hospital, Sykesville   Death: 2 May 1944
    Mort: W.B. Hilton
    Burial: 5 May 1944
    No marker

Monocacy Cemetery, Beallsville, Montgomery County, Maryland   41

Site 11 Henry Curtis Baker   Mort: W.B. Hilton   Place: Frederick Hospital
         Birth: 25 Jan 1903   Death: 14 May 1949   Burial: 16 May 1949
Site 12 Ethel Irene Baker   w/o Henry Baker
         Birth: 27 Jun 1904   Death: 7 Jan 1986   Burial: 10 Jan 1986

Lot: 33 Upper   Owner: George Welch
Site 1   Child of George Welch   Burial: 21 Apr 1910   No marker

Lot: 34 Upper   Owner: Miscellaneous
Site 1   Mary Effie Kidd   w/o William Frazier Kidd, age 92 yrs
         No marker   Death: 19 Jun 1992   Burial: 23 Jun 1992
Site 2   Errol Wilson Jeffcoat   h/o Frances (Mickey) Chisolm Jeffcoat
         Birth: 1917   Death: 8 Sep 1983   Burial: 13 Sep 1983
Site 4   Isabel C. Chisolm   w/o Julian J. Chisolm, age 92
         Birth: 1900   Death: 13 Sep 1992   Burial: 19 Sep 1992
Site 4   Julian J. Chisolm   Mort: Hilton   Place: Bethesda
         Birth: 1895   Death: 21 Feb 1965   Burial: 24 Feb 1965
Site 4   Edna Ann Chisholm Rohman   No marker
         Birth: 16 Dec 1926   Death: 23 Mar 1995   Burial: 6 Sep 1995

Lot: 35   Owner: Norman Cole
Site 1   Norman R. Cole   TS: MD Pvt US Army WWII
         Birth: 17 Mar 1912   Death: 26 Jul 1973   Burial: 30 Jul 1973
Site 2   Hazel M. Wood   Mort: W.W. Chambers   Place: Washington, DC
         Birth: 1905   Death: 10 Jun 1947   Burial: 13 Jun 1947
Site 3   Ida Cole Wood   Mort: W.T. Hilton & Sons
         Birth: 1888   Death: 1918   Burial: 8 Nov 1919
         Disintered from Congressional Cemetery, Washington, DC
Site 4   Norman Cole   Place: Washington, DC
         Birth: 1882   Death: 6 Aug 1938   Burial: 9 Aug 1938
         Mort: W.W. Chambers   h/o Ida C. Cole
Site 5   Mary Margaret Brooks   Mort: W.W. Chambers   Place: Washington, DC
         Birth: 1907   Death: 20 Feb 1943   Burial: 24 Feb 1943
Site 7   Sadie VanHorn   No marker   Mort: P.J. Saffell
         Place: Washington, DC   Death: 21 Apr 1923   Burial: 23 Apr 1923
Site 8   Ellis Kendall   No marker   Mort: W.W. Deal
         Place: Baltimore   Death: 26 Mar 1924   Burial: 29 Mar 1924
Site 9   Martha A. Kendall Andrews   Mort: H.B. Nevins
         Place: Terra Cotta   Death: 8 Feb 1921   Burial: 10 Feb 1921
         1st husband- Ellis Kendall   No marker

Lot: 36 Lower   Owner: Richard T. & Zora A. Young
Site   Agnes E. Young   Mort: Hilton & Hall
         Place: Frederick   Death: 17 Aug 1913   Burial: 19 Aug 1913
         w/o William LeRoy Young   No marker
Site   William Leroy Young   Mort: A.G. Frey
         Place: Washington, DC   Death: 8 Dec 1913   Burial: 10 Dec 1913
         h/o Agnes E. Young   No marker

Site 3 Richard Thomas Young   On stone with Zora Dove Young
        Birth: 1906   Death: 24 Sep 1977   Burial: 28 Sep 1977
Site 5 Ernest A. Young   No marker   Mort: C.E. Cline & Son
        removed from Frederick   Death: 29 Nov 1943   Burial: 11 Dec 1943

Lot: 36 Upper   Owner: A.B. Shreve
Site 2 Esther B. Trundle   illegible   Mort: Chas. E. Roberts
        Birth: 23 Apr 1786   Death: 24 Oct 1834   Burial: 6 May 1916
        w/o Daniel T. Trundle   Removed from Shreve burying ground
Site 3 Daniel T. Trundle   TS: Age 53-0-1   Mort: Chas. E. Roberts
        Birth: 13 Mar 1778   Death: 17 Mar 1831   Burial: 6 May 1916
        h/o Esther B. Trundle   Removed from Shreve burying ground
Site 4 Benjamin F. Shreve Jr.   No marker   Place: Washington, DC
        Birth: 28 Nov 1831   Death: 23 Mar 1916   Burial: 25 Mar 1916
        Mort: W.T. Hilton & Sons   s/o Mary & Benjamin F. Shreve
Site 5 Miss Mary E. Shreve   illegible   Mort: Chas. E. Roberts
        Birth: 2 Aug 1844   Death: 4 Feb 1862   Burial: 1 Apr 1916
        d/o Mary & Benjamin Shreve   Removed from Shreve burying ground
Site 6 Mary Elizabeth Trundle Shreve   Mort: Chas. E. Roberts
        Birth: 26 Mar 1811   Death: 23 Oct 1855   Burial: 1 Apr 1916
        d/o Daniel & Esther Belt Trundle   Removed from Shreve burying ground
        TS: w/o Benjamin Shreve, age 44-6-27
Site 6 Benjamin F. Shreve   illegible   Mort: Chas. E. Roberts
        Birth: 15 Mar 1804   Death: 25 Sep 1861   Burial: 1 Apr 1916
        h/o Mary Elizabeth Trundle Shreve   Removed from Shreve burying ground

Lot: 37   Owner: Ezra Cole
Site   Alice C. Chalmers   No marker   Mort: W.W. Chambers
        Place: Washington, DC   Death: 3 May 1944   Burial: 6 May 1944
Site   John Morris Cole   Burial: 15 Mar 1904   Age 1 month, No marker
Site 2 Richard Cole   No marker   Mort: W.B. Hilton
        Place: Washington, DC   Death: 8 Feb 1942   Burial: 11 Feb 1942
Site 4 Martha Ann Cole   Place: Sellman
        Birth: 1844   Death: 24 Feb 1917   Burial: 26 Feb 1917
        Mort: W.T. Hilton & Sons   TS: w/o Ezra E. Cole
Site 6 Ezra E. Cole   h/o Martha Ann Cole
        Birth: 1843   Death: 1902   Burial: 2 Mar 1902

Lot: 38 Upper   Owner: Maria Pettit
Site   Joyce Ann Steele   Child No marker   Mort: Hutchison & Son
        Place: Prince Frederick Death: 20 Apr 1950   Burial: 22 Apr 1950
Site 1 Frank E. Steele   No marker
                                 Death: 8 Aug 1975   Burial: 12 Aug 1975
Site 2 Mary A. Steele   Mort: Lee Funeral Home Place: Washington, DC
        Birth: 1894   Death: 11 Sep 1962   Burial: 14 Sep 1962
Site 3 Maria Cole Pettitt   Place: Washington, DC
        Birth: 23 Apr 1870   Death: 10 Feb 1938   Burial: 13 Feb 1938
        Mort: W.W. Chambers Co.   On stone with Charles F. Pettitt

Site 4 Charles F. Pettitt   Place: Washington, DC
        Birth: 4 Apr 1868   Death: 22 Feb 1936   Burial: 25 Feb 1936
        Mort: W.W. Deal   h/o Maria Cole Pettitt
Site 5 Helen M. Brill   Mother
        Birth: 17 Apr 1899   Death: 23 Jan 1977   Burial: 26 Jan 1977

Lot: 40 Owner: John R. & George Edward Spates
Site 3 Dorothy Ruth Spates   No marker   Place: Comus
        Birth: 1912   Death: 29 Jan 1962   Burial: 1 Feb 1962
        Mort: Hilton   w/o Edward Spates
Site 4 George Edward Spates   Death: 31 May 1986   No marker
Site 9 Robert Gordon Hagan   h/o Janet Spates Hagan
        Birth: 25 Mar 1937   Death: 4 Jul 1984   Burial: 7 Jul 1984
Site 10 Roger William Spates   s/o John R. & Janette Spates
        Birth: 25 Dec 1939   Death: 12 May 1992   Burial: 15 May 1992
Site 11 Jeanette C. Spates   Birth: 1915   Death: 7 Mar 1995
Site 12 John R. Spates   h/o Jeanette C. Spates
        Birth: 22 Oct 1910   Death: 15 Apr 1995   Burial: 17 Apr 1995

Lot: 41 Lower Owner: Frederick & Patricia Swain
Site 3 Virginia M. Swain   On stone with Robert L. Swain
        Birth: 16 Oct 1915   Death: 6 Jun 1992   Burial: 11 Jun 1992
Site 4 Robert L. Swain   Place: Bethesda
        Birth: 20 Sep 1905   Death: 3 Jun 1967   Burial: 6 Jun 1967
        Mort: Tyson Wheeler   h/o Virginia M. Swain

Lot: 41 Upper Owner: Sidney E. Dixon
Site 3 Esther Macie Dixon   Place: Frederick, MD
        Birth: 23 Jul 1908   Death: 29 Oct 1962   Burial: 1 Nov 1962
        Mort: M.R. Etchison & Son   On stone with Sidney E. Dixon
Site 4 Sidney E. Dixon   h/o Esther M. Dixon
        Birth: 19 Dec 1902   Death: 13 Nov 1979   Burial: 16 Nov 1979

Lot: 42 Lower Owner: Miscellaneous
Site 1 James Newman Brown Dulcan   h/o Suzanne P. Dulcan
        Birth: 1 Oct 1944   Death: 2 Jun 1989   Burial: 5 Jun 1989

Lot: 42 Upper Owner: Edith C. & Jack T. Lambert, Jr.
Site 4 Jasper Thomas Lambert   On stone with Edith Carlin Lambert
        Birth: 16 Nov 1930   Death: 8 Aug 1986   Burial: 11 Aug 1986

Lot: 43 Lower Owner: Marion W. & Helen R. Beall
Site 4 Charles Wilson Beall   Mort: Hilton   Place: Bethesda, MD
        Birth: 11 Sep 1942   Death: 11 Oct 1967   Burial: 13 Oct 1967
        TS: s/o Helen R. & Marion W. Beall, MD SP4 444 Trans. Co. WWII
Site 5 Helen Rutter Beall   No marker   w/o Marion W. Beall
        Birth: 23 Mar 1922   Death: 6 Sep 1976   Burial: 9 Sep 1976
Site 6 Marion W. Beall   No marker   h/o Helen Rutter Beall
        Birth: 21 Sep 1914   Death: 21 May 1974   Burial: 23 May 1974

Monocacy Cemetery, Beallsville, Montgomery County, Maryland

Lot: 43 Upper   Owner: Mary Pool Dronenburg
Site 4 Harry Nicholas Dronenburg   Mort: Wm. Hilton   Place: Frederick, MD
        Birth: 2 Aug 1924   Death: 7 Jun 1968   Burial: 10 Jun 1968
        h/o Mary Poole Dronenburg   TS: MD TEC 5 42 Car Depot GPAAF WWII
Site 6 Howard M. Smith   TS: COX US Navy WWII
        Birth: 16 Jul 1926   Death: 31 Jul 1989   h/o Mary P. Dronenburg

Lot: 44 Lower   Owner: Miscellaneous
Site 1 Lewis Bohannon Hamlett   Place: Silver Spring, MD
        Birth: 31 Aug 1915   Death: 16 Jun 1968   Burial: 19 Jun 1968
        Mort: Warner Pumphrey   TS: Distict of Columbia HA1 USNR WWII
Site 1 Margaret Ann Hamlett   On stone with Lewis Bohannon Hamlett
        Birth: 23 Dec 1907   Death: 31 Mar 1995   Burial: 3 Apr 1995
Site 5 Robert L. Paxson Jr.   TS: US Army   h/o Betty Pearson Paxson
        Birth: 27 Oct 1934   Death: 7 Mar 1980   Burial: 11 Mar 1980

Lot: 44 Upper   Owner: Frederick & Patricia Swain
Site 4 Patricia Ann Swain   On stone with Frederick O. Swain
        Birth: 8 Aug 1941   Death: 16 Dec 1990   Burial: 19 Dec 1990

Lot: 46 Upper   Owner: Miscellaneous
Site 4 Dorothy Edna Clements Ferril   On stone with Dale Ray Ferril
        Birth: 11 May 1917   Death: 28 Nov 1993   Burial: 3 Dec 1993

Addition to A

Lot: 1   Owner: James T. Trundle
Site 1   William Bryan Trundle   h/o Helen Kessler Trundle
         Birth: 20 Jun 1904   Death: 29 May 1974   Burial: 1 Jun 1974
Site 2   Helen Kessler Trundle   w/o William B. Trundle
         Birth: 28 Dec 1907   Death: 16 May 1979   Burial: 19 May 1979
Site 3   William Bryan Trundle Jr.   s/o William B. & Helen K. Trundle
         Birth: 3 Jul 1935   Death: 6 Oct 1979   Burial: 10 Oct 1979
Site 7   Americus Dawson Trundle   Mort: Wm. Hilton   Place: Bethesda, MD
         Birth: 2 Aug 1883   Death: 4 Jan 1971   Burial: 7 Jan 1971
Site 8   Gail Dawson Trundle   Place: Silver Spring
         Birth: 30 Mar 1925   Death: 6 Oct 1930   Burial: 8 Oct 1930
         Mort: John R. Wright   d/o Dawson Trundle
Site 10 Elizabeth Ellen Chiswell Trundle   Place: near Poolesville
         Birth: 1 Nov 1843   Death: 21 Sep 1918   Burial: 23 Sep 1918
         Mort: Hilton & Hall   w/o James Trundle
Site 12 James Thomas Trundle   Place: Poolesville
         Birth: 23 Feb 1841   Death: 16 Feb 1918   Burial: 18 Feb 1918
         Mort: Hilton & Hall   h/o Elizabeth Ellen Chiswell Trundle

Monocacy Cemetery, Beallsville, Montgomery County, Maryland 45

Lot: 2 Owner: Mrs. Henry Young
Site 1 Rebecca Ardella Young Place: Washington, DC
 Birth: 1873 Death: 16 Dec 1964 Burial: 17 Dec 1964
 Mort: Robert A. Pumphrey On stone with Sites 2,3, & 4
Site 2 Mary E. Cissel Young d/o Henry & M.A. Young Reinterment
 Birth: 26 Oct 1872 Death: 2 Sep 1873 Burial: 12 Nov 1896
Site 3 Edwin M. Young s/o Sarah E. & Henry Young Reinterment
 Birth: 1861 Death: 1862 Burial: 12 Nov 1896
Site 4 Sarah E. Young w/o Henry Young Reinterment of family
 Birth: 31 Dec 1831 Death: 1861 Burial: 12 Nov 1896
Site 5 Henry Young Jr. Place: Poolesville
 Birth: 18 Aug 1829 Death: 27 Jul 1918 Burial: 29 Jul 1918
 Mort: Hilton & Hall h/o Sara E. Young
Site 6 Martha Ann Cissel Young Place: Poolesville
 Birth: 1839 Death: 1 Jun 1924 Burial: 3 Jun 1924
 Mort: Hilton & Hall On stone with Henry Young, Jr.
Site 12 Henry Cissel Young Mort: Gawler & Sons Place: Washington, DC
 Birth: 16 Sep 1879 Death: 26 Dec 1969 Burial: 29 Dec 1969

Lot: 3 Owner: George D. Jones
Site 1 Ara Lee Hicks Jones On stone with George Lawrence Jones
 Birth: 11 Jan 1897 Death: 23 Sep 1982 Burial: 27 Sep 1982
Site 2 George Lawrence Jones h/o Ara Lee Hicks Jones
 Birth: 10 Jan 1895 Death: 25 Jul 1981 Burial: 28 Jul 1981
Site 3 George Darby Jones Place: Dickerson
 Birth: 6 Dec 1866 Death: 23 Jan 1922 Burial: 25 Jan 1922
 Mort: Hilton & Hall h/o Evie Wales Jones & Alethea Brewer
Site 4 Evie Wales Jones 1st w/o George Darby Jones
 Birth: 4 Mar 1866 Death: 1 Mar 1906 Burial: 3 Mar 1906
Site 5 Lee Allnutt Jones Mort: W.B. Hilton Place: Olney
 Birth: 18 Nov 1892 Death: 6 Dec 1959 Burial: 9 Dec 1959
 s/o George D. & Evie Wales Jones TS: MD PVT Co G 71st Inf WWI
Site 9 Charles W. Ferris TS: US Air Force Korea
 Birth: 1930 Death: 1991 Burial: 31 Jul 1992
Site 10 Infant Burgner Death: 3 Nov 1995 Cause: Stillborn
 No marker

Lot: 4 Owner: B.F. Pyles
Site 1 William Franklin Dade Birth: 29 Jan 1828 Burial: 14 Sep 1905
Site 2 Michael Brunner Death: 3 Apr 1848 TS: Age 78 yrs
Site 3 Elizabeth Brunner Death: 28 Jul 1842 TS: Age 59 yrs
Site 4 Joseph Brunner Birth: 14 Aug 1803 Death: 12 Jun 1874
Site 5 Lydia Brunner illegible Age 61-6-19
 Birth: 24 Jan 1806 Death: 5 Jul 1866
Site 6 Catherine Brunner Birth: 1 Jul 1802 Death: 21 Apr 1877
 illegible
Site 6 Joseph B. Pyles Age 30-1-1
 Birth: 1 Apr 1833 Death: 2 May 1863

Monocacy Cemetery, Beallsville, Montgomery County, Maryland

Site 8 Benjamin Franklin Pyles   h/o Sara R. Pyles
        Birth: 18 Nov 1840   Death: 17 Aug 1896   Burial: 18 Aug 1896
Site 9 Sarah R. Pyles   Place: Barnesville
        Birth: 11 Feb 1840   Death: 3 Apr 1919   Burial: 5 Apr 1919
        Mort: W.T. Hilton & Sons   TS: w/o Benjamin Franklin Pyles
Site 11 Hilleary Piles   Death: 30 March 1866   TS: Age 63 yrs
Site 12 Matilda Piles   Birth: 5 Jan 1805   Death: 24 Dec 1890
        w/o Hilleary Piles, age 85-11-19

Lot: 5 Owner: Washington Waters White
Site 2 Frances White Karger   Place: Washington, DC
        Birth: 20 Jul 1898   Death: 23 May 1960   Burial: 25 May 1960
        Mort: Robert A. Pumphrey   d/o Washington W. White
Site 3 Washington W. White   Birth: 4 Nov 1858   Burial: 5 Dec 1903

Lot: 6 Owner: William Gassaway
Site 1 William Augustus Gassaway   h/o Mary Elizabeth Gassaway
        Birth: 11 Sep 1837   Death: 3 Oct 1909   Burial: 15 Oct 1909
Site 2 Mary Elizabeth Gassaway   On stone with William Augustus Gassaway
        Birth: 7 Mar 1843   Death: 31 Aug 1905   Burial: 2 Spe 1905
Site 3 Sallie Cummins Griggs   TS: w/o Rev. Walter Porter Griggs
        Birth: 25 Nov 1861   Death: 15 Oct 1896
        d/o William A. & Mary Elizabeth Gassaway
Site 4 Rev. Walter Porter Griggs   Mort: Hilton & Hall
        Birth: 24 Aug 1858   Death: 29 May 1930   Burial: 1 Jun 1930
        Place: Poolesvile   h/o Sallie Cummins Gassaway Griggs
Site 5 Rev. Walter Gassaway Griggs Mort: Striffler-Hamby   Place: Columbus, GA
        Birth: 1896   Death: 3 Jan 1955   Burial: 7 Jan 1955
Site 7 Florence McNeir   id/o Rev. R.S. McNeir   No marker
                                                            Burial: 3 Jun 1900
Site 8 Bowie Barton Waters   Mort: R.W. Pumphrey   Place: Germantown
        Birth: 7 Oct 1940   Death: 11 Feb 1942   Burial: 13 Feb 1942
Site 9 Bowie Jennings Waters   Mort: Robert A. Pumphrey   Place: Rockville
        Birth: 14 Sep 1908   Death: 13 Dec 1963   Burial: 16 Dec 1963

Monocacy Cemetery, Beallsville, Montgomery County, Maryland   47

Row B

Lot: 1 Owner: Mrs. J. Sprigg Poole (1 stone in lot)
- Site 9 Annie Evelyn Poole   Mort: Almus R. Speare   Place: Washington, DC
  Birth: 1858   Death: 30 Apr 1936   Burial: 2 May 1936
- Site 10 J. Sprigg Poole   Mort: W.R. Pumphrey   Place: Rockville
  Birth: 1846   Death: 11 Sep 1914   Burial: 13 Sep 1914
- Site 11 Martha Sprigg Poole
  Birth: 1890   Death: 23 May 1972   Burial: 26 May 1972
- Site 12 Katherine Riggs Poole   Birth: 1891   Death: 11 Oct 1982

Lot: 2 Owner: Mrs. Rebecca Poole
- Site 3 William D. Poole   TS: Age 61-7-26   h/o Rebecca Poole
  Birth: 8 Aug 1801   Death: 3 Apr 1869
- Site 4 Rebecca Poole   TS: w/o William D. Poole, age 71-8-0
  Death: 29 Dec 1880   Burial: 31 Dec 1880
- Site 5 Miss Martha Poole   TS: Age 49-1-28
  Death: 17 Sep 1888   Burial: 19 Sep 1888
- Site 6 Miss Mary Margaret Dickerson   TS: Age 76-9-23
  Death: 7 Oct 1888   Burial: 9 Oct 1888
- Site 8 Rosa Lee Hopkins Poole   w/o Nathan D. Poole
  Death: 4 Mar 1911   Burial: 7 Mar 1911
- Site 9 Nathan Dickerson Poole   h/o Virginia Lee Poole
  Birth: 8 Jan 1845   Death: 5 Nov 1 912   Burial: 7 Nov 1912
- Site 10 Virginia Lee Poole
  Birth: 12 Sep 1850   Death: 7 Sep 1895   Burial: 10 Sep 1895
  TS: w/o Nathan Dickerson Poole, d/o Thomas S. & Sallie L. Hopkins

Lot: 3 Owner: W.W. Poole
- Site 1 Gertrude Poole   TS: d/o W.W. & Avilda Poole
  Birth: 9 Mar 1861   Death: 5 Dec 1861
- Site 2 Avilda Poole   TS: w/o W.W. Poole
  Birth: 8 Jan 1834   Death: 29 Sep 1894   Burial: 9 Oct 1894
- Site 3 William Wallace Poole   h/o Sarah Agnes Poole
  Birth: 1 Nov 1833   Death: 19 May 1899   Burial: 22 May 1899
- Site 4 Sarah Agnes Poole   TS: w/o W.W. Poole
  Birth: 8 Nov 1847   Death: 13 Mar 1905   Burial: 16 Mar 1905
- Site 8 Rosalie Poole Thomas
  Birth: 20 Apr 1866   Death: 12 Jun 1905   Burial: 14 Jun 1905
  TS: w/o Rev. Henry Thomas, d/o Wm.W. & Avilda Poole
- Site 9 Rev. Henry Thomas   Place: Hyattsville
  Birth: 1852   Death: 26 Feb 1921   Burial: 28 Feb 1921
  Mort: F. Gaschs Sons   h/o Rosalie Poole Thomas

Lot: 4 Owner: Mrs. Sarah Jones
- Site 2 S. Agnes Jones Poole   No dates on stone   Burial: 12 May 1905
  d/o Thomas L. & Mary T. Jones   Reinterment

Monocacy Cemetery, Beallsville, Montgomery County, Maryland

Site 2 Edwin Jones Burial: 12 May 1905 Reinterment
  No dates on stone
Site 2 Josephine Jones d/o Thomas L. & Mary T. Jones Reinterment
  No dates on stone Burial: 12 May 1905
Site 2 Martha E. Jones d/o Thomas L. & Mary T. Jones Reinterment
  No dates on stone Burial: 12 May 1905
Site 2 Mary Tomsey Jones d/o Thomas L. & Mary T. Jones Reinterment
  No dates on stone Burial: 12 May 1905
Site 2 Poole Jones s/o Thomas L. & Mary T. Jones Reinterment
  Not on stone Burial: 12 May 1905
Site 2 Sprigg Jones No dates on stone Burial: 12 May 1905
Site 3 Thomas L. Jones h/o Mary Tomsey Poole Jones Reinterment
  Birth: 12 Dec 1811 Death: 2 Jan 1873 Burial: 12 May 1905
Site 3 Mary Tomsey Jones TS: w/o Thomas L. Jones, d/o ? & Prissa Poole
  Birth: 23 Jun 1821 Death: 16 Feb 1849 TS: Age 27-?-26
Site 4 Mrs. Sarah Poole Jones Age 92
  Birth: 16 Mar 1812 Death: 12 Feb 1905 Burial: 15 Feb 1905
Site 6 Mary M. Jones Birth: 19 Sep 1834 Death: 1868
Site 8 Priscilla John Jones Mort: Hilton & Hall Place: Poolesville
  Birth: 8 Dec 1835 Death: 16 Feb 1921 Burial: 18 Feb 1921
Site 9 Frederick Reginald Freemont Jones
  Birth: 1854 Death: 18 Mar 1911 Burial: 20 Mar 1911
  On stone with Mary M. Jones & Priscella John Jones

Lot: 5 Owner: W. Henry Cooley
Site 1 William Henry Cooley Place: Washington, DC
  Birth: 3 Aug 1843 Death: 2 Dec 1921 Burial: 4 Dec 1921
  Mort: W.T. Hilton & Sons TS: h/o Maria E. Belt Cooley
Site 2 Maria E. Cooley Place: Washington, DC
  Birth: 3 Dec 1844 Death: 1 Nov 1926 Burial: 3 Nov 1926
  Mort: W.W. Deal & Co. TS: w/o William Henry Cooley
Site 3 Horace Cooley Death: 1886 Infant
Site 4 Wynona Cooley Birth: 1880 Death: 1885
Site 5 Magie E. Cooley d/o William Henry & Maria E. Belt Cooley
  Birth: 3 Jan 1872 Death: 3 Jan 1876 Burial: 5 Jan 1876
Site 6 Mollie D. Cooley Death: Mar 1871 illegible
  d/o William Henry & Maria Belt Cooley, age 4 mo.
Site 6 Mast Clark Cooley Born & Died: 1889 Burial: 28 Dec 1889
  is/o William Henry & Maria Belt Cooley
Site 7 H. Herbert Cooley Place: Washington, DC
  Birth: 1868 Death: 6 Jan 1934 Burial: 9 Jan 1934
  Mort: S.H. Hines Co. s/o William Henry & Maria Belt Cooley
Site 8 James Henry Brodnax Place: Washington, DC
  Birth: 1865 Death: 18 Jan 1940 Burial: 20 Jan 1940
  Mort: S.H. Hines Co. h/o Minnie Cooley Brodnax
Site 9 Minnie Cooley Brodnax Place: Washington, DC
  Birth: 1875 Death: 13 Jul 1955 Burial: 16 Jul 1955
  Mort: S.H. Hines Co. On stone with James H. Brodnax

Lot: 6 Owner: Dr. Edward Wootton

Site 1 Dr. Turner Wootton
Birth: 14 Feb 1797 Death: 18 Sep 1855
Place: Washington, DC

Site 2 Roland Wootton
Mort: Deal
Birth: 19 Apr 1881 Death: 22 Dec 1961 Burial: 25 Dec 1961
h/o Bettie Wootton

Site 3 Dr. Edward Wootton
Birth: 1839 Death: 1910 Burial: 31 Mar 1910
Place: Poolesville

Site 4 Bettie Wootton
Birth: 1844 Death: 20 Nov 1932 Burial: 22 Nov 1932
Mort: Hilton & Hall w/o Dr. Edward Wootton

Site 5 Bettie Hampton Wootton
Place: Silver Spring
Birth: 2 Nov 1903 Death: 26 Apr 1933 Burial: 28 Apr 1933
Mort: Warner E. Pumphrey d/o N. & E. Wootton

Site 8 Lutie Wootton Death: 2 Mar 1871
TS: d/o Dr. E. & Bettie Wootton, age 0-2-8

Site 9 Bettie Wootton Death: 5 Jul 1872
d/o Dr. E. & Bettie Wootton, age 0-11-10

Site 10 Alan Wootton Death: 15 Nov 1876 Burial: 16 Nov 1876
TS: s/o Dr. E. & Bettie Wootton, age 0-11-23

Site 11 Alice Wootton Death: 2 Sep 1877 Burial: 3 Sep 1877
TS: d/o Dr. E. & Bettie Wootton, age 0-5-10

Site 12 Hugh Hampton Wootton Death: 4 Jun 1887 Burial: 5 Jun 1885
TS: s/o Dr. E. & Bettie Wootton, age 3-7-15

Site 12 Henry Edgar Wootton TS: Eldest s/o Dr. Edward & Bettie Wootton
Birth: 4 Sep 1867 Death: 15 Dec 1887 Burial: 17 Dec 1885

Lot: 7 Owner: Dr. Edward Wootton

Site 1 Mildred Thornton Chiswell
Place: Silver Spring
Birth: 8 Dec 1904 Death: 17 Jul 1952 Burial: 20 Jul 1952
Mort: W.B. Hilton d/o Thomas F. & Eloise Chiswell, age 47

Site 2 Thomas Franklin Chiswell
Place: Silver Spring
Birth: 1871 Death: 7 Mar 1955 Burial: 9 Mar 1955
Mort: W.B. Hilton h/o Eloise W. Chiswell

Site 3 Eloise Wootton Chiswell
Place: Silver Spring
Birth: 16 Sep 1873 Death: 20 Nov 1956 Burial: 23 Nov 1956
Mort: W.B. Hilton h/o Thomas F. Chiswell

Site 4 Albert Wootton Mort: Robert A. Pumphrey Place: Rockville
Birth: 29 Jun 1882 Death: 24 Nov 1954 Burial: 26 Nov 1954

Site 5 Josephine Dawson Wootton w/o Albert Wootton
Birth: 4 Jan 1888 Death: 27 Dec 1980 Burial: 30 Dec 1980

Site 6 Emma V. Wootton d/o Albert & Josephine Wootton, age 76 yrs
Birth: 3 May 1918 Death: 25 Apr 1995 Burial: 6 May 1995

Site 7 Norman Wootton
Place: Silver Spring
Birth: 1869 Death: 14 Feb 1940 Burial: 17 Feb 1940
Mort: Warner E. Pumphrey h/o Edith Chiswell Wootton

Site 8 Edith Chiswell Wootton w/o Norman Wootton
Birth: 1882 Death: 5 Aug 1973 Burial: 7 Aug 1973

Monocacy Cemetery, Beallsville, Montgomery County, Maryland

Site 10 Lola H. Wootton
    Birth: 1911   Death: 29 Nov 1958
    Mort: W.E. Pumphrey
    Place: Colesville
    Burial: 2 Dec 1958
    On stone with Norman D. Wootton, Jr.
Site 11 Mary Sheppe Wootton   Age 78 yrs
    Birth: 1914   Death: 11 Sep 1993   Burial: 15 Sep 1993
    On stone with William Turner Wootton

Lot: 8 Owner: Jesse Veirs
Site 1 Jesse Veirs   illegible   h/o Sophia Veirs, age 77 yrs
    Birth: 13 May 1793   Burial: 19 Mar 1871
Site 2 Sophia Veirs   illegible   Burial: 23 Dec 1875
    w/o Jesse Veirs, age 64 yrs
Site 3 Mollie E. Veirs   d/o Jesse & Sophia Veirs, age 28 yrs
    illegible   Death: 25 Jan 1877   Burial: 27 Dec 1877
Site 4 Elijah Veirs   Son of Jesse Viers
    Birth: 9 Jan 1846   Death: 4 Feb 1900   Burial: 6 Feb 1900
Site 5 Miss Lavinia C. Veirs
    Birth: 14 Mar 1833   Death: 24 Mar 1904   Burial: 26 Mar 1904
Site 7 Miss L. Dorcas Veirs   TS: Age 52 yrs
    Death: 22 Nov 1905   Burial: 24 Nov 1905
Site 8 William S. Veirs
    Birth: 8 Aug 1837   Death: 1 Mar 1908   Burial: 6 Mar 1908
Site 9 Maria Louisa Veirs   TS: Age 76 yrs
    Death: 7 Feb 1912   Burial: 9 Feb 1912
Site 10 Miss Rose Anna Veirs   TS: Age 86 yrs   Mort: Hilton & Hall
    Place: Poolesville   Death: 6 Apr 1928   Burial: 8 Apr 1928
Site 11 Minerva Jane Veirs   TS: Age 84 yrs   Mort: Hilton & Hall
    Place: Poolesville   Death: 6 Aug 1930   Burial: 8 Aug 1930

Lot: 9 Owner: Mrs. C.C. & Webb Pleasant (No stones in lot)
Site 2 Basil Brook Pleasant   Burial: 24 Oct 1902
    Age 71 years   Reinterment
Site 3 Harriet Newel Pleasant   Burial: 24 Oct 1902
    w/o D.S. Pleasant, age 27 years   Reinterment
Site 4 Miflion Pleasant   Burial: 24 Oct 1902
    Age 2 years   Reinterment
Site 5 Deborah Pleasant   Burial: 24 Oct 1902
    Age 2 years   Reinterment
Site 6 Charles Henry Crab Orme   Burial: 24 Oct 1902
    Age 49 years   Reinterment
Site 7 Deborah Brook Orme   Burial: 24 Oct 1902
    Age 38 years   Reinterment
Site 8 Richard I. Orme   Burial: 24 Oct 1902
    Age 19 years   Reinterment
Site 9 Catheran Eliza Orme   Burial: 24 Oct 1902
    Age 2 years   Reinterment
Site 10 Phoebe Anna Orme   Burial: 24 Oct 1902
    Age 4 years   Reinterment

Monocacy Cemetery, Beallsville, Montgomery County, Maryland

| Site 11 | Edgar Thomas Orme | | Burial: 24 Oct 1902 |
| | Age 2 years | | Reinterment |

Lot: 10 Owner: Phillip Reed

Site	Daughter of Phillip Reed	No marker	Burial: 22 May 1881
Site	Child of Richard Stallings	No marker	Burial: 8 Apr 1878
Site	Child of Richard Stallings	No marker	Burial: 23 Jul 1876
Site	Richard S. Stallings	No marker	Burial: 15 Feb 1911
Site 3	Miss Mary Geneva Reed	Mort: R.W. Pumphrey	Place: Washington, DC
	Birth: 1855	Death: 1 Dec 1940	Burial: 4 Dec 1940
Site 4	Amanda Reed		w/o Philip Reed
	Birth: 1809	Death: 1879	Burial: 26 Nov 1880
Site 5	Philip Reed Sr.		h/o Amanda Reed
	Birth: 1804	Death: 1873	Burial: 1 Feb 1873
Site 6	Sarah Ann Reed		
	Birth: 1835	Death: 1872	Burial: 1872
Site 7	James William Works	Mort: M.R. Etchison & Sons	Place: Adamstown
	Birth: 1864	Death: 6 Jan 1942	Burial: 8 Jan 1942
Site 9	John William Stallings	No marker	Mort: William Cook
	Place: Baltimore	Death: 22 Dec 1940	Burial: 24 Dec 1940
Site 10	Eleanor Stallings	No marker	Mort: M.R. Etchison &
	Place: Adamstown	Death: 8 Apr 1928	Burial: 10 Apr 1928
Site 11	George Thomas Elliott	Mort: George Weber	Place: Philadelphia, PA
	Birth: 1879	Death: 23 Apr 1935	Burial: 25 Apr 1935

Lot: 11 Owner: Warner Bolinger

Site	Mr. Barthommea Beall	No marker	Burial: 4 Nov 1877
Site 3	William. H. Bolinger		
	Birth: 27 Feb 1836	Death: 26 Sep 1883	Burial: 28 Sep 1883
Site 4	Mary Bolinger	Death: 28 Oct 1879	
	TS: w/o Warner Bolinger, age 66-15-0		
Site 5	Warner Bolinger		h/o Mary Bolinger, age 63-6-5
	Birth: 20 Apr 1814	Death: 15 Nov 1877	Burial: 16 Nov 1877
Site 9	A. L. Bolinger	illegible	Mort: Hilton & Hall
	Place: Portsmouth, VA	Death: 26 Nov 1916	Burial: 28 Nov 1916
	h/o Emma J. Bolinger, age 67-4-2		
Site 10	Emma Jane Bolinger	illegible	Burial: 20 Mar 1912
	TS: w/o A.L. Bolinger, age about 60 yrs.		
Site 11	Clayton Lewis Bolinger		s/o A.L. & E.J. Bolinger
	Birth: 1 Nov 1877	Death: 7 Apr 1878	Burial: 8 Apr 1978
Site 11	Ethel Bolinger	illegible	d/o A.L. & E.J. Bolinger
	Birth: 3 Apr 1881	Death: 28 Jun 1881	Burial: 29 Jun 1881
Site 12	Wilbur Warner Bolinger	illegible	s/o A.L. & E.J. Bolinger
	Birth: 21 Sep 1874		Burial: 21 Sep 1824
Site 12	Elsie May Bolinger	illegible	i/o A.L. & E.J. Bolinger
	Birth: 3 Jul 1879		Burial: 17 Feb 1880

Lot: 12 Lower   Owner: P.F. Leapley (No stones in lot)
   Site   Child of P. F. Leapley   Burial: 30 Jul 1889
   Site   Child of P. F. Leapley   Burial: 6 Sep 1888

Lot: 12 Upper   Owner: B.F. Reed (No dates on stones)
   Site   Child of B. F. Reed   No marker   Burial: 5 Aug 1873
   Site 1   Benjamin Franklin Reed Burial: 20 Aug 1874   Father
   Site 2   Susan Rebecca Reed   Death: 21 Jan 1907   Burial: 24 Jan 1907
   Site 3   Bertie & Charlie Reed   Age 2 mo
   Site 4   Helen Smallwood Reed   Mort: S.H. Hines & Co.
            Place: Washington   Death: 24 Jul 1930   Burial: 26 Jul 1930
   Site 6   Ada Reed   Mort: R.Kent Smith
            Place: Lake Worth, FL   Death: 6 Jan 1959   Burial: 9 Jan 1959

Lot: 13   Owner: Thomas N. Gott
   Site 2   Daughter Gott   d/o Dr. Richard T. Gott
            Birth: 24 Nov 1874   Death: 24 Nov 1874
   Site 2   Dr. Richard T. Gott
            Birth: 17 Oct 1844   Death: 26 Nov 1908   Burial: 28 Nov 1908
   Site 3   Benjamin N. Gott   Mort: K.E. Ryan   Place: Washington, DC
            Birth: 29 Oct 1856   Death: 20 May 1928   Burial: 23 May 1928
   Site 4   Anna Mary Scholl Gott   Place: Silver Spring
            Birth: 23 Apr 1859   Death: 20 May 1935   Burial: 22 May 1935
            Mort: Warner E. Pumphrey   TS: w/o Benjamin N. Gott
   Site 5   Miller Aiken Cassedy   Place: Rockville
            Birth: 8 Oct 1887   Death: 10 Feb 1948   Burial: 12 Feb 1948
            Mort: Warner E. Pumphrey   h/o Mabel Claire Cassedy
   Site 6   Mable Claire Cassedy   TS: nee Gott   Place: Silver Spring
            Birth: 10 Apr 1889   Death: 31 Dec 1941   Burial: 3 Jan 1942
            Mort: Warner E. Pumphrey   On stone with Miller Aiken Cassedy
   Site 7   Thomas Harold Davis   illegible   Burial: 24 Aug 1872
            s/o Arundel T. & Sallie E. Davis, age 3-1-5
   Site 8   Sarah Ellen Davis   Place: Washington, DC
            Birth: 29 Jun 1846   Death: 25 Jan 1936   Burial: 27 Jan 1936
            Mort: Joseph F. Birch Sons   w/o Arundel Thomas Davis
   Site 9   Arundel Thomas Davis   Place: Washington, DC
            Birth: 1847   Death: 8 Feb 1937   Burial: 10 Feb 1937
            Mort: Jos. F. Burch's Sons   h/o Sarah Ellen Gott Davis, age 90
   Site 10 Eleanor Elgin Coates   Place: Washington, DC
            Birth: 1874   Death: 19 Nov 1958   Burial: 22 Nov 1958
            Mort: S.H. Hines Co.   On stone with Clarence J. Coates
   Site 11 Clarence J. Coates   Place: Washington, DC
            Birth: 1876   Death: 21 Nov 1956   Burial: 23 Nov 1956
            Mort: S.H. Hines Co.   h/o Eleanor Coates
   Site 12 Mary Collison Chiswell   Mort: Hilton
            Place: Frederick   Death: 12 Sep 1961   Burial: 14 Sep 1961

Monocacy Cemetery, Beallsville, Montgomery County, Maryland   53

Lot: 14 Owner: Thomas N. Gott
Site 1 William C. Gott   Place: Gaithersburg
        Birth: 14 Dec 1847   Death: 31 Jul 1937   Burial: 2 Aug 1937
        Mort: Ernest C. Gartner TS: s/o Thomas N. & Eleanor W. Gott
Site 2 Eugenia Gott   Place: Licksville
        Birth: 13 Jan 1854   Death: 18 Dec 1934   Burial: 20 Dec 1934
        Mort: Hilton & Hall   TS: d/o Thomas N. & Eleanor W. Gott
Site 3 Ann Mary Gott   Place: Licksville
        Birth: 28 Mar 1850   Death: 25 Feb 1922   Burial: 28 Feb 1922
        Mort: Hilton & Hall   TS: d/o Thomas N. & Eleanor W. Gott
Site 4 Thomas Norris Gott   TS: h/o Eleanor White Gott
        Birth: 1 Apr 1818   Death: 5 Sep 1903   Burial: 7 Sep 1903
Site 5 Eleanor White Gott   w/o Thomas Norris Gott
        Birth: 18 Sep 1822   Death: 17 Jan 1897   Burial: 19 Jan 1897
Site 6 Eleanor Chiswell Bourke   Mort: Etchinson & Sons
        Place: Frederick, MD   Death: 29 May 1969   Burial: 3 Jun 1969
Site 8 Eugenia G. Chiswell   Place: Frederick   Mort: Hilton & Hall
        Birth: 16 Sep 1883   Death: 6 Mar 1933   Burial: 9 Mar 1933
        TS: d/o John A. & E. Susan Chiswell
Site 9 Elizabeth Susan Gott Chiswell   Place: Licksville
        Birth: 21 Jul 1852   Death: 3 Dec 1926   Burial: 9 Dec 1926
        Mort: Hilton & Hall   TS: w/o John A. Chiswell
Site 10 John A. Chiswell   Mort: Hilton & Hall   Place: Licksville
        Birth: 30 Dec 1851   Death: 7 Jun 1924   Burial: 8 Jun 1924
Site 11 Margaret White Chiswell   Place: Licksville
        Birth: 7 Dec 1887   Death: 11 Jan 1919   Burial: 13 Jan 1919
        Mort: Hilton & Hall   TS: d/o John A. & E. Susan Chiswell

Lot: 15 Owner: E.D. Cruit
Site 1 Alice Maude Cruit   Place: Washington, DC
        Birth: 1871   Death: 24 Jun 1937   Burial: 26 Jun 1937
        Mort: Geo. W. Wise Co.   d/o Charlotte E. & Edwin D. Cruit
Site 2 Charlotte E. Cruit   Place: Washington, DC
        Birth: 1838   Death: 13 Jun 1924   Burial: 16 Jun 1924
        Mort: Geo W. Wise Co.   w/o Edwin D. Cruit
Site 3 Edwin D. Cruit   Place: Washington, DC
        Birth: 1836   Death: 25 Mar 1921   Burial: 28 Mar 1921
        Mort: H.O. Sheppard   h/o Charlotte E. Cruit
Site 5 Thomas D. Cruit   Place: Tewksbury, MA
        Birth: 1877   Death: 5 Oct 1918   Burial: 11 Oct 1918
        Mort: W.T. Hilton & Sons s/o Edwin D. & Charlotte E. Cruit
Site 7 Charlotte C. Cruit   Place: Poolesville
        Birth: 1914   Death: 16 Jan 1915   Burial: 18 Jan 1915
        Mort: Hilton & Hall   TS: d/o L.R. & C.M. Cruit
Site 8 Alice Nora Cruit   Place: Poolesville
        Birth: 1920   Death: 25 Jan 1921   Burial: 26 Jan 1921
        Mort: Hilton & Hall   TS: d/o Luther R. & C.M. Cruit

Monocacy Cemetery, Beallsville, Montgomery County, Maryland

Site 9 Edith Ellen Cruit
    Birth: 1866   Death: 20 Jul 1950
    Mort: Joseph T. Burch Sons
    Place: Washington, DC
    Burial: 23 Jul 1950
    d/o Charlotte E. & Edwin D. Cruit

Site 10 Russell C.H. Cruit
    Birth: 1882   Death: 31 Mar 1957
    Mort: Chambers
    Place: Washington, DC
    Burial: 3 Apr 1957
    s/o Edwin D. & Charlotte E. Cruit

Lot: 16 Owner: Richard Pyles (One stone)

Site 2 William C. Pyles
    Place: Poolesville   Death: 24 Nov 1929
    Mort: Hilton & Hall   Burial: 26 Nov 1929

Site 3 Richard Pyles   Birth: Jan 1820   Death: Mar 1875

Site 4 Susan Pyles   Birth: Apr 1823   Death: Jun 1898

Site 5 Mary V. (Jennie) Pyles   Mort: Hilton & Hall
    Place: Poolesville   Death: 15 Mar 1932   Burial: 17 Mar 1932

Site 6 John R. Pyles   Death: 31 Mar 1940   Burial: 31 Mar 1940

Site 7 Lola Wade Grimes   d/o C.T. & Mary Grimes, age 4 yrs 4 mo
    No marker   Death: 2 Jan 1889   Burial: 4 Jan 1889

Lot: 17 Owner: J.T. Fletchall

Site 1 William Thomas Fletchall   s/o John T. & Mary S. Fletchall
    TS: Age 2 yrs   Death: 27 Feb 1856

Site 2 Harriet Eleanor Fletchall   Death: 7 May 1853
    d/o John T. & Mary S. Fletchall   TS: Age 10 mo

Site 3 John Fletchall   s/o John T. & Mary S. Fletchall
    Birth: 26 Mar 1851   Death: 26 Mar 1851

Site 4 John T. Fletchall   h/o Mary S. Fletchall   TS: Age 69 yrs 4 mo
    Death: 11 Dec 1893   Burial: 12 Dec 1893

Site 5 Mary S. Fletchall   Death: 30 May 1903
    TS: w/o of John Fletchall, age 77-8-0

Site 6 George Walter Fletchall   TS: Age 52 yrs
    s/o John T. Fletchall   Death: 14 Apr 1903   Burial: 16 Apr 1903

Lot: 18 Owner: Miscellaneous

Site   Richard Mortimer Williams   h/o Rose Anderson   Removed to Rockville
    Birth: 13 Mar 1841   Death: 16 Jun 1882   Burial: 18 Jun 1882

Site 6 Richard Walter Allnutt   h/o Elizabeth Brown Allnutt
    Birth: 31 Jan 1907   Death: 19 Mar 1982   Burial: 23 Mar 1982

Site 7 Rachael Chiswell White   TS: w/o Benjamin White, age 68 yrs
    Birth: 7 Mar 1794   Death: 7 Mar 1862   Burial: 7 Mar 1862

Site 8 Benjamin White   w/o Rachael Chiswell White   s/o Nathan
    Birth: 15 Oct 1786   Death: 15 Apr 1862   TS: Age 75 yrs 6 mo

Site 9 Hester Chiswell Williams   Place: Poolesville
    Birth: 1 Jun 1834   Death: 5 Feb 1917   Burial: 8 Feb 1917
    Mort: Hilton & Hall   TS: w/o R.W. Williams, age 82-8-1

Site 10 R. Walter Williams Sr.   TS: Age 75-8-10   h/o Hester C. Williams
    Birth: 21 Oct 1814   Death: 31 Jan 1890   Burial: 2 Feb 1890

Site 11 Joseph Kenneth Allnutt   h/o Evalyn Darby Allnutt
    Birth: 19 Aug 1903   Death: 6 Sep 1977   Burial: 9 Sep 1977

Monocacy Cemetery, Beallsville, Montgomery County, Maryland

Site 12 Evelyn Darby Allnutt Mort: Hilton Place: Frederick
Birth: 10 Feb 1905 Death: 22 Oct 1966 Burial: 25 Oct 1966
w/o Joseph Kenneth Allnutt, d/o Joseph N. & Mary C. Darby

Lot: 19 Owner: Dr. Thomas Shaeffer
Site Thomas L. Schaeffer Burial: 3 Jan 1873 Child, no marker
Site 1 Lelia N. Hilleary Mort: E. William Lamoreax Place: Baltimore
Birth: 15 Mar 1870 Death: 20 Sep 1956 Burial: 24 Sep 1956
On stone with Aldridge G. Hilleary
Site 2 Aldridge G. Hilleary Mort: W.R. Pumphrey Place: Silver Spring
Birth: 10 Dec 1860 Death: 25 Sep 1915 Burial: 27 Sep 1915
Site 3 Ella May Schaeffer TS: d/o Thomas H. & Eliz. Shaeffer
Birth: 2 Jan 1868 Death: 22 Jan 1869
Site 3 Margaret Elizabeth Schaeffer illegible d/o T.H. & E. Schaeffer
Birth: 1 May 1873 Death: 16 Aug 1901 Burial: 18 Aug 1901
Site 4 Margaret Elizabeth Schaeffer Place: Baltimore
Birth: 30 Nov 1840 Death: 16 Feb 1915 Burial: 18 Feb 1918
Mort: Hilton & Hall TS: w/o Dr. T.H. Schaeffer
Site 5 Dr. Thomas H. Schaeffer Death: 15 Jun 1888 Burial: 17 Jun 1888
Site 6 Margaret Estelle Jordan Place: Catonsville
Birth: 1 May 1873 Death: 8 Jul 1934 Burial: 28 Jul 1934
Mort: Wm. J. Tickner & Sons TS: w/o W.W. Jordan
Site 7 John Thomas Hilleary Mort: Henry W. Jenkins Place: Baltimore
Birth: 1904 Death: 21 Feb 1963 Burial: 25 Feb 1963

Lot: 20 Owner: Samuel Young
Site 1 Mary E.Y. Davis Birth: 1853 Burial: 14 Nov 1906
Site 2 Geno D. Weller Mort: Joseph F. Birch Place: Washington, DC
Birth: 1870 Death: 5 Aug 1934 Burial: 7 Aug 1934
Site 4 Mr. Samuel C. Young Birth: 1809 Burial: 19 Oct 1877
Site 5 Eugenia T. Young w/o Samuel C. Young
Birth: 1832 Death: 1907 Burial: 28 Aug 1907

Lot: 21 Owner: R.W. Stout
Site 1 Norman Lee Schneider h/o Eleanor Stout Schneider
Birth: 1924 Death: 17 May 1974 Burial: 21 May 1974
Site 2 Eleanor Stout Schneider w/o Norman L. Schneider
Birth: 23 Nov 1912 Death: 17 Apr 1980 Burial: 21 Apr 1980
Site 3 Annie Rebekah Stout Place: Poolesville
Birth: 1906 Death: 9 Dec 1920 Burial: 11 Dec 1920
Mort: Hilton & Hall d/o Robert W. & Claudia C. Stout
Site 4 Claudia C. Stout w/o Robert W. Stout
Birth: 1880 Death: 27 Aug 1972 Burial: 30 Aug 1972
Site 5 Robert W. Stout Place: Poolesville
Birth: 18 Jun 1861 Death: 10 Nov 1938 Burial: 12 Nov 1938
Mort: Hilton & Hall h/o Claudia C. Stout
Site 6 Mamie F. Stout Birth: 1875 Death: 1893

Lot: 22 Owner: D.J. Willard, 1st

Site	Name	Marker/Death	Burial
Site	Child of C.F.M. Willard	No marker	Burial: 17 Sep 1873
Site	Child of Harry Willard	No marker	Burial: 16 Oct 1906
Site 1	D. Josephus Willard Jr. Birth: 21 Feb 1873	s/o Dewalt J. & Sarah E. Willard, no marker Death: 30 Jun 1873	Burial: 2 Jul 1873 Place: Poolesville
Site 2	Dewalt Joseph Willard Birth: 1843 Mort: W.T. Hilton & Sons	Death: 24 Feb 1932	Burial: 26 Feb 1932 h/o Sarah E. Willard
Site 2	Sarah Etta Willard Birth: 1844 Mort: Hilton & Price	Death: 22 Jul 1933	Place: Poolesville Burial: 23 Jul 1933 TS: w/o Dewalt J. Willard
Site 3	Maurice Willard Birth: 1876 Mort: Hilton & Price	Death: 14 Dec 1934	Place: Fountainville, PA Burial: 18 Dec 1934 s/o Dewalt & Sarah Willard
Site 4	George D. Willard Birth: 1868 Mort: W.B. Hilton	Death: 19 Sep 1948	Place: Bethesda Burial: 22 Sep 1948 h/o Mary M. Willard
Site 5	Mary M. Farr Willard Birth: 1863 Mort: W.B. Hilton	Death: 15 Jul 1950	Place: Rockville Burial: 17 Jul 1950 w/o George D. Willard
Site 6	Earnest Garfield Willard Birth: 1881 Mort: Wm. B. Hilton	Death: 30 Aug 1968	Place: Frederick, MD Burial: 31 Aug 1968 s/o D.J. & Sarah E. Willard

Lot: 23 Owner: J.S. Stallings

Site	Child of John Stallings	No marker	Burial: 15 Jun 1894
Site	Child of Robert L. Stallings	No marker	Burial: 3 Sep 1889
Site 1	Mrs. Rebecca S. Hillard	Death: 12 Jan 1894	Burial: 15 Jan 1894
Site 6	Lucy Stallings	Death: 11 Nov 1880	w/o John S. Stallings Burial: 12 Nov 1880

Lot: 24 Owner: A.T. Hempstone

Site 1	William Hempstone	No marker	MD MIL REV War
Site 2	Harriet B. Hempstone Birth: 10 May 1821	Death: 2 Jan 1881	w/o A.T. Hempstone Burial: 4 Jan 1881 h/o Harriet Hempstone
Site 3	Armstead T. Hempstone Birth: 28 Jul 1814	Death: 8 Apr 1894	
Site 3	Christie D. Hempstone TS: d/o Armistead T. & Harriet B. Hempstone	Birth: 5 May 1850	Death: 2 May 1886
Site 4	Harry D. Hempstone Birth: 30 Nov 1853	Death: 11 Aug 1900	Burial: 13 Aug 1900 Place: Poolesville
Site 5	William A. Hempstone Birth: 1855	Mort: Hilton & Hall Death: 3 Jul 1929	Burial: 5 Jul 1929 Place: Washington, DC
Site 6	Lutie A. Norris Hempstone Birth: 24 Oct 1862 Mort: Wm. R. Pumphrey	Death: 28 Feb 1944	Burial: 1 Mar 1944 w/o William A. Hempstone

Lot: 25 Owner: F.M. Griffith

Site 1 Herbert Marple Hurtt
    Birth: 5 Jul 1877 Death: 7 Apr 1907 Burial: 9 Apr 1907
Site 2 Bessie E. G. Hurtt Mort: S.H. Hines Co. Place: Washington, DC
    Birth: 17 Jun 1877 Death: 6 Sep 1961 Burial: 9 Sep 1961
    TS: w/o Herbert M. Hurtt
Site 7 Nathan Cook Dickerson TS: In his 82nd year
    Death: 14 May 1891 Burial: 16 May 1891
Site 8 Elizabeth Dickerson Griffith TS: w/o F.M. Griffith
    Birth: 26 Jun 1836 Death: 6 Apr 1904 Burial: 9 Apr 1904
Site 9 Francis Moore Griffith
    Birth: 14 Jun 1831 Death: 20 Jan 1908 Burial: 23 Jan 1908
    h/o Elizabeth D. Griffith, s/o Greenbury & Prudence Jones Griffith
Site 10 Mrs. Christie A. Dickerson TS: In her 72nd year
    Death: 20 Jun 1884 Burial: 22 Jun 1884
Site 11 Nathan C.D. Dickerson
    Birth: 26 Oct 1859 Death: 16 Feb 1905 Burial: 20 Feb 1905
Site 12 Francis M. Griffith Jr.
    Birth: 10 Jun 1870 Death: 8 Dec 1889 Burial: 11 Dec 1889

Lot: 26 Owner: J. Alonzo Padgett

Site 1 Maymie A. Padgett Mort: Hilton & Hall Place: Poolesville
    Birth: 1873 Death: 19 Jan 1938 Burial: 21 Jan 1938
Site 2 Edwin Earl Padgett Mort: W.T. Hilton & Sons Place: Dickerson
    Birth: 1882 Death: 4 Jan 1919 Burial: 6 Jan 1919
    TS: Death: 1918
Site 3 James Alonzo Padgett TS: Death: 1915 Place: Dickerson
    Birth: 1843 Death: 27 Aug 1916 Burial: 29 Aug 1916
    Mort: W.T. Hilton & Sons h/o Jane R. Padgett
Site 4 Jane R. Padgett w/o J. Alonzo Padgett
    Birth: 1850 Death: 1908 Burial: 25 Sep 1908
Site 5 Elsie Padgett d/o J. Alonzo & Elsie Padgett
    Birth: 10 Mar 1880 Death: 1880 Burial: 10 Mar 1881
Site 6 Della M. Padgett
    Birth: 1872 Death: 1883 Burial: 27 May 1883
Site 6 Infant Son Wolfe TS: s/o N.H. & D.M. Wolfe
    Birth: 1913 Death: 1913
Site 7 Mary Frances Padgett w/o Algernon J. Padgett
    Birth: 1886 Death: 12 Dec 1971 Burial: 14 Dec 1971
Site 8 Algernon J. Padgett Place: Frederick
    Birth: 1878 Death: 13 Mar 1927 Burial: 16 Mar 1927
    Mort: W.T. Hilton & Sons h/o Mary Frances Padgett
Site 9 Dunbar D. Padgett Mort: Wm. R. Pumphrey Place: Takoma Park
    Birth: 1895 Death: 1943
Site 10 Frank H. Padgett Mort: Hilton Place: Frederick
    Birth: 1891 Death: 17 Sep 1957 Burial: 19 Sep 1957

Monocacy Cemetery, Beallsville, Montgomery County, Maryland

Site 11 Dora Padgett Wolfe
    Birth: 1874   Death: 5 May 1940
    Mort: W.B. Hilton
Place: State Sanatorium
Burial: 7 May 1940
w/o Norman H. Wolfe

Site 12 Norman Hyatt Wolfe
    Birth: 1882   Death: 21 Mar 1969
    Mort: Wm. Hilton
Place: Takoma Park, MD
Burial: 24 Mar 1969
h/o Dora Padgett Wolfe

Lot: 27 Owner: R.J. Cooley, Jr.

Site   Mrs. Annie Willett Cooley   No marker
         Birth: 1863   Burial: 19 Sep 1884
Site   Child of Robert J. Cooley Sr.   No marker   Burial: 20 Jun 1895
Site   Robert T. Cooley Jr.   No marker
         Birth: 1849   Burial: 19 Apr 1907

Lot: 28 Owner: Elias Price

Site 1 Gertrude V. Price   Place: Poolesville
         Birth: 1876   Death: 16 Jul 1947   Burial: 17 Jul 1947
         Mort: W.B. Hilton   d/o Elias & Mary F. Price
Site 2 Mary Frances Price   Place: Poolesville
         Birth: 15 Feb 1844   Death: 21 Dec 1936   Burial: 23 Dec 1936
         Mort: Hilton & Hall   w/o Elias Price, age 92
Site 3 Elias Price   h/o Mary F. Price
         Birth: 14 Feb 1840   Death: 24 Jul 1904   Burial: 26 Jul 1904
Site 4 Infant Penn   Mort: W.R. Pumphrey
         Place: Rockville   Death: 27 Jan 1921   Burial: 28 Jan 1921
         i/o Melvin S. & Ethel Penn   No marker
Site 4 Melvin Stanley Penn   Mort: Robt. Pumphrey   Place: Silver Spring, MD
         Birth: 14 Jul 1891   Death: 25 Aug 1970   Burial: 28 Aug 1970
         TS: h/o Sarah Ethel Price Penn
Site 5 Sarah Ethel Price Penn   Place: Rockville
         Birth: 27 Oct 1878   Death: 29 Sep 1946   Burial: 2 Oct 1946
         Mort: W.R. Pumphrey   TS: w/o Melvin S. Penn
Site 7 Carrie Norma Poe   Place: Washington, DC
         Birth: 1881   Death: 1 Oct 1955   Burial: 4 Oct 1955
         Mort: W.W. Chambers   d/o Elias & Mary F. Price
Site 8 Clara L. Price   Place: Washington, DC
         Birth: 1871   Death: 15 May 1951   Burial: 17 May 1951
         Mort: Hunteman Funeral Home   d/o Elias & Mary F. Price, age 80
Site 10 Cora Price   Place: Washington, DC
         Birth: 1873   Death: 1 Mar 1959   Burial: 4 Mar 1959
         Mort: Chambers Co.   d/o Elias & Mary F. Price
Site 11 Lilly Belle Price Gattis
         Birth: 5 Dec 1888   Death: 29 Dec 1981   Burial: 31 Jan 1981

Lot: 29 Owner: Hanson & son Tom Miles

Site   Child Miles   No marker   c/o Thomas H. Miles
                                                Burial: 9 Dec 1894
Site   Mary Katherine Miles   No marker   Mort: A.G. Carlisle
         Place: Clarksburg   Death: 27 Oct 1916   Burial: 28 Oct 1916

Monocacy Cemetery, Beallsville, Montgomery County, Maryland 59

Site 1 Infant Miles   No marker   s/o H.T. & M.C. Miles
                                                                    Burial: Jul 1885
Site 2 M. M. Miles   No marker
Site 3 Howard Montgomery Miles   Place: Olney
        Birth: 12 Sep 1879   Death: 17 Dec 1952   Burial: 20 Dec 1952
        Mort: Ernest C. Gartner   h/o Della Mae Miles
Site 4 Della Mae Miles   Place: Clarksburg
        Birth: 29 Apr 1882   Death: 10 Nov 1959   Burial: 12 Nov 1959
        Mort: E.C. Gartner   w/o Howard M. Miles
Site 8 Elvira M. Miles   w/o James H. Miles   TS: Age 90 years
                                Death: 30 Jul 1899   Burial: 1 Aug 1899
Site 9 James Hanson Miles   h/o Elvira M. Miles   TS: Age 81 yrs
                                Death: 5 May 1891   Burial: 7 May 1891
Site 10 Hanson T. Miles   Place: Clarksburg
        Birth: 25 Mar 1850   Death: 18 Jun 1926   Burial: 20 Jun 1926
        Mort: E.C. Gartner   h/o Mary Catharine Miles
Site 11 Mary Catherine Miles   Place: Clarksburg
        Birth: 23 May 1855   Death: 11 Feb 1917   Burial: 13 Feb 1917
        Mort: A.G. Carlisle   w/o Hanson T. Miles

Lot: 30 Owner: Zach T. Reed (No stones in lot)
Site   Charles C. Reed   Burial: 31 Oct 1907   No marker
Site   Ruth Elizabeth Reed   No marker   Mort: F. Gasch Sons
         Place: Mt. Rainer   Death: 7 Sep 1936   Burial: 9 Sep 1936
Site   Child of Thomas I. Reed Burial: 31 Jul 1897   No marker
Site   Zachariah F. Reed   Burial: 9 Aug 1912   No marker
Site 9   Mary F. Walker   No marker   Mort: W.W. Chambers
         Place: Washington, DC Death: 5 Apr 1942   Burial: 8 Apr 1942
Site 10 Charles E. Walker   No marker   Mort: Lee & Sons
         Place: Washington, DC Death: 9 Aug 1956   Burial: 13 Aug 1956
Site 11 Belle Williams   No marker   Mort: W.W. Chambers
         Place: Washington, DC Death: 19 Apr 1954   Burial: 22 Apr 1954

Lot: 31 Owner: George F. Cooley
Site 1   George Jacob Bodmer
         Birth: 19 Jul 1917   Death: 26 Feb 1995   Burial: 1 Mar 1995
Site 2   Dorothy Cooley Bodmer   w/o George J. Bodmer
         Birth: 21 Apr 1917   Death: 10 Feb 1985   Burial: 12 Feb 1985
Site 3   Betty Columbia Wood Cooley   Place: Beallsville
         Birth: 1879   Death: 14 Sep 1965   Burial: 16 Sep 1965
         Mort: Hilton   w/o George F. Cooley
Site 4   George Fulton Cooley   Place: Beallsville, MD
         Birth: 1880   Death: 15 Nov 1967   Burial: 18 Nov 1967
         Mort: Hilton   h/o Betty C. Wood Cooley
Site 7   Kristin Georgeann Hoffacker   i/o Larry & Ginger Bodmer Hoffacker
         Birth: 30 May 1979   Burial: 4 Jun 1979   Cause: Stillborn

Lot: 32 Owner: Charles Kohlhoss

Site 1 Ellen Jane Kohlhoss TS: w/o Charles Kohlhoss I
  Birth: 1840 Death: 1893 Burial: 13 Feb 1893
Site 2 Charles Kohlhoss I Place: Poolesville
  Birth: 1840 Death: 28 Apr 1914 Burial: 30 Apr 1914
  Mort: Hilton & Hall h/o Ellen Jane Kohloss
Site 3 Mrs. Christie A. Carlisle
  Birth: 1814 Death: 1901 Burial: 23 Sep 1901
Site 4 C. E. Munsey Kohlhoss Place: Washington, DC
  Birth: 1869 Death: 23 Nov 1921 Burial: 25 Nov 1921
  Mort: W.T. Hilton & Sons s/o Ellen Jane & Charles Kohlhoss I
Site 5 Minnie (Carrie) S. Kohlhoss Place: Poolesville
  Birth: 1880 Death: 19 Feb 1945 Burial: 21 Feb 1945
  Mort: W.B. Hilton On stone with Harry Kohlhoss
Site 6 Harry Kohlhoss Place: Poolesville
  Birth: 1874 Death: 24 Mar 1957 Burial: 26 Mar 1957
  Mort: Hilton h/o Minnie S. Kohlhoss
Site 10 Charles Edward Kohlhoss Jr. On stone with Winifred Steiner Kohlhoss
  Birth: 9 Mar 1929 Death: 28 Jan 1983 Burial: 1 Feb 1983
  s/o Charles E. & Emma H. Kohlhoss
Site 11 Charles E. Kohlhoss Sr.
  Birth: 21 Sep 1901 Death: 17 Jul 1972 Burial: 20 Jul 1972
Site 12 Emma Mae Thornton Haller Kohlhoss On stone with Charles E. Kohlhoss
  Birth: 29 Mar 1907 Death: 1 Dec 1994 Burial: 5 Dec 1994

Lot: 33 Owner: John T. Hawkins

Site Charles Hawkins Jr. No marker Mort: W.T. Hilton & Sons
  Place: Boyds Death: 21 Mar 1927 Burial: 21 Mar 1927
Site Lucille Hawkins Mort: W.R. Pumphrey
  Place: Unity Death: 27 Aug 1919 Burial: 29 Aug 1919
  Cause: Stillborn No marker
Site 1 Myra Lorraine Hawkins Place: Quince Orchard
  Birth: 19 Jul 1923 Death: 3 Jun 1924 Burial: 6 Jun 1924
  Mort: W.T. Hilton & Sons TS: d/o A.R. & Clara M. Hawkins
Site 2 Laura F. Hawkins Mort: W.T. Hilton & Sons Place: Clarksburg
  Birth: 6 Nov 1859 Death: 21 Oct 1923 Burial: 23 Oct 1923
  On stone with John T. & Annie Elizabeth Hawkins
Site 3 Annie Elizabeth Hawkins Place: Boyds R.F.D.
  Birth: 23 Aug 1838 Death: 5 Mar 1915 Burial: 7 Mar 1915
  Mort: W.T. Hilton & Sons TS: w/o John T. Hawkins
Site 4 John T. Hawkins Place: Clarksburg
  Birth: 1 Jan 1835 Death: 28 Oct 1915 Burial: 31 Oct 1915
  Mort: W.T. Hilton & Sons h/o Annie E. Hawkins
Site 5 Clara M. Hawkins Place: Frederick
  Birth: 1889 Death: 20 Apr 1962 Burial: 23 Apr 1962
  Mort: E.C. Gartner On stone with Algie Raymond Hawkins

Monocacy Cemetery, Beallsville, Montgomery County, Maryland

Site 6	Algie Raymond Hawkins		Place: Bethesda
	Birth: 1884	Death: 3 Feb 1963	Burial: 6 Feb 1963
	Mort: E.C. Gartner		h/o Clara S. Hawkins
Site 11	Joseph Charles Hawkins	No marker	Mort: Warner E.
	Place: Kensington	Death: 11 Jan 1947	Burial: 14 Jan 1947
Site 12	Mrs. Catherine E. (Kate) Bennett		
	Birth: 6 Nov 1871	Death: 21 Oct 1906	Burial: 26 Oct 1906

Lot: 34 Owner: Henry E. Soper

Site 1	Mollie P. Soper		Place: Mt. Ranier
	Birth: 1868	Death: 20 May 1945	Burial: 22 May 1945
	Mort: Wm. J. Nalley		On stone with Henry E. Soper
Site 2	Henry E. Soper		Place: Cheverly
	Birth: 1868	Death: 4 Sep 1949	Burial: 6 Sep 1949
	Mort: Wm. Nalley		h/o Mollie P. White Soper
Site 3	Edward Wade Steele Jr.	No marker	Mort: F. Gaschs & Sons
	Place: Brentwood	Death: 20 Apr 1924	Burial: 22 Apr 1924
Site 4	Paul Mackley Soper	illegible	s/o Henry & Mollie P. Soper
	Birth: 25 May 1906	Death: 14 May 1907	Burial: 16 May 1907
Site 5	Alice Louise Haller Soper		Place: Prince Fred.
	Birth: 1 Jun 1903	Death: 30 Mar 1969	Burial: 2 Apr 1969
	On stone with Lingan D. Soper		
Site 6	Lingan Dow Soper		h/o Alice Haller Soper
	Birth: 24 Jan 1900	Death: 15 Jul 1980	Burial: 18 Jul 1980

Lot: 35 Lower Owner: James Eaton

Site 1	Lillian P. Benson	Mort: Lee's Crematory	Place: Cheverly, MD
	No marker	Death: 22 Mar 1967	Burial: 26 Mar 1967
Site 1	William P. Benson		No marker
		Death: 22 Mar 1967	Burial: 26 Mar 1967
Site 1	Miss Fannie A. Polen	No marker	Age 67 yrs
		Death: 27 Jan 1910	Burial: 29 Jan 1910
Site 2	Ella May Eaton		Place: Washington, DC
	Birth: 16 May 1886	Death: 9 Feb 1927	Burial: 12 Feb 1927
	Mort: Timothy Hanlon		TS: w/o James H. Eaton
Site 3	James H. Eaton		Place: Washington, DC
	Birth: 1868	Death: 2 Mar 1929	Burial: 6 Mar 1929
	Mort: W.W. Deal		h/o Ella May Eaton
Site 4	Lawrence Campbell Eaton		TS: MD PVT US Army WWII
	Birth: 30 May 1907	Death: 18 Mar 1972	Burial: 22 Mar 1972
Site 5	Fannie Eaton Grubb		No marker
	Birth: 27 Feb 1905	Death: 4 Mar 1985	Burial: 22 Mar 1985

Lot: 35 Upper Owner: Reginald Cross

Site	Emma Irene Cross		Place: Rockville
	Birth: 1877	Death: 24 Feb 1947	Burial: 26 Feb 1947
	Mort: W.R. Pumphrey		w/o Reginald Whalen Cross
Site 1	Reginald Whalen Cross	Place: Phoenix, AZ	h/o Emma Irene Cross
	Birth: 1875	Death: 9 Jun 1960	Burial: 14 Jun 1960

Site 2 Reginald Whalen Cross Jr.   Burial: 6 Oct 1909
        TS: s/o Emma Irene & Reginald Whalen Cross   illegible
Site 3 Charles Upton Cross   No marker   Mort: Fitzgerald Funeral Home
        Place: Washington, DC   Death: 26 Jul 1964   Burial: 30 Jul 1964
Site 5 Blanche Virginia Cross Campbell   Place: Cheverly
        Birth: 1912   Death: 17 Nov 1952   Burial: 20 Nov 1952
        Mort: Robert A. Pumphrey   nee Cross

Lot: 36 Owner: R. Edwin Jones
Site 1 Frederick Jones   TS: PVT US Army WWII
        Birth: 24 May 1910   Death: 30 Dec 1988   Burial: 4 Jan 1989
Site 3 Richard Edwin Jones   h/o Anna Elizabeth Jones Place: Paramount, WA
        Birth: 7 Feb 1873   Death: 3 Jan 1951   Burial: 5 Jan 1951
Site 4 Anna Elizabeth Jones   Place: Buckeystown
        Birth: 15 Apr 1875   Death: 6 Feb 1962   Burial: 9 Feb 1962
        Mort: Hilton   w/o Richard Edwin Jones
Site 5 Laura Kathleen Jones   Place: Hagerstown
        Birth: 31 Oct 1911   Death: 8 Aug 1916   Burial: 10 Aug 1916
        Mort: W.T. Hilton & Sons   TS: d/o R.E. & A.E. Jones
Site 6 Richard Edwin Jones Jr.   s/o R.E. & Anna E. Jones
        Birth: 19 Jan 1907   Death: 1 May 1907   Burial: 6 May 1907
Site 6 Herbert Leon Jones   c/o R.E. & A.E. Jones
        Birth: 26 May 1879   Death: 10 Jul 1899   Burial: 11 Jul 1899
Site 7 Annabel Lee Tillett   d/o John W. & Isabella Dean Tillett
        Birth: 16 Jun 1892   Death: 22 May 1980   Burial: 27 May 1980
Site 10 Mary Alta Jones   d/o A.G. & B.J. Jones   Reinterment
        Birth: 14 Oct 1869   Death: 15 Jun 1873   Burial: 22 Jun 1909
Site 11 Anna Virginia Gott Jones   Place: Dickerson
        Birth: 28 Mar 1845   Death: 25 Feb 1922   Burial: 28 Feb 1922
        Mort: W.T. Hilton & Sons   TS: w/o Benjamin John Jones
Site 12 Benjamin John Jones
        Birth: 24 Oct 1840   Death: 7 May 1909   Burial: 9 May 1909
        h/o Anna Virginia Gott Jones   TS: Pvt Co. B 36th VA Cavalry CSA

Lot: 37 Owner: Mrs. Howard White
Site 2 Winfield Scott Powers   Place: Jenkinstown, PA
        Birth: 1885   Death: 11 Mar 1957   Burial: 15 Mar 1957
        Mort: J.E. Heerbeg   h/o Virgie Lee Powers
Site 3 Virgie Leo Powers   Place: Washington, DC
        Birth: 1884   Death: 7 Oct 1970   Burial: 10 Oct 1970
        Mort: Robt. Wilhelm   On stone with Winfield Scott Powers
Site 4 Thomas White   Mort: W.T. Hilton & Sons   Place: Baltimore
        Birth: 1886   Death: 12 Apr 1921   Burial: 13 Apr 1921
Site 5 Alice V. White   Mort: W.T. Hilton & Sons Place: St. Elmo, VA
        Birth: 1857   Death: 25 Aug 1916   Burial: 27 Aug 1916
Site 6 Howard White
        Birth: 1857   Death: 1904   Burial: 14 Jan 1904

Monocacy Cemetery, Beallsville, Montgomery County, Maryland   63

Lot: 38 Upper   Owner: L.W. Poole
Site 1 Baby of Lewis Poole
Site 2 Nettie White Poole   Death: 2 Jul 1909   TS: d/o Lewis W. Poole
Site 3 Eleanor N. White Poole   Mort: W.R. Pumphrey Place: Frederick Hospital
        Birth: 12 Apr 1873   Death: 25 Dec 1944   Burial: 27 Dec 1944
        On stone with Lewis W. Poole
Site 4 Lewis W. Poole   Mort: Hilton & Price   Place: Boyds
        Birth: 12 Jun 1869   Death: 1 Jul 1936   Burial: 4 Jul 1936
Site 5 Lucretia W. Poole   Mort: W.T. Hilton & Sons   Place: Buck Lodge
        Birth: 15 Sep 1849   Death: 17 May 1913   Burial: 19 May 1913
        TS: w/o Richard K. Poole
Site 6 Richard K. Poole   Mort: W.R. Pumphrey   Place: Rockville
        Birth: 15 Sep 1847   Death: 2 Nov 1930   Burial: 5 Nov 1930

Lot: 39 Upper   Owner: John B. & Marie J. Offutt
Site 3 George Edward Offutt   Place: Poolesville
        Birth: 17 Nov 1944   Death: 17 Nov 1944   Burial: 18 Nov 1944
        Mort: W.B. Hilton   s/o Linwood T. & Helen W. Offutt
Site 3 Infant Son Offutt   Place: Barnesville
        Birth: 16 Aug 1940   Death: 20 Aug 1940   Burial: 20 Aug 1940
        Mort: W.B. Hilton   s/o L.T. & Helen W. Offutt
Site 3 Marie Moore Offutt   Place: Poolesville
        Birth: 30 Apr 1928   Death: 30 Apr 1928   Burial: 1 May 1928
        Mort: Hilton & Hall   TS: d/o John B. & Marie J. Offutt
Site 4 Roger Delano Offutt   Place: Poolesville
        Birth: 5 Jun 1935   Death: 5 Jun 1935   Burial: 6 Jun 1935
        Mort: Wm. B. Hilton   TS: s/o J.B. & Marie J. Offutt
Site 5 John B. Offutt   h/o Marie J. Offutt
        Birth: 28 Dec 1889   Death: 14 Mar 1975   Burial: 17 Mar 1975
Site 6 Marie Jones Offutt   w/o John B. Offutt
        Birth: 15 Jul 1895   Death: 8 Mar 1988   Burial: 9 Mar 1988

Lot: 40 Lower   Owner: Mrs. Albert Dixon
Site   Betty Welch   No marker   Mort: M.R. Etcherson & Son
        Place: New York   Death: 19 Jun 1940   Burial: 22 Jun 1940
Site 2 John Paul Dixon   No marker   Mort: M.R. Etchison
        Place: Sykesville   Death: 24 Nov 1965   Burial: 30 Nov 1965
Site 3 Margaret F. Dixon   Mort: M.R. Etchison & Sons   Place: Frederick
        Birth: 1869   Death: 26 Feb 1936   Burial: 29 Feb 1936
        On stone with Albert Sidney Dixon
Site 4 Albert Sidney Dixon   Mort: M.R. Etchison & Son   Place: Frederick
        Birth: 1866   Death: 5 Feb 1953   Burial: 7 Feb 1953
Site 5 Calvin S. Dixon   Death: Jan 1919   Burial: 18 Sep 1935
        Mort: Chas. Roberts   Removed from Pooles tract, Dickerson
Site 5 Rebecca Studebaker   Death: Mar 1921   Burial: 18 Sep 1935
        Mort: Chas. Roberts   Removed from Pooles Tract, Dickerson, MD

Lot: 40 Upper   Owner: Mary T. & Lawrence Guthrie
Site 3 Lawrence Rawlin Guthrie   h/o Mary Tuthill Guthrie
        Birth: 11 Sep 1881   Death: 19 Mar 1974   Burial: 22 Mar 1974
Site 4 Mary Cornelia Tuthill Guthrie   w/o Lawrence R. Guthrie
        Birth: 25 Nov 1885   Death: 10 May 1972   Burial: 13 May 1972

Lot: 41 Lower   Owner: Julian D. & Rosalie J. Freeman
Site 3 Rosalie Jones Freeman   No marker   w/o Dr. Julian D. Freeman
        Birth: 20 Jan 1908   Death: 14 May 1995   Burial: 18 May 1995

Lot: 41 Upper   Owner: Estate of Willson C. Poole
Site 3 Lois Wilson Poole   w/o Willson C. Poole
        Birth: 28 Jun 1902   Death: 23 Nov 1986   Burial: 26 Nov 1986
Site 4 Willson Clarke Poole   Place: Frederick Hospital
        Birth: 1898   Death: 2 Apr 1958   Burial: 4 Apr 1958
        Mort: Hilton   h/o Lois Poole

Lot: 42 Lower   Owner: Miscellaneous
Site 1 Earl William Rowe   No marker   Mort: Hilton
        Place: Dickerson   Death: 20 Dec 1960   Burial: 22 Dec 1960
Site 2 Steven Mark Cregger   No marker, baby   Mort: Hilton
        Place: Bethesda   Death: 20 Nov 1963   Burial: 21 Nov 1963
Site 2 Twin B Baby boy Johnson   Mort: Hilton
        Place: Bethesda   Death: 21 Jun 1964   Burial: 23 Jun 1964
        s/o Robert Johnson   No marker
Site 2 Twin A Baby boy Johnson   Mort: Hilton
        Place: Bethesda   Death: 21 Jun 1964   Burial: 23 Jun 1964
        s/o Robert Johnson   No marker
Site 2 Baby boy Kitts   Grandson of Irvin Kitts Mort: Hilton
        Place: Olney   Death: 2 Nov 1964   Burial: 3 Nov 1964
        No marker
Site 2 Sharon Lee Parker   Place: Silver Spring
        Birth: 27 Nov 1964   Death: 29 Nov 1964   Burial: 30 Nov 1964
        Mort: Hilton   d/o Theodore C. Parker Jr.
Site 3 David Wayne Allen   No marker   Mort: Hilton
        Place: Dawsonville   Death: 3 Feb 1965   Burial: 5 Feb 1965
Site 5 Richard G. Claggett   On stone with Minnie Mae Flood Claggett
        Birth: 17 Jan 1916   Death: 25 Sep 1985   Burial: 27 Sep 1985
Site 6 William Foust Vance   h/o Janet Vance, age 51 yrs
        Birth: 12 Sep 1943   Death: 7 Jun 1995   Burial: 12 Jun 1995

Lot: 42 Upper   Owner: James A. & Louise H. Richardson
Site 4 James Augustine Richardson   Place: Washington, DC
        Birth: 28 Feb 1902   Death: 2 Aug 1961   Burial: 5 Aug 1961
        Mort: Robert A. Pumphrey w/o Louise H. Richardson (Mrs. Arthur Hurd)

Lot: 43 Lower   Owner: Clinton F. Well, Jr.
Site   Clinton F. Wells Sr.   h/o Elizabeth W. Wells
        Birth: 1892   Death: 1961

Monocacy Cemetery, Beallsville, Montgomery County, Maryland   65

Site	Elizabeth Wells		On stone with Clinton F. Wells
Site	Birth: 1893	Death: 1965	
Site	Whitfield Wesley Wells	Birth: 27 May 1883	Death: 27 Dec 1970

Lot: 43 Upper Owner: Mrs. Elsie Phillips & Mrs. Eugene Dixon
Site 1 Elsie Fink Phillips   Mort: Robert A. Pumphrey   Place: Kensington
        Birth: 1895   Death: 18 Nov 1962   Burial: 20 Nov 1962
Site 2 Clara Edith Fink
        Birth: 28 Feb 1897   Death: 18 Oct 1995   Burial: 30 Oct 1995

Lot: 44 Lower Owner: Miscellaneous
Site 1 Mary Louise Stream Cline   Mort: Hilton   Place: Frederick
        Birth: 16 Jun 1939   Death: 9 Aug 1960   Burial: 12 Aug 1960
Site 2 Ruth V. Stream Grimes   Mort: Hilton   Place: Baltimore
        Birth: 25 Sep 1931   Death: 12 Feb 1967   Burial: 15 Feb 1967
Site 3 Elizabeth Ann Halmos   On stone with Eugene E. Halmos
        Birth: 2 Jan 1916   Death: 7 Jan 1984   Burial: 11 Jan 1984
Site 5 Therese R. Smolley   On stone with Donald M. Smolley
        Birth: 12 May 1944   Death: 26 Feb 1985   Burial: 28 Feb 1985
Site 6 Carl Joseph Haller   h/o Sally Shelton Haller
        Birth: 14 Apr 1905   Death: 20 Apr 1992   Burial: 3 May 1994
Site 6 Sally Shelton Haller   On stone with Joseph Carl Haller
        Birth: 8 Sep 1907   Death: 26 Apr 1994   Burial: 3 May 1994

Lot: 44 Upper Owner: Donald E. Jeffers
Site 2 Richard W. Jeffers   On stone with Blanche P. Jeffers
        Birth: 18 Jan 1921   Death: 29 Jun 1987   Burial: 2 Jul 1987
Site 3 Julia E. Jeffers   On stone with Mark Pulliam Jeffers
        Birth: 9 Nov 1898   Death: 9 Jul 1993   Burial: 12 Jul 1993
Site 4 Mark Pulliam Jeffers   Place: Bethesda
        Birth: 23 Jan 1895   Death: 12 Dec 1958   Burial: 15 Dec 1958
        Mort: Hilton   h/o Julia E. Jeffers

Lot: 45 Upper Owner: Frank Fisher
Site 1 Frank S. Fisher   Birth: 9 Sep 1908   Death: 19 Apr 1993
Site 2 Helen D. Fisher   w/o Frank Fisher, age 77 yrs
        Birth: 18 Jul 1914   Death: 4 May 1992   Burial: 19 May 1992

Addition to B

Lot: 1 Owner: Arthur C. Hersberger
Site 9 Arthur Cropley Hersberger   Place: Barnesville
        Birth: 16 Feb 1876   Death: 1 Sep 1945   Burial: 3 Sep 1945
        Mort: W.B. Hilton   h/o Verlinda Jones Hersberger
Site 10 Verlinda Jones Hersberger   Place: Paeonian Springs, VA
        Birth: 14 Oct 1874   Death: 12 Jun 1950   Burial: 15 Jun 1950
        Mort: Lloyd Slack   w/o Arthur Cropley Hersberger
Site 11 John A. Hersberger Jr.   Place: Dawsonville   Mort: Hilton
        Birth: 22 Nov 1947   Death: 17 Jun 1965   Burial: 21 Jun 1965
        s/o John A. & Cecilia Dronenberg Hersberger

Lot: 2 Lower Owner: W. Wallace Poole
Site 2 Virginia Poole Wallace   Place: Walter Reed
        Birth: 1909   Death: 15 Jun 1969   Burial: 18 Jun 1969
        Mort: Cawkes Funeral Home   d/o Wallace & Carrie Poole
Site 3 William Wallace Poole III   Place: Washington, DC
        Birth: 1906   Death: 31 Mar 1932   Burial: 2 Apr 1932
        Mort: W.T. Hilton & Sons   s/o Wallace & Carrie Poole
Site 4 William Wallace Poole   Place: Silver Spring
        Birth: 1874   Death: 9 Apr 1957   Burial: 12 Apr 1957
        Mort: Hilton   h/o Carrie Williams Poole
Site 5 Carrie Williams Poole   Place: Poolesville
        Birth: 1874   Death: 13 Mar 1930   Burial: 15 Mar 1930
        Mort: Hilton & Hall   w/o William Wallace Poole
Site 6 John W. Poole   s/o William Wallace & Carrie Williams Poole
        Birth: 1907   Death: 1908   Burial: 29 Jan 1908

Lot: 2 Upper Owner: Miscellaneous
Site 3 Helen Pyles Darby   On stone with John Riggs Darby
        Birth: 18 Jun 1913   Death: 22 Aug 1995   Burial: 25 Aug 1995
Site 4 John Riggs Darby   h/o Helen Pyles Darby
        Birth: 18 Jan 1910   Death: 10 Jun 1988   Burial: 14 Jun 1988

Lot: 3 Owner: Frederick S. Poole
Site   Child of F.W. Poole   No marker   Burial: 4 Jun 1900
Site 2 Walter Williams   Place: Richmond
        Birth: 1872   Death: 16 Sep 1946   Burial: 18 Sep 1946
        Mort: Bennett Funeral Home   h/o Anna Poole Williams
Site 3 Anna Poole Williams   Place: Richmond, VA
        Birth: 1874   Death: 4 Sep 1946   Burial: 6 Sep 1946
        Mort: Bennett Funeral Home   TS: w/o Walter Williams
Site 6 Louise W. Hankins   Birth: 1859   Burial: 16 Mar 1909
Site 7 John Dickerson Poole   s/o John & Sallie Poole
        Birth: 4 Sep 1828   Death: 6 Jan 1876   Burial: 7 Jan 1876
Site 8 Richard Poole   Birth: 1843   Burial: 15 Jan 1906

Monocacy Cemetery, Beallsville, Montgomery County, Maryland

Site 9 Florence P. Poole Mort: Hilton & Hall Place: Richmond, VA
Birth: 1844 Death: 23 Jul 1930 Burial: 25 Jul 1930
Site 11 Mary Douglas Poole Hankins Mort: Hilton & Hall Place: Richmond, VA
Birth: 1871 Death: 11 Feb 1939 Burial: 13 Feb 1939
Site 12 Louie Hankins Mort: A.W. Bennett Co. Place: Richmond, VA
Birth: 1859 Death: 2 May 1938 Burial: 3 May 1938

Lot: 4 Lower Owner: Ethel F. Gott
Site 1 Arthur Lee Jones
Birth: 21 Jan 1920 Death: 31 Dec 1973 Burial: 4 Jan 1974
Site 3 Ethel Fenwick Wood Gott Place: Silver Spring
Birth: 30 Dec 1881 Death: 4 Dec 1957 Burial: 7 Dec 1957
Mort: Hilton w/o John Forest Gott
Site 3 John Forest Gott Place: Barnesville
Birth: 10 Sep 1879 Death: 27 Jan 1953 Burial: 30 Jan 1953
Mort: W.B. Hilton h/o Ethel Wood Gott

Lot: 4 Upper Owner: Gertrude Gough & Ethel F. Gott
Site 1 Dr. R. Vinton Wood h/o Virginia A. Wood Reinterment
Birth: 26 Jun 1845 Death: 3 Feb 1889 Burial: 5 Jul 1897
TS: Age 44-5-7
Site 2 Virginia Ann Wood TS: Age 88-7-12 Place: Barnesville
Birth: 17 Feb 1847 Death: 29 Sep 1935 Burial: 1 Oct 1935
Mort: W.B. Hilton w/o Dr. R. Vinton Wood
Site 3 Katie Wood Death: 26 Aug 1879 Burial: 5 Jul 1897
TS: d/o Dr. R. Vinton & Virginia A. Wood, age 1-5-17 Reinterment

Row C

Lot: 0 Owner: Nathan Talbott
Site 1 Henrietta B. Talbott   No dates on stone   Burial: 19 Jan 1908
Site 2 Nathan T. Talbott   h/o Sarah P. Talbott
        Birth: 19 Nov 1819   Death: 13 Oct 1902   Burial: 15 Oct 1902
Site 3 Sarah P. Talbott   TS: w/o Nathan T. Talbott
        Birth: 21 Feb 1829   Death: 7 Oct 1892

Lot: 1 Owner: J. Montgomery Veirs
Site 1 Georgia Lee Veirs   illegible   Burial: 25 Jul 1865
        TS: s/o J.M. & L. Veirs, age 1-9-21
Site 2 J. Montgomery Veirs   TS: Age 59-1-5
                                Death: 8 Oct 1891   Burial: 9 Oct 1891
Site 3 Elizabeth A. Veirs   Mort: W.T. Hilton & Sons   Place: Oakland, CA
        Birth: 1843   Death: 4 Jan 1930   Burial: 13 Jan 1930

Lot: 2 Owner: John Henry Williams
Site   Child of John Henry Williams   No marker   Burial: 5 Sep 1873
Site 1   Sarah (Sallie) White Williams   Place: Poolesville
         Birth: 15 Jan 1849   Death: 7 Mar 1928   Burial: 9 Mar 1928
         Mort: Hilton & Hall   w/o John Henry Williams
Site 2   John Henry Williams   h/o Sarah White Williams
         Birth: 2 May 1842   Death: 7 Nov 1909   Burial: 9 Nov 1909
Site 3   Mary Chiswell Williams   Place: Poolesville
         Birth: 22 Aug 1875   Death: 25 Dec 1918   Burial: 27 Dec 1918
         Mort: Hilton & Hall   d/o John Henry & Sallie White Williams
Site 7   Anne Elizabeth Williams Edmonston   TS: w/o William E. Edmonston
         Birth: 26 May 1870   Death: 1 Mar 1976   Burial: 6 Mar 1976
         d/o John Henry & Sallie White Williams
Site 8   Dr. Francis T. Williams   s/o John Henry & Sallie William Place: Frederick
         Birth: 5 Mar 1887   Death: 9 Dec 1966   Burial: 12 Dec 1966
Site 10 Sarah John Williams Ward   Mort: R.A. Pumphrey   Place: Sykesville
         Birth: 10 Mar 1881   Death: 14 Jan 1963   Burial: 16 Jan 1963
         d/o John Henry & Sallie White Williams   On stone with Wilson S. Ward
Site 11 Wilson Stewart Ward   Place: Rockville
         Birth: 28 Aug 1879   Death: 28 Jun 1939   Burial: 30 Jun 1939
         Mort: W.R. Pumphrey   h/o Sarah John Williams Ward
Site 12 Vernon Williams   s/o John H. & Sarah Williams
         Birth: 1 Dec 1868   Death: 6 Jan 1869

Lot: 3 Owner: Howard Griffith
Site 2   Julia G. Cissel   Place: Darnestown
         Birth: 4 Sep 1853   Death: 11 Dec 1924   Burial: 13 Dec 1924
         Mort: Pumphrey & Sons   On stone with R. Humphrey Cissel
Site 3   R. Humphrey Cissel   h/o Julia G. Cissel
         Birth: 14 Jun 1849   Death: 6 Dec 1911   Burial: 8 Dec 1911

Site 4	William Howard Cissel	TS: s/o R.H. & Julia Cissel, age 24 yrs 1 mo	
		Death: 5 Jul 1900	Burial: 7 Jul 1900
Site 5	Georgie Newton Cissel		TS: s/o R.H. & Julia Cissel
	Birth: 13 Apr 1883	Death: 19 Apr 1888	
Site 6	Elmo Cissel	Death: 16 Aug 1886	Burial: 20 Aug 1886
	TS: is/o Humphry Cissel, age 3 days		
Site 9	Harry W. Griffith		Place: Raleigh, NC
	Birth: 3 Jan 1890	Death: 15 Nov 1936	Burial: 18 Nov 1936
	Mort: W.R. Pumphrey		No marker
Site 12	Charles LeRoy Cissel	Mort: W.R. Pumphrey	Place: Washington, DC
	Birth: 9 Jan 1897	Death: 8 Aug 1922	Burial: 11 Aug 1922

Lot: 4 Owner: Howard Griffith

Site	Child of William Griffith	Burial: 23 Nov 1890	No marker
Site 1	Lutie Griffith	Mort: W.R. Pumphrey	Place: Washington, DC
	Birth: 1884	Death: 11 Jan 1933	Burial: 14 Jan 1933
	On stone with Charles Greenberry & Carolina V. Griffith		
Site 2	Charles Greenberry Griffith	Place: Rockville	
	Birth: 1849	Death: 5 Nov 1931	Burial: 7 Nov 1931
	Mort: Warner Pumphrey	h/o Carolina V. Hempstone Griffith	
Site 3	Carolina V. Hempstone Griffith		Place: Poolesville
	Birth: 1853	Death: 26 Apr 1914	Burial: 28 Apr 1914
	Mort: W.T. Hilton & Sons	w/o Charles Greenberry Griffith	
Site 4	Raymond Griffith	Death: 18 Mar 1892	Burial: 21 Mar 1892
	TS: s/o Charles & Carolina V. Griffith, age0-8-10		
Site 5	Bettie Griffith	TS: d/o Charles G. & Carolina V. Griffith	
	Birth: 29 Aug 1875	Death: 29 Aug 1875	
Site 5	Willie Griffith	TS: s/o Charles G. & Carolina V. Griffith	
	Birth: 29 Aug 1875	Death: 23 Nov 1876	Burial: 24 Nov 1876
Site 6	Harriet Griffith Bastable	Mort: Robert A. Pumphrey	Place: Rockville
	Birth: 15 Jan 1877	Death: 9 Mar 1949	Burial: 12 Mar 1949
	TS: w/o Alvin B. Bastable	d/o Charles G. & Caroline V. Griffith	
Site 7	Angelica C. Griffith		w/o Howard Griffith Sr.
	Birth: 14 Feb 1830	Death: 16 Sep 1899	Burial: 18 Sep 1899
Site 8	Howard Griffith Sr.	TS: h/o Angelica C. Griffith & Sarah N. Griffith	
	Birth: 20 Mar 1821	Death: 5 Mar 1897	Burial: 7 Mar 1897
Site 9	Sarah Newton Griffith	Birth: 18 Sep 1822	Burial: 19 Mar 1859
	TS: w/o Howard Griffith Sr., d/o William & Sarah Chiswell, age 34-6-0		
Site 10	Prudence Griffith	Death: 7 Dec 1881	
	TS: w/o Maj. Greenberry Griffith, age 85-1-2		
Site 11	Jemima A. Griffith	Birth: 29 Dec 1814	Death: 21 Jul 1872

Lot: 5 Lower Owner: Hugh Miles

Site 2	Mary C. Miles	d/o James U. & Sarah A. Miles, age 9-5-6	
	Birth: 8 Sep 1855	Death: Mar 1865	Burial: 1 Apr 1865
Site 3	Sarah A. Miles	Birth: 14 Apr 1832	Death: 13 Jan 1905
	TS: w/o James U. Miles, age 72-7-29		
Site 4	James U. Miles	h/o Sarah A. Miles	TS: age 80-2-20
	Birth: 8 Oct 1831	Death: 7 Jan 1912	Burial: 9 Jan 1912

Lot: 5 Upper   Owner: Mrs. Mary E. Benson
Site   Elizabeth Benson   Burial: 25 Aug 1873   No marker
Site   Thomas P.B. Benson   Burial: 22 Jul 1873   No marker
Site 1   Henrietta Benson (Nettie)   m/o Bruce Benson   Place: Cabin John
          Birth: 16 Jan 1869   Death: 20 Dec 1940   Burial: 22 Dec 1940
          Mort: W.B. Pumphrey   On stone with Wm. H. Benson
Site 2   William H. Benson   Place: Bethesda
          Birth: 10 Sep 1862   Death: 20 Mar 1948   Burial: 22 Mar 1948
          Mort: W.R. Pumphrey   h/o Henrietta Benson, f/o Bruce Benson
Site 3   Mary M. Benson   Birth: 23 Feb 1833   Death: 1 Jun 1872
          d/o Thomas R. & Isabella A. Benson
Site 4   Allen M. Benson   h/o Mary E. Benson
          Birth: 1824   Death: 1897   Burial: 13 Sep 1897
Site 5   Mary E. Benson   TS: w/o Allen Benson
          Birth: 7 Mar 1834   Death: 22 Apr 1878   Burial: 24 Apr 1878

Lot: 6   Owner: R.T. Hillard (One stone in lot)
Site 2   Robert T. Hillard   1st w Jane S. Hillard, 2nd w Cecelia V. Hillard
          Birth: 1832   Death: 1896   Burial: 24 Jun 1896
Site 3   Jane S. Hillard   Burial: 1850
          1st w/o Robert T. Hillard   No dates on stone
Site 4   Edward C. Hillard   Burial: 11 Jan 1877   No dates on stone
          TS: s/o R.T. & Jane S. Hillard
Site 5   Cecelia V. Hillard   No marker   Place: Leesburg, VA
          Birth: 1850   Death: 19 Dec 1915   Burial: 21 Dec 1915
          Mort: Lloyd Slack   2nd w/o R.T. Hillard
Site 6   Carroll E. Hillard   Birth: 1876   Burial: 1876
          TS: s/o Robert T. & Cecelia V. Hillard

Lot: 7   Owner: W.W. Metzger
Site 2   Andrew James Baxter   h/o Frances Metzger Baxter
          Birth: 1836   Death: 1902
Site 2   Frances Metzger Baxter   Place: Granville, OH
          Birth: 1836   Death: 2 Apr 1920   Burial: 4 Apr 1920
          Mort: Hilton & Hall   On stone with Andrew James Baxter
Site 3   Alice A. Metzger Kraft   TS: w/o J.G. Kraft
          Birth: 17 Apr 1844   Death: 27 Apr 1872
Site 4   Charles Metzger   TS: s/o William & Harriet Metzger
          Birth: 17 Jun 1848   Death: 27 Sep 1898   Burial: 29 Sep 1898
Site 5   Hannah Virginia Metzger   TS: d/o William & Harriet Metzger
          Birth: 4 Oct 1832   Death: 25 Jan 1895   Burial: 28 Jan 1895
Site 6   George Metzer   Death: 5 Mar 1872
          TS: s/o William & Harriet Metzger
Site 8   Percival Metzger   Mort: Harry L. Slye   Place: Washington, DC
          Birth: 22 Feb 1855   Death: 19 Nov 1922   Burial: 22 Nov 1922
Site 9   Nathan T. Metzger   TS: s/o William & Harriet Metzger
          Birth: 11 Jun 1842   Death: 23 Oct 1875

Monocacy Cemetery, Beallsville, Montgomery County, Maryland 71

Site 10 Philip Metzger TS: s/o William & Harriet Metzger
 Birth: 8 Jan 1846 Death: 29 Mar 1862
Site 11 Harriet Morehead Trail Metzger TS: w/o William Metzger, age 94 yrs
 Birth: 22 Feb 1811 Death: 23 Sep 1894 Burial: 25 Sep 1894
Site 12 William Metzger Birth: 17 Oct 1805 Death: 19 Aug 1874
 h/o Harriet Morehead Trail Metzger TS: s/o Jacob & Christana M. Metzger

Lot: 8 Lower Owner: C.D. Heffner
Site 1 Catherine Jennie Leapley Place: Olney
 Birth: 1858 Death: 4 Oct 1953 Burial: 6 Oct 1953
 Mort: W.B. Hilton d/o George N. & Margaret A. Leapley
Site 2 George Franklin Leapley Place: Poolesville
 Birth: 1854 Death: 24 Apr 1937 Burial: 27 Apr 1937
 Mort: Hilton & Hall s/o Margaret A. & George N. Leapley
Site 3 Margarett Avilda Leapley Place: Poolesville
 Birth: 1851 Death: 31 Mar 1935 Burial: 2 Apr 1935
 Mort: Hilton & Hall d/o George N. & Margaret A.D. Leapley
Site 4 Margaret A.D. Leapley Death: 26 Jan 1859
 TS: w/o George N. Leapley, age 31 yrs
Site 5 George N. Leapley Death: 15 Dec 1876 Burial: 17 Dec 1876
 h/o Margaret A.D. Leapley TS: Age 65 yrs
Site 6 George Randolph Leapley Death: 7 Dec 1852
 TS: s/o George N. & Margaret Leapley, age 18 mo
Site 7 Joseph Adolphus Hughes
 Birth: 17 Apr 1844 Death: 20 Sep 1907 Burial: 22 Sep 1907
Site 8 Daniel T. Heffner TS: In his 60th year
 Death: 29 Jan 1876 Burial: 30 Jan 1875
Site 9 Catharine Huges Burial: 15 Nov 1874 TS: In her 75th year

Lot: 8 Upper Owner: John Merchant
Site 1 Mrs. Susannah Mulligan
 Birth: 24 Sep 1780 Death: 23 May 1873 Burial: 24 May 1873
Site 2 Margaret E. Merchant Death: 3 Nov 1883 Burial: 5 Nov 1883
 TS: w/o John O. Merchant, age 57-7-21
Site 3 John O. Merchant h/o Margaret E. Merchant TS: Age 94 yrs
 Death: 4 Feb 1907 Burial: 5 Feb 1907
Site 6 Andrew Roscoe Strange illegible s/o Andrew & Susan Strange
 Birth: 31 May 1882 Death: 4 Dec 1898 Burial: 6 Dec 1898

Lot: 9 Owner: Thomas Fyffe
Site 2 Thomas E. Fyffe Only s/o Thomas E. & Mary E. Fyffe
 Birth: 28 Mar 1872 Death: 5 Aug 1873 Burial: 6 Aug 1873
Site 3 Agnes Willet Fyffe c/o Thomas Fyffe
 Birth: 17 Sep 1882 Death: 10 Mar 1890 Burial: 11 Mar 1890
Site 4 Bettie Tolle Birth: 2 Mar 1869 Death: 4 Apr 1896
 TS: w/o Henry C. Tolle, d/o Thomas & M.E. Fyffe
Site 5 Mary E. Fyffe Place: Poolesville
 Birth: 10 Nov 1847 Death: 3 May 1929 Burial: 5 May 1929
 Mort: Hilton & Hall TS: w/o Thomas Fyffe

Monocacy Cemetery, Beallsville, Montgomery County, Maryland

Site 6 Thomas Fyffe   Birth: 28 Aug 1841   Death: 16 Oct 1908
Site 6 Benjamin Richard Fyffe   Mort: Hilton & Hall   Place: Poolesville
        Birth: 24 May 1890   Death: 14 Jan 1920   Burial: 16 Jan 1920
Site 7 Sarah Aldah Fyffe   Mort: John C. Mitchell Sons Place: Baltimore
        Birth: 1875   Death: 25 Jun 1947   Burial: 27 Jun 1947
Site 8 Mary Gertrude Pope   Place: Washington, DC
        Birth: 3 Oct 1870   Death: 16 Jun 1921   Burial: 18 Jun 1921
        Mort: Hilton & Hall   TS: w/o B.F. Pope, d/o Thomas & M.E. Fyffe
Site 9 John Thomas Fyffe, Sr.
        Birth: 5 Apr 1906   Death: 1 Dec 1977   Burial: 3 Dec 1977
Site 10 Martha Cooley Fyffe   On stone with John Thomas Fyffe Sr.
        Birth: 5 Aug 1908   Death: 26 Aug 1980   Burial: 28 Aug 1980
Site 12 Isaac Fyffe   c/o Thomas H. & Elizabeth Fyffe
        Birth: 2 Apr 1839   Death: 2 Mar 1892

Lot: 10 Lower   Owner: William Cissel
Site 2 America Williams   d/o Colmore & Mariel Howard Williams
        Birth: 3 Jun 1835   Death: 2 Sep 1854
Site 3 Colmore W. Williams   w/o Mariel Howard Williams
        Birth: 21 Feb 1787   Death: 11 Apr 1857
Site 4 Mariel H. Williams   TS: w/o Colmore Williams
        Birth: 7 Feb 1799   Death: 4 Jan 1875
Site 5 Sarah Ann E. Williams   d/o Colmore & Mariel Howard Williams
        Birth: 21 Mar 1821   Death: 11 Feb 1853
Site 6 Catherine Amelia Williams   Place: Brunswick
        Birth: 7 Jan 1831   Death: 27 Jan 1925   Burial: 19 Jan 1925
        Mort: C.H. Feeks & Sons   d/o Colmore & Mariel Howard Williams

Lot: 10 Upper   Owner: William Cissel
Site 1 William Cissel   h/o Rachael S. Cissell   TS: Age 79-7-6
        Birth: 9 Aug 1803   Death: 15 Mar 1883   Burial: 1 Sep 1896
        Reinterment of family
Site 2 Rachael S. Cissel   Wife of William Cissell   Reinterment
        Birth: 12 Aug 1812   Death: 8 Jun 1861   Burial: 1 Sep 1896
        Stone down and broken
Site 3 Elizabeth Cissel   Death: 8 Dec 1835   Burial: 1 Sep 1896
        TS: Daughter of William & Rachael S. Cissel Age 2-10-2   Reinterment
Site 4 Philip A. Cissell   Death: 6 Mar 1858   Burial: 1 Sep 1896
        TS: s/o William & Rachel S. Cissell, age 26-11-28   Reinterment
Site 5 Philip A. Cissel Sr.   TS: Age 63-8-9   Reinterment
                                        Death: 6 Nov 1861   Burial: 1 Sep 1896
Site 6 Beckie Jones   Death: 6 Aug 1862   Burial: 1 Sep 1896
        d/o A. Jackson & Sallie C. Jones, age 0-15-11
Site 6 Mary Eleanor Cissel   Mort: Hilton & Hall   Place: Washington, DC
        Birth: 22 Jan 1845   Death: 4 Apr 1926   Burial: 6 Apr 1926

Lot: 11   Owner: William T. Walter
Site   Maurice Walter   No marker   Burial: 5 Dec 1892
Site   Miss Stella Walter   No marker   Burial: 12 Apr 1911

Site 2	Mary Ann Walter		
	Birth: 1892	Death: 1 Sep 1914	Burial: 4 Sep 1914
Site 3	William T. Walter		No marker
	Birth: 1828		Burial: 18 Mar 1909
Site 4	Mrs. Thomas Walter	No marker	Burial: 8 Dec 1877
Site 5	E. Walter	No marker	
Site 6	Mrs. A. M. Benson	No marker	Burial: 25 Mar 1899
Site 8	W. T. Walter	No marker	Burial: 1861
Site 9	L. C. Walter	No marker	Burial: 1866
Site 10	Ida Walter Boxer	No marker	Mort: Martin W. Hysong
	Place: Washington, DC	Death: 12 Jul 1932	Burial: 15 Jul 1932
Site 11	John S. Boxer	Mort: Martin W. Hysong	Place: Washington, DC
	Birth: 1850	Death: 22 Mar 1927	Burial: 25 Mar 1927

Lot: 12 Owner: G.B.F. Walter

Site	John W. Conley	No marker	Burial: 6 Sep 1877
Site	Miss Lucinda Grimes	No marker	Burial: 19 Sep 1895
Site 1	Andrew K. Milne	Mort: S.H. Hines Co	Place: Washington, DC
	Birth: 1852	Death: 2 May 1947	Burial: 5 May 1947
Site 2	Mary E. Milne	Mort: S.H. Hines & Co	Place: Washington, DC
	Birth: 1865	Death: 24 Jun 1947	Burial: 27 Jun 1947
Site 5	Abbie Mae Colwell		Place: Washington, DC
	Birth: 1872	Death: 2 Feb 1952	Burial: 5 Feb 1952
	Mort: S.H. Hines Co.		Age 79
Site 6	John Paul Jones	Mort: S.H. Hines Co	Place: Washington, DC
	Birth: 1898	Death: 6 Jan 1932	Burial: 8 Jan 1932
Site 7	George T. Walter	Mort: W.T. Hilton & Sons	Place: Dickerson
	Birth: 1868	Death: 11 Jan 1925	Burial: 13 Jan 1925
Site 8	Mary Ann Walter		Place: Dickerson
	Birth: 1840	Death: 1 Sep 1915	Burial: 4 Sep 1915
	Mort: Hilton & Hall	On stone with George B.F. & George T. Walter	
Site 9	George B.F. Walter		Place: Dickerson
	Birth: 1837	Death: 14 Jul 1916	Burial: 16 Jul 1916
	Mort: W.T. Hilton & Sons		h/o Mary Ann Walter
Site 10	Walter Gant Jones		w/o F.C. & Abbie Walter Jones
	Birth: 27 Apr 1895	Death: 2 Feb 1896	Burial: 5 Feb 1896
Site 11	Elsie May Milne		id/o Andrew & Mary Milne
	illegible	Death: 27 Sep 1893	Burial: 28 Sep 1893
Site 12	Nettie Walter	d/o G.B.F. & Mary A. Walter, age 11 mo 1 day	
	illegible	Death: 22 Jun 1877	Burial: 23 Jun 1877

Lot: 13 Owner: James P. Walter

Site	Mrs. Nettie Barnes	No marker	Burial: 12 Jun 1896
Site	Daniel Walter	No marker	Burial: 23 Dec 1892
Site	Miss Dora Walter	No marker	Burial: 11 Mar 1901
Site	Miss Elizabeth Walter	No marker	Burial: 29 Aug 1894
Site	Mrs. Harriet L. Walter	No marker	Burial: 19 Jul 1905
Site	Child of James Walter	No marker	Burial: 21 Aug 1880
Site	James P. Walter	No marker	Burial: 21 Oct 1900

Monocacy Cemetery, Beallsville, Montgomery County, Maryland

Site   Child of James P. Walter   No marker   Burial: 23 Aug 1873
Site   Jesse Walter   Burial: 19 Sep 1881   c/o James P. Walters
       No marker
Site 5 John W. Connelly   Mort: W.T. Hilton   Place: Washington, DC
       Birth: 1850   Death: 19 Jun 1915   Burial: 22 Jun 1915
Site 6 Margaret E. Connelly   Mort: S.H. Hines Co.   Place: Washington, DC
       Birth: 1858   Death: 13 Nov 1930   Burial: 16 Nov 1930

Lot: 14 Owner: George Smith
Site 1 George Washington Hunter Smith Jr.   s/o G.W.H. & Mary E. Rice Smith
       Birth: 12 May 1849   Death: 9 Dec 1872   Burial: 11 Dec 1872
Site 2 Mary E. Rice Smith   On stone with Major G.W. Smith Sr.
       Birth: 21 Jun 1818   Death: 10 Feb 1874   Burial: 12 Feb 1874
Site 3 George Washington Hunter Smith Sr.
       Birth: 12 Mar 1812   Death: 21 Apr 1898   Burial: 22 Apr 1898
Site 7 Cleopatra Elgin   d/o C.F. & H.D. Smith Elgin
       Birth: 1875   Death: 1877   Burial: 31 Dec 1877
Site 8 Helen Douglas Smith Elgin   On stone with Charles Fenton Elgin
       Birth: 1837   Death: 29 Mar 1911   Burial: 30 Mar 1911
Site 9 Charles Fenton Elgin   Place: Poolesville
       Birth: 1832   Death: 5 Apr 1914   Burial: 8 Apr 1914
       Mort: Hilton & Hall   h/o Helen Douglas Smith Elgin
Site 10 John Thomas Elgin   Place: Poolesville
       Birth: 23 Sep 1869   Death: 29 Aug 1952   Burial: 31 Aug 1952
       Mort: W.B. Hilton   s/o Charles F. & Helen S. Elgin, age 82
Site 11 Jessie Virginia Elgin Ritchey   Mort: Wm. B. Hilton   Place: Sykesville
       Birth: 23 Aug 1873   Death: 1 Feb 1966   Burial: 6 Feb 1966
       w/o Charles A. Ritchey, d/o Charles F. & Helen S. Elgin
Site 12 Edward Wootton Elgin   Place: Poolesville
       Birth: 19 Nov 1871   Death: 21 Jul 1959   Burial: 23 Jul 1959
       Mort: Hilton   s/o Charles F. & Helen S. Elgin

Lot: 15 Owner: T.W. Poole
Site   Child of Mr. F. H. Poole   No marker   Burial: 2 Jul 1898
Site 4 John P. Handley   Mort: C.C. Carty   Place: Frederick
       Birth: 5 Sep 1901   Death: 26 Oct 1918   Burial: 28 Oct 1918
       TS: s/o Charles F. & Sarah P. Handley   Age 1-3-10
Site 5 William Trail Hempstone Poole   s/o William & Harriet Hempstone Poole
       Birth: 16 Sep 1821   Death: 29 Jun 1881   Burial: 30 Jun 1881
Site 6 William Poole   Death: 29 Jun 1878   Burial: 29 Jun 1881
       s/o Joseph & Mary McCauley Poole, h/o Harriet Hempstone Poole
       TS: In his 91st year
Site 7 Harriet Thomas Poole   TS: d/o T.homas H. & Christie E. Poole
       Birth: 25 Aug 1879   Apr 1880   Burial: 12 May 1880
Site 8 Christie E. Poole   TS: [2nd] w/o T.H. Poole
       Birth: 14 Feb 1811   Death: 9 Dec 1898   Burial: 11 Dec 1898
Site 9 Thomas H. Poole
       Birth: 14 Jun 1823   Death: 21 Apr 1891   Burial: 22 Mar 1891
       h/o Sarah Ann Fisher Poole & Christie Fisher Poole

Monocacy Cemetery, Beallsville, Montgomery County, Maryland

Site 10 Sarah Ann Fisher Poole   TS: [1st] w/o Thomas H. Poole
         Birth: 31 Jan 1819   Death: 19 Jan 1875
Site 11 William Thomas Poole   s/o Thomas Henry & Sarah Ann Fisher Poole
         Birth: 23 Dec 1856   Death: 27 Mar 1909   Burial: 30 Mar 1909
Site 12 Austin B. Handley   Death: 7 Sep 1912
         TS: s/o Charles F. & Sarah F. Handley, age 1-2-10

Lot: 16 Owner: William Edmund & Anna Lee Freeman
Site 1   William Edmund Freeman   Place: Washington, DC
         Birth: 1887   Death: 15 Feb 1955   Burial: 17 Feb 1955
         Mort: C.E. Cline & Son   h/o Anna Lee Poole Freeman
Site 2   Anna Lee Poole Freeman   Place: Chevy Chase
         Birth: 26 Jul 1888   Death: 11 Feb 1961   Burial: 14 Feb 1961
         Mort: Robert A. Pumphrey   w/o William E. Freeman
Site 3   Charles Edgar Poole   Mort: C.E. Cline   Place: Chevy Chase
         Birth: 26 Sep 1854   Death: 23 Dec 1937   Burial: 24 Dec 1937
Site 4   Laura Virginia Hays Poole Mort: C.E. Cline   Place: Adamstown
         Birth: 1859   Death: 26 Jan 1930   Burial: 29 Jan 1930
Site 5   Elsie May Poole   d/o Charles E. Poole
         Birth: 10 Aug 1880   Death: 21 Sep 1881   Burial: 23 Sep 1881
Site 7   James Franklin Poole   h/o Ann Elizabeth Hoskinson
         Birth: 18 Aug 1831   Death: 1901   Burial: 26 Mar 1901
Site 8   Annie Hoskinson Poole   w/o James Franklin Poole
         Birth: 4 May 1837   Death: 1910   Burial: 9 Jun 1910
Site 10 William Edmund Freeman Jr.
         Birth: 11 Feb 1914   Death: 2 Aug 1990   Burial: 6 Aug 1990
Site 11 Frank Leven Poole
         Birth: 16 Oct 1863   Death: 6 May 1865   Burial: 1865
Site 12 William Vernon Poole   No marker   s/o T.W. Poole
         Birth: 20 Jan 1861   Death: 28 May 1877   Burial: 29 May 1877

Lot: 17 Owner: John Jones
Site 1   John Frederick Jones   TS: s/o John & Mary M. Jones
         Birth: 27 Jun 1874   Death: 4 Aug 1875
Site 2   Agnes Estelle Jones   TS: d/o John & Mary M. Jones, age 1-9-0
         illegible   Death: 16 Sep 1890   Burial: 17 Sep 1890
Site 3   Reginald Sprigg Jones   TS: s/o John & Mary M. Jones, age 12 yrs
                                   Death: 10 Feb 1907   Burial: 12 Feb 1907
Site 4   Mary Hays Jones   Place: Braddock Heights
         Birth: 19 Feb 1849   Death: 10 Nov 1929   Burial: 12 Nov 1929
         Mort: M.R. Etchison   TS: w/o John Jones
Site 5   John Jones   Place: Poolesville
         Birth: 22 Nov 1838   Death: 3 Apr 1916   Burial: 6 Apr 1916
         Mort: Hilton & Hall   h/o Mary Hays Jones
Site 6   Miss Mary Poole Jones   Mort: M.R. Etcherson Place: Braddock Heights
         Birth: 16 Nov 1875   Death: 4 Jul 1940   Burial: 6 Jul 1940
Site 7   Hays Jones   Burial: 1 Nov 1909
         is/o L.H. & M.K. Jones   No marker

Site 8 Mrs. E. Medora Jones   Mort: Wm. B. Hilton   Place: Florida
        Birth: 8 Nov 1879   Death: 20 Jan 1966   Burial: 24 Jan 1966

Lot: 18 Owner: T.W. Hyde
Site 2 Priscilla John Poole   Death: 27 Jul 1909   Burial: 29 Jul 1909
        TS: w/o Reginald Poole, d/o Leonard & Eliza Hays, age 74 yrs
Site 3 Reginald Poole   h/o Priscilla J. Poole   Burial: 11 Apr 1861
        TS: s/o Dr. Thomas H. & Sarah F. Poole, age 28-1-7
Site 4 Dr. John Sprigg Poole   TS: s/o Dr. Thomas & E.W. Poole
        Birth: 20 Oct 1862   Death: 23 Apr 1904   Burial: 25 Apr 1904
Site 5 Georgia Rebecca Poole   Mort: H.S. Bailey   Place: Darlington
        Birth: 27 Aug 1868   Death: 9 Sep 1941   Burial: 11 Sep 1941
        TS: w/o Dr. John Sprigg Poole
Site 7 Jane Clark Poole   TS: d/o Dr. Thomas & Sarah A. Poole
        Birth: 31 Aug 1835   Death: 7 Sep 1837   Burial: 31 Aug 1835
Site 8 Sarah A.E. Willson Poole   TS: w/o Dr. Thomas Sprigg Poole
        Birth: 15 Apr 1808   Death: 21 Jan 1844
Site 9 Dr. Thomas Sprigg Poole   h/o Evelyn Wales Hyde Poole
                                      Death: 17 Mar 1870   TS: Age 66 yrs
Site 10 Evelyn Wailes Hyde Poole   TS: w/o Dr. Thomas Sprigg Poole, age 83 yrs
                                      Death: 25 Nov 1904   Burial: 27 Nov 1904
Site 11 Miss Mary (Mame) Wilson Poole
        Birth: 20 Jul 1854   Death: 29 Nov 1884   Burial: 2 Dec 1884

Lot: 19 Owner: Thomas W. Poole
Site 1 Miss Catherine (Katie) V. Poole   On stone with Thomas H. Poole
        Birth: 1 Jan 1866   Death: 20 Dec 1883   Burial: 23 Dec 1883
Site 2 Thomas H. Poole   Birth: 9 Nov 1847   Death: 20 May 1861
Site 3 Thomas W. Hyde   Age 92 years
        Birth: 2 Feb 1797   Death: 31 Jul 1887
Site   Emily Wailes Hyde   TS: w/o Thomas W. Hyde
        Birth: 1 Jun 1799   Death: 19 Oct 1836
Site 3 Alice Poole Gott   TS: w/o Richard Gott
        Birth: 1 Oct 1851   Death: 12 Jan 1913   Burial: 15 Jan 1913

Lot: 20 Owner: Mary Fisher
Site   Herbert Y. Fisher   No marker   Burial: 9 Dec 1880
Site   Mrs. Mary Fisher   No marker   Burial: 8 Apr 1885
Site   Child of R. J. Isherwood   No marker   Burial: 9 Apr 1884
Site 4 Joseph R. Fisher   Death: 17 Apr 1862   Burial: 9 Dec 1880
        h/o Mary V. Fisher   TS: Age 43-2-2   Reinterment
Site 5 Martin Fisher Sr.   Death: 18 Feb 1832   Burial: 9 Dec 1880
        h/o Pricilla Poole Fisher   TS: Age 37 yrs   Reinterment
Site 6 Pricilla Poole Fisher   TS: w/o Martin Fisher, age 81-9-0
                                      Death: 3 Feb 1880   Burial: 5 Feb 1880
Site 10 Herbert I. Fisher   s/o Joseph R. & Mary V. Fisher
        Birth: 21 Jan 1812   Death: 16 Jun 1912
Site 10 Joseph R. Fisher   s/o Joseph R. & Mary V. Fisher   Reinterment
        Birth: 29 Jun 1815   Death: 13 Jul 1816   Burial: 9 Dec 1880

Monocacy Cemetery, Beallsville, Montgomery County, Maryland

Site 11 John G. Fisher   s/o Joseph R. & Mary V. Fisher   Reinterment
        Birth: 8 Jul 1851   Death: 31 Jul 1851   Burial: 9 Dec 1880

Lot: 21 Owner: Richard G. White
Site 1 Thomas Oliver White   Mort: Hilton & Price   Place: Bradenton, FL
        Birth: 20 Aug 1862   Death: 15 Dec 1934   Burial: 18 Dec 1934
Site 2 Annie (Nannie) E. White   Place: Barnesville
        Birth: 25 Nov 1861   Death: 7 Feb 1926   Burial: 9 Feb 1926
        Mort: W.T. Hilton & Sons   TS: w/o Thomas Oliver White
Site 5 Richard G. White   TS: Age 52-2-17   h/o Huldah A. Piles White
        Birth: 22 Oct 1826   Death: 3 Jan 1879   Burial: 5 Jan 1879
Site 6 Huldah A. Piles White   w/o Richard G. White
        Birth: 28 Sep 1830   Death: 19 Dec 1910   Burial: 21 Dec 1910
Site 7 Laura V. White   Mort: Pierce Bros   Place: Los Angeles, CA
        Birth: 2 Jan 1886   Death: 21 May 1968   Burial: 27 May 1968
Site 9 Albert White   No dates   Burial: 13 Aug 1879
        TS: s/o Richard G. & H.A. White, age 2-8-16
Site 10 Herndon White   No dates   Death: 13 Aug 1879
        s/o Richard G. & H.A. White, age 3-8-13

Lot: 22 Owner: Peter Joseph Stang
Site   Child of Joseph H. Stang   No marker   Burial: 1 Oct 1881
Site   Child of Joseph H. Stang   No marker   Burial: 21 Nov 1882
Site 2 Henrietta Stang   2nd w/o P.J. Stang
        Birth: 7 Dec 1853   Death: 13 Sep 1877
Site 4 Martin J. Stang   Stone broken   Father
        Birth: 26 Sep 1848   Death: 31 Oct 1885
Site 5 Anna Stang   illegible   TS: w/o Joseph Stang
                               Death: 7 Feb 1897   Burial: 8 Feb 1897
Site 7 Oscar Francis Stang   No marker   Mort: Wm. Hilton
        Place: Jefferson, MD   Death: 6 Apr 1971   Burial: 9 Apr 1971
Site 8 Peter J. Stang   Place: Dawsonville
        Birth: 7 Jun 1851   Death: 31 Mar 1922   Burial: 2 Apr 1922
        Mort: Hilton & Hall   h/o Annie O. Stang & Henrietta Stang
Site 9 Anna Ollive Stang   Place: Dawsonville
        Birth: 5 Oct 1865   Death: 18 Oct 1944   Burial: 21 Oct 1944
        Mort: W.B. Hilton   TS: [1st] w/o Peter J. Stang
Site 10 Walter Hoffman Stang   s/o Peter & Annie O. Stang
        Birth: 12 Jan 1888   Death: 3 Feb 1888   Burial: 5 Feb 1886
Site 11 Edward Ludwig Stang   Birth: 29 Dec 1890   Burial: 27 Dec 1906
        illegible   s/o Peter Joseph & Annie O. Stang

Lot: 23 Owner: Adolphus Lindig
Site   Mrs. Anna L. Lindig   No marker   Burial: 10 May 1911
Site 1 Frederick J. Lindig   s/o A. & Anna S. Lindig
        Birth: 2 Apr 1880   Death: 30 Aug 1881   Burial: 31 Aug 1881
Site 2 Estelle Lindig   d/o Adolph & Anna S. Lindig
        Birth: 5 Feb 1883   Death: 8 Feb 1884   Burial: 9 Feb 1884

Site 3 Anna S. Lindig   TS: c/o Adolph & Anna Lindig
        Birth: 7 Nov 1844   Death: 8 May 1884   Burial: 13 May 1884
Site 4 Adolph Lindig
        Birth: 23 Dec 1835   Death: 10 Mar 1902   Burial: 12 Mar 1902
Site 5 Katie Lindig Moran   w/o William J. Moran   No marker
                                  Death: 25 Jan 1975   Burial: 29 Jan 1975
Site 6 William J. Moran   h/o Katie Lindig Moran
        Birth: 16 May 1877   Death: 16 Jan 1903   Burial: 17 Jan 1903
Site 7 Frank Gerald McGovern-Pearthree   Place: Washington, DC
        Birth: 1 Oct 1929   Death: 7 Apr 1942   Burial: 10 Apr 1942
        Mort: Harold J. Faltavull   s/o Evelyn McGovern Pearthree
Site 8 Gerald McGovern   Mort: W.T. Hilton & Sons
        Place: Baltimore   Death: 6 May 1917   Burial: 19 May 1917
        h/o Lottie Lindig McGovern   TS: Age 51 yrs
Site 9 Gerald McGovern   No marker   s/o Gerald & Lottie McGovern
        Birth: 30 Nov 1903   Burial: 3 Dec 1903
Site 10 Charlotte (Lottie) Wilhelminia McGovern   Mort: Peter Whaley
        Birth: 1871   Death: 11 Feb 1964   Burial: 13 Feb 1964
        Place: Lewes, DE
Site 11 Kathleen Moran Ropp   No marker   Mort: Lee Funeral Home
        Place: Montgomery Co.   Death: 27 Jun 1952   Burial: 30 Jun 1952
Site 12 Anna Lindig   Place: Washington, DC
        Birth: 5 Mar 1877   Death: 30 Aug 1934   Burial: 1 Sep 1934
        Mort: H.C. Taltawell   TS: c/o Adolph & Anna Lindig

Lot: 24 Owner: Mrs. Frank Elgin
Site 2 Franklyn Estelle Elgin   Mort: E.S. McCaveland   Place: Springfield, PA
        Birth: 3 Jul 1899   Death: 1 Mar 1968   Burial: 5 Mar 1968
        d/o William Franklin & Estelle White Elgin
Site 3 Mary Estelle Elgin   Place: Deleware, PA
        Birth: 18 Dec 1861   Death: 27 Feb 1963   Burial: 2 Mar 1963
        Mort: E.S. McCooland   w/o Dr. William Franklin Elgin
Site 4 Dr. William Franklin Elgin   Place: Glenolden, PA
        Birth: 16 Sep 1861   Death: 18 Apr 1938   Burial: 21 Apr 1938
        Mort: Oliver H. Bair Co.   h/o Mary Estelle White Elgin
Site 5 Mary Ellen Elgin Senat   d/o Dr. Frank & Mary Estelle Elgin
        Birth: 9 Dec 1889   Death: 16 Feb 1987   Burial: 17 Feb 1987
Site 7 Harry Spencer Brewer   TS: Dad   On stone with Edith Fink Brewer
        Birth: 16 Jun 1922   Death: 20 Oct 1989   Burial: 7 Apr 1990

Lot: 25 Owner: Mrs. R.T. Pyles
Site 1 Lotta V. Pyles   Place: Baltimore
        Birth: 19 Nov 1879   Death: 10 Jul 1956   Burial: 12 Jul 1956
        Mort: Stewart & Mowen   TS: d/o Richard & Frances Pyles
Site 2 Dr. Richard Grover Pyles   Place: Baltimore
        Birth: 3 May 1885   Death: 2 May 1935   Burial: 5 May 1935
        Mort: Hilton & Price   TS: s/o Richard T. & Frances E. Pyles
Site 3 Richard T. Pyles   h/o Frances E. Pyles   TS: Age 57-3-27
        Birth: 16 Jan 1812   Death: 13 May 1889   Burial: 14 May 1889

Monocacy Cemetery, Beallsville, Montgomery County, Maryland

Site 4 Frances Ellen Pyles Mort: W.T. Hilton & Sons Place: Barnesville
        Birth: 21 Mar 1847 Death: 4 Jan 1919 Burial: 6 Jan 1919
        TS: w/o Richard T. Pyles, age 71-9-13
Site 7 Percy Lee Pyles Place: Baltimore
        Birth: 15 Nov 1871 Death: 27 Oct 1932 Burial: 30 Oct 1932
        Mort: W.T. Hilton & Sons TS: s/o Richard T. & Francis E. Pyles
Site 8 Mary Jane Hawkins Mother, age 84 yrs
        Stone down & broken Death: 25 Sep 1906 Burial: 27 Sep 1906
Site 9 Claggett Pyles
        Birth: 27 Dec 1859 Death: 30 Jul 1911 Burial: 1 Aug 1911
Site 10 Mary V. Pyles Mort: Stewart & Nemen Co. Place: Baltimore
        Birth: 18 Aug 1871 Death: 31 Oct 1937 Burial: 2 Nov 1937

Lot: 26 Owner: John W. Brown
Site   Infant of Herbert Brown No marker Mort: Brown Bros.
        Place: Barnesville Death: 18 Mar 1922 Burial: 18 Mar 1922
Site 2 William Clifton Brown Death: 30 Jan 1894 Burial: 1 Feb 1894
        h/o Mollie Darby Brown TS: Age 40-5-1
Site 3 Mollie Darby Brown Place: Barnesville
        Birth: 1854 Death: 11 Sep 1928 Burial: 13 Sep 1928
        Mort: W.T. Hilton & Sons On stone with William Clifton Brown
Site 4 William Clifton Brown Place: Frederick
        Birth: 8 Feb 1882 Death: 17 Nov 1939 Burial: 19 Nov 1939
        Mort: W.B. Hilton h/o Emily Darby Brown Clark
Site 5 Emily Darby Brown Clark Place: Poolesville
        Birth: 1880 Death: 7 May 1960 Burial: 10 May 1960
        Mort: Hilton w/o William Clifton Brown
Site 7 John W. Brown Place: Barnesville
        Birth: 28 Nov 1826 Death: 17 Apr 1913 Burial: 19 Apr 1913
        Mort: W.T. Hilton & Sons h/o Mary E. Brown
Site 8 Mary Elizabeth Brown Place: Barnesville
        Birth: 10 Oct 1829 Death: 8 Feb 1929 Burial: 10 Feb 1929
        Mort: W.T. Hilton & Sons w/o John W. Brown, Age 99
Site 10 Sarah Elizabeth Brown Mort: W.B. Hilton Place: Kensington
        Birth: 4 Mar 1857 Death: 22 Apr 1955 Burial: 25 Apr 1955
Site 11 Hatton Darby Brown Place: Barnesville
        Birth: 2 Jan 1890 Death: 26 May 1961 Burial: 29 May 1961
        Mort: Hilton h/o Mary Poole Brown
Site 12 Mary Poole Brown w/o Hatton Darby Brown
        Birth: 2 Aug 1890 Death: 20 Mar 1978 Burial: 22 Mar 1978

Lot: 27 Owner: Zachariah G. Cooley
Site   Child of Mr. Claude Cooley No marker Burial: 8 Apr 1899
Site   Child of R.S. & Blanch J. Corley No marker Burial: 16 May 1908
Site 3 Zachariah G. Cooley Mort: W.T. Hilton & Sons Place: Dickerson
        Birth: 21 May 1849 Death: 24 Sep 1928 Burial: 25 Sep 1928
Site 4 Martha Maria Cooley Place: Dickerson
        Birth: 1 Apr 1853 Death: 19 Feb 1929 Burial: 21 Feb 1929
        Mort: W.T. Hilton & Sons TS: w/o Zachariah G. Cooley

80 Monocacy Cemetery, Beallsville, Montgomery County, Maryland

Site 5 Isabella Virginia Cooley
Place: Gaithersburg Death: 18 Dec 1963 Mort: Ernest A. Gartner Burial: 21 Dec 1963
Site 6 William Smith Cooley Death: 11 Aug 1973 Burial: 15 Aug 1973
Site 7 Nettie L. Compher TS: w/o Samuel P. Compher
Birth: 3 Jun 1876 Death: 30 Dec 1906 Burial: 2 Jan 1907
Site 8 Samuel P. Compher Birth: 16 Sep 1873 No death date on stone
Site 9 Eva May Compher Death: 16 Mar 1918 Burial: 20 Mar 1918
Place: West Palm Beach, FL Mort: W.T. Hilton & Sons
Site 10 Claude O. Cooley h/o Laura J. Cooley
Birth: 1874 No death date on stone
Site 11 Laura J. Cooley TS: Death 1937 Place: Dickerson
Birth: 1869 Death: 24 Apr 1938 Burial: 26 Apr 1938
Mort: W.B. Hilton On stone with Claude O. Cooley
Site 12 Gladys Lee Cooley d/o Claude & June Cooley
Birth: 21 Jul 1897 Death: 7 Mar 1899 Burial: 9 Mar 1899

Lot: 28 Lower   Owner: S.H. Cator
Site 1 Carrie W. Cator Place: Washington, DC
Birth: 1 Jan 1890 Death: 23 Aug 1952 Burial: 29 Aug 1952
Mort: S.H. Hines On stone with Richard T. Cator
Site 1 Richard T. Cator Place: Washington, DC
Birth: 11 Feb 1887 Death: 16 Feb 1971 Burial: 19 Feb 1971
Mort: Lanaham Funeral Home h/o Carrie W. Cator
Site 3 Mary R. Rogers Place: Washington, DC
Birth: 6 May 1884 Death: 3 Jul 1942 Burial: 6 Jul 1942
Mort: S.H. Hines Co. On stone with William J. Rogers
Site 3 William J. Rogers Place: Washington, DC
Birth: 9 Sep 1888 Death: 9 Mar 1932 Burial: 11 Mar 1932
Mort: S.H. Hines Co. h/o Mary R. Rogers
Site 4 Miss Mary Lilly Moulden Mort: Hilton & Hall Place: Washington, DC
Birth: 1858 Death: 1 Nov 1915 Burial: 3 Nov 1915
Site 5 Margaret S. Cator Place: Washington, DC
Birth: 1851 Death: 10 Jan 1915 Burial: 13 Jan 1915
Mort: Hilton & Hall Sites 4, 5, & 6 on one stone w/o Samuel H. Cator
Site 6 Samuel H. Cator Birth: 1851 Death: 1890

Lot: 28 Upper   Owner: C.O. McIntosh
Site 2 Annie Maria McIntosh Mort: S.H. Hines Co. Place: Washington, DC
Birth: 1862 Death: 26 Dec 1927 Burial: 28 Dec 1927
Site 3 Anne Virginia McIntosh Mort: L.W. Hines Co. Place: Washington, DC
Birth: 1895 Death: 7 Jul 1926 Burial: 9 Jul 1926
Site 4 Infant Hough Mort: S.H. Hines Co.
Place: Washington, DC Death: 11 Oct 1940 Burial: 12 Oct 1940
i/o Mortimer & Margaret Tetlow Hough No marker
Site 6 R. Etna Moulden
Birth: 1855 Death: 30 Oct 1882 Burial: 1 Nov 1882

Monocacy Cemetery, Beallsville, Montgomery County, Maryland

Lot: 29 Owner: Clinton Brown
Site 1 Sallie M. Brown   Mort: Robt. A. Pumphrey   Place: Bethesda
        Birth: 23 Feb 1880   Death: 21 Jan 1969   Burial: 24 Jan 1969
Site 2 Sarah Catherine Selby   Place: Dickerson
        Birth: 1858   Death: 18 Jan 1930   Burial: 20 Jan 1930
        Mort: Waner E. Pumphrey   TS: Mother
Site 3 Annie M. Brown   Mort: W.T. Hilton & Sons   Place: Sellman
        Birth: 29 Jan 1855   Death: 29 Apr 1919   Burial: 1 May 1919
Site 4 Andrew Clinton Brown   Mort: W.T. Hilton & Sons   Place: Barnesville
        Birth: 29 Feb 1852   Death: 27 Nov 1922   Burial: 29 Nov 1922
Site 5 William Curtis Brown   Mort: W.R. Pumphrey   Place: New York
        Birth: 25 Dec 1859   Death: 24 May 1938   Burial: 27 May 1938
Site 9 James W. Brown   Birth: 23 Aug 1876   Death: 8 Feb 1892
Site 10 Anna Virginia Carlisle   Mort: W.R. Speare   w/o James William Carlisle
        Birth: 20 Apr 1848   Death: 20 Nov 1905   Burial: 22 Apr 1925
        Moved here from Rock Creek Cemetery, Washington, DC
Site 11 James William Carlisle   Place: Washington, DC
        Birth: 24 May 1842   Death: 20 Apr 1925   Burial: 22 Apr 1925
        Mort: W.R. Speare Co.   h/o Anna V. Carlisle

Lot: 30 Owner: B.F. Sparrough
Site 2 Harry F. Garrett   Place: Baltimore
        Birth: 1877   Death: 15 Apr 1929   Burial: 17 Apr 1929
        Mort: Wm. H. Sardo & Co.   w/o Addie F. Garrett
Site 3 Addie Florence Garrett   Place: Arlington
        Birth: 1877   Death: 9 Mar 1952   Burial: 12 Mar 1952
        Mort: Deal Funeral Home   w/o Henry F. Garrett
Site 4 Catherine A. Sparrough   TS: w/o Benjamin F. Sparrough, age 36-6-22
        Birth: 2 Feb 1852   No death date on stone   Burial: 26 Aug 1888
Site 5 Benjamin F. Sparrough   Place: Washington, DC
        Birth: 19 Aug 1844   Death: 9 May 1914   Burial: 12 May 1914
        Mort: Hilton & Hall   h/o Catharine A. Sparrough

Lot: 31 Lower Owner: Mrs. Alice Beacht
Site   Mollie Beacht   No marker   Mort: M.R. Etchison &
                                  Death: 4 Oct 1933   Burial: 6 Oct 1933
        Place: Montevue Hospital   w/o Charles M. Beacht,
Site 2 Nora Shipley   Place: Rocky Ridge
        Birth: 17 Feb 1874   Death: 18 Jul 1952   Burial: 21 Jul 1952
        Mort: Roy W. Barber   Age 78   On stone with Frank S. Shipley
Site 3 Frank Sterling Shipley   Place: Walkersville
        Birth: 5 Jan 1866   Death: 29 Jul 1954   Burial: 2 Aug 1954
        Mort: G.C. Baron   h/o Nora Shipley
Site 4 Miss Effie B. Beacht   No death on stone   Burial: 11 Oct 1903
        TS: d/o Charles & Mollie Beacht, age 21-7-7
Site 6 Charles M. Beacht   Age 44-3-3
        illegible   Death: 14 Dec 1898   Burial: 17 Dec 1898

Monocacy Cemetery, Beallsville, Montgomery County, Maryland

Lot: 31 Upper   Owner: William Felix Veirs (No stones in lot)
- Site Benjamin Franklin Veirs   Death: 23 May 1911   Burial: 23 May 1911
- Site Mrs. Emiline Veirs   Death: 7 Aug 1896   Burial: 7 Aug 1896
- Site Lorenzo Veirs   Death: 7 May 1909   Burial: 7 May 1909
- Site Turner Veirs   No marker   Mort: Hilton & Hall
   Place: Poolesville   Death: 2 Aug 1917   Burial: 3 Aug 1917

Lot: 32   Owner: C. Fields
- Site C. G. Fields   No marker   Burial: 4 Feb 1892
- Site Charlie Fields and 2 children   No marker   Burial: 16 Apr 1894
- Site Child of Clayton Fields   No marker   Burial: 12 Dec 1902
- Site Son of Mr. C. Fields   No marker   Burial: 30 Sep 1896
- Site 3 Helen Elizabeth Betson   Mort: Geo W. Peters
   Place: Baltimore   Death: 13 Oct 1918   Burial: 16 Oct 1918
   TS: d/o H.C. & S.W. Betson, age 3-3-2
- Site 4 Child Betson   c/o H.C. & S.W. Betson   No marker
- Site 4 Clayton Betson   Mort: Hilton & Price
   Place: Martinsburg   Death: 10 Sep 1933   Burial: 11 Sep 1933
   s/o H.C. & Sallie Fields Betson   No marker
- Site 4 Helen M. Fields   d/o C.S. & Frances Fields, age 0-3-25
   illegible   Death: 25 Aug 1910   Burial: 26 Aug 1910
- Site 5 Armstead (Army) W. Fields   Place: Bethesda
   Birth: 17 May 1892   Death: 12 Jun 1958   Burial: 14 Jun 1958
   Mort: Hilton   s/o Clayton S. & Frances Fields
- Site 6 Clayton Spencer Fields Jr.   Mort: Deal   Place: Washington, DC
   Birth: 7 Jul 1897   Death: 29 Feb 1956   Burial: 3 Mar 1956
- Site 6 Gladys Mae Fields   On stone with Clayton S. Fields
   Birth: 17 Feb 1901   Death: 4 Jan 1991   Burial: 9 Jan 1991
- Site 7 Roger E. Fields   Place: Bethesda
   Birth: 9 Jun 1893   Death: 20 Sep 1945   Burial: 21 Sep 1945
   Mort: W.W. Chambers   s/o Clayton S. & Frances Fields
- Site 8 Frances W. Fields Nunnally   Mort: Hilton & Price   Place: Martinsburg
   Birth: 10 Jan 1900   Death: 8 Dec 1935   w/o Brick Nunnally
- Site 9 Clayton S. Fields   Place: Martinsburg
   Birth: 11 Jun 1857   Death: 18 Mar 1927   Burial: 21 Mar 1927
   Mort: Hilton & Hall   h/o Frances W. Fields
- Site 10 Frances W. Fields   Place: Washington, DC
   Birth: 19 Feb 1866   Death: 27 Jan 1929   Burial: 29 Jan 1929
   Mort: T. Hanlin   w/o Clayton S. Fields, Sr.

Lot: 33 Lower   Owner: Marion Riley
- Site Child of Marion Riley   No marker   Burial: 19 Aug 1900
- Site Child of Marion Riley   No marker   Burial: 15 Sep 1899
- Site 1 Effie Savilla Riley   TS: d/o Marion & Agnes Riley
   Birth: 4 Aug 1897   Death: 17 Sep 1890   Burial: 4 Aug 1897
- Site 3 Marion Riley   Mort: W.B. Hilton
   Place: Dickerson   Death: 19 Feb 1943   Burial: 22 Feb 1943
   h/o Agnes Riley   No marker

Monocacy Cemetery, Beallsville, Montgomery County, Maryland 83

Site 2 Agnes Riley Mort: W.T. Hilton & Sons
        Place: Dickerson Death: 16 Feb 1925 Burial: 18 Feb 1925
        w/o Marion Riley No marker

Lot: 33 Upper Owner: Miscellaneous
Site 1 Horace Truman Clothier Mort: W.B. Hilton Place: Beltsville
        Birth: 1891 Death: 22 Jan 1951 Burial: 25 Jan 1951
Site 3 Joseph Z. Haller Place: Frederick
        Birth: 1873 Death: 23 Feb 1951 Burial: 25 Feb 1951
        Mort: W.B. Hilton w/o Gertrude Titus Haller
Site 4 Alice Gertrude Titus Haller Place: Poolesville
        Birth: 1873 Death: 24 May 1952 Burial: 26 May 1952
        Mort: W.B. Hilton Age 79 On stone with Joseph S. Haller
Site 5 John H. Allnutt No marker
        Birth: 13 Nov 1813 Death: 2 Apr 1900 Burial: 4 Apr 1900

Lot: 34 Lower Owner: Miscellaneous
Site 1 Carl T. Fisher Mort: Hilton Place: Poolesville
        Birth: 2 Dec 1902 Death: 17 Feb 1967 Burial: 20 Feb 1967
        h/o Ruth Fega Fisher, s/o Jacob T. & Lelia H. Fisher
Site 2 Ruth Fega Fisher On stone with Carl T. Fisher
        Birth: 6 Feb 1903 Death: 13 Aug 1972 Burial: 16 Aug 1972
Site 3 George Westley Manaia h/o Barbara Repass Manaia
        Birth: 1936 Death: 14 Oct 1976 Burial: 30 Oct 1976
Site 4 Infant Stang No marker
Site 5 Annie May Stang Place: Jefferson
        Birth: 28 Apr 1856 Death: 23 May 1934 Burial: 26 May 1934
        Mort: M.R. Etchison Son On stone with Joseph F. Stang
Site 6 Joseph F. Stang h/o Annie M. Stang
        Birth: 29 Apr 1856 Death: 10 Apr 1901 Burial: 12 Apr 1901

Lot: 34 Upper Owner: Mrs. Richard Collier
Site 2 Richard H. Collier Place: Dickerson Mort: W.T. Hilton & Sons
        Birth: 30 Apr 1865 Death: 17 Aug 1917 Burial: 19 Aug 1917
Site 3 Theresa Collier Mort: S.H. Hines Co. Place: Washington, DC
        Birth: 1870 Death: 4 Jul 1955 Burial: 7 Jul 1955
Site 4 Marcus S. Collier Mort: S.H. Hines Place: Washington, DC
        Birth: 1891 Death: 5 Mar 1936 Burial: 8 Mar 1936
Site 5 Mary Louise Collier Mort: Robt. A. Pumphrey Place: Bethesda
        Birth: 1896 Death: 6 Feb 1969 Burial: 8 Feb 1969
Site 6 Carrie M. Collier
        Birth: 8 Apr 1890 Death: 8 Oct 1980 Burial: 11 Oct 1980

Lot: 35 Upper Owner: Frederick Stang
Site 3 Frederick A. Stang No marker Mort: Ernest C. Gartner
        Place: Washington Grove Death: 27 May 1944 Burial: 30 May 1944
Site 4 Robert L. Stang Death: 30 Dec 1882 Burial: 26 Apr 1904
        TS: s/o Frederick & Rose Stang, age 4-11-0

Monocacy Cemetery, Beallsville, Montgomery County, Maryland

Site 5 Rose Mossburg Stang Death: 15 Apr 1903 Burial: 17 Apr 1903
 TS: w/o Frederick G. Stang, age 50-4-8
Site 6 Frederick C. Stang Mort: Ernest C. Gartner Place: Rockville
 Birth: 13 Mar 1846 Death: 19 Jul 1928 Burial: 21 Jul 1928

Lot: 36 Lower Owner: Cornelius Soper
Site Child of Cornelius Soper No marker Burial: 29 Mar 1905
Site 4 Oliver Soper Mort: W.B. Hilton Place: Poolesville
 Birth: 2 Nov 1877 Death: 25 Jul 1948 Burial: 27 Jul 1948
Site 5 Elias R. Soper   Burial: 9 Mar 1908
 h/o Mollie Soper   No marker
Site 6 Mollie Soper   Mort: F. Gash & Sons
 Place: Maple Grove Death: 30 Sep 1921 Burial: 2 Oct 1921
 w/o Elias Soper   No marker

Lot: 36 Upper Owner: John T. Heffner
Site 1 John T. Heffner illegible Age 59 yrs
   Death: 28 Jul 1906 Burial: 30 Jul 1906
Site 2 Addie Welling Heffner No marker Mort: W.B. Hilton
 Place: Dickerson Death: 25 Dec 1948 Burial: 27 Dec 1948
Site 3 Marjorie A. Heil No marker Mort: H.J. Taltavull
 Place: Washington, DC Death: 13 Dec 1945 Burial: 16 Dec 1945
Site 4 Robert Heil No marker Mort: Deal Funeral Home
 Place: Washington, DC Death: 23 Jun 1951 Burial: 28 Jun 1951
Site 6 Leonard D. White No marker Mort: Hilton
 Place: Baltimore, MD Death: 8 Jan 1967 Burial: 11 Jan 1967

Lot: 37 Lower Owner: Mrs. Annie Beever
Site 1 Child Norris   No marker
Site 3 Kathleen S. Norris Place: Washington, DC Mort: Warner E.
 Birth: 6 Ma 1924 Death: 7 Aug 1935 Burial: 7 Aug 1935
 TS: d/o James & Anna G. Norris   No marker
Site 5 James Marshall Norris Place: Olney Mort: Warner E.
 Birth: 8 Jul 1874 Death: 31 Aug 1941 h/o Ann G. Norris
Site 6 Annie G. Norris Beever   TS: Mother
 Birth: 29 Apr 1886 Death: 7 Jun 1980 Burial: 11 Jun 1980

Lot: 37 Upper Owner: G.E. Waesche
Site 3 Alice Lakin Waesche   Place: Suitland
 Birth: 1876 Death: 12 Mar 1961 Burial: 15 Mar 1961
 Mort: Lee Funeral Home On stone with George Ernest Waesche
Site 4 George Ernest Waesche   Place: District Heights
 Birth: 1876 Death: 1 Sep 1934 Burial: 3 Sep 1934
 Mort: W.W. Deale   h/o Alice Lakin Waesche

Lot: 38 Lower Owner: Benjamin White
Site 1 Mason Wilbur Gray III   Place: Frederick
 Birth: 19 Oct 1916 Death: 30 Sep 1950 Burial: 2 Oct 1950
 Mort: W.B. Hilton   h/o Florence Jones White Gray

Monocacy Cemetery, Beallsville, Montgomery County, Maryland

Site 3 Sarah Graves White   w/o Benjamin White Jr.
        Birth: 14 May 1885   Death: 18 Jan 1975   Burial: 21 Jan 1975
Site 4 Benjamin White Jr.   h/o Sarah Graves White
        Birth: 23 Sep 1875   Death: 17 Apr 1976   Burial: 20 Apr 1976

Lot: 38 Upper   Owner: Dr. E.W. White
Site 3 Florence Pyles White   Place: Frederick, MD
        Birth: 6 Jun 1882   Death: 13 Apr 1968   Burial: 16 Apr 1968
        Mort: Wm. Hilton   w/o Elijah W. White
Site 4 Dr. Elijah Wootton White   Place: Poolesville
        Birth: 5 Mar 1882   Death: 29 May 1942   Burial: 31 May 1942
        Mort: W.B. Hilton   h/o Florence Pyles White
Site 5 Elijah Wootton White Jr.   h/o Catherine Boland White
        Birth: 1 Aug 1916   Death: 30 Oct 1990   Burial: 5 Nov 1990
Site 6 Catherine Boland White   w/o Elijah W. White Jr.
        Birth: 25 Feb 1915   Death: 28 Nov 1985   Burial: 3 Dec 1985

Lot: 39 Lower   Owner: Mrs. Pauline Clothier
Site 4 Sarah Pauline Hays Clothier   Place: Washington, DC
        Birth: 1 Jun 1892   Death: 1 Oct 1954   Burial: 4 Oct 1954
        Mort: W.B. Hilton   On stone with Archie Ball Clothier
Site 5 Archie Ball Clothier   Place: Silver Spring, MD
        Birth: 20 Sep 1894   Death: 27 Apr 1968   Burial: 30 Apr 1968
        Mort: Warner Pumphrey   h/o Pauline Hays Clothier
        TS: Dist. of Col. Mech 644 Aero SQ WWI

Lot: 39 Upper   Owner: Miscellaneous
Site 1 James Brawner Nicholson Jr.   h/o Elizabeth White Nicholson
        Birth: 6 Oct 1908   Death: 7 Jun 1979   Burial: 11 Jun 1979
Site 5 John Stinson Lacey   h/o Mary Fisher Lacey
        Birth: 22 Oct 1907   Death: 8 Aug 1995   Burial: 12 Aug 1995
Site 6 Mary Fisher Lacey   Age 73 yrs   On stone with John Stinson Lacey
        Birth: 5 Sep 1912   Death: 31 Aug 1986   Burial: 11 Sep 1986

Lot: 40   Owner: Edgar B. Chiswell
Site 2 M/Sgt. Thomas H. Chiswell   TS: Died in France
        Birth: 28 Apr 1920   Death: 19 Jan 1946   Burial: 30 Oct 1948
        Mort: W.B. Hilton   s/o Edgar B. & Haddie Smith Chiswell
Site 3 Haddie Smith Chiswell   Place: Poolesville
        Birth: 26 Aug 1885   Death: 3 Jun 1957   Burial: 5 Jun 1957
        Mort: Hilton   w/o Edgar B. Chiswell
Site 4 Edgar B. Chiswell   h/o Haddie Smith Chiswell Place: Lynchburg, VA
        Birth: 16 Sep 1885   Death: 6 Jan 1957   Burial: 8 Jan 1957
Site 10 Wayland Whitney Sweeney Jr.   TS: Lt. Col. US Army 1941-1946
        Birth: 26 Jan 1913   Death: 9 Jul 1990   Burial: 12 Jul 1990
        h/o Kathryn Leigh Chiswell Sweeney, age 75 yrs

Lot: 41 Owner: J.C. & Mary L. White

Site 3 Mary Lucile White
    Birth: 27 Dec 1880   Death: 30 May 1964
    Mort: Hilton
    Place: Frederick
    Burial: 1 Jun 1964
    w/o Joseph Collinson White

Site 4 Joseph Collinson White
    Birth: 21 Jan 1874   Death: 9 Sep 1947
    Mort: W.B. Hilton
    Place: Buckeystown
    Burial: 12 Sep 1947
    w/o Mary Lucile White

Site 9 Edna Donahoe Moore
    Birth: 30 Jun 1919   Death: 5 Mar 1986
    w/o J. Collinson Moore
    Burial: 11 Mar 1986

Site 10 Joseph Collinson Moore
    Birth: 6 Apr 1910   Death: 14 Apr 1993   Burial: 17 Apr 1993

Lot: 42 Owner: Miscellaneous

Site 1 William Marshall White
    Birth: 20 Oct 1908   Death: 4 Apr 1991
    h/o Eleanor Linthicum White
    Burial: 8 Apr 1991

Site 2 Eleanor Linthicum White   Birth: 11 Dec 1908   Death: 8 Feb 1993

Lot: 44 Lower Owner: Miscellaneous

Site 6 Harry Oscar Osborne   TS: MM1 US Navy WWII
    Birth: 3 Jan 1921   Death: 16 Apr 1992   Burial: 20 Apr 1992
    On stone with Louise H. Osborne

Lot: 44 Upper Owner: Miscellaneous

Site 4 Freda Bryant Watson   On stone with George Hugh Watson
    Birth: 1 Feb 1916   Death: 14 Oct 1994   Burial: 19 Oct 1994

Site 5 George Hugh Watson   h/o Freda B. Watson
    Birth: 25 Feb 1914   Death: 3 Jan 1992   Burial: 7 Jan 1992

Monocacy Cemetery, Beallsville, Montgomery County, Maryland   87

Row D

Lot: 0   Owner: Thomas P. Spates
Site 1   Elizabeth Ann Fields   Place: Rockville
         Birth: 19 Oct 1830   Death: 7 May 1913   Burial: 9 May 1913
         Mort: W.R. Pumphrey   TS: w/o Jetson G. Fields
Site 2   Jetson G. Fields   h/o Elizabeth A. Fields
         Birth: 4 Jun 1821   Death: 4 Dec 1903   Burial: 6 Dec 1903

Lot: 1   Owner: Mrs. Henry Spreadbury
Site 1   John Thomas Burrows   TS: Age 55 years
                                   Death: 13 Sep 1891   Burial: 15 Sep 1891
Site 2   Mrs. Elizabeth Spreadbury Burrows   TS: In her 69th year
                                   Death: 17 Feb 1898   Burial: 18 Feb 1898
Site 3   Henry Spreadbury   TS: Age 53 yrs
                                   Death: 11 Apr 1882   Burial: 15 Apr 1883

Lot: 2   Owner: George C. Fisher
Site   Mr. Martin Fisher   No marker   Burial: 31 Mar 1890
Site 1   Albert Boyd Fisher   Place: Point of Rocks
         Birth: 1 Aug 1871   Death: 5 Jul 1938   Burial: 7 Jul 1938
         Mort: M.R. Etchison & Son   h/o Laura Willare Fisher
Site 2   Laura Willard Fisher   Place: Frederick
         Birth: 14 Jan 1876   Death: 29 Apr 1951   Burial: 1 May 1951
         Mort: C.E. Cline & Sons   TS: w/o Albert B. Fisher
Site 3   George W. Spates
         Birth: Sep 1825   Death: 18 Mar 1883   Burial: 31 Mar 1883
Site 4   Ann Boyd Spates   TS: w/o George W. Spates
         Birth: 4 Nov 1825   Death: 24 Dec 1878   Burial: 26 Dec 1878
Site 6   Albert Boyd Fisher Jr.   Place: Pittsburgh
         Birth: 1903   Death: 28 Sep 1964   Burial: 5 Oct 1964
         Mort: Sherman Crematory   h/o Ruth Fisher
Site 6   Ruth M. Fisher   Age 77 yrs   TS: w/o Albert Boyd Fisher, Jr.
         Birth: 1902   Death: 30 Jul 1979   Burial: 2 Aug 1979
Site 7   Anita Willard Fisher   Place: Braddock Heights
         Birth: 20 Jan 1913   Death: 30 Jul 1913   Burial: 31 Jul 1913
         Mort: W.T. Hilton & Sons   d/o A.B. & L.W. Fisher
Site 8   Agnes Lauretta Fisher   d/o A.B. & L.W. Fisher
         Birth: 29 Jun 1907   Death: 5 Mar 1910   Burial: 8 Mar 1910
Site 9   George C. Fisher   TS: Age 63-3-24   h/o Sarah Agnes Fisher
         Birth: 11 Mar 1838   Death: 5 Jun 1901   Burial: 7 Jun 1901
Site 10 Sarah Agnes Fisher   Place: Point of Rocks
         Birth: 20 Jul 1851   Death: 13 Jan 1916   Burial: 15 Jan 1916
         Mort: W.T. Hilton & Sons   On stone with George C. Fisher
Site 11 Lulu Fisher   Death: 26 Oct 1876   Burial: 27 Oct 1876
         TS: d/o George C. & S. Agnes Fisher. age0-11-26

Lot: 3 Owner: Jonathan B. Benson

Site Jonathan Benson Death: 10 Sep 1873 Burial: 16 Sep 1873
      No marker
Site Mr. George Johnson No marker Burial: 12 Feb 1895
Site Alice May Miles Death: 13 Aug 1882 Burial: 13 Aug 1882
      d/o James R. & Sarah L. Miles, age 2-2-5 No marker
Site Charles Edgar Miles Death: 9 Sep 1888 Burial: 11 Sep 1888
      s/o James R. & Sarah L. Miles, age 6-8-20 No marker
Site Jonathan B. Miles Burial: 30 Apr 1886
      s/o James R. & Sarah L. Miles, age 9-10-19 No marker
Site 2 Leon S. Leslie h/o Bernice E. Leslie
      Birth: 28 Jun 1901 Death: 10 Jul 1974 Burial: 13 Jul 1974
Site 3 Bernice Elizabeth Leslie On stone with Leon S. Leslie
      Birth: 25 Sep 1909 Death: 14 Dec 1987 Burial: 16 Dec 1987
Site 6 Maurice W. Downs Mort: Warner E. Pumphrey
      Birth: 14 Aug 1906 Death: 8 May 1966 Burial: 11 May 1966
Site 7 James Robert Downs TS: TEC4 US Army WWII
      Birth: 22 Feb 1922 Death: 4 May 1982 Burial: 8 May 1982
Site 8 Clara N. Downs On stone with James Robert Downs
      Birth: 11 Apr 1924 Death: 22 Jan 1981
      TS: 2nd marker gives birth as 11 Apr 1923
Site 9 James R. Miles Place: Beallsville
      Birth: 18 Dec 1844 Death: 6 Nov 1914 Burial: 8 Nov 1914
      Mort: Hilton & Hall h/o Sarah L. Miles
Site 10 Sarah Lucretia Mossburg Miles Place: Claysville
      Birth: 10 May 1847 Death: 28 Dec 1922 Burial: 30 Dec 1922
      Mort: W.R. Pumphrey TS: w/o James R. Miles
Site 11 Maurice C. Downs h/o Sarah F. Downs
      Birth: 7 Feb 1885 Death: 17 Aug 1971 Burial: 20 Aug 1971
Site 12 Sarah F. Downs On stone with Maurice C. Downs
      Birth: 21 Jun 1885 Death: 9 Dec 1971 Burial: 13 Dec 1971

Lot: 4 Owner: Benjamin R. Poole

Site Child of Charlie Poole No marker Burial: 9 Oct 1894
Site 1 Ann Eliza Elgin TS: Age 96
      Death: 14 Dec 1905 Burial: 17 Dec 1905
Site 2 Thomas Jefferson Poole Place: Sykesville
      Birth: 7 Mar 1920 Death: 18 Apr 1962 Burial: 21 Apr 1962
      Mort: Hilton TS: s/o John E. & Laura Poole
Site 3 Jane Elgin Poole Mort: W.R. Pumphrey
      Place: Bethesda Death: 27 Jun 1917 Burial: 29 Jun 1917
      TS: w/o Benjamin R. Poole, age 83-9-19
Site 4 Benjamin R. Poole h/o Jane Elgin Poole TS: Age 75 yrs
      Birth: 6 May 1831 Death: 16 May 1906 Burial: 18 May 1906
Site 5 Charles J. Poole Death: 21 Oct 1894 Burial: 23 Oct 1894
      TS: s/o Jane & Benjamin Poole, age 28-11-14
Site 6 James Harvey Poole Death: 6 May 1874
      TS: s/o Jane & Benjamin Poole, age 3-11-21

Monocacy Cemetery, Beallsville, Montgomery County, Maryland

Site 6	Raymond Lee Poole		Place: Martinsburg
	Birth: 1 May 1928	Death: 4 May 1928	Burial: 5 May 1928
	Mort: Hilton & Hall		TS: s/o B.R. & C.K.E. Poole
Site 6	John Elgin Poole Jr.	No marker	Mort: W.B. Hilton
		Death: 3 Mar 1944	Burial: 4 Mar 1944
	Place: Montgomery Co., Hospital		s/o John E. Pool 2nd
Site 7	A. Myrtle Poole		TS: d/o J.E. & L.E. Poole, age 1-3-28
	Birth: 29 Apr 1909	Death 27 Aug 1910	Burial: 30 Aug 1910
Site 8	W. Walter Poole		TS: s/o J.E. & L.E. Poole, age 6-11-18
	Birth: 1906	Death: 11 Apr 1913	Burial: 12 Apr 1913
Site 9	Laura Ellen Reed Poole		Place: Silver Spring
	Birth: 9 Oct 1881	Death: 2 Oct 1961	Burial: 5 Oct 1961
	Mort: Hilton		TS: 2nd w/o John E. Poole
Site 10	John Elgin Poole		Place: Martinsburg
	Birth: 5 Sep 1863	Death: 30 Jan 1929	Burial: 1 Feb 1929
	Mort: Hilton & Hall	h/o Anna Elgin Poole & Laura Reed Poole	
Site 11	Anna Elgin Poole		Burial: 25 May 1900
	Birth: 22 Dec 1869	Death: 23 May 1900	TS: w/o John Elgin Poole
	d/o John O. & Martha Elgin		
Site 12	Mildred Poole Smith		d/o John E. & Laura Poole
	Birth: 1 Dec 1907	Death: 5 Dec 1991	Burial: 10 Dec 1991

Lot: 5 Owner: Benoni Allnutt

Site 1	Nathan B. Allnutt		s/o Benoni & Emily Allnutt
	Birth: 6 Dec 1882	Death: 5 Sep 1889	
Site 2	Sadie Allnutt		d/o Benoni & Emily Allnutt
	Birth: 27 Aug 1876	Death: 9 Nov 1890	Burial: 11 Nov 1890
Site 3	Emily Dawson Allnutt		TS: w/o Benoni Allnutt
	Birth: 15 Apr 1835	Death: 21 Oct 1908	Burial: 24 Oct 1908
Site 4	Benoni Allnutt		h/o Emily Dawson Allnutt
	Birth: 2 Jan 1835	Death: 30 May 1899	Burial: 31 May 1899
Site 5	Nellie (Eleanor) Allnutt		
	Birth: 1861	Death: 2 Sep 1923	Burial: 4 Sep 1923
Site 10	Lawrence E. Allnutt	Mort: W.B. Hilton	Place: Frederick Hospital
	Birth: 1872	Death: 1 May 1948	Burial: 3 May 1948
Site 11	Benoni D. Allnutt	Mort: W.B. Hilton	Place: Frederick
	Birth: 18 Nov 1872	Death: 9 Mar 1941	Burial: 12 Mar 1941

Lot: 6 Owner: Benjamin Allnutt

Site 1	Rachel Ann Allnutt	Mort: Hilton	Place: Germantown
	Birth: 23 Nov 1870	Death: 25 Aug 1963	Burial: 28 Aug 1963
Site 2	Albert S. Allnutt		
	Birth: 7 Dec 1867	Death: 1 Apr 1898	Burial: 3 Apr 1898
Site 3	Rachel White Allnutt		Place: Dawsonville
	Birth: 25 Nov 1835	Death: 7 Mar 1926	Burial: 9 Mar 1926
	Mort: Hilton & Hall		TS: w/o Benjamin W. Allnutt
Site 4	Benjamin White Allnutt		Place: Dawsonville
	Birth: 4 Dec 1837	Death: 16 Feb 1915	Burial: 18 Feb 1915
	Mort: W.T. Hilton & Sons		h/o Rachael W. Allnutt

Monocacy Cemetery, Beallsville, Montgomery County, Maryland

Site 7 Benjamin W. Allnutt   s/o Benj. & Rachael W. Allnutt
    Birth: 1 Nov 1869   Death: 15 Nov 1869
Site 7 Infant Allnutt   TS: d/o Benjamin & Rachael W. Allnutt
    Birth & Death: 12 Aug 1882   Burial: 15 Aug 1882
Site 7 Lawrence Allnutt   infant s/o Benj. & Rachael W. Allnutt
    Birth: 2 Sep 1873   Death: 12 Sep 1873
Site 10 Henry White Allnutt   Place: Germantown
    Birth: 14 Jan 1875   Death: 20 Sep 1956   Burial: 22 Sep 1956
    Mort: W.B. Hilton   h/o Jane Williams Allnutt
Site 11 Jane Williams Allnutt   w/o Henry White Allnutt
    Birth: 14 May 1887   Death: 1 Sep 1978   Burial: 4 Sep 1978
Site 12 Benjamin W. Allnutt   s/o Henry White & Jane Williams Allnutt
    Birth: 19 Aug 1919   Death: 2 Jun 1976   Burial: 5 Jun 1976

Lot: 7 Owner: Edward J. Chiswell
Site 1 Infant Chiswell   No marker   id/o E.L. & Naomi Chiswell
Site 3 Evie W. Chiswell   Mort: Warner E. Pumphrey   Place: Dickerson
    Birth: 3 Oct 1840   Death: 22 Nov 1937   Burial: 24 Nov 1937
    On stone with Lieut. Edward Jones Chiswell
Site 4 Lieut. Edward J. Chiswell   h/o Evie W. Chiswell
    Birth: 2 Jun 1836   Death: 21 Sep 1906   Burial: 23 Sep 1906
Site 5 Naomi North Chiswell   Place: Dickerson
    Birth: 23 May 1875   Death: 18 Oct 1942   Burial: 20 Oct 1942
    Mort: Warner E. Pumphrey   On stone with Edward Lee Chiswell
Site 6 Edward Lee Chiswell   Place: Silver Spring
    Birth: 19 Mar 1873   Death: 17 Oct 1946   Burial: 21 Oct 1946
    Mort: Warner E. Pumphrey   h/o Naomi North Chiswell
Site 12 Edward Fowler Chiswell
    Birth: 9 Sep 1913   Death: 7 Sep 1977   Burial: 10 Sep 1977
    s/o Edward L. & Naomi N. Chiswell, h/o Helen Chiswell

Lot: 8 Owner: Benjamin F. White
Site 1 Margaret A. White   TS: w/o Benjamin Franklin White
    Birth: 8 May 1828   Death: 20 Dec 1891   Burial: 22 Dec 1891
Site 2 Benjamin Franklin White   TS: Age 61-1-0   h/o Margaret A. White
    Birth: 1 Aug 1826   Death: 31 Aug 1887   Burial: 1 Sep 1887
Site 5 Ella R. Whitmore White   Place: Dickerson
    Birth: 1857   Death: 9 Feb 1927   Burial: 11 Feb 1927
    Mort: W.T. Hilton & Sons   TS: w/o Mansfield White
Site 6 Mansfield White   Place: Dickerson
    Birth: 1859   Death: 30 Jan 1951   Burial: 1 Feb 1951
    Mort: W.B. Hilton   h/o Ella Whitmore White, age 92
Site 7 Charles Muzzy Tipton   Place: Rockville
    Birth: 1885   Death: 13 Dec 1955   Burial: 16 Dec 1955
    Mort: W.B. Hilton   h/o Elizabeth White Tipton
Site 8 Elizabeth White Tipton   w/o Charles Muzzy Tipton
    Birth: 22 Sep 1896   Death: 26 Jun 1982   Burial: 28 Jun 1982
Site 9 Henry Whitmore White   h/o Mary Ethel Garner White
    Birth: 15 Jan 1893   Death: 16 Jun 1980   Burial: 19 Jun 1980

Monocacy Cemetery, Beallsville, Montgomery County, Maryland

Site 10	Mary Ethel Garner White		w/o Henry White
	Birth: 14 Jun 1903	Death: 11 Jan 1984	Burial: 14 Jan 1984
Site 11	Wellstood White	TS: Col. US Army WWI	h/o Rosalie Carr
	Birth: 22 Oct 1885	Death: 18 Nov 1980	Burial: 24 Nov 1980
Site 12	Rosalie Carr White		w/o Wellstood W. White
	Birth: 5 Feb 1888	Death: 26 Mar 1987	Burial: 31 Mar 1987

Lot: 9 Owner: Mrs. Sarah Dawson

Site 1 Mrs. Martha Dawson Waters
 Birth: 4 Mar 1842   Death: 12 May 1903   Burial: 14 May 1903
 On stone with Thomas Waters & Miss Mary Margaret Dawson

Site 2 Thomas Waters   Mort: W.R. Pumphrey   Place: Washington, DC
 Birth: 1 Nov 1835   Death: 12 Mar 1914   Burial: 14 Mar 1914

Site 3 Frederick A. Dawson   Age 74
 Birth: 22 Jul 1833   Death: 22 Jul 1907   Burial: 24 Jul 1907

Site 4 Mrs. Susan A. Dawson
 Birth: 7 Jul 1828   Death: 21 Mar 1908   Burial: 23 Mar 1908
 On stone with Frederick A. Dawson & Miss Adelaide Louisa Dawson

Site 7 William Edward Dawson   Reinterment
 Birth: 1850   Death: 8 Aug 1850   Burial: 26 Nov 1879
 TS: s/o Benoni & Sarah Dawson, age 1-9-20

Site 8 Joseph Henry Dawson   TS: s/o Benoni & Sarah Dawson, age 21-1-20
         Death: 20 Mar 1851   Burial: 26 Nov 1879

Site 9 Laura A. Dawson   Reinterment
 Birth: 27 Apr 1839   Death: 6 Aug 1841   Burial: 26 Nov 1879
 TS: d/o Benoni & Sarah Dawson, age 2-3-10

Site 10 Robert Thomas Dawson   Birth: 1844   Death: 11 Sep 1874
 TS: s/o Dr. Benoni & Sarah Newton Jones Dawson, age 30-2-14

Site 11 Miss Adelaide Louisa Dawson
 Birth: 20 Sep 1846   Death: 12 Jul 1910   Burial: 14 Jul 1910
 d/o Dr. Benoni & Sarah Newton Jones Dawson

Site 12 Sarah Newton Jones Dawson   TS: w/o Benoni Dawson, age 71 yrs 24 days
         Death: 17 Apr 1879   Burial: 18 Apr 1879

Site 13 Benoni Dawson   Reinterment
 Birth: 27 Oct 1797   Death: 11 Jan 1851   Burial: 26 Nov 1879
 h/o Sarah Newton Jones Dawson, age 53-2-19

Site 14 Miss Mary Margaret Dawson   d/o Dr. Benoni & Sarah Newton Jones Dawson
 Birth: 3 Aug 1837   Death: 6 May 1888   Burial: 7 Jun 1888

Lot: 10 Owner: Mrs. Mary E. Chiswell

Site 1 William Chiswell   Mort: Hilton & Hall   Place: Seneca
 Birth: 4 Mar 1841   Death: 3 Apr 1921   Burial: 4 Apr 1921
 s/o Thomas Fletchall & Mary Eleanor Jones Chiswell

Site 2 Thomas Fletchall Chiswell   Birth: 10 Sep 1810   Death: 7 May 1851
 h/o Mary Eleanor Jones Chiswell   TS: s/o William & Sarah Chiswell

Site 3 Mary Eleanor Jones Chiswell   TS: w/o Thomas Fletchall Chiswell
 Birth: 31 Mar 1810   Death: 27 Jan 1873   Burial: 30 Jan 1873

Site 4 Margaret White   Place: Poolesville
        Birth: 26 Jan 1846   Death: 17 Jul 1925   Burial: 19 Jul 1925
        Mort: Hilton & Hall   TS: w/o Samuel C. White, age 79-5-21
Site 5 Samuel C. White   Reinterment
        Birth: 17 Aug 1841   Death: 3 Aug 1873   Burial: 19 Dec 1900
        TS: s/o Dr. Stephen N.C. & Elizabeth White, age 31-11-16
Site 8 Mary Elizabeth Chiswell   d/o T.F. & M.E. Chiswell
        Birth: 30 Mar 1839   Death: 9 Sep 1839

Lot: 11 Owner: John A. Jones
Site 2 Infant Jones   Place: Dickerson
        Birth: 2 Dec 1920   Death: 2 Dec 1920   Burial: 3 Dec 1920
        Mort: W.T. Hilton & Sons   TS: i/o John A. & Mamie P. Jones
Site 3 Edward Wilkerson Jones   Place: Dickerson
        Birth: 12 Jul 1869   Death: 5 Jun 1915   Burial: 7 Jun 1915
        Mort: Hilton & Hall   s/o John A. & Rose D. Jones
Site 4 William A. Jones   TS: s/o John A. & Rose D. Jones, age 14 mo.
        Birth: 9 Aug 1872   Death: 8 Jul 1873   Burial: 9 Jul 1873
Site 5 Rose M. Darby Jones   w/o John A. Jones
        Birth: 9 Oct 1834   Death: 9 May 1896   Burial: 10 May 1896
Site 6 John Augustus Jones Sr.   h/o Rose M. Darby Jones
        Birth: 28 Sep 1821   Death: 17 Jan 1896   Burial: 17 Jan 1896
Site 8 John Augustus Jones III
        Birth: 17 Jan 1911   Death: 29 Aug 1983   Burial: 1 Sep 1983
        s/o John A. Jones Jr. & Mamie Pyles Jones, h/o Elsie Gross Jones
Site 9 Mamie Pyles Jones   Place: Poolesville, MD
        Birth: 27 Sep 1879   Death: 9 Jun 1968   Burial: 11 Jun 1968
        Mort: W. Hilton   w/o John A. Jones
Site 10 John A. Jones Jr.   Place: Frederick
        Birth: 10 Dec 1878   Death: 4 Jan 1961   Burial: 6 Jan 1961
        Mort: Hilton   h/o Mamie Pyles Jones
Site 11 Bettie Jones Newman   d/o John A. & Mamie P. Jones
        Birth: 5 Oct 1905   Death: 12 Feb 1990   Burial: 16 Feb 1990

Lot: 12 Lower Owner: John A. Jones
Site 1 Sarah Jones   TS: w/o Edward Jones, age 73-6-4   Reinterment
        Birth: 2 Nov 1742   Death: 6 May 1816   Burial: 28 Nov 1895
Site 2 Edward Jones Jr.   TS: Age 53-6-17
        Birth: 8 May 1737   Death: 25 Jan 1790   Burial: 28 Nov 1895
        h/o Sarah White Jones   Reinterment
Site 3 Edward Jones   Reinterment
        Birth: 1 Jun 1812   Death: 3 Dec 1835   Burial: 28 Nov 1895
        w/o Joseph James Wilkerson & Ann Newton Chiswell Jones
Site 4 Miss Elizabeth Jones   d/o Joseph H. & Ann V. Jones
        Birth: 25 May 1831   Death: 19 Aug 1894   Burial: 20 Aug 1894
Site 5 Ann Mildred Jones Cummings   TS: w/o Franklin Cummings
        Birth: 14 Apr 1824   Death: 22 Apr 1909   Burial: 23 Apr 1909
Site 6 William Jones   s/o Joseph & Ann Jones   Reinterment
        Birth: 10 Feb 1817   Death: 17 Aug 1844   Burial: 28 Nov 1895

Site 6 Anne Newton Chiswell Jones
Birth: 15 Nov 1786   Death: 5 Jan 1857   Burial: 28 Nov 1895
w/o Joseph James Wilkerson Jones   Reinterment
Site 6 Joseph James Wilkerson Jones
Birth: 18 May 1776   Death: 15 Dec 1840   Burial: 28 Nov 1895
h/o Anne Newton Chiswell Jones   Reinterment

Lot: 12 Upper Owner: Fred A. Dawson
Site 1 Robert Doyne Dawson   TS: s/o Thomas & Elizabeth Dawson, age 66-1-3
Birth: 10 Jul 1758   Death: 13 Aug 1824
Site 2 Sarah Newton Chiswell Dawson   Reinterment
Birth: 29 May 1754   Death: 13 Nov 1806   Burial: 20 May 1905
TS: w/o Robert Doyne Dawson, d/o Stephen N. & Sarah Chiswell
Site 3 George Washington Dawson Reinterment
Birth: 28 Nov 1799   Death: 26 Dec 1874   Burial: 11 Feb 1880
TS: s/o Robert & Sarah Dawson, age 75-1-0
Site 4 Mary Elizabeth Dawson   Reinterment
Birth: 22 Jul 1794   Death: 4 Feb 1852   Burial: 11 Feb 1880
TS: d/o Robert & Sarah Dawson, age 57-6-13
Site 5 Joseph N. Dawson   Reinterment
Birth: 20 Feb 1796   Death: 10 Jul 1869   Burial: 11 Feb 1880
TS: s/o Robert & Sarah Dawson, age 73-4-20
Site 6 Mary Elizabeth McLeod   Death: 20 May 1852   Burial: 28 Nov 1895
TS: d/o P.H. & M.C. MacLeod, age 6 yrs 3 mo 21 days   Reinterment
Site 6 Joseph Wilkinson McLeod   TS: s/o P.H. & M.C. McLeod, age 4-0-23
Reinterment   Death: 23 Jul 1852   Burial: 28 Nov 1895

Lot: 13 Owner: John T. Norris
Site   F. M. Norris   No marker   Burial: 14 Sep 1905
Site 1 James Elmer Norris   Mort: Jos. B. Wright   Place: Washington, DC
Birth: 1877   Death: 1 Jul 1928   Burial: 3 Jul 1928
Site 2 Warren King Norris   b. 1 Jul 1865 (Family Bible)
Birth: 1864   Death: 1909
Site 3 John T. Norris
Birth: 1832   Death: 1898   Burial: 11 Aug 1898
Site 4 Margaret A. Norris   No marker
Death: 4 May 1908   Burial: 4 May 1908
Site 4 Margaret Ann King Norris   w/o John T. Norris
Birth: 13 Mar 1840   Death: 1908   Burial: 28 May 1909
Site 5 Marion A. Norris   Birth: 26 Aug 1866   Death: 1906
Site 6 Clinton A. Norris
Birth: 14 Oct 1868   Death: 1892   Burial: 16 May 1892
Site 7 Cora Norris Gott   Mort: R. A. Pumphrey   Place: Washington, DC
Birth: 1871   Death: 8 Oct 1950   Burial: 11 Oct 1950
Site 10 A. Mabel Mae Norris Christmas   On stone with Margaret Ann Norris Forest
Birth: 25 Jan 1861   Death: 1951   sister/o M.A. Forrest
Site 10 Margaret Ann Norris Forrest   Mort: Pearsons   Place: 3305 18th St., N.W.
Birth: 1873   Death: 21 Oct 1966   Burial: 24 Oct 1966

Monocacy Cemetery, Beallsville, Montgomery County, Maryland

Site 11 Julius Crawford Forrest
     Place: Falls Church, VA
Site 12 Charles Olin Norris
     Birth: 1879
     No marker
     Death: 15 Dec 1972
     Mort: J.R. Wright Co.
     Death: 8 Feb 1931
     Mort: O.C. Pearson
     Burial: 17 Dec 1972
     Place: Washington, DC
     Burial: 10 Feb 1931

Lot: 14 Owner: W.C. Hoskinson

Site 3 Walter B. Hoskinson — Mort: Wm. B. Hilton — Place: Lonaconing, MD
     Birth: 6 May 1879 — Death: 15 Oct 1966 — Burial: 18 Oct 1966
Site 4 Thomas Hoskinson — Mort: Hilton & Hall — Place: Poolesville
     Birth: 19 Feb 1852 — Death: 23 Sep 1931 — Burial: 25 Sep 1931
Site 5 Mary Gertrude Hoskinson — Mort: Hilton & Hall — Place: Poolesville
     Birth: 22 Feb 1854 — Death: 27 Oct 1923 — Burial: 29 Oct 1923
Site 6 John Fletchall Hoskinson — c/o Thomas Hoskinson
     Birth: 19 Aug 1890 — Death: 4 Nov 1890 — Burial: 5 Nov 1890
Site 7 William T. Hoskinson — Mort: Hilton & Hall — Place: Washington, DC
     Birth: 8 Oct 1877 — Death: 18 Dec 1935 — Burial: 21 Dec 1935
Site 8 William C. Hoskinson — Mort: Hilton & Hall — Place: Poolesville
     Birth: 7 Feb 1850 — Death: 18 Feb 1934 — Burial: 20 Feb 1934
Site 9 Dorcas A. Hoskinson — Birth: 23 Jan 1826 — Burial: 20 Oct 1875
Site 10 Lula B. Hoskinson — Mort: Hilton — Place: Bethesda
     Birth: 12 Jun 1885 — Death: 1 Dec 1962 — Burial: 4 Dec 1962
Site 11 Stella G. Hoskinson
     Birth: 14 Aug 1883 — Death: 18 Aug 1977 — Burial: 22 Aug 1977
Site 12 Mary Dorcas Hoskinson — Mort: Hilton — Place: Poolesville
     Birth: 3 Mar 1881 — Death: 8 Oct 1965 — Burial: 11 Oct 1965

Lot: 15 Owner: Sons & Heirs of William T. Jones

Site 1 John J. Isaac Jones — TS: s/o William & Airy Ann Jones
     Birth: 23 Oct 1838 — Death: 13 Dec 1897 — Burial: 15 Dec 1897
Site 2 William Thomas Jones — TS: s/o William & Airy Ann Jones
     Birth: 22 Aug 1833 — Death: 27 Dec 1910 — Burial: 28 Dec 1910
Site 7 William Jones Sr. — TS: Age 76-4-5 — h/o Airy Ann Jones
     Birth: 31 Jan 1800 — Death: 5 Jun 1876
Site 8 Airy Ann Jones — TS: Relict of William Jones Sr.
     Birth: 12 May 1802 — Death: 1 Sep 1876 — Burial: 3 Jul 1876
Site 9 Columbia Jones — TS: d/o William & Airy Ann Jones
     Birth: 20 Jun 1835 — Death: 20 Feb 1882 — Burial: 22 Feb 1882
Site 10 Miss Airy Ann Jones — TS: d/o William & Airy Ann Jones
     Birth: 2 Sep 1829 — Death: 27 Jul 1888 — Burial: 29 Jul 1888

Lot: 16 Owner: Charles Sellman

Site 1 Charles Sellman — TS: Age 54-0-15 — h/o Lucy Veirs Sellman
     Birth: 19 Apr 1848 — Death: 5 May 1902 — Burial: 7 May 1902
Site 2 Lucy Veirs Sellman — TS: w/o Charles Sellman, age 58-10-27
     Birth: 8 Apr 1854 — Death: 5 Mar 1913 — Burial: 7 Mar 1913
Site 3 Howard Maynard Sellman — TS: Age 39-8-18 — Place: Poolesville
     Birth: 19 Jun 1885 — Death: 7 Mar 1925 — Burial: 9 Mar 1925
     Mort: Hilton & Hall — s/o Charles & Lucy Veirs Sellman

Monocacy Cemetery, Beallsville, Montgomery County, Maryland

Site 5 Charles Sellman   Death: 4 Feb 1881   Burial: 6 Feb 1881
        TS: s/o Charles & Lucy Sellman, age 5-9-24
Site 6 William Sellman   TS: s/o Charles & Lucy Sellman, age 0-5-7
                                  Death: 21 Jun 1877   Burial: 23 Jun 1877
Site 9 Roger B. Sellman   TS: Age 73-1-14   Place: Harrisburg, PA
        Birth: 2 Apr 1883   Death: 16 May 1956   Burial: 19 May 1956
        Mort: W.Orville Kimmel   s/o Charles & Lucy Sellman
Site 10 Throop Ainsworth   TS: s/o J.T. & Mary Sellman Ainsworth
        Birth: 11 Oct 1896   Death: 27 Jul 1897   Burial: 29 Jul 1897
Site 11 Child of J.T. & Mary Sellman Ainsworth   illegible
                                                              Burial: 10 Oct 1904
Site 12 Infant son of J.T. & Mary Sellman Ainsworth   No marker
                                                              Burial: 9 May 1895

Lot: 17 Owner: Dr. S. Olin White
Site   Sarah White Richey   w/o Dr. Stephen Olin Richey
                                  Death: 19 Jan 1880   Burial: 21 Jan 1880
Site   Dr. Steven Olin Richey   Place: Washington, DC
        Birth: 1849   Death: 8 Oct 1919   Burial: 12 Oct 1919
        Mort: Jos. Gawlers Sons   h/o Sarah White Richey

Lot: 18 Owner: Thomas H. White
Site 2 Mary Ellen White   TS: [1st] w/o Thomas H. White
        Birth: 14 Oct 1834   Death: 26 May 1890   Burial: 27 Aug 1890
Site 3 Thomas H. White   Mort: W.T. Hilton & Sons   Place: Glenolden, PA
        Birth: 20 Sep 1831   Death: 19 Jan 1930   Burial: 22 Jan 1930
        h/o Mary Ellen White & Laura R. White
Site 5 Laura R. White   Place: Glenden, PA
        Birth: 11 Sep 1850   Death: 22 Feb 1926   Burial: 24 Feb 1926
        Mort: W.T. Hilton & Sons   TS: 2nd w/o Thomas H. White
Site 5 Thomas Henry White Jr.   TS: s/o T.H. & L.R. White
        Birth: 22 Nov 1895   Death: 22 Nov 1895   Burial: 23 Nov 1895
Site 5 Henry White   s/o T.H. & L.R. White
        Birth: 24 Feb 1858   Death: 23 Mar 1862
Site 5 Willis White   s/o T.H. & L.R. White   Reinterment
        Birth: 26 Sep 1859   Death: 2 Aug 1863   Burial: 23 Jun 1880
Site 6 Oliver C. White   s/o T.H. & M.E. White
        Birth: 14 May 1878   Death: 22 Jun 1880   Burial: 23 Jun 1880
Site 7 Alvin E. White   w/o Joseph T. White
        Birth: 1896   Death: 1898   Burial: 27 Feb 1898
Site 8 Alvin H. White   Mort: Roy W. Barber   Place: Washington Grove
        Birth: 1927   Death: 8 Feb 1929   Burial: 10 Feb 1929
Site 9 Sallie Estella White   Mort: Roy W. Barber   Place: Washington Grove
        Birth: 27 Nov 1868   Death: 5 Jan 1929   Burial: 9 Jan 1929
Site 10 Joseph T. White   Mort: Roy W. Barber   Place: Washington Grove
        Birth: 1863   Death: 14 Oct 1933   Burial: 17 Oct 1933
Site 11 Amy R. White   Mort: Barber   Place: Washington, DC
        Birth: 1893   Death: 15 Feb 1971   Burial: 18 Feb 1971

Site 12 William Rodney White   Mort: Roy W. Barber   Place: Washington Grove
         Birth: 1890   Death: 6 Sep 1953   Burial: 8 Sep 1953
Site 12A Maurice White   Birth: 20 Jun 1875   Death: 31 Jul 1876

Lot: 19 Owner: J. Collison White
Site   Child of J. Collison White   No marker   Burial: 24 Apr 1894
Site 1 Edward C. White   Death: 8 Apr 1878
        TS: s/o John C. & A.T.G. White
Site 3 Grace Boteler White   Place: Dawsonville
        Birth: 24 Apr 1841   Death: 20 Mar 1917   Burial: 22 Mar 1917
        Mort: W.T. Hilton & Sons   On stone with J. Collison White
Site 4 John Collison White   h/o Grace Boteler White
        Birth: 3 Dec 1833   Death: 29 Aug 1910   Burial: 30 Aug 1910
Site 7 Helen Catherine White   Death: 20 Jul 1904   Burial: 22 Jul 1904
        TS: d/o Henry (Harry) B. & Sarah E. White, age 2-2-5
Site 9 Elizabeth Virginia White Moore   On stone with John William Moore
        Birth: 16 May 1882   Death: 2 Nov 1977   Burial: 4 Nov 1977
Site 10 John William Moore   Place: Boyds
        Birth: 27 Jan 1866   Death: 1 Apr 1954   Burial: 3 Apr 1954
        Mort: W.B. Hilton   h/o E. Virginia White Moore

Lot: 20 Owner: Joseph C. White
Site 2 Edith B. White
        Birth: 8 Apr 1899   Death: 29 Aug 1984   Burial: 1 Sep 1984
Site 3 Sarah Elizabeth White   Place: Baltimore
        Birth: 17 Nov 1873   Death: 5 Feb 1960   Burial: 8 Feb 1960
        Mort: W.B. Hilton   On stone with Harry B. White
Site 4 Harry B. White   Place: Boyds
        Birth: 31 Mar 1870   Death: 27 Jul 1950   Burial: 30 Jul 1950
        Mort: W.B. Hilton   h/o Sarah Elizabeth White
Site 5 Mary C. White   w/o Joseph C. White
        Birth: 14 Jun 1804   Death: 4 Oct 1890   Burial: 5 Oct 1890
Site 6 Joseph Collison White   h/o Mary C. White   Reinterment
        Birth: 15 Aug 1798   Death: 6 Dec 1886   Burial: 27 May 1890
Site 7 Mary Ruth Dade   Death: 11 Sep 1863   Burial: 1 Jun 1899
        c/o Alexandra Dade   TS: Age 8-4-6   Reinterment
Site 8 Thomas Collison Dade   Death: 27 Oct 1863   Burial: 1 Jun 1899
        c/o Alexandra Dade   TS: Age 0-8-6
Site 9 Alonzo Dade   Death: 30 Jun 1871   Burial: 1 Jun 1899
        c/o Alexandra Dade   TS: Age 0-4-20   Reinterment
Site 11 Serena Elizabeth Dade   Death: 4 Feb 1863   Burial: 1 Jun 1899
        c/o Alexandra Dade   TS: Age 3-0-12   Reinterment
Site 12 Wade Hampton Dade   Death: 12 Feb 1863   Burial: 1 Jun 1899
        c/o Alexandra Dade   TS: Age 1-5-2   Reinterment

Lot: 21 Owner: Mrs. Mary Gott
Site 1 Nellie McDonald Gott   Place: Baltimore
        Birth: 1874   Death: 2 Jun 1944   Burial: 5 Jun 1944
        Mort: W.B. Hilton   TS: w/o Richard Brook Gott

Monocacy Cemetery, Beallsville, Montgomery County, Maryland 97

Site 2	Richard Brook Gott		Place: Sykesville
	Birth: 1874	Death: 18 May 1961	Burial: 20 May 1961
	Mort: Hilton		h/o Nellie McDonald Gott
Site 4	Mary E. Gott		TS: w/o Richard Gott, Sr.
	Birth: 10 Apr 1816	Death: 29 Sep 1886	
Site 5	Richard Gott, Sr.		h/o Mary E. Gott
	Birth: 24 Oct 1807	Death: 23 Aug 1853	Burial: 29 Aug 1886
Site 6	Susan A. Gott		TS: d/o Richard & Mary E. Gott, in her 22nd year
	Birth: 16 Jan 1840	Death: 2 Mar 1862	
Site 7	M. Luella Gott	illegible	TS: d/o J.S. & F.E. Gott
		Death: 21 Sep 1888	Burial: 22 Sep 1888
Site 8	Samuel Roger Gott	Mort: W.T. Hilton & Sons	Place: Sykesville
	Birth: 23 Jun 1882	Death: 28 May 1919	Burial: 30 May 1919
Site 9	Florence E. Gott	Mort: W.T. Hilton & Sons	Place: Dickerson
	Birth: 1851	Death: 27 Sep 1921	Burial: 30 Sep 1921
Site 10	John S. Gott	Mort: W.T. Hilton & Sons	Place: Dickerson
	Birth: 1848	Death: 17 Aug 1923	Burial: 19 Aug 1923

Lot: 22 Owner: Benjamin F. Dyson

Site	Child of Benjamin F. Dyson	No marker	Burial: 14 Oct 1881
Site 1	William Jerry Dyson	Mort: Roy W. Barber	Place: Olney
	Birth: 12 Oct 1869	Death: 4 Feb 1946	Burial: 6 Feb 1946
Site 2	Matilda T. Dyson	Mort: W.T. Hilton & Sons	Place: Dawsonville
	Birth: 30 Nov 1874	Death: 11 Feb 1926	Burial: 14 Feb 1926
	On stone with William Jerry Dyson & Mary J. Dyson		
Site 3	Eddy Dyson	Death: 7 Aug 1880	
	s/o Benjamin F. Dyson		TS: Age 1-4-7
Site 4	Elijah V. Dyson	Death: 13 Aug 1871	
	s/o B.F. & C. Dyson		TS: Age 4 mo.
Site 5	Paul Dyson	Mort: W.B. Hilton	Place: Frederick Hospital
	Birth: 12 Oct 1877	Death: 4 Dec 1944	Burial: 6 Dec 1944
Site 7	Mary J. Dyson	Mort: Hilton & Hall	Place: Dawsonville
	Birth: 31 Aug 1865	Death: 12 Jan 1934	Burial: 14 Jan 1934
Site 8	Catherine Jane Dyson		TS: w/o Benjamin F. Dyson
	Birth: 7 Jul 1838	Death: 27 Mar 1912	Burial: 29 Mar 1912
Site 9	Benjamin F. Dyson		h/o Catherine Jane Dyson
	Birth: 7 May 1829	Death: 5 Dec 1910	Burial: 8 Dec 1910
Site 10	Joseph B.P. Dyson	Mort: W.T. Hilton & Sons	Place: Dawsonville
	Birth: 1 Feb 1864	Death: 10 Feb 1930	Burial: 13 Feb 1930

Lot: 23 Owner: Thomas Milford

Site 2	Jennie Milford	Mort: Hilton & Hall	Place: Poolesville
	Birth: 15 Apr 1862	Death: 11 Nov 1937	Burial: 13 Nov 1937
	On stone with Mary Ella and Cora V. Milford		
Site 3	Mary Ella Milford	Mort: Hilton & Hall	Place: Poolesville
	Birth: 16 Oct 1856	Death: 21 Apr 1932	Burial: 23 Apr 1932
Site 4	Cora V. Milford	Mort: Hilton & Hall	Place: Fulton, MO
	Birth: 12 Jul 1872	Death: 11 Jan 1929	Burial: 14 Jan 1929

Monocacy Cemetery, Beallsville, Montgomery County, Maryland

Site 5 Thomas Milford
  Birth: 5 Jun 1816   Death: 7 Jan 1884   Burial: 8 Jan 1884
Site 6 Mrs. Cleyland Milford   On stone with Thomas Milford
  Birth: 18 Jun 1826   Death: 9 Jun 1894   Burial: 11 Jun 1894
Site 7 Henry B. Veirs
  Birth: 6 Sep 1833   Death: 13 Apr 1903   Burial: 15 Apr 1903
Site 9 Samuel B. Milford, DDS   Mort: W.B. Hilton   Place: Frederick Hospital
  Birth: 5 Feb 1864   Death: 10 Jun 1956

Lot: 24 Owner: Aaron B. Hersberger
Site   Infant Son Hersberger   TS: 1884
Site   Infant Son Hersberger   TS: 1874
Site 1 Infant Son Hersberger
  Birth: 9 Sep 1872   Burial: 1872   No marker
Site 2 Hesterell Hersberger   c/o A.B. Hersberger
  Birth: 12 Aug 1882   Death: 15 Oct 1882   Burial: 17 Oct 1882
Site 3 Son of A. B. Hersburger   Birth: 1883   Burial: 24 Jul 1883
        No marker
Site 4 Julia Eliza Hersberger   Mort: Hilton   Place: Poolesville
  Birth: 22 Aug 1878   Death: 7 May 1960   Burial: 11 May 1960
Site 6 Sarah Hersberger Griffith   Place: Rockville
  Birth: 14 Nov 1883   Death: 3 Mar 1967   Burial: 6 Mar 1967
  Mort: R.A. Pumphrey   On stone with A. Hempstone Griffith
Site 6 Armistead Hempstone Griffith   Place: Rockville
  Birth: 29 Jan 1881   Death: 7 Nov 1943   Burial: 9 Nov 1943
  Mort: W.B. Hilton   h/o Sarah Hersberger Griffith
Site 8 Nell Rebecca Hersburger   Mort: Hilton & Hall   Place: Washington, DC
  Birth: 4 Feb 1889   Death: 15 May 1925   Burial: 17 May 1925
Site 9 Hester Ann Hersberger   Place: Poolesville
  Birth: 25 Apr 1846   Death: 28 Apr 1921   Burial: 1 May 1921
  Mort: W.T. Hilton & Sons   On stone with Aaron B. Hersberger
Site 10 Aaron B. Hersberger   h/o Hester A. Hersberger
  Birth: 7 Mar 1836   Death: 2 Jan 1907   Burial: 4 Jan 1907
Site 11 Anna B. Hersberger Winstead   No marker   Mort: H.R. Brown
  Place: Washington, DC   Death: 16 Dec 1966   Burial: 19 Dec 1966

Lot: 25 Owner: Wesley Magaha
Site   Child of Mr. Wesley Magaha   No marker   Burial: 4 Oct 1898
Site 1 Walter S. Magaha   TS: Age 45-9-6
  Birth: 17 Apr 1855   Death: Death: 23 Jan 1900   Burial: 29 Jan 1901
Site 2 Savilla Magaha   illegible   w/o John Magaha
  Birth: 11 Jul 1827   Burial: 25 Mar 1890
Site 3 John Magaha   h/o Savilla Magaha
  Birth: 1 Jul 1822   Death: 1 Dec 1891   Burial: 3 Dec 1891
Site 4 Emma S. Moxley   TS: w/o Marion E. Moxley
  Birth: 15 Oct 1879   Death: 10 Aug 1901   Burial: 12 Aug 1901
Site 5 Maria H. Magaha   TS: w/o John Wesley Magaha, age 35-2-0
                       Death: 13 Dec 1881   Burial: 15 Feb 1881

Monocacy Cemetery, Beallsville, Montgomery County, Maryland

Site 8 John Wesley Magaha   No marker   Place: Poolesville
        Birth: 3 Oct 1898   Death: 18 Nov 1920   Burial: 20 Nov 1920
        Mort: Hilton & Hall   c/o John & Manzella Magaha
Site 9 Manzella E. Magaha & child   TS: w/o J.W. Magaha
        Birth: 21 Jan 1861   Death: 25 Oct 1902   Burial: 26 Oct 1902

Lot: 26 Owner: William Taylor
Site 1 James William Taylor   TS: s/o J.W. & Sarah R. Taylor
        Birth: 19 Aug 1848   Death: 23 Oct 1849
Site 2 Ann Mary Taylor   TS: d/o J.H. & Sarah R. Taylor, age 3-6-0
        Birth: 27 Mar 1846   Death: 27 Sep 1849
Site 3 Sarah Jane Taylor   Birth: 15 Nov 1843   Death: 28 Sep 1849
        TS: d/o J.H. & Sarah R. Taylor, age 5-10-13
Site 4 Sarah R. Taylor   No marker   w/o John W. Taylor, age 84
                                    Death: 28 Sep 1905   Burial: 30 Sep 1905
Site 5 John W. Taylor   Death: 5 Jul 1876   h/o Sarah R. Taylor
        TS: s/o Asbury & Rhoda Taylor, age 59-8-6
Site 6 John Henry Ward   Place: Washington, DC
        Birth: 1861   Death: 14 Aug 1944   Burial: 17 Aug 1944
        Mort: W.B. Hilton   h/o Claudia Ward
Site 6 Claudia Ward   Place: Washington, DC
        Birth: 1865   Death: 10 Aug 1951   Burial: 14 Aug 1951
        Mort: Deal Funeral Home   TS: w/o John Henry Ward, age 86
Site 7 Annie L. Robertson   TS: w/o George Robertson, age 72-9-10
        Birth: 14 Feb 1836   Death: 24 Oct 1908   Burial: 26 Oct 1908
Site 8 George Robertson   TS: Age 66-10-19   h/o Annie L. Robertson
        Birth: 21 Feb 1831   Death: 10 Jan 1897   Burial: 12 Jan 1897
Site 10 Ruth E. Seyferth   Stone down, illegible Place: Barnesville
        Birth: 7 Feb 1851   Death: 6 Apr 1935   Burial: 9 Apr 1935
        Mort: Hilton & Price   TS: w/o Oswald Seyferth
Site 11 Oswald Seyferth   Place: Clarksburg
        Birth: 4 Jun 1839   Death: 22 Nov 1920   Burial: 25 Nov 1920
        Mort: W.T. Hilton & Sons   Stone down, illegible
Site 12 Child of Seymorus Conwell   No marker   Burial: 30 May 1884

Lot: 27 Owner: Heirs of Thomas J. Shreve
Site   Henry Chandler Heffner   No marker
        Birth: 3 Mar 1868   Death: 13 Aug 1868   Burial: 20 Jun 1916
        Mort: Chas. E. Roberts   Removed from Shreve buring ground
Site   Jacob Henry Heffner   No marker
        Birth: 4 Jun 1863   Death: 4 Jun 1863   Burial: 20 Jun 1916
        Mort: Chas. E. Roberts   Removed from Shreve buring ground
Site   John Thomas Heffner   No marker   Mort: Chas. E. Roberts
        Burial: 20 Jun 1916   Removed from Shreve buring ground
Site   David H. Trundle   No marker
        Birth: 9 Jan 1808   Death: 21 May 1847   Burial: 20 Jun 1916
        Mort: Chas. E. Roberts   Removed from Shreve buring ground
Site   James E. Trundle   No marker   Mort: Chas. E. Roberts
        Burial: 20 Jun 1916   Removed from Shreve buring ground

Site 2	Miss Clara Stephen Heffner		TS: Age 47 yrs
	Birth: 10 Jun 1864	Death: 23 Jun 1911	Burial: 25 Jun 1911
Site 3	John T. Heffner	h/o Martha J. Heffner	TS: Age 66 yrs
	Birth: 12 Jan 1839	Death: 14 Jul 1905	Burial: 16 Jul 1905
Site 4	Martha J. Heffner		Place: Washington, DC
	Birth: 28 Apr 1841	Death: 1 Aug 1933	Burial: 3 Aug 1933
	Mort: W.W. Chambers		TS: w/o John T. Heffner
Site 5	Clarisa A. Trundle		w/o David Henry Trundle
	Birth: 20 Jul 1811	Death: 7 Apr 1885	Burial: 9 Apr 1885
Site 6	Sarah E. Atwell		No marker
		Death: 22 Aug 1905	Burial: 20 Jun 1916
Site 9	Claudia Stella H. Shreve	TS: Age 73-8-17	Place: Takoma Park
	Birth: 16 Jul 1881	Death: 11 Apr 1952	Burial: 14 Apr 1952
	Mort: W.B. Hilton	On stone with Thomas J. Shreve, age 70	
Site 10	Thomas J. Shreve		Place: Dickerson
	Birth: 12 Jul 1870	Death: 1 Feb 1940	Burial: 5 Feb 1940
	Mort: W.B. Hilton		h/o Stella H. Shreve

Lot: 28 Lower   Owner: Mary Margaret Poole

Site	Mary M. Poole	No marker	Burial: 28 Aug 1907
Site	Raymond Poole		No marker
	Birth: 1865		Burial: 2 Nov 1895
Site 2	Anna Mae Poole		Place: Frederick Hospital
	Birth: 9 Oct 1937	Death: 20 Sep 1949	Burial: 22 Sep 1949
	Mort: W.B. Hilton		Age 11
Site 3	Emma R. Poole	Death: 13 Dec 1904	
	TS: d/o B.E. & Mary C. Poole, age 6-2-18		
Site 4	Francis Marion Poole	On stone with Virginia Young Poole, age 77 yrs	
	Birth: 1901	Death: 12 Aug 1979	Burial: 15 Aug 1979
Site 5	Sarah Agnes Beall Poole		Place: Poolesville
	Birth: 2 Mar 1875	Death: 3 Jun 1947	Burial: 5 Jun 1947
	Mort: W.B. Hilton		TS: w/o Charles I. Poole
Site 6	Charles Irving Poole		Place: Burdein
	Birth: 18 Jul 1869	Death: 20 May 1928	Burial: 22 May 1928
	Mort: Hilton & Hall		h/o Sarah Agnes Beall Poole

Lot: 28 Upper   Owner: Hazel Hickman

Site	Allie Hickman	No marker	Burial: 13 Jan 1906
Site	Hazel Hickman	No marker	Burial: 15 Jan 1909
Site	Mrs. Lula Hickman	No marker	Burial: 7 Nov 1901
Site	Mollie Magaha Hickman	No marker	w/o Hazel Hickman
			Burial: 7 Aug 1898
Site	Purnell Hickman	s/o Hazel Hickman	No marker
			Burial: 18 Sep 1899
Site 4	Blanche Hickman		d/o Hazel Hickman, age 1 mo 2 days
	No marker	Death: 29 Dec 1884	Burial: 30 Dec 1884
Site 6	Margaret A. Hickman		TS: w/o William T. Hickman
	Birth: 29 Mar 1818	Death: 20 Mar 1900	Burial: 21 Mar 1900

Monocacy Cemetery, Beallsville, Montgomery County, Maryland   101

Lot: 29 Owner: Robert Cooley, Sr. (No stones in this lot)
Site Mr. Brown Cooley   Burial: 29 May 1893
Site Child of Calvin Cooley   Burial: 31 Jul 1894
Site Mrs. Eugene Cooley   Burial: 25 Mar 1898
Site Eugene Cooley   h/o Mary A. Cooley   Mort: Hilton & Hall
      Place: Libby Hospital   Death: 30 Jun 1913   Burial: 2 Jul 1913
Site Miss Lucy Cooley   Burial: 11 May 1896
Site Martin S. Cooley   Mort: W.W. Deal
      Place: Silver Spring   Death: 10 Jun 1930   Burial: 13 Jun 1930
Site Mary A. Cooley   w/o Robert J. Cooley   Burial: 5 Mar 1901
Site Robert J. Cooley   s/o of Ann & James Cooley
      Birth: 8 Mar 1820   Burial: 11 Apr 1911
Site Mr. Sid Cooley   Burial: 15 Dec 1909

Lot: 30 Owner: Isaac Thomas Jones
Site 3 Arthur Jones   No marker   Mort: W.T. Hilton & Sons
        Place: Washington, DC   Death: 29 Jul 1917   Burial: 31 Jul 1917
Site 4 Mary Leona Jones   TS: w/o Isaac Thomas Jones
        Birth: 17 Apr 1840   Death: 20 Apr 1901   Burial: 22 Apr 1901
Site 5 Isaac Thomas Jones   TS: h/o Mary Leona Jones
        Birth: 10 Dec 1831   Death: 17 Apr 1885

Lot: 31 Lower   Owner: M.J. Morningstar
Site 1 Infant Fisher   No marker   d/o C.A. & Anna M. Fisher
                                Death: 17 Mar 1900   Burial: 18 Mar 1900
Site 3 Bessie I. Morningstar   Place: Frederick
        Birth: 30 Mar 1887   Death: 23 May 1924   Burial: 25 May 1924
        Mort: Hilton & Hall   TS: [1st] w/o Muriel J. Morningstar
Site 4 Murel J. Morningstar   Mort: W.B. Hilton   Place: Poolesville
        Birth: 27 Jan 1885   Death: 22 Jul 1954   Burial: 26 Jul 1954
        h/o Bessie I. Morningstar & Emma M. Morningstar
Site 5 Emma M. J. Morningstar   Place: Poolesville
        Birth: 26 Jun 1888   Death: 14 Apr 1962   Burial: 17 Apr 1962
        Mort: Hilton   TS: w/o Murrel. Morningstar
Site 6 Elizabeth M. Morningstar (Bet)   d/o M.J. Morningstar
        Birth: 13 Feb 1929   Death: 28 Feb 1995   Burial: 3 Mar 1995

Lot: 31 Upper   Owner: E.A. Morningstar
Site 1 Susie E. Morningstar   illegible   Burial: 31 Apr 1892
        w/o Edward A. Morningstar, age 18-10-0
Site 2 Minnie Irene Kremer   Mort: W.T. Hilton   Place: Washington, DC
        Birth: 1886   Death: 16 Sep 1920   Burial: 18 Sep 1920
Site 3 Della Virginia Morningstar Mort: S.H. Hines Co. Place: Washington, DC
        Birth: 18 Feb 1875   Death: 28 May 1950   Burial: 31 May 1950

Monocacy Cemetery, Beallsville, Montgomery County, Maryland

Lot: 32 Owner: Mr. & Mrs. A.L. Specht
Site 1 Minnie G. Havener   Burial: 10 Jan 1892   TS: w/o Phillip A. Havener
        Dates illegible
Site 2 Iva Viola Havener   illegible   d/o Phillip A. Havener
        Birth: 27 Oct 1895   Death: 31 Oct 1895   Burial: 5 Oct 1897
Site 8 Lewis Edward Specht   Place: Frederick
        Birth: 5 May 1895   Death: 5 Jan 1955   Burial: 8 Jan 1955
        Mort: C.E. Cline & Son   h/o Alice S. Specht
Site 9 Alice M. Specht   Place: Buckeystown
        Birth: 4 Apr 1873   Death: 18 Sep 1939   Burial: 20 Sep 1939
        Mort: C.E. Cline & Son   w/o Lewis Edward Specht
Site 10 Lewis Altha L. Specht
        Birth: 12 Jun 1868   Death: 20 Jan 1940   Burial: 22 Jan 1940

Lot: 33 Owner: W.L. Chambers
Site 1 Louise Lanier Chambers   Place: Washington DC
        Birth: 6 Nov 1885   Death: 10 Feb 1918   Burial: 11 Feb 1918
        Mort: W.T. Hilton & Sons TS: d/o William L. & Laura L. Chambers
Site 2 Laura Ligon Chambers   Mort: W.T. Hilton & Sons
        Place: Sellman   Death: 13 Jul 1918   Burial: 15 Jul 1918
        w/o Judge William Lee Chambers   No marker
Site 3 William Lee Chambers   Mort: Hilton & Price
        Place: Sellman   Death: 26 Aug 1933   Burial: 28 Aug 1933
        h/o Laura Ligon Chambers   No marker

Lot: 34 Owner: W.L. Chambers
Site   Hathaway Chambers   No marker   Place: Sellman
        Birth: 7 Jan 1916   Death: 5 Apr 1916   Burial: 6 Apr 1916
        Mort: W.T. Hilton & Sons
Site   Infant of William H. Chambers No marker   Mort: Hilton & Hall
        Place: Frederick   Death: 7 Aug 1918   Burial: 8 Aug 1918
Site   David Clopton   No marker   Mort: W.W. Chambers
        Place: Washington, DC   Death: 8 Jan 1933   Burial: 10 Jan 1933
Site 2 William Lea Chambers   Mort: W.T. Hilton & Sons
        Place: Sellman   Death: 4 Jan 1914   Burial: 4 Jan 1914
        s/o William & Hathaway Chambers
Site 3 Annie Laurie Chambers   d/o William & Hathaway Chambers
        Birth: 21 Jun 1910   Death: 11 Sep 1910   Burial: 12 Sep 1910
Site 8 D. Clopton Chambers   No marker   Place: near Charlestown, WV
        Mort: M.J. Strider   Death: 21 Sep 1923   Burial: 23 Sep 1923

Lot: 35 Lower Owner: Nora S. Meem & Dorothy M. Stanton
Site 1 Stanley Stanton   No marker   h/o Dorothy Meem Stanton
                                  Death: 1 Dec 1995   Burial: 9 Dec 1995
Site 2 Dorothy Meem Stanton   No marker   Age 87 yrs
                                  Death: 3 Jul 1993   Burial: 6 Jul 1993

Monocacy Cemetery, Beallsville, Montgomery County, Maryland

Site 3 Nora Sellman Meem
    Birth: 20 Sep 1872   Death: 14 Sep 1960
    Mort: W.B. Hilton
    Place: Staunton, VA
    Burial: 17 Sep 1960
    w/o Harry C. Meem
Site 4 Harry Cloriviere Meem
    Birth: 14 Jul 1870   Death: 8 Jul 1940
    Mort: W.B. Hilton
    Place: Dickerson
    Burial: 11 Jul 1940
    h/o Nora Sellman Meem

Lot: 35 Upper   Owner: Sidney S. Hawkins
Site 1 Annie Elizabeth Hawkins   No marker
    Birth: 2 Dec 1915   Death: 18 Jan 1996   Burial: 22 Jan 1996
Site 2 Wilson S. Hawkins   Place: Washington, DC
    Birth: 1914   Death: 9 Jan 1959   Burial: 12 Jan 1959
    Mort: Gartner   s/o Sidney Smith & Mary Case Hawkins
Site 3 Mary Case Hawkins   Place: Rockville
    Birth: 1877   Death: 23 Feb 1957   Burial: 25 Feb 1957
    Mort: Gartner   On stone with Sidney Smith Hawkins
Site 4 Sidney Smith Hawkins   Place: Rockville
    Birth: 1879   Death: 22 Mar 1954   Burial: 25 Mar 1954
    Mort: Ernest C. Gartner   h/o Mary Case Hawkins

Lot: 36 Lower   Owner: William L. White
Site 1 William Lingin White Jr.   s/o William L. & Mary Bowman White
    Birth: 10 Nov 1916   Death: 7 Nov 1983   Burial: 9 Nov 1983
    On stone with Margaret L. White
Site 2 Child of William L. White Jr. No marker   Mort: W.B. Hilton
    Place: Barnesville   Death: 6 Jun 1939   Burial: 7 Jun 1939
Site 2 Baby girl White   No marker   Mort: W.B. Hilton
    Place: Olney   Death: 7 Dec 1953   Burial: 8 Dec 1953
    d/o William L. White, Jr.
Site 3 Mary Virginia Bowman White   Place: Barnesville
    Birth: 1876   Death: 29 Dec 1943   Burial: 1 Jan 1944
    Mort: W.B. Hilton   w/o William Lingham White
Site 4 William Lingham White   Place: Gaithersburg
    Birth: 13 Jan 1872   Death: 19 May 1939   Burial: 21 May 1939
    Mort: W.B. Hilton   h/o Mary Virginia Bowman White
Site 5 Eleanor White Thurston
    Birth: 1904   Death: 26 Oct 1970   Burial: 28 Oct 1970
    Mort: Tyson Wheeler   w/o Robert Lamont Thurston
Site 6 Robert Lamont Thurston   h/o Mary Eleanor White
    Birth: 7 Jul 1904   Death: 19 Mar 1986   Burial: 22 Mar 1986

Lot: 36 Upper   Owner: Mrs. W.F. Mattingly
Site 3 Evelyn Gertrude Mattingly   Place: Washington, DC
    Birth: 5 Mar 1880   Death: 15 Mar 1950   Burial: 17 Mar 1950
    Mort: Robert A. Pumphrey   w/o William Francis Mattingly
Site 4 William Francis Mattingly   Place: Dist Lee, VA   Mort: Reaguer
    Birth: 23 Oct 1875   Death: 22 Aug 1936   Burial: 24 Aug 1936
Site 6 Howard W. Henderson   Mort: W.R. Pumphrey   Place: Washington, DC
    Birth: 19 Jun 1909   Death: 7 Jan 1936   Burial: 9 Jan 1936

Lot: 37 Lower   Owner: Mrs. Jessie Wood

Site 2 Stanford Edward Wood
Birth: 3 Aug 1910   Death: 15 Dec 1940   Place: Frederick   Burial: 17 Dec 1940
Mort: W.B. Hilton   s/o Alfred Worth & Jessie P. Wood

Site 3 Jessie Phillips Wood
Birth: 6 Sep 1884   Death: 19 Feb 1967   Place: Kensington   Burial: 22 Feb 1967
Mort: Hilton   w/o Alfred Worth Wood

Site 4 Albert Worth Wood
Birth: 16 Mar 1874   Death: 6 Jul 1941   Place: Barnesville   Burial: 8 Jul 1941
Mort: W.B. Hilton   h/o Jessie Phillips Wood

Site 6 Karl William Ochs   On stone with Hazel Wood Ochs
Birth: 4 May 1904   Death: 15 May 1988   Burial: 18 May 1988

Lot: 37 Upper   Owner: Miscellaneous

Site 2 Leslie Lee Ross   Mort: F. Gasche & Son   Place: Washington, DC
Birth: 8 Aug 1936   Death: 5 Feb 1940   Burial: 8 Feb 1940

Site 3 Edward Seabrook Hull   Mort: Gawler   Place: Arlington, VA
Birth: 1899   Death: 29 Mar 1969   Burial: 2 Apr 1969

Site 5 Claudia K. Ellen Johnson Poole
Birth: 1 Oct 1906   Death: 25 Sep 1995   Burial: 27 Sep 1995
On stone with Raymond Benjamin Poole & son, Franklin E. Poole

Site 6 Raymond Benjamin Poole   h/o Ellen Johnson Poole
Birth: 8 Jun 1904   Death: 13 Apr 1981   Burial: 16 Apr 1981

Lot: 38 Lower   Owner: Charles R. Israel & Son

Site 1 Alice Grace Israel   Place: Sykesville
Birth: 13 Aug 1890   Death: 6 Sep 1956   Burial: 8 Sep 1956
Mort: E.C. Gartner   w/o Charles R. Israel

Site 2 Charles Reid Israel   Place: Boyds
Birth: 5 Nov 1885   Death: 19 Oct 1949   Burial: 21 Oct 1949
Mort: Ernest C. Gartner   h/o Grace Israel

Site 3 Charles F. Israel
Birth: 21 Aug 1912   Death: 16 Jul 1971   Burial: 21 Jul 1971
s/o Charles R. & A. Grace Israel, h/o Lillian B. Hoyle Israel

Lot: 39 Upper   Owner: Helen C. Burdette

Site 3 Lloyd Wilkens Burdette   TS: S SGT US Army WWII
Birth: 9 Dec 1916   Death: 27 Aug 1991   Burial: 31 Aug 1991
On stone with Helen Carlisle Burdette, age 74 yrs

Lot: 40 Upper   Owner: Helen C. Burdette

Site 1 Susan Campbell Burdette
Birth: 16 Nov 1957   Death: 4 May 1994   Burial: 4 May 1994

Row E

Lot: 0 Owner: Joseph N. Allnutt
A stone at the front of this lot states: *"These slabs were removed from the graveyard at Mother's Delight"*

Site 1 Eleanor Allnutt   Death: 29 Oct 1832   TS: In her 82nd yr
Site 2 Lawrence Allnutt   Death: 18 May 1825   TS: In his 76th yr
Site 3 Benoni Allnutt   Birth: 5 Nov 1785   Death: 4 Aug 1859
        TS: Age 73 years
Site 3 Edwin Allnutt   TS: s/o Eleanor & Laurence Allnutt, in his 21st yr
        Birth: 27 Feb 1833   Death: 9 Oct 1853
Site 5 Eleanor Allnutt   Death: 22 May 1860
        TS: w/o Laurence Allnutt, in her 58th yr
Site 6 Laurence Allnutt   TS: Age 63-6-14   h/o Eleanor White Allnutt
        Birth: 6 Feb 1796   Death: 20 Aug 1859
Site 7 Verlinder Allnutt   Death: 3 Sep 1831
        TS: w/o James Allnutt, age 76-7-7
Site 7 James Allnutt   Death: 21 Feb 1838   h/o Verlinder Allnutt
        TS: age 86-4-6
Site 8 Jane D. Perry   TS: d/o James & Verlinda Allnutt
        Birth: 1 Aug 1782   Death: 12 Oct 1857
Site 9 Basil Darby   s/o George & Verlinda Darby
        Birth: 27 Mar 1824   Death: 25 Oct 1850
Site 10 Verlinda Darby   Birth: 28 Apr 1791   Death: 16 Mar 1851
        TS: d/o Laurence & Eleanor Allnutt, w/o George Darby
Site 11 George Darby   Birth: 17 Mar 1799   Death: 30 Nov 1866
        h/o Verlinda Darby   TS: s/o Basil & Rebecca Darby
Site 12 Rebecca Dawson Darby   TS: w/o Thomas Darby, age 27 years
        Birth: 29 Jan 1795   Death: 16 Jun 1822
Site 13 Mary Doyne Dawson   Death: 7 Feb 1784
        TS: d/o Robert & Sarah Dawson, in her 13th year
Site 14 William Cyrus Dawson   TS: In his 13th yr. Mort: Benson Allnutt
                               Death: 14 Dec 1824   Burial: 10 Nov 1924
Site 15 Elizabeth Dawson   Mort: Benson Allnutt
        TS: In her 57th yr. Death: 14 Feb 1839   Burial: 10 Nov 1924
Site 16 William Dawson   Mort: Benson Allnutt   TS: In his 33rd yr.
                               Death: 23 Sep 1816   Burial: 10 Nov 1924

Lot: 1 Owner: Joseph N. Allnutt
Site 3 Emily Dawson Allnutt
        Birth: 12 Oct 1901   Death: 2 Oct 1986   Burial: 4 Oct 1986
Site 4 Sadie Lucile Allnutt   Place: Springfield Hospital
        Birth: 20 Nov 1891   Death: 14 Feb 1948   Burial: 17 Feb 1948
        Mort: W.R. Pumphrey   d/o Lucie Williams & Joseph N. Allnutt
Site 5 Walter Doyne Allnutt   TS: s/o Lucie Williams & Joseph N. Allnutt
        Birth: 3 Mar 1899   Death: 20 Oct 1899   Burial: 13 Oct 1899

Monocacy Cemetery, Beallsville, Montgomery County, Maryland

Site 6 Dorothy Williams Allnutt TS: d/o Lucie Williams & Joseph N. Allnutt
Birth: 9 Jun 1895 Death: 20 Aug 1896
Place: Silver Spring
Site 7 Lucie Williams Allnutt
Birth: 15 Feb 1869 Death: 7 Feb 1948 Burial: 9 Feb 1948
Mort: W.R. Pumphrey w/o Joseph N. Allnutt
Site 8 Joseph N. Allnutt Place: Poolesville
Birth: 19 Jan 1864 Death: 10 Jul 1957 Burial: 13 Jul 1957
Mort: R.A. Pumphrey h/o Lucie Williams Allnutt

Lot: 2 Owner: Nathan W. Allnutt
Site 1 Margaret Eleanor Allnutt No marker Burial: 1 Apr 1899
d/o N.S. & M.G. Allnutt
Site 4 Samuel E. Veirs Stone down h/o Valeria Wailes Veirs
Birth: 13 Sep 1848 Death: 9 May 1885 Burial: 11 May 1885
Site 5 Valeria Wailes Veirs TS: w/o Samuel E. Veirs
Birth: 16 May 1852 Death: 14 Mar 1911 Burial: 16 Mar 1911
Site 6 Margaret Allnutt Darby Place: Ijamsville
Birth: 22 Mar 1873 Death: 15 Jul 1944 Burial: 18 Jul 1944
Mort: W.B. Hilton TS: w/o Milton G. Darby
Site 7 Milton George Darby Place: Dawsonville
Birth: 7 Mar 1859 Death: 7 Nov 1931 Burial: 9 Nov 1931
Mort: Hilton & Hall h/o Margaret Allnutt Darby
Site 8 S. Eleanor Burroughs Death: 23 Dec 1886
TS: only d/o George & Rebecca Burroughs, age 80 yrs.

Lot: 3 Owner: Nathan W. Allnutt
Site 2 Margaret E. White Allnutt Place: Dawsonville
Birth: 3 Aug 1831 Death: 30 Jun 1920 Burial: 2 Jul 1920
Mort: Hilton & Hall On stone with Nathan White Allnutt
Site 3 Nathan White Allnutt h/o Margaret Ellen White Allnutt
Birth: 16 Dec 1826 Death: 24 Oct 1901 Burial: 27 Oct 1901
Site 4 Estelle Allnutt TS: d/o Nathan White & Margaret E. Allnutt
Birth: 3 Nov 1857 Death: 21 Jul 1862
Site 5 Joseph Frank Allnutt
Birth: 1890 Death: 15 Nov 1976 Burial: 17 Nov 1976
Site 6 Margaret Allnutt TS: d/o Nathan White & Margaret E. Allnutt
Birth: 6 Apr 1884 Death: 9 Apr 1884
Site 6 Sarah Allnutt TS: d/o Nathan White & Margaret E. Allnutt
Birth: 6 Apr 1884 Death: 10 Apr 1884
Site 7 Elzey D. Allnutt Place: Silver Spring
Birth: 1896 Death: 19 Apr 1966 Burial: 22 Apr 1966
Mort: Warner E. Pumphrey w/o Arthur W. Allnutt
Site 8 Arthur W. Allnutt Place: Washington, DC
Birth: 1896 Death: 19 Nov 1950 Burial: 21 Nov 1950
Mort: S.H. Hines Husband of Elzey D. Allnutt
Site 9 Anna Chiswell Allnutt Place: Dawsonville
Birth: 3 Jul 1858 Death: 19 Oct 1939 Burial: 21 Oct 1939
Mort: Hilton & Hall On stone with Edwin R. Allnutt

Site 10 Edwin R. Allnutt   Place: Dawsonville
         Birth: 26 Jan 1854   Death: 9 May 1920   Burial: 11 May 1920
         Mort: Hilton & Hall   h/o Anna Chiswell Allnutt
Site 11 Eleanor Allnutt   TS: Infant/o Edwin R. & Anna Chiswell Allnutt
         Birth: 8 Apr 1888   Death: 10 Apr 1888   Burial: 11 Apr 1888
Site 12 Oscar Allnutt   s/o Edwin R. & Anna Chiswell Allnutt
         Birth: 16 Nov 1881   Death: 2 Feb 1883   Burial: 3 Feb 1883

Lot: 4 Owner: Samuel Dyson
Site 3 Joseph Dyson   On stone with Samuel Dyson
         Birth: 23 Nov 1827   Death: 29 Mar 1898   Burial: 31 Mar 1898
Site 4 Samuel Dyson
         Birth: 5 Dec 1811   Death: 26 Mar 1882   Burial: 27 Mar 1882

Lot: 5 Owner: Mrs. Rachael White
Site 2 Evelina Wailes White   TS: w/o Nathan S. White, age 69-11-13
         Birth: 13 Jul 1801   Death: 6 Jun 1871   Burial: 31 May 1881
         Reinterment
Site 3 Nathan Smith White II   TS: Age 83-4-23   h/o Evelina W. White
         Birth: 28 Feb 1798   Death: 5 May 1881   Burial: 6 May 1881
Site 4 Rachael Ann White   d/o Nathan Smith & Evelina Wailes White
         Birth: 1 May 1838   Death: 27 Sep 1885
Site 5 Emily Catherine Wailes White Saunders   TS: w/o John Saunders, age 50-0-28
         Birth: 30 Aug 1833   Death: 27 Sep 1883   Burial: 28 Sep 1883
Site 6 John Saunders   h/o Emily White Saunders
         Birth: 29 Dec 1816   Death: 3 May 1884   Burial: 5 May 1884

Lot: 6 Owner: Thomas D. Darby
Site   Child of Frank Williams   No marker   Reinterment
                                   Death: 16 Jul 1898   Burial: 16 Sep 1903
Site 1 Thomas Dawson Darby Jr.   Mort: W.B. Hilton   Place: Frederick
         Birth: 29 Oct 1867   Death: 21 Jun 1940   Burial: 23 Jun 1940
         s/o Thomas Dawson & Sarah Elizabeth Darby
Site 2 Benoni Dawson Darby   illegible
         Birth: 13 Dec 1871   Death: 27 Mar 1871   Burial: 23 Aug 1881
         s/o Thomas Dawson & Sarah Elizabeth Dawson Darby
Site 2 George Dawson Darby   illegible
         Birth: 7 Mar 1865   Death: 6 Jun 1865   Burial: 23 Aug 1881
         s/o Thomas Dawson & Sarah Elizabeth Dawson Darby
Site 2 Sarah Ann Valinda Darby   illegible
         Birth: 9 Jan 1874   Death: 16 Aug 1874   Burial: 23 Aug 1881
         d/o Thomas Dawson & Sarah Elizabeth Dawson Darby
Site 2 Susan Augusta Darby   illegible
         Birth: 17 May 1866   Death: 16 Aug 1866   Burial: 23 Aug 1881
         d/o Thomas Dawson & Sarah Elizabeth Dawson Darby
Site 3 Thomas Dawson Darby   TS: age 68-0-20
         Birth: 15 May 1826   Death: 5 Jun 1894   Burial: 6 Jun 1894
         h/o Sarah Elizabeth Dawson Darby

Monocacy Cemetery, Beallsville, Montgomery County, Maryland

Site 4 Sarah Elizabeth Darby   On stone with Thomas Dawson Darby
        Birth: 1 Jan 1831   Death: 19 Mar 1910   Burial: 21 Mar 1910
Site 5 Mary Louise Steward   Mort: W.B. Hilton   Place: State Hospital
        Birth: 21 May 1876   Death: 14 Jan 1940   Burial: 16 Jan 1940
        d/o Thomas D. & Sarah Elizabeth Dawson Darby, w/o Willard Gilbert Steward
Site 6 Bessie Dawson Darby   Place: Barnesville
        Birth: 29 Aug 1862   Death: 8 Feb 1940   Burial: 10 Feb 1940
        Mort: W.B. Hilton   Unmarried
Site 7 Daughter Darby   Cause: Stillborn   Place: Dawsonville
        Birth: 26 Mar 1919   Death: 26 Mar 1919   Burial: 27 Mar 1919
        Mort: Hilton & Hall   TS: d/o Joseph N. & Mary C. Darby
Site 8 Edward Spencer Darby   Place: Dawsonville
        Birth: 21 Feb 1917   Death: 21 Feb 1917   Burial: 23 Feb 1917
        Mort: Hilton & Hall   TS: s/o Joseph N. & Mary C. Darby
Site 8 Mary Eleanor Darby   TS: d/o Joseph N. & Mary C. Darby
        Birth: 28 Feb 1911   Death: 28 Feb 1911   Burial: 2 Mar 1911
Site 10 Mary Eleanor Chiswell Darby   Place: Takoma Park
        Birth: 4 Jul 1880   Death: 26 May 1952   Burial: 28 May 1952
        Mort: W.B. Hilton   w/o Joseph N. Darby
Site 11 Joseph Newton Darby   Place: Takoma Park
        Birth: 5 Jan 1864   Death: 15 Sep 1951   Burial: 18 Sep 1951
        Mort: W.B. Hilton   h/o Mary Eleanor Chiswell Darby, age 87
Site 12 Robert Doyne Darby   Mort: Hilton   Place: Bethesda (Hosp)
        Birth: 4 Aug 1869   Death: 1 Mar 1962   Burial: 3 Mar 1962
        s/o Thomas Dawson & Sarah Elizabeth Dawson Darby

Lot: 7 Owner: William P. Dawson
Site 1 Nicholas Lowe Dawson   h/o Cyanne Prince Dawson
        Birth: 21 Jul 1804   Death: 17 Apr 1890
Site 2 Cyanne Prince Dawson   TS: w/o Nicholas Lowe Dawson
        Birth: 1 Sep 1819   Death: 30 Oct 1895   Burial: 1 Nov 1895
Site 3 Charles E. Dawson
        Birth: 27 Jun 1863   Death: 1 Jan 1910   Burial: 23 Jan 1910
Site 4 William P. Dawson   Mort: W.R. Pumphrey   Place: Washington, DC
        Birth: 21 Jan 1853   Death: 16 Jul 1918   Burial: 18 Jul 1918
Site 5 Emma C. Dawson   Mort: W.R. Pumphrey   Place: Rockville
        Birth: 18 Aug 1854   Death: 15 Jan 1940   Burial: 17 Jan 1940
        On stone with William P. Dawson
Site 8 Corinne D. Duff   Mort: W.R. Pumphrey   Place: Germantown
        Birth: 23 Nov 1883   Death: 2 May 1925   Burial: 4 May 1925
Site 9 Nicholas Lowe Dawson   Mort: Wm. R. Pumphrey   Place: Baltimore
        Birth: 23 Apr 1885   Death: 16 Sep 1944   Burial: 21 Sep 1944
Site 10 Virginia Mays Dawson   On stone with William Veirs Dawson
        Birth: 1896   Death: 18 Jul 1975   Burial: 21 Jul 1975
Site 11 William Veirs Dawson   Place: Gaithersburg
        Birth: 17 Jun 1890   Death: 26 Feb 1959   Burial: 28 Feb 1959
        Mort: Robert A. Pumphrey   h/o Virginia Mays Dawson

Monocacy Cemetery, Beallsville, Montgomery County, Maryland

Site 12 Thomas G. Dawson   Mort: R.W. Pumphrey   Place: Darnestown
Birth: 26 Mar 1858   Death: 28 Mar 1932   Burial: 31 Mar 1932

Lot: 8 Lower   Owner: Miscellaneous
Site 1 Carrie Newsom Pessou   Mort: Hilton & Hall   Place: Washington, DC
Birth: 23 Feb 1865   Death: 28 Jan 1922   Burial: 1 Feb 1922
Site 2 Jane H. Kinney   Mort: W.R. Pumphrey   Place: Washington, DC
Birth: 7 Sep 1893   Death: 20 Feb 1926   Burial: 22 Feb 1926

Lot: 8 Upper   Owner: L.B. Wynne
Site   Wife of Lewis B. Wynne Sr.   No marker   Burial: 16 Feb 1898
Site 3 Rev. Lewis B. Wynne   h/o Harriet J. Wynne
Birth: 30 Jun 1815   Death: 3 Feb 1883   Burial: 5 Feb 1883
TS: born KY, Minister of Primitive Baptist Church, died at College ?, DC
Site 4 Harriet J. Wynne   Death: 30 Apr 1898   w/o Lewis B. Wynne

Lot: 9   Owner: Robert Carter
Site   Child of Burrel Carter   No marker   Burial: 20 Feb 1891
Site   Child of Mr. Joseph Carter   No marker   Burial: 11 Mar 1893
Site 2 Elizabeth Ann Carter   On stone with George Henry Carter
Birth: 4 May 1826   Death: 4 Apr 1907   Burial: 6 Apr 1907
Site 3 George Henry Carter   h/o Elizabeth Ann Carter
Birth: 8 Sep 1822   Death: 7 Jun 1902   Burial: 9 Jun 1902
Site 4 Miss Laura A.G. Carter   illegible   Burial: 23 May 1877
Site 5 Joseph L. Carter
Birth: 8 Oct 1889   Death: 19 Dec 1971   Burial: 23 Dec 1971
Site 6 Miss Molly Carter   No marker   Burial: 23 Apr 1890
Site 7 Anna Lucille Carter   Mort: Warner E. Pumphrey   Place: Silver Spring
Birth: 14 Nov 1883   Death: 6 Oct 1956   Burial: 9 Oct 1956
On stone with John Jacob Carter
Site 8 John Jacob Carter   Mort: W.T. Hilton & Sons   Place: Hyattsville
Birth: 20 Feb 1883   Death: 4 Aug 1919   Burial: 6 Aug 1919
Site 9 David H. Carter   Death: 14 May 1906   Burial: 16 May 1906
TS: s/o Joseph E. & Mary V. Carter, age 21-0-9
Site 10 Grover C. Carter   Death: 7 Mar 1893   Burial: 11 Mar 1893
TS: s/o Joseph E. & Mary V. Carter, age 4 mo.
Site 10 Mary E. Carter   Death: 11 Sep 1901   Burial: 15 Sep 1901
TS: d/o Joseph E. & Mary V. Carter, age 1-2-0
Site 11 Mary Virginia Carter   Place: Sellman
Birth: 3 Nov 1861   Death: 18 Sep 1931   Burial: 20 Sep 1931
Mort: W.T. Hilton & Sons   TS: w/o Joseph E. Carter
Site 12 Joseph E. Carter   Mort: C.E. Cline & Son   Place: Frederick
Birth: 20 Mar 1855   Death: 21 Jan 1939   Burial: 24 Jan 1939
h/o Mary V. Carter   No death date on stone

Lot: 10   Owner: Henry Hickerson
Site   Child of J.B.L. Hickerson   No marker   Burial: 14 Jan 1902
Site   Infant of M. C. Hickerson   No marker   Burial: 13 Oct 1907
Site   Sophie C. Hickerson   No marker   Burial: 26 May 1911

Monocacy Cemetery, Beallsville, Montgomery County, Maryland

Site 3 Elizabeth Frances Hickerson　　　　　　　Place: Culpepper, VA
　　　　Birth: 30 Aug 1830　　Death: 28 Jan 1920　　Burial: 30 Jan 1920
　　　　Mort: W.R. Pumphrey　w/o Henry C. Hickerson　　Stone down
Site 4 Henry C. Hickerson　　　　　　　h/o Elizabeth Frances Hickerson
　　　　Birth: 30 Jul 1829　　Death: 12 Apr 1894　　Burial: 14 Apr 1894
Site 5 Miss Marcie W. Hickerson　Death: 14 Oct 1889　Burial: 16 Oct 1889
　　　　TS: d/o Henry & Elizabeth Hickerson, age 17-3-9
Site 6 Virgil M. Hickerson　　Death: 24 Mar 1880　　Burial: 25 Mar 1880
　　　　TS: s/o Henry & Elizabeth E. Hickerson, age 23-6-16
Site 8 Clara V. Hickerson　　　　　　　　　Place: Frederick, MD
　　　　Birth: 19 Dec 1876　　Death: 2 Oct 1969　　Burial: 4 Oct 1969
　　　　Mort: Dailey's Funeral Home　　On stone with Lindsay R. Hickerson
Site 9 Lindsay R. Hickerson　　　　　　　　Place: Washington, DC
　　　　Birth: 23 Oct 1863　　Death: 7 Mar 1943　　Burial: 9 Mar 1943
　　　　Mort: Wm. R. Pumphrey　　　　　　h/o Clara V. Hickerson
Site 10 Catherine S. Hickerson　No marker　　Burial: 29 Oct 1910
　　　　d/o Lindsay R. & Clara V. Hickerson, age0-6-25
Site 10 Lucy Francis Hickerson　No marker　　Mort: W.R. Pumphrey
　　　　Place: Rockville　　Death: 20 Feb 1914　　Burial: 23 Feb 1914
　　　　d/o Lindsay R. & Clara V. Hickerson, age 2-1-0
Site 11 Henry V. Hickerson　　No marker　　Burial: 12 Jan 1909
Site 11 Mary L. Hickerson　　　No marker　　Burial: 22 Jul 1907
　　　　d/o Lindsay R. & Clara V. Hickerson, age 2-20-0

Lot: 11　Owner: L.A. Darby
Site 2 Susan Elizabeth Darby　Mort: Hilton & Hall　Place: Dawsonville
　　　　Birth: 10 Jan 1861　　Death: 5 Oct 1937　　Burial: 7 Oct 1937
　　　　d/o Lawrence Allnutt & Sallie Ann Chiswell Darby
Site 3 Grace Newton Darby　　Mort: Hilton & Hall　Place: Clarendon, VA
　　　　Birth: 27 Jun 1863　　Death: 15 Aug 1931　　Burial: 17 Aug 1931
　　　　d/o Lawrence Allnutt & Sallie Anne Chiswell Darby
Site 4 Mary Verlinda Darby　　Mort: Hilton & Hall　　Place: Dawsonville
　　　　Birth: 14 Oct 1857　　Death: 24 Dec 1924　　Burial: 26 Dec 1924
　　　　d/o Lawrence Allnutt & Sallie Anne Chiswell Darby
Site 5 Sallie Anne Chiswell Darby　　　　　　　Place: Dawsonville
　　　　Birth: 13 Mar 1834　　Death: 24 Jun 1913　　Burial: 26 Jun 1913
　　　　Mort: Hilton & Hall　　　　　w/o Lawrence Allnutt Darby
Site 6 Lawrence Allnutt Darby Sr.　　　　　　　Place: Dawsonville
　　　　Birth: 1 Jan 1829　　Death: 22 Nov 1914　　Burial: 24 Nov 1914
　　　　Mort: Hilton & Hall　　　　h/o Sallie Anne Chiswell Darby
Site 9 Roger William Darby　Mort: W.B. Hilton　Place: Dawsonville
　　　　Birth: 27 Feb 1878　　Death: 28 Jun 1950　　Burial: 30 Jun 1950
　　　　s/o Lawrence Allnutt & Sallie Anne Chiswell Darby
Site 10 Edward Darby　　Mort: W.B. Hilton　Place: Frederick Hospital
　　　　Birth: 20 Sep 1868　　Death: 8 Apr 1945　　Burial: 10 Apr 1945
　　　　s/o Lawrence Allnutt & Sallie Anne Chiswell Darby

Monocacy Cemetery, Beallsville, Montgomery County, Maryland   111

Lot: 12   Owner: George Brewer

Site 3 Ida Ann Brewer Irwin   On stone with Reginald H. Irwin
        Birth: 17 Feb 1933   Death: 6 Sep 1996   Burial: 12 Sep 1996
Site 4 Reginald Herbert Irwin   h/o Ida Ann Shreve Irwin
        Birth: 17 Aug 1914   Death: 28 Mar 1988   Burial: 31 Mar 1988
Site 5 Daniel Herbert Shreve   Place: Washington, DC
        Birth: 3 Apr 1893   Death: 10 Jan 1954   Burial: 13 Jan 1954
        Mort: Robert A. Pumphrey   h/o Margaret Brewer Shreve
Site 6 Margaret Brewer Shreve   On stone with Daniel Herbert Shreve
        Birth: 19 Jul 1889   Death: 3 Feb 1991   Burial: 7 Feb 1991
Site 7 Miss Emily Young   Birth: 14 Aug 1832   Burial: 12 Dec 1905
Site 7 Dr. William Brewer   TS: Age 84-2-20   Mort: Chas. E. Roberts
        Birth: 24 Jul 1777   Death: 14 Oct 1861   Burial: 11 Apr 1916
        h/o Mary R. Brewer   Removed from burying ground
Site 8 Mary R. Brewer   Mort: Chas. E. Roberts
        Birth: 13 Dec 1782   Death: 2 Feb 1867   Burial: 11 Apr 1916
        TS: w/o Dr. William Brewer, age 84-1-25 Removed from burying ground
Site 9 Joseph Brewer   TS: Age 50-9-23   Mort: Chas. E. Roberts
        Birth: 17 May 1812   Death: 10 Mar 1863   Burial: 11 Apr 1916
        h/o Warnetta Brewer   Removed from burying ground
Site 10 Warnetta Brewer   Mort: Chas. E. Roberts
        Birth: 9 Oct 1815   Death: 12 Dec 1859   Burial: 11 Apr 1916
        TS: w/o Joseph Brewer, age 44-2-3   Removed from burying ground
Site 11 Camillus Brewer   TS: Age 21-3-4
        Birth: 22 Jun 1817   Death: 1838

Lot: 13   Owner: George Brewer

Site   Cornellus Brewer   No marker   Mort: Chas. E. Roberts
        Burial: 11 Apr 1916   Removed from burying ground
Site 1 Ida White Brewer   No marker   d/o William G. & Ida White Brewer
        Birth: 21 Sep 1882   Death: 27 Sep 1882   Burial: 28 Sep 1882
Site 2 Infant Brewer   No marker   s/o William G. & Ida White Brewer
        Birth: 15 Apr 1886   Burial: 17 May 1886
Site 3 Ida White Brewer   Place: Dickerson
        Birth: 2 Jul 1852   Death: 29 Jul 1930   Burial: 30 Jul 1930
        Mort: Hilton & Hall   TS: w/o William G. Brewer
Site 4 William G. Brewer   Place: Dawsonville   Mort: W.B. Hilton
        Birth: 15 Jan 1850   Death: 6 Dec 1944   Burial: 9 Dec 1944
Site 5 Aletha T. Brewer   TS: Age 73-7-27   On stone with George Brewer
        Birth: 12 Feb 1826   Death: 9 Oct 1899   Burial: 11 Oct 1899
Site 6 George W. Brewer   h/o Aletha T. Brewer
        Birth: 9 Feb 1822   Death: 4 Jun 1908   Burial: 6 Jun 1908

Lot: 14   Owner: Dr. N. Brewer

Site 1 Unit Rasin   Place: Philadelphia
        Birth: 3 Jan 1882   Death: 6 May 1951   Burial: 9 May 1951
        Mort: John R. Henderson   h/o Martha D. Rasin

Site 2 Martha Davis Rasin   Place: Whitemarsh
        Birth: 3 May 1878   Death: 21 Feb 1960   Burial: 23 Feb 1960
        Mort: Kirk & Nice   TS: w/o Unit Rasin
Site 3 Ruth E.W. Jones Brewer   Death: 25 Jun 1905   Burial: 26 Jun 1905
        TS: w/o Dr. N. Brewer, d/o Daniel & Mary Jones, age 67 yrs.
Site 4 Dr. Nicholas Brewer   h/o Martha Plater Williams Brewer
        Birth: 29 Aug 1818   Death: 25 Sep 1880   Burial: 27 Sep 1880
Site 5 Martha Plater Brewer   Death: 2 Mar 1851   Burial: 8 Jul 1881
        TS: d/o E.W. Williams, Esq., w/o Dr. Nicholas Brewer, age 23-11-0
        Moved to Monocacy 1881
Site 6 Jane Plater Brewer Davis   Death: 7 Jan 1891   Burial: 9 Jan 1891
        TS: d/o Dr. N. & Martha Plater Brewer, w/o James Lynn Davis, age 40 yrs.
Site 6 James Lynn Davis   Death: 29 Jan 1903   Burial: 1 Feb 1903
        TS: s/o James L. & E.G. Davis, age 54-10-10   h/o Jane Plater Brewer Davis
Site 7 Nannie Hamner Davis   Birth: 19 Dec 1885   Death: 28 Apr 1893
        TS: Age 7-4-9   On stone with Mary Brewer Davis
Site 8 Hubert Nelson Hicks   Mort: W.B. Hilton   Place: Frederick
        Birth: 4 Feb 1886   Death: 5 Oct 1954   Burial: 7 Oct 1954
        TS: h/o Jennie Lynn Davis Hicks (no dates for Jennie)
Site 10 Arthur Brewer   Death: 22 Jan 1866   Burial: 8 Jul 1881
        TS: s/o Dr. N. & Martha Plater Brewer, age 15-7-2 Moved to Monocacy 1881
Site 11 William Brewer   Death: 31 Aug 1854   Burial: 8 Jul 1881
        TS: s/o Dr. N. & Martha Plater Brewer, age 10 mo
        Moved to Monocacy   No dates on stone
Site 12 Jane Davis Hicks   w/o Hubert Nelson Hicks   Mort: Hilton
        Place: Braddock Heights Death: 11 Jun 1962   Burial: 13 Jun 1962
        No marker see Hubert, Site 8
Site 12 Mary Brewer Davis   Mort: F. Gasch's Sons   Place: Hyattsville, MD
        Birth: 25 Oct 1881   Death: 2 Mar 1968   Burial: 4 Mar 1968

Lot: 15 Owner: Dr. N. Brewer
Site 2 Daniel T. Jones   h/o Mary Sellman Jones, age 86 yrs
                                 Death: 4 Feb 1897   Burial: 6 Feb 1897
Site 3 Mary Sellman Jones   On stone with Daniel T. Jones
        Birth: 1817   Death: 8 Feb 1897   Burial: 10 Feb 1897
        TS: Age 80 yrs, married 62 years

Lot: 16 Owner: W.O. Sellman
Site 1 Infant Sellman   i/o W.O. & Ann P. Sellman, age 7 mo 6 days
        No marker   Death: 5 Jul 1859   Burial: 2 Aug 1884
Site 2 Gassaway Sellman   s/o W.O. & Ann P. Sellman   Reinterment
        No marker   Death: 6 Feb 1862   Burial: 2 Aug 1884
Site 3 William Sellman   s/o W.O. & Ann P. Sellman   Reinterment
        Birth: 30 Aug 1839   Death: 1 Jul 1859   Burial: 2 Aug 1884
Site 4 Ann Priscilla Woodward Poole Sellman
        Birth: 6 Jul 1818   Burial: 9 Feb 1890
        TS: w/o William O. Sellman, age 71-7-3
Site 5 Capt. William Oliver Sellman   TS: Age 69-11-18   h/o Ann P. Sellman
        Birth: 5 Aug 1814   Death: 23 Jul 1884   Burial: 24 Jul 1884

Site 8 Anita Dora Clapperton
        Birth: 20 May 1890   Death: 7 Mar 1983   Burial: 10 Mar 1983
Site 9 Nannie Estelle Donn   Mort: W.E. Lees & Son   Place: Washington, DC
        Birth: 1860   Death: 11 May 1934   Burial: 14 May 1934
Site 10 Frances Cookman Donn   Mort: J.W. Lee & Co. Removed from Washington
        Birth: 1842   Death: 1908   Burial: 23 Nov 1932
Site 11 Lewis L. Sellman
        Birth: 1852   Death: 1904   Burial: 23 Jul 1904

Lot: 17 Owner: F.O. Sellman
Site   Benjamin G. Sellman   Death: 25 Feb 1851   Burial: 30 Sep 1881
        is/o Frederick & Damaris Sellman   No marker   Reinterment
Site 2 Oliver Gassaway Sellman   Stone down   Burial: 26 Oct 1898
        TS: s/o Frederick & Damaris Sellman   Age 32 yrs 6 days
Site 3 Susan G. Sellman
        Birth: 24 Jun 1839   Death: 30 Jan 1862   Burial: 30 Sep 1881
        TS: d/o Gassaway & Juletter Sellman, age 22-7-6   Reinterment
Site 4 Juletter Sellman   Age 43 yrs 2 mo 9
        Birth: 3 Jan 1811   Death: 12 Mar 1854   Burial: 30 Sep 1881
        TS: w/o Gassaway Sellman, d/o Major T.& Christey A. Gittings
Site 5 Gassaway Sellman   h/o Juletter Sellman   Reinterment
        Birth: 4 Feb 1811   Death: 6 Apr 1857   Burial: 30 Sep 1881
        TS: Age 46-2-2
Site 11 Damaris Almira Sellman   TS: w/o Frederick Oliver Sellman
        Birth: 4 Apr 1843   Death: 4 Sep 1912   Burial: 6 Sep 1912
Site 12 Frederick Oliver Sellman   h/o Damaris Almira Sellman
        Birth: 19 Sep 1842   Death: 20 Feb 1904   Burial: 22 Feb 1904

Lot: 18 Owner: William G. Wall
Site 1 Mary Catherine Wall   Mort: W.T. Hilton & Sons   Place: Boyds
        Birth: 6 Jan 1849   Death: 7 Jul 1932   Burial: 10 Jul 1932
Site 2 Lawrence Dade Wall   Place: Henderson, NC
        Birth: 1881   Death: 15 Oct 1927   Burial: 17 Oct 1927
        Mort: W.T. Hilton & Sons   h/o Virginia B. Wall
Site 3 Laura E. Kendall
        Birth: 23 Apr 1847   Death: 12 Sep 1899   Burial: 14 Sep 1899
Site 4 Malcolm Wall   TS: s/o William E. & Mary C. Wall
        Birth: 28 Dec 1877   Death: 26 Aug 1888   Burial: 28 Aug 1888
Site 5 Maze Wall   illegible   d/o William E. & Mary C. Wall
        Birth: 7 Jan 1883   Death: 28 Jun 1884   Burial: 29 Jun 1884

Lot: 19 Owner: William G. Wall
Site 2 Helen Wessel Wall   Mort: Robert A. Pumphrey   Place: Bethesda
        Birth: 22 Jan 1884   Death: 5 Nov 1953   Burial: 7 Nov 1953
Site 3 William Guy Wall   Mort: W.B. Hilton   Place: Indianapolis, IN
        Birth: 7 Aug 1875   Death: 16 Jan 1941   Burial: 20 Jan 1941
Site 4 Annie M. Dade   Mort: Hilton & Price   Place: Boyds
        Birth: 2 Dec 1852   Death: 7 Nov 1935   Burial: 9 Nov 1935

Site 5 William Edwards Wall   Mort: W.T. Hilton & Sons   Place: New York
        Birth: 27 Jul 1846   Death: 26 Jul 1929   Burial: 29 Jul 1929
Site 9 Lt. Robert Dade Wall   Mort: W.B. Hilton   SFI40R, TS: Lt. US Army
        Birth: 17 Sep 1921   Death: 25 Feb 1945   Burial: 7 May 1949
        TS: s/o Laurence D. & Virginia Wall, killed in action, Luzon, P.I.
Site 10 Virginia Blanks Wall   Mort: Hilton   TS: w/o Lawrence D. Wall
        Birth: 1893   Death: 1 Jul 1966   Burial: 4 Jul 1966

Lot: 20 Owner: Benjamin C. Gott
Site 1 Marguerite Hayden Gott   Age 81 yrs
        Birth: 4 Jun 1903   Death: 1 Apr 1985   Burial: 5 Apr 1985
Site 2 Richard V. Gott   h/o Lillian Pearl Gott
        Birth: 18 May 1907   Death: 27 Jul 1978   Burial: 30 Aug 1978
Site 3 Dorothy Gott Brosius   Mort: Wm. Hilton   Place: Bethesda, MD
        Birth: 1903   Death: 14 Jan 1968   Burial: 16 Jan 1968
Site 3 Lillian Pearl Gott   Place: Rockville
        Birth: 25 Dec 1877   Death: 23 Apr 1940   Burial: 25 Apr 1940
        Mort: W.B. Hilton   2nd w/o James Perry Gott
Site 4 James Perry Gott   Place: Washington, DC
        Birth: 17 Feb 1861   Death: 11 Feb 1937   Burial: 13 Feb 1937
        Mort: W.B. Hilton   h/o Annie Laurie Covington Gott
Site 5 Annie Laurie Covington Gott   w/o James Perry Gott
        Birth: 16 Feb 1864   Death: 30 Nov 1896   Burial: 2 Dec 1896
Site 7 James Gott Allnutt   Place: Baltimore
        Birth: 1921   Death: 20 Oct 1921   Burial: 22 Oct 1921
        Mort: W.T. Hilton & Sons   s/o Ernest & Lucille Allnutt
Site 8 Ernest C. Allnutt Jr.   Birth: 1918   s/o Ernest & Lucille Gott Allnutt
Site 8 Ernest C. Allnutt   Place: Baltimore
        Birth: 1884   Death: 13 Jan 1928   Burial: 16 Jan 1928
        Mort: W.T. Hilton & Sons   h/o Lucille Allnutt
Site 9 Lucille Gott Allnutt   Place: Baltimore, MD
        Birth: 1887   Death: 12 Oct 1968   Burial: 21 Oct 1968
        Mort: Robert Pumphrey   w/o Ernest C. Allnutt
Site 10 Elizabeth L. Allnutt Gott   Place: Annapolis
        Birth: 18 Sep 1867   Death: 23 Feb 1969   Burial: 25 Jun 1969
        Mort: John M. Taylor & Sons   w/o Benjamin C. Gott
Site 11 Benjamin C. Gott   Place: Annapolis
        Birth: 20 Apr 1866   Death: 12 Sep 1946   Burial: 14 Sep 1946
        Mort: John M. Taylor & Son   h/o Elizabeth L. Gott
Site 12 Benjamin C. Gott   TS: s/o Benjamin C. & Elizabeth L. Gott
        Birth: 14 Apr 1903   Death: 2 Aug 1904

Lot: 21 Owner: Benjamin C. Gott
Site 2 Elizabeth Beall Gott   Mort: Joseph Gawler   Place: Washington, DC
        Birth: 26 Feb 1871   Death: 21 Nov 1970   Burial: 24 Nov 1970
Site 3 Mariel Rebecca Gott   Mort: W.T. Hilton & Sons   Place: Rockville
        Birth: 17 May 1837   Death: 15 Mar 1927   Burial: 17 Mar 1927
Site 4 Benjamin C. Gott
        Birth: 28 May 1814   Death: 23 Apr 1885   Burial: 26 Apr 1885

Monocacy Cemetery, Beallsville, Montgomery County, Maryland   115

Site 6 Ann E. Gott   Death: 10 Oct 1885
Site 11 Nathan E. Gott   Mort: W.T. Hilton & Sons   Place: near Boyds
        Birth: 13 Jul 1868   Death: 11 Oct 1917   Burial: 13 Oct 1917
Site 12 Annie Warfield Gott   Place: Fairfax Co.
        Birth: 15 Sep 1873   Death: 5 Jan 1964   Burial: 7 Jan 1964
        Mort: Robert A. Pumphrey   On stone with Nathan E. Gott

Lot: 22   Owner: Charles F. Darby
Site 1 Bettie I. Vaughn   Mort: W.T. Hilton & Sons   Place: Silver Spring
        Birth: 1840   Death: 12 Jan 1925   Burial: 14 Jan 1925
Site 2 Nellie Vaughn Darby   d/o S.V. & Charles R. Darby
        Birth: 11 Nov 1886   Death: 1 Feb 1886
Site 3 William Hendren Darby   s/o Sarah V. & Charles R. Darby
        Birth: 10 Sep 1882   Death: 18 Oct 1889   Burial: 20 Oct 1889
Site 4 Sarah Virginia Darby   Place: Barnesville
        Birth: 1855   Death: 17 Nov 1922   Burial: 20 Nov 1922
        Mort: W.T. Hilton & Sons   w/o Charles R. Darby
Site 5 Charles R. Darby   Mort: W.T. Hilton & Sons   Place: Barnesville
        Birth: 1855   Death: 19 Jun 1920   Burial: 21 Jun 1920
Site 6 Anne Louise Hendron   No marker   Mort: W.B. Hilton
        Place: Riverdale   Death: 21 Nov 1946   Burial: 24 Nov 1946

Lot: 23   Owner: Samuel Darby
Site 3 Mary Jane Darby   w/o Samuel Darby
        Birth: 24 Jul 1820   Death: 20 Mar 1897   Burial: 21 Mar 1897
Site 4 Samuel C. Darby   h/o Mary Jane Darby
        Birth: 3 Jan 1824   Death: 14 Dec 1897   Burial: 14 Dec 1897
Site 5 Samuel Porter Darby   No marker   Mort: John Harmison
        Place: Washington, DC   Death: 11 Jan 1959   Burial: 13 Jan 1959
Site 7 Sallie Darby   d/o Mary Jane & Samuel Darby
                                Death: 21 Mar 1862   illegible
Site 8 John E. Darby   s/o Mary Jane & Samuel Darby
        Birth: 24 Jan 1852   Death: 30 Sep 1874   illegible
Site 9 Zachary T. Darby   Death: 11 Aug 1874   No marker

Lot: 24   Owner: John W. Darby
Site 2 Eva W. Darby   Birth: 6 Jul 1849   Death: Oct 1873
Site 3 Ellen R. Darby   TS: w/o John W. Darby, age 76-5-16
        Birth: 16 Sep 1819   Death: 11 Mar 1896   Burial: 14 Mar 1896
Site 4 John W. Darby   TS: Age 66-11-14   h/o Ellen R. Darby
        Birth: 8 Mar 1822   Death: 22 Feb 1889   Burial: 24 Feb 1889
Site 5 Ellen Ruth Iglehart   Mort: W.B. Hilton   Place: Barnesville
        Birth: 2 Dec 1856   Death: 19 Sep 1938   Burial: 20 Sep 1938
Site 6 Basil R. Iglehart   Mort: Ernest C. Gartner   Place: Gaithersburg
        Birth: 5 Feb 1851   Death: 23 Dec 1935   Burial: 26 Dec 1935
Site 8 Nellie Hall Darby   TS: [1st] w/o Richard Edwin Darby
        Birth: 10 Apr 1864   Death: 30 Nov 1897   Burial: 1 Dec 1897

Site 9 Richard Edwin Darby   Place: Barnesville
        Birth: 10 Dec 1862   Death: 18 Sep 1938   Burial: 20 Sep 1938
        Mort: W.B. Hilton   h/o Nellie Hall Darby
Site 10 Cora John Darby   Place: Barnesville
        Birth: Apr 1863   Death: 28 Jan 1926   Burial: 1 Feb 1926
        Mort: W.T. Hilton & Sons   TS: [2nd] w/o Richard Edwin Darby
Site 11 Infant Daughter Darby   d/o R. Edwin & Cora J. Darby
        Birth: 6 Oct 1907   Death: 9 Oct 1907   Burial: 11 Oct 1907
Site 12 Ruth Ellen Darby   Mort: W.T. Hilton   Place: Washington, DC
        Birth: 27 Dec 1902   Death: 14 May 1919   Burial: 17 May 1919

Lot: 25 Owner: Remus Darby
Site 1 Ruth Ellen Darby   TS: d/o Nettie & Remus R. Darby
        Birth: 17 Dec 1890   Death: 10 May 1897   Burial: 11 May 1897
Site 2 Infant Darby   TS: d/o Nettie & Remus R. Darby, age 12 days
                                    Death: 16 Jan 1887
Site 3 Nettie Darby   TS: [1st] w/o Remus R. Darby
        Birth: 26 Aug 1858   Death: 24 May 1893   Burial: 25 May 1893
Site 4 Remus R. Darby   Place: Barnesville
        Birth: 1847   Death: 10 Jul 1916   Burial: 12 Jul 1916
        Mort: W.T. Hilton & Sons   h/o Nettie Darby
Site 5 Clara F. Darby   Place: Gaithersburg
        Birth: 4 Aug 1860   Death: 14 Dec 1938   Burial: 16 Dec 1938
        Mort: Ernest C. Gartner   TS: [2nd] w/o Remus R. Darby
Site 8 Lawrence Jones Darby
        Birth: 22 Sep 1898   Death: 4 Jun 1987   Burial: 6 Jun 1987
Site 9 William Robert Griffith   s/o William F. & Alice D. Griffith, age 53 yrs
        Birth: 26 Mar 1931   Death: 3 Jan 1985   Burial: 5 Jan 1985
Site 9 Mary Arlene Lowe Griffith Reed
        Birth: 28 Oct 1946   Death: 3 Dec 1995   Burial: 7 Dec 1995
Site 10 William Franklin Griffith   h/o Alice Darby Griffith
        Birth: 1899   Death: 17 Jan 1978   Burial: 20 Jan 1978
Site 11 Alice Darby Griffith   On stone with William Franklin Griffith, age 95 yrs
        Birth: 29 Mar 1900   Death: 4 Oct 1995   Burial: 7 Oct 1995

Lot: 26 Owner: H. Clay Burch
Site 2 Francis E. Burch   TS: CSA
        Birth: 1823   Death: 1898F   Burial: 14 Apr 1898
Site 3 Mrs. William Mossburg   Burial: 10 Apr 1881   No marker
Site 4 Mrs. Harriet Burch   Burial: 28 Jan 1906   No marker
Site 5 Mrs. Mary R. Burch   Place: Olney Hospital
        Birth: 8 Aug 1864   Death: 19 Sep 1929   Burial: 21 Sep 1929
        Mort: W.T. Hilton & Sons   TS: w/o Henry C. Burch
Site 6 Henry Clay Burch   Mort: Hilton & Hall   Place: Olney
        Birth: 14 Apr 1854   Death: 19 Dec 1930   Burial: 21 Dec 1930

Lot: 27 Owner: Miscellaneous
Site 1 Howard Eugene Poole   h/o Willie Webster
        Birth: 5 Sep 1903   Death: 3 Feb 1978   Burial: 8 Feb 1978

Monocacy Cemetery, Beallsville, Montgomery County, Maryland   117

Site 2 Lelia Ellinor Poole Mossburg   Place: Bethesda, MD
        Birth: 20 Oct 1892   Death: 20 Apr 1970   Burial: 23 Apr 1970
        Mort: Joseph Gawler   w/o Charles Henry Mossburg
Site 3 Charles Henry Mossburg   Place: Bethesda
        Birth: 1891   Death: 31 Aug 1942   Burial: 2 Sep 1942
        Mort: Warner E. Pumphrey   h/o Lelia E. Mossburg
Site 5 Jean Charles Edmond Blanchard
        Birth: 19 Oct 1812   Death: 18 Oct 1891   Burial: 21 Dec 1891
Site 6 Joseph Franklin Cummings Jr.   h/o Ann Mildred Jones Cummings
        Birth: 16 Jul 1851   Death: 30 Mar 1912   Burial: 2 Apr 1912

Lot: 28 Owner: Albert Edward Young
Site 1 George Llewellyn Young   TS: s/o Llewellyn & Stella M. Young, age 0-1-29
        Birth: 11 Nov 1909   Death: 9 Dec 1910   Burial: 11 Dec 1910
Site 2 Stella M. Young   Place: Dickerson
        Birth: 20 Mar 1877   Death: 1 Apr 1946   Burial: 4 Apr 1946
        Mort: W.B. Hilton   w/o Llewellyn Young
Site 3 Lewellyn Young   Place: Beallsville
        Birth: 19 Nov 1874   Death: 22 Jul 1935   Burial: 24 Jul 1935
        Mort: Hilton & Hall   h/o Stella M. Young
Site 4 Mary Bertha Young   Mort: S.H. Hines   Place: Washington, DC
        Birth: 27 Jul 1870   Death: 13 Apr 1937   Burial: 15 Apr 1937
Site 5 Madeline Louise Roberts Young   On stone with Albert Edward Young
        Birth: 16 Oct 1914   Death: 17 Sep 1994   Burial: 20 Sep 1994
        d/o Joseph Edward & Carrie Peters Roberts
Site 6 Albert Edward Young   h/o Madeline L. Young
        Birth: 29 Feb 1908   Death: 27 Sep 1973   Burial: 1 Oct 1973
Site 10 Carrie Frances Roberts   w/o Joseph Roberts
        Birth: 8 Mar 1899   Death: 10 Jul 1985   Burial: 13 Jul 1985
Site 11 Emma D. Young   TS: Mother   Place: Rockville, MD
        Birth: 15 Jan 1879   Death: 14 Mar 1971   Burial: 16 Mar 1971
        Mort: Tyson Wheeler   On stone with John W. Young
Site 12 John William Young   TS: Father   Place: Montgomery Co.
        Birth: 14 Jan 1869   Death: 27 Jul 1929   Burial: 30 Jul 1929
        Mort: W.R. Pumphrey   h/o Emma D. Young

Lot: 29 Lower   Owner: John W. Hickman
Site 1 Clara Poole Elliott   Place: Washington, DC
        Birth: 27 Aug 1930   Death: 18 Feb 1953   Burial: 21 Feb 1953
        Mort: Robert A. Pumphrey   w/o Grafton Elliott
Site 2 Clarence L. Norris
        Birth: 10 Dec 1907   Death: 6 Oct 1982   Burial: 9 Oct 1982
Site 3 Hazel Hickman Norris   w/o Clarence Norris
        Birth: 10 May 1911   Death: 15 May 1983   Burial: 17 May 1983
Site 4 Carolyn R. Hickman   No marker
        Birth: 4 Feb 1913   Death: 26 Mar 1997   Burial: 2 Apr 1997
Site 5 Beulah M. Hickman   Place: Olney
        Birth: 10 Mar 1887   Death: 3 May 1967   Burial: 7 May 1967
        Mort: Hilton   w/o John W. Hickman

Site 6 John W. Hickman Place: Poolesville
Birth: 12 Sep 1887   Death: 17 Dec 1966   Burial: 21 Dec 1966
Mort: Hilton   h/o Beulah M. Hickman

Lot: 29 Upper   Owner: Lester Young
Site 1 Roger Raymond Poole   Place: Bethesda
Birth: 29 Aug 1903   Death: 12 Feb 1944   Burial: 14 Feb 1944
Mort: W.B. Hilton   h/o Alta Bertha Young Poole
Site 3 Nellie V. Hickman Young   Place: Sellman
Birth: 9 Sep 1892   Death: 26 Jun 1913   Burial: 28 Jun 1913
Mort: Hilton & Hall   d/o Hazel H. Hickman   TS: w/o Lester S. Young
Site 4 Lester S. Young   Mort: W.B. Hilton   Place: Frederick
Birth: 4 Sep 1885   Death: 23 Jul 1960   Burial: 25 Jul 1960
Site 5 Theodore Hazel Young   No marker
Birth: 30 Dec 1911   Death: 18 Feb 1996   Burial: 20 Feb 1996

Lot: 30   Owner: Charles T. Cooley
Site 1 Charles L. Cooley   No marker
Death: 23 Feb 1976   Burial: 26 Feb 1976
Site 2 Beulah Frances Cooley   No marker   Mort: Robert A.
Place: Bethesda   Death: 19 Oct 1960   Burial: 21 Oct 1960
Site 3 Elgie N. Cooley   No marker
Birth: 5 Jul 1896   Death: 25 Dec 1980   Burial: 28 Dec 1980
Site 4 Sterling T. Cooley   Mort: Warner E. Pumphrey   Place: Rockville
Birth: 1902   Death: 10 Feb 1934   Burial: 14 Feb 1934
On stone with Charles T. & May Etta Cooley
Site 5 May Etta Cooley   Place: Frederick Co., VA
Birth: 1877   Death: 3 Mar 1964   Burial: 7 Mar 1964
Mort: Warner & Pumphrey   TS: w/o Charles T. Cooley
Site 6 Charles T. Cooley   Place: Capital View
Birth: 1869   Death: 7 Jul 1930   Burial: 10 Jul 1930
Mort: Warner E. Pumphrey   h/o Mary E. Cooley
Site 7 Charles L. Cooley   On stone with Barbara A. Cooley
Birth: 24 Jan 1928   Death: 20 Jan 1989   Burial: 23 Jan 1989
Site 11 Annie Cooley Curtis   On stone with Robert Elmer Curtis
Birth: 2 Feb 1909   Death: 5 Aug 1981
Site 12 Robert Elmer Curtis   h/o Annie Cooley Curtis
Birth: 26 Jul 1903   Death: 26 Sep 1972   Burial: 29 Sep 1972

Lot: 31   Owner: J.T. Reid
Site 2 S. Elizabeth Grunwell   Mort: W.R. Pumphrey   Place: Boyds
Birth: 26 Jul 1880   Death: 28 Dec 1947   Burial: 31 Dec 1947
On stone with Nannie R. & John T. Reid
Site 3 Nannie R. Reid   TS: w/o John T. Reid   Place: Olney
Birth: 7 Jan 1870   Death: 8 Dec 1951   Burial: 11 Dec 1951
Mort: Robert A. Pumphrey   Age 81
Site 4 John T. Reid   Place: Boyds
Birth: 7 Jan 1863   Death: 16 Feb 1937   Burial: 19 Feb 1937
Mort: W.R. Pumphrey   h/o Nannie R. Reid

Monocacy Cemetery, Beallsville, Montgomery County, Maryland

Site 5 Ethel Reid Linthicum On stone with Charles Gorman Linthicum
       Birth: 25 Jan 1894   Death: 4 Feb 1980   Burial: 7 Feb 1980
Site 6 Charles Gorman Linthicum
       Birth: 30 Apr 1893   Death: 3 Apr 1983   Burial: 6 Apr 1983

Lot: 32   Owner: Eva L. Aud
Site 1 Kathleen Louise Aud
       Birth: 7 Nov 1903   Death: 16 Sep 1988   Burial: 20 Sep 1988
Site 2 Susan E. Aud   d/o Eva Louise & Trujean Handy Aud
       Birth: 3 Aug 1905   Death: 1 Sep 1978   Burial: 4 Sep 1978
Site 3 Eva Louise Aud   Place: Silver Spring, MD
       Birth: 3 Oct 1879   Death: 9 Mar 1970   Burial: 12 Mar 1970
       Mort: Tyson Wheeler   On stone with Trujean Handy Aud
Site 4 Trujean Handy Aud   Mort: W.R. Pumphrey   Place: Rockville
       Birth: 10 Nov 1870   Death: 23 Apr 1940   Burial: 26 Apr 1940

Lot: 33 Lower   Owner: H.H. Heflin
Site 2 Herbert Marshall Heflin   Place: Brunswick
       Birth: 18 Oct 1906   Death: 19 Jan 1941   Burial: 22 Jan 1941
       Mort: W.B. Hilton   h/o Ethel Payne Heflin
Site 3 Maggie L. Heflin
       Birth: 18 Apr 1885   Death: 26 Feb 1968   Burial: 1 Mar 1968
       Mort: Tyson Wheeler   On stone with Herbert H. Heflin
Site 4 Herbert H. Heflin   Place: Bethesda (Hosp)
       Birth: 10 Apr 1880   Death: 18 Feb 1962   Burial: 21 Feb 1962
       Mort: Tyson Wheeler   h/o Maggie L. Heflin
Site 5 Carrie Gibson Heflin   d/o Herbert H. & Maggie L. Heflin
       Birth: 7 Jun 1913   Death: 17 Apr 1989   Burial: 21 Apr 1989

Lot: 33 Upper   Owner: Grace K. Molby
Site 3 Grace Kelly Molby   Place: Washington, DC
       Birth: 9 Mar 1875   Death: 6 Nov 1965   Burial: 10 Nov 1965
       Mort: Gawler   w/o Frank Lewis Molby
Site 4 Frank Lewis Molby   Place: Beallsville
       Birth: 10 Mar 1867   Death: 28 Feb 1939   Burial: 3 Mar 1939
       Mort: W.B. Hilton   h/o Grace Kelly Molby
Site 5 Richard VanDyke Molby   Place: Frederick
       Birth: 24 Nov 1895   Death: 21 Oct 1943   Burial: 23 Oct 1945
       Mort: W.B. Hilton   s/o Grace Kelly & Frank Lewis Molby

Lot: 34 Upper   Owner: Jeannie E.T. McClasson
Site 4 Jeannie E.T. McClasson   Age 62 yrs
                                  Death: 21 Sep 1991   Burial: 28 Sep 1991

Monocacy Cemetery, Beallsville, Montgomery County, Maryland

Row F

Lot: 0   Owner: John F. Waesche
- Site   Wife of Thomas Waesche and child   No marker   Burial: 6 Sep 1891
- Site 1 Margaret Belt Waesche   Mort: S.H. Hines Co.   Place: Washington, DC
  Birth: 1868   Death: 15 Mar 1950   Burial: 18 Mar 1950
- Site 2 J. Richard Waesche   Place: Frederick   Mort: Hilton & Hall
  Birth: 1872   Death: 7 Mar 1938   Burial: 9 Mar 1938
- Site 3 M. Elizabeth Waesche   Place: Washington, DC
  Birth: 1875   Death: 23 Dec 1939   Burial: 25 Dec 1939
  Mort: W.B. Hilton   w/o J. Richard Waesche
- Site 4 John F. Waesche   Place: Beallsville
  Birth: 5 Oct 1834   Death: 5 Apr 1923   Burial: 8 Apr 1923
  Mort: Hilton & Hall   h/o Margaret Elizabeth Waesche
- Site 5 Margaret Elizabeth Waesche   TS: w/o John F. Waesche
  Birth: 31 Aug 1891   Death: 30 Aug 1891
- Site 6 Ann Amelia Belt
  Birth: 25 Aug 1819   Death: 29 Sep 1855   Burial: 8 Nov 1900
  TS: w/o John R. Belt, d/o William & Elizabeth Eagle   Reinterment
- Site 6 Charles E. Waesche   No marker   s/o John F. & M.E. Waesche
  Birth: 7 Jan 1879   Burial: Mar 1879
- Site 7 William H. Waesche   Mort: Hilton & Hall   Place: Poolesville
  Birth: 21 Feb 1832   Death: 26 Sep 1913   Burial: 28 Sep 1913
- Site 8 Joseph F. Smith   Mort: John S. Rhodes   Place: St. Petersburg, FL
  Birth: 1 Jun 1878   Death: 10 Aug 1954   Burial: 14 Aug 1954
- Site 9 Annie E. Smith   Place: Washington, DC
  Birth: 27 Feb 1833   Death: 1 Apr 1947   Burial: 3 Apr 1947
  Mort: S.H. Hines Co.   On stone with Joseph F. Smith
- Site 12 Infant of John F. Waesche   illegible   Burial: 14 Mar 1879

Lot: 1   Owner: Dr. B.E. Hughes
- Site 1 Margaret Hughes Halvosa   On stone with Albert C. Halvosa
  Birth: 1897   Death: 22 Jul 1982   Burial: 26 Jul 1982
- Site 2 Elizabeth E. Hughes   d/o B.E. & C.E. Hughes   Reinterment
  Birth: 14 Nov 1866   Death: 12 Aug 1867   Burial: 28 Apr 1884
- Site 2 Preston Brooks Hughes   s/o B.E. & C.E. Hughes   Reinterment
  Birth: 29 May 1871   Death: 27 Jul 1872   Burial: 28 Apr 1884
- Site 3 Dr. Benjamin E. Hughes   Death: 26 Apr 1880   Burial: 28 Apr 1884
  w/o Catherine S. Hughes   TS: Age 61-8-1
- Site 4 Catherine S Hughes   TS: w/o Dr. Benj. E. Hughes
  Birth: 3 Nov 1825   Death: 20 Feb 1903
- Site 5 Edgar Hughes   Mort: W.R. Pumphrey   Place: Washington, DC
  Birth: 6 Apr 1857   Death: 1 Jun 1929   Burial: 3 Jun 1929
- Site 7 John Edward Lewis   Place: Olney, MD
  Birth: 12 May 1892   Death: 25 Nov 1970   Burial: 28 Nov 1970
  Mort: Olin Molesworth   TS: MD PVT Co F 63 Infantry WWI

Monocacy Cemetery, Beallsville, Montgomery County, Maryland

Site 8 Mary Hughes Lewis On stone with John Edward Lewis
        Birth: 11 Mar 1895 Death: 17 Oct 1989 Burial: 19 Oct 1989
Site 9 George Edward Hughes Place: Clarksburg
        Birth: 17 Jul 1854 Death: 7 Aug 1927 Burial: 9 Aug 1927
        Mort: E.C. Gartner h/o Louisa Dutrow Hughes
Site 10 Louisa Dutrow Hughes Place: Clarksburg
        Birth: 26 Jul 1853 Death: 24 Oct 1933 Burial: 26 Oct 1933
        Mort: E.C. Gartner TS: w/o George E. Hughes
Site 12 Albert C. Halvosa Place: Ranson, WV
        Birth: 1903 Death: 12 Mar 1969 Burial: 15 Mar 1969
        Mort: John H. Enders h/o Margaret Hughes Halvosa

Lot: 2 Owner: Isaac Young
Site 1 Irene Young d/o Isaac & Margaret Young Reinterment
        Birth: 11 Jan 1870 Death: 25 Jul 1870 Burial: 28 Apr 1884
        TS: Age 0-6-4
Site 2 Elle Lee Young illegible
        id/o Isaac & Margaret Young Burial: 28 Apr 1884
Site 3 Isaac Young h/o Margaret R. Young Treasurer of the Board
        Birth: 25 Jan 1828 Death: 7 Apr 1895 Burial: 9 Apr 1895
Site 4 Margaret R. Young TS: w/o Isaac Young
        Birth: 18 Aug 1829 Death: 1 Jul 1906 Burial: 3 Jul 1906
Site 7 Joseph T. Chiswell Jr. Son of Joseph Chilswick
        Birth: 1897 Death: 1898 Burial: 21 Jan 1898
Site 8 Ruby A. Chiswell
        Birth: 1904 Death: 1911 Burial: 17 Jan 1911
Site 9 Linda Young Chiswell Mort: Hilton & Hall Place: Washington, DC
        Birth: 1864 Death: 9 Feb 1914 Burial: 11 Feb 1914
Site 10 Joseph T. Chiswell
        Birth: 18 Sep 1855 Death: 1912 Burial: 4 May 1912
Site 11 Olivia Marguerite Chiswell
        Birth: 18 Jul 1892 Death: 12 Jul 1983 Burial: 14 Jul 1983

Lot: 3 Owner: Robert Sellman
Site   Child of Robert Sellman Sr. No marker Burial: 15 Dec 1881
Site 1 Lizzie Gould Sellman Death: 2 Mar 1889 Burial: 4 Mar 1889
        d/o Robert Sellman, age 0-8-14 No marker
Site 2 Helen G. Sellman No marker Burial: 7 Mar 1887
        d/o Robert Sellman, age 1-0-12
Site 3 Willie Sellman No marker
Site 4 William Arthur Sellman TS: s/o Robert & Sarah Sellman
        Birth: 25 Jan 1852 Death: 2 Aug 1852
Site 4 Wallace Sellman TS: s/o Robert & Sarah Sellman
        Birth: 2 Nov 1842 Death: 22 May 1863
Site 5 Serena Dade Sellman TS: [2nd] w/o Robert Sellman Sr.
        Birth: 31 Jan 1814 Death: 9 Nov 1891 Burial: 11 Nov 1891
Site 6 Robert Sellman Sr. Death: 29 Jul 1886
        h/o Sarah Ann Sellman & Serena Dade Sellman TS: Age 67-9-2

Site 6 Sarah Ann Sellman   TS: [1st] w/o Robert Sellman
         Birth: 31 May 1823   Death: 20 Sep 1852
Site 7 Miss Mary Serena Sellman   TS: d/o Alonzo & S. Belle Sellman
         Birth: 15 Jul 1876   Death: 10 Mar 1904   Burial: 12 Mar 1904
Site 8 S. Belle Sellman   Place: Baltimore, MD
         Birth: 23 Jul 1845   Death: 9 Jan 1917   Burial: 10 Jan 1917
         Mort: W.T. Hilton & Sons   TS: w/o Alonzo Sellman
Site 9 Alonzo Sellman
         Birth: 17 Sep 1844   Death: 27 Oct 1878   Burial: 27 Oct 1878
         h/o S. Belle Sellman   TS: s/o Robert & Sarah Sellman
Site 10 Minnie Sellman West   Place: Philadelphia
         Birth: 10 Aug 1873   Death: 7 May 1947   Burial: 10 May 1947
         Mort: John R. Henderson   TS: d/o Alonzo & S. Belle Sellman
Site 11 William Arthur Sellman   Place: Springfield, PA
         Birth: 17 May 1875   Death: 24 Aug 1961   Burial: 8 Sep 1961
         Mort: J.Malcolm Henderson   TS: s/o Alonzo & S. Belle Sellman

Lot: 4 Owner: Charles Waters
Site 1 Perry Davis Waters   TS: s/o Charles H. & Ella Yates Waters
         Birth: 26 Jun 1885   Death: 22 Apr 1888   Burial: 23 May 1886
Site 2 Allnutt Hess Waters   Death: 27 Aug 1889   Burial: 28 Aug 1889
         TS: s/o Dr. Charles H. & Ella Yates Waters, age 1-6-5
Site 3 Eleanor Allnutt Waters   Death: 9 Aug 1890
         TS: d/o Dr. Charles H. & Ella Yates Waters, age 0-10-23
Site 4 Alice May Allnutt Waters
         Birth: 12 Sep 1873   Death: 17 Sep 1893   Burial: 22 Sep 1893
         TS: d/o Dr. Charles H. & Ella Yates Waters, age 20-0-10
Site 8 Charles Lewis Waters, MD Mort: M.W. Hysong   Place: Washington, DC
         Birth: 11 Mar 1879   Death: 17 Jun 1931   Burial: 19 Jun 1931
Site 9 Ella Yates Waters   Place: Washington, DC
         Birth: 21 Feb 1848   Death: 2 Jun 1921   Burial: 4 Jun 1921
         Mort: W.R. Pumphrey   TS: w/o Charles H. Waters MD
Site 10 Dr. Charles H. Waters   Mort: W.R. Pumphrey Place: Washington, DC
         Birth: 1 Jul 1849   Death: 21 Jan 1920   Burial: 25 Jan 1920
         h/o Ella Yates Waters   TS: A Primitive Baptist Minister
Site 12 Alta Waters   Mort: M. Gaghan
         Death: 13 Sep 1967   Burial: 15 Sep 1967   No marker
Site 12 Paul Yates Waters   No marker   Mort: Warner E.
         Place: Silver Spring   Death: 5 Jun 1940   Burial: 7 Jun 1940

Lot: 5 Owner: Vernon Hempstone
Site   Child of Vernon Hempstone No marker   Burial: 3 Apr 1880
Site 1 Townley Hempstone   s/o Vernon Hempstone, twin
         Birth: 23 Jun 1888   Death: 23 Jun 1888   Burial: 20 Sep 1888
Site 2 Vernon Stanley Hempstone   s/o Vernon Hempstone, twin
         Birth: 23 Jun 1888   Death: 23 Jun 1888   Burial: 20 Sep 1888
Site 3 Ann Elizabeth Poole Hempstone   Place: Rockville
         Birth: 31 Aug 1855   Death: 15 Oct 1922   Burial: 17 Oct 1922
         Mort: Hilton & Hall   w/o Vernon Hempstone

Site 4　Vernon Hempstone　　　　　　　　　　　Place: Poolesville
　　　　Birth: 16 Jan 1851　　Death: 2 Jan 1929　　Burial: 5 Jan 1929
　　　　Mort: Hilton & Hall　　h/o Ann Elizabeth Poole Hempstone
Site 5　Robert Whitney Hempstone　Mort: Wm. Hilton　Place: Frederick, MD
　　　　Birth: 22 Jun 1893　　Death: 9 Feb 1970　　Burial: 12 Feb 1970

Lot: 6　Owner: Mrs. S.A. Morrison
Site　　Carlton Lee Christie　　No marker　　Mort: Geo M. Gartner
　　　　Place: Gaithersburg　　Death: 21 Nov 1924　Burial: 22 Nov 1924
Site 1　Charles Morrison　　　　TS: s/o Charles V. & Mary F. Morrison
　　　　Birth: 1 Jul 1892　　Death: 22 Sep 1892　　Burial: 24 Sep 1892
Site 1　George V. Morrison　　Death: 22 Apr 1899　　Burial: 23 Apr 1899
　　　　TS: s/o Charles V. & Mary F. Morrison, age 2 days
Site 2　Mary Frances Morrison　　　　　　　　　　Place: Poolesville
　　　　Birth: 14 Jan 1868　　Death: 20 Mar 1947　Burial: 22 Mar 1947
　　　　Mort: W.B. Hilton　　　　TS: w/o Charles V. Morrison
Site 3　Charles V. Morrison　　　　　　　　　　　Place: Poolesville
　　　　Birth: 2 Dec 1867　　Death: 25 May 1915　Burial: 28 May 1915
　　　　Mort: Hilton & Hall　　　h/o Mary Frances Morrison
Site 4　Sarah A. Morrison　　TS: w/o James W. Morrison, age 54-1-21
　　　　Birth: 10 Sep 1844　　Death: 1 Nov 1898　　Burial: 3 Nov 1898
Site 5　Barbara M. Connelly　　Birth: 11 Jun 1813　　Death: 6 Jun 1887

Lot: 6A　Owner: Mrs. Mary Porter
Site 2　Mrs. Mary E. Porter　　　　　　　　　　　TS: Age 89-7-4
　　　　　　　　　　　　　　　Death: 4 Jul 1906　　Burial: 5 Jul 1906
Site 3　Miss Willie E. Porter　　　　　　　　　　TS: Age 42 yrs
　　　　　　　　　　　　　　　Death: 6 Apr 1883　　Burial: 8 Apr 1883

Lot: 7　Owner: William Thomas Poole
Site 1　Mabel Poole Warfield　　　　　　　　　　Place: Barnesville
　　　　Birth: 11 Apr 1895　　Death: 11 Mar 1941　Burial: 13 Mar 1941
　　　　Mort: W.B. Hilton　　　　TS: d/o A. & M. Poole
Site 2　Eleanor Leonard Poole　　　　　TS: w/o William T. Poole
　　　　Birth: 19 Nov 1831　　Death: 20 Oct 1891　Burial: 22 Oct 1891
Site 3　Algernon Poole　　　　illegible　　　　　s/o A. & M. Poole
　　　　Birth: 2 Dec 1891　　Death: 16 Mar 1892　Burial: 18 Mar 1892
Site 5　William Thomas Poole
　　　　Birth: 1 Nov 1830　　Death: 2 Mar 1884　　Burial: 5 Mar 1884
Site 12　Leonard Hays Poole
　　　　Birth: 1858　　　　　Death: 11 Feb 1912　Burial: 11 Feb 1912

Lot: 8　Owner: F.B. & S. Hempstone
Site　　Edward Alton Nichols　　　s/o Charles S. & Louise H. Nichols
　　　　Birth: 14 Feb 1869　　Death: 6 Mar 1869
Site 1　Daisy Louise Nichols　　　d/o Charles S. & Louise H. Nichols
　　　　Birth: 3 Jun 1886　　Death: 2 Apr 1902　　Burial: 4 Apr 1902
　　　　TS: Age 15-10-0

124 Monocacy Cemetery, Beallsville, Montgomery County, Maryland

Site 2 Charles S. Nichols   h/o Louise H. Nichols
       Birth: 29 Jun 1845   Death: 24 Feb 1907   Burial: 26 Feb 1907
Site 3 Louise H. Nichols   w/o Charles S. Nichols
       Birth: 1847   Death: 1908   Burial: 26 Feb 1908
Site 4 Flavius Braden Hempstone   Mort: W.T. Hilton & Sons   Place: New York
       Birth: 29 May 1850   Death: 17 Jun 1924   Burial: 18 Jun 1924
Site 5 Mary M. Hempstone   TS: Mother [of Samuel Harris Hempstone]
       Birth: 1813   Death: 8 Jul 1891   Burial: 11 Jun 1891
       TS: Death: 1892
Site 6 Samuel Harris Hempstone TS: Brother   s/o Mary M. Hempstone
       Birth: 1844   Death: 1888   Burial: 10 Mar 1886
Site 12 Snowden Lee Hempstone   Mort: W.T. Hilton & Sons   Place: Bardonia, NY
        Birth: 9 Jun 1852   Death: 3 Jan 1929   Burial: 5 Jan 1929

Lot: 9 Owner: Mrs. Leah Chiswell
Site 1 Elizabeth Ellen Chiswell   Place: Poolesville
       Birth: 23 Nov 1852   Death: 17 Jul 1951   Burial: 19 Jul 1951
       Mort: W.B. Hilton   On stone with Sarah P. Chiswell   Age 98
Site 2 Sarah P. Chiswell   Mort: Hilton & Hall   Place: Poolesville
       Birth: 10 Apr 1850   Death: 21 Jan 1921   Burial: 23 Jan 1921
Site 3 George Walter Chriswell
       Birth: 6 Mar 1819   Death: 10 Jun 1882   h/o Leah Griffith Chriswell
Site 4 Leah Griffith Chiswell   On stone with George Walter Chriswell
       Birth: 21 Mar 1826   Death: 1 Dec 1891   Burial: 2 Dec 1891
Site 5 Sarah Chiswell   Death: 20 Mar 1863
       TS: w/o William Chiswell, in her 76th yr
Site 6 William Chiswell   TS: Age 63-8-12
       Birth: 26 Jan 1783   Death: 8 Oct 1846
Site 10 Leah Griffith White   Mort: Thomas F. Murrey   Place: Washington, DC
        Birth: 1887   Death: 28 Oct 1938   Burial: 31 Oct 1938
Site 11 Lulu Helen Chiswell   TS: Age 60-9-15   Place: Washington, DC
        Birth: 12 Apr 1859   Death: 27 Jan 1920   Burial: 30 Jan 1920
        Mort: W.R. Pumphrey   w/o William Greenbury Chiswell
Site 12 William Greenbury Chiswell   TS: Age 55-10-14   h/o Lulu Helen Chriswell
        Birth: 13 Feb 1848   Death: 27 Dec 1903   Burial: 30 Dec 1903

Lot: 10 Owner: Mrs. E.J.C. & Thomas Oxley
Site 1 Viletter Oxley   w/o Edward Oxley
       Birth: 13 Sep 1824   Death: 10 Apr 1892   Burial: 1 Apr 1892
Site 2 Miss Louisa V. Oxley
       Birth: 28 Feb 1854   Death: 10 Jul 1894   Burial: 11 Jul 1894
Site 3 John E. Oxley
       Birth: 7 Nov 1846   Death: 10 Dec 1907   Burial: 13 Dec 1907
Site 4 Mary A. Oxley
       Birth: 26 Apr 1860   Death: 4 Mar 1905   Burial: 7 Mar 1905
Site 5 Emily J.C. Oxley   Death: 21 Jan 1887
       TS: w/o Thomas Oxley, in her 66th yr
Site 6 Thomas Oxley   TS: Age 72-24-0
                                   Death: 10 Apr 1889   Burial: 12 Apr 1889

Monocacy Cemetery, Beallsville, Montgomery County, Maryland

Site 8 Robert W. Oxley   Mort: Hilton & Hall   Place: Dickerson
        Birth: 16 Mar 1862   Death: 18 Sep 1939   Burial: 20 Sep 1939
Site 9 Elizabeth C. Oxley   Mort: Hilton & Hall   Place: Dickerson
        Birth: 5 Feb 1849   Death: 3 Apr 1919   Burial: 5 Apr 1919
Site 10 Sallie E. Oxley   Death: 1 Mar 1887
        TS: w/o Edgar F. Oxley, age 41-11-6
Site 11 Edgar F. Oxley   Place: Martinsburg
        Birth: 17 Nov 1844   Death: 20 Nov 1915   Burial: 22 Nov 1915
        Mort: Hilton & Hall   h/o Sallie E. Oxley

Lot: 11 Owner: Mrs. Margaret Smoot
Site 1 Harriet Ann Smoot   Place: Vienna, VA
        Birth: 1861   Death: 3 Jul 1955   Burial: 5 Jul 1955
        Mort: W.W. Chambers   On stone with Henry G. Smoot
Site 2 Henry G. Smoot   Mort: H.A. Sager   Place: Ryan, VA
        Birth: 1858   Death: 23 Oct 1918   Burial: 26 Oct 1918
Site 3 Margaret A. White Smoot   Place: Washington, DC
        Birth: 1830   Death: 25 Dec 1912   Burial: 27 Dec 1913
        Mort: Hilton & Hall   TS: w/o Robert W. Smoot
Site 4 Robert W. Smoot   h/o Margaret A. White Smoot
        Birth: 1823   Death: 9 Aug 1883   Burial: 11 Aug 1883
Site 8 Helen W. Fillebrown   w/o Robert Fillebrown
        Birth: 1910   Death: 20 May 1993   Burial: 24 May 1993
Site 9 Henry Clay Fillebrown   Death: 5 Sep 1904
        TS: s/o Thomas C. & Julia Fellebrown, age 0-1-10
Site 10 Thomas C. Fillebrown   Place: Washington, DC
        Birth: 1872   Death: 20 Aug 1936   Burial: 24 Aug 1936
        Mort: W.W. Chambers   h/o Julia M. Fillebrown
Site 11 Julia M. Fillebrown   Place: Washington, DC
        Birth: 11 Jan 1875   Death: 21 Jun 1940   Burial: 24 Jun 1940
        Mort: W.W. Chambers Co.   On stone with Thomas C. Fillebrown

Lot: 12 Owner: William L. Brunner
Site   Mrs. Della Trundle   Burial: 27 Jul 1895   No marker
Site 3 William L. Brunner   h/o Julia M. Brunner
        Birth: 10 Jul 1835   Death: 27 Nov 1906   Burial: 29 Nov 1906
Site 4 Julia A.M. Brunner   Place: Washington Grove
        Birth: 20 Feb 1841   Death: 17 Sep 1924   Burial: 20 Sep 1924
        Mort: W.T. Hilton & Sons   TS: w/o William L. Brunner
Site 5 George W. Brunner   TS: s/o William L. & Julia M. Brunner
        Birth: 26 Mar 1864   Death: 8 Apr 1889   Burial: 9 Apr 1889
Site 6 Malista C. Brunner   TS: d/o Wm. L. & Julia M. Brunner
        Birth: 1880   Death: 1886
Site 8 Jennings Bryan Phillips   Place: Barnesville
        Birth: 27 Mar 1900   Death: 9 Oct 1944   Burial: 12 Oct 1944
        Mort: W.B. Hilton   h/o Mary Brunner Phillips
Site 9 Malista C. Brunner   Place: Barnesville
        Birth: 1900   Death: 10 Aug 1918   Burial: 12 Aug 1918
        Mort: W.T. Hilton & Sons   TS: d/o A.E. & Catherine E. Brunner

Site 10 Americus E. Brunner　　　　　　　　　　　Place: State Sanitorium
　　　　Birth: 31 Dec 1861　　Death: 31 May 1937　　Burial: 3 Jun 1937
　　　　Mort: W.B. Hilton　　　　　　　　　　　　h/o Catherine E. Brunner
Site 11 Catherine E. Brunner　　　　　　　　　　　Place: Barnesville
　　　　Birth: 29 Oct 1877　　Death: 2 Jul 1917　　Burial: 4 Jul 1917
　　　　Mort: W.T. Hilton & Sons　　　　　　　　　TS: w/o Americus E. Brunner
Site 12 George William Brunner　　　　　　　　　　Place: State San., MD
　　　　Birth: 1899　　　　　Death: 19 Mar 1916　　Burial: 22 Mar 1916
　　　　Mort: Hilton & Hall　　　　　TS: s/o A.E. & Catherine E. Brunner

Lot: 13 Owner: John B. Byrd
Site 1 Mary Jane Byrd　　　　　　　　　　　　　　Place: Rockville
　　　　Birth: 1874　　　　　Death: 14 May 1953　　Burial: 17 May 1953
　　　　Mort: W.B. Hilton　　　　　　　　　　　　d/o John B. & Sallie T. Byrd
Site 2 Elsie May Byrd　　　　　　　　　　　　　　Place: Frederick
　　　　Birth: 1881　　　　　Death: 20 Aug 1949　　Burial: 23 Aug 1949
　　　　Mort: W.B. Hilton　　　　　　　　　　　　d/o John B. & Sallie T. Byrd
Site 3 Miss Annie Byrd　　　　　　　　　　　　　Place: Rockville
　　　　Birth: 1870　　　　　Death: 1 Mar 1923　　Burial: 4 Mar 1923
　　　　Mort: Hilton & Hall　　　　　　　　　　　d/o John B. & Sallie T. Byrd
Site 4 John B. Byrd Jr.　　　　　　　　　　　　　Place: Dawsonville
　　　　Birth: 1877　　　　　Death: 15 May 1916　　Burial: 19 May 1916
　　　　Mort: Hilton & Hall　　　　　　　　　　　s/o John B. & Sallie T. Byrd
Site 5 Miss Clara Byrd　　　　　　　　　　　　　On stone with John B. Byrd, Jr.
　　　　Birth: 5 Aug 1868　　Death: 13 Jan 1903　　Burial: 15 Jan 1903
Site 6 William L. Byrd
　　　　Birth: 1884　　　　　Death: 1884　　　　　TS: Infant
Site 7 Elizabeth (Betty) Byrd Milford　　　　　　Mort: W.B. Hilton
　　　　Birth: 1872　　　　　Death: 28 Dec 1955　　Burial: 30 Dec 1955
　　　　w/o Dr. S.B. Milford, d/o John B. & Sallie T. Byrd　　Place: Rockville
Site 8 George W. Byrd　　　　　　　　　　　　　　Place: Dawsonville
　　　　Birth: 1866　　　　　Death: 11 May 1936　　Burial: 13 May 1936
　　　　Mort: Wm. Hilton　　　　　　　　　　　　　s/o John B. & Sallie T. Byrd
Site 9 Samuel D. Byrd　　　　　　　　　　　　　　Place: Frederick
　　　　Birth: 1863　　　　　Death: 21 Jul 1926　　Burial: 23 Jul 1926
　　　　Mort: Hilton & Hall　　　　　　　　　　　s/o John B. & Sallie T. Byrd
Site 10 Sallie T. Veirs Byrd　　TS: Mother　　　　Place: Dawsonville
　　　　Birth: 1845　　　　　Death: 6 Aug 1916　　Burial: 8 Aug 1916
　　　　Mort: Hilton & Hall　　　　　　　　　　　On stone with John B. Byrd
Site 11 John B. Byrd　　　　　TS: Father　　　　　h/o Sallie T. Byrd
　　　　Birth: 4 Oct 1829　　Death: 24 Oct 1904　　Burial: 25 Oct 1904

Lot: 14 Owner: Charles M. Williams
Site 　Child of Charles M. Williams　No marker　　Burial: 11 Aug 1883
Site 　Child of Charles M. Williams　No marker　　Burial: 3 Jun 1879
Site 2 Dorsey Waters Williams　　　　　　　　　　Place: Frederick, MD
　　　　Birth: 9 Aug 1880　　Death: 1 Jun 1971　　Burial: 3 Jun 1971
　　　　Mort: Wm. Hilton　　　s/o Charles McGill & Jane Waters Williams

Site 3 Charles McGill Williams   Place: Poolesville
        Birth: 9 Oct 1852   Death: 16 Jan 1924   Burial: 18 Jan 1924
        Mort: Hilton & Hall   h/o Jane Waters Williams
Site 4 Prudence Jane Waters Williams   Place: Poolesville
        Birth: 6 Sep 1853   Death: 27 Jan 1923   Burial: 29 Jan 1923
        Mort: Hilton & Hall   w/o Charles McGill Williams
Site 5 Emily Howard Williams   d/o C.M. & J.W. Williams, age 2 mo
        illegible   Death: 2 Jun 1877   Burial: 3 Jun 1877
Site 6 Emily Howard Waters   TS: w/o H.W. Dorsey Waters
        Birth: 6 Dec 1818   Death: 1 Oct 1903
Site 7 Arthur White Williams   s/o Charles M. & Jane Water Williams
        Birth: 28 Sep 1892   Death: 21 Sep 1976   Burial: 23 Sep 1976
Site 9 Emily Byron Williams Oxley   w/o Thomas Cummings Oxley
        Birth: 9 Dec 1889   Death: 15 Mar 1981   Burial: 18 Mar 1981
Site 10 Thomas Cummings Oxley   h/o Emily Williams Oxley
        Birth: 7 Jan 1889   Death: 13 Dec 1980   Burial: 17 Dec 1980

Lot: 15   Owner: J. Thomas Chiswell
Site 3 Joseph Thomas Chiswell Jr.   Place: Dawsonville
        Birth: 9 Jun 1849   Death: 24 Mar 1931   Burial: 26 Mar 1931
        Mort: Hilton & Hall   h/o Caroline Hilleary Chiswell
Site 4 Caroline Hilleary White Chiswell   Place: Poolesville
        Birth: 5 Jan 1850   Death: 26 Jan 1919   Burial: 28 Jan 1919
        Mort: Hilton & Hall   TS: w/o Joseph Thomas Chiswell, Jr.
Site 5 Sallie D. Chiswell   Death: 26 Nov 1884   Burial: 27 Nov 1884
        d/o Thomas & Caroline Hilleary Chiswell, age 21 days   No marker
Site 6 Maggie M. Chiswell   Death: 18 Oct 1883   Burial: 19 Sep 1883
        TS: d/o Thomas & Caroline Hilleary Chiswell, age 12 days
Site 7 Elizabeth Goldsmith Burke No marker   Place: Camp Hill, PA
        Birth: 28 Mar 1882   Death: 24 Nov 1922   Burial: 26 Nov 1922
        Mort: W.T. Hilton & Sons   w/o Thomas Hilleary Chiswell
Site 8 Thomas Hilleary Chiswell No marker   Place: St. Pertersburg, FL
        Birth: 19 Dec 1880   Death: 28 Oct 1954   Burial: 13 Nov 1954
        Mort: John S. Rhodes   h/o Elizabeth Burke Chiswell

Lot: 16   Owner: Martin U. & Edward White
Site 1 Laura A. White   Death: 7 Sep 1890
        TS: [2nd] w/o J.T. White, age 29-9-11
Site 3 Anna F. White   Death: 18 Jul 1887   Burial: 20 Jul 1885
        TS: [1st] w/o Joseph T. White, age 35-6-24
Site 4 Ida D. White   Birth: 7 May 1877   Death: 15 Apr 1886
Site 5 Emma F. White   Birth: 10 Nov 1883   Death: 30 Nov 1885
Site 6 Robert N. White   s/o Joseph T. White   TS: Age 10 days
                                 Death: 18 Jul 1882   Burial: 19 Jul 1882
Site 12 Joseph Thomas White   No marker   Burial: 14 Aug 1904
        s/o Joseph T. & Margaret White
Site 16 Joseph T. White   Place: Washington, DC
        Birth: 1854   Death: 11 Jun 1927   Burial: 14 Jun 1927
        Mort: M.K. Zerkle   h/o Laura A. White

Lot: 19 Owner: James M. Dawson
- Site   James M. Dawson Jr.   Birth: 2 Dec 1871   Death: 12 Dec 1871
- Site   James P. Dawson   Birth: 18 Mar 1858   Death: 31 Oct 1863
- Site 2 Virginia O. Dawson   No marker   Place: Springfield Hospital
                                  Death: 12 Sep 1955   Burial: 14 Sep 1955
- Site 3 Mary E. Dawson   Mort: Hilton & Hall   Place: Ardmore, OK
          Birth: 1860   Death: 8 Jul 1913   Burial: 12 Jul 1913
- Site 4 Mrs. Louisa V. Dawson
          Birth: 5 Apr 1829   Death: 23 Nov 1906   Burial: 25 Nov 1906
- Site 5 James M. Dawson Jr.   h/o Louisa Hepburn Dawson
          Birth: 13 Sep 1812   Death: 1 Aug 1888   Burial: 12 Aug 1888

Lot: 20 Owner: George R. Hays
- Site 2 Mary Emma Wiggins
          Birth: 15 Jan 1868   Death: 3 Feb 1913   Burial: 6 Feb 1913
          w/o Joseph St. Clair Wiggins, d/o G.R. & Sarah A. Hays
- Site 3 Sarah A. Hays   w/o George R. Hays
          Birth: 1830   Death: 1894   Burial: 17 Jan 1894
- Site 4 George R. Hays   h/o Sarah A. Hays
          Birth: 1827   Death: 1888   Burial: 14 Nov 1888
- Site 5 Otho T. Hays
          Birth: 1861   Death: 1884   Burial: 5 Apr 1884
- Site 9 Samuel Edward Hays   Mort: A.K. Coffman   Place: Indian Springs
          Birth: 1873   Death: 6 Sep 1932   Burial: 8 Sep 1932
- Site 10 Sarah Ida Hays   Mort: A.K. Coffman   Place: Hagerstown
          Birth: 1863   Death: 26 Apr 1927   Burial: 29 Apr 1927

Lot: 21 Owner: M.Thomas Pyles
- Site 1 Sarah Ellen (Nellie) Brewer Pyles   On stone with Joseph Brunner Pyles
          Birth: 9 Jun 1880   Death: 1 Nov 1981   Burial: 4 Nov 1981
- Site 2 Joseph Brunner Pyles   Place: Frederick
          Birth: 27 Jan 1877   Death: 26 Sep 1948   Burial: 28 Sep 1948
          Mort: W.B. Hilton   h/o Nellie Brewer Pyles
- Site 3 Ann Elizabeth (Bettie) Williams Pyles   TS: [1st] w/o Michael Thomas Pyles
          Birth: 20 Jun 1849   Death: 25 Mar 1887
- Site 4 Michael Thomas Pyles
          Birth: 6 Mar 1843   Death: 10 Oct 1907   Burial: 13 Oct 1907
          h/o Ann Elizabeth (Bettie) Williams Pyles & Mary Florence Williams Pyles
- Site 5 Mary Florence Williams Pyles   Place: Poolesville
          Birth: 2 Nov 1838   Death: 30 May 1924   Burial: 1 Jun 1924
          Mort: Hilton & Hall   TS: [2nd] w/o Michael Thomas Pyles
- Site 6 Edwin Pyles   Mort: Hilton & Hall   Place: Dawsonville
          Birth: 16 Apr 1850   Death: 1 Sep 1920   Burial: 3 Sep 1920
- Site 9 Emma Williams Pyles   Place: Rockville, MD
          Birth: 7 Jan 1879   Death: 11 Nov 1967   Burial: 14 Nov 1967
          Mort: Hilton   w/o Walter Williams Pyles

Site 10 Walter Williams Pyles   Place: Poolesville
         Birth: 2 Jul 1878   Death: 5 Jul 1934   Burial: 8 Jul 1934
         Mort: Hilton & Hall   h/o Emma Talbott Williams Pyles
Site 11 Beatrice Howard Pyles   w/o Thomas W. Pyles
         Birth: 22 May 1921   Death: 9 Dec 1978   Burial: 15 Dec 1978
Site 12 Thomas Walter Pyles   h/o Beatrice Howard Pyles & Mary Haskell Downs
         Birth: 20 Apr 1917   Death: 11 Aug 1991   Burial: 14 Aug 1991

Lot: 22 Owner: Arthur Williams
Site 3 John T. Williams   h/o Sarah (Sadie) Newton Cissell
         Birth: 21 Jan 1884   Death: 20 May 1972   Burial: 24 May 1972
Site 4 James Dawson Williams   Mort: W.R. Pumphrey   Place: Kensington
         Birth: 28 Oct 1882   Death: 16 Oct 1918   Burial: 18 Oct 1918
Site 5 Annie E. Dawson Williams   Place: Kensington
         Birth: 21 Dec 1856   Death: 14 May 1934   Burial: 16 May 1934
         Mort: W.R. Pumphrey   w/o Arthur Williams
Site 6 Arthur Williams   Place: Kensington
         Birth: 21 Sep 1853   Death: 15 Mar 1923   Burial: 18 Mar 1923
         Mort: W.R. Pumphrey   h/o Annie Elizabeth Dawson Williams
Site 9 Julia Elizabeth Williams   Place: Olney
         Birth: 5 Dec 1907   Death: 31 Dec 1934   Burial: 2 Jan 1935
         Mort: W.R. Pumphrey   d/o John T. & Sadie Cissell Williams
Site 10 Sarah (Sadie) Newton Cissell Williams   Place: Beallsville
         Birth: 18 Dec 1884   Death: 22 Dec 1946   Burial: 24 Dec 1946
         Mort: W.R. Pumphrey   w/o John Thomas Williams

Lot: 23 Owner: Americus Dawson
Site 1 James H. Jones   Place: Rockville
         Birth: 14 Aug 1848   Death: 12 Aug 1924   Burial: 14 Jul 1924
         Mort: W.R. Pumphrey   h/o Katie Barbee Jones
Site 2 Katie Barbee Jones   Place: Fairfax, VA
         Birth: 8 Oct 1864   Death: 19 Aug 1948   Burial: 21 Aug 1948
         Mort: W.R. Pumphrey   On stone with James H. Jones
Site 4 Rachael White Trundle Dawson   TS: w/o Americus Dawson
         Birth: 20 Jan 1840   Death: 21 Apr 1910   Burial: 24 Apr 1910
Site 5 Americus Dawson   Death: 5 Jun 1891   Burial: 8 Jun 1891
         h/o Rachael White Trundle Dawson   TS: Age 71-5-16
Site 7 A. Dawson Jones   illegible   s/o J.H. & K.B. Jones, no marker
         Birth: 1 Apr 1889   Death: 17 Oct 1880   Burial: 19 Oct 1889
Site 8 Kirtley Jones   Place: Baton Rouge, LA
         Birth: 21 Aug 1893   Death: 20 Jul 1931   Burial: 24 Jul 1931
         Mort: Warner E. Pumphrey   s/o James H. & Katie Barbee Jones

Lot: 24 Owner: Robert Sellman
Site 1 Ruth Sellman   TS: Age 75-3-0
         Birth: 9 Dec 1780   Death: 9 Mar 1862   Burial: 2 Aug 1884
Site 2 William M. Sellman   TS: Age 71-11-0 h/o Ruth Sellman, Reinterment
         Birth: 1 Feb 1786   Death: 31 Dec 1857   Burial: 2 Aug 1884

Lot: 25 Lower   Owner: Henry Rinehart
- Site   Mrs. Henry Rinehart   Burial: 27 Feb 1889   No marker
- Site   Henry Rinehart   Burial: 27 Aug 1890   No marker

Lot: 25 Upper   Owner: R.W. Holland
- Site 1   Horatio Trundle   No marker   Mort: W.T. Hilton & Sons
  Place: Dickerson   Death: 19 Sep 1925   Burial: 22 Sep 1925
- Site 2   Richard Waters Holland
  Birth: 27 Apr 1819   Death: 26 Feb 1898   Burial: 28 Feb 1898
- Site 3   John W. Holland   Place: Dickerson
  Birth: 1840   Death: 18 Nov 1922   Burial: 21 Nov 1922
  Mort: W.T. Hilton & Sons   h/o Emily Ann Trundle Holland
- Site 4   Emily A. Holland   Place: Dickerson
  Birth: 1847   Death: 30 Nov 1916   Burial: 2 Dec 1916
  Mort: A.G. Carlisle   On stone with John W. Holland & C. Ernest Holland
- Site 6   C. Ernest Holland   Mort: A.G. Carlisle   Place: Dickerson
  Birth: 1872   Death: 16 Sep 1917   Burial: 19 Sep 1917
- Site 6   James B. Holland   No marker   Mort: Chambers
  Place: Washington, DC   Death: 26 Dec 1956   Burial: 28 Dec 1956

Lot: 26   Owner: James T. Trundle
- Site 1   Clara I. Trundle   d/o Perry L.T. Trundle   Reinterment
  Birth: Sep 1855   Death: 2 Feb 1859   Burial: 29 Jun 1896
- Site 2   Anna Virginia Trundle   d/o Perry L.T. Trundle   Reinterment
  Birth: 5 Oct 1839   Death: 30 Apr 1844   Burial: 29 Jun 1896
- Site 3   Barbara E. Trundle   w/o Perry L.T. Trundle   Reinterment
  Birth: 9 Nov 1816   Death: 11 Jun 1884   Burial: 29 Jun 1896
- Site 4   Perry L.J. Trundle   h/o Barbara Dawson Trundle   Reinterment
  Birth: 8 Mar 1817   Death: 13 Feb 1881   Burial: 29 Jun 1896
- Site 9   Miss Ella H. Bouic
  Birth: 8 Oct 1876   Death: 14 Aug 1900   Burial: 16 Aug 1900
- Site 10   Susan E. Bouic   w/o John P. Bouic
  Birth: 10 Apr 1849   Death: 5 Apr 1900   Burial: 6 Apr 1900
- Site 11   John Peter Bouic   h/o Susan E. Bouic
  Birth: 23 Jan 1825   Death: 6 Nov 1895   Burial: 8 Nov 1895
- Site 12   Lelia May Bouic   TS: d/o John Peter & Susan E. Bouic
  Birth: 5 May 1878   Death: 21 Feb 1891   Burial: 24 Feb 1891

Lot: 27   Owner: Charles M. Butler
- Site 1   Elspet Garen Butler   Mort: Hilton
  Place: Kensington   Death: 14 Oct 1959   Burial: 17 Oct 1959
  w/o Richard Butler   No marker
- Site 3   Margaret E. Trundle   Place: Dickerson
  Birth: 2 Aug 1848   Death: 5 Jul 1913   Burial: 7 Jul 1913
  Mort: Hilton & Hall   TS: w/o Robertus Trundle
- Site 4   Robertus Trundle   h/o Margaret E. Trundle
  Birth: 12 Sep 1845   Death: 15 Apr 1889   Burial: 17 Apr 1889
- Site 4   Mamie E. Trundle   TS: d/o Robertus & Mary E. Trundle
  Birth: 29 Nov 1871   Death: 27 Jul 1872

Monocacy Cemetery, Beallsville, Montgomery County, Maryland   131

Site 6 George W. Butler
 Birth: 1844   Death: 1890   TS: CSA
         Burial: 15 Jan 1890
Site 8 Kathleen Mable Butler   Place: Washington, DC
 Birth: 20 Aug 1907   Death: 31 Jan 1928   Burial: 2 Feb 1928
 Mort: W.R. Pumphrey   TS: d/o Richard T. & Emma Reese Butler
Site 9 Emma Reese Butler   Mort: Waner E.
 Place: Silver Spring   Death: 9 Jan 1930   Burial: 11 Jan 1930
 2nd w/o Richard T. Butler   No marker
Site 10 Richard T. Butler   Mort: Robert A.
 Place: Potomac   Death: 11 Jan 1952   Burial: 14 Jan 1952
 h/o Emma Reese Butler, age 82   No marker
Site 11 Rosa E. Butler   TS: [1st] w/o Richard T. Butler
 Birth: 23 Jul 1870   Death: 19 Dec 1903   Burial: 22 Dec 1903

Lot: 28 Lower   Owner: William G. McKeever & John E. Darby
Site 3 Gertrude Hyatt Darby   w/o John Edwin Darby
 Birth: 9 Feb 1876   Death: 25 Mar 1972   Burial: 28 Mar 1972
Site 4 John Edwin Darby   h/o Gertrude H. Darby
 Birth: 17 Sep 1884   Death: 1 Aug 1975   Burial: 4 Aug 1975
Site 5 Antionette Darby McKeever   w/o William Galen McKeever
 Birth: 8 Sep 1908   Death: 1 Jul 1975   Burial: 9 Jul 1975
Site 6 William Galen McKeever   h/o Antionette Darby McKeever
 Birth: 22 Oct 1900   Death: 8 Nov 1986   Burial: 12 Nov 1986

Lot: 28 Upper   Owner: Mrs. Maude Waters
Site 1 Maria Elizabeth Lorain Waters Mort: Gartner Place: Gaithersburg, MD
 Birth: 8 Oct 1895   Death: 19 Dec 1970   Burial: 22 Dec 1970
Site 3 Maud Estelle Getzendanner Waters   Place: Gaithersburg
 Birth: 4 Apr 1868   Death: 28 Dec 1930   Burial: 31 Dec 1930
 Mort: E.C. Gartner   TS: w/o Charles Clark Waters
Site 4 Charles Clark Waters Mort: Ernest C. Gartner Place: Gaithersburg
 Birth: 2 Jul 1866   Death: 31 Jan 1934   Burial: 3 Feb 1934
 TS: s/o William A. Waters, MD   h/o Maude Estelle Getzendanner Waters
Site 6 Dr. Joseph T. Getzendanner TS: Age 58-4-15 Moved from Frostburg
 Birth: 4 May 1817   Death: 19 Sep 1875   Burial: 6 Dec 1897
Site 6 Mary Jane Getzendanner   TS: w/o Dr. Joseph T. Getzendanner
 Birth: 21 Aug 1844   Death: 19 Sep 1907   Burial: 21 Jun 1901

Lot: 29   Owner: Thomas Rawlins
Site 1 Miss Margaret C. Rawlins   TS: d/o Joshua H. & Laura L. Rawlins
 Birth: 12 Sep 1876   Death: 8 Oct 1907   Burial: 12 Oct 1907
Site 2 Laura Lee Rawlins   TS: w/o Joshua H. Rawlins
 Birth: 3 Dec 1848   Death: 9 Mar 1910
Site 3 Joshua H. Rawlins   Place: Redland
 Birth: 1847   Death: 13 Feb 1918   Burial: 15 Feb 1918
 Mort: A.G. Carlisle   h/o Laura Lee Rawlins
Site 4 C. Jane Rawlins   TS: Age 73-1-16   Mort: W.R. Pumphrey
 Place: Redland   Death: 18 Aug 1917   Burial: 20 Aug 1917

Monocacy Cemetery, Beallsville, Montgomery County, Maryland

Site 5	Thomas Rawlins		TS: Age 87-5-20
		Death: 20 Aug 1891	Burial: 28 Aug 1891
Site 6	Jane R. Rawlins		On stone with Thomas Rawlins
		Death: 15 Oct 1848	Age 38-7-29
Site 7	Ellen R. Higgins	No marker	Mort: Hilton
	Place: PA	Death: 19 Jun 1967	Burial: 22 Jun 1967
Site 7	Joseph R. Higgins	No marker	Mort: Hilton
	Place: PA	Death: 19 Jun 1967	Burial: 22 Jun 1967
Site 8	Rose Clagett Wright		TS: d/o Rush L. & Rachael E. Wright
	Birth: 23 Jul 1911	Death: 29 Oct 1912	Burial: 31 Oct 1912
Site 9	Rachel Ella Wright		Place: Gaithersburg
	Birth: 15 Aug 1874	Death: 8 Feb 1942	Burial: 12 Feb 1942
	Mort: Roy W. Barber		TS: w/o Rush L. Wright
Site 10	Rush Lee Wright		Place: Dallas, TX
	Birth: 6 Jan 1870	Death: 30 Jul 1956	Burial: 4 Aug 1956
	Mort: Allan D. Compbell Sr.		h/o Rachael Ella Wright

Lot: 30   Owner: John W. Darby Jr.

Site 1	Baby Darby	illegible	Burial: 30 Sep 1891
	c/o John W. Darby Jr. & Virginia L. Darby		
Site 2	Infant Ward		Place: Montgomery County Hospital
	Birth: 1924	Death: 27 May 1924	Burial: 28 May 1924
	Cause: Stillborn	Mort: William H. Ward	
	TS: s/o William H. & Virginia Darby Ward		
Site 3	Virginia L. Darby		Place: Gaithersburg
	Birth: 25 Jun 1865	Death: 23 Feb 1914	Burial: 25 Feb 1914
	Mort: A.G. Carlisle		TS: w/o John W. Darby Jr.
Site 4	John W. Darby Jr.		h/o Virginia L. Darby
	Birth: 20 May 1859	Death: 19 Nov 1910	Burial: 22 Nov 1910
Site 5	Virginia Darby Ward		On stone with William H. Ward
	Birth: 29 Apr 1893	Death: 4 Jun 1973	Burial: 6 Jun 1973
Site 6	William Harrison Ward		h/o Virginia Darby Ward
	Birth: 17 Feb 1898	Death: 29 Feb 1980	Burial: 4 Mar 1980

Lot: 31   Owner: Spahr Bros

Site	Miss Isabel Spahr	Burial: 11 Apr 1902	No marker
Site	Mr. M. R. Spahr	Burial: 13 Mar 1896	No marker

Lot: 32   Owner: Charles Larman

Site	Charles A. Larman	No marker	Mort: M.R. Etchison &
	Place: Frederick	Death: 24 Feb 1934	Burial: 26 Feb 1934
Site	Child of Edward Larman	Burial: 29 Mar 1906	No marker
Site	James R. Larman	No marker	Mort: W.T. Hilton & Sons
	Place: Boyds	Death: 12 Dec 1929	Burial: 14 Dec 1929
Site	John W. Larman	No marker	Mort: Hilton & Hall
	Place: Washington, DC	Death: 21 Jul 1916	Burial: 23 Jul 1916
Site 5	Mary A. Larman		TS: w/o Charles Larman, age 66-10-4
		Death: 3 Jan 1902	Burial: 5 Jan 1902

Monocacy Cemetery, Beallsville, Montgomery County, Maryland   133

```
Site 6   Charles Larman                              h/o Mary A. Larman, age 67 yrs
                                   Death: 2 Jan 1892
Site 7   Infant of George Larman   No marker         Mort: W.T. Hilton & Sons
         Place: Barnesville        Death: 3 Feb 1914 Burial: 5 Feb 1914
Site 9   Bessie Violet Larman      No marker         Mort: Hilton
         Place: Boyds              Death: 19 Oct 1962 Burial: 22 Oct 1962
Site 10  George F. Larman          No marker         Mort: W.B. Hilton
         Place: Frederick          Death: 14 Feb 1943 Burial: 16 Feb 1943
Site 11  Benjamin H. Larman        No marker         Mort: Wm. Hilton
         Place: Bethesda, MD       Death: 26 Mar 1969 Burial: 29 Mar 1969
```

Lot: 33 Lower   Owner: Mrs. J.J. Umstead
```
Site 3   Sallie E. White Umstead                     Place: Frederick
         Birth: 10 Jul 1880        Death: 11 Nov 1966 Burial: 13 Nov 1966
         Mort: M.R. Etchison                         w/o John J. Umstead
Site 4   John J. Umstead                             Place: Dickerson
         Birth: 29 Jan 1872        Death: 17 Mar 1941 Burial: 19 Mar 1941
         Mort: W.B. Hilton                           h/o Sallie E. Umstead
Site 5   Frances Ella Umstead      Mort: W.B. Hilton Place: Bethesda
         Birth: 23 Aug 1868        Death: 26 Feb 1945 Burial: 28 Feb 1945
```

Lot: 33 Upper   Owner: C.C. Creger
```
Site     Baby Boy Shry             No marker         Mort: J.B. Beall
         Place: Olney              Death: 4 Sep 1934 Burial: 5 Sep 1934
Site 2   Lettie Argirtha Creger    Mort: Hilton & Hall Place: Laytonsville
         Birth: 17 May 1898        Death: 24 Mar 1925 Burial: 25 Mar 1925
Site 3   Margaret R. L. Creger     TS: w/o Charles C. Creger  Mort: Hilton & Hall
         Place: Martinsburg        Death: 21 May 1923 Burial: 22 May 1923
Site 4   Charles C. Creger                           Place: Thurmont
         Birth: 3 May 1878         Death: 6 Aug 1944 Burial: 9 Aug 1944
         Mort: M.J. Creager & Son                    h/o Margaret L. Creger
Site 5   Floyd Bascum Creger                         Place: Olney, MD
         Birth: 31 Dec 1901        Death: 9 Jan 1971 Burial: 12 Jan 1971
         Mort: Gartner                               h/o Margie A. Creger
Site 6   Margie A. Creger                            On stone with Floyd B. Creger
         Birth: 17 Jun 1911        Death: 26 Jan 1995 Burial: 30 Jan 1995
```

Lot: 34 Lower   Owner: Thomas H. Carter
```
Site 3   Carrie Virginia Carter                      Place: Frederick
         Birth: 3 Dec 1884         Death: 3 Jan 1942 Burial: 6 Jan 1942
         Mort: M.R. Etchison & Son              On stone with Thomas H. Carter
Site 4   Thomas H. Carter                            Place: Frederick, MD
         Birth: 23 Jan 1881        Death: 27 Aug 1967 Burial: 30 Aug 1967
         Mort: Etchison                              h/o Carrie V. Carter
Site 5   Maude M. Carter                             Mort: Feete Funeral Home
         Place: Frederick, MD      Death: 24 Sep 1968 Burial: 27 Sep 1968
         w/o Thomas H. Carter, d/o John William & Cora Hawes     No marker
```

Lot: 34 Upper Owner: Notley H. & Mary B. Davis

Site 1 John Dutrow Linthicum
Birth: 1881 Death: 8 Aug 1953
Mort: W.L. Burdette
Place: Dickerson
Burial: 11 Aug 1953
h/o Leona Davis Linthicum

Site 2 Leona May D. Linthicum
Birth: 1885 Death: 9 Oct 1960
Mort: M.R. Etchison
Place: Poolesville
Burial: 11 Oct 1960
On stone with John Dutrow Linthicum

Site 3 Harriet A. Hays Davis
Birth: 22 Apr 1861 Death: 22 Apr 1925
Mort: W.T. Hilton & Sons
Place: Adamstown
Burial: 25 Sep 1925
TS: w/o John Wallace Davis

Site 4 John Wallace Davis
Birth: 17 Aug 1854 Death: 6 Aug 1933
Mort: Hilton & Price
Place: Adamstown
Burial: 8 Aug 1933
h/o Harriet A. Hays Davis

Site 5 Mary Brosius Davis
Birth: 23 Mar 1886 Death: 19 Apr 1968
Mort: W.M. Hilton
Place: Olney, MD
Burial: 22 Apr 1968
On stone with Notley Hays Davis

Site 6 Notley Hays Davis
Birth: 1883 Death: 1 Jun 1953
Mort: W.B. Hilton
Place: Barnesville
Burial: 4 Jun 1953
h/o Mary Brosius Davis

Lot: 35 Upper Owner: Mrs. William J. Brosius

Site 3 Louise D. Brosius
Birth: 1886 Death: 19 Oct 1968
Mort: Wm. Hilton
Place: Frederick, MD
Burial: 21 Oct 1968
On stone with J. William Brosius

Site 4 John William Brosius
Birth: 14 Nov 1884 Death: 18 Jun 1945
Mort: W.B. Hilton
Place: Winchester
Burial: 21 Jun 1945
h/o Louise D. Brosius

Lot: 36 Lower Owner: Lottie M. McGovern

Site 37 Anna L. McGovern
Birth: 30 Nov 1903 Death: 4 Mar 1980
No marker
Burial: 6 Mar 1980

Lot: 36 Upper Owner: Douglas & Grace Horine

Site 2 Douglas Edwin Horine
Birth: 21 Nov 1911 Death: 13 May 1982
h/o Grace Umstead Horine
Burial: 17 May 1982

Site 3 Bessie E. Horine
Birth: 8 Oct 1889 Death: 28 Jul 1945
Mort: W.B. Hilton
Place: Frederick Hospital
Burial: 31 Jul 1945
w/o John Phillip Horine

Site 4 John Philip Horine
Birth: 24 Jan 1889 Death: 7 Jun 1968
Mort: W. Hilton
Place: Bethesda, MD
Burial: 10 Jun 1968
h/o Bessie E. Horine

Lot: 37 Lower Owner: Whorton & Shreve

Site 3 Earl Thomas Shreve
Birth: 15 Nov 1909 Death: 16 Dec 1965
Mort: Hilton
Place: Baltimore
Burial: 18 Dec 1965
h/o Virginia F. Shreve

Site 4 Edna Louise Shreve Whorton
Birth: 29 Mar 1907 Death: 7 Nov 1983
w/o Bradford Whorton
Burial: 11 Nov 1983

Monocacy Cemetery, Beallsville, Montgomery County, Maryland   135

Site 5 Bradford Whorton   h/o Edna L. Shreve Whorton Place: Takoma Park
        Birth: 30 Apr 1900   Death: 30 May 1966   Burial: 3 Jun 1966

Lot: 38 Lower   Owner: Ralph A. Gilchrist
Site 3 Eleanor Waters Gilchrist   Mort: Robert A. Pumphrey Place: Washington, DC
        Birth: 1893   Death: 5 Apr 1951   Burial: 7 Apr 1951
Site 4 Ralph Alexander Gilchrist   h/o Eleanor Waters Gilchrist
        Birth: 1896   Death: Mar 1983   Burial: 5 Mar 1983

Lot: 38 Upper   Owner: Miscellaneous
Site 2 James G. Titus   Place: Bethesda, MD
        Birth: 12 Dec 1914   Death: 17 Apr 1967   Burial: 20 Apr 1967
        Mort: Hilton   h/o Elizabeth Jarrels Titus Watkins
Site 3 Robert Alexander Bobb   s/o Mrs. Jesse M. Lane
        Birth: 1 Mar 1952   Death: 23 Aug 1979   Burial: 28 Aug 1979
Site 4 Jesse Melvin Lane   Mort: Hilton   Place: Bethesda
        Birth: 1909   Death: 2 Sep 1966   Burial: 5 Sep 1966
Site 5 Leona F. Wolfrey   Place: Rockville, MD
        Birth: 19 Oct 1889   Death: 29 May 1970   Burial: 2 Jun 1970
        Mort: R. Pumphrey   On stone with Bert B. Wolfrey
Site 6 Bert B. Wolfrey   Place: Bethesda
        Birth: 1 Jan 1899   Death: 24 Mar 1967   Burial: 29 Mar 1967
        Mort: Pumphrey   h/o Leona F. Wolfrey

Lot: 39 Upper   Owner: Ralph A. Gilchrist
Site 1 Samuel Dever Waters   Mort: R.A. Pumphrey   Place: Washington, DC
        Birth: 1891   Death: 10 Sep 1964   Burial: 10 Oct 1964

Lot: 40   Owner: Miscellaneous
Site 1 Thomas Matthew King   h/o Mary Magaline King
        Birth: 27 Jun 1908   Death: 19 Dec 1978   Burial: 22 Dec 1978
Site 2 Mary Magaline Burriss King   On stone with Thomas Matthew King
        Birth: 30 Mar 1906   Death: 19 Aug 1989   Burial: 29 Aug 1989
Site 3 Irene V. Orme   On stone with Charles M. Orme
        Birth: 1898   Death: 2 Aug 1985   Burial: 6 Aug 1985
Site 4 Charles M. Orme   Mort: Molesworth   Place: Frederick, MD
        Birth: 7 Mar 1892   Death: 14 Jul 1970   Burial: 17 Jul 1970
        h/o Irene Orme   TS: MD PFC Co. A 304 Supply Tn WWI
Site 5 Wallace Muir   Place: Boyds, MD   Mort: Wm. Hilton
        Birth: 30 Oct 1906   Death: 5 Apr 1968   Burial: 8 Apr 1968
Site 6 Dorothy Troth Muir   w/o Wallace Muir
        Birth: 31 Jul 1905   Death: 6 Jun 1988   Burial: 10 Jun 1988

Lot: 41 Upper   Owner: Maurice Waters & Jean Knox Chiswell
Site 4 Maurice Waters Chiswell   h/o Jean Knox Chiswell
        Birth: 28 May 1927   Death: 23 Feb 1993   Burial: 1 Mar 1993

Row F North

Lot: 1 Owner: Howard Griffith, Jr
Site   Infant Clark   Mort: Warner E.
        Place: Washington, DC   Death: 9 Jul 1931   Burial: 9 Jul 1931
        i/o Morrison & Blanche Griffith Clark   No marker
Site 3 Lutie Brewer Griffith   TS: [1st] w/o Howard Griffith
        Birth: 19 Aug 1876   Death: 20 Feb 1904 Burial: 22 Feb 1904
Site 4 Howard Griffith   Place: Warmer E. Pumphrey
        Birth: 22 Jun 1878   Death: 27 Dec 1942 Burial: 29 Dec 1942
        h/o Luttie Brewer Griffith & Elizabeth Perry Griffith
Site 5 Elizabeth Perry Griffith   Place: Bethesda
        Birth: 17 Feb 1879   Death: 10 Dec 1959 Burial: 12 Dec 1959
        Mort. Robert A. Pumphrey   TS: [2nd] w/o Howard Griffith Jr.
Site 7 Estelle Perry Lee   Mort: W.R. Pumphrey Place: Bethesda
        Birth: 14 Aug 1871   Death: 7 Jan 1949   Burial: 9 Jan 1949
Site 10 Thomas Perry Griffith
        Birth: 27 Jul 1913   Death: 7 Apr 1986   Burial: 10 Apr 1986
Site 11 Charles Howard Griffith   On stone with Gustava Lamond Griffith
        Birth: 30 Aug 1907   Death: 19 Feb 1997 Burial: 22 Feb 1997

Lot: 2 Owner: Mrs. Baker Nicholson
Site 2 Franklin B. Nicholson   Mort: W.T. Hilton & Sons Place: Atlantic City
        Birth: 7 Mar 1893   Death: 15 Sep 1915 Burial: 18 Sep 1915
Site 3 Elizabeth Ann Nicholson   Mort: W.T. Hilton & Sons Place: Dickerson
        Birth: 1851   Death: 24 Jan 1926 Burial: 26 Jan 1926
Site 4 Lawrence Baker Nicholson
        Birth: 16 Mar 1846   Death: 1 Jul 1904   Burial: 4 Jul 1904
Site 5 Lawrence B. Nicholson
        Birth: 22 Mar 1879   Death: 20 Sep 1911 Burial: 23 Sep 1911
Site 6 William Douglas Nicholson
        Birth: 7 Jul 1918   Death: 25 May 1988 Burial: 15 Jun 1988
        s/o Arthur P. & Susan Virginia Oland Nicholson
Site 7 Susan Virginia C. Nicholson w/o Arthur P. Nicholson
        Birth: 2 Feb 1886   Death: 7 Jul 1973   Burial: 9 Jul 1973
Site 8 Arthur Purnell Nicholson   Place: Dickerson
        Birth: 10 Dec 1885   Death: 9 Jan 1919   Burial: 8 Jan 1919
        Mort: W.T. Hilton & Sons   h/o Susan Virginia Nicholson
Site 10 Linwood Burton Nicholson   Mort: W.B. Hilton   Place: Dickerson
        Birth: 27 Apr 1874   Death: 19 Sep 1954 Burial: 21 Sep 1954
Site 12 Arthur Baker Nicholson
        Birth: 29 Oct 1915   Death: 14 Jun 1986 Burial: 18 Jun 1986

Lot: 3 Lower Owner: Linwood T. & Frances L. Jones
Site 1 Leona Madelin Jones Taylor
        Birth: 20 Oct 1903   Death: 9 Oct 1984   Burial: 12 Oct 1984

Site 3 Frances Lavinia Jones   Place: Hagerstown
        Birth: 11 Dec 1903   Death: 7 Mar 1962   Burial: 10 Mar 1962
        Mort: E.C. Gartner   TS: w/o Linwood T. Jones
Site 4 Linwood Thomas Jones   h/o Frances L. Jones
        Birth: 17 Nov 1891   Death: 9 Aug 1974   Burial: 12 Aug 1974

Lot: 3 Upper   Owner: Adelia L. Jones
Site 2 Maurice R. Jones   Mort: Timothy Hanlon   Place: Washington, DC
        Birth: 1898   Death: 2 Aug 1942   Burial: 8 Aug 1942
Site 3 Adelia L. Jones   Place: Clarksburg
        Birth: 10 Apr 1874   Death: 19 Jun 1945   Burial: 22 Jun 1945
        Mort: W.B. Hilton   TS: w/o John R. Jones
Site 4 John Rufus Jones   Place: Dickerson
        Birth: 7 Aug 1865   Death: 12 Dec 1930   Burial: 15 Dec 1930
        Mort: W.T. Hilton & Sons   h/o Adelia L. Jones
Site 5 Leo Lawrence Jones   Death: 4 Mar 1905   Burial: 7 Mar 1905
        s/o John R. & Adelia L. Jones   TS: Age 0-10-24

Lot: 4 Owner: W.M. Williams
Site 3 William McKendree Williams   Place: Boyds
        Birth: 14 Sep 1875   Death: 10 Jun 1948   Burial: 12 Jun 1948
        Mort: W.R. Pumphrey   h/o Sarah White Williams
Site 4 Sarah White Williams   Place: Bethesda
        Birth: 17 Jul 1880   Death: 16 Aug 1949   Burial: 19 Aug 1949
        Mort: Robert A. Pumphrey   w/o William McKendree Williams
Site 5 Robert M. Williams   h/o Rebecca Gott Williams
        Birth: 22 Jul 1904   Death: 1955   Burial: 16 Sep 1995
Site 6 Rebecca Gott Williams   w/o Robert Williams
        Birth: 20 Mar 1905   Death: 5 Jul 1994   Burial: 12 Sep 1994
Site 9 Bradford Nelson Headley   Place: Bethesda
        Birth: 27 Mar 1888   Death: 12 Apr 1956   Burial: 14 Apr 1956
        Mort: Robert A. Pumphrey   h/o Anna Williams Headley
Site 10 Anna Louise W. Headley   w/o Bradford Nelson Headley
        Birth: 16 Sep 1899   Death: 31 Jan 1997   Burial: 1 Feb 1997
Site 12 Bradford Nelson Headley Jr.   Place: Boyds
        Birth: 12 Oct 1922   Death: 23 Oct 1929   Burial: 25 Oct 1929
        Mort: Pumphrey & Sons   s/o Bradford N. & Anna Williams Headley

Lot: 5 Owner: Dr. J.Harris Stonestreet
Site 1 Edward Francis Giddings   Place: Barnesville
        Birth: 1905   Death: 1934   Burial: 19 Feb 1934
        Mort: Hilton & Price   h/o Virginia Giddings
Site 2 Virginia Stonestreet Giddings   w/o Edward F. Giddings
        Birth: 18 Jul 1900   Death: 28 Dec 1978   Burial: 2 Jan 1979
Site 3 Gertrude Worthington Stonestreet Gough   Place: Barnesville
        Birth: 1876   Death: 12 Jan 1960   Burial: 14 Jan 1960
        Mort: W.B. Hilton   1st w/o Dr. J. Harris Stonestreet
Site 4 Dr. J. Harris Stonestreet   h/o Gertrude Worthington Stonestreet
        Birth: 17 Aug 1862   Death: 13 Jan 1909   Burial: 15 Jan 1909

138 Monocacy Cemetery, Beallsville, Montgomery County, Maryland

Site 5 Joseph Harris Stonestreet Place: Barnesville
   Birth: 1905 Death: 24 May 1957 Burial: 27 May 1957
   Mort: Hilton h/o Mae Montgomery Stonestreet
Site 6 Mae Montgomery Stonestreet w/o Joseph Harris Stonestreet
   Birth: 8 Sep 1903 Death: 8 Aug 1980 Burial: 11 Aug 1980

Lot: 6 Owner: E.C. Hersperger
Site 3 Webb Sellman Hersperger Place: Darnestown
   Birth: 1 Mar 1902 Death: 18 Jun 1933 Burial: 20 Jun 1933
   Mort: Hilton & Hall h/o Virginia Gatrell Hersperger
Site 9 Elmer Clayton Hersperger Place: Dickerson
   Birth: 5 Sep 1866 Death: 22 Sep 1941 Burial: 24 Sep 1941
   Mort: W.B. Hilton h/o Anna P. Hersperger
Site 10 Anna P. Hersperger Place: Poolesville
   Birth: 1879 Death: 28 Apr 1923 Burial: 30 Apr 1923
   Mort: Hilton & Hall TS: w/o Elmer C. Hersperger
Site 11 Evelyn Hersperger Anderson w/o Alde Anderson
   Birth: 14 Nov 1904 Death: 1 Jan 1984 Burial: 3 Jan 1984
Site 12 Alde B. Anderson h/o Evelyn Hersperger
   Birth: 15 Mar 1897 Death: 3 Sep 1973 Burial: 6 Sep 1973

Lot: 7 Owner: Andrew F. Small
Site 4 Andrew F. Small
   Birth: 9 Jun 1856 Death: 3 Aug 1910 Burial: 6 Aug 1910

Lot: 8 Upper Owner: Albert Ballenger
Site 1 Lillie May Ballenger Place: Frederick Hospital
   Birth: 28 May 1879 Death: 10 Nov 1942 Burial: 12 Nov 1942
   Mort: W.B. Hilton w/o Ernest B. Ballenger
Site 2 Ernest B. Ballenger TS: Father Place: Clarksburg
   Birth: 25 Feb 1872 Death: 9 Jul 1941 Burial: 11 Jul 1941
   Mort: W.B. Hilton h/o Lillie May Ballenger
Site 3 Sarah A. Ballenger TS: w/o Albert Ballenger
   Birth: 27 Jun 1848 Death: 25 Jun 1909 Burial: 27 Jun 1909
Site 4 Albert Ballenger Place: Dickerson
   Birth: 6 Jun 1847 Death: 13 Jun 1920 Burial: 15 Jun 1920
   Mort: W.T. Hilton & Sons h/o Sarah A. Ballenger
Site 5 Luther Albert Ballenger Jr. Mort: W.T. Hilton & Sons Place: Dickerson
   Birth: 7 Apr 1875 Death: 5 Oct 1921 Burial: 7 Oct 1921
Site 6 Lena Ballenger Oden Mort: W.B. Hilton Place: Sykesville
   Birth: 1 Aug 1877 Death: 29 May 1941 Burial: 31 May 1941
   TS: Father

Row G

Lot: 1 Owner: Harry Williams

Site 1 Mary Whaling Williams   Place: Sykesville
         Birth: 1893   Death: 15 Feb 1960   Burial: 18 Feb 1960
         Mort: W.B. Hilton   w/o Henry Ralph Williams
Site 2 Henry Ralph Williams   Place: Cumberland, MD
         Birth: 27 Mar 1896   Death: 25 Feb 1968   Burial: 28 Feb 1968
         Mort: Wm. Hilton   h/o Mary Whaling Williams
Site 3 Nellie White Williams   Place: Poolesville
         Birth: 6 Oct 1867   Death: 7 Jun 1946   Burial: 10 Jun 1946
         Mort: W.B. Hilton   w/o Harry M. Williams
Site 4 Harry McGill Williams   Place: Poolesville
         Birth: 25 Aug 1867   Death: 15 Sep 1950   Burial: 18 Sep 1950
         Mort: W.B. Hilton   h/o Nellie White Williams
Site 5 Elizabeth Stinson Williams Birth: 1907   2nd w/o Henry Ralph Williams
Site 9 Margaret Williams Gray   w/o Gustavus Robert Gray
         Birth: 2 Jan 1894   Death: 20 Sep 1990   Burial: 24 Sep 1990
Site 10 Gustavus Robert Gray   TS: Death: 1951   Place: Poolesville
         Birth: 1889   Death: 4 Jan 1950   Burial: 6 Jan 1950
         Mort: W.B. Hilton   h/o Margaret Williams Gray

Lot: 2 Owner: Horace Davis

Site 1 Mrs. Nannie Davis Carr   TS: w/o Arthur B. Carr
         Birth: 10 May 1879   Death: 12 May 1905   Burial: 14 May 1905
Site 2 Child Davis   Mort: Hilton & Hall
         Place: Poolesville   Death: 9 Sep 1913   Burial: 10 Sep 1913
         c/o Frank & Susie Davis   No marker
Site 2 Mary Emma Davis   Place: Poolesville
         Birth: 16 Dec 1855   Death: 25 Apr 1932   Burial: 27 Apr 1932
         Mort: Hilton & Hall   w/o Horace M. Davis
Site 3 Horace M. Davis   Place: Poolesville
         Birth: 11 Jun 1851   Death: 9 Oct 1936   Burial: 11 Oct 1936
         Mort: Hilton & Hall   h/o Mary Emma Davis
Site 4 Dr. Horace M. Davis   Place: Baltimore
         Birth: 15 Jul 1881   Death: 8 Feb 1935   Burial: 20 Feb 1935
         Mort: John O. Mitchell Sons   h/o Lucie Dodson Davis
Site 5 Lucie Dodson Davis   Place: Los Altos. CA
         Birth: 2 Oct 1878   Death: 16 Feb 1965   Burial: 19 Feb 1965
         Mort: Hays   On stone with Dr. Horace M. Davis
Site 7 Carolyne Virginia Davis   TS: d/o Frank I. & Susie G. Davis
         Birth: 17 Oct 1909   Death: 26 Jul 1910   Burial: 27 Jul 1910
Site 9 Susie Griffith Davis   w/o Frank Isaac Davis
         Birth: 23 Jun 1886   Death: 15 Jun 1975   Burial: 18 Jun 1975
Site 10 Frank Isaac Davis   Place: Rockville
         Birth: 4 Sep 1885   Death: 7 Feb 1960   Burial: 10 Feb 1960
         Mort: Robert A. Pumphrey   h/o Susie Griffith Davis

Monocacy Cemetery, Beallsville, Montgomery County, Maryland

Site 11 Charles Horace Davis On stone with Mabel Coatsworth Davis
 Birth: 20 Nov 1911 Death: 28 Nov 1987 Burial: 3 Dec 1987

Lot: 3 Owner: Lawrence Chiswell
Site 1 Lawrence Newton Brewer s/o Stephen Newton & Ruth Chiswell Brewer
 Birth: 19 Oct 1928 Death: 25 Jun 1996 Burial: 28 Jun 1996
Site 2 Ruth Chiswell Brewer w/o Stephen Newton Brewer
 Birth: 1900 Death: 28 Apr 1989 Burial: 1 May 1989
Site 3 Stephen Newton Brewer h/o Ruth Chiswell Brewer
 Birth: 2 Jun 1897 Death: 18 Jun 1974 Burial: 20 Jun 1974
Site 4 James Burch Brewer Place: Detroit
 Birth: 29 Oct 1892 Death: 23 Jul 1955 Burial: 28 Jul 1955
 Mort: Ted C. Sullivan h/o Mary Brewer
Site 5 Mary McDonnell Brewer w/o James Burch Brewer
 Birth: 1888 Death: 15 Sep 1984 Burial: 18 Sep 1984
Site 7 Marjorie Waters Chiswell w/o Maurice H. Chiswell
 Birth: 1898 Death: 27 Oct 1973 Burial: 30 Oct 1973
Site 8 Maurice H. Chiswell Place: Gaithersburg
 Birth: 1896 Death: 17 Jan 1966 Burial: 19 Jan 1966
 Mort: Ernest C. Gartner h/o Marjorie Waters Chiswell
Site 9 Hattie Hersperger Chiswell Place: Frederick
 Birth: 1874 Death: 29 Jan 1960 Burial: 1 Feb 1960
 Mort: W.B. Hilton w/o Lawrence A. Chiswell
Site 10 Lawrence A. Chiswell Place: Barnesville
 Birth: 1869 Death: 1 Aug 1937 Burial: 3 Aug 1937
 Mort: W.B. Hilton h/o Hattie Hersperger Chiswell
Site 11 Constance Chiswell Hilton w/o William Brosius Hilton
 Birth: 3 Apr 1906 Death: 7 Oct 1982 Burial: 11 Oct 1982
Site 11 William Brosius Hilton No marker h/o Constance Chiswell Hilton
 Birth: 26 Apr 1903 Death: 24 Feb 1977 Burial: 28 Feb 1977

Lot: 4 Owner: Dr. Byron W. Walling
Site 1 Child Walling c/o Dr. Byron W. & Emily W. Walling
  Death: 23 Nov 1883 Burial: 23 Nov 1883
Site 2 Emily W. Walling w/o Dr. Byron W. Walling
 Birth: 29 Aug 1858 Death: 9 Feb 1908 Burial: 11 Feb 1908
Site 3 Dr. Byron W. Walling Place: Poolesville
 Birth: 6 Aug 1852 Death: 14 Nov 1938 Burial: 16 Nov 1938
 Mort: Hilton & Hall h/o Emily W. Walling
Site 4 Katherine Walling Thompson Place: Braddock Heights
 Birth: 8 Mar 1891 Death: 1 Jan 1962 Burial: 3 Jan 1962
 Mort: Hilton w/o Sidney Thompson
Site 5 Sidney Thompson Place: Washington, DC
 Birth: 13 Oct 1893 Death: 2 Jun 1958 Burial: 6 Jun 1958
 Mort: Hilton h/o Katherine Walling Thompson
Site 7 Baby Girl Thompson No marker Mort: Robert A.
 Place: Bethesda Death: 22 Jan 1957 Burial: 24 Jan 1957
 d/o Sidney & Virginia Mae Stonestreet Thompson

Monocacy Cemetery, Beallsville, Montgomery County, Maryland 141

Site 12 Marne Stewart Thompson   Place: Frederick
        Birth: 9 Sep 1922   Death: 13 May 1953   Burial: 15 May 1953
        Mort: M.R. Etchison & Son   1st w/o Byron W. Thompson

Lot: 5 Owner: Mrs. Willie Magruder or Rudolph Beall
Site   Dorothy Gott Beall   No marker
                                 Death: 5 Oct 1912   Burial: 5 Oct 1912
Site   Rebecca Schoole Beall   No marker
                                 Death: 6 Aug 1912   Burial: 6 Aug 1912
Site   Rudolph Gott Beall   No marker
                                 Death: 5 May 1909   Burial: 5 May 1909
Site 1 Henry Brooks Beall
        Birth: 1904   Death: 29 Sep 1904   Burial: 29 Sep 1904
Site 3 Caroline Eleanor Beall   Place: Halethorpe, MD
        Birth: 28 Jan 1884   Death: 15 Oct 1970   Burial: 17 Oct 1970
        Mort: Ernest Gartner   On stone with Marion T. Beall
Site 4 Marion T. Beall   Place: Baltimore
        Birth: 30 Apr 1877   Death: 1 Jun 1963   Burial: 4 Jun 1963
        Mort: Ernest C. Gartner   h/o Caroline Eleanor Beall
Site 5 Eliza C. West Beall   Mort: Hilton & Hall   Place: Poolesville
        Birth: 1835   Death: 1 Feb 1917   Burial: 3 Feb 1917
Site 6 William Rudolph Beall   Birth: 1835   Burial: 16 Mar 1906
Site 7 E. Rudolph Beall   Mort: Hilton & Hall   Place: Poolesville
        Birth: 1876   Death: 5 Nov 1913   Burial: 7 Nov 1913
Site 8 Barbara Jean Chapman   Mort: Snellings   Place: Portsmouth, VA
        Birth: 16 Aug 1941   Death: 6 Jan 1942   Burial: 7 Jan 1942
        d/o Robert & Mabel Chapman   On stone with Robert H. Chapman, Jr.
Site 8 Robert H. Chapman Jr.   Place: Md. Route 28
        Birth: 5 Feb 1942   Death: 18 Nov 1948   Burial: 20 Nov 1948
        Mort: W.R. Pumphrey   s/o Robert & Mabel Chapman
Site 9 Douglas B. Linde   Mort: E.C. Gartner   Place: Baltimore
        Birth: 5 Oct 1946   Death: 7 Oct 1946   Burial: 7 Oct 1946
Site 10 Dorothy Anne Beall Chapman   TS: d/o Robert H. & Mabel C. Chapman
        Birth: 8 Aug 1953   Death: 15 Aug 1953   Burial: 17 Aug 1953
Site 11 Caroline B. Fitzsimmons Birth: 1913   On stone with Paul Fitzsimmons
Site 12 Paul B. Fitzsimmons   h/o Caroline B. Fitzsimmons
        Birth: 1910   Death: 1990

Lot: 6 Owner: Scott Rice
Site   Elvira M. Reamy   No marker   Mort: W.T. Hilton & Sons
        Place: Washington, DC   Death: 28 Jan 1920   Burial: 30 Jan 1920
Site   Miss Leona Rice   Burial: 4 Apr 1908   No marker
Site   Margaret A. Rice   No marker   Mort: W.T. Hilton & Sons
        Place: Washington, DC   Death: 6 Apr 1917   Burial: 9 Apr 1917
Site   Marker to 6 children of W.S. & Annie C. Rice, no dates, see 6 below
        Child of Scott Rice   i/o W.S. & Annie C. Rice   Burial: 6 Apr 1900
Site   Child of Scott Rice   i/o W.S. & Annie C. Rice   Burial: 22 Jun 1892
Site   Child of Scott Rice   c/o W.S. & Annie C. Rice   Burial: 12 Sep 1884
Site   Child of Scott Rice   i/o W.S. & Annie C. Rice   Burial: 23 Aug 1894

Site	Child of Scott Rice	i/o W.S. & Annie C. Rice	Burial: 20 Aug 1896
Site	Child of Scott Rice	i/o W.S. & Annie C. Rice	Burial: 1 Oct 1898
Site	William O. Rice	Burial: 9 May 1907	No marker
Site 3	Annie C. Rice	TS: w/o Winfield Scott Rice, age 85-4-2, and infant	
	Birth: 4 Oct 1866	Death: 6 Feb 1902	Burial: 8 Feb 1902
Site 8	Richard Alonzo Rice	Age 86	Mort: Hill & Johnson
	Place: Salesburg	Death: 11 Feb 1952	Burial: 14 May 1952
	No marker	[I transcribed dates from Interrment Books as May]	

Lot: 7 Lower   Owner: Charles E. Poole

Site 1	James Robert Poole		Place: Dickerson
	Birth: 12 Jul 1924	Death: 17 Sep 1924	Burial: 18 Sep 1924
	Mort: W.T. Hilton & Sons		TS: s/o Walter S. & M.R. Poole
Site 1	Maynard S. Poole	Death: 14 May 1910	
	TS: s/o Walter S. & M.R. Poole, age 2 days		
Site 1	Rachel A. Poole		Place: Dickerson
	Birth: 12 Jul 1924	Death: 20 Sep 1924	Burial: 21 Sep 1924
	Mort: W.T. Hilton & Sons		TS: d/o Walter S. & M.R. Poole
Site 1	Thomas W. Poole	TS: s/o Walter S. & M.R. Poole, age 12 days	
		Death: 25 Apr 1911	Burial: 26 Apr 1911
Site 2	Infant of Harry Stottlemyer	No marker	Mort: Hilton & Price
	Place: Dickerson	Death: 24 Jun 1933	Burial: 25 Jun 1933
Site 3	Raymond W. Collins	No marker Child	Mort: W.W. Chambers
	Place: Washington, DC	Death: 19 Jan 1945	Burial: 21 Jan 1945
Site 3	Robert L. Collins	No marker Child	Mort: W.W. Chambers
	Place: Washington, DC	Death: 26 Jun 1934	Burial: 28 Jun 1934
Site 4	Samuel Dixon Poole	Mort: W.B. Hilton	Place: Darnestown
	Birth: 16 Aug 1888	Death: 19 Sep 1942	Burial: 21 Sep 1942
Site 5	Rachael Virginia Poole	TS: w/o Charles E. Poole, age 54-9-14	
		Death: 23 Nov 1904	Burial: 24 Nov 1904
Site 6	Charles E. Poole		TS: Age 61-8-12
	h/o Rachael V. Poole	Death: 15 Feb 1908	Burial: 17 Feb 1908

Lot: 7 Upper   Owner: J.R. Lillard

Site	Miss Bessie B. Lillard		
	Birth: 1890	Death: 1905	Burial: 29 Jun 1905
Site	Ernest L. Lillard		
	Birth: 1874	Death: 1913	Burial: 17 Jan 1913
Site	James R. Lillard	Mort: W.R. Pumphrey	Place: Sykesville
	Birth: 1848	Death: 28 Jul 1920	Burial: 30 Jul 1920
Site	Mary Ellen Lillard		w/o J.R. Lillard
	Birth: 1851	Death: 1904	Burial: 31 Aug 1904
Site	William E. Lillard		
	Birth: 1879	Death: 1902	Burial: 14 Jul 1902

Monocacy Cemetery, Beallsville, Montgomery County, Maryland   143

Lot: 8   Owner: William Waesche
Site 1 John William Waesche   Death: 16 Feb 1901   Burial: 18 Feb 1901
        TS: s/o William L. & Mamie A. Waesche, age 0-9-14
Site 4 Martha Waesche Anderson   On stone with Martin Anderson
        Birth: 17 May 1895   Death: 2 Apr 1976   Burial: 21 Apr 1976
Site 5 Martin Anderson   h/o Martha Waesche Anderson
        Birth: 19 Aug 1888   Death: 27 Feb 1972   Burial: 1 Mar 1972
Site 6 William L. Waesche   TS: Age 39-5-16
        Birth: 7 May 1863   Death: 23 Oct 1902   Burial: 26 Oct 1902

Lot: 9   Owner: Charles Luhn
Site 1 Alice Elizabeth Luhn   Place: Ijamsville
        Birth: 23 Jul 1855   Death: 10 May 1950   Burial: 14 May 1950
        Mort: W.B. Hilton   On stone with George C. Luhn
Site 2 George Christopher Luhn Jr.   Place: Dickerson
        Birth: 14 Nov 1856   Death: 20 Nov 1935   Burial: 22 Nov 1935
        Mort: M.R. Etchison   h/o Alice E. McLain Luhn
Site 3 William Alexander Luhn   Mort: W.B. Hilton   Place: Frederick
        Birth: 27 Jul 1869   Death: 19 Feb 1949   Burial: 21 Feb 1949
        s/o George Christopher & Anna Elizabeth Sellman Luhn
Site 4 Charles McLain Luhn Jr. Mort: W.T. Hilton & Sons Place: Dickerson
        Birth: 1880   Death: 10 Jan 1919   Burial: 11 Jan 1919
Site 5 Sarah Catherine McLain Luhn TS: w/o Charles Andrew Luhn   Reinterment
        Birth: 23 Mar 1857   Death: 10 Aug 1880   Burial: 18 Jun 1901
Site 6 Charles Andrew Luhn   Place: Frederick
        Birth: 31 Dec 1849   Death: 20 Jun 1942   Burial: 23 Jun 1942
        Mort: C.E. Cline & Son   h/o Catherine McLain Luhn
Site 7 Katherine Lee Thomas   Place: Frederick
        Birth: 22 Jan 1890   Death: 13 Jul 1960   Burial: 15 Jul 1960
        Mort: W.B. Hilton   On stone with Albert Melvin Thomas
Site 8 Albert Melvin Thomas   h/o Katherine Lee Thomas
        Birth: 13 Jul 1884   Death: 12 Jan 1973   Burial: 15 Jan 1973
Site 9 Annie Elizabeth Sellman Luhn   Mort: Chas. E. Roberts
        Birth: 25 Nov 1825   Death: 22 Jun 1911   Burial: 13 Sep 1937
        On stone with George C. Luhn   Removed from Dickerson
Site 10 George Christopher Luhn Sr.   Mort: Chas. E. Roberts
        Birth: 17 Aug 1920   Death: 22 Jan 1896   Burial: 13 Sep 1937
        h/o Annie E. Luhn   Removed from Dickerson

Lot: 10 Owner: Miscellaneous
Site 1 Frances Hoyle Lyddane   On stone with Charles William Lydanne
        Birth: 13 Aug 1912   Death: 7 Nov 1996   Burial: 9 Nov 1996
Site 2 Charles William Lyddane   h/o Frances H. Lydanne
        Birth: 19 May 1908   Death: 1978   Burial: 11 Nov 1978
Site 4 Sallie Coleman Schaeffer   Place: Germantown
        Birth: 1860   Death: 2 Jan 1949   Burial: 5 Jan 1949
        Mort: Ernest C. Gartner   On stone with Frank Gallion Schaeffer

Site 5	Frank Gallion Schaeffer		Place: Germantown
	Birth: 1859	Death: 23 Oct 1938	Burial: 25 Oct 1938
	Mort: Ernest C. Gartner		h/o Sallie Coleman Schaeffer
Site 6	Thomas Murray Schaeffer	No marker	s/o Sallie & Frank Schaeffer
	Birth: 2 Dec 1901	Death: 10 Aug 1902	Burial: 13 Aug 1902
Site 7	Cosmos M. Harding	No dates on stone	Mort: Hilton & Hall
	Place: Germantown	Death: 29 Jan 1919	Burial: 31 Jan 1919
Site 10	Frank William Schaeffer		
	Birth: 28 Sep 1899	Death: 23 Nov 1983	Burial: 2 Dec 1983
Site 11	Ira Montgomery Hall		Place: Gaithersburg
	Birth: 3 Dec 1884	Death: 29 Nov 1954	Burial: 1 Dec 1954
	Mort: Robert A. Pumphrey		w/o Emily Lydanne Hall
Site 12	William A. Schaeffer	Mort: Hilton & Hall	Place: Germantown
	Birth: 31 Jan 1831	Death: 23 Jan 1917	Burial: 25 Jan 1917

Lot: 11 Owner: William Schaeffer

Site 1	Samuel Nelson Clugston	Place: Seneca	Mort: Ernest C. Gartner
	Birth: 1856	Death: 15 Apr 1937	Burial: 18 Apr 1937
Site 3	Edith Clugston Schaeffer		Place: Rockville, MD
	Birth: 1884	Death: 24 Mar 1968	Burial: 27 Mar 1968
	Mort: Francis Barber		2nd w/o William Light Schaeffer
Site 4	William Light Schaeffer	Mort: Ernest C. Gartner	Place: near Dawsonville
	Birth: 1858	Death: 20 Apr 1937	Burial: 23 Apr 1937
	h/o Edith Clugston Schaeffer & Katie L. Schaeffer		
Site 5	Katie L. Schaeffer		Place: Seneca
	Birth: 1862	Death: 7 Jul 1914	Burial: 9 Jul 1914
	Mort: Hilton & Hall		TS: [1st] w/o William Light Schaeffer
Site 6	Joseph E. Jennings		Reinterment
	Birth: 1861	Death: 1890	Burial: 30 Oct 1902
Site 9	Clara C. Jennings		Place: Washington, DC
	Birth: 27 Jun 1881	Death: 8 Mar 1970	Burial: 11 Mar 1970
	Mort: Tyson Wheeler		w/o Charles C. Jennings
Site 10	Charles C. Jennings		Place: Bethesda, MD
	Birth: 19 Jan 1888	Death: 9 Jun 1971	Burial: 12 Jun 1971
	Mort: Tyson Wheeler		h/o Clara C. Jennings
Site 11	Mrs. Sarah L. Jones		
	Birth: 1836	Death: 1910	Burial: 19 Feb 1911
Site 12	Charles H. Jones		Reinterment
	Birth: 1855	Death: 1886	Burial: 30 Oct 1902

Lot: 12 Lower Owner: Newton White & Bros.

Site 2	Bessie S. White		w/o Julian N. White
	Birth: 13 Aug 1904	Death: 11 Oct 1989	Burial: 16 Oct 1989
Site 3	Julian N. White	Mort: John N. Taylor & Sons	Place: Annapolis
	Birth: Jun 1901	Death: 30 Aug 1965	Burial: 2 Sep 1965
Site 4	Mary (Mamie) Everline Pratt	Place: Centreville	Mort: Barton Bros.
	Birth: 1867	Death: 8 Feb 1950	Burial: 10 Feb 1950
Site 5	Joseph Newton White	Mort: Hilton & Hall	Place: near Hall
	Birth: 1853	Death: 15 Jan 1921	Burial: 17 Jan 1921

Monocacy Cemetery, Beallsville, Montgomery County, Maryland   145

Lot: 12 Upper   Owner: Dr. Charles Pratt
Site 1 Arthur White   Mort: W.B. Hilton   Place: Poolesville
        Birth: 14 Nov 1854   Death: 13 Feb 1941   Burial: 19 Feb 1941
Site 2 B. Frank White   Mort: Hilton & Hall   Place: Washington, DC
        Birth: 1851   Death: 23 May 1931   Burial: 25 May 1931
Site 3 Mary Elizabeth White Pratt   Place: Morgantown, WV
        Birth: 21 Aug 1856   Death: 18 Feb 1939   Burial: 21 Feb 1939
        Mort: H.A. Davidson   On stone with Charles E. Pratt, MD
Site 4 Charles E. Pratt, MD   Place: Adamstown
        Birth: 27 Dec 1851   Death: 2 Oct 1916   Burial: 4 Oct 1916
        Mort: Hilton & Hall   h/o Mary Elizabeth White Pratt

Lot: 13   Owner: John D. Bowman
Site 2 Frederick Bowman   Death: 19 May 1884   Burial: 2 Nov 1909
        TS: s/o R.H. & E.J. Bowman   Reinterment
Site 3 Elizabeth Jane Darby Bowman   TS: w/o R.H. Bowman
        Birth: 9 Jan 1845   Death: 28 Jan 1909   Burial: 31 Jan 1909
Site 4 Richard H. Bowman   Place: Rockville
        Birth: 28 Feb 1841   Death: 5 Mar 1914   Burial: 7 Mar 1914
        Mort: A.G. Carlisle   h/o Elizabeth Jane Darby Bowman
Site 9 Evelyn T. Bowman   Place: Rockville
        Birth: 25 Dec 1885   Death: 19 Nov 1953   Burial: 21 Nov 1953
        Mort: Robert A. Pumphrey   TS: w/o J. Darby Bowman
Site 10 John Darby Bowman   Place: Rockville
        Birth: 30 Nov 1880   Death: 28 May 1954   Burial: 31 May 1954
        Mort: Robert A. Pumphrey   h/o Evelyn T. Bowman

Lot: 14   Owner: Robert E. Stout
Site 3 Mary A. Herbert   Mort: W.R. Pumphrey   Place: Cabin John
        Birth: 27 May 1850   Death: 2 Mar 1921   Burial: 4 Mar 1921
Site 4 Bessie M. Stout   Mort: Deal   Place: Washington, DC
        Birth: 10 Oct 1883   Death: 3 Aug 1947   Burial: 6 Aug 1947
Site 5 Harry L. Stout   Mort: W.W. Ulrich   Place: Washington, DC
        Birth: 14 Nov 1881   Death: 22 Jun 1927   Burial: 24 Jun 1927

Lot: 15   Owner: L.C. Young
Site 2 Mary Ryan Young   Mort: R.A. Pumphrey   Place: Washington, DC
        Birth: 1900   Death: 15 Jan 1959   Burial: 19 Jan 1959
Site 3 Harriet Oden Young   Mort: Martin W. Hysong   Place: Washington, DC
        Birth: 28 Sep 1861   Death: 11 Nov 1938   Burial: 14 Nov 1938
Site 4 Ludwick Craven Young   Place: Washington, DC
        Birth: 31 Oct 1841   Death: 7 Nov 1930   Burial: 9 Nov 1930
        Mort: W.T. Hilton & Sons   h/o Virginia Saunders
Site 5 Joy Young Rogers   Place: Washington, DC
        Birth: 1891   Death: 10 Dec 1953   Burial: 12 Dec 1953
        Mort: S.H. Hines Co.   On stone with Merrill Rogers
Site 6 Merrill Rogers   Place: Washington, DC
        Birth: 1892   Death: 1 Nov 1964   Burial: 4 Nov 1964
        Mort: Robert A. Pumphrey   h/o Joy Rogers

Site 9 Louise Bayard Young   d/o Ludwick Craven & Harriet Oden Young
        Birth: 8 Oct 1892   Death: 23 Mar 1988   Burial: 27 Apr 1988
Site 10 Frances Oden   No dates on stone   Mort: W.T. Hilton & Sons
        Place: Washington, DC   Death: 23 Apr 1933   Burial: 24 Apr 1933
Site 11 Matilda Nesbit Young   No death date on stone
        Birth: 14 Apr 1898   Death: 1 Apr 1989   Burial: 4 Apr 1989

Lot: 16 Lower   Owner: Charles S. Butler
Site 2 George R. Butler   On stone with Cinderella Titus Butler
        Birth: 15 Sep 1907   Death: 9 Nov 1979   Burial: 12 Nov 1979
Site 3 Hattie Alice Butler   Place: Dickerson
        Birth: 12 Dec 1875   Death: 4 May 1949   Burial: 7 May 1949
        Mort: W.B. Hilton   On stone with Charles S. Butler
Site 4 Charles Spates Butler   Place: Dickerson
        Birth: 11 Jan 1868   Death: 20 Jan 1961   Burial: 24 Jan 1961
        Mort: Hilton   h/o Hattie A. Butler

Lot: 16 Upper   Owner: Harry L. Butler
Site 2 Lucile Butler   TS: d/o Harry L. & Jennie Brunner Butler
        Birth: 7 Mar 1901   Death: 13 Jul 1902   Burial: 15 Jul 1902
Site 3 Jennie I. Brunner Butler   TS: w/o Harry L. Butler
        Birth: 9 Jul 1878   Death: 14 May 1909   Burial: 26 May 1909
Site 4 Harry Lee Butler   Place: near Rockville
        Birth: 23 Apr 1871   Death: 17 Oct 1914   Burial: 20 Oct 1914
        Mort: Hilton & Hall   h/o Jennie Brunner Butler
Site 5 Charles Martin Butler   h/o Virginia Clark Butler
        Birth: 16 Dec 1903   Death: 24 Apr 1972   Burial: 26 Apr 1972
Site 6 Virginia Clark Butler   Mort: Hilton   w/o Charles Martin Butler
        Birth: 27 Oct 1910   Death: 23 Nov 1989   Burial: 27 Nov 1989

Lot: 17   Owner: Charles Oxley
Site 2 C. Gilbert Oxley   No marker
        Birth: 4 Mar 1891   Death: 19 May 1911   Burial: 22 May 1911
Site 3 Annie E. Oxley   TS: [1st] w/o Charles W. Oxley
        Birth: 12 Jan 1857   Death: 4 Mar 1912   Burial: 6 Mar 1912
Site 4 Charles W. Oxley   Place: Poolesville
        Birth: 17 Aug 1856   Death: 28 Jan 1929   Burial: 30 Jan 1929
        Mort: Hilton & Hall   h/o Annie E. Oxley & Catharine A. Oxley
Site 5 Catharine A. Oxley   Place: Poolesville
        Birth: 24 May 1861   Death: 22 Jul 1925   Burial: 24 Jul 1925
        Mort: Hilton & Hall   TS: [2nd] w/o Charles W. Oxley
Site 7 Erwin Brown Staggs   d/o J. Herbert & Elizabeth Oxley Brown
        Birth: 2 Mar 1924   Death: 22 Oct 1978   Burial: 25 Oct 1978
Site 8 J. Herbert Brown   Place: Frederick
        Birth: 4 Feb 1885   Death: 2 Jan 1929   Burial: 4 Jan 1929
        Mort: Hilton & Hall   h/o Elizabeth Oxley Brown
Site 9 Elizabeth Oxley Brown   w/o J. Herbert Brown
        Birth: 12 Jun 1893   Death: 25 Feb 1982   Burial: 27 Feb 1982

Monocacy Cemetery, Beallsville, Montgomery County, Maryland   147

Site 12 Katherine E. Oxley Lazell   Mort: Hilton & Hall   Place: Lansing, MI
         Birth: 18 Oct 1887   Death: 8 Jan 1916   Burial: 12 Jan 1916

Lot: 18 Lower   Owner: Frederick Reed
Site   Clara I. Reed   No marker   Mort: W.R. Pumphrey
        Place: Rockville   Death: 4 Jul 1923   Burial: 6 Jul 1923
Site   Dorothy Beatrice Reed   No marker   Mort: W.R. Pumphrey
        Place: Washington   Death: 9 Jan 1931   Burial: 12 Jan 1931
Site   Etta Prescott Reed   No marker   Mort: W.R. Pumphrey
        Place: Rockville   Death: 23 Feb 1923   Burial: 25 Feb 1923
Site   Gertie Reed   Burial: 16 Sep 1912   No marker
Site   Helen Louise Reed   No marker   Mort: W.R. Pumphrey
        Place: Gaithersburg   Death: 31 May 1934   Burial: 3 Jun 1934
Site   Lewis T. Reed   No marker   Mort: W.R. Pumphrey
        Place: Rockville   Death: 30 Apr 1923   Burial: 1 May 1923
Site   Woodrow W. Reed   Mort: Hilton & Hall
        Place: Poolesville   Death: 1 Sep 1913   Burial: 2 Sep 1913
        Child of Frederick Reed   No marker
Site 1 George Lawrence Oaks   No marker   Mort: W.R. Pumphrey
        Place: Owings Mills   Death: 30 Jul 1941   Burial: 30 Jul 1941
Site 2 Infant twins of Forest Oaks No marker   Mort: Forest Oaks
        Place: Potomac   Death: 22 Jul 1925   Burial: 23 Jul 1925
Site 4 Upton D. Reed   TS: US Coast Guard WWII
        Birth: 4 Mar 1921   Death: 26 Sep 1992   Burial: 30 Sep 1992
Site 5 Mattie Ella Reed   Place: Gaithersburg
        Birth: 31 May 1883   Death: 6 Jul 1947   Burial: 9 Jul 1947
        Mort: W.R. Pumphrey   w/o Frederick A. Reed
Site 6 Frederick A. Reed   h/o Mattie Ella Reed
        Birth: 20 Sep 1879   Death: 24 Mar 1977   Burial: 28 Mar 1977

Lot: 18 Upper   Owner: Mrs. Thomas Hickman
Site 1 Nancy Lee Hickman   Place: Frederick
        Birth: 28 Jul 1942   Death: 5 Aug 1942   Burial: 6 Aug 1942
        Mort: W.B. Hilton   TS: d/o Thomas T. & E.A. Hickman
Site 2 Miss Ida Marie Hickman   Mort: Hilton   Place: Buckeystown
        Birth: 1883   Death: 26 Sep 1959   Burial: 29 Sep 1959
        On stone with Thomas A. Hickman & Mary Ida Trundle Hickman
Site 3 Mary Ida Trundle Hickman   Mort: Hilton & Hall   Place: Poolesville
        Birth: 1853   Death: 23 Feb 1920   Burial: 25 Feb 1920
Site 4 Thomas A. Hickman
        Birth: 1843   Death: 1912   Burial: 16 Mar 1912
Site 5 Thomas T. Hickman   Place: Dickerson
        Birth: 7 Apr 1885   Death: 9 Mar 1941   Burial: 12 Mar 1941
        Mort: W.B. Hilton   h/o Della Trundle Hickman
Site 6 Della Trundle Hickman   w/o Thomas T. Hickman
        Birth: 25 Jul 1895   Death: 10 Nov 1985   Burial: 12 Nov 1985

Lot: 19 Owner: Dr. Vernon Dyson

Site 3 Lena M. Dyson
    Birth: 7 May 1872   Death: 15 Aug 1940   Place: Laytonsville
    Mort: Roy W. Barber   Burial: 17 Aug 1940
    TS: w/o Vernon H. Dyson, MD
Site 4 Vernon H. Dyson, MD   Place: Olney
    Birth: 24 Dec 1866   Death: 5 Oct 1947   Burial: 7 Oct 1947
    Mort: Roy W. Barber   h/o Lena M. Dyson
Site 10 Benjamin Franklin Dyson   Mort: Hilton & Hall   Place: Dawsonville
    Birth: 1868   Death: 28 Dec 1923   Burial: 30 Dec 1923

Lot: 20 Owner: Isaac Fyffe

Site 2 Evelyn Darby Fyffe   Mort: Hilton & Hall   Place: Poolesville
    Birth: 1910   Death: 4 May 1913   Burial: 5 May 1913
Site 3 Elizabeth Darby Fyffe   Place: Poolesville
    Birth: 25 Jul 1874   Death: 19 Nov 1956   Burial: 21 Nov 1956
    Mort: W.B. Hilton   w/o Isaac Fyffe, nee Darby
Site 4 Isaac Fyffe   Mort: W.B. Hilton   Place: Poolesville
    Birth: 27 May 1874   Death: 6 Aug 1947   Burial: 8 Aug 1947
Site 6 Carroll Thomas Chiswell   h/o Mary Fyffe Chiswell
    Birth: 28 Mar 1899   Death: 16 Apr 1982   Burial: 19 Apr 1982
Site 7 Robert M. Elsdon   Mort: M.W. Hysong   Place: Washington, DC
    Birth: 16 Jun 1910   Death: 3 Nov 1947   Burial: 5 Nov 1947
Site 9 Minnie May Fyffe Penn   Place: Laurel
    Birth: 18 Feb 1874   Death: 3 Jan 1952   Burial: 5 Jan 1952
    Mort: Deuitt Donaldson   Age 77
Site 10 Walter B. Fyffe   Mort: Hilton & Hall   Place: Poolesville
    Birth: 19 Jan 1878   Death: 15 Sep 1919   Burial: 17 Sep 1919
Site 12 Bruce Harry Elsdon   Mort: DeWitt Donaldson   Place: Laurel
    Birth: 20 Mar 1945   Death: 5 Feb 1963   Burial: 8 Feb 1963

Lot: 21 Lower Owner: Mrs. Joseph White

Site 4 Rose Alberta L. Allison
    Birth: 28 Mar 1891   Death: 20 Jan 1984   Burial: 7 Dec 1984
Site 5 Creszensa L. White   Place: Spring Garden, PA
    Birth: 26 Nov 1884   Death: 18 Dec 1963   Burial: 20 Dec 1963
    Mort: Strack & Strine   w/o Joseph Meade White, MD
Site 6 Joseph Meade White MD   Mort: W.B. Hilton   Place: Poolesville
    Birth: 6 Sep 1871   Death: 12 May 1949   Burial: 15 May 1949
    h/o Crezensa L. White   TS: Virginia, Major Med. Corps.

Lot: 21 Upper Owner: S.F. Maxwell

Site 3 Maggie Blance Maxwell
    Birth: 1877   Death: 1895   Burial: 10 Nov 1915
    Mort: W.T. Hilton & Sons   Removed from Mt. Pleasant
Site 4 Sarah Frances Beall Maxwell   Place: Clarksburg, WV
    Birth: 1851   Death: 11 Aug 1926   Burial: 13 Aug 1926
    Mort: W.T. Hilton & Sons   TS: w/o James Stevenson Maxwell

Monocacy Cemetery, Beallsville, Montgomery County, Maryland   149

Site 5 James Stevenson Maxwell   Mort: W.T. Hilton & Sons
        Birth: 1844   Death: 1892   Burial: 10 Nov 1915
        h/o Sarah Frances Beall Maxwell   Removed from Mt. Pleasant
Site 6 Emma Maxwell Beall   Mort: W.B. Hilton   Place: Boyds
        Birth: 1851   Death: 1 Jan 1946   Burial: 4 Jan 1946

Lot: 22 Owner: Hays D. Poole
Site 1 Prissilla W. Poole   Mort: Charles E. Roberts
        Birth: 21 Apr 1780   Death: 2 May 1866   Burial: 6 Oct 1917
        TS: w/o John Poole Sr.   Removed from F.P. Hays farm
Site 2 John Poole, Sr.   TS: In his 59th yr   Mort: Charles E. Roberts
                              Death: 30 Mar 1828   Burial: 6 Oct 1917
        h/o Prissilla W. Poole   Removed from F.P. Hays farm
Site 3 Elisha Howard   TS: In his 84th yr   Mort: Charles E. Roberts
        Death: 27 Apr 1874   h/o Eleanor Howard   Burial: 5 Oct 1917
                              Removed from Barnesville Methodist Church
Site 4 Eleanor Howard   Mort: Charles E. Roberts
        Birth: 12 Jul 1791   Death: 8 Feb 1873   Burial: 5 Oct 1917
        TS: w/o Capt. Elisha Howard   Removed from Barnesville Methodist Church
Site 5 Eliza Medora Hays Howard   Mort: Charles E. Roberts
        Birth: 11 Dec 1836   Death: 18 Jan 1859   Burial: 5 Oct 1917
        d/o Leonard & Eliza Hays   Removed from Barnesville Methodist Church
        Howard not on stone   Dates illegible
Site 6 Eliza Hays   Mort: Charles E. Roberts
        Birth: 28 Jun 1807   Death: 21 Jul 1874   Burial: 5 Oct 1917
        w/o Leonard Hays   Removed from Barnesville Methodist Church
Site 6 Leonard Hays   TS: Age 70-8-25   Mort: Charles E. Roberts
        Birth: 30 Jul 1793   Death: 24 Apr 1864   Burial: 5 Oct 1917
        h/o Eliza Hays   Removed from Barnesville Methodist Church
Site 7 Margaret D. Poole   illegible   Mort: Charles E. Roberts
        Birth: 18 Jun 1837   Death: 12 Apr 1838   Burial: 9 Oct 1917
        d/o William D. & Rebecca Poole   Removed from F.P. Hays farm
Site 8 Elizabeth D. Poole   Mort: Charles E. Roberts
        Birth: 11 Feb 1831   Death: 28 Dec 1831   Burial: 9 Oct 1917
        TS: d/o William D. & Rebecca Poole   Removed from F.P. Hays farm
Site 9 Martha Deborah Poole   Mort: Charles E. Roberts
        Birth: 23 Jun 1821   Death: 29 Oct 1838   Burial: 9 Oct 1917
        TS: d/o John & Prissilla Woodward Sprigg Poole
        Removed from F.P. Hays farm
Site 10 Mary E. Poole   Mort: Charles E. Roberts
        Birth: 4 Sep 1811   Death: 9 Oct 1846   Burial: 9 Oct 1917
        TS: w/o Isaac R. Poole, age 35 years   Removed from F.P. Hays farm
Site 11 Isaac R. Poole   h/o Mary E. Poole   Mort: Charles E. Roberts
        Birth: 26 Jul 1815   Death: 18 Sep 1844   Burial: 6 Oct 1917
        TS: s/o John & Priscilla Poole   Removed from F.P. Hays farm

Monocacy Cemetery, Beallsville, Montgomery County, Maryland

Site 12 Sally Poole
Birth: 22 Aug 1836 Death: 22 Aug 1836
TS: w/o John Poole, d/o Nathan & Margaret Simpson?
Dates illegible, rest almost illegible
Mort: Charles E. Roberts
Burial: 6 Oct 1917
Removed from F.P. Hays farm

Site 12A John Poole III TS: Age 48 years Mort: Charles E. Roberts
Birth: 16 Aug 1801 Death: 27 Sep 1849 Burial: 6 Oct 1917
h/o Sally Poole Removed from F.P. Hays farm

Lot: 23 Lower Owner: Dorothy Mumford

Site 3 Dorothy L. Mumford Birth: 1888 TS: w/o John M. Mumford
Site 4 John M. Mumford Place: Dickerson
Birth: 1881 Death: 3 Jul 1917 Burial: 5 Jul 1917
Mort: W.T. Hilton & Sons h/o Dorothy L. Mumford

Lot: 23 Upper Owner: Samuel E. Jewel

Site 1 Elizabeth Blanchard Jewel Mort: F. Gaschs Sons Place: Riverdale, MD
Birth: 29 Mar 1914 Death: 8 Jan 1959 Burial: 10 Jan 1959
Site 2 Mamie E. Jewel Mort: Hilton & Hall
Place: Poolesville Death: 18 Feb 1918 Burial: 20 Feb 1918
TS: d/o Samuel E. & Edna L. Jewel, age 12-11-8
Site 3 Edna Leola Jewel Place: Hyattsville
Birth: 11 Jul 1880 Death: 26 Mar 1961 Burial: 28 Mar 1961
Mort: F. Gasch Sons w/o Samuel Edgar Jewel
Site 4 Samuel Edgar Jewell Place: Hyattsville
Birth: 8 Aug 1882 Death: 15 Aug 1962 Burial: 17 Aug 1962
Mort: F. Gasch & Sons h/o Edna Leola Jewel
Site 5 Grace Magaha Jewel Moulden Moulden not on stone
Birth: 10 Sep 1913 Death: 14 Sep 1989 Burial: 18 Sep 1989

Lot: 24 Owner: Rosser E. Butler

Site 1 Lula C. Butler Place: Germantown, MD
Birth: 14 Dec 1882 Death: 14 Nov 1970 Burial: 17 Nov 1970
Mort. Wm. Hilton d/o Charles M. & Frances Thomas Butler
Site 2 Rosser Eugene Butler Mort: Hilton Place: Poolesville
Birth: 10 Jun 1887 Death: 12 Jul 1964 Burial: 14 Jul 1964
s/o Charles M. & Frances Thomas Spates Butler
Site 3 Frances Thomas Spates Butler Place: Cabin John
Birth: 4 Aug 1847 Death: 2 Jul 1918 Burial: 4 Jul 1918
Mort: W.R. Pumphrey TS: w/o Charles M. Butler
Site 4 Charles Martin Butler Place: Cabin John
Birth: 15 May 1843 Death: 12 Apr 1918 Burial: 14 Apr 1918
Mort: W.R. Pumphrey h/o Frances Thomas Spates Butler
Site 5 William George Butler Mort: W.B. Hilton Place: Poolesville
Birth: 20 Jun 1879 Death: 11 Mar 1948 Burial: 13 Mar 1948
s/o Charles M. & Frances Thomas Spates Butler
Site 6 Corrie F. Butler Mort: W.B. Hilton Place: Poolesville
Birth: 23 Oct 1876 Death: 12 Mar 1953 Burial: 16 Mar 1953
d/o Charles M. & Frances Thomas Butler

Monocacy Cemetery, Beallsville, Montgomery County, Maryland   151

Site 7 Wesley M. VanDerCook
        Birth: 8 Feb 1910   Death: 10 Jan 1974   Burial: 14 Jan 1974
        h/o Helen Butler VanDercook   TS: Maryland S SGT Army WWII
Site 9 Ruth Ann Butler   w/o J. Gorman Butler
        Birth: 16 Jul 1891   Death: 14 Mar 1983   Burial: 17 Mar 1983
Site 10 Joseph Gorman Butler   Mort: W.B. Hilton   Place: Frederick
        Birth: 4 Aug 1884   Death: 18 Mar 1951   Burial: 21 Mar 1951
        s/o Charles M. & Frances Thomas Butler, h/o Ruth Butler
Site 11 Lucille Irene Cox Butler   w/o Gorman Lee Butler
        Birth: 23 Mar 1917   Death: 15 Feb 1988   Burial: 18 Feb 1988
Site 12 Gorman Lee Butler   h/o Lucille Cox Butler
        Birth: 27 Aug 1918   Death: 6 Jun 1986   Burial: 9 Jun 1986

Lot: 25 Owner: C.R. Young
Site 2 Jessie Lowe Young
        Birth: 1921   Death: 21 Nov 1992   Burial: 27 Nov 1992
Site 3 Courtney Richard Young Jr. Mort: Falls Church   Place: Arlington, VA
        Birth: 1918   Death: 6 Mar 1968   Burial: 9 Mar 1968
Site 4 Zourie Petzman Young   Mort: W.T. Hilton   Place: Washington, DC
        Birth: 1900   Death: 13 Oct 1918   Burial: 15 Oct 1918
Site 5 Courtney Richard Young, Sr.
        Birth: 1897   Death: 7 Feb 1975   Burial: 10 Feb 1975

Lot: 26 Owner: M.E. Wade
Site 1 Courtney Anne Wade   Mort: Hilton
        Place: Bethesda NIH   Death: 20 Feb 1958   Burial: 22 Feb 1958
Site 2 J. Paul Wade   Mort: W.B. Hilton
        Place: Boyds   Death: 4 Oct 1946   Burial: 6 Oct 1946
Site 3 Zourie P. Wade   Mort: W.B. Hilton
        Place: Buck Lodge   Death: 13 Apr 1946   Burial: 15 Apr 1946
        w/o M. Eugene Wade   TS: Mother
Site 4 Marcellus Eugene Wade   Mort: W.T. Hilton & Sons
        Place: Washington, DC   Death: 15 Jan 1928   Burial: 18 Jan 1928
        h/o Zourie P. Wade   TS: Father
Site 5 Crawford Francis Wade   Mort: Hilton
        Place: Frederick   Death: 19 Apr 1964   Burial: 21 Apr 1964
Site 6 Emma Frances Wade   Mort: W.B. Hilton
        Place: Boyds   Death: 19 May 1948   Burial: 22 May 1948
Site 10 Marcellus Eugene Wade Jr.   Mort: Robert A.
        Place: Bethesda   Death: 14 Mar 1954   Burial: 17 Mar 1954

Lot: 27 Owner: Robert Young
Site 1 William (Tom) M. Young   Mort: Robert A. Pumphrey   Place: Bethesda
        Birth: 1892   Death: 23 Jul 1955   Burial: 26 Jul 1955
Site 2 Mary Ethel Young   Mort: W.T. Hilton & Sons Place: Washington, DC
        Birth: 1894   Death: 12 Apr 1920   Burial: 14 Apr 1920
Site 3 Lucy Anna Young   Mort: W.B. Pumphrey   Place: Boyds
        Birth: 1864   Death: 15 Mar 1936   Burial: 18 Mar 1936

Site 4 Robert L. Young   Mort: Wm. R. Pumphrey   Place: Boyds
        Birth: 1862   Death: 27 Aug 1937   Burial: 30 Aug 1937
Site 5 Alice Irene Young
        Birth: 26 May 1903   Death: 9 May 1992   Burial: 12 May 1992
Site 6 Lucy Ann Y. Wettengel
        Birth: 8 Aug 1905   Death: 11 Mar 1983   Burial: 15 Mar 1983

Lot: 28 Lower Owner: Mrs. Marguerite Gossard
Site 1 Leonard Upton Young   Place: Frederick
        Birth: 19 Oct 1925   Death: 2 Oct 1929   Burial: 3 Oct 1929
        Mort: W.T. Hilton & Sons   TS: s/o J.M. & M.E. Young
Site 2 John Mortimer Young   Mort: E.C. Gartner   Place: Silver Spring, MD
        Birth: 10 Nov 1899   Death: 10 Jan 1967   Burial: 13 Jan 1967
        h/o Marguerite E. Young, s/o Llewellyn & Stella Young
Site 3 Marguerite E. Knott Gossard   On stone with John Mortimer Young
        Birth: 24 Mar 1899   Death: 26 Aug 1973   Burial: 29 Aug 1973
        widow of Frank Gossard, d/o William D. & Annie Blance Carlin Knott
Site 4 Isaih Franklin Gossard   Mort: W.T. Hilton & Sons   Place: Beallsville
        Birth: 26 Dec 1895   Death: 4 Oct 1920   Burial: 6 Oct 1920
Site 5 John Rodney Young   No marker
        Birth: 1 Jul 1930   Death: 6 Jul 1996   Burial: 10 Jul 1996

Lot: 28 Upper Owner: Arthur L. Orme
Site 2 Arthur T. Orme   No marker   Child   Mort: W.B. Hilton
        Place: Washington, DC   Death: 24 Apr 1935   Burial: 25 Apr 1935
Site 3 Laura E. Orme   Mort: Chambers Co.   Place: Washington, DC
        Birth: 22 Apr 1875   Death: 6 Aug 1956   Burial: 9 Aug 1956
Site 4 William A. Orme   Mort: S.H. Hines Co.   Place: Washington, DC
        Birth: 5 Nov 1864   Death: 3 Feb 1933   Burial: 6 Feb 1934
Site 5 George Ervin Orme   On stone with Mary A. Orme
        Birth: 7 Oct 1903   Death: 9 Jul 1971   Burial: 12 Jul 1971

Lot: 29 Owner: Edwin R. Allnutt
Site 2 Edwin Ruthvin Allnutt Jr.   Place: Dawsonville
        Birth: 1925   Death: 30 Nov 1938   Burial: 2 Dec 1938
        Mort: Hilton & Hall   s/o Edwin R. & Carrie Williams Allnutt
Site 3 Carrie Williams Allnutt   w/o Edwin Ruthvin Allnutt
        Birth: 11 Apr 1895   Death: 28 Jun 1987   Burial: 1 Jul 1987
Site 4 Edwin Ruthvin Allnutt   Place: Dawsonville
        Birth: 26 May 1892   Death: 28 Dec 1958   Burial: 31 Dec 1958
        Mort: Hilton   h/o Carrie Williams Allnutt

Lot: 30 Lower Owner: Eliza Reid
Site 2 William Oakley Reid   Place: Hagerstown, MD
        Birth: 31 Jan 1905   Death: 24 Jan 1971   Burial: 26 Jan 1971
        Mort: Minnich Funeral Home   On stone with Nina G. Reid
Site 3 Alice Irene Young Reid   Place: Buck Lodge
        Birth: 1868   Death: 22 Jun 1938   Burial: 24 Jun 1938
        Mort: W.R. Pumphrey   TS: Mother

Monocacy Cemetery, Beallsville, Montgomery County, Maryland   153

Site 5 James F. Dailey   Age 83 yrs.
        Birth: 18 Apr 1901   Death: 4 Mar 1985   Burial: 6 Mar 1985

Lot: 30 Upper   Owner: Eliza Reid
Site 2 Mark Reid   On stone with Marion M. Reid   Age 80 yrs
        Birth: 13 Jul 1916   Death: 4 Dec 1996   Burial: 13 Dec 1996
Site 3 Eliza Estelle Young Reid Mort: W.R. Pumphrey   Place: Chevy Chase
        Birth: 1876   Death: 6 Feb 1935   Burial: 9 Feb 1935
Site 4 Stephen A. Reid   Mort: Wm. R. Pumphrey   Place: Chevy Chase
        Birth: 1870   Death: 17 Jan 1944   Burial: 20 Jan 1944
Site 5 Reuel W. Elton
        Birth: 9 May 1890   Death: 11 Jun 1980   Burial: 19 Jun 1980
Site 6 Ellen Reid Elton   On stone with Reuel W. Elton
        Birth: 1903   Burial: 23 Dec 1983

Lot: 31 Lower   Owner: M.A. Munger
Site   Infant Miller   No marker   Mort: W.R. Pumphrey
        Place: Washington, DC   Death: 9 Nov 1933   Burial: 10 Nov 1933
Site 1 Martha Rose Hilleary Surber   Mort: W.R. Pumphrey Place: Rockville
        Birth: 16 Aug 1852   Death: 12 May 1936   Burial: 14 May 1936
Site 2 Georgia Surber Munger   Mort: Robert A. Pumphrey   Place: Rockville
        Birth: 15 Sep 1876   Death: 3 Apr 1958   Burial: 5 Apr 1958
Site 3 Marvin Arthur Munger   Mort: Robert A. Pumphrey   Place: Sykesville
        Birth: 30 Dec 1872   Death: 17 Jan 1959   Burial: 20 Jan 1959
Site 5 Isabelle Miller   No marker   Burial: 30 Dec 1987
Site 6 Norman Egbert Miller   No marker   Mort: Robert A.
        Place: Bethesda   Death: 21 Apr 1965   Burial: 24 Apr 1965

Lot: 31 Upper   Owner: J.B. Munger
Site 2 Cora Ellen Munger   Place: Poolesville
        Birth: 18 Jul 1868   Death: 16 May 1952   Burial: 19 May 1962
        Mort: W.B. Hilton   Age 83
Site 3 Eliza Munger   Mort: Hilton & Hall   Place: Poolesville
        Birth: 1842   Death: 6 Jan 1924   Burial: 8 Jan 1924
Site 4 John B. Munger
        Birth: 17 Apr 1842   Death: 18 Sep 1941   Burial: 20 Sep 1941
Site 5 A. Beulah Mae Munger   Mort: Hilton   Place: Poolesville
        Birth: 12 Dec 1881   Death: 8 Jan 1961   Burial: 10 Jan 1961

Lot: 32   Owner: George W. Brewer
Site 3 Bettie Williams Brewer   Place: Poolesville
        Birth: 6 Jan 1883   Death: 2 Sep 1954   Burial: 4 Sep 1954
        Mort: W.B. Hilton   w/o George W. Brewer
Site 4 George W. Brewer   Place: Poolesville
        Birth: 3 Sep 1878   Death: 12 Nov 1950   Burial: 14 Nov 1950
        Mort: W.B. Hilton   h/o Bettie Williams Brewer
Site 5 Charles M. Brewer   TS: PFC US Army WWII
        Birth: 15 Jul 1908   Death: 30 Mar 1984   Burial: 3 Apr 1984

Lot: 33 Owner: Dr. R.W. Williams

Site 6 William Griffith Perry — is/o William & Jane Williams Perry
  Birth: 6 Nov 1987 Death: 10 Feb 1988 Burial: 15 Feb 1988
Site 9 Mable White Williams Place: Dickerson
  Birth: 6 Jun 1887 Death: 15 Jul 1920 Burial: 17 Jul 1920
  Mort: Hilton & Hall w/o Dr. R.W. Williams
Site 10 Dr. Roger W. Williams Place: Poolesville, MD
  Birth: 23 May 1885 Death: 5 Jul 1970 Burial: 8 Jul 1970
  Mort: Wm. Hilton h/o Mabel White Williams
Site 11 Roger Walter Williams Jr. h/o Mary Shaw Brown Williams
  Birth: 25 Feb 1914 Death: 10 Feb 1987 Burial: 14 Feb 1987

Lot: 34 Owner: John A. Jones

Site 1 Pauline Jones Cissel
  Birth: 1 Aug 1898 Death: 1978 Burial: 15 May 1978
Site 2 William Griffith Cissel Mort: W. Ruben Pumphrey Place: Darnestown
  Birth: 1895 Death: 20 Jun 1930 Burial: 22 Jun 1930
  TS: Maryland 304 Corps Sanitary Train 79 Div
Site 5 Clara Manakee Dyson Place: Kensington
  Birth: 1875 Death: 3 Apr 1939 Burial: 5 Apr 1939
  Mort: W.R. Pumphrey TS: w/o Harry K. Manakee
Site 6 Harry K. Manakee Mort: W.W. Chambers
  Place: Washington, DC Death: 10 Sep 1931 Burial: 12 Sep 1931
Site 7 Edna Manakee Jones Place: Washington, DC
  Birth: 1871 Death: 25 Feb 1940 Burial: 27 Feb 1940
  Mort: W.R. Pumphrey On stone with John A. Jones
Site 8 John A. Jones Place: Washington, DC
  Birth: 1870 Death: 31 Aug 1959 Burial: 3 Sep 1959
  Mort: S.H. Hines Co. h/o Edna M. Jones
Site 9 Margarete A. Jones On stone with Earl Manakee Jones
  Birth: 1902 Death: 1978 Burial: 1 Dec 1978
Site 10 Earl Manakee Jones h/o Margrette A. Jones
  Birth: 27 Jun 1900 Death: 19 Dec 1990 Burial: 22 Dec 1990

Lot: 35 Lower Owner: John Davis, Jr.

Site 1 Margaret J. Davis w/o John W. Davis
  Birth: 12 Apr 1893 Death: 11 Sep 1988 Burial: 14 Sep 1988
Site 2 Harriet Jane Davis Mort: W.T. Hilton & Sons Place: near Thurston
  Birth: 1921 Death: 19 Oct 1923 Burial: 21 Oct 1923
Site 3 John W. Davis Jr.
  Birth: 8 Oct 1887 Death: 20 Jul 1971 Burial: 22 Jul 1971
Site 5 Minnie Abigail Hayes
  Birth: 23 May 1890 Death: 5 Jun 1980 Burial: 9 Jun 1980
Site 6 Virginia Lorraine Hays Mort: Wm. Hilton Place: CA
  Birth: 31 Jul 1919 Death: 6 Jun 1970 Burial: 16 Jun 1970

Lot: 35 Upper Owner: Joseph Gray

Site 1 Adeline Gray Mort: Warner E. Pumphrey Place: Darnestown
  Birth: 1848 Death: 8 Dec 1937 Burial: 11 Dec 1937

Monocacy Cemetery, Beallsville, Montgomery County, Maryland   155

Site 2	Jerome B. Gray		Place: Travilah
	Birth: 1850	Death: 27 Sep 1923	Burial: 29 Sep 1923
	Mort: George M. Gartner		h/o Martha Kelly Gray
Site 2	Martha Kelley Gray	TS: w/o Jerome B. Gray, buried Ebenezer, VA	
	Birth: 1844	Death: 1890	
Site 3	Ida Cooley Gray		Place: Kensington
	Birth: 1872	Death: 20 Jan 1960	Burial: 23 Jan 1960
	Mort: Tyson Wheeler		On stone with Joseph B. Gray
Site 4	Joseph B. Gray		Place: Olney
	Birth: 1871	Death: 8 Oct 1959	Burial: 10 Oct 1959
	Mort: Gartner Funeral Home		h/o Ida Cooley Gray
Site 5	Miss Della M. Holmes	Mort: Tyson Wheeler	Place: Kensington, MD
	Birth: 18 Jul 1878	Death: 9 Aug 1968	Burial: 12 Aug 1968
Site 6	Pearl M. Brown	Mort: Tyson Wheeler	Place: Salsbury
	Birth: 2 Jun 1898	Death: 9 Mar 1969	Burial: 12 May 1969

Lot: 36 Lower   Owner: R.E. White

Site 3	Helen V. White	Mort: W.B. Hilton	Place: Washington, DC
	Birth: 25 Jan 1906	Death: 25 Jun 1943	Burial: 27 Jun 1943

Lot: 36 Upper   Owner: Benjamin J. Hays

Site 3	Mary E. Hayes Hardy	Mort: W.B. Hilton	Place: Baltimore
	Birth: 6 Jun 1927	Death: 5 Oct 1956	Burial: 8 Oct 1956
Site 4	Mary Eloise Hays Gott Millard	Mort: W.B. Hilton	Place: Baltimore
	Birth: 4 Feb 1887	Death: 26 Jul 1955	Burial: 29 Jul 1955
Site 5	Thomas Preston Hayes		TS: CBM US Navy WWII
	Birth: 20 Jan 1910	Death: 25 Nov 1981	Burial: 28 Nov 1981

Lot: 37   Owner: James H. Norris

Site 2	James Walter Norris		Place: State Sanatorium
	Birth: 14 Jul 1887	Death: 4 Nov 1924	Burial: 7 Nov 1924
	Mort: W.T. Hilton & Sons		On stone with Clifton Hershey Norris
Site 4	Clifton Hershey Norris	Mort: W.T. Hilton	Place: Washington, DC
	Birth: 2 Jan 1892	Death: 23 Oct 1918	Burial: 26 Oct 1918
Site 5	William Eugene Hauver Jr.		TS: LT SG US Navy WWII
	Birth: 26 Nov 1913	Death: 13 Jan 1984	Burial: 20 Jan 1984
Site 7	Frank W. Dahn		Place: Bethesda
	Birth: 1879	Death: 2 Jun 1958	Burial: 4 Jun 1958
	Mort: Robert A. Pumphrey		h/o Norrine Norris Dahn
Site 8	Norrine Norris Dahn		On stone with Frank W. Dahn
	Birth: 1893	Death: 20 Jun 1972	Burial: 23 Jun 1972
Site 9	Nonie E. Norris		Place: Boyds
	Birth: 1870	Death: 24 Sep 1956	Burial: 26 Sep 1956
	Mort: W.B. Hilton		On stone with James Henry Norris
Site 10	James Henry Norris		Place: Boyds
	Birth: 1863	Death: 28 Apr 1947	Burial: 30 Apr 1947
	Mort: W.B. Hilton		h/o Nonnie E. Norris

Lot: 38 Lower   Owner: Mrs. Grayson C. Dade

Site 1 Frank Bond Dade   Mort: Holloman & Brown   Place: Norfolk, VA
        Birth: 1892   Death: 9 Mar 1956   Burial: 12 Mar 1956
Site 2 John Liston Dade   Mort: R.A. Mattingly   Place: Washington, DC
        Birth: 1889   Death: 10 Aug 1945   Burial: 14 Aug 1945
Site 3 Viola Dade   Mort: W.R. Pumphrey   Place: Washington, DC
        Birth: 1866   Death: 20 Jan 1940   Burial: 22 Jan 1940
Site 4 Charles Grason Dade   Mort: W.R. Speare Co.   Place: Washington, DC
        Birth: 1859   Death: 28 Aug 1924   Burial: 30 Aug 1924
Site 5 Thomas Dade   No marker   Mort: Robt. Pumphrey
        Place: Wheaton, MD   Death: 14 Apr 1968   Burial: 23 Apr 1968

Lot: 38 Upper   Owner: H.W. Lewis

Site 2 Mildred Lewis Brosius   Age 96 yrs.
        Birth: 1898   Death: 15 Mar 1994   Burial: 26 Mar 1994
Site 3 Sarah (Sallie) M. Lewis   Place: Gaithersburg
        Birth: 1862   Death: 17 Jan 1933   Burial: 19 Jan 1933
        Mort: W.R. Pumphrey   On stone with William Motzer Lewis
Site 4 William Motzer Lewis   Mort: W.R. Pumphrey   Place: Gaithersbur
        Birth: 1856   Death: 20 May 1934   Burial: 23 May 1934

Lot: 39   Owner: W. LeRoy Darby

Site 3 Laura Allnutt Darby   w/o William LeRoy Darby
        Birth: 26 Apr 1896   Death: 28 Dec 1989   Burial: 30 Dec 1989
Site 4 William LeRoy Darby   Place: Washington Grove
        Birth: 13 Sep 1896   Death: 29 Mar 1963   Burial: 1 Apr 1963
        Mort: Francis H. Barber
Site 5 Natalie A. Darby   Mort: W.T. Hilton & Sons Place: Dawsonville
        Birth: 4 Jul 1921   Death: 22 Aug 1922   Burial: 23 Aug 1922

Lot: 40 Lower   Owner: Luther E. Cecil

Site 4 Mary C. Cecil   Place: Barnesville
        Birth: 5 May 1849   Death: 16 Oct 1918   Burial: 18 Oct 1918
        Mort: W.T. Hilton & Sons   TS: w/o Luther E. Cecil
Site 5 Luther E. Cecil   Mort: W.T. Hilton & Sons Place: Barnesville
        Birth: 9 Sep 1846   Death: 18 May 1919   Burial: 20 May 1919
Site 6 Clara L. Cecil   No marker   Mort: Howard H. Hubbard
        Place: Baltimore   Death: 20 Aug 1958   Burial: 25 Aug 1958

Lot: 40 Upper   Owner: Lyttleton S. Poole

Site 3 Deborah Jane Poole   Place: Forest Glen
        Birth: 20 Nov 1886   Death: 28 Oct 1918   Burial: 30 Oct 1918
        Mort: A.G. Carlisle   TS: w/o Lyttleton S. Poole
Site 4 Lyttleton Stewart Poole   Place: Buck Lodge
        Birth: 13 Apr 1881   Death: 3 Feb 1937   Burial: 6 Feb 1937
        Mort: W.R. Pumphrey   h/o Debora Jane Poole

Lot: 41   Owner: Dr. W.L. Lewis

Site 3 Margaret Darby Lewis — Place: Olney
Birth: 15 Nov 1870   Death: 15 Mar 1952   Burial: 18 Mar 1952
Mort: Robert A. Pumphrey   w/o Dr. William Latave Lewis, age 81
TS: d/o Laurence Allnutt & Sallie Chiswell Darby

Site 4 William Latane Lewis, MD   Mort: W.R. Pumphrey   Place: Kensington
Birth: 19 Dec 1860   Death: 12 Jul 1933   Burial: 14 Jul 1933
h/o Margaret Darby Lewis   TS: s/o Thomas Waring & Anne Ursula Lewis

Lot: 43 Lower   Owner: Whitaker, Huey & Carter

Site 1 Beulah Whitaker   Mort: Lee Funeral Home   Place: Kensington
Birth: 25 Sep 1868   Death: 16 May 1959   Burial: 19 May 1959

Site 2 Theresa Whitaker   Mort: Lee Funeral Home   Place: Alta Vista
Birth: 2 May 1871   Death: 11 Mar 1952   Burial: 13 Mar 1952

Site 3 Hester E. Trundle Whitaker   Place: Washington, DC
Birth: 23 Aug 1836   Death: 19 Jan 1925   Burial: 22 Jan 1925
Mort: W.T. Hilton & Sons   TS: w/o A.L. Whitaker

Site 4 A. L. Whitaker   Mort: W.T. Hilton & Sons
Birth: 1 Jul 1829   Death: 4 Nov 1906   Burial: 21 Jul 1926
h/o Hester E. Trundle Whitaker   Removed from Frankfort, Ind.

Site 5 Harriet Elizabeth Whitaker   Mort: W.T. Hilton   Place: Washington, DC
Birth: 17 Sep 1857   Death: 8 Sep 1929   Burial: 10 Sep 1929

Lot: 43 Upper   Owner: Emma H. Lupton

Site 6 John William Vinson   No marker   Mort: W.B. Hilton
Place: Gaithersburg   Death: 18 Mar 1951   Burial: 21 Mar 1951

Lot: 44 Lower   Owner: J.M. & M.M. Savage

Site 1 Joseph M. Savage   h/o Margaret M. Savage
Birth: 5 Oct 1895   Death: 27 Oct 1975   Burial: 31 Oct 1931

Site 2 Margaret M. Savage   Place: Washington, DC
Birth: 1 Sep 1905   Death: 10 May 1969   Burial: 13 May 1969
Mort: Tyson Wheeler   On stone with Joseph M. Savage

Site 3 Geneva M. Nash   No marker   Mort: W.W. Deal
Place: Washington, DC   Death: 9 Jun 1930   Burial: 12 Jun 1930

Site 4 George F. Savage   No marker   Mort: Hilton
Place: Olney   Death: 16 Dec 1964   Burial: 19 Dec 1964

Site 5 Ronald G. Moler   On stone with Edna D. Moler
Birth: Oct 1908   Death: 15 Mar 1983   Burial: 18 Mar 1983

Lot: 44 Upper   Owner: Mrs. Irving J. Ballenger

Site 3 Nellie Holland Ballenger Benson   Benson not on stone   Place: Olney
Birth: 1888   Death: 12 Jul 1964   Burial: 15 Jul 1964
Mort: E.C. Gartmer   TS: [1st] w/o Irving J. Ballenger

Site 4 Carol Hope Ballenger   No marker   Mort: Ernest C. Gartner
Place: Clarksburg   Death: 29 Apr 1943   Burial: 2 May 1943
with Irving T. Ballenger

Monocacy Cemetery, Beallsville, Montgomery County, Maryland

Site 4 Irving Thompson Ballenger
Birth: 1890 Death: 5 Jan 1919
Mort: W.T. Hilton & Sons
Place: Dickerson
Burial: 7 Jan 1919
h/o Nellie Holland Ballenger

Site 5 Nellie Irving Nichols
Birth: 22 Apr 1919 Death: 5 Dec 1982
On stone with Joseph D. Nichols
Burial: 8 Dec 1982

Site 6 Joseph Deets Nichols
Birth: 10 Mar 1919 Death: 6 Sep 1978
h/o Nellie I. Nichols TS: TEC 5 US Army WWII
Burial: 9 Sep 1978

Lot: 45 Lower Owner: Mrs. Oscar T. Cecil

Site 1 Florence M. Gibson Mort: Wm. G. Nalley Place: Baltimore
Birth: 16 May 1865 Death: 16 Nov 1942 Burial: 18 Nov 1942
TS. w/o Robert F. Gibson

Site 2 Robert F. Gibson Mort: W.T. Hilton & Sons Place: Sellman
Birth: 6 May 1861 Death: 13 Sep 1931 Burial: 16 Sep 1931

Site 3 Selma G. Cecil Place: Baltimore
Birth: 5 Aug 1884 Death: 24 Jan 1966 Burial: 26 Jan 1966
Mort: Seltz Funeral Home On stone with Oscar T. Cecil

Site 4 Oscar T. Cecil Mort: W.T. Hilton & Sons Place: Barnesville
Birth: 20 May 1871 Death: 30 Dec 1922 Burial: 1 Jan 1923

Lot: 45 Upper Owner: Mrs. Thomas S. Fisher

Site 3 Mary E. Fisher Place: Kensington
Birth: 3 Sep 1870 Death: 2 Nov 1950 Burial: 4 Nov 1950
Mort: Robert A. Pumphrey On stone with Thomas S. Fisher

Site 4 Thomas S. Fisher Mort: W.T. Hilton & Sons Place: Bucklodge
Birth: 10 Feb 1873 Death: 6 Sep 1920 Burial: 8 Sep 1920

Site 5 George Allnutt Fisher Birth: 16 Feb 1898 Burial: 17 Mar 1973

Lot: 46 Lower Owner: James T. Reed, Jr.

Site 1 James T. Reed Jr. No marker Mort: Robert A.
Place: Washington, DC Death: 12 May 1956 Burial: 16 May 1956

Site 2 Etta Mallie Reed Mort: R.A. Pumphrey Place: Washington, DC
Birth: 19 Feb 1891 Death: 15 Dec 1953 Burial: 18 Dec 1953

Site 3 James T. Reed Mort: Robert A. Pumphrey Place: Washington
Birth: 11 Sep 1883 Death: 8 Jan 1961 Burial: 12 Jan 1961

Site 4 Robert O. Reed Mort: Hilton & Hall Place: Frederick
Birth: 19 Nov 1893 Death: 16 Dec 1924 Burial: 20 Dec 1924

Site 5 Harriet A. Reed Duley Mort: W.B. Hilton Place: Dickerson
Birth: 26 Mar 1861 Death: 10 May 1945 Burial: 15 May 1945
TS: Duley not on stone

Site 6 Thomas J. Reed Mort: Hilton & Hall Place: Martinsburg
Birth: 25 Sep 1846 Death: 23 Feb 1924 Burial: 26 Feb 1924

Lot: 47 Upper Owner: James T. Reed, Jr.

Site 8 Wayne D. Reed Mort: Robert A. Place: Washington, DC
Birth: 14 Feb 1955 Death: 24 Mar 1955 Burial: 26 Mar 1955

Site 11 Greeta I. Reid On stone with Robert D. Reid
Birth: 6 Jul 1937 Death: 30 Aug 1973 Burial: 4 Sep 1973

Monocacy Cemetery, Beallsville, Montgomery County, Maryland

Lot: 48 Lower   Owner: Miscellaneous
- Site 3 Edna Earle Hersberger   w/o Marshall Hersberger
  - Birth: 10 Apr 1880   Death: 6 Mar 1972   Burial: 9 Mar 1972
- Site 4 Marshall Hersberger   Place: Bethesda
  - Birth: 22 Mar 1880   Death: 23 Jun 1957   Burial: 26 Jun 1957
  - Mort: Hilton   h/o Edna Earle Hersberger
- Site 5 Ellen Kneesi   On Carpenter stone
  - Birth: 22 Feb 1942   Death: 27 Jun 1994   Burial: 30 Jun 1994

Lot: 49 Lower   Owner: R. Edgar Stephens
- Site 1 Mary Lou Stephens
  - Birth: 19 Mar 1925   Death: 23 Feb 1997   Burial: 27 Feb 1997
- Site 2 George Russell Earl   Mort: Molesworth   Place: Rockville
  - Birth: 24 May 1888   Death: 10 Dec 1966   Burial: 13 Dec 1966
  - TS: Colorado SGT US Marine Corps WWI
- Site 3 Essie R. Stephens Earl   w/o R. Edgar Stephens & George R. Earl
  - Birth: 10 Apr 1893   Death: 13 Feb 1980   Burial: 16 Feb 1980
- Site 4 Robert Edgar Stephens   Place: Baltimore
  - Birth: Dec 1886   Death: 20 Nov 1954   Burial: 23 Nov 1954
  - Mort: Olin L. Molesworth   h/o Esther Cooley Stephens
- Site 5 Esther Cooley Stephens   Place: Takoma Park
  - Birth: 1873   Death: 20 Feb 1954   Burial: 22 Feb 1954
  - Mort: Warner E. Pumphrey   w/o Robert Edgar Stephens
- Site 6 Ernest Paul Hogman   Mort: Warner E. Phumprey   Place: Takoma Park
  - Birth: 1882   Death: 24 Sep 1961   Burial: 26 Sep 1961

Lot: 49 Upper   Owner: Algie Morningstar
- Site 1 Harriet Mornigstar Hanson
  - Birth: 1905   Death: 1989   Burial: 1 Apr 1989
  - w/o Joseph S. Hanson, sister of Thomas Morningstar
- Site 2 Joseph S. Hanson   TS: LCDR US Navy WWII
  - Birth: 1905   Death: 1977   Burial: 28 Oct 1977
- Site 3 Fanny Maude Morningstar   TS: Mother   Place: Barnesville
  - Birth: 1879   Death: 31 Oct 1948   Burial: 2 Nov 1948
  - Mort: W.B. Hilton   w/o Algie T. Morningstar
- Site 4 Algie Thomas Morningstar   Place: Barnesville
  - Birth: 1879   Death: 22 Sep 1958   Burial: 24 Sep 1958
  - Mort: Hilton   h/o Fannie Maude Morningstar
- Site 5 Arthur Sylvester Morningstar   Place: Bethesda
  - Birth: 1910   Death: 11 Sep 1960   Burial: 15 Sep 1960
  - Mort: Tyson Wheeler   TS: Father

Lot: 50   Owner: Mrs. Sadie T. Hoyle
- Site 3 Sarah Trussell Hoyle   Place: Dickerson
  - Birth: 17 Feb 1875   Death: 19 Oct 1947   Burial: 21 Oct 1947
  - Mort: W.B. Hilton   w/o Franklin Jones Hoyle
- Site 4 Franklin Jones Hoyle   Place: Bethesda
  - Birth: 1 Jun 1870   Death: 20 Oct 1960   Burial: 22 Oct 1960
  - Mort: W.B. Hilton   h/o Sarah Trussell Hoyle

Monocacy Cemetery, Beallsville, Montgomery County, Maryland

Site 5 Margaret Bowers Hoyle
        Birth: 9 Dec 1918   Death: 30 Jan 1981
Site 7 Joseph Henry Hoyle   Place: Silver Spring, MD
        Birth: 9 Jan 1914   Death: 4 Apr 1970   Burial: 7 Apr 1970
        Mort: Robert Pumphrey   s/o Franklin Jones & Sadie Trussell Hoyle

Lot: 51 Lower Owner: John & Elva Cooper
Site 1 John H. Cooper
        Birth: 28 Mar 1911   Death: 27 Jun 1985   Burial: 29 Jun 1985
Site 2 Frances L. Cooper   Age 19   Place: Washington, DC
        Birth: 25 Nov 1932   Death: 9 Jan 1952   Burial: 11 Jan 1952
        Mort: Deal Funeral Home   TS: d/o John H. & Elva G. Cooper
Site 3 Elva G. Cooper   w/o John Hartzell Cooper
        Birth: 26 Apr 1909   Death: 3 Sep 1980   Burial: 6 Sep 1980

Lot: 51 Upper Owner: James M. Belcher
Site 2 Corp. Claude Hicks Belcher   Place: Korea
        Birth: 9 Jan 1929   Death: 12 Feb 1950   Burial: 9 Dec 1951
        Mort: W.B. Hilton   Age 22 TS: Maryland 38 INF 2 INF DIV Korea
Site 3 James Walter Belcher   h/o Mattie B. Belcher
        Birth: 25 Mar 1886   Death: 7 Feb 1978   Burial: 20 Feb 1978
Site 4 Mattie B. Belcher   Place: Frederick, MD
        Birth: 30 May 1904   Death: 25 Jun 1969   Burial: 27 Jun 1969
        Mort: Wm. Hilton   On stone with James Walter Belcher
Site 5 Alberta M. Belcher   Mort: Hilton   Place: Bethesda
        Birth: 7 Jun 1927   Death: 22 Jun 1965   Burial: 24 Jun 1965

Lot: 52 Lower Owner: Donald M. Shry
Site 3 Bessie Mae Shry   Place: Westminster
        Birth: 1891   Death: 19 May 1967   Burial: 22 May 1967
        Mort: D.D. Harlzle & Son   On stone with Nelson F. Shry
Site 4 Nelson Fillmore Shry   Place: Union Bridge
        Birth: 1887   Death: 21 Dec 1951   Burial: 24 Dec 1951
        Mort: D.D. Hartzler & Son   h/o Bessie M. Shry

Lot: 52 Upper Owner: Gaines, Wall & Fitzgerald
Site 1 Charles W. Fitzgerald   h/o Virginia Jones Fitzgerald
        Birth: 6 May 1899   Death: 21 Feb 1982   Burial: 26 Feb 1982
Site 2 Virginia Jones Fitzgerald   w/o Charles Fitzgerald
        Birth: 12 Nov 1895   Death: 1 Apr 1987   Burial: 4 May 1987
Site 4 Nena J. Wall
        Birth: 11 Nov 1890   Death: 3 Aug 1982   Burial: 9 Aug 1982

Lot: 53 Owner: William P. Hunter
Site 1 Harriet A. Littlefield   Not buried at Monocacy, name on stone
        Birth: 1806   Death: 1892 On stone with George E. Littlefield
Site 2 George E. Littlefield   Mort: Chambers Co.   Place: Washington, DC
        Birth: 1881   Death: 11 Mar 1959   Burial: 14 Mar 1959

Monocacy Cemetery, Beallsville, Montgomery County, Maryland   161

Site 3 Mattie L. Hunter   Place: Silver Spring
        Birth: 14 Sep 1882   Death: 14 Jun 1962   Burial: 16 Jun 1962
        Mort: W.W. Chambers   w/o William P. Hunter
Site 4 William Pierce Hunter   Place: Beallsville
        Birth: 22 Nov 1877   Death: 16 Aug 1955   Burial: 18 Aug 1955
        Mort: W.B. Hilton   h/o Mattie L. Hunter
Site 9 Catherine B. White Hunter   w/o William Pierce Hunter Jr.
        Birth: 7 Apr 1912   Death: 2 Jul 1989   Burial: 5 Jul 1989
Site 10 William Pierce Hunter Jr.   Place: Cumberland, MD
        Birth: 11 Aug 1911   Death: 5 Nov 1970   Burial: 7 Nov 1970
        Mort: Tyson Wheeler   h/o Catherine White Hunter
Site 11 Mary Victoria Weller   Place: Frederick
        Birth: 7 Oct 1885   Death: 14 Jun 1962   Burial: 16 Jun 1962
        Mort: Hilton   On stone with Parker L. Weller
Site 12 Parker L. Weller   Place: Braddock Heights
        Birth: 28 Feb 1875   Death: 2 Dec 1958   Burial: 4 Dec 1958
        Mort: Hilton   h/o Mary Victoria Weller

Lot: 54 Lower   Owner: C.E. Knill, Jr.
Site 3 Annie Neal Knill   Place: Sellman
        Birth: 23 Sep 1918   Death: 7 Sep 1954   Burial: 9 Sep 1954
        Mort: W.B. Hilton   w/o Charles E. Knill Jr.

Lot: 54 Upper   Owner: Mary Morningstar
Site 1 Catherine M. Dill
        Birth: 5 Jun 1907   Death: 26 Jan 1992   Burial: 30 Jan 1992
Site 2 Elmer B. Dill   Mort: Pumphrey   Place: Takoma Park, MD
        Birth: 11 Jan 1908   Death: 2 Oct 1969   Burial: 4 Oct 1969
Site 5 Agnes Honore Morningstar   Place: Barnesville
        Birth: 13 Sep 1874   Death: 15 Aug 1965   Burial: 17 Aug 1965
        Mort: Hilton   TS: Mother   w/o Edgar John Morningstar
Site 6 Edgar John Morningstar   TS: Father   Place: Frederick
        Birth: 5 Jul 1875   Death: 29 Apr 1954   Burial: 1 May 1954
        Mort: W.B. Hilton   h/o Agnes Honore Morningstar

Lot: 55 Lower   Owner: Anna Poole
Site 3 Sarah Anna Beall Poole   On stone with John Ethan Poole
        Birth: 24 Jul 1909   Death: 5 May 1992   Burial: 14 May 1992
Site 4 John Ethan Poole   Place: Dickerson
        Birth: 15 Feb 1897   Death: 29 Mar 1957   Burial: 30 Mar 1957
        Mort: Hilton   h/o Anna Beall Poole

Lot: 55 Upper   Owner: Miscellaneous
Site 2 Rev. James Lee Shannon
        Birth: 23 Sep 1918   Death: 1 Apr 1988   Burial: 5 Apr 1988
        s/o Adam S. & Margaret B. Shannon, h/o Catherine Fry Shannon
Site 3 Margaret B. (Maggie) Shannon   Place: Bethesda
        Birth: 1888   Death: 7 Dec 1960   Burial: 10 Dec 1960
        Mort: Hilton   w/o Adam S. Shannon

Site 4 Adam S. Shannon   Place: Barnesville
        Birth: 1886   Death: 25 Sep 1956   Burial: 27 Sep 1956
        Mort: W.B. Hilton   h/o Margaret B. Shannon
Site 6 Adam S. Shannon, Jr.   h/o Ethel Grubb Shannon
        Birth: 29 Dec 1916   Death: 8 Aug 1985   Burial: 10 Aug 1985

Lot: 56 Lower Owner: William E. Aud
Site 3 Grace Susan Aud   Place: Poolesville
        Birth: 22 Jul 1921   Death: 8 Jan 1957   Burial: 11 Jan 1957
        Mort: Hilton   w/o William E. Aud

Lot: 56 Upper Owner: Thomas E. Cole
Site 2 Margaret Ann Cole
        Birth: 28 Aug 1933   Death: 8 Nov 1990   Burial: 12 Nov 1990
Site 3 Bertha M. Cole   Place: Frederick Hospital
        Birth: 25 Mar 1913   Death: 13 Apr 1954   Burial: 16 Apr 1954
        Mort: W.B. Hilton   On stone with Thomas E. Cole & Maggie E. Cole
Site 4 Thomas E. Cole   h/o Bertha M. Cole
        Birth: 17 Sep 1907   Death: 11 Dec 1977   Burial: 14 Dec 1977
Site 5 Maggie E. Cooley Cole Birth: 7 Feb 1912 2nd w/o Thomas E. Cole

Lot: 57 Upper Owner: James H. & Jean A. Fling
Site 6 James Montgomery Boswell Jr.   h/o Helen Heeter Boswell
        Birth: 10 Oct 1912   Death: 28 Nov 1993   Burial: 1 Dec 1993

Lot: 58 Upper Owner: Miscellaneous
Site 6 Robert F. Snyder   No marker   Death: 12 Jan 1993

Row H

Lot: 1 Lower   Owner: Mrs. Mamie Jones
Site 2 Sarah E. Corcoran Hamill   Place: Washington, DC
          Birth: 1858   Death: 21 Aug 1927   Burial: 23 Aug 1927
          Mort: W.R. Pumphrey   TS: w/o Henry Phelps Hamill
Site 4 Rev. Henry Phelps Hamill   Place: Washington, DC
          Birth: 1853   Death: 4 Jul 1931   Burial: 6 Jul 1931
          Mort: Warner E. Pumphrey   TS: 50 years Methodist Preacher

Lot: 1 Upper   Owner: Franklin Williams
Site 3 Francis G. Williams   TS: s/o F.T. & Mary L. Williams
          Birth: 25 Jun 1898   Death: 16 Jul 1898   Burial: 16 Jul 1898
          Reinterment - 16 Sep 1903
Site 4 Mary Louise Dawson Williams   Place: Rockville
          Birth: 21 Jun 1855   Death: 13 Jul 1932   Burial: 15 Jul 1932
          Mort: W.R. Pumphrey 2nd w/o Francis T. Williams
Site 5 Francis T. Williams
          Birth: 30 Aug 1845   Death: 3 Nov 1906   Burial: 7 Nov 1906
          h/o Mary L. Dawson Williams & Georgia Griffith Williams
Site 6 Georgia Griffith Williams   Death: 16 Mar 1891   Burial: 17 Mar 1891
          TS: [1st] w/o Francis T. Williams, age 39-4-5   Reinterment - 16 Sep 1903
Site 7 Julia May Williams   TS: d/o Francis T. & Georgia Griffith Williams
          Birth: 17 Nov 1882   Death: 20 Nov 1882   Burial: 20 Nov 1882
          Reinterment - 16 Sep 1903

Lot: 2   Owner: Mrs. William H. Dickerson
Site   Edwin Trundle Dickerson   Mort: Tickner   Place: Baltimore
          Birth: 6 Nov 1878   Death: 5 Feb 1958   Burial: 10 Feb 1958
          TS: h/o Jennie R. Bier Dickerson, Judge of Supreme Bench, Baltimore City
Site 1 C. Milton Dickerson   Mort: Wm. G. Tickner & Son   Place: Baltimore
          Birth: 24 Nov 1867   Death: 16 Apr 1943   Burial: 19 Apr 1943
Site 2 Edith Dickerson   TS: Daughter   Place: Baltimore
          Birth: 7 Sep 1870   Death: 14 Dec 1933   Burial: 18 Dec 1933
          Mort: Wm. Cook   d/o William H. & Elizabeth Dickerson
Site 3 Elizabeth Ellen Trundle Dickerson   TS: Mother   Place: Baltimore
          Birth: 28 Nov 1842   Death: 16 Sep 1926   Burial: 18 Sep 1926
          Mort: William Cook   On stone with William Harrison Dickerson
Site 4 William Harrison Dickerson   h/o Elizabeth Ellen Trundle Dickerson
          Birth: 28 Jun 1838   Death: 19 Jul 1912   Burial: 21 Jul 1912
Site 5 Lillian Dickerson   Place: Baltimore
          Birth: 24 Dec 1871   Death: 15 Dec 1951   Burial: 18 Dec 1951
          Mort: Wm. J. Tickner   Age 79
Site 7 Charles Milton Dickerson   No marker
          Birth: 13 Aug 1867   Death: 29 Nov 1944
Site 8 Martha H. Dickerson   No marker
          Birth: 23 Aug 1870   Death: 4 Jun 1944

Monocacy Cemetery, Beallsville, Montgomery County, Maryland

Site 9 Eugenia T. Dickerson   No marker
        Birth: 16 Apr 1877   Death: 15 Jul 1897
Site 10 Alonzo Dickerson   No marker
        Birth: 14 Sep 1874   Death: 21 Aug 1879
Site 11 George H. Dickerson   No marker   h/o Myrtle M. Dickerson
        Birth: 3 Jun 1871   Death: 23 Apr 1960
Site 12 Myrtle M. Dickerson   No marker   w/o George H. Dickerson
        Birth: 2 Dec 1878   Burial: 6 Feb 1922

Lot: 3 Owner: L.B. Johnson

Site 1 Myrtle M. Johnson   Place: Washington, DC
        Birth: 2 Dec 1878   Death: 26 Feb 1922   Burial: 1 Mar 1922
        Mort: W.T. Hilton & Sons   TS: w/o George H. Johnson
Site 2 George Haslip Johnson   Place: Frederick
        Birth: 3 Jun 1871   Death: 23 Apr 1960   Burial: 25 Apr 1960
        Mort: M.R. Etchison   h/o Myrtle M. Johnson
Site 3 Alonzo Johnson   Reinterment
        Birth: 14 Sep 1874   Death: 21 Aug 1879   Burial: 21 Aug 1904
Site 4 Miss Eugenia Tyson Johnson   Reinterment
        Birth: 16 Apr 1877   Death: 15 Jul 1897   Burial: 21 Aug 1904
Site 5 Martha H. Johnson   Mort: W.W. Chambers   Place: Washington, DC
        Birth: 23 Aug 1870   Death: 4 Jun 1941   Burial: 7 Jun 1941
Site 6 Charles M. Johnson   Mort: S.H. Hines Co.   Place: Washington, DC
        Birth: 13 Aug 1867   Death: 29 Nov 1944   Burial: 2 Dec 1944
Site 7 Laura E. Schwerin   Mort: J. Wm. Lees   Place: Washington, DC
        Birth: 30 Apr 1873   Death: 18 Feb 1937   Burial: 20 Feb 1937
Site 8 Miss Mattie B. Johnson   Mort: Etchison   Place: Hillsboro, VA
        Birth: 30 Sep 1878   Death: 14 Jul 1968   Burial: 16 Jul 1968
Site 9 Sarah C. Johnson   Mort: W.T. Hilton & Sons   Place: Comus
        Birth: 24 Feb 1843   Death: 15 Nov 1917   Burial: 17 Nov 1917
Site 10 Levin B. Johnson   Mort: W.T. Hilton & Sons   Place: Comus
        Birth: 2 Dec 1839   Death: 31 Aug 1929   Burial: 2 Sep 1929

Lot: 4 Owner: William T. Jones

Site   Eleanor Woodward Jones   No dates on stone   Burial: 14 Sep 1903
        TS: d/o William T. & Achsah Waters Jones   Reinterment
Site   John Blake Jones   No dates on stone   Burial: 14 Sep 1903
        TS: s/o William T. & Achsah Waters Jones   Reinterment
Site   Nannie Jones   TS: d/o W.T. & E.R. Jones   Reinterment
        Birth: 5 Apr 1869   Death: 22 Jul 1877   Burial: 14 Sep 1903
Site 1 Mary (Mamie) McCubbin Jones   Place: Kensington
        Birth: 1863   Death: 8 Nov 1937   Burial: 11 Nov 1937
        Mort: W.R. Pumphrey
Site 2 Achsah D. Waters Jones   TS: [1st] w/o William T. Jones   Reinterment
        Birth: 25 Feb 1825   Death: 14 Apr 1866   Burial: 14 Sep 1903
Site 3 William T. Jones
        Birth: 27 Sep 1822   Death: 5 May 1903   Burial: 8 May 1903
        h/o Achsah Waters Jones & Elizabeth R. Jones   Reinterment

Monocacy Cemetery, Beallsville, Montgomery County, Maryland   165

Site 4	Elizabeth R. Jones		TS: [2nd] w/o William T. Jones
	Birth: 16 Aug 1833	Death: 27 Apr 1905	Burial: 30 Apr 1905
Site 9	Charles C. Jones		Place: Bethesda
	Birth: 24 Aug 1899	Death: 11 Sep 1957	Burial: 13 Sep 1957
	Mort: R.A. Pumphrey		s/o Clara C. & Eugene Jones
Site 10	Clara Conley Jones		Place: Frederick
	Birth: 30 May 1872	Death: 24 Dec 1943	Burial: 28 Dec 1943
	Mort: Wm. R. Pumphrey		TS: w/o Eugene Jones
Site 11	Eugene Jones, MD		Place: Washington, DC
	Birth: 27 Sep 1873	Death: 22 Sep 1931	Burial: 23 Sep 1931
	Mort: W.R. Pumphrey		h/o Clara Conley Jones

Lot: 5   Owner: Howard Spates (1 Stone in lot)

Site	Clara C. Spates	Birth: 12 Nov 1886	Death: 24 Nov 1886
Site	Nellie Elizabeth Spates	Birth: 21 Feb 1890	Death: 12 Aug 1890
Site 1	Howard Jetson Spates	Mort: W.R. Pumphrey	Place: Logan
	Birth: 23 Jul 1877	Death: 11 Apr 1938	Burial: 13 Apr 1938
Site 2	William Outerbridge Spates	Mort: W.R. Pumphrey	Place: Rockville
	Birth: 9 Oct 1878	Death: 4 Jul 1918	Burial: 7 Jul 1918
Site 3	Anna R. Shaw	No marker	Mort: Alfred Rose
	Place: Philadelphia, PA	Death: 10 Apr 1971	Burial: 14 Apr 1971
Site 4	Richard Fremont Spates	Mort: Hilton & Hall	Place: Poolesville
	Birth: 17 May 1850	Death: 10 Feb 1930	Burial: 11 Feb 1930
Site 5	Clara Elizabeth Karn Spates		w/o Richard Fenton Spates
	Birth: 30 Sep 1859	Death: 9 Nov 1905	Burial: 12 Nov 1905
Site 6	Franklin Pearce Spates		Place: Minteir Hot Springs
	Birth: 29 Feb 1853	Death: 6 Dec 1927	Burial: 13 Dec 1927
	Mort: W.R. Pumphrey	TS: Death 1930, resident of Silver City, NM	
Site 7	Elizabeth Lucille Backman		No marker
		Death: 4 Dec 1982	Burial: 6 Dec 1982
Site 11	Annie Essie Spates	w/o Joseph Roger Spates	No marker
		Death: 28 Mar 1975	Burial: 31 Mar 1975
Site 12	Joseph Roger Spates		Place: Takoma Park
	Birth: 8 Nov 1881	Death: 4 Sep 1950	Burial: 4 Sep 1950
	Mort: W.B. Hilton		h/o Annie E. Spates

Lot: 6   Owner: Claggett Hilton & Thomas Story

Site 1	Alonnie Brosius Hilton		Place: Frederick
	Birth: 14 Aug 1874	Death: 18 Dec 1950	Burial: 20 Dec 1950
	Mort: M.R. Etchison & Son	w/o Claggett C. Hilton	
Site 2	Claggett C. Hilton		Place: Frederick
	Birth: 24 Feb 1867	Death: 4 Jan 1933	Burial: 6 Jan 1933
	Mort: W.R. Pumphrey		h/o Alonnie Brosius Hilton
Site 3	Frances R. Snyder Hilton		w/o W.T. Hilton
	Birth: 5 Nov 1830	Death: 16 Jun 1912	Burial: 19 Jun 1912
Site 4	Mr. W. T. Hilton		h/o Frances R. Hilton, age 80
	Birth: 31 May 1829	Death: 26 Jan 1909	Burial: 28 Jan 1909
Site 5	Henry Mortimer Hilton	Mort: Hilton & Price	Place: Barnesville
	Birth: 9 Jan 1854	Death: 18 Sep 1934	Burial: 20 Sep 1934

Site 6 Sarah Elizabeth Hilton
        Birth: 31 Dec 1832   Death: 14 Dec 1907   Burial: 16 Dec 1907
Site 7 Mary S. Fields
        Birth: 15 Oct 1871   Death: 25 May 1910   Burial: 27 May 1910
Site 8 Frank W. Story   Mort: Ruback   Place: Norwalk, OH
        Birth: 22 Jun 1873   Death: 24 May 1956   Burial: 26 May 1956
Site 9 Thomas S. Story   Mort: W.T. Hilton & Sons Place: Barnesville
        Birth: 15 May 1835   Death: 8 Mar 1914   Burial: 8 Mar 1914
Site 10 Sidonia Francis Story   Mort: Hilton & Hall   Place: Barnesville
        Birth: 13 Jul 1858   Death: 27 Jan 1917   Burial: 29 Jan 1917
Site 11 Edward H. Story   Mort: Wm. Hilton   Place: Silver Spring, MD
        Birth: 23 Oct 1891   Death: 5 Jun 1970   Burial: 8 Jun 1970
Site 12 Mary W. Story   d/o Henry Wingert & Lillian Story
        Birth: 20 May 1899   Death: 14 Feb 1991   Burial: 22 Feb 1991

Lot: 7 Owner:
Site 3 Lillian Elizabeth Jones Mort: W.B. Hilton   Place: Silver Spring
        Birth: 6 Sep 1882   Death: 10 Feb 1939   Burial: 13 Feb 1939
        w/o Lawrence B. Jones   Disinterred 8 Nov 1984
        Moved to Gates of Heaven Cemetery, Silver Spring, MD   No marker
Site 4 Lawrence Beall Jones   Mort: Hilton & Price   Place: Dickerson
        Birth: 11 Oct 1875   Death: 31 Jan 1934   Burial: 3 Feb 1934
        h/o Lillian Elizabeth Jones   Disinterred 8 Nov 1984
        Moved to Gates of Heaven Cemetery, Silver Spring, MD   No marker
Site 5 Infant Jones   Mort: C.E. Cline   Place: Frederick City Hospital
        Birth: 26 Jun 1916   Death: 26 Jun 1916   Burial: 27 Jun 1916
        i/o Lawrence B. & Lillian Jones   Disinterred 8 Nov 1984
        Moved to Gates of Heaven Cemetery, Silver Spring, MD   No marker

Lot: 7 Lower   Owner: Samuel Creighton & Lawrence R. Jones
Site 9 Constance Beulah Nicholson Jones   Place: Dickerson
        Birth: 1889   Death: 3 Jun 1931   Burial: 5 Jun 1931
        Mort: W.T. Hilton & Sons   1st w/o Samuel Creighton Jones
Site 10 Samuel Creighton Jones   Mort: W.B. Hilton   Place: Frederick Hospital
        Birth: 1888   Death: 3 Nov 1944   Burial: 6 Nov 1944
        h/o Constance Beulah Nicholson Jones & Kathryn Soper
Site 11 Myrna Livingston Jones Clark   Place: Riverdale, MD
        Birth: 1923   Death: 11 Apr 1970   Burial: 14 Apr 1970
        Mort: Wm. Hilton   TS: w/o Henry T. Clark Jr.

Lot: 7 Upper   Owner: Mary Ann & J. Maurice Carlisle, Jr.
Site 4 Mary Ann Poole Carlisle   w/o J. Maurice Carlisle, Jr.
        Birth: 10 Jun 1936   Death: 18 Jun 1991   Burial: 21 Jun 1991

Lot: 8 Owner: Notley & G. Hays
Site 1 May Hays   Place: Buckeystown
        Birth: 10 Aug 1849   Death: 10 Sep 1918   Burial: 13 Sep 1918
        Mort: Mr. R. Etchison   TS: d/o T.L. & M.P. Hays

Monocacy Cemetery, Beallsville, Montgomery County, Maryland

Site 2 William Notley Hays
    Birth: 18 Mar 1834
    Death: 9 Feb 1909
    TS: s/o Samuel S. & Annie R. Hays
    Burial: 11 Feb 1909

Site 3 Harriet A. Hays Baker
    Birth: 5 Apr 1830
    Death: 23 May 1906
    TS: d/o S.S. Sr. & Annie Hays, w/o Edward Baker
    Burial: 25 May 1906

Site 4 Samuel Simmons Hays
    Birth: 2 Apr 1826
    Death: 16 Jul 1910
    TS: s/o S.S. Sr. & Annie B. Hays
    Burial: 18 Jul 1910

Site 5 Virginia Hays Anderson
    Birth: 1851
    Death: 28 Apr 1930
    Mort: W.T. Hilton & Sons
    Place: Adamstown
    Burial: 1 May 1930

Site 7 Thomas L. Hays
    Birth: 20 Nov 1816
    Death: 4 Oct 1873
    Mort: Chas. E. Roberts
    h/o Mary T. Hays
    TS: Age 56-10-14
    Burial: 5 May 1930
    Reinterment

Site 8 Mary T. Hays
    Death: 9 Apr 1884
    TS: w/o Thomas L. Hays, age 58-1-21
    Mort: Chas. E. Roberts
    Burial: 5 May 1930
    Reinterment

Lot: 9 Owner: Abraham Harris

Site 1 Harvey Joseph Harris
    Birth: 5 Mar 1880
    Death: 23 Oct 1951
    Mort: W.B. Hilton
    Place: Germantown
    Burial: 26 Oct 1951
    Age 70

Site 2 Nettie Irene Harris
    Birth: 13 Feb 1874
    Death: 23 Mar 1939
    Mort: W.B. Hilton
    Place: Dickerson
    Burial: 25 Mar 1939
    d/o Abraham & Mary T. Harris

Site 3 Mary E. Taylor Harris
    Birth: 1846
    Mort: W.T. Hilton & Son
    Death: 28 Dec 1932
    Place: Barnesville
    Burial: 31 Dec 1932
    TS: w/o Abraham Simmons Harris

Site 4 Abraham Simmons Harris
    Birth: 13 Mar 1834
    Death: 31 Jan 1907
    TS: Age 72-9-18
    Burial: 2 Feb 1907

Site 5 Charles Abner Harris
    Place: Sykesville
    No marker
    Death: 19 Jun 1953
    Mort: W.B. Hilton
    Burial: 22 Jun 1953

Site 11 Estelle Mae Harris
    Birth: 27 Aug 1889
    Mort: B.Lee Feete
    Death: 6 Dec 1960
    Place: Frederick
    Burial: 9 Dec 1960

Site 12 Alfred John Harris
    Birth: 7 Feb 1887
    Mort: C.H. Feete
    Death: 25 Feb 1950
    Place: Martinsburg, WV
    Burial: 28 Feb 1950

Lot: 10 Owner: H.B. Fawley

Site Child of H. C. Brown
    No marker
    Burial: 5 Aug 1904

Site 1 Infant Fawley
    Place: Travilah
    Cause: Stillborn
    No marker
    Death: 20 May 1939
    Mort: W.B. Hilton
    Burial: 20 May 1939
    i/o H.O. & H.L. Fawley

Site 1 Lillian Lee Fawley
    Birth: 9 Apr 1899
    Death: 3 Apr 1921
    Mort: Hilton & Hall
    Place: Poolesville
    Burial: 5 Apr 1921
    TS: w/o Harry B. Fawley

Site 2 Harry B. Fawley
    Birth: 12 Sep 1893
    Death: 18 Mar 1944
    Mort: W.B. Hilton
    Place: Olney
    Burial: 21 Mar 1944
    h/o Lillian Lee Fawley

Site 3 Margaret Anne Fawley
    Birth: 5 Feb 1857
    Death: 23 Dec 1938
    Mort: Hilton & Hall
    Place: Travilah
    Burial: 27 Dec 1938
    TS: w/o William B. Fawley

Site 4 William B. Fawley   Place: Travilah
        Birth: 12 Dec 1853   Death: 7 May 1939   Burial: 9 May 1939
        Mort: Hilton & Hall   h/o Margaret Anne Fawley
Site 7 Chasi David Fawley   Death: 26 Aug 1907   Burial: 27 Aug 1907
        s/o H. Berkley & Virgie O. Fawley, age 1-2-18   illegible
Site 7 Virgie Fawley   Death: 18 Jul 1909   Burial: 19 Jul 1909
        d/o H.B. & Virgie O. Fawley, age 0-3-2   illegible
Site 7 Infant Shoemaker   Cause: Stillborn   Place: Washington, DC
        Birth: 1 Jun 1938   Death: 1 Jun 1938   Burial: 2 Jun 1938
        Mort: W.R. Pumphrey   i/o J.W. & Louise F. Shoemaker   illegible
Site 8 Virgie O. Fawley   Mort: Tyson Wheeler   Place: Gaithersburg, MD
        Birth: 12 Feb 1884   Death: 4 Feb 1971   Burial: 6 Feb 1971
Site 9 Harland B. Fawley   Place: Bethesda
        Birth: 7 Jan 1882   Death: 8 Apr 1964   Burial: 11 Apr 1964
        Mort: Tyson Wheeler   h/o Virgie O. Fawley
Site 10 James William Shoemaker   h/o Louise M. Fawley Shoemaker
        Birth: 8 Feb 1914   Death: 20 Nov 1977   Burial: 22 Nov 1977
Site 11 Louise M. Fawley Shoemaker   TS: w/o James William Shoemaker
        Birth: 19 Sep 1911   Death: 20 Oct 1990   Burial: 24 Oct 1990

Lot: 11 Owner: T.R. Hall
Site 4 Mortimer Beecher Hall   Mort: John M. Oakey Inc. Place: Roanoke, VA
        Birth: 1875   Death: 8 Jul 1937   Burial: 10 Jul 1937
Site 7 Louis Taliaferro Headley   Place: Baltimore
        Birth: 3 Jan 1890   Death: 15 Jan 1942   Burial: 18 Jan 1942
        Mort: William Cook   h/o Claire Williams Headley
Site 8 Claire Williams Headley   w/o Lewis T. Headley
        Birth: 21 Apr 1891   Death: 13 Apr 1979   Burial: 16 Apr 1979
Site 9 Thomas Randolph Hall III
        Birth: 11 Nov 1907   Death: 31 Dec 1976   Burial: 31 Dec 1979
        s/o T.R. & Beulah White Hall   TS: Buried in Golconda, IL
Site 10 Thomas Randolph Hall   Place: Poolesville
        Birth: 1871   Death: 12 Dec 1927   Burial: 14 Dec 1927
        Mort: Hilton & Hall   h/o Beulah White Hall
Site 11 Beulah White Hall   Place: Culpepper, VA
        Birth: 24 Feb 1880   Death: 5 Dec 1969   Burial: 8 Dec 1969
        Mort: Wm. Hilton   w/o Thomas Randolph Hall
Site 12 Elizabeth Owens Hall   Mort: Hilton & Hall   Place: St. Louis, MO
        Birth: 1906   Death: 23 Feb 1940   Burial: 27 Feb 1940

Lot: 12 Owner: Harvey White
Site 1 Eleanor May Jones
        Birth: 12 Jan 1910   Death: 3 Dec 1984   Burial: 5 Dec 1984
        TS: d/o George D. Jones & Alethea Brewer Jones White
Site 2 Alethea Brewer Jones White
        Birth: 20 Jan 1875   Death: 7 Jan 1979   Burial: 10 Jan 1979
        TS: [w/o George D. Jones & 3rd] w/o Harvey J. White

Monocacy Cemetery, Beallsville, Montgomery County, Maryland   169

Site 3 Ida Dyson White   Place: Poolesville
        Birth: 24 Jul 1872   Death: 19 Oct 1919   Burial: 21 Oct 1919
        Mort: Hilton & Hall   TS: [1st] w/o Harvey J. White
Site 4 Harvey Jones White   Mort: W.B. Hilton   Place: Pooesville
        Birth: 9 Mar 1869   Death: 28 Feb 1950   Burial: 2 Mar 1950
        h/o Ida Dyson White, Nannie Poole White & Alethea B. White
Site 5 Nannie Poole White   Place: Poolesville
        Birth: 10 Nov 1869   Death: 8 Feb 1928   Burial: 10 Feb 1928
        Mort: Hilton & Hall   TS: [2nd] w/o Harvey J. White
Site 7 Elizabeth Darnell Jones   Mort: Chas. Roberts
                                Death: 28 Nov 1863   Burial: 15 May 1920
        TS: w/o John Jones, Sr., age 61 yrs   Removed from private burial ground
Site 7 John Jones Sr.   TS: age 68 yrs   Mort: Chas. Roberts
                                Death: 16 Feb 1870   Burial: 15 May 1920
        h/o Elizabeth Darnell Jones   Removed from private burial ground
Site 9 Matilda Thompson White   On stone with Byron Dyson White
        Birth: 1 May 1901   Death: 21 Feb 1986   Burial: 25 Feb 1986
Site 10 Byron Dyson White, MD   Place: Frederick
        Birth: 10 Feb 1895   Death: 5 Feb 1963   Burial: 8 Feb 1963
        Mort: Hilton   h/o Matilda Thompson White

Lot: 13 Owner: W.W. Williams
Site 1 Helen Williams   Place: Poolesville
        Birth: 1915   Death: 3 Jul 1915   Burial: 3 Jul 1915
        Mort: W.T. Hilton & Sons   Baby
Site 2 Richard Poole Williams
        Birth: 9 Sep 1908   Death: 26 Sep 1910   Burial: 28 Sep 1910
Site 3 Frances Poole Williams   Place: Kensington
        Birth: 2 Feb 1878   Death: 8 Feb 1958   Burial: 10 Feb 1958
        Mort: Hilton   w/o William W. Williams
Site 4 William White Williams   Place: Washington, DC
        Birth: 2 Apr 1877   Death: 9 Jan 1926   Burial: 11 Jan 1926
        Mort: W.T. Hilton & Sons   h/o Frances Poole Williams
Site 5 William Edward Williams   Place: Bethesda, MD
        Birth: 16 May 1912   Death: 14 May 1971   Burial: 17 May 1971
        Mort: Robt. Pumphrey   h/o Ann Perry Williams
Site 6 Ann Perry Williams   w/o William E. Williams, age 80 yrs
        Birth: 1914   Death: 5 Apr 1995   Burial: 8 Apr 1995

Lot: 14 Owner: Edward S. Emerson
Site 2 Worthington B. Emerson   On stone with Georgiana & Edward S. Emerson
        Birth: 26 Jan 1881   Death: 9 Jul 1881   Burial: 30 Jan 1911
Site 3 Georgiana Emerson   w/o Edward Simpson Emerson
        Birth: 8 Apr 1850   Death: 19 Mar 1907   Burial: 30 Jan 1911
Site 4 Edward Simpson Emerson   Place: Washington, DC
        Birth: 9 Sep 1849   Death: 18 Sep 1914   Burial: 21 Sep 1914
        Mort: W.T. Hilton & Sons   h/o Georgiana Emerson

Monocacy Cemetery, Beallsville, Montgomery County, Maryland

Site 5 Maurice A. Emerson　　　　　　　　　　　　　Place: Washington, DC
　　　　Birth: 1 Jan 1871　　　Death: 14 Oct 1949　　Burial: 16 Oct 1949
　　　　Mort: S.H. Hines Co.　　　　　　　　　　　h/o Etta Bready Emerson
Site 6 Etta Bready Emerson　　　　　　　　　　　TS: w/o Maurice A. Emerson
　　　　Birth: 14 Nov 1874　　Death: 22 Mar 1973　　Burial: 26 Mar 1973
Site 8 Grover C. Emerson　　　Mort: Chevy Chase　　Place: Washington, DC
　　　　Birth: 1887　　　　　Death: 3 Nov 1954　　Burial: 6 Nov 1954
Site 9 Lulu Thompson Emerson　Mort: S.H. Hines Co.　Place: Washington, DC
　　　　Birth: 1884　　　　　Death: 3 May 1940　　Burial: 5 May 1940
Site 10 Benjamin Lee Emerson　Mort: S.H. Hines Co.　Place: Washington, DC
　　　　Birth: 1883　　　　　Death: 4 Apr 1933　　Burial: 6 Apr 1933
Site 11 Della Jones Emerson Burlingame　Mort: Everly　Place: Arlington, VA
　　　　Birth: 1876　　　　　Death: 15 Apr 1967　　Burial: 17 Apr 1967
Site 12 Frederick H. Burlingame　Mort: W.T. Hilton　Place: Washington, DC
　　　　Birth: 1863　　　　　Death: 1 Jan 1920　　Burial: 4 Jan 1920

Lot: 15　Owner: Mrs. George W. Bosley
Site 3 Annie Laura Brown Bosley　　　　　　　　　Place: Gaithersburg
　　　　Birth: 1861　　　　　Death: 24 Feb 1940　　Burial: 27 Feb 1940
　　　　Mort: Roy W. Barber　　　　　　　On stone with George W. Bosley
Site 4 George W. Bosley　　　　　　　　　　　　Place: Baltimore
　　　　Birth: 1856　　　　　Death: 29 Jul 1913　　Burial: 31 Jul 1913
　　　　Mort: Hilton & Hall　　　　　　　h/o Annie L. Brown Bosley
Site 6 Gerald Marvin Rotruck　　　　　On stone with Edythe Orme Rotruck
　　　　Birth: 2 Sep 1916　　Death: 5 Apr 1984　　Burial: 9 Apr 1984
Site 8 Charles L. Orme　　TS: "Lindy"　On stone with Jean Muir Orme
　　　　Birth: 3 Oct 1927　　Death: 16 May 1995　　Burial: 19 May 1995
Site 11 Myrtle E. Fregoing　　　　　　　　　Mort: Herman M. Snyder
　　　　Place: Damascus　　Death: 10 Aug 1938　　Burial: 12 Aug 1938
　　　　d/o Wilbur Luhn　　　　　　　　　　　　　　　No marker
Site 12 Child of Wilber Luhn　　　　　　　　　　　　　No marker

Lot: 16　Owner: H.C. Darby
Site 2 Elizabeth Darby　　　　　　　　d/o Harry C. & Katie D. Darby
　　　　Birth: 1911　　　　　Death: 1911　　　　Burial: 13 Jul 1911
Site 3 Katie Dyson Darby　　　　　　　　　　　　Place: Germantown
　　　　Birth: 1 Sep 1876　　Death: 18 Oct 1961　　Burial: 20 Oct 1961
　　　　Mort: Hilton　　　　　　　　　　　　　　w/o Harry C. Darby
Site 4 Harry Clay Darby　　　　　　　　　　　　　Place: Ijamsville
　　　　Birth: 5 Sep 1872　　Death: 11 Feb 1954　　Burial: 13 Feb 1954
　　　　Mort: W.B. Hilton　　　　　　　　　　　h/o Katie Dyson Darby
Site 5 Irene Darby Wynn　　Mort: J.Arthur Walter (Hilton)　Place: Suitland
　　　　Birth: 5 May 1912　　Death: 3 Jul 1962　　Burial: 7 Jul 1962
Site 7 Catherine Vaughn Darby　　　　　d/o Harry C. & Katie D. Darby
　　　　Birth: 9 Nov 1910　　Death: 19 Oct 1978　　Burial: 21 Oct 1978
Site 8 Harry Dunbar Darby, Jr.　　　　　　　　　　Place: Beallsville
　　　　Birth: 1947　　　　　Death: 4 Oct 1955　　Burial: 6 Oct 1955
　　　　Mort: W.B. Hilton　　　　　　　s/o H.D. & Debora Tienny Darby

Monocacy Cemetery, Beallsville, Montgomery County, Maryland   171

Lot: 17 Lower   Owner: Miscellaneous
Site   Eugene E. Cissel   Mort: Roy W. Barber   Place: Washington Grove
        No marker   Death: 23 Apr 1928   Burial: 25 Apr 1928
Site 1 Flora Mae Whisman Hurt   On stone with Stewart C. Whisman
        Birth: 1913   Death: 12 Apr 1993
Site 2 Stewart C. Whisman   Place: Bethesda, MD
        Birth: 1912   Death: 29 Jun 1966   Burial: 1 Jul 1966
        Mort: Hilton   h/o Flora Whisman
Site 3 Ward Alexander Fulton   h/o Jennie Coleman Fulton
        Birth: 30 Nov 1898   Death: 28 Mar 1980   Burial: 1 Apr 1980
Site 4 Jennie Coleman Fulton   On stone with Ward Alexander Fulton
        Birth: 1 May 1898   Death: 29 Feb 1981   Burial: 3 Mar 1981

Lot: 17 Upper   Owner: G.B. Remsburg (1 stone, no dates)
Site   Clara Remsburg   Mort: Hilton & Hall   Place: Poolsville
        Birth: 30 Jun 1864   Death: 26 May 1913   Burial: 27 May 1927
Site   Daniel Steven Remsburg   Mort: W.B. Hilton   Place: Washington, DC
        Birth: 2 Nov 1866   Death: 5 Jun 1936   Burial: 8 Jun 1936
Site   Daniel T. Remsburg
Site   Samuel Young Remsburg   Mort: Hilton & Hall
        Place: Poolesville   Death: 17 Jul 1931   Burial: 19 Jul 1931
Site   William Remsburg
Site   Drucilla Trundle Young   Mort: Hilton & Hall
        Place: Poolesville   Death: 22 Dec 1921   Burial: 24 Dec 1921
Site   Mary Young   No marker
Site 1 George Brewer Remsburg   Mort: Hilton   Place: Boyds, MD
                                    Death: 1 Jun 1962   Burial: 4 Jun 1962

Lot: 18 Lower   Owner: Frank E. & Elizabeth Cubitt
Site 2 John Allen Cubitt   Mort: Hilton & Hall   Place: Poolesville
        Birth: 1873   Death: 30 Jun 1930   Burial: 2 Jul 1930
Site 3 Mary Christine Cubitt   Mort: Hilton & Hall   Place: Poolesville
        Birth: 7 Feb 1853   Death: 30 Apr 1926   Burial: 2 May 1926
        TS: w/o George W. Cubitt
Site 4 George Washington Cubitt   Mort: Hilton & Hall   Place: Poolesville
        Birth: 24 Mar 1845   Death: 26 Sep 1937   Burial: 28 Sep 1937
Site 5 Elizabeth Rebecca Luhn Cubitt   Place: Frederick, MD
        Birth: 12 Feb 1891   Death: 9 Jan 1971   Burial: 12 Jan 1971
        Mort: Wm. Hilton   On stone with Frank E. Cubitt
Site 6 Frank Edward Cubitt   h/o Elizabeth Rebecca Luhn Cubitt
        Birth: 29 Jul 1889   Death: 21 Aug 1986   Burial: 23 Aug 1986

Lot: 18 Upper   Owner: Mrs. James O. Cubitt
Site 1 William Wilson Payne   Place: Bethesda, MD
        Birth: 25 Nov 1906   Death: 18 Jan 1971   Burial: 21 Jan 1971
        Mort: Tyson Wheeler   h/o Ruby Cubitt Payne
Site 2 Ruby Cubitt Payne   w/o William Wilson Payne
        Birth: 7 Jun 1905   Death: 29 Dec 1996   Burial: 31 Dec 1996

172 Monocacy Cemetery, Beallsville, Montgomery County, Maryland

Site 3 Millard O. Cubitt Mort: Hilton & Hall Place: Poolesville
 Death: 28 Sep 1928 Burial: 30 Sep 1928
 TS: s/o James O. & Carrie V. Cubitt, age 22-1-9
Site 4 James O. Cubitt Mort: W.T. Hilton & Sons
 Place: Georgetown Death: 11 Jun 1914 Burial: 13 Jun 1914
 h/o Carrie V. Cubitt TS: Age 36-9-23
Site 5 Rodney William Cubitt
 Birth: 1908 Death: 27 Sep 1992 Burial: 2 Oct 1992
Site 5 Twin Daughters Payne No marker Mort: Hilton & Hall
 Place: Frederick Death: 20 Nov 1928 Burial: 21 Nov 1928
 d/o Wilson W. & Ruby C. Payne

Lot: 19 Owner: John W. Turner
Site Elnor Frances Bussard No marker Mort: C.C. Carty
 Place: Frederick Death: 29 Sep 1917 Burial: 1 Oct 1917
Site 2 Enos C. Bussard Mort: W.T. Hilton & Sons
 Place: Sykesville Death: 21 Jan 1916 Burial: 26 Jan 1916
 TS: s/o William W. & Margaret A. Bussard, age 32-0-16
Site 3 William W. Bussard Place: Barnesville
 Birth: 10 Jul 1848 Death: 10 Sep 1934 Burial: 12 Sep 1934
 Mort: Hilton & Price h/o Margaret A. Bussard
Site 4 Margaret A. Bussard Place: Frederick
 Birth: 29 Feb 1860 Death: 31 Oct 1921 Burial: 2 Nov 1921
 Mort: Thomas P. Price TS: w/o William W. Bussard
Site 5 John William Turner h/o Zelma C. Turner
 Birth: 9 Aug 1905 Death: 7 May 1978 Burial: 10 May 1978
Site 6 Zelma Catherine Turner On stone with John William Turner
 Birth: 5 Nov 1908 Death: 24 Aug 1993 Burial: 27 Aug 1983
Site 10 John W. Bussard Mort: M.L. Creager Place: State Sanatorium
 Birth: 12 Oct 1889 Death: 30 Dec 1919 Burial: 1 Jan 1920
Site 11 Oliver P. Turner Place: Frederick
 Birth: 16 Apr 1865 Death: 4 Aug 1950 Burial: 7 Aug 1950
 Mort: C.E. Cline & Son h/o Isabel Irene Turner
Site 12 Isabel Irene Turner Place: Frederick
 Birth: 29 Jan 1881 Death: 1 Jun 1933 Burial: 4 Jun 1933
 Mort: C.E. Cline & Son TS: w/o Oliver P. Turner
Site 13 George Raymond Bowers Mort: C.E. Cline Place: Baltimore
 Birth: 7 May 1921 Death: 11 Aug 1928 Burial: 13 Aug 1928

Lot: 20 Owner: Harry Savage
Site Hazel Rudolph Knott No marker Mort: W.T. Hilton & Sons
 Place: Barnesville Death: 8 Dec 1927 Burial: 9 Dec 1927
Site Harry R. Savage No marker Mort: Hilton & Hall
 Place: Poolesville Death: 6 Sep 1913 Burial: 8 Sep 1913
Site 1 Helen Savage No marker Mort: W.T. Hilton & Sons
 Place: Barnesville Death: 23 Jul 1922 Burial: 24 Jul 1922
Site 1 Leonard Michael Upton Savage No marker Mort: W.T. Hilton & Sons
 Place: Chevy Chase Death: 20 Oct 1929 Burial: 21 Oct 1929

Monocacy Cemetery, Beallsville, Montgomery County, Maryland   173

Site 3 Martha Virginia Ruby   On stone with LeRoy Edward Savage
        Birth: 10 Aug 1911   Death: 28 Oct 1987   Burial: 30 Oct 1987
Site 4 LeRoy Edward Savage
        Birth: 1 Dec 1913   Death: 1 Jul 1986   Burial: 3 Jul 1986
Site 7 Martha E. Savage   Place: Darnstown
        Birth: 1855   Death: 16 Sep 1922   Burial: 18 Sep 1922
        Mort: W.R. Pumphrey   On stone with George D. Savage
Site 8 George D. Savage   Place: Darnestown
        Birth: 1849   Death: 31 Jan 1934   Burial: 2 Feb 1934
        Mort: W.R. Pumphrey   h/o Martha E. Savage
Site 9 Harry R. Savage   Place: Boyds
        Birth: 1879   Death: 22 Jan 1956   Burial: 25 Jan 1956
        Mort: W.B. Hilton   h/o Osie Bertha Savage
Site 10 Osie Bertha Savage   Place: Boyds
        Birth: 1891   Death: 1 Feb 1960   Burial: 3 Feb 1960
        Mort: W.B. Hilton   On stone with Harry R. Savage
Site 11 Kenneth S. Savage   Place: Bethesda, MD
        Birth: 22 Jul 1933   Death: 9 Jul 1968   Burial: 12 Jul 1968
        Mort: Tyson Wheeler   On stone with Greta M. Savage

Lot: 21 Lower   Owner: Roy Bodmer
Site 1 John Davis Bodmer   Place: Beallsville
        Birth: 30 Jan 1926   Death: 1 Aug 1935   Burial: 3 Aug 1935
        Mort: Hilton & Hall   s/o Roy & Mollie Bodmer
Site 2 Marjorie G. Bodmer   Mort: Hilton & Hall
        Place: Frederick   Death: 31 Jan 1918   Burial: 2 Feb 1918
        TS: d/o Roy & Mollie M. Bodmer, age 3-1-18
Site 3 William Eugene Bodmer   Place: Frederick
        Birth: 18 Dec 1936   Death: 21 Jan 1948   Burial: 23 Jan 1948
        Mort: W.B. Hilton   TS: s/o William L. & Catherine R. Bodmer
Site 4 Henry LeRoy Bodmer   TS: Roy   Place: Rockville
        Birth: 13 Nov 1887   Death: 2 Jun 1948   Burial: 5 Jun 1948
        Mort: W.B. Hilton   h/o Mollie Cubitt Bodmer
Site 5 Mollie M. Cubitt Bodmer   w/o Henry LeRoy Bodmer
        Birth: 20 Jun 1887   Death: 23 Dec 1977   Burial: 26 Dec 1977
Site 6 Catherine Ricketts Bodmer   On stone with William LeRoy Bodmer
        Birth: 26 Jan 1914   Death: 24 Apr 1994   Burial: 26 Apr 1994
Site 6 William LeRoy Bodmer
        Birth: 14 Jul 1913   Death: 11 Jun 1984   Burial: 15 Jun 1984

Lot: 21 Upper   Owner: John W. Poole
Site   Eugene H. Poole   No marker   Mort: Warner E.
        Place: Washington, DC   Death: 20 Jun 1939   Burial: 23 Jun 1939
Site   Effie Allnutt Poole   Mort: Warner E.
        Place: Hyattsville   Death: 22 Jan 1936   Burial: 24 Jan 1936
        w/o John William Poole   No marker
Site   John Hanson Poole
        Birth: 4 Mar 1886   Death: 22 Jul 1909   Burial: 17 Aug 1909

Monocacy Cemetery, Beallsville, Montgomery County, Maryland

Site John William Poole II   Mort: Warner E.
      Place: Sykesville   Death: 12 Feb 1932   Burial: 15 Feb 1932
      h/o Effie Allnutt Poole   No marker
Site 2 Raymond Jerome Poole   Mort: F. Gaschs Sons   Place: Hyattsville
      Birth: 1895   Death: 17 Nov 1916   Burial: 20 Nov 1916
Site 5 Benjamin F. Poole Sr.   Mort: W. E. Pumphrey   Place: Washington, DC
      Birth: 2 Apr 1882   Death: 9 May 1949   Burial: 12 May 1949
Site 6 Mamie L. Poole   Place: Washington, DC
      Birth: 29 Nov 1884   Death: 14 Mar 1952   Burial: 17 Mar 1952
      Mort: Francis J. Collins   w/o Benjamin F. Poole

Lot: 22   Owner: Jacob Bodmer
Site 1 Miss Mary Catherine Bodmer   Sister of Jacob Bodmer, age 14 yrs
      Birth: 28 Dec 1860   Death: 27 Mar 1874   Burial: 28 Mar 1874
Site 2 Carrie Melissa Wiles Bodmer Mort: W.B. Hilton   Place: Mt. Rainier
      Birth: 30 May 1861   Death: 29 Mar 1939   Burial: 1 Apr 1939
Site 3 Lyda Bodmer   Place: Poolesville
      Birth: 7 Jun 1890   Death: 14 Jul 1928   Burial: 26 Jul 1928
      Mort: Hilton & Hall   d/o J & C. Wiles Bodmer
Site 4 Jacob Bodmer   Mort: Hilton & Hall   Place: Poolesville
      Birth: 18 May 1856   Death: 26 Sep 1928   Burial: 29 Sep 1928
Site 7 Carrie Bodmer Chiswell   On stone with Dr. George William Chiswell
      Birth: 16 Dec 1893   Death: 14 Mar 1978   Burial: 15 Mar 1978
Site 8 Dr. George William Chiswell   h/o Carrie Bodmer Chiswell
      Birth: 23 Sep 1892   Death: 9 Jan 1987   Burial: 12 Jan 1987
Site 11 Jessie Vernia Zittle   Mort: W.R. Pumphrey   Place: Silver Spring
      Birth: 30 Aug 1868   Death: 9 Apr 1929   Burial: 10 Apr 1929
Site 12 Consuelo N. Bellman   Mort: Hilton & Hall   Place: Poolesville
      Birth: 28 Oct 1899   Death: 16 Feb 1917   Burial: 19 Feb 1917

Lot: 23   Owner: George E. Nicholson
Site 4 Donald Hubert Nicholson   s/o Wilfred D. & Gladys Nicholson
      Birth: 1938   Death: 1980   Burial: 12 Dec 1980
Site 4 Wilfred Donald Nicholson   Place: Bethesda, MD
      Birth: 1918   Death: 26 Dec 1967   Burial: 29 Dec 1967
      Mort: Wm. Hilton   h/o Gladys Nicholson
Site 5 Thomas Newton Ward   Mort: W.B. Hilton
      Place: Comus   Death: 19 Apr 1936   Burial: 20 Apr 1936
      s/o J.V. & Annie E. Ward, age 3 weeks
Site 7 David T. Ward   h/o Rebecca Nicholson Ward
      Birth: 22 Sep 1897   Death: 5 Feb 1976   Burial: 9 Feb 1976
Site 8 Alice Rebecca Nicholson Ward   On stone with David T. Ward
      Birth: 25 Mar 1906   Death: 15 Sep 1983   Burial: 17 Sep 1983
Site 9 George E. Nicholson   Place: Comus
      Birth: 9 May 1877   Death: 19 May 1936   Burial: 21 May 1936
      Mort: W.B. Hilton   h/o Mary C. Nicholson
Site 10 Mary C. Nicholson   Place: Poolesville, MD
      Birth: 1882   Death: 13 Mar 1970   Burial: 16 Mar 1970
      Mort: Wm. Hilton   w/o George E. Nicholson

Monocacy Cemetery, Beallsville, Montgomery County, Maryland 175

Site 11 Mary Myrtle Nicholson Ward On stone with Elmer Charles Ward Sr.
       Birth: 1 Mar 1912   Death: 17 Apr 1987   Burial: 20 Apr 1987
Site 12 Elmer Charles Ward, Sr.
       Birth: 7 Oct 1907   Death: 19 Sep 1986   Burial: 22 Sep 1986

Lot: 24 Owner: J.V. Nicholson
Site   Annie Elener Ward   No marker   Mort: W.T. Hilton & Sons
        Place: Frederick   Death: 12 Aug 1931   Burial: 12 Aug 1931
Site 3 Martha Nicholson   Place: Comus
        Birth: 18 Aug 1843   Death: 11 Feb 1934   Burial: 14 Feb 1934
        Mort: Hilton & Price   TS: w/o John L. Nicholson
Site 4 John L. Nicholson   Place: Bucklodge
        Birth: 9 Apr 1845   Death: 5 May 1917   Burial: 7 May 1917
        Mort: W.T. Hilton & Sons   h/o Martha Nicholson
Site 6 Martha Jane Nicholson Dillehay   Place: Comus
        Birth: 12 Dec 1868   Death: 24 Feb 1932   Burial: 27 Feb 1932
        Mort: W.T. Hilton & Sons   TS: Jennie
Site 8 Vernon Leroy Nicholson   s/o J. Vernon & Annie V. Nicholson
        Birth: 14 Mar 1908   Death: 15 Jan 1995   Burial: 19 Jan 1995
Site 9 Annie V. Heffner Nicholson   Place: Frederick, MD
        Birth: 14 Sep 1885   Death: 16 Apr 1970   Burial: 20 Apr 1970
        Mort: M.R. Etchison   w/o John Vernon Nicholson
Site 10 John Vernon Nicholson   Place: Frederick, MD
        Birth: 20 May 1880   Death: 10 Jul 1970   Burial: 14 Jul 1970
        Mort: Etchison & Sons   h/o Annie Heffner Nicholson

Lot: 25 Owner: Charles E. Roberts
Site   Baby girl Roberts   No marker   Mort: George A. Roberts
        Place: Beallsville   Death: 28 Apr 1943   Burial: 28 Apr 1943
Site 1 Viola E. Baker   Mort: Wm. Hilton
        Place: Sellman, MD   Death: 21 Apr 1971   Burial: 24 Apr 1971
        w/o William R. Baker   No marker
Site 1 William R. Baker   Mort: Wm. Hilton   Place: Sellman, MD
        Birth: 4 May 1924   Death: 21 Apr 1971   Burial: 23 Apr 1971
        h/o Viola Whisman Baker, CPL US Army WWII   No marker
Site 2 Maggie M. Roberts   Place: Beallsville
        Birth: 11 Jan 1882   Death: 26 Jun 1938   Burial: 28 Jun 1938
        Mort: Hilton & Hall   TS: [2nd] w/o Charles E. Roberts
Site 3 Charles Edward Roberts   Place: Beallsville
        Birth: 17 Aug 1872   Death: 11 Jul 1942   Burial: 13 Jul 1942
        Mort: W.B. Hilton   h/o Maggie M. Roberts
Site 4 Clara V. Roberts   Mort: C.E. Roberts   Place: Bakersville
        Birth: 19 Jan 1874   Death: 9 Sep 1897   Burial: 29 Jun 1932
        TS: [1st] w/o Charles E. Roberts   Reinterment
Site 5 Lorraine Roberts McKimmey   No marker
        Birth: 30 May 1930   Death: 31 Oct 1994   Burial: 4 Nov 1994
Site 9 Sean Russell Nicewarner   Death: 13 Jun 1996

Monocacy Cemetery, Beallsville, Montgomery County, Maryland

Site 10 Barbara Anne Roberts
Birth: 14 Jul 1927
Death: 13 Jul 1933
Mort: Hilton & Price
Place: Frederick
Burial: 16 Jul 1933
TS: d/o C.W. & Mildred Luhn Roberts

Site 11 Mildred Luhn Roberts
Birth: 15 Mar 1903 w/o Charles William Roberts

Site 12 Charles William Roberts
Birth: 7 Sep 1902
Death: 28 Nov 1969
Mort: Wm. Hilton
Place: Beallsville, MD
Burial: 1 Dec 1969
h/o Mildred Luhn Roberts

Lot: 26 Owner: Mrs. R.C. Carlisle

Site 1 Mason Lewis Frye
Birth: 25 Jul 1868
Mort: Hilton & Price
Death: 11 Feb 1936
Place: Dickerson
Burial: 14 Feb 1936

Site 2 Mary I. Frye
Birth: 5 Nov 1872
Mort: W.T. Hilton & Sons
Death: 11 Oct 1932
Place: Dickerson
Burial: 13 Oct 1932

Site 3 Frances C. Carlisle
Birth: 5 Dec 1852
Mort: W.T. Hilton & Sons
Death: 17 Dec 1923
Place: Dickerson
Burial: 19 Dec 1923
TS: w/o Richard C. Carlisle

Site 4 Richard C. Carlisle
Birth: 6 Jan 1849
Mort: W.T. Hilton & Sons
Death: 19 Jul 1921
Place: Dickerson
Burial: 21 Jul 1921

Site 5 Richard Vernon Carlisle
Birth: 23 Aug 1877
Mort: W.B. Hilton
Death: 2 Nov 1934
Place: Washington, DC
Burial: 5 Nov 1934

Site 6 Annie Edna Manion
Birth: 18 Dec 1874
Mort: W.L. Burdette
Death: 10 Apr 1950
Place: Frederick
Burial: 13 Apr 1930

Site 9 Bettie C. Fields Carlisle
Birth: 14 Sep 1898
Death: 29 Aug 1989
On stone with James Maurice Carlisle
Burial: 1 Sep 1989

Site 10 James Maurice Carlisle
Birth: 4 Mar 1889
Mort: Hilton
Death: 19 May 1959
Place: Dickerson
Burial: 22 May 1959
h/o Bettie Fields Carlisle

Site 11 Lucy Lavina Carlisle
Birth: 28 Mar 1880
Mort: Hilton
Death: 2 Aug 1958
Place: Dickerson
Burial: 5 Aug 1958

Site 12 William Vernon Manion
Birth: 9 Sep 1899
Mort: W.L. Burdette
Death: 7 Jun 1958
Place: Urbana
Burial: 10 Jun 1958

Lot: 27 Lower Owner: Homer Lilly

Site 1 Homer Johnston Lilly
Birth: 3 Sep 1899
Death: 25 Apr 1975

Site 2 Norma Marie Lilly Waters
Birth: 24 Nov 1911
Death: 25 Sep 1983
TS: Sister of Homer Johnston Lilly
Burial: 27 Sep 1983

Site 3 Bertha Jackson Lilly
Birth: 27 Nov 1880
Mort: M.R. Etchison & Sons
Death: 17 Oct 1933
Place: Monrovia
Burial: 20 Oct 1933
w/o Kelly J. Lilly

Site 4 Kelly J. Lilly
Birth: 18 May 1878
Mort: W.T. Hilton & Sons
Death: 13 Jun 1926
Place: Dickerson
Burial: 15 Jun 1926
h/o Bertha J. Lilly

Site 5 Thomsey W. Lilly Kay
Birth: Jul 1906
Death: 5 Mar 1981
Burial: 9 Mar 1981

Lot: 27 Upper Owner: John A. Beall

Site 1 Frank T. Beall
Birth: 21 Aug 1886
Mort: Deal
Death: 26 Jun 1953
Place: Washington, DC
Burial: 30 Jun 1953

Monocacy Cemetery, Beallsville, Montgomery County, Maryland 177

Site 2 Pearl A. Selena Beall
      Birth: 1886   Death: 24 Oct 1973   On stone with Marion W. Beall
      Burial: 27 Oct 1973
      Place: Poolesville
Site 3 Marion W. Beall
      Birth: 1876   Death: 27 Apr 1951   Burial: 29 Apr 1951
      Mort: W.B. Hilton   h/o Pearl Astlin Beall
Site 4 James Maurice Beall   No marker   Mort: W.B. Hilton
      Place: Poolesville   Death: 15 Jun 1946   Burial: 18 Jun 1946
Site 5 John Alvin Beall   Mort: Hilton & Hall   Place: Poolesville
      Birth: 1 Sep 1889   Death: 3 Nov 1925   Burial: 4 Nov 1925
Site 6 James M. Beall   Place: Georgetown Hospital
      Birth: 22 Jun 1845   Death: 29 Dec 1924   Burial: 1 Jan 1925
      Mort: Hilton & Hall   On stone with John Alvin Beall

Lot: 28 Lower   Owner: Charles W. Poole
Site 1 Edna Mildred Beall Poole   On stone with Charles Wade Poole, Jr.
      Birth: 31 Jan 1905   Death: 21 Aug 1995   Burial: 26 Aug 1995
Site 2 Charles Wade Poole Jr.
      Birth: 23 Jun 1898   Death: 1 Oct 1984   Burial: 6 Oct 1984
Site 3 James Alfred Poole   TS: "Hoppy"   Place: Taneytown, MD
      Birth: 17 Jan 1929   Death: 16 Apr 1968   Burial: 18 Apr 1968
      Mort: C.O. Fuss & Son   s/o Charles W. & Edna Poole
Site 4 Charles E. Poole   Place: Frederick
      Birth: 28 Jun 1923   Death: 6 Jun 1924   Burial: 8 Jun 1924
      Mort: Hilton & Hall   TS: s/o Charles W. & Edna M. Poole

Lot: 28 Upper   Owner: B.F. Shreve
Site 3 Laura Shreve   Place: Dickerson
      Birth: 8 Jun 1862   Death: 31 May 1924   Burial: 2 Jun 1924
      Mort: Hilton & Hall   TS: w/o Benjamin F. Shreve
Site 4 Benjamin F. Shreve   Place: Dickerson
      Birth: 8 Mar 1862   Death: 26 Apr 1947   Burial: 28 Apr 1947
      Mort: W.B. Hilton   h/o Laura Shreve
Site 5 Mary Virginia Johnson Fisk   On stone with Richard Carroll Fisk
      Birth: 9 Apr 1920   Death: 19 Mar 1995   Burial: 22 Mar 1995

Lot: 29 Lower   Owner: Joseph Tedore
Site 1 Dorothy Louise Tedore   No marker
      Birth: 28 Mar 1919   Death: 11 Apr 1987   Burial: 14 Apr 1987
Site 2 Thomas E. Tedore, Sr.   Mort: W.W. Chambers   Place: Washington, DC
      Birth: 18 Jan 1908   Death: 1 Apr 1953   Burial: 6 Apr 1953
Site 3 Bessie Cole Tedore   Place: Washington, DC
      Birth: 2 Feb 1887   Death: 16 Mar 1925   Burial: 20 Mar 1925
      Mort: W.W. Chambers   On stone with Joseph Tedore
Site 4 Joseph Tedore   Mort: W.W. Chambers   Place: Washington, DC
      Birth: 12 Dec 1877   Death: 16 Mar 1928   Burial: 19 Mar 1928
Site 5 Frances M. Calavetinos
      Birth: 4 Mar 1912   Death: 22 Sep 1995   Burial: 13 Oct 1995
Site 6 Genevieve Tedore   No marker   Burial: 20 Apr 1996

Lot: 29 Upper   Owner: E.P. Jones

Site 3 Mary Virginia Cornwell
      Birth: 20 Apr 1858   Death: 6 Mar 1935   TS: w/o John L. Cornwell   Burial: 7 Mar 1935
Site 4 Lottie C. Jones   Death: 7 Feb 1891
Site 5 Alfred Leroy Jones   No marker   Mort: W.T. Hilton & Sons
      Place: Dickerson   Death: 30 Oct 1924   Burial: 1 Nov 1924
      s/o Eugene P. & Lottie V. Jones
Site 5 LeRoy Albert Jones   TS: s/o E.P. & L.V. Jones
      Death: 24 Oct 1924   Burial: 30 Oct 1924
Site 6 Eugene Phillips Jones   Place: Gaithersburg
      Birth: 22 Jul 1865   Death: 11 Jun 1942   Burial: 13 Jun 1942
      Mort: Ernest C. Gartner   h/o Lottie C. Jones

Lot: 30 Lower   Owner: Charles A. Cole

Site 1 Charles Lee Cole   TS: Pvt US Army WWII
      Birth: 27 Jun 1920   Death: 28 Sep 1975   Burial: 1 Oct 1975
Site 1 William U. Cole   TS: US Army WWII
      Birth: 5 Jun 1915   Death: 11 Jan 1979   Burial: 17 Jan 1979
Site 2 Myrtle E. Cole   No marker   Mort: W.W. Deal Co.
      Place: Washington, DC   Death: 14 Jun 1928   Burial: 16 Jun 1928
Site   Joseph Franklin Kendale   TS: US Air Force
      Birth: 11 Oct 1937   Death: 9 Jul 1996
Site 3 Annie M. Cole   No marker   Mort: W.W. Chambers
      Place: Washington, DC   Death: 3 Feb 1936   Burial: 5 Feb 1936
Site 4 Charles Albert Cole   No marker   Mort: F. Gaschs Sons
      Place: Cottage City   Death: 30 Dec 1936   Burial: 2 Jan 1947

Lot: 31 Lower   Owner: Louise Ann Cannon

Site 1 Richard Carlisle Mejia, Sr.
      Birth: 30 Sep 1937   Death: 7 Dec 1992   Burial: 19 Dec 1992
Site 2 Paul Franklin Mejia
      Birth: 6 Nov 1938   Death: 28 Dec 1974   Burial: 3 Jan 1975
Site 3 George Richard Carlisle   No marker   Place: Washington, DC
      Birth: 25 Apr 1888   Death: 9 Sep 1931   Burial: 11 Sep 1931
      Mort: N.B. Nevin
Site 4 Helen C. Herring   Age 86 yrs
      Birth: 10 Feb 1909   Death: 23 Dec 1996   Burial: 26 Dec 1996

Lot: 31 Upper   Owner: Mrs. Alice Hughes

Site 3 Alice Julia Hughes   TS: w/o William Arthur Hughes
Site 4 William Arthur Hughes   Mort: Pumphrey & Sons   Place: Slade City, FL
      Birth: 1858   Death: 30 Oct 1929   Burial: 3 Nov 1929

Lot: 32 Lower   Owner: Lowe & Hammett

Site 2 Louis Richard Lowe   Mort: W.R. Pumphrey   Place: Washington, DC
      Birth: 10 May 1878   Death: 8 Aug 1931   Burial: 11 Aug 1931
Site 3 Nancy E. Hammett   Mort: W.R. Pumphrey   Place: Washington, DC
      Birth: 18 Aug 1898   Death: 6 Jan 1929   Burial: 8 Jan 1929

Monocacy Cemetery, Beallsville, Montgomery County, Maryland   179

Site 4 William F. Hammett
         Birth: 10 Sep 1886   Death: 27 Apr 1977   Burial: 30 Apr 1977
Site 5 Margaret Geiger Hammett   Mort: R.A. Pumphrey   Place: Silver Spring
         Birth: 1855   Death: 27 Apr 1950   Burial: 29 Apr 1950

Lot: 32 Upper   Owner: Kathleen & J. Hoyle Nevin
Site 1 Alice Nevin Talley   Age 85 yrs
         Birth: 27 Aug 1909   Death: 27 Jan 1995   Burial: 30 Jan 1995
Site 3 Katherine H. Nevin   No marker
                                   Death: 23 Jul 1972   Burial: 26 Jul 1972
Site 4 David John Nevin   No marker   Mort: W.W. Chambers
         Place: Washington, DC   Death: 5 Feb 1928   Burial: 8 Feb 1928
Site 5 James Hoyle Nevin   No marker   Mort: W.W. Chambers
         Place: Washington, DC   Death: 27 Aug 1931   Burial: 31 Aug 1931

Lot: 33   Owner: Mrs. Ollie Stowers
Site 3 Ollie I. Stowers   Mort: Money & King   Place: Vienna, VA
         Birth: 10 Mar 1881   Death: 9 Oct 1959   Burial: 13 Oct 1959
Site 4 John W. Stowers   Mort: W.T. Hilton & Sons   Place: Frederic
         Birth: 12 Oct 1877   Death: 30 Sep 1928   Burial: 2 Oct 1928
Site 5 George W. Stowers   Mort: W.E. Pumphrey   Place: Washington, DC
         Birth: 16 Jan 1905   Death: 8 May 1959   Burial: 12 May 1959
Site 6 Mattie Arbanna Whipp
         Birth: 16 Jan 1905   Death: 28 Aug 1984   Burial: 1 Sep 1984

Lot: 34 Lower   Owner: J. Guy Arrington
Site 1 Harriet Arrington Ware   Age 86 yrs   On stone with Clayton Ellms Ware
         Birth: 27 Sep 1902   Death: 24 May 1989   Burial: 27 May 1989
Site 2 Clayton Ellms Ware
         Birth: 4 Feb 1901   Death: 14 Oct 1990   Burial: 19 Oct 1990
Site 3 Bessie V. Arrington   w/o John Thomas Arrington
         Birth: 1874   Death: 11 Nov 1971   Burial: 13 Nov 1971
Site 4 John Thomas Arrington   Place: Washington, DC
         Birth: 1864   Death: 16 Jan 1935   Burial: 19 Jan 1935
         Mort: Harry L. Slye   h/o Bessie V. Arrington
Site 5 Audrey Virginia Kenyon   No marker
         Birth: 6 Mar 1911   Death: 10 Jun 1991   Burial: 14 Jun 1991
Site 6 Robert Rowlodge Kenyon   Place: Washington, DC
         Birth: 25 Jan 1911   Death: 7 May 1968   Burial: 10 May 1968
         Mort: Tyson Wheeler   TS: MD SK3 USNR WWII

Lot: 34 Upper   Owner: Charles C. Orme
Site 3 Daisy D. Orme   Place: Barnesville
         Birth: 10 Aug 1876   Death: 6 Feb 1934   Burial: 8 Feb 1934
         Mort: W.R. Pumphrey   TS: w/o Charles C. Orme
Site 4 Charles Clinton Orme   Place: Barnesville
         Birth: 21 May 1871   Death: 10 Sep 1957   Burial: 13 Sep 1957
         Mort: Hilton   h/o Daisy D. Orme

180   Monocacy Cemetery, Beallsville, Montgomery County, Maryland

Site 5 Nettie Mae Orme LaGasse   Place: Gainesville, FL
       Birth: 9 Feb 1910   Death: 8 Nov 1968   Burial: 14 Nov 1968
       Mort: Tyson Wheeler   On stone with Alfred Henri LaGasse

Lot: 35 Lower   Owner: Mrs. Leona Josephine Reed
Site 1 Richard Randolph Reed   Mort: Hilton & Hall
       Place: Poolesville   Death: 30 Jan 1938   Burial: 31 Jan 1938
       s/o Clifford & Hattie Reed   No marker
Site 2 Dewey Alton Reed   Place: Poolesville
       Birth: 1913   Death: 18 Jan 1945   Burial: 20 Jan 1945
       Mort: W.B. Hilton   s/o Russell C. & Leona J. Reed
Site 3 Leona Josephine Reed   TS: Mother   Place: Frederick
       Birth: 1879   Death: 15 May 1962   Burial: 17 May 1962
       Mort: Hilton   w/o Russell C. Reed
Site 4 Russell C. Reed   TS: Father   Place: Poolesville
       Birth: 1878   Death: 29 May 1936   Burial: 31 May 1936
       Mort: Hilton & Hall   h/o Leona Josephine Reed
Site 5 Cecil Layman Reed   Place: Frederick
       Birth: 1902   Death: 11 May 1956   Burial: 14 May 1956
       Mort: W.B. Hilton   s/o Russell C. & Leona J. Reed

Lot: 35 Upper   Owner: Herman Frye
Site 2 Herman Leon Frye Jr.   Place: Dickerson
       Birth: 5 Dec 1938   Death: 18 Dec 1938   Burial: 20 Dec 1938
       Mort: W.B. Hilton   TS: s/o Herman Leon & Nina E. Frye
Site 3 Nina E. Frye   On stone with Herman Leon Frye
       Birth: 11 Apr 1901   Death: 20 May 1993   Burial: 24 May 1993
Site 4 Herman Leon Frye   h/o Nina E. Frye
       Birth: 17 May 1900   Death: 12 May 1975   Burial: 18 May 1975

Lot: 36   Owner: Ort Pierce & J.F. Nicholson
Site 6 William O. Carlisle   No marker   Mort: S.H. Hines Co.
       Place: Washington, DC   Death: 5 Jan 1936   Burial: 8 Jan 1936

Lot: 37 Lower   Owner: William M. Carlin
Site 2 Infant Carlin   Place: Frederick
       Birth: 25 Jan 1936   Death: 25 Jan 1936   Burial: 29 Jan 1936
       Mort: Hilton & Price   TS: d/o Wm. & V.M. Carlin
Site 3 Virgie M. Carlin   On stone with William Melvin Carlin
       Birth: 21 Mar 1899   Death: 12 Feb 1990   Burial: 16 Feb 1990
Site 4 William Melvin Carlin   h/o Virgie M. Carlin
       Birth: 2 Sep 1898   Death: 27 Jul 1978   Burial: 31 Jul 1978

Lot: 37 Upper   Owner: Wm. Christian Beck
Site 1 Katherine Hughes Beck   w/o William Christian Beck Jr.
       Birth: 1892   Death: 16 Aug 1975   Burial: 19 Aug 1975
Site 2 William Christian Beck Jr.   Place: Charles Town, WV
       Birth: 1894   Death: 22 Mar 1970   Burial: 26 Mar 1970
       Mort: Melvin Strider Co.   h/o Katherine Hughes Beck

Monocacy Cemetery, Beallsville, Montgomery County, Maryland   181

Site 3	Nellie Saxton Beck	TS: Mother	Place: Washington, DC
	Birth: 1867	Death: 12 Dec 1945	Burial: 17 Dec 1945
	Mort: Wm. R. Pumphrey		w/o William Christian Beck
Site 4	William Christian Beck	TS: Father	Place: Washington, DC
	Birth: 1865	Death: 12 Dec 1937	Burial: 15 Dec 1937
	Mort: W.R. Pumphrey		h/o Nellie Saxton Beck
Site 5	Marjorie Saxton Beck	Mort: R.A. Pumphrey	Place: Washington, DC
	Birth: 1905	Death: 10 Jun 1965	Burial: 14 Jun 1965

Lot: 38 Lower   Owner: Mrs. Charles T. Brosius

Site 1	Dorothy Brosius Koss		On stone with Joseph P. Koss
	Birth: 3 Dec 1922	Death: 20 Jan 1985	Burial: 22 Jan 1985
Site 2	Charles T. Brosius Jr.		h/o Ellen Brosius, age 74 yrs
	Birth: 20 Nov 1916	Death: 10 Dec 1990	Burial: 15 Dec 1990
Site 2	Ellen Ayers Brosius	Age 67 yrs.	On stone with Charles T. Brosius
	Birth: 2 Sep 1916	Death: 9 May 1984	Burial: 12 May 1984
Site 2	Julia L. Ayers Burroughs	No marker	m/o Ellen Ayers Brosius
	Birth: 9 Jul 1893	Death: 21 Mar 1989	Burial: 27 Mar 1989
Site 3	Genevieve T. Darby Brosius		Place: Silver Spring, MD
	Birth: 23 Feb 1888	Death: 15 Jun 1970	Burial: 18 Jun 1970
	Mort: Wm. Hilton		w/o Charles T. Brosius
Site 4	Charles Thomas Brosius		Place: Lime Kiln
	Birth: 27 Mar 1879	Death: 19 Apr 1938	Burial: 21 Apr 1938
	Mort: W.B. Hilton		h/o Genevieve T. Brosius
Site 5	Charles T. Brosius IV		
	Birth: 8 Jul 1940	Death: 13 Dec 1996	Burial: 16 Dec 1996

Lot: 38 Upper   Owner: John Wakeman Ayers

Site 1	Julia L. Ayers		On stone with John Wakeman Ayers
	Birth: 9 Jul 1893	Death: 20 Mar 1989	
Site 2	John Wakeman Ayers		Place: Bridgeport, WV
	Birth: 29 Apr 1888	Death: 12 Mar 1936	Burial: 14 Mar 1936
	Mort: W.W. Bartlett		h/o Julia L. Ayers
Site 4	John F. Blood		On stone with Hester Ayers Blood
	Birth: 13 Aug 1917	Death: 20 Nov 1985	Burial: 23 Nov 1985

Lot: 39 Lower   Owner: Mrs. Arthur Dunningan

Site 1	William Penn Bryant	TS: US Army WWII	h/o Janice Dunnigan Bryant
	Birth: 27 Dec 1924	Death: 28 Apr 1992	Burial: 1 May 1992
Site 3	Bess Blanche Leffel Dunnigan		w/o Arthur B. Dunnigan
	Birth: 28 Feb 1886	Death: 29 Nov 1980	Burial: 1 Dec 1980
Site 4	Arthur Blaine Dunnigan	Mort: W.B. Hilton	Place: Poolesville
	Birth: 22 Nov 1894	Death: 24 Sep 1942	Burial: 26 Sep 1942

Lot: 39 Upper   Owner: Lawrence Price

Site	Rebecca Price Starkey	Birth: 1918	Death: 1984
Site 3	Deborah Jane Price	Mort: W.B. Hilton	Place: Washington, DC
	Birth: 1892	Death: 8 Aug 1938	Burial: 11 Aug 1938
	w/o Lawrence H. Price		

Site 4 Laurence Hilton Price   Place: Frederick, MD
        Birth: 1892   Death: 23 Aug 1970   Burial: 26 Aug 1970
        Mort: Wm. Hilton   h/o Deborah Jane Price
Site 6 Jessie Virginia Price Mort: W.B. Hilton   Place: Frederick Hospital
        Birth: 1860   Death: 13 Jan 1944   Burial: 15 Jan 1944

Lot: 40 Lower   Owner: William G. Baker
Site 3 David T. Jones   Removed from Mothers Delight
        Mort: Chas. E. Roberts   Death: 7 Apr 1855   Burial: 13 Nov 1928
        TS: s/o David T. & M.J. Jones, age 1-7-6   Cause: Membranous Croup
Site 4 Ann Maria Jones   Removed from Mothers Delight
        Mort: Chas. E. Roberts   Death: 19 Aug 1846   Burial: 13 Nov 1928
        TS: d/o David W. & Mary Ann Jones, age 5-9-25   Cause: Mercury Poisening
Site 5 Laura Virginia Jones   Age 18-9-17   Mort: Chas. E. Roberts
        Birth: 26 Jun 1845   Death: 12 Apr 1864   Burial: 13 Nov 1928
        d/o David T. & Mary Ann Jones   Cause: Typhoid Fever
        Removed from Mothers Delight
Site 6 Mary Ann Jones   Removed from Mothers Delight
        Mort: Chas. E. Roberts   Death: 18 Aug 1855   Burial: 13 Nov 1928
        TS: Consort of David T. Jones, age 40-4-26   Cause: Dysentery

Lot: 40 Upper   Owner: W.C. Garbers (No stones in lot)
Site 1 Helen Embrey   Mort: Fred Garbers   Place: Washington, DC
        Birth: 1928   Death: 3 May 1969   Burial: 7 May 1969
Site 2 David Theodore Roosevelt Garbers   Mort: W.B. Hilton
        Place: Frederick   Death: 15 Feb 1936   Burial: 16 Feb 1936
        Infant   No marker
Site 3 Margaret Clark   No marker   Mort: Wm. Reuben Pumphrey
        Place: Tampa, FL   Death: 8 Nov 1942   Burial: 12 Nov 1942

Lot: 41 Lower   Owner: H.T. Waesche
Site 4 Hugh Henry Waesche   Mort: Lotz Funeral Home Place: Roanoke, VA
        Birth: 1904   Death: 23 Apr 1969   Burial: 28 Apr 1969
Site 5 Henry Theodore Waesche   Place: Washington, DC
        Birth: 1870   Death: 5 Dec 1955   Burial: 8 Dec 1955
        Mort: Warner E. Pumphrey   h/o Lucy Peyton Waesche
Site 6 Lucy Peyton Waesche   Place: Washington, DC
        Birth: 1870   Death: 11 Apr 1927   Burial: 13 Apr 1927
        Mort: Henry Slye   On stone with Henry Theodore Waesche

Lot: 41 Upper   Owner: William G. Baker
Site 1 Thomas Dawson   Mort: Chas. E. Roberts
        Birth: 20 Feb 1787   Death: 15 Apr 1852   Burial: 13 Nov 1928
        TS: s/o Robert D. & Sarah Newton Dawson, age 65-1-25   Cause: Unknown
        Removed from Mothers Delight
Site 2 Susanah H. Dawson   Age 37-5-15   Mort: Chas. E. Roberts
        Cause: Unknown   Death: 1 May 1826   Burial: 13 Nov 1928
        Removed from Mothers Delight

Monocacy Cemetery, Beallsville, Montgomery County, Maryland

Site 3 Susan Dawson TS: In her 57th yr Cause: Blood Poisening
Mort: Chas. E. Roberts Death: 23 Nov 1880 Burial: 13 Nov 1928
Removed from Mothers Delight

Site 4 Eleanor Dawson Age 69-0-16 Cause: Appoplexy
Birth: 12 Feb 1869 Death: 28 Feb 1878 Burial: 13 Nov 1928
Mort: Chas. E. Roberts Removed from Mothers Delight

Site 5 Ann Dawson Mort: Chas. E. Roberts
Cause: Unknown Death: 5 Mar 1854 Burial: 13 Nov 1928
TS: w/o James M. Dawson, in her 74th yr. Removed from Mothers Delight

Site 6 James M. Dawson TS: Age 91-7-0 Mort: Chas. E. Roberts
Birth: 11 Jun 1775 Death: 11 Jan 1867 Burial: 12 Nov 1928
h/o Mrs. Ann Dawson Cause: Senile Dysentery
Removed from Mothers Delight

Lot: 42 Lower Owner: Mrs. Rachael Rush

Site 1 Mervale B. Russell
Birth: 16 Dec 1913 Death: 17 May 1992 Burial: 21 May 1992

Site 2 Lynne R. Day
Birth: 18 Jun 1938 Death: 15 Dec 1988 Burial: 19 Dec 1988

Site 3 Rachael Gott Rush On stone with Emerson Stone Rush
Birth: 1906 Death: 1990 Burial: 12 Jun 1990

Site 4 Emerson Stone Rush Place: Cleveland, OH
Birth: 1892 Death: 4 May 1942 Burial: 7 May 1942
Mort: Mills & Son & Rafer h/o Rachael Gott Rush

Lot: 42 Upper Owner: Virginia & Edwin Cruitt

Site 3 Katherine W. Cruit Place: Baltimore
Birth: 1887 Death: 15 Jan 1955 Burial: 18 Jan 1955
Mort: G. Howard Strong w/o Luther Cruit

Site 4 Luther Reed Cruit Place: Poolesville
Birth: 1876 Death: 3 Jan 1942 Burial: 5 Jan 1942
Mort: W.B. Hilton h/o Katherine W. Cruit

Lot: 43 Lower Owner: Miscellaneous

Site 3 Kitty Morrissey Wacker Place: Stoveham, ME
Birth: 19 Jul 1884 Death: 25 Aug 1959 Burial: 28 Aug 1959
Mort: Clarence B. Huff w/o John Frederick Wacker

Site 4 John Frederick Herman Wacker Place: Arlington, VA
Birth: 10 Apr 1886 Death: 25 Jul 1941 Burial: 28 Jul 1941
Mort: W.R. Pumphrey h/o Kitty Morrissey Wacker

Lot: 43 Upper Owner: Ernest Offutt

Site 3 Lucy Morrissey Offutt Place: Washington, DC
Birth: 14 Feb 1888 Death: 4 Dec 1953 Burial: 7 Dec 1953
Mort: Fitzgerald Funeral Home On stone with William Ernest Offutt

Site 4 William Ernest Offutt Place: Washington, DC
Birth: 12 Oct 1887 Death: 10 Mar 1955 Burial: 12 Mar 1955
Mort: Fitzgerald Funeral Home h/o Lucy Morrissey Offutt

Monocacy Cemetery, Beallsville, Montgomery County, Maryland

Lot: 44 Lower   Owner:Miscellaneous
- Site 1 Samuel Robert Huey   h/o Hester Carter Huey
  - Birth: 7 Oct 1893   Death: 9 Apr 1984   Burial: 12 May 1984
- Site 2 Hester Carter Huey   On stone with Samuel Robert Huey
  - Birth: 27 Nov 1895   Death: 30 Mar 1975   Burial: 2 Apr 1975
- Site 3 Virginia M. Whitaker Carter   Place: Washington, DC
  - Birth: 9 Jul 1866   Death: 31 May 1929   Burial: 3 Jun 1929
  - Mort: H.W. Deal   TS: w/o Samuel Henry Carter
- Site 4 Samuel Henry Carter   Place: Washington, DC
  - Birth: 31 Dec 1868   Death: 27 Dec 1926   Burial: 29 Dec 1926
  - Mort: W.W. Deal Co.   h/o Virginia M. Whitaker Carter
- Site 5 Frances Carter Hazelwood   On stone with Fred Hazelwood
  - Birth: 30 Dec 1898   Death: 23 Dec 1994   Burial: 4 Jan 1995
- Site 6 Fred Hazelwood   h/o Frances Carter Hazelwood
  - Birth: 4 Apr 1899   Death: 20 Jul 1987   Burial: 23 Jul 1987

Lot: 44 Upper   Owner: Henry Kennedy
- Site 3 Henry Kennedy   Birth: 22 Feb 1869   h/o Emma I. Kennedy
- Site 4 Emma I. Kennedy   Place: Frederick
  - Birth: 31 Mar 1863   Death: 6 Mar 1927   Burial: 8 Mar 1927
  - Mort: W.T. Hilton & Sons   TS: w/o Henry Kennedy

Lot: 45 Lower   Owner: Anna A. Thomas
- Site 1 C. Anna Babington   Birth: 1906
- Site 3 Harriet A. Babington   Place: Bethesda
  - Birth: 28 Apr 1878   Death: 23 Apr 1966   Burial: 27 Apr 1966
  - Mort: Joseph Gawler   TS: w/o George L. Babington
- Site 4 Anna Hays Trundle Thomas   Place: Rockville
  - Birth: 12 Mar 1844   Death: 21 Apr 1925   Burial: 23 Apr 1925
  - Mort: W.T. Hilton & Sons   TS: w/o Levin Thomas
- Site 5 Charles P. Thomas   Mort: Robert A. Pumphrey   Place: Takoma Park
  - Birth: 1875   Death: 4 Nov 1965   Burial: 8 Nov 1965

Lot: 46 Lower   Owner: William A. Daniel
- Site   Baby boy Painter   No marker   Mort: W.B. Hilton
  - Place: Frederick Hospital Death: 25 Aug 1945   Burial: 26 Aug 1945
- Site 1 Garland Edward Painter   On stone with Elizabeth Daniel Painter
  - Birth: 24 Oct 1917   Death: 28 Jan 1997   Burial: 30 Jan 1997
- Site 3 Mansfield White Daniel   TS: US Army WWII   h/o Mary White Daniel
  - Birth: 13 Jun 1918   Death: 20 Mar 1994   Burial: 23 Mar 1994
- Site 4 Elsie White Daniel   Place: Bethesda, MD
  - Birth: 24 Apr 1889   Death: 24 Aug 1969   Burial: 26 Aug 1969
  - Mort: Wm. Hilton   w/o William A. Daniel
- Site 5 Lt. William Aglionby Daniel Jr.   Mort: Wm. B. Hilton
  - Place: Orlando, FL   Death: 20 Aug 1943   Burial: 30 Aug 1943
  - s/o William A. & Elsie W. Daniel   TS: Age 26 yrs., MD 2 Lieut. Air Corps
- Site 6 William Aglionby Daniel   Place: Frederick
  - Birth: 11 Jul 1878   Death: 1 Nov 1965   Burial: 4 Nov 1965
  - Mort: Hilton   h/o Elsie White Daniel

Lot: 46 Upper Owner: Miscellaneous

Site 2 Marco M. Whisman
Birth: 8 Oct 1884 Death: 21 Apr 1971
Mort: Wm. Hilton
Place: Sellman, MD
Burial: 23 Apr 1971
h/o Perline E. Whisman

Site 2 Perlina E. Whisman
Birth: 13 Apr 1885 Death: 21 Apr 1971
Mort: Wm. Hilton
Place: Sellman, MD
Burial: 23 Apr 1971
TS: w/o Marco M. Whisman

Site 3 Ruth H. Young Davis
Birth: 25 Jul 1912 Death: 23 Jun 1987
On stone with Jesse Wilson Davis
Burial: 26 Jun 1987

Site 4 Jesse Wilson Davis
Birth: 23 Nov 1912 Death: 21 May 1976
h/o Ruth H. Young Davis
Burial: 25 May 1976
TS: CPL US Army WWII

Site 5 Charles E. Benson
Birth: 1871 Death: 26 Nov 1955
Mort: Robert A. Pumphrey
Place: Cabin John
Burial: 29 Nov 1955
h/o Addie S. Benson

Site 6 Addie S. Benson
Birth: 1875 Death: 6 Nov 1942
Mort: Wm. Reuben Pumphrey
Place: Cabin John
Burial: 9 Nov 1942
On stone with Charles E. Benson

Lot: 47 Lower Owner: Miscellaneous

Site 1 Ernest Randall
Place: New York Death: 19 May 1967
No marker Mort: Robert E. Wilhelm
Burial: 22 May 1967

Site 3 Jesse D. Kauffman
Birth: 12 May 1908
Mort: W.B. Hilton Death: 16 Mar 1946
Place: Frederick Hospital
Burial: 18 Mar 1946

Site 5 Annie V. Titus
Birth: 1877 Death: 7 Dec 1968
Mort: Wm. Hilton
Place: Poolesville, MD
Burial: 9 Dec 1968
On stone with John Franklin Titus

Site 6 John Franklin Titus
Birth: 1877 Death: 18 Jun 1945
Mort: W.B. Hilton
Place: Poolesville
Burial: 21 Jun 1945
w/o Annie V. Titus

Lot: 47 Upper Owner: Mrs. Thomas deBeck

Site 2 Gail Wade deBeck
Birth: 1895 Death: 28 Feb 1980
w/o Thomas O. deBeck
Burial: 1 Mar 1980

Site 3 Baby boy deBeck
Place: York, PA Death: 14 Jun 1965
No marker Mort: Strack & Strine
Burial: 17 Jun 1965

Site 3 Thomas O. deBeck
Birth: 1897
Mort: Wm. R. Pumphrey Death: 23 Mar 1944
Place: Bethesda
Burial: 26 Mar 1944

Lot: 48 Owner: Dewalt J. Willard

Site 3 Delmah Dutrow Willard
Birth: 13 Mar 1879 Death: 25 Nov 1956
Mort: W.B. Hilton
Place: Poolesville
Burial: 28 Nov 1956
w/o Harry L. Willard

Site 4 Harry L. Willard
Birth: 23 Aug 1871 Death: 30 Jul 1943
Mort: W.B. Hilton
Place: Poolesville
Burial: 1 Aug 1943
h/o Delmah Dutrow Willard

Site 5 Dewalt Joseph Willard Sr.
Birth: 26 Aug 1909 Death: 24 Jul 1991
s/o Harry L. & Delmah Dutrow Willard
Burial: 27 Jul 1991

Monocacy Cemetery, Beallsville, Montgomery County, Maryland

Lot: 49 Lower   Owner: C.W. Rutter & C.R. Beall
Site 3 Charles Henry Rutter   Place: Bethesda
        Birth: 15 Jun 1905   Death: 10 Jul 1966   Burial: 13 Jul 1966
        Mort: Hilton   h/o Nellie Beall Rutter
Site 4 Phillip Henry Rutter   Age 6 days   Place: Frederick
        Birth: 29 Dec 1951   Death: 4 Jan 1952   Burial: 6 Jan 1952
        Mort: W.B. Hilton   TS: s/o C.H. & Nellie N. Rutter
Site 5 Gertrude Downs Rutter   w/o John W. Rutter
        Birth: 27 Aug 1883   Death: 29 Aug 1979   Burial: 31 Aug 1979
Site 6 John W. Rutter   Place: Poolesville
        Birth: 4 Sep 1877   Death: 27 Mar 1958   Burial: 29 Mar 1958
        Mort: Hilton   h/o Gertrude Downs Rutter

Lot: 49 Upper   Owner: Annie Leah Davison
Site 1 Thomas Clinton Hawkins   Place: Bethesda
        Birth: 11 Mar 1869   Death: 27 Jan 1946   Burial: 29 Jan 1946
        Mort: Warner E. Pumphrey   TS: Father
Site 2 Annie Gertrude Hawkins   Place: Washington, DC
        Birth: 12 Nov 1870   Death: 27 May 1947   Burial: 29 May 1947
        Mort: Warner E. Pumphrey   TS: Mother
Site 3 Alice Georgeanna H. Frazier   Mort: Rinaldi   Place: Washington, DC
        Birth: 12 Jul 1911   Death: 28 Jul 1955   Burial: 2 Aug 1955
Site 4 Rebecca F. Adkins   Mort: Takoma F.H.   Place: Washington, DC
        Birth: 1912   Death: 13 Dec 1968   Burial: 16 Dec 1968
Site 5 Claude S. Adkins   Mort: Takoma Park F.H.   Place: Washington, DC
        Birth: 1905   Death: 29 Dec 1968   Burial: 31 Dec 1968
Site 6 John R. Hawkins
        Birth: 6 Feb 1908   Death: 13 Jan 1980   Burial: 16 Jan 1980

Lot: 50 Lower   Owner: Mrs. Nina Tetlow
Site 1 Mortimer B. Hough   h/o Margaret Tetlow Hough
        Birth: 6 Feb 1908   Death: 19 Jan 1980   Burial: 23 Jan 1980
        TS: Birth: 1911, MM 1 US Navy WWII, Korea
Site 2 Margaret Gertrude Tetlow Hough   w/o Mortimer B. Hough, age 80 yrs
        Birth: 1913   Death: 16 Oct 1993   Burial: 23 Oct 1993
Site 3 Nora R. Tetlow   Place: Rockville
        Birth: 1882   Death: 8 May 1956   Burial: 10 May 1956
        Mort: Robert A. Pumphrey   On stone with Stanley C. Tetlow
Site 4 Stanley C. Tetlow   Place: Rockville
        Birth: 1881   Death: 19 May 1952   Burial: 21 May 1952
        Mort: Robert A. Pumphrey   h/o Nora C. Tetlow

Lot: 50 Upper   Owner: Denzil Raymond Fike
Site 4 Marilou Jones
        Birth: 12 Jul 1941   Death: 15 Nov 1991   Burial: 19 Nov 1991
Site 5 Denzil Raymond Fike
        Birth: 28 Oct 1898   Death: 20 Feb 1991   Burial: 23 Feb 1991
Site 6 Mary E. Fike   Mort: W. E. Pumphrey   Place: Washington, DC
        Birth: 2 Oct 1901   Death: 6 Jun 1950   Burial: 9 Jun 1950

Lot: 51 Lower   Owner: L.E. Johnson
Site 2 Luther Eugene Johnson Jr.   Place: Frederick
        Birth: 29 Apr 1949   Death: 20 Sep 1954   Burial: 23 Sep 1954
        Mort: W.B. Hilton   TS: s/o L. Eugene & Mary E. Johnson
Site 4 Luther Eugene Johnson Sr. On stone with Mary Elizabeth Roberson Johnson
        Birth: 5 May 1926   Death: 18 Mar 1997   Burial: 22 Mar 1997
Site 5 Grace E. White Roberson   On stone with Newton Gilbert Roberson
        Birth: 3 Oct 1905   Death: 5 Apr 1995   Burial: 8 Apr 1995
Site 6 Newton Gilbert Roberson   h/o Grace E. White Roberson
        Birth: 23 Oct 1904   Death: 10 Jan 1972   Burial: 13 Jan 1972

Lot: 51 Upper   Owner: Frank E. Morton
Site 2 Claude David Morton   Place: Frederick
        Birth: 3 Jul 1945   Death: 31 Jan 1953   Burial: 2 Feb 1953
        Mort: W.B. Hilton   TS: s/o Frank E. & Lola E. Morton
Site 3 Lola E. Morton   On stone with Frank Edwin Morton
        Birth: 17 Apr 1907   Death: 12 Jun 1982   Burial: 15 Jun 1982
Site 4 Frank Edwin Morton   h/o Lola E. Morton
        Birth: 9 Mar 1909   Death: 14 May 1975   Burial: 16 May 1975

Lot: 52 Lower   Owner: Zora V. Dixon
Site 3 Zora Viola Dixon   On stone with Eberly T. Dixon
        Birth: 1887   Death: 2 Mar 1975   Burial: 4 Mar 1975
Site 4 Eberly Thomas Dixon   Place: Frederick Hospital
        Birth: 1871   Death: 14 Oct 1953   Burial: 17 Oct 1953
        Mort: W.B. Hilton   h/o Zora Viola Dixon

Lot: 52 Upper   Owner: Nellie T. Jones
Site 2 William T. Jones   Birth: 5 Dec 1919   Death: 28 Jun 1990
Site 3 Nellie Jane Titus Jones   Place: Poolesville
        Birth: 8 Jul 1881   Death: 1 Nov 1959   Burial: 3 Nov 1959
        Mort: Hilton   w/o Louis J. Jones
Site 4 Louis John Jones   Place: Bethesda
        Birth: 3 Oct 1881   Death: 15 Apr 1952   Burial: 17 Apr 1952
        Mort: W.B. Hilton   h/o Nellie Titus Jones, age 71

Lot: 53 Lower   Owner: Miscellaneous
Site 7 Peggy Janet Gibson   Mort: W.B. Hilton   Place: Bethesda Hospital
        Birth: 20 Jan 1960   Death: 19 Feb 1960   Burial: 22 Feb 1960
Site 7 Michele Rene Baugher   Place: Anchorage, Alaska
        Birth: 24 Jan 1961   Death: 24 Jan 1961   Burial: 3 Feb 1961
        Mort: USAF Mortuary   TS: d/o Thomas H. & Patricia M. Baugher
Site 7 Nikki C. Baugher   No marker   Mort: USAF Mortuary
                                 Death: 16 Oct 1961   Burial: 24 Oct 1961
        Place: Anchorage, Alaska   d/o Thomas H. & Patricia M. Baugher
Site 8 Betty Jo Justus   Infant   No marker   Mort: Hilton
        Place: Baltimore   Death: 14 Jul 1962   Burial: 16 Jul 1962

188 Monocacy Cemetery, Beallsville, Montgomery County, Maryland

Site 8 Linda Sue Harvey   Place: Silver Spring
        Birth: 26 Apr 1964   Death: 26 Apr 1964   Burial: 26 Apr 1964
        Mort: Hilton   d/o Charles & Neva Harvey
Site 9 Cleveland C. Smith   Mort: Hilton   Place: Bethesda
        Birth: 1882   Death: 12 Mar 1961   Burial: 15 Mar 1961
Site 10 Edward W. Titus   Mort: Hilton   Place: Bethesda
        Birth: 17 Jan 1907   Death: 12 Aug 1959   Burial: 15 Aug 1959
Site 11 Sarah E. Ludwig Grubb   w/o Carroll E. Grubb   Mort: W.R. Pumphrey Jr.
        Place: Reading, PA   Death: 20 Jun 1931   Burial: 23 Jun 1931
Site 12 Carrol Edgar Grubb   h/o Sarah E. Grubb   Mort: Phil. H. Fairchild
        Place: Ft. Lauderdale, FL Death: 24 May 1958   Burial: 27 May 1958

Lot: 53 Upper Owner: Hays & Hill
Site 2 Alice R. Cole Hays   On stone with Frederick Albert Hays
        Birth: 24 Nov 1919   Death: 29 Sep 1990   Burial: 3 Oct 1990
Site 3 Frederick Albert Hays   Place: Washington, DC
        Birth: 1889   Death: 21 Oct 1959   Burial: 23 Oct 1959
        Mort: Deal (Hilton)   h/o Alice Hays
Site 5 Eleanor Medora Hays Hill   Place: Atlanta, GA
        Birth: 1875   Death: 29 May 1959   Burial: 1 Jun 1959
        Mort: H.M. Patterson & Son   On stone with Hugh P. Hill Sr.
Site 6 Hugh Peter Hill Sr.   Place: Atlanta, GA
        Birth: 1873   Death: 13 Feb 1964   Burial: 17 Feb 1964
        Mort: H.M. Paterson & Son   h/o Eleanor Medora Hays Hill

Lot: 54 Owner: William S. Bowling
Site 5 St. Clair Brooke Bowling   Place: Washington, DC
        Birth: 25Mar 1909   Death: 5 Mar 1957   Burial: 7 Mar 1957
        Mort: R.A. Pumphrey   w/o William Sinclair Bowling
Site 6 William Sinclair Bowling
        Birth: 28 Mar 1908   Death: 3 May 1984   Burial: 9 May 1984
        Disinterred 25 Sep 1984, moved to Ignatius Cemetery, Port Tobacco, MD

Lot: 55 Lower Owner: Fred & Luella J. Reed
Site 5 Frederick A. Reed Jr.
        Birth: 12 Jan 1910   Death: 19 Feb 1997   Burial: 22 Feb 1997
Site 6 Betty Lou Pifer
        Birth: 30 Nov 1933   Death: 3 Feb 1990   Burial: 6 Feb 1990

Lot: 55 Upper Owner: John & Janet Martin
Site 2 Joseph Alan Martin   Mort: W.E. Pumphrey   Place: Arlington
        Birth: 2 Jan 1960   Death: 21 Jan 1960   Burial: 22 Jan 1960
Site 4 John R. Martin
        Birth: 10 Nov 1929   Death: 5 Nov 1985   Burial: 7 Nov 1986

Lot: 56 Upper Owner: Miscellaneous
Site 2 Thomas Russell Kinna   Mort: Hilton   Place: Comus
        Birth: 4 Apr 1933   Death: 8 Feb 1959   Burial: 11 Feb 1959
        TS: MD FN US Navy   s/o Gladys Irene Morningstar Kinna

Monocacy Cemetery, Beallsville, Montgomery County, Maryland

Site 3 Gladys Irene Morningstar Kinna   TS: w/o Russell J. Kinna
        Birth: 14 Aug 1913   Death: 18 Dec 1978   Burial: 20 Dec 1978
Site 4 Russell J. Kinna
        Birth: 5 Apr 1911   Death: 26 Oct 1984   Burial: 30 Oct 1984
Site 5 Gregory Andrew Starkey   TS: Grandson
        Birth: 16 Nov 1922   Death: 8 Jan 1996   Burial: 16 Jan 1996

Lot: 57 Owner: John A. Backus
Site 6 Anne Griffith Backus   Birth: 11 May 1918   Death: 18 Jun 1993

Lot: 58 Upper Owner: Miscellaneous
Site 5 Hilda May Wolfrey   On stone with Phillip Lee Wolfrey
        Birth: 25 Sep 1920   Death: 19 Sep 1995   Burial: 22 Sep 1995
Site 6 Philip Lee Wolfrey   Birth: 12 May 1922   Death: 18 Jan 1993

Row I

Lot: 1 Owner: E.J. Zimmerman
Site 1 Susan B. Zimmerman   Death: 14 Jan 1906   Burial: 16 Jan 1906
        TS: d/o E.J. & Amanda M. Zimmerman, age 27-6-0
Site 2 Amanda M. E. Zimmerman   TS: w/o Edward J. Zimmerman, age 62 yrs
        Death: 5 Mar 1908   Burial: 8 Mar 1908
Site 3 Edward J. Zimmerman   Death: 6 Mar 1912   Burial: 9 Mar 1912
        h/o Amanda E. Zimmerman   TS: Age 67-11-14
Site 4 Harriett F.S. Zimmerman   Place: Glenelg
        Birth: 8 Nov 1867   Death: 21 Mar 1932   Burial: 23 Mar 1932
        Mort: Weir & Son   TS: d/o E.J. & Amanda M. Zimmerman
Site 5 D. Howard Zimmerman   Mort: M.R. Etchison &
        Place: Baitonsville Road   Death: 24 Feb 1930   Burial: 26 Feb 1930
        TS: s/o E.J. & Amanda M. Zimmerman, age 58-3-4
Site 6 Charles J. Zimmerman   Place: West Friendship
        Birth: 29 May 1875   Death: 7 Nov 1935   Burial: 10 Nov 1935
        Mort: Weir & Sons Inc.   TS: s/o E.J. & Amanda M. Zimmerman
Site 8 Maurice H. Zimmerman   Place: Mt. Airy
        Birth: 8 Nov 1880   Death: 19 May 1944   Burial: 22 May 1944
        Mort: C.M. Waltz   h/o Margaret A. Zimmerman
Site 9 Margaret A. Zimmerman   TS: w/o Maurice H. Zimmerman
        Birth: 8 Feb 1895   Death: 12 May 1979   Burial: 15 May 1979

Lot: 2 Lower   Owner: L.M. & Evelyn B. Mason
Site 3 Lyle Millan Mason, MD   Place: Washington, DC
        Birth: 4 May 1891   Death: 13 Feb 1957   Burial: 15 Feb 1957
        Mort: Hines   h/o Evelyne B. Mason
Site 4 Evelyne Brewer Mason   Place: Washington, DC
        Birth: 9 May 1895   Death: 4 Sep 1958   Burial: 6 Sep 1958
        Mort: Robert A. Pumphrey   On stone with Lyle M. Mason

Lot: 2 Upper   Owner: Joseph D. & Lillian B. Byrd
Site 3 Lillian Brewer Byrd   On stone with Joseph D. Byrd
        Birth: 25 Mar 1886   Death: 29 Dec 1974   Burial: 31 Dec 1974
Site 4 Joseph Dyson Byrd   Place: Boyds
        Birth: 2 Aug 1880   Death: 8 Jan 1958   Burial: 10 Jan 1958
        Mort: Hilton   h/o Lillian Brewer Byrd

Lot: 3 Owner: Harry D. Grubb
Site 2 Elizabeth Neer Grubb   Place: Poolesville
        Birth: 18 Aug 1875   Death: 2 Dec 1957   Burial: 6 Dec 1957
        Mort: Hilton   TS: d/o John E. & Margaretta C. Grubb
Site 3 Margaretta C. Grubb   Place: Poolesville
        Birth: 7 Nov 1849   Death: 5 Apr 1932   Burial: 7 Apr 1932
        Mort: W.R. Pumphrey   TS: w/o John Edgar Grubb
Site 4 John Edgar Grubb   h/o Margaretta C. Grubb
        Birth: 15 Feb 1850   Death: 27 Mar 1909   Burial: 29 Mar 1909

Monocacy Cemetery, Beallsville, Montgomery County, Maryland 191

Site 5 Leah Roberta (Berta) Grubb
    Birth: 14 Mar 1854   Death: 26 Mar 1919
    Mort: Hilton & Hall
    Place: Poolesville
    Burial: 28 Mar 1919
    TS: L. Berta Grubb
Site 6 Harold Dunbar Grubb
    Birth: 3 Nov 1917   Death: 9 Apr 1988
    w/o Harry & Bettie Grubb
    Burial: 12 Apr 1988
Site 10 Bettie Lorene Padgett Grubb
    Birth: 25 Oct 1884   Death: 24 Feb 1963
    Mort: Hilton
    Place: Frederick
    Burial: 26 Feb 1963
    On stone with Harry Daniel Grubb
Site 11 Harry Daniel Grubb
    Birth: 31 May 1885   Death: 11 Apr 1973
    h/o Bettie Lorene Padgett Grubb
    Burial: 14 Apr 1973
Site 12 Lola Annie Ray   No marker
    Place: Poolesville   Death: 14 Feb 1918
    Mort: Hilton & Hall
    Burial: 15 Feb 1918

Lot: 4 Owner: George W. Sauerwein (all on 1 stone in lot)
Site 1 Katie May Storm
    Birth: 1882   Death: 15 Mar 1906   Burial: 17 Mar 1906
Site 2 Catherine S. Sauerwein   Place: Washington, DC
    Birth: 1863   Death: 28 Dec 1939   Burial: 30 Dec 1939
    Mort: W.W. Chambers Co.   w/o George W. Sauerwein
Site 3 George W. Sauerwein   Place: Gaithersburg
    Birth: 1859   Death: 4 Jan 1923   Burial: 7 Jan 1923
    Mort: Geo M. Gartner   h/o Catherine S. Sauerwein
Site 4 Grace I. Ricketts   Place: Washington, DC
    Birth: 1897   Death: 7 Apr 1955   Burial: 9 Apr 1955
    Mort: W.W. Chambers   d/o George W. & Caterine S. Sauerwein
Site 5 Lucille F. Sauerwein   w/o George W. Sauerwein
    Birth: 1897   Death: 5 Feb 1992   Burial: 11 Feb 1992
Site 6 George William Sauerwein   h/o Lucille Sauerwein
    Birth: 1901   Death: 19 Nov 1971   Burial: 24 Nov 1971
Site 7 Nellie M. Storm   Mort: Hilton   Place: Sykesville
    Birth: 1887   Death: 31 Oct 1966   Burial: 31 Oct 1966
Site 8 Martin L. Storm   Mort: Ernest C. Gartner   Place: Darnestown
    Birth: 1888   Death: 12 Jul 1929   Burial: 14 Jul 1929
Site 9 Howard William Storm   Mort: Roy W. Barber   Place: Clarksburg
    Birth: 1915   Death: 4 Jul 1941   Burial: 6 Jul 1941
Site 10 Howard C. Sauerwein
    Birth: 1899   Death: 17 Mar 1974   Burial: 21 Mar 1974

Lot: 5 Owner: L.A. Darby, Jr.
Site 1 Alice Harrison Darby   w/o Albert Darby
    Birth: 22 Jan 1905   Death: 28 Nov 1985   Burial: 30 Nov 1985
Site 2 Albert Allnutt Darby   h/o Alice Harrison Darby
    Birth: 20 Oct 1904   Death: 1 Mar 1986   Burial: 4 Mar 1986
Site 4 Lawrence Allnutt Darby   Place: Frederick Hospital
    Birth: 19 Nov 1875   Death: 26 Jul 1949   Burial: 28 Jul 1949
    Mort: W.B. Hilton   h/o Julia A. Darby
Site 5 Julia Allnutt Darby   Place: Bethesda
    Birth: 20 Nov 1877   Death: 2 Nov 1956   Burial: 5 Nov 1956
    Mort: W.B. Hilton   w/o Lawrence A. Darby

Site 6 Lawrence Allnutt Darby Jr.   h/o Angela Elberth Darby
        Birth: 28 Aug 1908   Death: 5 Aug 1979   Burial: 8 Aug 1979

Lot: 6 Owner: Mrs. Cora L. Pollock
Site   Three children of G. Pollock   Burial: 18 Sep 1909   Removed
Site 2 George Findlay Pollock, Jr.   TS: WWI-WWII, Korea
        Birth: 5 Jun 1899   Death: 1 Mar 1989   Burial: 3 Mar 1989
Site 3 John Emory Pollock   Place: Bethesda
        Birth: 19 Jan 1892   Death: 21 Jun 1967   Burial: 23 Jun 1967
        Mort: R.A. Pumphrey   h/o Grace Dutrow Pollock
Site 5 Cora Lee Pollock   Place: Washington, DC
        Birth: 28 Jul 1867   Death: 4 Feb 1931   Burial: 7 Feb 1931
        Mort: W.R. Pumphrey   w/o George Findlay Pollock
Site 6 George Findlay Pollock   h/o Cora Lee Pollock
        Birth: 31 Dec 1860   Death: 6 Jul 1909   Burial: 9 Jul 1909
Site 6 Grace Amelia Pollock   w/o George Finley Pollock, age 97 yrs
        Birth: 8 Apr 1892   Death: 29 Sep 1989   Burial: 3 Oct 1989
Site 7 Richard J. Fulton, Sr. TS: US Navy WWII   h/o Jane Pollock Fulton
        Birth: 3 Apr 1926   Death: 31 Oct 1994   Burial: 5 Nov 1994
Site 8 Jane Pollock Fulton
        Birth: 20 Sep 1925   Death: 21 Oct 1993   Burial: 26 Oct 1993

Lot: 7 Owner: Mr. & Mrs. Robert Fulton
Site 9 Lulu Belle Dutrow   Place: Cockeyville
        Birth: 1870   Death: 23 Feb 1954   Burial: 26 Feb 1954
        Mort: Wm. Cook Inc.   w/o Hershey Dutrow
Site 10 B. Hershey Dutrow   Place: Boyds
        Birth: 1866   Death: 14 Mar 1924   Burial: 16 Mar 1924
        Mort: W.T. Hilton & Sons   h/o Lulu Belle Dutrow

Lot: 8 Owner: Charles Morningstar
Site 3 Annie Mary Morningstar   Place: Sykesville
        Birth: 1877   Death: 17 Nov 1949   Burial: 19 Nov 1949
        Mort: W.B. Hilton   On stone with Charles W. Morningstar
Site 4 Charles W. Morningstar   Place: Bethesda
        Birth: 1875   Death: 1 Apr 1960   Burial: 4 Apr 1960
        Mort: W.B. Hilton   h/o Annie Mary Morningstar
Site 7 Child of Charles Morningstar   No marker   Burial: 9 Jul 1909
Site 7 Infant Ward   No marker   Mort: W.T. Hilton & Sons
        Place: Frederick   Death: 3 May 1929   Burial: 4 May 1929
Site 8 Archie M. Morningstar   Burial: 24 Mar 1912   No marker

Lot: 9 Owner: George R. Astlin
Site 1 Elsie Matthews   No marker   Mort: Hilton & Hall
        Place: Poolesville   Death: 9 Aug 1915   Burial: 10 Aug 1915
Site 4 James B. Matthews   Mort: Hilton & Hall   Place: Poolesville
        Birth: 8 Feb 1856   Death: 4 Nov 1926   Burial: 6 Nov 1926

Monocacy Cemetery, Beallsville, Montgomery County, Maryland   193

Site 5	Mary M. Astlin		Place: Silver Spring
	Birth: 15 Apr 1859	Death: 15 Nov 1941	Burial: 17 Nov 1941
	Mort: Warner E. Pumphrey		TS: w/o George R. Astlin
Site 6	George R. Astlin	Death: 18 Jan 1908	Burial: 20 Jan 1908
	h/o Mary M. Astlin, age 58-8-12		
Site 7	Dora Luellen Burch		Place: Silver Sprin
	Birth: 9 Aug 1899	Death: 1 Dec 1920	Burial: 3 Dec 1920
	Mort: W.R. Pumphrey		TS: d/o C.W. & L.W. Burch
Site 8	Margaret Astlin Braady		
	Birth: 8 Jul 1911	Death: 3 Oct 1983	Burial: 6 Oct 1983
Site 9	Mary Ellen James		TS: Astlin on stone
	Birth: 24 Jan 1904	Death: 6 Jan 1983	Burial: 8 Jan 1983
Site 10	James Walter Astlin		h/o Mary B. Astlin
	Birth: 4 Aug 1908	Death: 8 Jun 1972	Burial: 12 Jun 1968
Site 11	Infant Astlin		Mort: Hilton & Hall
	Place: Washington DC	Death: 24 Dec 1918	Burial: 25 Dec 1918
	i/o James R. & Mary B. Astlin		No marker
Site 11	Mary B. Astlin		Place: Washington DC
	Birth: 8 May 1890	Death: 24 Dec 1918	Burial: 28 Dec 1918
	Mort: Hilton & Hall		On stone with James Richard Astlin
Site 12	James Richard Astlin		
	Birth: 12 Aug 1889	Death: 5 Feb 1980	Burial: 8 Feb 1980

Lot: 10 Lower   Owner: J.F. Loy

Site 1	Mary M. Loy	Mort: Olin Molesworth	Place: Olney, MD
	Birth: 1886	Death: 6 Feb 1968	Burial: 8 Feb 1968
Site 2	Claude Edgar Loy		
	Birth: 1889	Death: 29 Dec 1972	Burial: 1 Jan 1973
Site 3	Catherine Rebecca Loy		Place: Barnesville
	Birth: 1859	Death: 25 Feb 1945	Burial: 28 Feb 1945
	Mort: Roy W. Barber		TS: [2nd] w/o Joseph F. Loy
Site 4	Joseph F. Loy		Place: Clarksburg
	Birth: 1843	Death: 26 Nov 1917	Burial: 28 Nov 1917
	Mort: W.T. Hilton & Sons		h/o Catherine Loy & Mary C. Loy
Site 5	Minnie E. Loy		Place: Clarksburg
	Birth: 1876	Death: 3 Jan 1919	Burial: 5 Jan 1919
	Mort: W.T. Hilton & Sons		d/o Joseph Loy
Site 6	Mary C. Loy		TS: [1st] w/o Joseph F. Loy
	Birth: 1851	Death: 1884	

Lot: 10 Upper   Owner: Albert F. Loy

Site 1	Albert F. Loy	No marker	Mort: Wm. Hilton
	Place: Bethesda	Death: 6 Jan 1969	Burial: 9 Jan 1969
Site 2	Marie V. Loy	TS: d/o Albert F. & Lelia V. Loy, age 0-3-2	
		Death: 12 Aug 1909	Burial: 14 Aug 1909
Site 2	Mary V. Loy	Death: 19 Aug 1909	Burial: 22 Aug 1909
	TS: d/o Albert F. & Lelia V. Loy, age 0-3-15		

Site 3 Lelia V. Loy   Mort: Hilton
        Place: Bethesda   Death: 5 Apr 1958   Burial: 8 Apr 1958
        w/o Albert F. Loy   No marker
Site 4 Albert F. Loy   Mort: W.T. Hilton & Sons
        Place: Chevy Chase   Death: 17 Sep 1928   Burial: 19 Sep 1928
        h/o Lelia V. Loy   No marker
Site 6 Thomas Loy   No marker
        Birth: 1918   Death: 10 Aug 1974   Burial: 13 Aug 1974

Lot: 11 Lower Owner: Paul Roberson
Site 2 James Claud Goldsborough Jr.   s/o Eva Goldsborough White
        Birth: 28 Aug 1941   Death: 26 Aug 1990   Burial: 29 Aug 1990
Site 3 Mary Heffner Roberson   On stone with Paul Roberson
        Birth: 18 Sep 1898   Death: 24 Oct 1996   Burial: 28 Oct 1996
Site 4 Paul Roberson   Place: Dickerson
        Birth: 1896   Death: 9 Oct 1936   Burial: 11 Oct 1936
        Mort: Wm. B. Hilton   h/o Mary Heffner Roberson

Lot: 11 Upper Owner: Miscellaneous
Site 1 Annie E. Martin   Age 77   Place: Washington, DC
        Birth: 1874   Death: 16 Sep 1951   Burial: 19 Sep 1961
        Mort: W.K. Hunteman   On stone with Joseph A. Martin
Site 2 Joseph A. Martin   Place: Washington, DC
        Birth: 1867   Death: 19 Jul 1949   Burial: 23 Jul 1949
        Mort: W.K. Hunteman   h/o Annie E. Martin
Site 4 Bertha Orme   Place: Sykesville
        Birth: 1874   Death: 7 Feb 1950   Burial: 9 Feb 1950
        Mort: W.B. Hilton   On stone with Maurice Orme
Site 4 Maurice Orme   Place: Rockville
        Birth: 1861   Death: 29 Sep 1949   Burial: 1 Oct 1949
        Mort: W.B. Hilton   h/o Bertha Orme
Site 6 Allen S. Orme   Burial: 14 Nov 1909   No marker

Lot: 12 Lower Owner: Henry Ford
Site   Infant daughter Ford   TS: d/o J.? & ? Ford, born & died 27 Dec, 1916
Site 2 Infant of Henry Ford   Mort: Hilton & Hall   Place: Vienna, VA
        Birth: 27 Dec 1915   Death: 28 Dec 1915   Burial: 28 Dec 1915
        No marker
Site 3 Ida Mae Ford   Mort: W.B. Hilton   Place: Beallsville
        Birth: 1882   Death: 11 Feb 1954   Burial: 14 Feb 1954
Site 4 Henry W. Ford   Mort: Hamrick & Co.   Place: Staunton, VA
        Birth: 1870   Death: 26 Oct 1964   Burial: 29 Oct 1964
Site 5 Annie Eliza Simpson   Place: Vienna, VA
        Birth: 20 Jan 1855   Death: 12 Feb 1916   Burial: 14 Feb 1916
        Mort: Hilton & Hall   TS: w/o Henry R. Simpson
Site 6 Henry R. Simpson   Place: Beallsville
        Birth: 22 May 1857   Death: 9 May 1928   Burial: 11 May 1928
        Mort: Hilton & Hall   h/o Annie Eliza Simpson

Monocacy Cemetery, Beallsville, Montgomery County, Maryland   195

Lot: 12 Upper   Owner: James Ford
Site 1 Daniel F. Ford   Mort: Olin L. Molesworth   Place: Silver Spring
        Birth: 1872   Death: 22 Sep 1959   Burial: 23 Sep 1959
Site 2 John J. Ford   Age 25 yrs 8 mo
                                  Death: 16 Sep 1910   Burial: 17 Sep 1910
Site 3 Ellen F. Ford   TS: w/o James Ford, age 82 yrs   Mort: Hilton & Hall
        Place: Beallsville   Death: 21 Nov 1929   Burial: 24 Nov 1929
Site 4 James Ford   Mort: Hilton & Hall
        Place: Beallsville   Death: 16 May 1913   Burial: 18 May 1913
        h/o Ellen F. Ford, age 72 yrs   Stone down

Lot: 13 Lower   Owner: B.F. Roberson
Site   Winona Roberson   No marker   Mort: Hilton & Price
        Place: Dickerson   Death: 24 Mar 1934   Burial: 25 Mar 1934
Site 2 David Franklin Roberson   Mort: W.B. Hilton
        Place: Dickerson   Death: 1 Oct 1951   Burial: 4 Oct 1951
        s/o Mary F. & Benjamin F. Roberson, age 50   No marker
Site 3 Mary F. Roberson   Place: Dickerson
        Birth: 1862   Death: 16 Mar 1927   Burial: 18 Mar 1927
        Mort: G.W. Peters   TS: w/o Benjamin F. Roberson
Site 4 Benjamin F. Roberson   Place: Dickerson
        Birth: 1857   Death: 6 Oct 1935   Burial: 8 Oct 1935
        Mort: W.B. Hilton   h/o Mary F. Roberson

Lot: 13 Upper   Owner: E.D. Mobley
Site 2 Mattie Marie Offutt
        Birth: 2 Apr 1893   Death: 15 Feb 1975   Burial: 19 Feb 1975
Site 3 Cornelia Carter Stang Mobley   TS: w/o Ernest Dorsey Mobley, age 46-1-25
        former w/o Martin Stang   Death: 22 Mar 1911   Burial: 24 Mar 1911
Site 4 Ernest Dorsey Mobley   Mort: W.W. Chambers
        Place: Washington, DC   Death: 9 Mar 1946   Burial: 12 Mar 1946
        h/o Mary E. Nicholson & Cornelia Carter Stang   No marker
Site 5 Agnes Jane Offutt Hottinger   On stone with Virgil Hottinger
        Birth: 1920   Death: 30 Apr 1992

Lot: 14   Owner: Owen Wright
Site   Child of Owen Wright   No marker   Burial: 11 Jun 1911
Site 2 Child of Owen Wright   Burial: 31 Mar 1913
        Cause: Stillborn   No marker
Site 5 Nettie E. Wright   Place: Silver Spring
        Birth: 25 Jun 1891   Death: 20 Oct 1966   Burial: 25 Oct 1966
        Mort: R.A. Pumphrey   w/o Owen F. Wright
Site 6 Owen F. Wright   Place: Westminster
        Birth: 9 Jul 1884   Death: 10 May 1954   Burial: 12 May 1954
        Mort: W.B. Hilton   h/o Nettie E. Wright
Site 7 Laura L. Wright   Place: Poolesville
        Birth: 9 Feb 1884   Death: 11 May 1950   Burial: 14 May 1950
        Mort: W.B. Hilton   w/o John R. Wright

Monocacy Cemetery, Beallsville, Montgomery County, Maryland

Site 8 John Robert Wright
    Birth: 15 Feb 1881   Death: 8 Dec 1957
    Mort: C.O. Fuss & Son
    Place: Taneytown
    Burial: 10 Dec 1957
    h/o Laura L. Wright

Site 9 Margaret America Ann Wright
    Birth: 9 Nov 1884   Death: 24 Aug 1918
    Mort: Hilton & Hall
    Place: Frederick
    Burial: 27 Aug 1918
    On stone with Samuel P. Wright

Site 10 Samuel P. Wright
    Birth: 12 Aug 1845   Death: 7 Jul 1922
    Mort: M.R. Etchison
    Place: Brunswick
    Burial: 9 Jul 1922
    h/o Margaret Wright

Site 11 Ida Marie Wright Feeney
    Birth: 5 Feb 1878   Death: 17 Jan 1963
    Mort: Pierce Bros.
    Place: Los Angeles, CA
    Burial: 22 Jan 1963
    w/o John A. Feeney

Site 12 John A. Feeney
    Birth: 17 Jul 1873   Death: 23 Mar 1949
    Mort: Warner E. Pumphrey
    Place: Silver Spring
    Burial: 26 Mar 1949
    h/o Ida Marie Wright Feeney

Lot: 15 Lower   Owner: George W. Long

Site   George W. Long   Birth: 1874
    h/o Mary Carpenter Long & Elizabeth Long
    Not buried in Monocacy

Site 2 Elizabeth A. Long
    Birth: 1882   Death: 25 Oct 1944
    Mort: S.H. Hines Co.
    Place: Washington, DC
    Burial: 27 Oct 1944
    2nd w/o George W. Long

Site 3 Mable C. Wainwright
    Birth: 1910   Death: 5 May 1932
    Mort: W.W. Chambers Co.
    Place: Washington, DC
    Burial: 7 May 1932
    TS: d/o Mary C. & George W. Long

Site 4 Mary Carpenter Long
    Birth: 1872   Death: 19 Feb 1917
    Mort: Hilton & Hall
    Place: Poolesville
    Burial: 21 Feb 1917
    w/o George W. Long

Lot: 15 Upper   Owner: Ernest B. Poole

Site 1 Melvin M. Poole
    Birth: 26 Aug 1886   Death: 9 Mar 1935
    Mort: W.R. Pumphrey
    Place: Washington, DC
    Burial: 12 Mar 1935
    TS: Brother

Site 2 Helen Poole   Mort: W.T. Hilton & Sons
    Birth: 15 May 1916   Death: 27 Jan 1917
    Place: Washington, DC
    Burial: 29 Jan 1917

Site 5 Daisy F. Poole
    Birth: 10 Feb 1887   Death: 5 Sep 1951
    Mort: Robert A. Pumphrey
    Place: Washington, DC
    Burial: 8 Sep 1951
    w/o Ernest Bollen Poole, age 64

Site 6 Ernest Bollen Poole
    Birth: 7 Aug 1890   Death: 18 Jun 1966
    Mort: Pearsons
    Place: Falls Church, VA
    Burial: 29 Jun 1966
    h/o Daisy F. Poole

Lot: 16   Owner: William E. Roberson

Site 1 Edward V. Roberson
    Birth: 1909   Death: 14 Apr 1941
    Mort: W.B. Hilton
    Place: Sykesville
    Burial: 16 Apr 1941
    s/o William Edgar Roberson

Site 2 James Sedrick Roberson   Mort: W.T. Hilton & Sons
    Place: Dickerson   Death: 9 Apr 1915
    Burial: 11 Apr 1915
    h/o Rosa May Roberson
    No marker

Monocacy Cemetery, Beallsville, Montgomery County, Maryland

Site 3 Rosa May Roberson Mort: W.T. Hilton & Sons
 Place: Ashville, NC Death: 9 Nov 1917 Burial: 12 Nov 1917
 w/o James Sedrick Roberson No marker
Site 4 William Edgar Roberson Mort: Hilton Place: Dickerson
 Birth: 1884 Death: 26 Dec 1960 Burial: 29 Dec 1960
Site 5 Ruth Margaret Roberson w/o William E. Roberson
 Birth: 20 Aug 1896 Death: 13 Oct 1983 Burial: 15 Oct 1983
Site 8 Kevin Ellsworth Roberson Place: Frederick Hospital
 Birth: 15 Jun 1957 Death: 16 Jun 1957 Burial: 18 Jun 1957
 Mort: Hilton TS: s/o Ellis L. & Barbara T. Roberson

Lot: 17 Owner: Ira T. Sears
Site 2 Florence Ellen Sears Mort: M.R. Etchison Place: near Greenfield
 Birth: 1873 Death: 19 Jan 1943 Burial: 22 Jan 1943
Site 3 Sarah Jane Sears Mort: Geo W. Peters Place: Dickerson
 Birth: 1848 Death: 2 Jul 1921 Burial: 4 Jul 1921
 TS: w/o William Thomas Sears
Site 4 William Thomas Sears Mort: Geo. W. Peters Place: Frederick
 Birth: 1844 Death: 6 Jun 1916 Burial: 8 Jun 1916
Site 5 Edward Charles Sears Place: Sears Road Co., Frederick
 Birth: 1885 Death: 3 Aug 1955 Burial: 6 Aug 1955
 Mort: M.R. Etchison & Son
Site 8 Faith Virginia Sears Mort: W.R. Etchison & Son Place: Adamstown
 Birth: 1940 Death: 23 Dec 1948 Burial: 27 Dec 1948
 TS: d/o Fulton D. & Dorothy P. Sears
Site 9 Willie Millard Sears
 Birth: 1902 Death: 23 Dec 1984 Burial: 27 Dec 1984
Site 11 Ira Thomas Sears Mort: M.R. Etchison & Son Place: Dickerson
 Birth: 1877 Death: 20 May 1955 Burial: 23 May 1955
Site 11 Lottie V. Sears Place: Frederick
 Birth: 12 Jun 1878 Death: 15 Feb 1940 Burial: 18 Feb 1940
 Mort: M.R. Etcherson & Son On stone with Ira Thomas Sears

Lot: 18 Owner: James B. Elgin
Site 1 Fannie C. Elgin Mort: Hilton & Hall
 Place: Falls Church, VA Death: 27 Feb 1934 Burial: 2 Mar 1934
 d/o James B. & Sarah Elgin TS: age 62-2-4
Site 3 Sarah Taylor Elgin Mort: Hilton & Hall
 Place: Poolesville Death: 12 Feb 1917 Burial: 13 Feb 1917
 TS: w/o James B. Elgin, age 78-7-16
Site 4 James B. Elgin Mort: Hilton & Hall
 Place: Dunloring, VA Death: 27 Jun 1920 Burial: 29 Jun 1920
 h/o Sarah Elgin TS: age 81-2-12
Site 5 Hattie K. Elgin Place: Washington, DC
 Birth: 24 Feb 1868 Death: 21 Jan 1947 Burial: 25 Jan 1947
 Mort: Huntemans Funeral Home d/o James B. & Sarah Taylor Elgin
Site 10 Charles Ogelbie Elgin Place: Dunn Loring, VA
 Birth: 22 Mar 1870 Death: 11 Nov 1948 Burial: 13 Nov 1948
 Mort: O.C. Pearson s/o James B. & Sarah Taylor Elgin

Monocacy Cemetery, Beallsville, Montgomery County, Maryland

Site 11 Elizabeth Elgin Black Ware d/o Charles O. Elgin
 No marker Death: 18 Nov 1988 Burial: 22 Nov 1988
Site 12 Harvey O. Black Place: Washington, DC
 Birth: 23 May 1900 Death: 26 May 1936 Burial: 28 May 1936
 Mort: W.W. Chambers h/o Elizabeth Elgin Black

Lot: 19 Owner: A.G. Elgin

Site 2 Clifford Howard Elgin Place: Washington, DC
 Birth: 18 May 1912 Death: 8 Apr 1934 Burial: 10 Apr 1934
 Mort: Hilton & Hall s/o Diana C. & Arthur G. Elgin
Site 3 Diana Carpenter Elgin Place: Poolesville
 Birth: 23 Aug 1881 Death: 27 Nov 1920 Burial: 29 Nov 1920
 Mort: Hilton & Hall TS: [1st] w/o Arthur G. Elgin
Site 4 Arthur Gorman Elgin Mort: Hilton Place: Frederick
 Birth: 4 Oct 1877 Death: 6 Mar 1959 Burial: 9 Mar 1959
 h/o Diana Carpenter Elgin & Mary Aldridge Elgin
Site 5 Mary Aldridge Elgin Place: Frederick, MD
 Birth: 7 Sep 1896 Death: 24 Jul 1970 Burial: 27 Jul 1970
 Mort: Wm. Hilton 2nd w/o Arthur Gorman Elgin
Site 7 Emily Blandford Elgin Place: Rockville
 Birth: 17 Sep 1911 Death: 30 May 1955 Burial: 2 Jun 1955
 Mort: Robert A. Pumphrey TS: [1st] w/o John Edward Elgin
Site 8 John Edward Elgin TS: CPL US Army WWII Army Air Corps
 Birth: 17 Mar 1908 Death: 25 May 1984 Burial: 29 May 1984
Site 11 Mary Elizabeth Elgin Mann Place: Sykesville
 Birth: 25 Sep 1865 Death: 17 Dec 1957 Burial: 19 Dec 1957
 Mort: Hilton On stone with Arthur Howard Mann, Jr., MD
Site 12 Arthur Howard Mann Jr., MD Place: Sykesville Hospital
 Birth: 29 Oct 1869 Death: 26 Sep 1919 Burial: 28 Sep 1919
 Mort: Hilton & Hall h/o Mary Elgin Mann

Lot: 20 Owner: William H. Sears

Site 2 Miss Marjorie V. Sears
 Birth: 1 Jun 1904 Death: 29 Jun 1976 Burial: 1 Jul 1976
Site 3 Airy V. Sears w/o William H. Sears
 Birth: 22 Nov 1878 Death: 22 Feb 1979 Burial: 24 Feb 1979
Site 4 William Henry Sears Place: Dickerson
 Birth: 28 Mar 1872 Death: 21 Aug 1939 Burial: 24 Aug 1939
 Mort: W.B. Hilton h/o Airy Sears
Site 5 William Linwood Sears Place: Bethesda, MD
 Birth: 29 Nov 1900 Death: 12 Jan 1971 Burial: 16 Jan 1971
 Mort: Wm. Hilton h/o Ella Umstead Sears
Site 7 Catherine E. Beall Mort: W. E. Pumphrey Place: Washington, DC
 Birth: 1 Mar 1882 Death: 18 Mar 1940 Burial: 20 Mar 1940
Site 9 Ella Sears Eader w/o Paul L. Eader
 Birth: 11 Nov 1907 Death: 10 May 1995 Burial: 13 May 1995
Site 10 Paul L. Eader h/o Ella Sears Eader
 Birth: 25 Aug 1915 Death: 21 Oct 1987 Burial: 24 Oct 1987

Monocacy Cemetery, Beallsville, Montgomery County, Maryland

Lot: 21 Owner: Elias Beall

Site 2 William H. Beall Mort: W.T. Hilton Place: Washington, DC
        Birth: 28 Mar 1872 Death: 21 May 1917 Burial: 23 May 1917
        TS: s/o Erwin O. & Bessie Frances Beall, age 8-3-14

Site 3 Erwin O. Beall Place: Alexandria
        Birth: 12 Jun 1887 Death: 10 Mar 1967 Burial: 14 Mar 1967
        Mort: Cunningham h/o Bessie Frances Beall

Site 4 Bessie Frances Beall On stone with Erwin O. Beall
        Birth: 18 Aug 1887 Death: 13 Feb 1972 Burial: 16 Feb 1972

Site 6 Golden Ellsworth Williams On stone with Ida F. Beall Williams
        Birth: 28 Nov 1903 Death: 9 Apr 1974 Burial: 11 Apr 1974

Site 7 Ruth Ellen Beall Compher Place: Poolesville
        Birth: 3 Jul 1894 Death: 27 May 1954 Burial: 29 May 1954
        Mort: W.B. Hilton On stone with Zachariah M. Compher

Site 8 Zachariah M. Compher Place: Frederick, MD
        Birth: 20 Nov 1884 Death: 9 Jan 1969 Burial: 13 Jan 1969
        Mort: Wm. Hilton h/o Ruth Beall Compher

Site 9 Carrie T. Beall Place: Georgetown Hospital
        Birth: 29 Apr 1878 Death: 14 Oct 1919 Burial: 16 Oct 1919
        Mort: W.T. Hilton & Sons TS: w/o John William Beall

Site 10 John William Beall Place: Poolesville
        Birth: 19 Sep 1881 Death: 21 Apr 1957 Burial: 24 Apr 1957
        Mort: Hilton h/o Carrie T. Beall

Site 11 Ida Beall Place: Poolesville
        Birth: 8 Jun 1857 Death: 1 Apr 1921 Burial: 3 Apr 1921
        Mort: Hilton & Hall TS: w/o Elias Beall

Site 12 Elias Beall Place: Poolesville
        Birth: 27 Mar 1859 Death: 9 Nov 1938 Burial: 11 Nov 1938
        Mort: Hilton & Hall h/o Ida Beall

Lot: 22 Owner: R.D. Poole

Site 3 Adaline G. Poole Place: Washington, DC
        Birth: 1887 Death: 11 Nov 1968 Burial: 14 Nov 1968
        Mort: Simmons Bros. On stone with Reginald D. Poole

Site 4 Reginald D. Poole Place: Washington, DC
        Birth: 1883 Death: 24 Aug 1961 Burial: 28 Aug 1961
        Mort: Simmons Bros. h/o Adaline G. Poole

Lot: 23 Lower Owner: Miscellaneous

Site 4 Frank B. Cowell Mort: W.T. Hilton & Sons Place: Shawomet, RI
        Birth: 20 Dec 1880 Death: 10 Oct 1918 Burial: 14 Oct 1918

Lot: 23 Upper Owner: Mrs. O.K. Poole

Site 1 Hallie G. Walker Mort: Gartner Place: Bethesda, MD
        Birth: 13 Mar 1910 Death: 29 Aug 1969 Burial: 2 Sep 1969
        On stone with William Hughes Walker & Mable P. Walker

Site 1 William Hughes Walker Place: Olney
        Birth: 27 Aug 1901 Death: 24 Jan 1962 Burial: 27 Jan 1962
        Mort: E.C. Gartner h/o Hallie Walker

Monocacy Cemetery, Beallsville, Montgomery County, Maryland

Site 2 Mable P. Walker Mort: E.C. Gartner Place: Washington, DC
       Birth: 4 Feb 1904 Death: 24 May 1948 Burial: 28 May 1948
Site 3 Katie Dorsey Poole TS: w/o Oscar K. Poole Mort: Gartner Funeral
       Place: Takoma Park Death: 17 Feb 1946 Burial: 20 Feb 1946
Site 4 Oscar K. Poole Place: Washington DC
       Birth: 7 Feb 1875 Death: 21 Aug 1918 Burial: 23 Aug 1918
       Mort: W.T. Hilton & Sons h/o Katie D. Poole

Lot: 24 Owner: William H. Larman
Site 1 Joseph Edgar Larman Mort: W.B. Hilton Place: Boyds
       Birth: 19 Nov 1907 Death: 7 Sep 1941 Burial: 9 Sep 1941
Site 2 William Edward Larman Place: Frederick
       Birth: 1866 Death: 14 Dec 1938 Burial: 17 Dec 1938
       Mort: W.B. Hilton On stone with Mary A. G. & William H. Larman
Site 3 Mary Anna George Larman Place: Boyds
       Birth: 1845 Death: 23 Jan 1926 Burial: 25 Jan 1926
       Mort: W.T. Hilton & Sons TS: w/o William H. Larman
Site 4 William H. Larman Place: Buck Lodge
       Birth: 1842 Death: 17 Mar 1923 Burial: 19 Mar 1923
       Mort: W.T. Hilton & Sons h/o Mary George Anna Larman
Site 5 Fannie Elizabeth Larman Mort: W.B. Hilton Place: Boyds
       Birth: 15 Jul 1867 Death: 9 Mar 1946 Burial: 12 Mar 1946
Site 6 William B. Benson Mort: W.H. Hilton Place: Bethesda, MD
       Birth: 1890 Death: 14 Dec 1968 Burial: 16 Mar 1968
Site 7 Frank E. Larman Mort: W.W. Chambers Place: Washington, DC
       Birth: 27 Oct 1896 Death: 3 Oct 1944 Burial: 6 Oct 1944
Site 8 William Clifton Larman Mort: Deal Place: Washington, DC
       Birth: 20 Aug 1894 Death: 22 Jul 1957 Burial: 25 Jul 1957
       TS: Veteran of WWI

Lot: 25 Owner: Mrs. Joseph Waters
Site 4 Doris Hammond Waters Mort: W.R. Pumphrey Place: Washington
       Birth: 1915 Death: 2 Jan 1916 Burial: 5 Oct 1925
       [c/o] On stone with Joseph Waters Disinterred from Washington, DC
Site 4 Joseph Henry Waters Mort: W.R. Pumphrey Place: Pittsburg
       Birth: 1885 Death: 28 Jul 1925 Burial: 28 Sep 1925

Lot: 26 Owner: C.H. Stouffer
Site 2 Albert F. Stouffer No marker Mort: J. Arthur Walters
       Place: Washington, DC Death: 4 Nov 1943 Burial: 8 Nov 1943
Site 3 Georgia A. Stouffer TS: Mother Place: Washington
       Birth: 3 Mar 1865 Death: 17 Oct 1925 Burial: 19 Oct 1925
       Mort: Perry & Walsh w/o Charles H. Stouffer
Site 4 Charles Henry Stouffer TS: Father Place: Takoma Park
       Birth: 26 Nov 1866 Death: 26 Jul 1942 Burial: 28 Jul 1942
       Mort: J. Arthur Walters h/o Georgia A. Stouffer
Site 5 Charles H. Stouffer Jr. s/o C.H. & Georgia A. Stouffer
       Birth: 17 Sep 1897 Death: 28 Dec 1976 Burial: 3 Jan 1977
Site 6 Grace Stouffer No marker Burial: 14 Jul 1990

Monocacy Cemetery, Beallsville, Montgomery County, Maryland   201

Site 12 Grace Murphy   No marker   Age 65 yrs
                               Death: 19 Oct 1988   Burial: 21 Oct 1988

Lot: 27 Lower   Owner: L.F. Loy
Site 1 Roy William Swank   Place: Frederick
       Birth: 25 Jul 1908   Death: 26 Jan 1954   Burial: 29 Jan 1954
       Mort: W.B. Hilton   s/o W.S. & J.H. Swank, unmarried
Site 2 Mary J. Hilton   Place: Dickerson
       Birth: 1837   Death: 2 Dec 1926   Burial: 4 Dec 1926
       Mort: W,T, Hilton & Sons   w/o Rufus E.G. Hilton
Site 3 Rufus E.G. Hilton   Birth: 1840   Death: 1897
Site 4 Luther F. Loy   No marker   Mort: W.T. Hilton & Sons
       Place: Dickerson   Death: 18 Jun 1931   Burial: 21 Jun 1931
Site 5 Jessie Irene H. Swank   Place: Dickerson
       Birth: 6 Apr 1879   Death: 22 Mar 1941   Burial: 22 Mar 1941
       Mort: W.B. Hilton   w/o William S. Swank
Site 6 William Samuel Swank   Place: Dickerson
       Birth: 5 Jan 1879   Death: 23 Nov 1950   Burial: 26 Nov 1950
       Mort: W.B. Hilton   h/o Jessie H. Swank

Lot: 27 Upper   Owner: E.J. Wynne
Site 1 Ethel Virginia Wynne   Place: Dickerson
       Birth: 1916   Death: 10 Dec 1932   Burial: 12 Dec 1932
       Mort: Hilton & Hall   d/o Edward J. & Ida L. Wynne
Site 2 James Wiley Wynne   Place: Dickerson
       Birth: 17 Jan 1912   Death: 17 Aug 1926   Burial: 19 Aug 1926
       Mort: Hilton & Hall   s/o Ida L. & Edward J. Wynne
Site 3 Ida Lake Wynne   Mort: Hilton & Hall   Place: Dickerson
       Birth: 1882   Death: 17 Sep 1938   Burial: 18 Sep 1938
       On stone with Edward J. Wynne
Site 4 Edward Johnson Wynne   Place: Poolesville
       Birth: 1873   Death: 12 Apr 1942   Burial: 14 Apr 1942
       Mort: W.B. Hilton   h/o Ida L. Wynne
Site 6 Lola Imogene Wynne   Birth: 28 Sep 1923   Death: 2 Apr 1988
       On stone with Ralph W. Wynne

Lot: 28   Owner: S.H. Hurt
Site 1 Sallie Bone Hurt   Place: Poolesville
       Birth: 15 Dec 1840   Death: 1 Feb 1926   Burial: 3 Feb 1926
       Mort: Hilton & Hall   w/o George W. Hurt
Site 2 George W. Hurt   Place: Poolesville
       Birth: 12 Jan 1841   Death: 28 Jun 1932   Burial: 30 Jun 1932
       Mort: Hilton & Hall   h/o Sallie Bone Hurt
Site 7 Emma R. Lambert Hurt   Place: Brunswick
       Birth: 22 Nov 1875   Death: 10 Apr 1953   Burial: 12 Apr 1953
       Mort: W.B. Hilton   w/o John Stephen Hurt
Site 8 John Stephen Hurt   Place: Bethesda
       Birth: 12 Dec 1868   Death: 1 Apr 1959   Burial: 2 Apr 1959
       Mort: Hilton   h/o Emma Lambert Hurt

Monocacy Cemetery, Beallsville, Montgomery County, Maryland

Site 9 Della M. Hurt
         Birth: 24 Jun 1898   Death: 6 May 1991   Burial: 8 May 1991
Site 10 Eugene William Hurt   Place: Rockville
         Birth: 25 Jul 1894   Death: 21 Dec 1958   Burial: 23 Dec 1958
         Mort: Hilton   TS: Pvt. Co. A 108 MG BN Virginia, WWI

Lot: 29   Owner: Miss Mary H. Robertson
Site 1 Warrick W. Stephens Hefner   Place: Akron, OH
         Birth: 1866   Death: 29 Jun 1928   Burial: 3 Jul 1928
         Mort: W.W. Deal Co.   h/o Kathryn Robertson Hefner
Site 2 Kathryn Robertson Hefner   Place: Washington, DC
         Birth: 1885   Death: 4 Nov 1948   Burial: 6 Nov 1948
         Mort: S.H. Hines Co.   TS: w/o Warrick W. Stephens Hefner
Site 3 Elizabeth Cameron Robertson   Place: Washington
         Birth: 1854   Death: 8 Jan 1931   Burial: 10 Jan 1931
         Mort: O.B. Jenkins   TS: w/o Robert Robertson
Site 4 Robert Robertson   Mort: O.B. Jenkins   Place: Washington, DC
         Birth: 1847   Death: 25 Apr 1929   Burial: 27 Apr 1929
Site 7 Mary H. Robertson   Mort: Paul D. Sconell   Place: Henbley, OH
         Birth: 1889   Death: 28 Dec 1955   Burial: 31 Dec 1955

Lot: 30 Lower   Owner: John M. Sullivan
Site 1 Alexandra W. Sullivan   Mort: Doly Bros.   Place: Detroit
         Birth: 27 Jul 1886   Death: 8 May 1929   Burial: 7 Aug 1929
Site 2 Louisa J. Sullivan   Place: Laytonsville
         Birth: 16 Jun 1861   Death: 22 May 1932   Burial: 24 May 1932
         Mort: Roy W. Barber   w/o John M. Sullivan
Site 3 John M. Sullivan   Mort: Roy W. Barber   Place: Laytonsville
         Birth: 4 Sep 1857   Death: 17 Sep 1931   Burial: 19 Sep 1931
Site 5 Susie F. Sullivan Perell   Place: Brookville
         Birth: 24 Jan 1894   Death: 18 Feb 1939   Burial: 20 Feb 1939
         Mort: W.B. Hilton   w/o Samuel Perill, d/o John M. Sullivan

Lot: 30 Upper   Owner: George R. Elkins (No stones in lot)
Site 2 Texanna Elkins Potter   No marker   Mort: W.B. Hilton
         Place: Poolesville   Death: 9 Apr 1953   Burial: 12 Apr 1953
Site 3 Catherine Elkins   w/o George R. Elkins   Mort: W.B. Hilton
         Place: Poolesville   Death: 30 Nov 1945   Burial: 3 Dec 1945
Site 4 George R. Elkins   h/o Catherine Elkins   Mort: Hilton & Hall
         Place: Martinsburg   Death: 15 Dec 1928   Burial: 18 Dec 1928
Site 5 Joseph Milton Elkins   No marker   Mort: Hilton & Hall
         Place: Poolesville   Death: 30 Mar 1934   Burial: 1 Apr 1934

Lot: 31   Owner: O.B. Cooley
Site 1 John Bernard Cooley   Place: Washington, DC
         Birth: 5 Jun 1911   Death: 24 May 1931   Burial: 26 May 1931
         Mort: E.C. Gartner   s/o Lucie E. & Otho B. Cooley

Site 2	Lucy Elizabeth Cooley	TS: Mother	Place: Bethesda
	Birth: 27 Mar 1885	Death: 23 Nov 1956	Burial: 27 Nov 1956
	Mort: Warner E. Pumphrey	w/o Otho B. Cooley	
Site 3	Otho B. Cooley	TS: Father	Place: Kensington, MD
	Birth: 10 Apr 1878	Death: 12 Dec 1967	Burial: 15 Dec 1967
	Mort: Arthur Walters		
Site 7	Sandra L. Cooley		Place: Baltimore
	Birth: 2 Aug 1944	Death: 14 Feb 1945	Burial: 17 Feb 1945
	Mort: J. Arthur Walters		d/o Earl Calvert Cooley
Site 8	Earl Calvert Cooley		TS: PVT US Army WWII
	Birth: 22 May 1922	Death: 1 Sep 1977	Burial: 6 Sep 1977

Lot: 32 Lower   Owner: Howard Roberson

Site 1	James W. Holland		h/o Daisy Bussard Holland
	Birth: 11 Apr 1908	Death: 28 Oct 1978	Burial: 31 Oct 1978
Site 2	Daisy Elizabeth Bussard Holland		Place: Silver Spring
	Birth: 18 Nov 1907	Death: 30 Jun 1962	Burial: 3 Jul 1962
	Mort: Warner E. Pumphrey		w/o James W. Holland
Site 4	Howard Calvin Roberson	Mort: Hilton	Place: Dickerson
	Birth: 31 Jul 1885	Death: 9 Jul 1961	Burial: 12 Jul 1961
Site 4	Mary E. Roberson		w/o Howard Calvin Roberson
	Birth: 22 Feb 1893	Death: 8 Apr 1980	Burial: 11 Apr 1980

Lot: 32 Upper   Owner: George D. Brown

Site 1	Christine G. Holland		No marker
	Birth: 8 Aug 1917	Death: 14 Mar 1997	Burial: 17 Mar 1997
Site 2	David H. Brown		Place: Brunswick, MD
	Birth: 13 Mar 1921	Death: 19 Dec 1970	Burial: 22 Dec 1970
	Mort: Feete Funeral Home		w/o Annie K. & George D. Brown
Site 3	Annie K. Brown		Place: Frederick, MD
	Birth: 11 Aug 1884	Death: 4 Jul 1970	Burial: 7 Jul 1970
	Mort: Feete Funeral Home		w/o George D. Brown
Site 4	George David Brown		Place: Dickerson
	Birth: 21 Feb 1885	Death: 6 Dec 1931	Burial: 9 Dec 1931
	Mort: W.T. Hilton & Sons		h/o Annie K. Brown
Site 5	Elizabeth W. Bussard		Place: Dickerson
	Birth: 18 Jan 1858	Death: 22 Jan 1934	Burial: 25 Jan 1934
	Mort: Hilton & Price		TS: :Bettie" Mother
Site 6	Robert Lee Bussard	Mort: Feete Funeral Home	Place: Brunswick
	Birth: 4 Feb 1883	Death: 18 Jun 1963	Burial: 21 Jun 1963

Lot: 33 Lower   Owner: Mrs. Effie Fox

Site 1	Ivan Hedge		h/o Matilda Fox Hedge, age 86 yrs
	Birth: 2 Jan 1904	Death: 12 Mar 1991	Burial: 15 Mar 1991
Site 2	Matilda Fox Hedge		On stone with Ivan Hedge
	Birth: 24 Apr 1904	Death: 11 Dec 1988	Burial: 15 Dec 1988
Site 3	Effie C. Munger Fox		On stone with Thomas B. Fox
	Birth: 1878	Death: 1 Jul 1975	Burial: 5 Jul 1975

Site 4 Thomas Benton Fox   Place: Poolesville
        Birth: 1872   Death: 8 May 1934   Burial: 11 May 1934
        Mort: W.R. Pumphrey   h/o Effie Mungar Fox
Site 5 Margaret Fox Poole   Place: Havre De Grace
        Birth: 19 Aug 1906   Death: 27 Oct 1943   Burial: 29 Oct 1943
        Mort: W.B. Hilton   d/o T.B. & Effie M. Fox

Lot: 33 Upper   Owner: Mrs. Elsie Bussard
Site 1 John Maurice Bussard   Place: Thurmont
        Birth: 3 Dec 1949   Death: 3 Dec 1949   Burial: 4 Dec 1949
        Mort: W.L. Creager & Son   TS: s/o W.J. & Ophelia L. Bussard
Site 2 Charles Arthur Bussard Mort: M.R. Etchison   Place: GA
        Birth: 1920   Death: 12 Nov 1966   Burial: 16 Nov 1966
        TS: US Army WWII
Site 3 Elsie Naomi Bussard   Mort: M.R. Etchison & Son   Place: Frederick
        Birth: 1895   Death: 1 Aug 1953   Burial: 4 Aug 1953
Site 4 Joseph Henry Bussard   Mort: M.R. Etchison & Son   Place: Frederick
        Birth: 1887   Death: 2 Mar 1933   Burial: 5 Mar 1933

Lot: 34 Owner: Mrs. Irene Perkins
Site 2 Sarah Elizabeth Norris Lindig   Place: St. Paul, MN
        Birth: 1869   Death: 28 Jun 1949   Burial: 2 Jul 1949
        Mort: W.B. Hilton   On stone with Henry M. Lindig, age 80
Site 3 Henry M. Lindig   Place: Washington, DC
        Birth: 1863   Death: 2 Apr 1946   Burial: 5 Apr 1946
        Mort: W.B. Hilton   h/o Sarah Elizabeth Norris Lindig
Site 4 Thomas Eldridge Perkins   Place: New York
        Birth: 4 Feb 1895   Death: 16 Jul 1933   Burial: 18 Jul 1933
        Mort: W.R. Pumphrey   h/o Irene Lindig Perkins
Site 7 Alma Dennie Lewis   Place: Washington, DC
        Birth: 23 Jan 1889   Death: 24 Jan 1962   Burial: 27 Jan 1962
        Mort: Robert A. Pumphrey   On stone with Irene Lindig Lewis
Site 8 Irene Lindig Lewis   c/o Thomas Eldridge Perkins & Alma D. Lewis
        Birth: 22 May 1893   Death: 4 Aug 1979   Burial: 9 Aug 1979

Lot: 35 Lower   Owner: C.R. Nichols
Site 1 Mary Elizabeth Woodward Mort: W.R. Pumphrey   Place: Bethesda
        Birth: 19 Feb 1873   Death: 9 Mar 1939   Burial: 12 Mar 1939
Site 3 Delma Bridget Nichols   Place: Bethesda
        Birth: 7 Oct 1880   Death: 20 Aug 1942   Burial: 23 Aug 1942
        Mort: Wm. Reuben Pumphrey   w/o Clinton R. Nichols
Site 4 Clinton R. Nichols   Place: Bethesda
        Birth: 1874   Death: 30 Apr 1965   Burial: 3 May 1965
        Mort: Robert A. Pumphrey   h/o Delma Bridget Nichols
Site 5 Florence Ellen Nichols   Mort: Wm. R. Pumphrey
        Place: Bethesda   Death: 6 Apr 1944   Burial: 9 Apr 1944
Site 6 George Frederick Nichols Mort: W.B. Hilton   Place: Frederick
        Birth: 25 May 1882   Death: 19 Dec 1941   Burial: 21 Dec 1941

Lot: 35 Upper   Owner: Mrs. Mary Ainsworth

Site 1 Judah T. Ainsworth   Place: Washington, DC
Birth: 9 Oct 1866   Death: 9 Oct 1948   Burial: 6 Nov 1948
Mort: J.Wm. Sees & Son   h/o Mary Sellman Ainsworth

Site 2 J. Trent Ainsworth   Place: Washington, DC
Birth: 1903   Death: 29 Dec 1936   Burial: 31 Dec 1936
Mort: W.B. Hilton   s/o Judah T. & Mary Sellman Ainsworth

Site 3 Mary Sellman Ainsworth   Place: Washington, DC
Birth: 6 Sep 1873   Death: 6 Apr 1948   Burial: 8 Apr 1948
Mort: S.H. Hines Co.   w/o Judah T. Ainsworth

Site 4 Ruth Sellman Ainsworth
Birth: 27 Feb 1898   Death: 22 May 1977   Burial: 24 May 1977

Lot: 36 Lower   Owner: Charles Ernest White

Site 1 Donald C. White DD   TS: US Army   s/o Charles E. & Abbie May White
Birth: 25 Mar 1915   Death: 19 Nov 1994   Burial: 7 Dec 1994

Site 2 John Collinson White   TS: Son   Place: Dawsonville
Birth: 1908   Death: 23 May 1937   Burial: 26 May 1937
Mort: W.B. Hilton   s/o Charles E. & Abbie May White

Site 3 Abbie May Specht White   TS: Mother   Place: Frederick
Birth: 1874   Death: 17 Mar 1964   Burial: 20 Mar 1964
Mort: Hilton   w/o Charles Ernest White

Site 4 Charles Ernest White   TS: Father   Place: Boyds
Birth: 1876   Death: 24 Oct 1944   Burial: 26 Oct 1944
Mort: W.B. Hilton   h/o Abbie May Specht White

Site 5 Betty White Reesch   Age 79 yrs   On stone with Albert D. Reesch,
Birth: 2 Aug 1911   Death: 23 Apr 1991   Burial: 26 Apr 1991

Site 6 Albert D. Reesch   h/o Bettie White Reesch
Birth: 29 Sep 1900   Death: 22 Apr 1982   Burial: 24 Apr 1982

Lot: 36 Upper   Owner: Marshall Morningstar

Site 1 Henry Milton Larman   No marker   Mort: E.C. Gartner
Place: Kensington   Death: 29 Sep 1948   Burial: 2 Oct 1948

Site 2 Elizabeth May Larman   No marker   Mort: W.B. Hilton
Place: Dickerson   Death: 30 Oct 1946   Burial: 2 Nov 1946

Site 3 Anna Mary Larman Morningstar   w/o Marshall Morningstar
Birth: 31 Aug 1897   Death: 5 Jan 1978   Burial: 9 Jan 1978

Site 4 Marshall C. Morningstar   Mort: W.B. Hilton   Place: Dickerson
Birth: 6 Apr 1897   Death: 25 Nov 1939   Burial: 27 Nov 1939

Site 5 Frances Elizabeth Norwood   No marker   Mort: W.B. Hilton
Place: Cooksville   Death: 24 Jul 1941   Burial: 26 Jul 1941

Site 6 Emma L. Fox   Birth: 5 Dec 1888   Death: 2 Apr 1937

Lot: 37 Lower   Owner: Joseph R. & James R. Cole

Site 3 Mary E. Cole   Place: Poolesville
Birth: 7 Nov 1885   Death: 14 Apr 1946   Burial: 16 Apr 1946
Mort: W.B. Hilton   TS: w/o John E. Cole

Site 4 John Edward Cole   Place: Barnesville
         Birth: 26 Apr 1877   Death: 13 Nov 1938   Burial: 16 Nov 1938
         Mort: W.B. Hilton   h/o Mary E. Cole
Site 5 Ellen M. Cole   Age 71 yrs   On stone with Leonard S. Cole
         Birth: 17 Oct 1913   Death: 3 Jun 1985   Burial: 7 Jun 1985
Site 5 Leonard S. Cole
         Birth: 21 Feb 1911   Death: 23 Mar 1974   Burial: 28 Mar 1974
Site 6 Douglas Raymond Cole   Mort: W.B. Hilton
         Place: Barnesville   Death: 3 Feb 1941   Burial: 4 Feb 1941
         Cause: Stillborn   No marker

Lot: 37 Upper   Owner: Montgomery E. Higgins
Site 3 Alice Cross Higgins   Place: Boyds
         Birth: 1854   Death: 3 May 1938   Burial: 5 May 1938
         Mort: W.B. Hilton   w/o James L. Higgins
Site 4 James L. Higgins   Place: Boyds
         Birth: 1851   Death: 12 Apr 1939   Burial: 14 Apr 1939
         Mort: W.B. Hilton   h/o Alice C. Higgins
Site 5 Maude Virginia Higgins   Mort: Hilton   Place: Washington, DC
         Birth: 1883   Death: 18 Feb 1961   Burial: 20 Feb 1961

Lot: 38 Lower   Owner: Miscellaneous
Site 1 Gordon Murdock Smith, MD   On stone with Lillian H. Smith
         Birth: 2 Jul 1918   Death: 24 Jun 1995   Burial: 27 Jun 1995
Site 2 Sophia E. Hubble   Place: Dickerson
         Birth: 9 Apr 1884   Death: 9 Jun 1939   Burial: 11 Jun 1939
         Mort: W.B. Hilton   w/o O.K. Hubble
Site 3 Otis Knox Hubble Sr.   Place: Baltimore
         Birth: 15 Feb 1882   Death: 21 Nov 1953   Burial: 23 Nov 1953
         Mort: W.B. Hilton   h/o Sophia E. Hubble
Site 5 Raymond Luther Catron   TS: S2 US Navy WWII
         Birth: 2 Mar 1926   Death: 26 Apr 1987   Burial: 1 May 1987
Site 6 William E. Ratliff
         Birth: 14 Dec 1911   Death: 24 Sep 1983   Burial: 27 Sep 1983

Lot: 38 Upper   Owner: Thomas H. Jarboe
Site 2 Thomas L. Jarboe   On stone with Ethel M. Jarboe
         Birth: 13 Feb 1912   Death: 21 Sep 1992   Burial: 25 Sep 1992
Site 3 Susie Ella Jarboe   Place: Darnestown
         Birth: 1880   Death: 21 Jun 1938   Burial: 23 Jun 1938
         Mort: W.R. Pumphrey   On stone with Thomas H. Jarboe
Site 4 Thomas H. Jarboe   Place: Washington, DC
         Birth: 1880   Death: 6 Jun 1951   Burial: 9 Jun 1951
         Mort: S.H. Hines Co.   h/o Susie Ella Jarboe
Site 5 Raymond H. Jarboe   Mort: Hines   Place: Washington, DC
         Birth: 1904   Death: 5 Feb 1967   Burial: 9 Feb 1967

Lot: 39 Lower   Owner: Burgess E. Dodson

Site 1 Upton Leon Dodson, Sr.   On stone with Mary L. Dodson
        Birth: 27 Oct 1923   Death: 25 Mar 1993   Burial: 27 Mar 1993
Site 3 Burgess E. Dodson   Place: Silver Spring
        Birth: 1904   Death: 15 Jul 1967   Burial: 18 Jul 1967
        Mort: R.A. Pumphrey   h/o Dollie T. Burgess
Site 4 Dollie T. Dodson   TS: Mother   Place: Bethesda
        Birth: 3 Nov 1904   Death: 16 Oct 1953   Burial: 20 Oct 1953
        Mort: Robert A. Pumphrey   w/o Burgess E. Dodson
Site 5 Robert Edison Dodson   Place: Bethesda
        Birth: 6 Sep 1937   Death: 9 Aug 1948   Burial: 11 Aug 1948
        Mort: W.R. Pumphrey   c/o Burgess E. & Dollie T. Dodson
Site 6 Ida Dodson   No marker   Mort: Warner E.
        Place: Baltimore   Death: 20 Oct 1944   Burial: 23 Oct 1944

Lot: 39 Upper   Owner: E.J. Morningstar & Grace McAuliffe

Site 2 Hazel Edgar Morningstar   Place: Washington, DC
        Birth: 1908   Death: 14 Nov 1939   Burial: 17 Nov 1939
        Mort: W.R. Pumphrey   s/o Mary Florine & Edgar J. Morningstar
Site 3 Mary Florine Morningstar   Place: Bethesda
        Birth: 1878   Death: 21 Sep 1955   Burial: 24 Sep 1955
        Mort: Robert A. Pumphrey   On stone with Edgar J. Morningstar
Site 4 Edgar J. Morningstar   Place: Bethesda
        Birth: 1888   Death: 4 Oct 1964   Burial: 7 Oct 1964
        Mort: Robert A. Pumphrey   h/o Mary Florine Morningstar
Site 5 Grace Morningstar McAuliffe   Place: Bethesda, MD
        Birth: 1911   Death: 2 Sep 1967   Burial: 5 Sep 1967
        Mort: R.A. Pumphrey   On stone with James Stephen McAuliffe
Site 6 James Stephen McAuliffe   h/o Grace Morningstar McAuliffe
        Birth: 16 Jan 1907   Death: 31 Oct 1996   Burial: 4 Nov 1996

Lot: 40 Lower   Owner: Walter Poole

Site 1 Harry L. Poole   TS: MD SFC US Army WWII, Korea
        Birth: 29 Sep 1925   Death: 15 Oct 1972   Burial: 19 Oct 1972
        s/o Mabel Rebecca & Walter S. Poole
Site 2 Walter Stone Poole Jr.   Place: Dickerson
        Birth: 1931   Death: 25 Feb 1945   Burial: 16 Mar 1945
        Mort: W.B. Hilton   s/o Mabel Rebecca & Walter Stone Poole
Site 3 Mabel Rebecca Poole   Place: Frederick
        Birth: 1889   Death: 16 Mar 1957   Burial: 19 Mar 1957
        Mort: Hilton   w/o Walter Stone Poole
Site 4 Walter Stone Poole   h/o Mabel Rebecca Poole
        Birth: 1883   Death: 12 Jun 1976   Burial: 16 Jun 1976

Lot: 40 Upper   Owner: Elmer Lee Cosgrave

Site 1 Child Cosgrave   No marker
Site 3 Frances C. Cosgrave   Place: Chas. E. Roberts
        Birth: 1886   Death: 1932   Burial: 27 Nov 1941
        Removed from Pooles tract, Dickerson, MD

Site 3 Rose Marie Cosgrave   Place: Chas. E. Roberts
        Birth: 1911   Death: 1913   Burial: 27 Nov 1941
        Removed from Pooles tract, Dickerson, MD
Site 4 William D. Cosgrave   Mort: W.R. Pumphrey   Place: Washington, DC
        Birth: 1874   Death: 15 Nov 1941   Burial: 17 Nov 1941
        On stone with Frances C. Cosgrave & Rose Marie Cosgrave

Lot: 41 Lower Owner: Miscellaneous
Site 3 Frances M. Wright   On stone with Robert Silas Wright
        Birth: 16 Sep 1913   Death: 20 Jun 1987   Burial: 22 Jun 1987
Site 4 Robert Silas Wright   Place: Hagerstown, MD
        Birth: 28 Aug 1908   Death: 29 Dec 1970   Burial: 2 Jan 1971
        Mort: Barton Funeral Home   h/o Frances M. Wright

Lot: 41 Upper Owner: Norman W. Ryman
Site 1 Minnie S. Ryman O'Donnell   On stone with Patrick O'Donnell
        Birth: 23 Nov 1895   Death: 13 Aug 1973   Burial: 15 Aug 1973
Site 2 Patrick O'Donnell   h/o Minnie S. O'Donnell
                               Death: 29 Mar 1978   Burial: 31 Mar 1978
Site 3 Cora A. Ryman   Place: Rockville
        Birth: 1873   Death: 25 Feb 1958   Burial: 27 Feb 1968
        Mort: Hilton   On stone with Homer K. Ryman
Site 4 Homer K. Ryman   Place: Hagerstown
        Birth: 1871   Death: 12 Oct 1958   Burial: 15 Oct 1958
        Mort: Hilton   h/o Cora A. Ryman

Lot: 42 Owner: Gilmer R. Hawkins
Site 2 Windsor T. Hawkins   Place: Frederick
        Birth: 25 Oct 1927   Death: 17 Mar 1935   Burial: 19 Mar 1935
        Mort: N.Z. Cramer   s/o Lucy Viola & Gilmer R. Hawkins
Site 3 Lucy Viola Hawkins   Place: Frederick
        Birth: 12 Mar 1893   Death: 27 Apr 1956   Burial: 30 Apr 1956
        Mort: M.R. Etchison & Son   w/o Gilmer R. Hawkins
Site 4 Gilmer Richard Hawkins   Place: Urbana
        Birth: 15 Jun 1891   Death: 5 Jul 1957   Burial: 8 Jul 1957
        Mort: Etchison   h/o Lucy Viola Hawkins
Site 5 David Hubert Hawkins   TS: US Army, Korea
        Birth: 11 Apr 1930   Death: 8 Dec 1981   Burial: 12 Dec 1981
        h/o Arlene Comegys Hawkins, s/o Gilmer & Viola Woodfield Hawkins

Lot: 43 Owner: George O. Holland
Site 2 Earl L. Holland   Place: Bethesda
        Birth: 23 Sep 1902   Death: 24 May 1949   Burial: 27 May 1949
        Mort: W.B. Hilton   s/o Annie M. & George O. Holland
Site 3 Annie Mary Holland   Place: Comus
        Birth: 27 Oct 1875   Death: 23 Aug 1947   Burial: 26 Aug 1947
        Mort: W.B. Hilton   w/o George O. Holland

Monocacy Cemetery, Beallsville, Montgomery County, Maryland   209

Site 4 George Otis Holland   Place: Dickerson
        Birth: 13 Oct 1874   Death: 2 May 1951   Burial: 5 May 1951
        Mort: W.B. Hilton   h/o Annie Mary Holland
Site 6 Bowie Frank Thompson   On stone with Nettie Lee Holland Thompson
        Birth: 21 Jan 1914   Death: 4 Oct 1986   Burial: 7 Oct 1986

Lot: 44 Lower   Owner: Miscellaneous
Site 1 Mary Reid Elsdon   Place: Washington, DC
        Birth: 1875   Death: 14 Sep 1952   Burial: 17 Sep 1952
        Mort: Chambers & Co.   On stone with Thomas Elsdon
Site 2 Thomas Elsdon   Place: Washington, DC
        Birth: 1874   Death: 26 Sep 1953   Burial: 29 Sep 1953
        Mort: W.W. Chambers   h/o Mary G. Reid Elsdon
Site 3 William Frazier Kidd   No marker   Mort: W.B. Hilton
        Place: Poolesville   Death: 27 Aug 1952   Burial: 30 Aug 1952
Site 4 Rebecca Wingate   Mort: W.B. Hilton
        Place: Poolesville   Death: 27 Jan 1948   Burial: 30 Jan 1948
        Mother of Grover C. Wingate   No marker
Site 5 Carrie E. Smith Catron Cole   Mort: Hardesty Funeral Home
        Place: Knoxville, TN   Death: 24 Nov 1970   Burial: 28 Nov 1970
        w/o James A. Catron   No marker
Site 6 James A. Catron   Place: Suburban Hospital
        Birth: 5 May 1899   Death: 8 Dec 1947   Burial: 10 Dec 1947
        Mort: W.B. Hilton   h/o Carrie E. Smith Catron

Lot: 44 Upper   Owner: R.M. Phelps
Site 2 Patricia Ann Phelps   Age 6 mo   Mort: W.R. Pumphrey
        Place: Washington, DC   Death: 6 Sep 1946   Burial: 7 Sep 1946
        No marker
Site 2 Stella Elizabeth Rutter
        Birth: 6 Mar 1910   Death: 10 Nov 1983   Burial: 18 Nov 1983
Site 5 Estella L. Phelps   Age 94 yrs On stone with Richard Martin Phelps
        Birth: 1898   Death: 5 Oct 1992   Burial: 7 Oct 1992
Site 6 Richard Martin Phelps   Mort: R.A. Pumphrey   Place: Bethesda
        Birth: 2 Jun 1887   Death: 29 Jun 1957   Burial: 2 Jul 1957
        h/o Estella L. Phelps   TS: PVT USA Dist. of Col. WWI

Lot: 45 Lower   Owner: Miscellaneous
Site 1 Carl R. Musser   Place: Boyds
        Birth: 1945   Death: 3 Nov 1951   Burial: 5 Nov 1951
        Mort: W.B. Hilton   s/o John Musser
Site 2 Woodrow Wilson Hunt   No marker
                                Death: 5 Mar 1973   Burial: 9 Mar 1973
Site 3 Dorothy Juanita Hunt   Mort: W.B. Hilton   Place: Edwards Ferry
        Birth: 1941   Death: 20 Jun 1955   Burial: 23 Jun 1955
Site 3 Katherine Sue Wilkins   Age 29
        Birth: 14 Nov 1963   Death: 26 Jan 1990   Burial: 8 Feb 1990
Site 4 Frances Lucille Hunt   Mort: W.B. Hilton   Place: Beallsville
        Birth: 1937   Death: 17 Jun 1951   Burial: 20 Jun 1951

Monocacy Cemetery, Beallsville, Montgomery County, Maryland

Site 5 Mary Stewart Pugh
Birth: 23 Apr 1885 Death: 7 Apr 1951
Mort: W.B. Hilton
Place: Bethesda
Burial: 9 Apr 1951
w/o David Pugh

Lot: 45 Upper   Owner: Miscellaneous
Site 1 Buna E. Groff
Birth: 19 Aug 1895 Death: 5 Mar 1973
Site 2 Morris Claire Groff
Birth: 12 Nov 1894 Death: 29 Apr 1949
Mort: W.B. Hilton
Site 3 Augusta Rogers Cassell
Birth: 1877 Death: 28 Jul 1971
Site 4 Robert N. Cassell
Birth: 1875 Death: 11 Jan 1950
Mort: W.L. Creager & Son
Site 5 Thomas N. Newton Mort: W.B. Hilton
Birth: 7 May 1859 Death: 26 Feb 1949
Site 5 Franklin Lee Smith Mort: W.B. Hilton
Birth: 1906 Death: 4 Jul 1949

On stone with Morris C. Groff
Burial: 8 Mar 1973
Place: Dawsonville
Burial: 3 May 1949
h/o Buna C. Groff
w/o Robert N. Cassell
Burial: 30 Jul 1971
Place: Baltimore
Burial: 13 Jan 1950
h/o Augusta Rogers Cassell
Place: Bethesda
Burial: 1 Mar 1949
Place: Washington, DC
Burial: 6 Jul 1949

Lot: 46 Lower   Owner: Miscellaneous
Site 1 Nellie Pearl Painter
Birth: 2 Apr 1888 Death: 24 Feb 1952
Mort: W.B. Hilton Age 63
Site 2 Clarence E. Painter
Birth: 30 May 1889 Death: 19 Apr 1975
Site 3 Joyce Anne Hunt Mort: W.B. Hilton
Birth: 11 Nov 1954 Death: 6 Apr 1955
Site 3 Robin Ellis Smith
Birth: 11 Dec 1953 Death: 9 Feb 1954
Mort: W.B. Hilton
Site 4 Thompson Gregory Neel Mort: W.B. Hilton
Birth: 7 Jun 1906 Death: 10 Sep 1953
Site 5 Pauline Eleanor Scott Age 42
Birth: 26 Jun 1909 Death: 25 Dec 1951
Mort: Francis J. Collins
Site 6 Clifton Harold Scott
Birth: 6 May 1908 Death: 24 Feb 1972
Site 6 Robert Edward Brady Age 81   No marker
Place: Takoma Park Death: 19 Nov 1951

Place: Frederick
Burial: 26 Feb 1952
On stone with Clarence E. Painter
h/o Nellie Pearl Painter
Burial: 21 Apr 1975
Place: Boyds
Burial: 7 Apr 1955
Place: Bethesda
Burial: 11 Feb 1954
s/o Franklin & Elizabeth C. Smith
Place: Bethesda
Burial: 12 Sep 1953
Place: Washington
Burial: 29 Dec 1951
On stone with Clifton Harold Scott,
h/o Pauline Eleanor Scott
Burial: 28 Dec 1972
Mort: W.B. Hilton
Burial: 21 Nov 1951

Lot: 46 Upper   Owner: Miscellaneous
Site 1 Annie Harrison Whisman
Birth: 5 Oct 1910 Death: 25 Oct 1950
Mort: W.B. Hilton
Site 2 Frank Whisman
Birth: 13 Aug 1907 Death: 8 Aug 1989
Site 3 Richard John Riley Mort: W.B. Hilton
Birth: 10 May 1896 Death: 26 May 1950

Place: Poolesville
Burial: 28 Oct 1950
On stone with Frank Whisman
h/o Annie Harrison Whisman
Burial: 10 Aug 1989
Place: Frederick Hospital
Burial: 29 May 1950

Monocacy Cemetery, Beallsville, Montgomery County, Maryland

Site 4 Samuel Stephen Shawver   Mort: W.B. Hilton
        Birth: 29 Jun 1927   Death: 27 Jan 1950   Burial: 30 Jan 1950
        s/o Charles E. & Vannie E. Shawver   TS: PFC CAC MD WWII
Site 5 Charles Stephen Shawver   Place: Frederick
        Birth: 27 May 1889   Death: 1 Aug 1965   Burial: 4 Aug 1965
        Mort: Hilton   h/o Vaennie E. Shawver
Site 5 Vaennie Elizabeth Leffel Shawver   On stone with Charles Stephen Shawver
        Birth: 3 Apr 1892   Death: 1 Jan 1979   Burial: 4 Jan 1979

Lot: 47   Owner: Miscellaneous
Site 1 Blanche McCloud Johnson   Place: Front Royal
        Birth: 20 Aug 1895   Death: 5 Feb 1953   Burial: 7 Feb 1953
        Mort: W.B. Hilton   On stone with Harry C. Johnson
Site 2 Harry C. Johnson   Place: Martinsburg, WV
        Birth: 22 Jun 1895   Death: 14 Jul 1953   Burial: 17 Jul 1953
        Mort: W.B. Hilton   h/o Blanche McCloud Johnson
Site 3 Jennette Smith   Place: Marriottsville
        Birth: 2 Jul 1950   Death: 11 Apr 1953   Burial: 14 Apr 1953
        Mort: Weer & Haight   d/o John H. & Martha Smith
Site 4 John Henry Smith   Mort: Weer & Haight   Place: Marriottsville
        Birth: 30 Apr 1904   Death: 8 Aug 1954   Burial: 10 Aug 1954
        h/o Martha Smith   TS: Pvt Co B 309 Inf. Md. WWII
Site 5 William W. Browning   No marker   Mort: W.B. Hilton
        Place: Martinsburg   Death: 10 Dec 1953   Burial: 12 Dec 1953
Site 6 Charles William Day   On stone with Mary Louise Brown Day
        Birth: 16 May 1918   Death: 25 Jan 1994   Burial: 29 Jan 1994
Site 6 Mary Louise Brown Day   2nd w/o Charles William Day
        Birth: 24 Feb 1918   Death: 27 Nov 1981   Burial: 30 Nov 1981
Site 6 Mary Elizabeth Day   Mort: W.B. Hilton   Place: Olny
        Birth: 1881   Death: 4 Jan 1954   Burial: 7 Jan 1954
Site 7 Margaret M. Gilliam   Place: Bluefield, WV
        Birth: 20 Sep 1879   Death: 17 Nov 1967   Burial: 21 Nov 1967
        Mort: Hilton   On stone with Ira H. Gilliam
Site 8 Ira Howard Gilliam   Place: Poolesville
        Birth: 2 Sep 1877   Death: 22 Jan 1954   Burial: 24 Jan 1954
        Mort: W.B. Hilton   h/o Margaret M. Gilliam
Site 9 Charles E. Fox Jr.   Mort: W.W. Chambers   Place: Washington, DC
        Birth: 6 Jun 1883   Death: 18 Jun 1954   Burial: 22 Jun 1954
Site 10 Martha Norm Smith   Place: Bethesda, MD
        Birth: 4 May 1922   Death: 3 Nov 1970   Burial: 4 Nov 1970
        Mort: Harry Haight   w/o John Henry Smith
Site 11 Thomas I. Lydard   Mort: W.B. Hilton   Place: Frederick
        Birth: 27 Jul 1901   Death: 26 Jan 1955   Burial: 29 Jan 1955
Site 12 Baby Boy Cregger   No marker   Mort: Deal Funeral Home
        Place: Washington, DC Death: 21 Aug 1959   Burial: 24 Aug 1959
Site 12 Esther Thelma Cregger   Place: Bethesda
        Birth: 1910   Death: 24 Feb 1955   Burial: 26 Feb 1955
        Mort: W.B. Hilton   w/o Ray Cregger

Lot: 48 Owner: Miscellaneous

Site 1 Kenneth Floyd Cregger
Place: Germantown
No marker
Death: 8 Apr 1953
Mort: W.B. Hilton
Burial: 10 Apr 1953

Site 3 Douglas Ray Leith
Birth: 23 Apr 1949
Mort: W.B. Hilton
Death: 10 May 1952
Place: Poolesville
Burial: 12 May 1952
Child

Site 3 Dewayne C. Barnhouse
Place: Baltimore
No marker
Death: 22 Nov 1966
Mort: F.H. Barber
Burial: 26 Nov 1966

Site 4 Margaret Beall
Place: Washington, DC
No marker
Death: 9 Apr 1952
Mort: Deal Funeral Home
Burial: 12 Apr 1952

Site 5 Jennie Marie Fowler
Birth: 15 Aug 1908
Mort: W.B. Hilton
Death: 27 Dec 1951
Place: Bethesda
Burial: 29 Dec 1951
Age 43

Site 6 Charles Grundy Fowler
Birth: 19 Apr 1907
Mort: Hilton
Death: 24 Feb 1967
Place: Frederick
Burial: 27 Feb 1967
h/o Jennie M. Fowler

Site 7 Armstead Matthews
Place: Sharon Home
No marker
Death: 24 Mar 1955
Mort: W.B. Hilton
Burial: 28 Mar 1955

Site 8 Temperance M. Benson
Birth: 19 Aug 1896
Mort: Robert A. Pumphrey
Death: 10 Nov 1955
Place: Rockville
Burial: 14 Nov 1955

Site 9 James Wade Benson
Birth: 18 May 1895
Mort: R.W. Pumphrey Place: Frederick Co., MD
Death: 27 Mar 1941
Burial: 30 Mar 1941

Site 10 Dorothy S. Ward
Birth: 23 Nov 1907
On stone with Carson W. Ward
Death: 25 Jun 1979
Burial: 27 Jun 1979

Site 11 Carson W. Ward
Birth: 1 Jan 1905
Death: 6 May 1990
h/o Dorothy S. Ward
Burial: 10 May 1990

Site 12 Annie E. Lawson
Place: Bethesda
w/o Alfred S. Lawson
Death: 9 Dec 1955
Mort: W.B. Hilton
Burial: 12 Dec 1955
No marker

Site 12 William Joseph Clements
Birth: 7 Jun 1882
Mort: Hilton Place: Gaithersburg
Death: 30 Nov 1960
Burial: 3 Dec 1960

Lot: 49 Owner: Miscellaneous

Site 1 Florence Allnutt Whittaker
Birth: 1900
Death: 1992
Age 92 yrs
Burial: 20 Jul 1992

Site 2 Frankie Alberta Williams
Birth: 6 Nov 1897
Mort: Robert G. Newberry
Death: 21 Sep 1961
Place: Wytheville, VA
Burial: 25 Sep 1961
On stone with Kelly Prevo Williams

Site 3 Kelly Prevo Williams
Birth: 17 Jun 1894
Death: 11 Aug 1971
h/o Frankie Alberta Williams
Burial: 13 Aug 1971

Site 4 Rachael Hunt
Place: Germantown
No marker
Death: 23 Apr 1961
Mort: Hilton
Burial: 26 Apr 1961

Site 6 Robert Lee Hash
Birth: 1889
Mort: Hilton
Death: 14 Dec 1963
Place: Dickerson
Burial: 16 Dec 1963
h/o Ella May Hash

Site 7 Claud Augustus Carter
Birth: 1907
Mort: Hilton
Death: 28 Jul 1963
Place: Poolesville
Burial: 31 Jul 1963

Site 8 Nora E. Ruble Mort: Wm. Hilton Place: Frederick, MD
  Birth: 1 May 1879 Death: 30 Nov 1970 Burial: 2 Dec 1970
  On stone with Elbert R. Ruble & A. Bertie Ruble
Site 9 Elbert K. Ruble   Place: Frederick
  Birth: 27 Feb 1883 Death: 15 Dec 1962 Burial: 18 Dec 1962
  Mort: Hilton   h/o Nora E. Ruble
Site 10 A. Bertie Ruble   Sister of Elbert K. Ruble
  Birth: 2 Mar 1880 Death: 29 Jun 1974 Burial: 2 Jul 1974
Site 11 Viola Clarihe Spencer   Mort: Hilton
  Place: Silver Spring Death: 3 Apr 1962 Burial: 6 Apr 1962
  w/o Sidney H. Spencer   No marker

Lot: 50 Owner: Miscellaneous

Site 1 William Clayton Betson   Place: Takoma Park
  Birth: 7 Dec 1916 Death: 19 Mar 1967 Burial: 22 Mar 1967
  Mort: Hilton TS: TSgt. Hq. Co. 2679 PW BN MD WWII
Site 2 Harry J. Davis
  Birth: 30 Jul 1891 Death: 23 Sep 1966 Burial: 26 Sep 1966
Site 3 Thomas P. Corse   Place: Bethesda
  Birth: 1961 Death: 6 Feb 1963 Burial: 8 Feb 1963
  Mort: Hilton s/o William & Barbara Corse
Site 3 Baby Corse   Mort: Hilton
  Place: Bethesda Death: 2 Mar 1964 Burial: 2 Mar 1964
  i/o William & Barbara Corse   No marker
Site 4 Edgar Carl Lamarr Mort: Hilton Place: Dickerson
  Birth: 14 Jan 1925 Death: 29 Dec 1962 Burial: 31 Dec 1962
Site 5 Edward Arlington Betson Mort: Hilton Place: Dickerson
  Birth: 28 Jan 1928 Death: 27 Nov 1962 Burial: 30 Nov 1962
  TS: Maryland Pvt. Co. C 288 Eng. Const. BN WWII
Site 6 Bertha Sartain Payne Ross   Place: Barnesville
  Birth: 22 Mar 1911 Death: 23 May 1961 Burial: 26 May 1961
  Mort: Hilton   Mother
Site 7 Charles H. Leppo   Mort: Wm. Hilton
  Place: Bethesda, MD Death: 25 Sep 1969 Burial: 29 Sep 1969
  f/o Joseph Leppo   No marker
Site 8 William F. Smith No marker Mort: Hilton
  Place: Bethesda Death: 8 May 1965 Burial: 12 May 1965
Site 9 James Preston Smith No marker Mort: Hilton
  Place: Sykesville Death: 15 Oct 1964 Burial: 21 Oct 1964
Site 10 Juanita B. Deadrick On stone with Raymond M. Deadrick
  Birth: 10 Aug 1897 Death: 31 May 1978 Burial: 2 Jun 1978
Site 10 Raymond M. Deadrick   Place: Frederick
  Birth: 9 Jul 1896 Death: 21 Jul 1965 Burial: 24 Jul 1965
  Mort: Hilton   h/o Juanita Deadrick
Site 12 Louise deCostella Hominal   Place: Poolesville
  Birth: 1873 Death: 16 May 1964 Burial: 19 May 1964
  Mort: Hilton Mother of Mrs. Warren E. Irvin

Lot: 51 Owner: Miscellaneous

Site 1 Gladys S. Haller
Birth: 1905 Death: 28 Jul 1967
Mort: Hilton
Place: Rockville, MD
Burial: 31 Jul 1967
On stone with Robert L. Haller

Site 2 Robert Lee Haller
Birth: 1911 Death: 6 Nov 1978
h/o Gladys S. Haller
Burial: 8 Nov 1978

Site 3 Robert L. Hunt No marker
Place: Bethesda, MD Death: 30 Sep 1967
Mort: Tyson Wheeler
Burial: 4 Oct 1967

Site 4 Marian E. Anderson Birth: 1912 On stone with Carl E. Anderson

Site 5 Carl E. Anderson
Birth: 1900 Death: 13 Oct 1967
Mort: Hilton
Place: Dickerson
Burial: 16 Oct 1967
h/o Marion E. Anderson

Site 6 Reginald W. Davis
Birth: 1909 Death: 1967 Burial: 27 May 1967

Site 8 Elizabeth Titus Moore
Birth: 14 Sep 1919 Death: 3 Nov 1988
On stone with Alvin Moore
Burial: 7 Nov 1988

Site 9 Alvin Moore
Birth: 18 May 1899 Death: 21 Jun 1972
h/o Elizabeth Titus Moore
Burial: 24 Jun 1972

Site 10 Alvin Dean Moore
Birth: 11 May 1953 Death: 17 Jun 1965
Mort: Hilton
Place: Dawsonville
Burial: 21 Jun 1965
s/o Elizabeth Titus & Alvin Moore

Site 12 Wendell Russell Tascher
Birth: 1898 Death: 24 Nov 1964
Mort: Hilton
Place: Rockville
Burial: 26 Nov 1964
h/o Evelyn A. Tascher

Lot: 52 Lower Owner: Miscellaneous

Site 7 Dave Joshua Anders
Birth: 3 Dec 1930 Death: 2 May 1964
Mort: Hilton
Place: Poolesville
Burial: 6 May 1964
h/o Julia Anders Hawkins

Site 8 Agnes Virginia Dixon Luhn
Birth: 6 Oct 1908 Death: 14 Sep 1988
On stone with Stonestreet W. Luhn
Burial: 15 Sep 1988

Site 9 Stonestreet W. Luhn
Birth: 17 Oct 1908 Death: 24 Sep 1966
Mort: Barber
h/o Agnes V. Luhn
Burial: 26 Sep 1966

Site 10 Lester Erwin Beall
Birth: 15 Jun 1909 Death: 25 May 1962
Mort: Francis H. Barber Place: Unity, MD
Burial: 28 May 1962

Site 11 Effie L. Johnson
Birth: 27 Jun 1907 Death: 7 Aug 1971
On stone with Thomas M. Johnson
Burial: 11 Aug 1971

Site 12 Thomas M. Johnson
Birth: 26 Mar 1905 Death: 4 Jan 1962
Mort: W.W. Chambers
Place: Washington, DC
Burial: 8 Jan 1962
h/o Effie L. Johnson

Lot: 52 Upper Owner: Jacob T. & Lelia G. Fisher

Site 1 Charles W. Fritz
Birth: 23 Mar 1905 Death: 17 Mar 1972
h/o Lana Fisher Fritz
Burial: 21 Mar 1972

Site 2 Lana Fisher Fritz
Birth: 31 Aug 1908 Death: 3 May 1986
On stone with Charles W. Fritz
Burial: 5 May 1986

Monocacy Cemetery, Beallsville, Montgomery County, Maryland   215

Site 3 Lelia Gertrude Fisher   Place: Frederick, MD
        Birth: 2 Mar 1881   Death: 8 Nov 1962   Burial: 20 Nov 1962
        Mort: Hilton   On stone with Jacob T. Fisher
Site 4 Jacob T. Fisher   Mort: Hilton   Place: Frederick, MD
        Birth: 17 Aug 1880   Death: 8 May 1967   Burial: 11 May 1967
Site 6 Eldon Matron Parrish   On stone with Glenda Fritz Parrish
        Birth: 18 Oct 1920   Death: 20 Oct 1994   Burial: 24 Oct 1994

Lot: 53 Lower Owner: Miscellaneous
Site 1 Mary A. Ricketts   No marker   Mort: Ernest C. Gartner
        Place: Bethesda, MD   Death: 24 Dec 1967   Burial: 28 Dec 1967
Site 2 John Charles Kohlenberg No marker   Mort: Gartner Funeral
        Place: Bethesda, MD   Death: 12 Dec 1968   Burial: 16 Dec 1968
Site 3 Milward F. Moore   Place: Silver Spring
        Birth: 1885   Death: 4 Mar 1969   Burial: 6 Mar 1969
        Mort: Wm. Hilton   Brother of Alvin Moore
Site 5 William Thomas Beall   Place: Bethesda, MD
        Birth: 13 Mar 1907   Death: 27 Sep 1970   Burial: 30 Sep 1970
        Mort: Robt. Pumphrey   h/o Evelyn Beall
Site 6 William Meredith Nicholson   Mort: E.C. Gartner   Place: Olney, MD
        Birth: 18 Feb 1884   Death: 31 May 1968   Burial: 2 Jun 1968

Lot: 53 Upper Owner: Robert H. Chapman
Site 4 Elizabeth Claire Chapman   Place: Washington, DC
        Birth: 9 Jul 1950   Death: 2 Nov 1962   Burial: 6 Nov 1962
        Mort: Robert A. Pumphrey   d/o Robert H. & Mabel B. Chapman
Site 5 Virginia Beall Temple   Mort: Ernest C. Gartner   Place: Bethesda
        Birth: 14 Sep 1814   Death: 15 Nov 1965   Burial: 17 Nov 1965
Site 6 Marcus L. Temple   Birth: 16 Apr 1912   Death: 28 Feb 1988

Lot: 54 Owner: Miscellaneous
Site 2 George Randall Beitzel   Place: Bethesda
        Birth: 11 Apr 1916   Death: 22 Jan 1967   Burial: 24 Jan 1967
        Mort: Hilton   On stone with Leora M. Beitzel
Site 3 Michael B. Justus   Mort: Hilton   Place: Frederick
        Birth: 9 Aug 1964   Death: 23 Jul 1966   Burial: 26 Jul 1966
Site 3 Richard Sexton   No marker   Mort: Wm. Hilton
        Place: Baltimore, MD   Death: 22 Nov 1968   Burial: 25 Nov 1968
Site 4 Alda Justus   No marker   Mort: Constance C. Hilton
        Place: Frederick   Death: 22 Mar 1966   Burial: 25 Mar 1966
Site 5 Kenneth P. Butt   On stone with M. Estelle Butt
        Birth: 28 Jun 1921   Death: 28 Jul 1993   Burial: 31 Jul 1993
Site 7 Roderick Gordon Smith   TS: US Navy
        Birth: 12 Jan 1932   Death: 19 Jul 1994   Burial: 22 Jul 1994
Site 8 Mark Steven Justus   No marker   Mort: Wm. Hilton
        Place: Washington, DC   Death: 27 Mar 1970   Burial: 30 Mar 1970
Site 8 Roy E. Young Jr.   No marker
        Birth: 18 Aug 1979   Death: 25 Feb 1980   Burial: 28 Feb 1980

Monocacy Cemetery, Beallsville, Montgomery County, Maryland

Site 11 Lucille Fox Dean On stone with Smith P. Dean
 Birth: 1901 Death: 10 Aug 1986 Burial: 14 Aug 1986
Site 12 Smith P. Dean Place: New York
 Birth: 1891 Death: 28 Jan 1968 Burial: 30 Jan 1968
 Mort: Wm. Hilton h/o Lucille Fox Dean

Lot: 55 Lower Owner: Miscellaneous
Site 1 Annie Ellis Nicholson w/o William Mardith Nicholson
 Birth: 22 Jun 1900 Death: 19 Oct 1981 Burial: 22 Oct 1981
Site 2 Reubin C. Wolfrey
 Birth: 12 Dec 1919 Death: 5 Jun 1977 Burial: 9 Jun 1977
Site 3 Michael Edward Newman Mort: Robt. Pumphrey Place: Bethesda, MD
 Birth: 16 May 1954 Death: 27 Dec 1970 Burial: 30 Dec 1970
Site 4 Grayson Edward Stottlemyer
 Birth: 12 Feb 1908 Burial: 1 May 1971 Mort: Robt. Pumphrey
Site 5 Charles R. Beall h/o Lucie Rutter Beall
 Birth: 14 Oct 1906 Death: 21 Aug 1988 Burial: 24 Aug 1988
Site 6 Lucie Frances Rutter Beall On stone with Charles Raymond Beall
 Birth: 2 Oct 1903 Death: 10 Jun 1987 Burial: 12 Jun 1978

Lot: 55 Upper Owner: Miscellaneous
Site 1 Norman D. Wootton
 Birth: 29 Dec 1908 Death: 27 Jun 1974 Burial: 1 Jul 1974
 h/o Tah-Wee-Nah M. Wootton, s/o Norman & Edith Wootton
Site 6 Oma M. Mills Place: Bethesda, MD
 Birth: 8 Feb 1925 Death: 9 Aug 1969 Burial: 13 Aug 1969
 Mort: Wm. Hilton On stone with Esker Mills

Lot: 56 Lower Owner: Miscellaneous
Site 1 Charles Upton Butt, Sr. Mort: Tyson Wheeler Place: Sykesville
 Birth: 15 Nov 1909 Death: 9 Aug 1969 Burial: 13 Aug 1969
Site 3 John Andrew Rice Mort: Wm. Hilton Place: Silver Spring, MD
 Birth: 1 Feb 1888 Death: 16 Nov 1968 Burial: 20 Nov 1968
 h/o Anna Beall Rice TS: s/o John Andrew & Anna Bell Smith Rice of SC
Site 5 Erna H. Leopold On stone with Max Leopold
 Birth: 1897 Death: 25 Feb 1977 Burial: 1 Mar 1977
Site 6 Max Leopold h/o Erna H. Leopold
 Birth: 1893 Death: 7 Nov 1974 Burial: 11 Nov 1974

Lot: 56 Upper Owner: Miscellaneous
Site 1 James H. Anderson Place: Silver Spring, MD
 Birth: 3 Jul 1915 Death: 14 Mar 1969 Burial: 17 Mar 1969
 Mort: Wm. Hilton h/o Mae Anderson (Whisman)
Site 2 Mae S. Whisman Anderson On stone with James M. Anderson
 Birth: 29 Apr 1918 Death: 13 Jul 1989 Burial: 15 Jul 1989
Site 3 Glen Allan Pullum
 Birth: 3 Aug 1956 Death: 23 Mar 1978 Burial: 4 May 1978

Site 5 Harry J. Stottlemeyer Sr.   Place: Frederick, MD
        Birth: 20 Jun 1905   Death: 12 Jan 1968   Burial: 13 Jan 1968
        Mort: Wm. Hilton   On stone with Mildred Poole Stottlemeyer
Site 6 Harry J. Stottlemeyer Jr. Mort: Wm. Hilton   Place: Bethesda, MD
        Birth: 18 May 1932   Death: 10 Jan 1968   Burial: 13 Jan 1968
        s/o Harry L. & Mildred P. Stottlemeyer, h/o Louise Stottlemeyer
        SGT CORP ENG MD Korea

Lot: 58 Upper   Owner: Miscellaneous

Site 2 Susie Mae Gordon   w/o Franklin D. Gordon, age 53 yrs
        Birth: 7 Dec 1940   Death: 17 Apr 1994   Burial: 19 Apr 1994
Site 6 David Barber Anderson   h/o Rosemary S. Anderson
        Birth: 1931   Death: 1995   Burial: 25 Jan 1995

Row K

Lot: 1   Owner: Charles E. Allnutt
- Site 1 Julia Miller Allnutt — d/o Charles E. & Effie M. Allnutt
  - Birth: 19 Oct 1904   Death: 5 Nov 1990   Burial: 12 Nov 1990
- Site 2 Charles Edward Allnutt Jr.   Place: Washington, DC
  - Birth: 20 Jan 1904   Death: 12 Apr 1962   Burial: 16 Apr 1962
  - Mort: Deal Funeral Home   s/o Charles E. & Effie M. Allnutt
- Site 3 Effie Miller Allnutt   Place: Seneca
  - Birth: 2 Jun 1873   Death: 25 Nov 1952   Burial: 28 Nov 1952
  - Mort: W.B. Hilton   w/o Charles E. Allnutt
- Site 4 Charles Edward Allnutt Sr.   Place: Seneca
  - Birth: 31 Oct 1869   Death: 5 Jan 1929   Burial: 7 Jan 1929
  - Mort: Hilton & Hall   h/o Effie Miller Allnutt
- Site 8 Guy Francis Allnutt   h/o Hilda Perry Allnutt
  - Birth: 27 Jan 1894   Death: 15 Mar 1982   Burial: 23 Mar 1982
- Site 9 Hilda Perry Allnutt   w/o Guy Francis Allnutt
  - Birth: 26 Nov 1902   Death: 23 Jan 1980   Burial: 26 Jan 1980

Lot: 2   Owner: Lewis P. Allnutt
- Site 1 Susan Allnutt Hibler   Place: Texas
  - Birth: 6 Sep 1904   Death: 20 Jan 1944   Burial: 25 Jan 1944
  - Mort: Barry Hagedon   On stone with C. Arthur Hibler
- Site 2 C. Arthur Hibler   Birth: 1 Mar 1902   h/o Susan Allnutt Hibler
- Site 3 Lutie Chiswell Allnutt   Place: Poolesville
  - Birth: 16 Sep 1879   Death: 18 Feb 1963   Burial: 21 Feb 1963
  - Mort: Hilton   w/o Lewis P. Allnutt
- Site 4 Lewis Phillip Allnutt   h/o Lutie Chiswell Allnutt
  - Birth: 2 Jan 1875   Death: 11 Jan 1978   Burial: 13 Jan 1978
- Site 8 Lewis Phillip Allnutt Jr.   h/o Evelyn Souder Allnutt
  - Birth: 25 Sep 1910   Death: 28 Aug 1989   Burial: 1 Sep 1989

Lot: 3   Owner: R.W. Allnutt
- Site 1 Americus Dawson Allnutt   Place: Washington, DC
  - Birth: 6 Dec 1919   Death: 5 Nov 1937   Burial: 7 Nov 1937
  - Mort: Warner E. Pumphrey   s/o Robert W. & Alice T. Allnutt
- Site 2 Thomas Dawson Allnutt   Place: Dawsonville
  - Birth: 7 Apr 1915   Death: 7 Apr 1915   Burial: 8 Apr 1915
  - Mort: Hilton & Hall   s/o Robert W. & Alice T. Allnutt
- Site 3 Alice Thomas Allnutt   Place: Dawsonville
  - Birth: 1875   Death: 31 Jul 1949   Burial: 3 Aug 1949
  - Mort: W.B. Hilton   w/o Robert W. Allnutt
- Site 4 Robert Wilkerson Allnutt   Mort: W.B. Hilton   Place: Dawsonville
  - Birth: 12 Apr 1866   Death: 27 Aug 1947   Burial: 29 Aug 1947
- Site 5 Annie Lee Allnutt   d/o Robert W. & Alice T. Allnutt
  - Birth: 11 May 1897   Death: 3 Apr 1978   Burial: 6 Apr 1978

Monocacy Cemetery, Beallsville, Montgomery County, Maryland   219

Site 5 Nelva Thomas Allnutt   d/o Robert W. & Alice T. Allnutt
        Birth: 28 Mar 1908   Death: 30 Mar 1979   Burial: 1 Apr 1979
Site 6 Emily Allnutt Loos   d/o Robert W. & Alice B. Allnutt
        Birth: 8 Aug 1904   Death: 25 Jan 1988   Burial: 4 Apr 1988
Site 7 Lucille Johnson Allnutt   Place: Bethesda
        Birth: 1916   Death: 22 Nov 1949   Burial: 25 Nov 1949
        Mort: W.B. Hilton   1st w/o Benoni D. Allnutt
Site 11 Benjamin Nourse Allnutt
        Birth: 1902   Death: 1 Jan 1972   Burial: 4 Jan 1972
        h/o Elsie Lee Chiswell, s/o Robert W. & Alice T. Allnutt
Site 12 James Russell Allnutt   Place: Dawsonville
        Birth: 1900   Death: 29 Dec 1966   Burial: 31 Dec 1966
        Mort: Hilton   s/o Robert W. & Alice T. Allnutt (unmarried)

Lot: 4 Owner: Mrs. F.A. Allnutt
Site 4 Frederick A. Allnutt   Place: Washington, DC
        Birth: 7 Jan 1868   Death: 31 Jul 1915   Burial: 2 Aug 1915
        Mort: A.G. Carlisle   h/o Ada Perry Allnutt
Site 5 Ada Perry Allnutt   Place: Washington, DC
        Birth: 23 Jul 1873   Death: 5 Jan 1964   Burial: 8 Jan 1964
        Mort: Robert A. Pumphrey   w/o Frederick A. Allnutt
Site 8 Frederick J. Kubeck   s/o Thomas & Eleanor Kubeck
        Birth: 27 Apr 1965   Death: 6 Jun 1988   Burial: 22 Jun 1988
Site 9 Gladys Bauserman Allnutt
        3 Oct 1901   Death: 21 Nov 1996   Burial: 29 Nov 1996
Site 10 Frederick A. Allnutt Jr.
        Birth: 18 Feb 1904   Death: 3 Feb 1973   Burial: 6 Feb 1973
        s/o F.A. & Ada Perry Allnutt, h/o Gladys Allnutt
Site 11 Eleanor Allnutt Sharkey
        Birth: 27 Dec 1901   Death: 20 Apr 1984   Burial: 24 Apr 1984
        w/o Thomas L. Sharkey, d/o F.A. & Ada P. Allnutt
Site 12 Thomas Leo Sharkey   Place: Chevy Chase
        Birth: 12 Apr 1899   Death: 27 Apr 1952   Burial: 30 Apr 1952
        Mort: Robert A. Pumphrey   h/o Eleanor Allnutt Sharkey

Lot: 5 Owner: Dr. L.F. Brooks
Site 1 Lois Brooks   d/o Lewis F. & M. Katherine Brooks
        Birth: 2 Jan 1909   illegible   Burial: 8 Aug 1909
Site 1 Mary Ann Brooks   Place: Poolesville
        Birth: 11 Feb 1931   Death: 4 Mar 1931   Burial: 7 Mar 1931
        Mort: Hilton & Hall   TS: d/o James E. & Anna M. Brooks
Site 1 Hilton Lawson Sheppard Jr.   Place: Washington, DC
        Birth: 19 Sep 1928   Death: 20 Sep 1928   Burial: 20 Sep 1928
        Mort: W.T. Hilton & Sons   TS: s/o Hilton L. & Minnie Brooks Shepherd
Site 2 Harold B. Brooks   Mort: Wm. B. Hilton   Place: Kensington, MD
        Birth: 14 May 1912   Death: 22 Oct 1970   Burial: 24 Oct 1970
        h/o Estelle White Brooks, s/o L.F. & Katherine Brooks

Monocacy Cemetery, Beallsville, Montgomery County, Maryland

Site 3 Mary Katherine Brooks   Place: Poolesville
        Birth: 17 Sep 1870   Death: 5 Dec 1958   Burial: 8 Dec 1958
        Mort: Hilton   On stone with Lewis Franklin Brooks
Site 4 Lewis Franklin Brooks   Place: Poolesville
        Birth: 9 Nov 1868   Death: 15 Mar 1934   Burial: 18 Mar 1934
        Mort: Hilton & Hall   h/o Mary Katherine Brooks
Site 5 Margaret Elizabeth Brooks Mort: W.B. Hilton   Place: Poolesville
        Birth: 17 May 1892   Death: 16 Oct 1952   Burial: 18 Oct 1952
        d/o Dr. L.F. & Mary Katherine Books, age 60
Site 12 Leo Franklin Brooks   Place: Washington, DC
        Birth: 15 Jul 1896   Death: 5 Dec 1964   Burial: 8 Dec 1964
        Mort: Hilton   s/o Dr. L.F. & Mary Katherine Brooks

Lot: 6 Owner: Mrs. Lawrence Allnutt
Site 1 Margaret Valeria Allnutt   TS: d/o Laurence A. & Ella T. Allnutt
        Birth: 3 Feb 1905   Death: 2 Jan 1907
Site 1 Ella J. Corbin   TS: Age 62 yrs.   Mort: Hilton & Hall
        Place: Dawsonville   Death: 1 Dec 1919   Burial: 3 Dec 1919
Site 2 Mildred Thomas Allnutt   TS: d/o Laurence A. & Ella T. Allnutt
        Birth: 21 Feb 1903   Death: 9 Mar 1905   Burial: 12 Mar 1905
Site 3 Mary Alice Jones   Mort: Hilton & Hall   Place: Dawsonville
        Birth: 11 Sep 1842   Death: 13 Nov 1919   Burial: 16 Nov 1919
Site 4 Ella V. Thomas Allnutt   Place: Kensington
        Birth: 21 Feb 1873   Death: 31 Oct 1959   Burial: 3 Nov 1959
        Mort: Robert A. Pumphrey   TS: w/o Lawrence A. Allnutt
Site 5 Lawrence A. Allnutt   Place: Dawsonville
        Birth: 19 Oct 1859   Death: 12 Aug 1930   Burial: 14 Aug 1930
        Mort: Hilton & Hall   h/o Ella V. Thomas Allnutt
Site 7 Arthur Carpenter Elgin   h/o Ellen Allnutt Elgin
        Birth: 29 Mar 1906   Death: 22 Nov 1982   Burial: 24 Nov 1982
Site 8 Ellen Allnutt Elgin   On stone with Arthur Carpenter Elgin
        21 Apr 1907   Death: 12 Jul 1996
Site 10 Franklin Thomas Allnutt   s/o Lawrence & Ella Thomas Allnutt
        Birth: 4 Mar 1904   Death: 2 Apr 1981   Burial: 4 Apr 1981
Site 12 James Laurence Allnutt   h/o Carolyn Canady
        Birth: 8 Jul 1915   Death: 11 Mar 1980   Burial: 14 Mar 1980

Lot: 7 Owner: Henry Miles
Site   Ellen Frances Miles   Place: Capitol Heights   Mort: Hilton & Hall
        Birth: 13 Dec 1874   Death: 16 Jul 1916   Burial: 20 Jul 1916
Site   John Jacob Miles   Place: Lunllad   Mort: W.H. Sardo Co.
        28 Nov 1907   Death: 1 Sep 1925   Burial: 2 Sep 1925

Lot: 8 Lower Owner: William Everhart
Site 4 Daniel H. Everhart   No marker   Mort: W.T. Hilton & Sons
        Place: Barnesville   Death: 12 Jun 1915   Burial: 14 Jun 1915

Monocacy Cemetery, Beallsville, Montgomery County, Maryland

Lot: 8 Upper   Owner: W.S. Beall (All on one stone)
Site 1 Alice Beall Frye   Place: Bethesda
        Birth: 1880   Death: 11 Mar 1963   Burial: 13 Mar 1963
        Mort: Hilton   w/o Howard Frye
Site 2 Howard Frye   Mort: Hilton   Place: Sykesville
        Birth: 1872   Death: 19 Oct 1964   Burial: 21 Oct 1964
Site 3 Christine Kohlhoss Clipper   Mort: W.H. Sardo Place: Washington
        Birth: 1902   Death: 24 Jul 1930   Burial: 26 Jul 1930
Site 4 Melissa Moulden Beall   w/o Winfield Scott Beall
        Birth: 1843   Death: 1930   Burial: 3 Aug 1911
Site 5 Winfield Scott Beall   Mort: Hilton & Hall   Place: Damascus
        Birth: 1848   Death: 6 Feb 1937   Burial: 8 Feb 1937
        Married Melissa Moulden Beall 26 Oct 1875
Site 6 Miss Caroline Frye   Place: Sykesville
        Birth: 1871   Death: 25 Jan 1957   Burial: 28 Jan 1957
        Mort: Hilton   sister/o Howard Frye

Lot: 9   Owner: Mrs. Annie Moxley
Site 1 Evertt Glenwood Moxley   Place: Clarksburg
        Birth: 5 Oct 1882   Death: 4 Feb 1952   Burial: 7 Feb 1952
        Mort: W.B. Hilton   s/o Annie & Thomas E. Moxley, age 70
Site 2 Oliver G. Moxley   illegible   Mort: Chas. E. Roberts
        Burial: 3 Mar 1915   s/o Annie & Thomas E. Moxley, age 10 yrs
        Removed from Mt. Pleasant, Dickerson, MD
Site 3 Annie E. Moxley   Place: Washington, DC
        Birth: 14 Jun 1849   Death: 27 Dec 1914   Burial: 30 Dec 1914
        Mort: Mr. Etchison   TS: w/o Thomas E. Moxley
Site 4 Thomas E. Moxley   Mort: Chas. E. Roberts
        Birth: 7 Feb 1845   Death: 5 Mar 1910   Burial: 3 Mar 1915
        h/o Annie E. Moxley   Removed from Mt. Pleasant, Dickerson, MD
Site 5 David Samuel Moxley   Place: Frederick, MD
        Birth: 4 Aug 1959   Death: 11 Apr 1967   Burial: 14 Apr 1967
        Mort: M.R. Etchison   TS: s/o George B. & Mabel M. Moxley
Site 6 George Bunkingham Moxley   h/o Mabel M. Moxley
        Birth: 10 May 1885   Death: 24 Nov 1977   Burial: 28 Nov 1977
Site 12 Joseph Winfield Cranford   Place: Olney
        Birth: 6 Jan 1880   Death: 9 Jun 1952   Burial: 12 Jun 1952
        Mort: W.B. Hilton   h/o Ida J. Moxley Cranford

Lot: 10 Lower   Owner: William H. Dickerson
Site 3 Moselle Jarboe Dickerson   Place: Rockville
        Birth: 1875   Death: 20 Feb 1957   Burial: 23 Feb 1957
        Mort: R.A. Pumphrey   TS: w/o William Harrison Dickerson
Site 4 William Harrison Dickerson   Place: Dickerson
        Birth: 1869   Death: 14 Dec 1930   Burial: 16 Dec 1930
        Mort: W.T. Hilton & Sons   h/o Moselle Jarboe Dickerson

Lot: 10 Upper Owner: William Price

Site 1 Evelyn Mae Henderson
  Birth: 4 Jul 1915 Death: 17 Oct 1984 Burial: 20 Oct 1984
              Place: Frederick
Site 3 Algerene Turner Price
  Birth: 16 Jul 1862 Death: 21 Mar 1919 Burial: 23 Mar 1919
  Mort: C.C. Carty   TS: w/o William T. Price
Site 4 William T. Price   Place: Washington, DC
  Birth: 1856 Death: 10 Oct 1943 Burial: 12 Oct 1943
  Mort: Chambers & Co.   h/o Algerene Turner Price

Lot: 11 Lower Owner: Frederick & Arthur Bowman

Site 2 William Arthur Bowman   Place: Springfield Hospital
  Birth: 1872 Death: 8 Jan 1952 Burial: 10 Jan 1952
  Mort: W.B. Hilton   Age 79
Site 4 Catherine E. Bowman Mort: Hilton & Price Place: Dickerson
  Birth: 1844 Death: 14 Nov 1934 Burial: 16 Nov 1934
Site 5 William Harrison Bowman Mort: Hilton & Hall Place: Poolesville
  Birth: 10 Jun 1842 Death: 31 Jul 1923 Burial: 2 Aug 1923
Site 6 Frederick E. Bowman Place: Boyds Mort: W.B. Hilton
  Birth: 1883 Death: 18 Jan 1942 Burial: 20 Jan 1942

Lot: 11 Upper Owner: Charles J. Norris

Site 1 Vera DeEtte Norris   On stone with Charles William Norris
  Birth: 15 Dec 1911 Death: 10 Aug 1985 Burial: 13 Aug 1985
Site 2 Charles William Norris, Sr.   Place: Bethesda, MD
  Birth: 15 Feb 1908 Death: 20 Dec 1967 Burial: 22 Dec 1967
  Mort: Wm. Hilton   h/o Vera DeEtte Norris
Site 3 Cora Ellen Norris   Place: Beallsville
  Birth: 9 Sep 1880 Death: 8 Oct 1966 Burial: 11 Oct 1966
  Mort: Wm. B. Hilton   w/o Charles J. Norris
Site 4 Charles J. Norris   Place: Poolesville
  Birth: 29 Feb 1871 Death: 4 Dec 1926 Burial: 7 Dec 1926
  Mort: Hilton & Hall   h/o Cora Ellen Noriis
Site 4 Charles William Norris Jr.   No marker
  Birth: 11 Nov 1956 Death: 11 Nov 1956 Burial: 11 Nov 1956
  Cause: Stillborn   s/o Charles William & Vera E. Norris
Site   Joni Lynn Norris Place: Washington Mort: Deal Funeral Home
  Birth & Death: 11 Oct 1956   Burial: 12 Oct 1956
  Cause: Stillborn   TS: Infant d/o Charles W. Norris Jr.
Site 5 Shirley Ann Norris   On stone with Charles W. Norris
  Birth: 6 Apr 1936 Death: 11 Feb 1989 Burial: 14 Feb 1989
Site 6 Charles William Norris Jr.   h/o Shirley Cubitt Norris
  Birth: 2 Jun 1934 Death: 31 May 1995 Burial: 3 Jun 1995

Lot: 12 Owner: Mrs. Marion Moxley

Site 1 Frank Moxley   Mort: W.T. Hilton & Sons
  Place: Dickerson Death: 27 Feb 1917 Burial: 1 Mar 1917
  TS: is/o Marion E. & Nanie E. Moxley, age 1-11-16

Site 2 Catherine Moxley Bittinger   Age 84 yrs.
  Birth: 1909   Death: 3 Feb 1994   Burial: 5 Feb 1994
Site 3 Nannie Estelle Moxley   Mort: Joseph F. Birch
  Place: Alexandria, VA   Death: 25 Nov 1959   Burial: 27 Nov 1959
  w/o Marion E. Moxley   TS: Age 80-10-27
Site 4 Marion E. Moxley   Mort: Hilton & Hall
  Place: Frederick   Death: 24 Jul 1917   Burial: 27 Jul 1917
  h/o Nannie E. Moxley   TS: Age 43-7-28
Site 5 Viola Moxley Allen   No marker
  Birth: 20 Mar 1913   Death: 31 Jul 1994   Burial: 1 Aug 1994
Site 7 Charles W. Magaha   No marker   Mort: Hilton & Hall
  Place: Poolesville   Death: 27 Dec 1919   Burial: 29 Dec 1919

Lot: 13 Lower   Owner: Joseph C. Hoyle
Site 1 Reid Leroy Hammann   h/o Anna Hoyle Hammann
  Birth: 21 Oct 1899   Death: 12 Sep 1971   Burial: 15 Sep 1971
Site 2 Anna Hoyle Hammann   w/o Reid Leroy Hammann
  Birth: 2 Mar 1900   Death: 11 Aug 1985   Burial: 16 Aug 1985
Site 3 Mary A. Hoyle   Place: Washington, DC
  Birth: 12 Aug 1874   Death: 11 Mar 1926   Burial: 13 Mar 1926
  Mort: W.T. Hilton & Sons   w/o Joseph C. Hoyle
Site 4 Joseph C. Hoyle   Place: Washington Home for
  Birth: 15 Feb 1868   Death: 4 Mar 1966   Burial: 7 Mar 1966
  Mort: S.H. Hines   h/o Mary A. Hoyle

Lot: 13 Upper   Owner: Elmer Hoyle
Site 2 Mary Lee Hoyle   Mort: W.T. Hilton & Sons
  Place: Frederick   Death: 27 Jan 1918   Burial: 30 Jan 1918
  d/o Alda B. & Elmer E. Hoyle, age 1-11-20
Site 3 Alda Brent Hoyle   Place: Gaithersburg, MD
  Birth: 15 Aug 1886   Death: 3 Dec 1969   Burial: 6 Dec 1969
  Mort: Ernest Gartner   w/o Elmer Eugene Hoyle
Site 4 Elmer Eugene Hoyle   Place: Washington Grove
  Birth: 17 Dec 1876   Death: 4 Aug 1964   Burial: 6 Aug 1964
  Mort: Ernest E. Gartner   h/o Alda Brent Hoyle

Lot: 14 Lower   Owner: Cleveland Cromwell
Site 1 Authur Hays Cromwell   Place: Poolesville
  Birth: 17 Jan 1905   Death: 1 Nov 1923   Burial: 3 Nov 1923
  Mort: Hilton & Hall   TS: s/o Cleveland & Mary E. Cromwell
Site 2 Pearl B. Cromwell   Mort: Chas. E. Roberts
  Birth: 31 Jul 1903   Death: 2 May 1908   Burial: 21 Oct 1918
  TS: d/o Cleveland & Mary E. Cromwell   Removed from Barnesville
Site 3 Mary Elizabeth Cromwell   Place: Poolesville
  Birth: 11 Jul 1873   Death: 7 Aug 1937   Burial: 10 Aug 1937
  Mort: Hilton & Hall   TS: w/o Cleveland Cromwell
Site 4 Cleveland Cromwell   Place: Germantown
  Birth: 4 Mar 1873   Death: 6 Nov 1952   Burial: 10 Nov 1952
  Mort: Ernest C. Gartner   h/o Mary Elizabeth Cromwell

Monocacy Cemetery, Beallsville, Montgomery County, Maryland

Lot: 14 Upper Owner: Miscellaneous
Site 3 Grace Olivia Cromwell   Place: Dickerson
        Birth: 13 Aug 1879   Death: 9 Feb 1962   Burial: 12 Feb 1962
        Mort: Hilton   On stone with Richard Cromwell
Site 4 Richard Cromwell   Place: Wheaton, MD
        Birth: 1880   Death: 2 Nov 1968   Burial: 2 Nov 1968
        Mort: Wm. Hilton   h/o Grace Olivia Cromwell

Lot: 15 Lower Owner: T.B. Lambert
Site 1 Martha A. Lambert
        Birth: 2 Oct 1896   Death: 4 Jul 1992   Burial: 7 Jul 1992
Site 2 Virginia F. Lambert   Place: Poolesville
        Birth: 7 Mar 1904   Death: 4 Mar 1920   Burial: 6 Mar 1920
        Mort: Hilton & Hall   TS: d/o T.B. & Viola V. Lambert
Site 3 Viola Virginia Lambert   Place: Dickerson
        Birth: 9 Apr 1866   Death: 8 Nov 1958   Burial: 11 Nov 1958
        Mort: Hilton   TS: w/o Thomas B. Lambert
Site 4 Thomas Benton Lambert   Place: Poolesville
        Birth: 16 Dec 1864   Death: 20 Oct 1935   Burial: 22 Oct 1935
        Mort: Warner E. Pumphrey   h/o Viola Virginia Lambert
Site 5 Mary Lambert Steele   On stone with Clarence Steele
        Birth: 25 Feb 1898   Death: 18 May 1991   Burial: 21 May 1991
Site 6 Clarence Fogleman Steele   h/o Mary Lambert Steele   Place: Frederick
        Birth: 14 Oct 1896   Death: 18 Apr 1958   Burial: 21 Apr 1958
        Mort: Hilton   TS: Maryland PVT Co. E 11 Ammunition TN WWI

Lot: 15 Upper Owner: Charles C. Reed
Site   Anna Reed   No marker   Mort: Clyde J. Nichols
        Place: Washington, DC   Death: 30 Jul 1928   Burial: 31 Jul 1928
Site 1 Infant of Charles C. Reed Sr. No marker   Mort: A.G. Carlisle
        Place: Washington Grove Death: 13 Oct 1918   Burial: 15 Oct 1918
Site 2 Infant Son Reed   Death: 1919   TS: s/o C.C. & Annie M. Reed
Site 3 Annie M. Allnutt Reed   On stone with Charles Clifton Reed Sr.
        Birth: 16 Aug 1898   Death: 1984
Site 4 Charles C. Reed Sr.   h/o Annie M. Reed
        Birth: 27 Apr 1889   Death: 1977   Burial: 24 Feb 1977
Site 5 Margaret Estelle Duffy   w/o Harold Arthur Duffy
        Birth: 7 Dec 1916   Death: 14 Sep 1995   Burial: 23 Sep 1995
Site 6 Harold Arthur Duffy
        Birth: 17 May 1912   Death: 13 Aug 1984   Burial: 17 Aug 1984

Lot: 16 Owner: T.L. Grubb
Site 2 Elizabeth Silcott   Mort: W.T. Hilton & Sons   Place: Beallsville
        Birth: 1836   Death: 23 Aug 1918   Burial: 24 Aug 1918
Site 3 Bertha A. Crissey   Mort: W.R. Pumphrey
        Place: Beallsville   Death: 21 Nov 1930   Burial: 23 Nov 1930
        w/o James B. Crissey   No marker

Monocacy Cemetery, Beallsville, Montgomery County, Maryland

Site 4 James Beverley Crissey   Place: Beallsville
        Birth: 19 Sep 1855   Death: 6 Nov 1922   Burial: 8 Nov 1922
        Mort: Hilton & Hall   h/o Bertha A. Crissy
Site 9 Margaret E. Grubb   Place: Beallsville
        Birth: 10 Feb 1882   Death: 6 Apr 1930   Burial: 8 Apr 1930
        Mort: W.T. Hilton & Sons   1st w/o Thomas L. Grubb
Site 10 Thomas L. Grubb   Mort: W.B. Hilton   Place: Frederick Hospital
        Birth: 28 Jul 1877   Death: 9 May 1950   Burial: 11 May 1950
        h/o Margaret E. Grubb & Catherine Chiswell Grubb, age 73
Site 11 Catherine Chiswell Grubb   Mort: Hilton   2nd w/o Thomas L. Grubb
        Birth: 18 Mar 1885   Death: 26 Jun 1966   Burial: 29 Jun 1966
Site 12 Byron Walling Chiswell   b/o Catherine Chiswell Grubb
        Birth: 6 Aug 1894   Death: 22 Jan 1974   Burial: 24 Jan 1974

Lot: 17 Lower   Owner: Miscellaneous
Site 2 Dr. Robert Kirsch   Mort: Hilton
        Birth: 1930   Death: 17 Aug 1996
Site 3 Ada C. Wood   Place: Charles Town
        Birth: 6 Nov 1882   Death: 12 Oct 1918   Burial: 14 Oct 1918
        Mort: W.T. Hilton & Sons   w/o Ernest P. Wood
Site 4 Ernest P. Wood   Place: Charles Town, WV
        Birth: 17 Sep 1872   Death: 12 Jan 1938   Burial: 16 Jan 1938
        Mort: Melvin T. Strider   h/o Ada C. Wood

Lot: 17 Upper   Owner: George B. Tobery (One stone in lot)
Site 1 George Prentice Tobery   Mort: John T. Newman   Place: Ocean City, NJ
        Birth: 20 Jul 1919   Death: 17 Jul 1963   Burial: 16 Jul 1963
        s/o Marie Roberson & George Basil Tobery
        TS: Maryland PFC 110 AAA GUN BN CAC WWII
Site 2 Dorothy Marie Tobery   Place: Dickerson
        Birth: 1918   Death: 3 Sep 1918   Burial: 5 Sep 1918
        Mort: W.T. Hilton & Sons   d/o George B. & Marie Roberson Tobery
Site 3 George Basil Tobery   h/o Marie Roberson Tobery
        Birth: 1890   Death: 1973   Burial: 18 Mar 1973
Site 4 Marie Roberson Tobery   w/o George Basil Tobery
        Birth: 27 Sep 1896   Death: 29 Jul 1987   Burial: 1 Aug 1987
Site 5 Carrie Roberson Nicholson   w/o Linwood Burton Nicholson
        Birth: 1886   Death: 1977   Burial: 10 Nov 1977

Lot: 18 Lower   Owner: Roy Wright
Site 2 Jacob Franklin Wright   Place: Fowblesburg
        Birth: 20 Dec 1919   Death: 21 May 1941   Burial: 23 May 1941
        Mort: J.F. Esline & Sons   TS: s/o Roy L. & Rella G. Wright
Site 3 Rella Grace Wright   Place: Westminster
        Birth: 5 Apr 1890   Death: 23 Sep 1940   Burial: 26 Sep 1940
        Mort: H. Bankard Sons   TS: w/o Roy L. Wright
Site 4 Lula Bee Wright   Place: Bucklodge
        Birth: 27 Apr 1921   Death: 27 Apr 1921   Burial: 28 Apr 1921
        Mort: W.T. Hilton & Sons   TS: d/o Roy L. & Rella G. Wright

Monocacy Cemetery, Beallsville, Montgomery County, Maryland

Site 4 Roy Leslie Wright
Birth: 17 Mar 1887 Death: 29 Dec 1964
Mort: J.E. Myers Jr.
Place: Hagerstown
Burial: 2 Jan 1965
h/o Rella Grace Wright

Site 5 Ida Madeline Mellott
Birth: 5 Apr 1867 Death: 30 Oct 1958
Mort: M.E. Dugan
Place: Beglerville, PA
Burial: 3 Nov 1958
w/o Jacob B. Mellott

Site 6 Jacob B. Mellott
Birth: 27 Oct 1864 Death: 7 Oct 1924
Mort: W.T. Hilton & Sons
Place: Buck Lodge
Burial: 7 Oct 1924
h/o Ida Madeline Mellott

Lot: 18 Upper   Owner: Charles O. Roberson

Site 2 Edith E. Roberson
Birth: 2 Aug 1920 Death: 2 Aug 1984
On stone with Marshall K. Roberson
Burial: 4 Aug 1984

Site 3 Marshall Knill Roberson
Birth: 5 May 1917 Death: 14 Apr 1986
Burial: 17 Apr 1986

Site 4 Charles O. Roberson
Birth: 18 Apr 1889 Death: 19 Jan 1964
Mort: Hilton
Place: Frederick
Burial: 21 Jan 1964

Site 5 Charles L. Roberson
Place: Barnesville Death: 30 Oct 1918
is/o Charles O. Roberson
Mort: W.T. Hilton & Sons
Burial: 31 Oct 1918
No marker

Lot: 19 Lower   Owner: Mrs. Andrew Phelps

Site   Edna Phelps   No marker
Place: Poolesville Death: 30 Aug 1923
Mort: Hilton & Hall
Burial: 30 Aug 1923

Site   Unnamed Cooper   No marker
Place: Washington, DC Death: 14 Oct 1933
Mort: Arthur Cooper
Burial: 16 Oct 1933

Site 1 Arthur Berkely Cooper
Birth: 2 Oct 1895 Death: 11 Jul 1963
Mort: Eackles Funeral Home   TS: Va PFC Co. B 301 BN Tank Corps WWI
Place: Martinsburg, WV
Burial: 13 Jul 1963

Site 3 Martha Annie Phelps Cooper
Birth: 25 Feb 1898 Death: 10 Dec 1954
Mort: Robert A. Pumphrey
Place: Takoma Park
Burial: 14 Dec 1954
nee Phelps

Site 4 Archie C. Phelps
Birth: 1885 Death: 15 Jan 1928
Mort: Geo. W. Wise Co.   On stone with Annie E. & Andrew Wilson Phelps
Place: Washington, DC
Burial: 18 Jan 1928

Site 5 Annie E. Phelps
Birth: 1861 Death: 12 Mar 1938
Mort: W.R. Pumphrey
Place: Washington, DC
Burial: 15 Mar 1938

Site 6 Andrew Wilson Phelps
Birth: 1853 Death: 1920
Mort: W.T. Hilton & Sons
Burial: 28 Sep 1921
Removed from Waughs Chapel

Lot: 19 Upper   Owner: Frances S. Wade

Site 1 Wallace Wade
Death: 6 Mar 1849
TS: is/o James Perry & Harriet Ann Wade
Mort: Chas. E. Roberts
Burial: 2 Sep 1937
Removed from Barnesville

Site 2 James Perry Wade Jr.
Removed from Barnesville   Death: 31 Aug 1858
TS: s/o James Perry Sr. & Harriet Ann Wade, age 1-2-10
Mort: Chas. E. Roberts
Burial: 2 Sep 1937

Monocacy Cemetery, Beallsville, Montgomery County, Maryland

Site 3 James Perry Wade Mort: Chas. E. Roberts
Birth: 7 Aug 1825 Death: 15 Apr 1858 Burial: 2 Sep 1937
TS: h/o Harriet Ann Wade, age 32 yrs. Removed from Barnesville

Site 4 Harriet Ann Wade Mort: Chas. E. Roberts
Birth: 16 Feb 1828 Death: 26 Jan 1906 Burial: 2 Sep 1937
TS: w/o James Perry Wade, d/o Jacob & Sarah Nichols
Removed from Barnesville

Site 5 Alice Wade Mort: Chas. E. Roberts
Birth: 10 Dec 1855 Death: 30 Oct 1889 Burial: 2 Sep 1937
TS: d/o James Perry & Harriet Ann Wade Removed from Barnesville

Site 6 Mary Eliza Wade Mort: Chas. E. Roberts
Birth: 1 Jun 1853 Death: 23 Feb 1937 Burial: 2 Sep 1937
TS: d/o James Perry & Harriet Ann Wade Removed from Barnesville

Lot: 20 Lower   Owner: Thomas H. Clements

Site 2 Infant Clements Mort: W.T. Hilton & Sons
Place: Washington, DC Death: 30 Jan 1920 Burial: 31 Jan 1920
i/o Thomas H. & Edna G Clements

Site 3 Edna G. Clements Place: Washington, DC
Birth: 1 Dec 1888 Death: 1 Feb 1920 Burial: 4 Feb 1920
Mort: W.T. Hilton & Sons w/o Thomas H. Clements

Site 4 Thomas Henry Clements Mort: J. Milton Bender Place: Gettysburg, PA
Birth: 28 Feb 1885 Death: 20 Sep 1959 Burial: 23 Spe 1959
h/o Edna G. Clements & Leona Waddell Clements

Site 5 Leona L. Waddell Clements 2nd w/o Thomas H. Clements
Birth: 18 Aug 1908 Death: 21 Aug 1989 Burial: 24 Aug 1989

Lot: 20 Upper   Owner: Mrs. George M. Burdette

Site 1 James T. Burdette Mort: Hilton
Death: 17 Jun 1975 Burial: 19 Jun 1975

Site 2 Otis McLelland Burdette Mort: Hilton Place: Wheaton
Birth: 2 Feb 1902 Death: 28 Dec 1965 Burial: 30 Dec 1965

Site 3 Infant of Mrs. Julia Mentzer No marker Mort: W.T. Hilton & Sons
Place: Dickerson Death: 21 Nov 1929 Burial: 22 Nov 1929

Site 3 Anna Eliza Smith Burdette Place: Dickerson
Birth: 9 Aug 1872 Death: 9 Jan 1919 Burial: 12 Jan 1919
Mort: W.T. Hilton & Sons On stone with George McClellan Burdette

Site 4 George McClellan Burdette Mort: W.T. Hilton & Sons Place: Dickerson
Birth: 12 Mar 1870 Death: 17 Dec 1918 Burial: 19 Dec 1918

Site 5 John Russell Burdette Place: Dickerson
Birth: 31 Mar 1901 Death: 22 Feb 1964 Burial: 26 Nov 1964
Mort: Hilton s/o Helen Mulligan Burdette

Lot: 21   Owner: Randolph Luhn

Site 3 Sarah Elizabeth Luhn Place: Sellman
Birth: 23 Jul 1858 Death: 10 Jul 1930 Burial: 12 Jul 1930
Mort: W.T. Hilton & Sons w/o Randolph Luhn

Site 4 Randolph Luhn   Place: Beallsville
        Birth: 29 Sep 1852   Death: 15 Feb 1940   Burial: 18 Feb 1940
        Mort: W.B. Hilton   h/o Sarah Elizabeth Luhn
Site 5 Clara Belle Luhn   Place: Olney, MD
        Birth: 11 Aug 1896   Death: 28 Jan 1970   Burial: 30 Jan 1970
        Mort: Olin Molesworth   w/o Lawrence W. Luhn
Site 6 Lawrence W. Luhn   h/o Clara Belle Luhn
        Birth: 11 Aug 1894   Death: 1 May 1976   Burial: 4 May 1976
Site 8 Hazel V. Luhn   Place: State Sanatorium
        Birth: 10 Sep 1915   Death: 24 Jul 1937   Burial: 27 Jul 1937
        Mort: W.B. Hilton   d/o Arthur P. & Bessie E. Luhn
Site 9 Elizabeth (Bessie) Ellen Luhn   Mort: Hilton & Hall   Place: Poolesville
        Birth: 14 Oct 1883   Death: 25 Jul 1921   w/o Arthur P. Luhn
Site 10 Arthur Price Luhn   Mort: W.B. Hilton   Place: Dickerson
        Birth: 9 Sep 1881   Death: 8 Feb 1950

Lot: 22 Lower   Owner: Dr. William C. Miller
Site 2 Alma Mae Miller   Place: Gaithersburg
        Birth: 9 Sep 1925   Death: 22 Jun 1931   Burial: 24 Jun 1931
        Mort: W.T. Hilton & Sons   On stone with Dr. William C. Miller
Site 3 William C. Miller, MD   Place: MD Carl. Hosp.
        Birth: 1 May 1880   Death: 24 Spe 1967   Burial: 27 Sep 1967
        Mort: Pumphrey   h/o Alma Mae Miller

Lot: 22 Upper   Owner: Lee Ford
Site   William H. Ford   Birth: 1920   Death: 1974
Site 1 Aubrey Thomas Ford
        Birth: Nov 1921   Death: 22 Nov 1983   Burial: 25 Nov 1983
Site 2 Infant of Lee Ford   No marker   Mort: W.R. Pumphrey
        Place: Glenmont   Death: 22 Aug 1922   Burial: 23 Aug 1922
Site 3 Mary Elizabeth Fox Ford   w/o Lee Ford
        Birth: 5 Jun 1889   Death: 8 Nov 1983   Burial: 11 Nov 1983
Site 4 Lee N. Ford   Mort: W.C. Mattingly   Place: Leonardtown
        Birth: 1880   Death: 12 Aug 1943   Burial: 15 Aug 1943
        h/o Mary Fox Ford
Site 5 Lottie E. Fox Ford   w/o Thomas Davis Ford
        Birth: 1893   Death: 1977   Burial: 4 Feb 1977
Site 6 Thomas Davis Ford   Place: Hyattsville
        Birth: 1882   Death: 16 Apr 1944   Burial: 19 Apr 1944
        Mort: W.W. Chambers   h/o Lottie E. Fox Ford

Lot: 23   Owner: Alfred Pearson
Site   Lily Ann Pearson   No marker   Mort: W.B. Hilton
        Place: Washington, DC   Death: 6 Jul 1937   Burial: 8 Jul 1937
Site 1 John A. Pearson   Mort: Hilton & Hall   Place: Cloppers
        Birth: 28 Dec 1896   Death: 18 Aug 1921   Burial: 20 Aug 1921
Site 2 Eugene H. Pearson   Mort: Hilton & Hall   Place: Cloppers
        Birth: 16 Jul 1899   Death: 18 Aug 1921   Burial: 20 Aug 1921

Monocacy Cemetery, Beallsville, Montgomery County, Maryland

Site 3 Lillian Anne Pearson   Place: Poolesville
        Birth: 7 Jun 1865   Death: 29 Sep 1928   Burial: 1 Oct 1928
        Mort: Hilton & Hall   w/o Alfred Pearson
Site 4 Alfred Pearson   Place: Adamstown
        Birth: 4 Sep 1859   Death: 9 Feb 1947   Burial: 12 Feb 1947
        Mort: W.B. Hilton   h/o Lillie A. Pearson
Site 5 Lula May Pearson Young   Mort: W.B. Hilton   Place: Frederick
        Birth: 28 Jun 1893   Death: 13 Oct 1952   Burial: 16 Oct 1952
        d/o Alfred & Lillie Pearson, w/o Ernest Lee Young, age 60
Site 6 Ernest Lee Young   s/o Lulu May Pearson Young
        Birth: 26 Jun 1926   Death: 8 Apr 1993
Site 7 Newton J. Covert
        Birth: 5 Oct 1889   Death: 15 Feb 1984   Burial: 18 Feb 1984
Site 8 Mabel Elizabeth Covert   w/o Newton U. Covert, age 46 yrs
        Birth: 21 Jul 1905   Death: 22 Jan 1996   Burial: 31 Jan 1996
Site 9 Harold Alfred Young   TS: Age 72 yrs.   Mort: Keeney & Basford
        Birth: 23 Jul 1924   Death: 22 Nov 1996   Burial: 25 Nov 1996
Site 10 Elsie Mae Pearson Gause DD   On stone with Walter R. Gause
        Birth: 4 Oct 1903   Death: 27 Dec 1994   Burial: 29 Dec 1994
Site 11 Ernest H. Pearson
        Birth: 4 Jun 1901   Death: 6 Jun 1987   Burial: 9 Jun 1987
Site 12 Charles Harold Pearson Jr.
        Birth: 24 Jan 1944   Death: 28 Oct 1984   Burial: 1 Nov 1984

Lot: 24 Lower   Owner: Maurice E. Ricketts
Site 1 Brenda Lou Selby Carter   Mort: Etchison & Sons   Place: Ijamsville, MD
        Birth: 11 Feb 1949   Death: 8 Dec 1969   Burial: 11 Dec 1969
Site 2 Helen Wilson Selby   Mort: W.B. Hilton   Place: Bethesda
        Birth: 16 Mar 1920   Death: 3 Jan 1956   Burial: 6 Jan 1955
Site 3 Bertha S. Warfield Ricketts   Mort: W.T. Hilton & Sons
        Birth: 20 Oct 1886   Death: 17 Mar 1922   Burial: 19 Mar 1922
        Place: Sandy Spring   TS: w/o Maurice E. Ricketts
Site 4 Maurice E. Ricketts   Mort: W.L. Burdette   Place: Hyattstown
        Birth: 2 Sep 1881   Death: 30 Jan 1961   Burial: 2 Feb 1961
        h/o Bertha Warfield Rickets
Site 5 Charles E. Ricketts   s/o Maurice E. & Bessie Warfield Ricketts
        Birth: 28 Oct 1904   Death: 28 Mar 1976   Burial: 1 Apr 1976
Site 6 Barbara J. Bowers   TS: Mother
        Birth: 2 Jun 1944   Death: 2 Feb 1986   Burial: 5 Feb 1986

Lot: 24 Upper   Owner: R.E. Johnson
Site   Marian L. Johnson   No marker   Mort: W.R. Pumphrey
        Place: Washington, DC   Death: 28 Sep 1936   Burial: 30 Sep 1936
Site   Marie Johnson   No marker   Mort: W.R. Pumphrey
        Place: Kensington   Death: 26 Jul 1921   Burial: 27 Jul 1921
Site 2 Baby Johnson   No marker   Mort: W.R. Pumphrey
        Place: Takoma Park   Death: 20 Jan 1937   Burial: 21 Jan 1937
Site 3 Sarah A. Johnson   No marker
        Birth: 4 Jul 1901   Death: 9 Jan 1983   Burial: 13 Jan 1983

230　　Monocacy Cemetery, Beallsville, Montgomery County, Maryland

```
Site 4  Richard Edwin Johnson    No marker              Place: Takoma Park
        Birth: 23 May 1898       Death: 29 Mar 1956     Burial: 2 Apr 1956
        Mort: Robert A. Pumphrey
Site 5  Maurice Allan Glick      No marker              Mort: Warner E.
        Place: Kensington        Death: 21 Jul 1961     Burial: 24 Jul 1961
```

Lot: 25 Owner: Charles W. Burch
```
Site 1  Infant Son Burch                                Mort: Warner E.
        Place: Washington, DC    Death: 17 Oct 1933     Burial: 17 Oct 1933
        TS: s/o Carroll A. & Edith M. Burch
Site 2  Francis Albert Burch                            Place: Silver Spring
        Birth: 27 Feb 1906       Death: 11 Nov 1925     Burial: 13 Nov 1925
        Mort: Pumphrey & Sons    TS: s/o Charles W. & Lulu W. Burch
Site 3  Lula W. Astlin Burch                            Place: Colesville
        Birth: 26 Apr 1880       Death: 1 Jul 1955      Burial: 4 Jul 1955
        Mort: Warner E. Pumphrey                        TS: w/o Charles W. Burch
Site 4  Charles W. Burch                                Place: Silver Spring
        Birth: 19 Apr 1873       Death: 27 Jun 1948     Burial: 30 Jun 1948
        Mort: Warner E. Pumphrey                        h/o Lulu Astlin Burch
Site 5  Salvatore Vincent Catalano (Sam)
        Birth: 26 Feb 1907       Death: 26 Jul 1971     Burial: 29 Jul 1971
        On stone with Dorothy Virginia Burch Catalano
Site 10 Myrtle Burch Hood                               w/o Wilbur C. Hood
        Birth: 11 Aug 1904       Death: 11 Sep 1977     Burial: 14 Sep 1977
Site 11 Elizabeth C. Burch                              On stone with George W. Burch
        Birth: 31 Jan 1905       Death: 27 Feb 1996     Burial: 2 Mar 1996
Site 12 George W. Burch                                 h/o Elizabeth C. Burch
        Birth: 18 Jan 1902       Death: 26 Apr 1973     Burial: 30 Apr 1973
```

Lot: 26 Lower Owner: Isaac & Tina Cubitt
```
Site 3  Edna Lee Dodd Cubitt                            On stone with Isaac Davis Cubitt
        Birth: 25 May 1901       Death: 21 Dec 1975     Burial: 23 Dec 1975
Site 4  Isaac Davis Cubitt       Mort: Hilton           Place: Bethesda
        Birth: 21 Aug 1891       Death: 15 Dec 1962     Burial: 18 Dec 1962
        h/o Edna Lee Dodd Cuitt  TS: Maryland Cook Co. C 326 Infantry WWI, PH
Site 6  John Isaac (Jack) Cubitt                        s/o Isaac D. & Edna L. Cubitt
        Birth: 22 Apr 1928       Death: 7 Feb 1994      Burial: 7 Feb 1994
        On stone with Dorothy A. Cubitt
```

Lot: 26 Upper Owner: William H. Dodd
```
Site 2  Harry H. Dodd            No marker              Place: Olney
        Birth: 1921              Death: 4 Sep 1926      Burial: 6 Sep 1926
        Mort: W.R. Pumphrey                    s/o Phoebe Ella & William H. Dodd
Site 3  Phebe Ella Dodd                                 Place: near Redland
        Birth: 12 Jun 1880       Death: 13 Dec 1925     Burial: 15 Dec 1925
        Mort: Pumphrey & Sons                           TS: w/o William H. Dodd
Site 4  William H. Dodd                                 Place: Leesburg, VA
        Birth: 21 May 1876       Death: 17 Jul 1943     Burial: 20 Jul 1943
        Mort: Lloyd Slack                               w/o Phoebe Ella Dodd
```

Monocacy Cemetery, Beallsville, Montgomery County, Maryland

Site 5 Ocie Ella Dodd   Mort: Tyson Wheeler   Place: Washington, DC
        Birth: 15 Jun 1903   Death: 30 Nov 1964   Burial: 3 Dec 1964
        d/o Phoebe Ella & William H. Dodd
        TS: Maryland PFC Womens Army Corp P WWII
Site 6 Virginia N. Dodd Greer   Place: Baltimore
        Birth: 4 Oct 1916   Death: 13 Jun 1965   Burial: 15 Jun 1965
        Mort: Tyson Wheeler   d/o Phoebe Ella & William H. Dodd

Lot: 27 Lower Owner: Charles E. Fox (No markers in lot)
Site   Martha Ellen Fox   No marker   Mort: W.B. Hilton
        Place: Washington, DC   Death: 26 Feb 1938   Burial: 1 Mar 1938
Site 1 Helen F. Turner   d/o Thomas Carter   Mort: W.T. Hilton & Sons
        Place: Baltimore   Death: 7 Jul 1931   Burial: 10 Jul 1931
Site 2 John Henry Fox   No marker   Mort: W.T. Hilton & Sons
        Place: State Sanatorium   Death: 13 Mar 1932   Burial: 16 Mar 1932
Site 3 Owen Stanley Fox   No marker   Mort: W.T. Hilton & Sons
        Place: Buck Lodge   Death: 25 Oct 1927   Burial: 28 Oct 1927
Site 4 Emma M. Fox   w/o Charles E. Fox   Mort: C.E. Cline & Son
        Place: Lime Kiln   Death: 3 Apr 1937   Burial: 4 Apr 1937
Site 5 Charles Edward Fox   h/o Emma M. Fox   Mort: W.B. Hilton
        Place: Silver Spring   Death: 9 Aug 1940   Burial: 12 Aug 1940
Site 6 George Fox   No marker   Mort: W.B. Hilton
        Place: Olney   Death: 30 Dec 1939   Burial: 2 Jan 1940

Lot: 27 Upper Owner: Charles E. Edward
Site   Baby Norwood   Mort: W.T. Hilton & Sons
        Place: Buck Lodge   Death: 6 Nov 1928   Burial: 7 Nov 1928
        c/o Edward Norwood   No marker
Site   Margaretta Norwood   No marker   Mort: W.R. Pumphrey
        Place: Quince Orchard   Death: 2 Jan 1940   Burial: 5 Jan 1940
Site 1 Luther Dodson   No marker   Mort: W.T. Hilton & Sons
        Place: Baltimore   Death: 17 Aug 1928   Burial: 19 Aug 1928
Site 3 Infant Norwood   Mort: W.T. Hilton & Sons
        Place: Frederick   Death: 11 Dec 1926   Burial: 13 Dec 1926
        i/o Edward & Lelia M. Norwood   No marker
Site 3 Lelia M. Norwood   Place: Frederick
        Birth: 24 Apr 1902   Death: 11 Dec 1926   Burial: 13 Dec 1926
        Mort: W.T. Hilton & Sons   TS: w/o B. Edward Norwood
Site 6 Bradley Norwood   Mort: W.T. Hilton & Sons
        Place: Buck Lodge   Death: 3 Jan 1929   Burial: 5 Jan 1929
        Father of Edward Norwood   No marker

Lot: 28 Owner: G.L. Hildebrand
Site 1 Raymond B. Harrison   Place: Washington, DC
        Birth: 1907   Death: 20 Jan 1959   Burial: 22 Jan 1959
        Mort: Robert A. Pumphrey   h/o Helen Hildebrand Harrison
Site 2 Helen Hildebrand Harrison   On stone with Raymond B. Harrison
        Birth: 1910   Death: 11 Sep 1977   Burial: 15 Sep 1977

232 Monocacy Cemetery, Beallsville, Montgomery County, Maryland

Site 3 Ruth Margaret Elizabeth Hildebrand Place: Dickerson
Birth: 1858   Death: 27 Nov 1926   Burial: 30 Nov 1926
Mort: M.R. Etchison   w/o George L. Hildebrand
Site 4 George Luther Hildebrand Mort: M.R. Etchison & Son   Place: Dickerson
Birth: 1859   Death: 11 Jun 1932   Burial: 14 Jun 1932
h/o Ruth Margaret Elizabeth Hildebrand
Site 5 Anna Mae Hildebrand   d/o G.L. & Ruth Davis Hildebrand
Birth: 1887   Death: 26 Mar 1978   Burial: 28 Mar 1978
Site 7 Austin M. Goodwin, Sr.   TS: RD 1 US Navy Korea
Birth: 15 Mar 1932   Death: 11 Apr 1987   Burial: 22 Apr 1987
Site 7 Nathan Davis Hildebrand   h/o Nellie Selby Hildebrand
Birth: 19 Jun 1885   Death: 4 Jul 1972   Burial: 6 Jul 1972
Site 8 Nellie Selby Hildebrand   On stone with Nathan Davis Hildebrand
Birth: 11 Jan 1892   Death: 30 Dec 1976   Burial: 3 Jan 1977
Site 9 Bertha Helen Hildebrand Painter   Place: Barnesville
Birth: 1892   Death: 29 May 1959   Burial: 1 Jun 1959
Mort: Hilton   On stone with Elmer Lee Painter
Site 10 Elmer Lee Painter   h/o Bertha Helen Hildebrand Painter
Birth: 1894   Death: 12 Apr 1977   Burial: 14 Apr 1977

Lot: 29 Owner: George A. Davis
Site 1 George F. Davis   Mort: W.R. Pumphrey   Place: Kensington
Birth: 8 Jan 1848   Death: 18 Jul 1928   Burial: 21 Jul 1928
Site 2 George Alfred Davis   Mort: Robert A.   Place: Bethesda
Birth: 1885   Death: 22 Nov 1955   Burial: 26 Nov 1955
h/o Margaret Nolia Davis
Site 3 Margaret Nolia Davis   Mort: R.A. Pumphrey
Place: Kensington, MD   Death: 19 Jul 1967   Burial: 22 Jul 1967
w/o George Alfred Davis   No marker
Site 4 Edith Miller   No marker   Mort: R.A. Pumphrey
Place: Bethesda   Death: 30 Jan 1957   Burial: 1 Feb 1957

Lot: 30 Owner: Dr. James Robert Hicks
Site 2 Robert K. Hicks   Mort: S.H. Hines Co.   Place: Washington, DC
Birth: 1900   Death: 6 Jul 1929   Burial: 8 Jul 1929
Site 3 Eliza Virginia Walker Hicks   Place: Dickerson
Birth: 1865   Death: 13 Sep 1955   Burial: 16 Sep 1955
Mort: M.R. Etchison & Son   w/o Dr. James Robert Hicks
Site 4 Dr. James Robert Hicks   Place: Dickerson
Birth: 1854   Death: 9 Jun 1933   Burial: 11 Jun 1933
Mort: Warner E. Pumphrey   h/o Eliza Virginia Walker Hicks
Site 5 Myra Hicks Howe   On stone with Dr. John Stewart Howe
Birth: 16 May 1905   Death: 26 Mar 1986   Burial: 29 Mar 1986
Site 6 John Stewart Howe MD
Birth: 8 May 1908   Death: 10 Mar 1989   Burial: 20 Mar 1989
Site 8 Saunders Lee Hicks   Place: Dickerson
Birth: 1861   Death: 19 Jan 1933   Burial: 21 Jan 1933
Mort: Warner Pumphrey   h/o Hattie Susan Walker Hicks

Monocacy Cemetery, Beallsville, Montgomery County, Maryland   233

Site 9 Hattie Susan Walker Hicks   Place: Dickerson
        Birth: 1876   Death: 7 Jul 1964   Burial: 9 Jul 1964
        Mort: Hilton   w/o Saunders Lee Hicks
Site 12 Arthur Gloyd Hoyle   On stone with Anna Lee Hoyle, age 84 yrs
        Birth: 17 Feb 1907   Death: 24 Jul 1991   Burial: 27 Jul 1991

Lot: 31 Lower   Owner: Miscellaneous
Site 2 Sarah Gertrude Matthews Poole   No marker   w/o John F. Poole Sr.
        Birth: 14 Jul 1967   Death: 30 Dec 1994   Burial: 4 Jan 1995
Site 3 John Franklin Poole III   s/o John F. Jr. & Gertrude Matthews Poole
        Birth: 28 Aug 1950   Death: 5 Aug 1981   Burial: 8 Aug 1981
Site 4 James Perry Spratt   Mort: S.H. Hines Co.   Place: Staunton, VA
        Birth: 27 Aug 1850   Death: 3 Jan 1931   Burial: 5 Jan 1931
Site 6 Charles Maynard Matthews Jr.   On stone with Ruby Mundy Matthews
        Birth: 15 Dec 1928   Death: 31 Jan 1981   Burial: 3 Feb 1981

Lot: 31 Upper   Owner: Sarah D. Spratt
Site 2 Alice L. Shawver   Mort: W.T. Hilton & Sons
        Place: Tazewell, VA   Death: 13 Sep 1931   Burial: 17 Sep 1931
        w/o Saunders Lee Shawver   No marker
Site 3 Sarah D.A. Spratt   Place: Bluefield, WV
        Birth: 1 Apr 1874   Death: 5 Jun 1943   Burial: 8 Jun 1943
        Mort: J.J. Greever   TS: w/o Harvey G. Spratt
Site 4 Harvey George Spratt   Place: Poolesville
        Birth: 16 Jun 1855   Death: 9 Aug 1929   Burial: 11 Aug 1929
        Mort: Hilton & Hall   h/o Sarah D.A. Spratt
Site 5 Sanders Lee Shawver   Mort: M.L. Creager &
        Place: Thurmont   Death: 25 Apr 1951   Burial: 27 Apr 1951
        h/o Alice L. Shawver   No marker

Lot: 32   Owner: Nathan S. Cooley
Site 1 Vernon Thomas Cooley   s/o Nathan S. & Lillie Sears Cooley
        Birth: 3 Mar 1912   Death: 28 Feb 1988   Burial: 2 Mar 1988
Site 2 Eldridge M. Cooley   Mort: W.T. Hilton   Place: Washington, DC
        Birth: 3 Aug 1905   Death: 23 Dec 1929   Burial: 26 Dec 1929
Site 3 Lillie May Cooley   Place: Germantown
        Birth: 11 Oct 1875   Death: 13 Nov 1964   Burial: 16 Nov 1964
        Mort: Hilton   w/o Nathan S. Cooley
Site 4 Nathan S. Cooley   Place: Dickerson
        Birth: 17 Apr 1871   Death: 28 May 1953   Burial: 31 May 1953
        Mort: W.B. Hilton   h/o Lillie May Cooley
Site 5 Alice May Cooley   Mort: W.B. Hilton   Place: Dickerson
        Birth: 13 Sep 1907   Death: 30 Nov 1953   Burial: 3 Dec 1953
Site 6 Royie G. Cooley   Mort: W.B. Hilton   Place: Dickerson
        Birth: 21 Jul 1898   Death: 22 Aug 1954   Burial: 24 Aug 1954
Site 7 Herbert William Cooley   TS: PFC US Army WWII
        Birth: 2 Feb 1914   Death: 31 Aug 1979   Burial: 5 Sep 1979

Lot: 33 Lower Owner: James S. Moore

Site 2 Helen Moore Zimmerman Mort: W.E. Pumphrey Place: Washington, DC
        Birth: 1 Oct 1906 Death: 26 Sep 1941 Burial: 28 Sep 1941
Site 3 Susan Ann Moore Mort: W.E. Pumphrey Place: Washington, DC
        Birth: 23 May 1878 Death: 2 Jan 1934 Burial: 4 Jan 1934
Site 4 James S. Moore Mort: W.E. Pumphrey Place: Washington, DC
        Birth: 7 Feb 1864 Death: 29 Feb 1936 Burial: 2 Mar 1936
Site 5 Barbara Moore Ladson   No marker
        Birth: 27 Mar 1918 Death: 24 Oct 1984 Burial: 26 Oct 1986
Site 6 Mildred Moore Harris Mort: R.W. Pumphrey Place: Washington, DC
        Birth: 1904 Death: 22 Mar 1942 Burial: 25 Mar 1942

Lot: 33 Upper Owner: Prentice Waddell

Site 1 Charles Maynard Matthews Sr.   h/o Isabell Waddell Matthews
        Birth: 9 Sep 1895 Death: 5 Dec 1977 Burial: 7 Dec 1977
Site 1 Isabell Mariah Matthews   On stone with Charles Matthews
        Birth: 27 Jul 1906 Death: 28 Dec 1989 Burial: 30 Dec 1989
Site 3 Sarah Anderson Waddell
        Birth: Apr 1889 Death: 27 May 1966 Burial: 30 May 1966
        Mort: Wm. B. Hilton   On stone with Prentice C. Waddell
Site 4 Prentice C. Waddell   Place: PA
        Birth: May 1884 Death: 23 Apr 1966 Burial: 25 Apr 1966
        Mort: Wm. B. Hilton   h/o Sarah Anderson Waddell
Site 5 Annie E. Waddell   Place: Poolesville
        Birth: 6 Aug 1912 Death: 13 Mar 1930 Burial: 15 Mar 1930
        Mort: Hilton & Hall   TS: d/o P.C. & Sarah Anderson Waddell
Site 6 Annie E. Waddell   Place: Washington, DC
        Birth: 1 Jul 1936 Death: 8 May 1939 Burial: 10 May 1939
        Mort: W.R. Pumphrey   TS: d/o Stewart & Dorothy Waddell

Lot: 34 Lower Owner: F.N. Pangle

Site 2 Helen Louise Pangle   Place: Leesburg, VA
        Birth: 1920 Death: 13 May 1934 Burial: 15 May 1934
        Mort: Hilton & Hall   d/o Frederick N. & Gracie Pearl Pangle
Site 3 Gracie Pearl Pangle   Place: Urbana
        Birth: 18 Jan 1890 Death: 26 Nov 1957 Burial: 29 Nov 1957
        Mort: Etchison   On stone with Frederick N. Pangle
Site 4 Frederick Newton Pangle   Place: Frederick
        Birth: 18 Oct 1888 Death: 2 Jul 1962 Burial: 6 Jul 1962
        Mort: M.R. Etchison & Son   h/o Gracie Pearl Pangle
Site 5 Pearl Elizabeth Pangle Reed   Place: Baltimore
        Birth: 19 Feb 1910 Death: 27 Oct 1964 Burial: 31 Oct 1964
        Mort: Etchison Funeral Home   On stone with Clownie Reed
Site 6 Clownie E. Reed   h/o Pearl Elizabeth Pangle Reed
        Birth: 10 Mar 1910 Death: 23 May 1987 Burial: 25 May 1987

Monocacy Cemetery, Beallsville, Montgomery County, Maryland   235

Lot: 34 Upper   Owner: Jim & George Thompson
Site 1 Fannie O. Thompson   Place: Poolseville
        Birth: 28 Nov 1863   Death: 7 Apr 1933   Burial: 9 Apr 1933
        Mort: Warner E. Pumphrey   On stone with James M. Thompson
Site 2 James M. Thompson   Place: Poolesville
        Birth: 27 Apr 1865   Death: 21 Oct 1943   Burial: 23 Oct 1943
        Mort: W.B. Hilton   h/o Fannie O. Thompson
Site 2 Wayne Eugene Thompson   No marker   Mort: M.R. Etchison
        Place: Frederick   Death: 5 Apr 1960   Burial: 8 Apr 1960
Site 3 George Sureace Keesee   h/o Georgia Gray Keesee, age 100 yrs
        Birth: 24 Dec 1893   Death: 25 Jul 1994   Burial: 28 Jul 1994
Site 4 Georgia Gray Keesee   Mort: W.E. Pumphrey   Place: Takoma Park
        Birth: 25 Jun 1898   Death: 18 Jul 1958   Burial: 21 Jul 1958
        On stone with George S. Keesee   d/o J.M. & F.O. Thompson
Site 5 Lois Jean Keesee   Mort: W.E. Pumphrey   Place: Dickerson
        Birth: 6 Jul 1929   Death: 13 Aug 1931   Burial: 14 Aug 1931

Lot: 35 Lower   Owner: George L. Reed, Jr.
Site   George L. Reed   Mort: W.R. Pumphrey   Place: Chevy Chase
        Birth: 2 Apr 1905   Death: 29 Jan 1938   Burial: 31 Jan 1938
Site 2 Thomas W. Boyce   Mort: W.R. Pumphrey   Place: Washington, DC
        Birth: 1 Jun 1885   Death: 11 Apr 1938   Burial: 18 Apr 1939
Site 5 Nena Reed Allnutt   w/o Herbert Thomas Allnutt
        Birth: 8 Jun 1908   Death: 26 Aug 1989   Burial: 29 Aug 1989
Site 6 Herbert Thomas Allnutt
        Birth: 26 Apr 1897   Death: 23 Mar 1975   Burial: 26 Mar 1975

Lot: 35 Upper   Owner: Raymond & Eva Lynch
Site 1 Martha E.K. Reed Grant   Place: Washington, DC
        Birth: 8 Oct 1908   Death: 2 May 1943   Burial: 2 May 1943
        Mort: Wm. Reuben Pumphrey   d/o Frederick A. & Martha L. Reed
Site 2 Martha L. Lynch   Mort: W.R. Pumphrey   Place: Washington, DC
        Birth: 14 Apr 1933   Death: 5 Jan 1937   Burial: 7 Jan 1937
Site 4 Raymond Joseph Lynch   No marker
        Birth: 19 Nov 1968   Death: 21 Jun 1996   Burial: 25 Jun 1996

Lot: 36 Lower   Owner: Mrs. Bettie M. Allnutt
Site 2 Warner Stutler Allnutt   s/o Bettie Maude & John Hanson Allnutt
        Birth: 1901   Death: 1966   Burial: 8 Sep 1966
Site 3 Edna Allnutt Patton   Place: Roanoke, VA
        Birth: 1899   Death: 10 Feb 1938   Burial: 12 Feb 1938
        Mort: John M. Oakey   d/o Bettie Maude & John Hanson Allnutt
Site 4 Bettie Maude Padgett Allnutt   Place: Arlington, VA
        Birth: 1875   Death: 27 Aug 1962   Burial: 29 Aug 1962
        Mort: Arlington Funeral Home   w/o John Hanson Allnutt
Site 5 John Hanson Allnutt   h/o Bettie Maude Padgett Allnutt
        Birth: 1867   Death: 1911   Burial: 4 Dec 1911

Monocacy Cemetery, Beallsville, Montgomery County, Maryland

Lot: 36 Upper   Owner: Mrs. William S. Smoot
Site 2 Brian William Smoot   TS: s/o William S. & Heidi D. Smoot
        Birth: 9 Nov 1975   Burial: 24 Jul 1979   Age 3 yrs
Site 3 Elizabeth Jones Smoot   Place: Alexandria, VA
        Birth: 18 May 1886   Death: 18 Dec 1969   Burial: 20 Dec 1969
        Mort: William B. Hilton   w/o William Sothoron Smoot
Site 4 William Sothoron Smoot   Place: Waterford, VA
        Birth: 2 Mar 1886   Death: 9 Sep 1936   Burial: 11 Sep 1936
        Mort: Lloyd Slack, VA   h/o Elizabeth Jones Smoot

Lot: 37 Lower   Owner: W.G. Warfield
Site 1 David D. Warfield   Mort: W.B. Hilton   Place: Dickerson
        Birth: 28 Sep 1928   Death: 25 Feb 1945   Burial: 15 Mar 1945
        Cause: Drowned in Dickerson Quarry   s/o William G. & Bettie E. Warfield
Site 2 Shirley Ann Warfield   Place: Frederick
        Birth: 23 Nov 1934   Death: 27 Dec 1939   Burial: 29 Dec 1939
        Mort: W.B. Hilton   d/o William G. & Bettie M. Warfield
Site 3 Bettie E. Warfield   Place: Comus
        Birth: 15 Mar 1891   Death: 28 Aug 1962   Burial: 30 Aug 1962
        Mort: Hilton   w/o William G. Warfield
Site 4 William G. Warfield   Place: Frederick
        Birth: 25 Feb 1883   Death: 10 Mar 1940   Burial: 13 Mar 1940
        Mort: W.B. Hilton   h/o Bettie E. Warfield

Lot: 37 Upper   Owner: Miscellaneous
Site 1 Margaret Luse Greer   Mort: Hilton   Place: Frederick
        Birth: 1893   Death: 4 Mar 1967   Burial: 8 Mar 1967
Site 2 Flora Elkins Shry Hitt   Mort: Wm. B. Hilton   Place: Bethesda
        Birth: 11 Sep 1882   Death: 10 Mar 1966   Burial: 14 Mar 1966
Site 3 Myra Munger Driver   Place: Buckeystown
        Birth: 1876   Death: 2 May 1964   Burial: 5 May 1964
        Mort: M.R. Etchison & Son   On stone with Charles W. Driver
Site 4 Charles Wilson Driver   Place: Frederick
        Birth: 1877   Death: 2 Sep 1938   Burial: 5 Sep 1938
        Mort: M.W. Etchison & Son   h/o Myra Munger Driver
Site 5 Reese A. Waddell   Place: Frederick
        Birth: 1877   Death: 16 Feb 1966   Burial: 19 Feb 1966
        Mort: Wm. B. Hilton   h/o Aura E. Waddell
Site 6 Aura Elmeda Waddell   On stone with Reese A. Waddell
        Birth: 1888   Death: 21 Oct 1973   Burial: 24 Oct 1973

Lot: 38 Lower   Owner: Thomas E. & Ena Luhn
Site 3 Thomas E. Luhn   Mort: Hunteman   Place: National Airport
        Birth: 24 Jan 1890   Death: 24 Oct 1949   Burial: 27 Oct 1949
        s/o George W. & Amelia Mae Reid Luhn, h/o Ena Luhn
Site 4 Helen Virginia Luhn   TS: d/o George W. & Amelia M. Luhn, age 0-6-26
        Birth: 4 May 1895   Death: 30 Dec 1895
Site 4 Leslie L. Luhn   TS: s/o George W. & Amelia May Luhn, age 0-6-5
        Birth: 5 Jan 1889   Death: 10 Jul 1989

Monocacy Cemetery, Beallsville, Montgomery County, Maryland   237

  Site 5 George W. Luhn   Place: Poolesville
          Birth: 26 Jun 1864   Death: 24 Jan 1940   Burial: 27 Jan 1940
          Mort: W.B. Hilton   h/o Amelia Mae Luhn
  Site 6 Amelia May Reid Luhn   Place: Paeonian Springs, VA
          Birth: 17 Apr 1868   Death: 26 Dec 1950   Burial: 29 Dec 1950
          Mort: W.B. Hilton   w/o George W. Luhn, age 82

Lot: 38 Upper   Owner: J.W. Heflin
  Site 2 Dorothy Lucile Heflin   Place: Olney, MD
          Birth: 20 Nov 1932   Death: 6 Jul 1938   Burial: 8 Jul 1938
          Mort: W.B. Hilton   d/o J.W. & Goldie M. Heflin
  Site 3 Goldie Matthews Heflin   On stone with John W. Heflin
          Birth: 15 Feb 1909   Death: 21 Jun 1996   Burial: 24 Jun 1996
  Site 4 John W. Heflin   h/o Goldie Matthews Heflin
          Birth: 12 Mar 1908   Death: 5 Mar 1996   Burial: 9 Mar 1996

Lot: 39 Lower   Owner: H.B. Barr
  Site 3 Harold Bryan Barr
          Birth: 1895   Death: 17 Feb 1978   Burial: 20 Feb 1978
          s/o William & Emma Whitman Barr, h/o Estelle Marie Barr
  Site 4 Estelle Marie Jamison Barr   On stone with Harold Bryan Barr
          Birth: 1902   Death: 19 Mar 1976   Burial: 22 Mar 1976
  Site 5 Emma Whitman Barr   Place: Barnesville
          Birth: 1867   Death: 7 Jan 1946   Burial: 9 Jan 1946
          Mort: W.B. Hilton   On stone with William L. Barr
  Site 6 William Lincoln Barr   Place: Barnesville
          Birth: 1864   Death: 12 May 1945   Burial: 14 May 1945
          Mort: W.B. Hilton   h/o Emma Whitman Barr

Lot: 39 Upper   Owner: Miscellaneous
  Site 1 Donnelly Sheppard   Mort: W.B. Hilton   Place: Dickerson
          Birth: 21 Oct 1893   Death: 23 Mar 1944   Burial: 25 Mar 1944
  Site 2 Ethel Moore King Brown   Place: Silver Spring
          Birth: 1908   Death: 14 Sep 1962   Burial: 17 Sep 1962
          Mort: Warner E. Pumphrey   w/o Luther Roland King
  Site 3 Luther Roland King   Place: Washington, DC
          Birth: 1891   Death: 22 Oct 1945   Burial: 25 Oct 1945
          Mort: Warner E. Pumphrey   h/o Ethel Moore (Brown)
  Site 4 Ollie D. Rullmann   Place: Gaithersburg
          Birth: 9 Mar 1891   Death: 2 Jun 1944   Burial: 5 Jun 1944
          Mort: W.B. Hilton   On stone with William Rullmann
  Site 5 William Rullmann   Place: Bethesda
          Birth: 4 Jun 1883   Death: 27 Dec 1945   Burial: 30 Dec 1945
          Mort: W.B. Hilton   h/o Ollie D. Rullmann
  Site 6 Thomas B. Gott   Place: Washington, DC
          Birth: 23 Apr 1885   Death: 15 Apr 1942   Burial: 18 Apr 1942
          Mort: R.W. Pumphrey   f/o Ruby Gott Tyler

Lot: 40 Lower Owner: Robert E. Rawlings
Site 3 Medora C. Rawlings   Mort: W.B. Hilton   Place: Beallsville
        Birth: 24 Sep 1898   Death: 8 Aug 1946   Burial: 10 Aug 1946
Site 6 Bessie O. Jeffery   Mort: W.B. Hilton   Place: Frederick Hospital
        Birth: 27 Feb 1871   Death: 3 Dec 1944   Burial: 5 Dec 1944

Lot: 40 Upper Owner: Mrs. Reginald C. Allnutt
Site 2 Jane Allnutt Nicolaisen
        Birth: 2 Dec 1925   Death: 28 Oct 1996   Burial: 1 Nov 1996
Site 3 Edna W. Allnutt   Wife of R. Cecil Allnutt
        Birth: 11 Apr 1898   Death: 11 Jan 1985   Burial: 14 Jan 1985
Site 4 Reginald Cecil Allnutt Mort: S.H. Hines Co.   Place: Washington, DC
        Birth: 17 Jul 1898   Death: 3 Oct 1944   Burial: 5 Oct 1944
Site 6 Shelly Rae Klippel
        Birth: 1963   Death: 1986   Burial: 26 Feb 1986

Lot: 41 Lower Owner: Mrs. Ada Cosgrave
Site 4 Grafton Eugene Poole   TS: PFC US Army WWII
        Birth: 11 Aug 1922   Death: 2 Jan 1981   Burial: 6 Jan 1981
Site 5 Ada Viola Cosgrave   Place: Bethesda, MD
        Birth: 1891   Death: 17 Dec 1967   Burial: 20 Dec 1967
        Mort: Robert Pumphrey   On stone with Lawrence Snowden Cosgrave
Site 6 Lawrence Snowden Cosgrave   Place: Bethesda
        Birth: 1890   Death: 9 Sep 1948   Burial: 12 Sep 1948
        Mort: W.R. Pumphrey   h/o Ada Viola Cosgrave

Lot: 41 Upper Owner: Telfair B. Dorsett
Site 3 Helen Elizabeth Jeffery Dorsett   On stone with Telfair Bowie Dorsett
        Birth: 26 Feb 1907   Death: 29 Nov 1986   Burial: 2 Dec 1986
Site   Telfair Bowie Dorsett Birth: 20 Jan 1900   Death: 25 Apr 1967

Lot: 42 Lower Owner: G. Grady Hubble
Site 1 Margaret I. Cole   d/o George Grady & Aubra Virginia Hubble
        Birth: 24 Jun 1920   Death: 10 Sep 1978   Burial: 13 Sep 1978
Site 2 Donald T. Hubble   Mort: W.B. Hilton   Place: Frederick Hospital
        Birth: 15 Dec 1935   Death: 23 Oct 1949   Burial: 25 Oct 1949
        s/o George Grady & Aubra Thompson Hubble
Site 3 Aubra Virginia Thompson Hubble   w/o George Grady Hubble
        Birth: 10 Jan 1899   Death: 21 Mar 1976   Burial: 23 Mar 1976
Site 4 George Grady Hubble   Place: Bethesda
        Birth: 20 Sep 1891   Death: 7 May 1963   Burial: 10 May 1963
        Mort: Hilton   h/o Aubra Thompson Hubble
Site 5 Erma Louise Hubble Brown   w/o Richard Haffen Brown, divorced
        Birth: 19 Feb 1922   Death: 6 Mar 1989   Burial: 7 Mar 1989

Lot: 42 Upper Owner: Mrs. Della M. Neel
Site 1 Mary M. Neel   Place: Wheaton, MD
        Birth: 25 Aug 1906   Death: 2 Mar 1968   Burial: 5 Mar 1968
        Mort: Wm. Hilton   w/o Herbert O. Neel

Monocacy Cemetery, Beallsville, Montgomery County, Maryland 239

Site 2 Herbert O. Neel   Mort: Deal   Place: Washington, DC
Birth: 30 Aug 1903   Death: 23 Aug 1959   Burial: 26 Aug 1959
h/o Mary M. Neel, s/o Lewis Wiley & Della M. Neel
Site 3 Della M. Strowers Neel   Place: Washington, DC
Birth: 29 Nov 1883   Death: 6 Jun 1951   Burial: 12 Jun 1951
Mort: S.H. Hines Co.   w/o Lewis Wiley Neel
Site 4 Lewis Wiley Neel   Place: Washington, DC
Birth: 10 Oct 1881   Death: 1 Oct 1948   Burial: 4 Oct 1948
Mort: S.H. Hines Co.   h/o Della M. Neel
Site 5 Samuel Robert Neel   s/o L. Wiley & Della M. Neel
Birth: 9 May 1914   Death: 28 Dec 1975   TS: Corp. US Army WWII
Site 6 Archie Clifton Neel Sr.
Birth: 25 Apr 1912   Death: 12 Mar 1977   Burial: 17 Mar 1977
s/o Lewis W. & Della M. Neel   TS: Pvt. US Army WWII

Lot: 43 Lower   Owner: Mrs. Annie Rippeon
Site 3 Annie Laurie Rippeon   w/o Floyd L. Rippeon Sr.
Birth: 2 Apr 1907   Death: 14 Jun 1995   Burial: 17 Jun 1995
Site 4 Floyd Leslie Rippeon Sr.   Place: Nectsville??
Birth: 7 Feb 1900   Death: 16 Dec 1950   Burial: 24 Dec 1950
Mort: G.C. Barton   Reinterment
Site 5 William M. Rippeon Sr.
Birth: 17 Dec 1934   Death: 23 Oct 1983   Burial: 29 Oct 1983

Lot: 43 Upper   Owner: Mrs. Oscar G. & C.M. Rhodes
Site 3 Florence Ann Rhodes Trout   w/o Oscar G. Rhodes
Birth: 7 Nov 1893   Death: 4 Oct 1993   Burial: 18 Oct 1993
Site 4 Oscar G. Rhodes   Place: Doclerspm
Birth: 6 Oct 1885   Death: 19 Feb 1951   Burial: 21 Feb 1951
Mort: W.B. Hilton   h/o Flora A. Rhodes
Site 5 Clinton Monroe Rhodes   Place: Bucklodge
Birth: 9 Dec 1875   Death: 20 May 1959   Burial: 23 May 1959
Mort: Hilton   b/o Oscar G. Rhodes
Site 6 William M. Rhodes   Mort: W.B. Hilton   Place: Baltimore
Birth: 12 Oct 1870   Death: 30 Sep 1955   Burial: 3 Oct 1955

Lot: 44   Owner: Walter M. Butler, Jr.
Site 2 Walter Mason Butler Jr.   Place: Dickerson
Birth: 26 Jun 1915   Death: 20 Mar 1952   Burial: 24 Mar 1952
Mort: W.B. Hilton   s/o Walter M. & Rosa Cubitt Butler, age 37
Site 3 Rosa May Cubitt Butler   Place: Sykesville
Birth: 26 Jan 1882   Death: 5 Oct 1960   Burial: 8 Oct 1960
Mort: W.B. Hilton   w/o Walter M. Butler, Sr.
Site 4 Walter Mason Butler   Place: Dickerson
Birth: 3 May 1871   Death: 23 Mar 1951   Burial: 26 Mar 1951
Mort: W.B. Hilton   h/o Rosa May Cubitt Butler
Site 5 Hollis Edward Hopkins Sr.   h/o Dorothy Butler Hopkins
Birth: 26 Jul 1918   Death: 14 Feb 1976   Burial: 17 Feb 1976

Lot: 45 Lower   Owner: Miscellaneous

Site 7 Clara L. Lowe   Mort: Hilton   On stone with Melvin George Lowe
  Birth: 15 Sep 1874   Death: 6 Aug 1966   Burial: 9 Aug 1966
Site 8 Melvin George Lowe   Mort: R. A. Pumphrey   Place: Washington, DC
  Birth: 11 Sep 1882   Death: 2 Jan 1956   Burial: 4 Jan 1956
Site 9 Hazel A. Ward   TS: Mother   w/o Arthur Harry Ward
  Birth: 5 Apr 1903   Death: 22 Apr 1988   Burial: 25 Apr 1988
Site 10 Arthur Harry Ward   TS: Father   Place: Arlington
  Birth: 1887   Death: 9 May 1956   Burial: 13 May 1956
  Mort: Everly Funeral Home
Site 10 Ollie Virginia Woods   Place: Frederick Hospital
  Birth: 18 Oct 1944   Death: 18 Oct 1944   Burial: 19 Oct 1944
  Mort: W.B. Hilton   d/o Robert W. & Mary Waddell Woods
Site 11 Mary Virginia Waddell Woods   On stone with Robert W. Woods, age 76 yrs
  Birth: 1913   Death: 18 Jun 1990   Burial: 21 Jun 1990
Site 12 Robert W. E. Woods   Place: Boyds
  Birth: 1911   Death: 5 Aug 1956   Burial: 8 Aug 1956
  Mort: W.B. Hilton   h/o Mary Waddell Woods

Lot: 45 Upper   Owner: Charles V. Willard

Site 3 Annie Catherine Cubitt Willard   Place: Sykesville
  Birth: 1 May 1884   Death: 4 Apr 1960   Burial: 7 Apr 1960
  Mort: W.B. Hilton   w/o Charles V. Willard
Site 4 Charles Victor Willard   Place: Beallsville
  Birth: 27 Jul 1884   Death: 7 Dec 1963   Burial: 9 Dec 1963
  Mort: Hilton   h/o Annie Catherine Cubitt Willard
Site 5 Ellis A. Willard   Place: Beallsville
  Birth: 8 Nov 1880   Death: 2 Dec 1954   Burial: 4 Dec 1954
  Mort: W.B. Hilton   Brother of Charles V. Willard

Lot: 46   Owner: Maurice E. Bradshaw

Site 3 Tressie E. Dove Bradshaw   No marker   Place: Baltimore
  Birth: 22 Apr 1914   Death: 12 Dec 1954   Burial: 15 Dec 1954
  Mort: G.C. Barton   w/o Maurice E. Bradshaw
Site 4 Maurice E. Bradshaw   No marker   h/o Tressie Dove Bradshaw
  Birth: 7 Jul 1906   Death: 21 Jun 1978   Burial: 23 Jun 1978

Lot: 47 Lower   Owner: Miscellaneous

Site 7 Florence Brooks Snyder   Place: Cumberland
  Birth: 1904   Death: 17 May 1964   Burial: 20 May 1964
  Mort: Byron Kight   On stone with Rev. Jacob H. Snyder
Site 8 Rev. Jacob H. Snyder   Place: Lancaster, PA
  Birth: 1896   Death: 12 Dec 1967   Burial: 16 Dec 1967
  Mort: Carl Reynolds   h/o Florence Brooks Snyder
Site 9 Virginia Reeder Hewitt   No marker   Mort: W.B. Hilton
  Place: Frederick   Death: 23 May 1960   Burial: 26 May 1960
Site 10 Winfield Scott Edwards   Mort: W.B. Hilton   Place: Bethesda
  Birth: 1876   Death: 8 Nov 1960   Burial: 10 Nov 1960

Monocacy Cemetery, Beallsville, Montgomery County, Maryland 241

Site 11 Helen Gilliam Holcomb
Birth: 27 Jan 1917 Death: 15 Oct 1958
Mort: Hilton
Place: Washington, DC
Burial: 18 Oct 1958
w/o Clem Lee Holcomb

Site 12 Thomas Larry Barnhouse No marker Mort: Hilton
Place: Dickerson Death: 30 Dec 1957 Burial: 2 Jan 1958

Lot: 47 Upper Owner: Martin L. Poole
Site 1 Martin LeRoy Poole s/o Charles Edward & Emma Gertrude Young Poole
Birth: 25 Feb 1913 Death: 24 Sep 1995 Burial: 28 Sep 1995

Site 2 William Alfred Poole Mort: Etchison Place: Frederick, MD
Birth: 28 Dec 1909 Death: 6 Mar 1970 Burial: 9 Mar 1970
s/o Charles E. & Emma Gertrude Young Poole

Site 3 Emma Gertrude Young Poole Mort: Etchison Place: Frederick Hospital
Birth: 27 Jun 1884 Death: 1 Apr 1957 Burial: 4 Apr 1957
d/o Alfred & Lavinia Darr Young, w/o Charles Edward Poole

Site 4 Charles Edward Poole Place: Hagerstown, MD
Birth: 11 Jan 1880 Death: 18 Nov 1969 Burial: 21 Nov 1969
Mort: Etchison & Sons h/o Emma Gertrude Young Poole

Lot: 48 Owner: Miscellaneous
Site 1 Rose Anne May Whisman No marker Mort: Hilton
Place: Poolesville Death: 3 Oct 1957 Burial: 5 Oct 1957

Site 1 Wanda Jean Barnhouse No marker Mort: Hilton
Place: Frederick Death: 25 Dec 1957 Burial: 27 Dec 1957

Site 1 Nicole Marie Webber No marker Burial: 12 Dec 1983
Cause: Stillborn d/o Sue Ann Weber

Site 2 Joe Early Taylor No marker Mort: Hilton
Place: Poolesville Death: 22 Jan 1958 Burial: 23 Jan 1958

Site 3 Ellis Saunders Kidd Mort: F.C. Higinbotham Place: Buckeystown
Birth: 9 Aug 1932 Death: 8 May 1965 Burial: 13 May 1965

Site 4 Walter Steve Kidd Place: Poolesville
Birth: 10 Jul 1893 Death: 31 Jul 1957 Burial: 2 Aug 1957
Mort: Hilton TS: OHIO Pvt 495 Aero Const. Squad WWI

Site 5 Pearl Rebecca Mulligan No marker
Death: 11 Dec 1976 Burial: 15 Dec 1976

Site 6 Linwood Samuel Price Place: Adamstown
Birth: 9 Dec 1915 Death: 11 Nov 1956 Burial: 15 Nov 1956
Mort: W.B. Hilton TS: Maryland PFC Co. B 757 MP BN WWII

Site 7 Martha Etta Dove Place: Dickerson
Birth: 4 Nov 1884 Death: 19 Aug 1962 Burial: 22 Aug 1962
Mort: M.R. Etchison & Son On stone with John Harvey Dove

Site 8 John Harvey Dove Place: Bethesda
Birth: 21 Sep 1877 Death: 25 Dec 1957 Burial: 28 Dec 1957
Mort: Roy W. Barber h/o Martha Etta Dove

Site 9 Ellis Lee Baker Mort: Hilton Place: Adamstown
Birth: 1923 Death: 14 Aug 1963 Burial: 17 Aug 1963

Site 10 William Claude Baker Jr. Mort: Hilton Place: Urbana
Birth: 1919 Death: 20 Aug 1957 Burial: 23 Aug 1957

Monocacy Cemetery, Beallsville, Montgomery County, Maryland

Site 11 Rose Baker Mort: Hilton Place: Adamstown
Birth: 1893 Death: 8 Jul 1961 Burial: 11 Jul 1961
On stone with William Claude Baker
Site 12 William Claude Baker Mort: Hilton Place: Buckeystown
Birth: 1892 Death: 28 Apr 1965 Burial: 1 May 1965

Lot: 49 Owner: Miscellaneous
Site 1 Barbara Lee Corse w/o William C. Corse
Birth: 1934 Death: 29 Jul 1971 Burial: 31 Jul 1971
Site 3 James Brent Clark No marker Mort: Robt. Pumphrey
Place: Washington, DC Death: 4 Dec 1966 Burial: 5 Dec 1966
Site 4 Alice L.H. Clark No marker Mort. Robert A.
Place: Washington, DC Death: 3 Feb 1962 Burial: 6 Feb 1962
Site 4 Elizabeth Clarke No marker age 94 yrs.
 Death: 26 Jan 1977 Burial: 2 May 1988
Site 5 Edward M. Hoffacker h/o Mary I. Hoffacker
Birth: 21 May 1903 Death: 27 Sep 1984 Burial: 29 Sep 1984
Site 6 Mary I. Hoffacker On stone with Edward M. Hoffacker
Birth: 22 Jan 1902
Site 7 Clemens Riley Holcomb s/o Helen Gilliam & Clem Lee Holcomb
Birth: 13 Jun 1945 Death: 2 Mar 1973 Burial: 6 Mar 1973
Site 8 George W. Binnix Sr.
Birth: 16 Sep 1894 Death: 19 Sep 1983 Burial: 23 Sep 1983
Site 11 Ralph Walker Ruble On stone with Elvira Rudasill Ruble
Birth: 17 Nov 1911 Death: 16 Jan 1973 Burial: 19 Jan 1973
Site 12 Floyd Smith No marker Mort: Wm. Hilton
Place: Sykesville, MD Death: 22 Feb 1970 Burial: 25 Feb 1970

Lot: 50 Lower Owner: Miscellaneous
Site 12 Clem Lee Holcomb h/o Helen Gilliam Holcomb
Birth: 26 May 1910 Death: 24 Feb 1974 Burial: 28 Feb 1974

Lot: 50 Upper Owner: Miscellaneous
Site 4 Perry Oliver Butt h/o Susanna Butt
Birth: 8 Jan 1929 Death: 27 Feb 1996 Burial: 1 Mar 1996
Site 4 Douglas Eugene Phillips Mort: Hilton
Birth: 7 Apr 1952 Death: 27 Jul 1995 Burial: 25 Jul 1995
Site 6 Joseph Eugene Kidd
Birth: 16 Aug 1953 Death: 14 Mar 1974 Burial: 16 Mar 1974

Lot: 51 Owner: Miscellaneous
Site 5 Leslie Jackson Randall No marker
 Death: 29 May 1976 Burial: 2 Jun 1976
Site 6 Alfred Lee Pearson s/o Alfred & Myrtle Pearson No marker
 Death: 28 Apr 1974 Burial: 4 May 1974

Lot: 52 Lower Owner: Miscellaneous
Site 4 Claire Elizabeth Painter Ruble d/o Nellie & Clarence Painter
Birth: 30 Nov 1914 Death: 21 May 1987 Burial: 25 May 1987
On stone with Elbert Kyle Ruble

Monocacy Cemetery, Beallsville, Montgomery County, Maryland

Site 5 Elbert Kyle Ruble   h/o Claire Painter Ruble
        Birth: 25 Mar 1913   Death: 3 Sep 1985   Burial: 6 Sep 1985
Site 6 Lester Franklin Carter   No marker   Mort: Etchison & Son
        Place: Frederick, MD   Death: 13 Apr 1971   Burial: 16 Apr 1971

Lot: 52 Upper   Owner: Miscellaneous
Site 1 Roger William Beall   No marker   Mort: W.W. Chambers
        Place: Silver Spring, MD Death: 27 Feb 1971   Burial: 3 Mar 1971
Site 4 Sallie Sutphin Tolbert Pridgen   TS: Mother
        Birth: 5 Jul 1916   Death: 14 Jun 1985   Burial: 14 Jun 1985
Site   Jannette Dean Tolbert   Birth: 11 Oct 1943   Death: 1 May 1990
        TS: Daughter   On stone with Sallie Sutphin Tolbert Pridgen
Site 5 Leonard N. Tolbert   Mort: Tyson Wheeler   Place: Bethesda, MD
        Birth: 1912   Death: 5 Jan 1971   Burial: 9 Jan 1971
Site 6 Arnold Melvin Williams   Place: Vallejo, CA
        Birth: 22 Sep 1926   Death: 3 Jun 1970   Burial: 8 Jun 1970
        Mort: Wm. Hilton   s/o Kelly P. Williams

Lot: 53 Lower   Owner: Miscellaneous
Site 1 Marie Ann Nicholson Atterton   Mort: Hilton
        Birth: 1934   Death: 11 Jul 1991
Site 4 Jerry Moore Leith   No marker   Death: 2 Jun 1994
Site 5 Ruth E. Leith   On stone with Thomas G. Leith, age 75 yrs
        Birth: 1 Jun 1913   Death: 7 Aug 1988   Burial: 10 Aug 1988
Site 6 David Harrison Leith   Mort: Wm. Hilton   Place: Bethesda, MD
        Birth: 9 Mar 1949   Death: 23 May 1971   Burial: 27 May 1971

Lot: 53 Upper   Owner: Miscellaneous
Site 1 Terry Annette Carr   d/o William H. Carr
        Birth: 6 Jul 1976   Death: 19 Nov 1976   Burial: 23 Nov 1976
Site 3 Harry Lee Mentzer   TS: Son
        Birth: 16 May 1923   Death: 10 Feb 1990   Burial: 14 Feb 1990
Site 4 Julia Ellen Mentzer   TS: Mother   On stone with Harry Lee Mentzer
        Birth: 2 Apr 1896   Death: 10 Jul 1971   Burial: 14 Jul 1971
Site 6 Jerry Lee Jarvis   Place: Frederick, MD
        Birth: 1949   Death: 24 Jan 1971   Burial: 26 Jan 1971
        Mort: Wm. Hilton   h/o Linda Moore Jarvis

Lot: 54 Lower   Owner: Miscellaneous
Site 6 John Edward Davidson Jr.
        Birth: 3 Jul 1946   Death: 12 Jul 1995   Burial: 14 Jul 1995

Lot: 55 Lower   Owner: Miscellaneous
Site 1 Frank W. Whisman Jr.   On stone with Ruth A. Whisman
        Birth: 23 Jul 1930   Death: 19 Dec 1991   Burial: 21 Dec 1991

Lot: 55 Upper   Owner: Miscellaneous
Site 3 William Crawford McGrady
        Birth: 6 Jan 1933   Death: 3 Nov 1995   Burial: 7 Nov 1995

Site 4 Mary E. McGrady   On stone with William Crawford McGrady
        Birth: 1941   Death: 1989   Burial: 23 May 1989

Lot: 56 Lower   Owner: Miscellaneous
Site 1 Joseph M. Deadrick
        Birth: 26 Jun 1928   Death: 29 Nov 1989   Burial: 2 Dec 1989
Site 2 Maurice Allen Downs
        Birth: 5 Jul 1952   Death: 11 Aug 1982   Burial: 16 Aug 1982
Site 3 Marie Edith Leppo Fogle   w/o Gilbert Fogle
        Birth: 1924   Death: 14 Dec 1989   Burial: 18 Dec 1989
Site 4 Thomas E. Newman
        Birth: 23 Feb 1929   Death: 14 Dec 1982   Burial: 18 Dec 1982
Site 5 Minnie Pearl Mumma   No marker
        Birth: 9 Mar 1949   Death: 23 Mar 1976   Burial: 27 Mar 1976
Site 6 Roland K. Stottlemyer   s/o Herbert Stottlemyer & Mrs. Helen Johnson
        Birth: 8 Jan 1910   Death: 14 Jan 1975   Burial: 18 Jan 1975

Lot: 56 Upper   Owner: Miscellaneous
Site 2 Minnie Pearl Smith Cole   w/o Paul M. Cole, age 61
        Birth: 1917   Death: 18 Jan 1979   Burial: 23 Jan 1979
Site 4 Julia Frances Linton
        Birth: 9 Apr 1928   Death: 14 Sep 1989   Burial: 18 Sep 1989
Site 5 Callie Frances Anders   On stone with Willie Anders
        Birth: 30 Jan 1907   Death: 27 Dec 1973   Burial: 31 Dec 1973
Site 6 Willie J. Anders   h/o Callie Frances Anders
        Birth: 1 Jun 1909   Death: 2 Aug 1994   Burial: 8 Aug 1994

Lot: 57 Upper   Owner: Virginia & Mable Gravely
Site 3 Hosley J. Gravely Jr.   On stone with Virginia M. Gravely
        Birth: 26 Apr 1930   Death: 9 May 1996   Burial: 18 May 1996

Monocacy Cemetery, Beallsville, Montgomery County, Maryland   245

Row L

Lot: 1 Lower   Owner: Charles W. Fawley
- Site 2 Charles William Fawley Jr.
  - Birth: 24 Jul 1905   Death: 1 Sep 1972   Burial: 4 Sep 1972
- Site 3 Ada Catherine Fawley   TS: Mother   Place: Poolesville
  - Birth: 1880   Death: 18 Jun 1935   Burial: 20 Jun 1935
  - Mort: Hilton & Hall   On stone with Charles W. Fawley, Sr.
- Site 4 Charles William Fawley Sr.   Place: Rockville
  - Birth: 1879   Death: 16 Dec 1961   Burial: 19 Dec 1961
  - Mort: Tyson Wheeler   TS: Father   h/o Ada Catherine Fawley
- Site 5 Eileen B. Fawley   On stone with Robert Berkley Fawley
  - Birth: 12 Feb 1901   Death: 20 Jul 1982   Burial: 23 Jul 1982
- Site 6 Robert Berkley Fawley   h/o Eileen B. Fawley
  - Birth: 11 Apr 1907   Death: 27 Aug 1979   Burial: 30 Aug 1979

Lot: 1 Upper   Owner: W.C. Campbell
- Site 3 William C. Campbell   Place: Charlottesville, VA
  - Birth: 16 Jun 1866   Death: 13 May 1948   Burial: 16 May 1948
  - Mort: Woodward Funeral Home   h/o Nell James Mundy Campbell
- Site 4 Nell James Mundy Campbell   Place: Staunton, VA
  - Birth: 22 Feb 1880   Death: 19 Sep 1954   Burial: 21 Sep 1954
  - Mort: Woodward Funeral Home   TS: w/o William C. Campbell

Lot: 2 Lower   Owner: Edwin L. & Dorothy H. Yates
- Site 1 Adelaide Reed Yates   Mort: W.H. Hines Co.   Place: Washington, DC
  - Birth: 23 Dec 1873   Death: 25 Mar 1941   Burial: 27 Mar 1941
- Site 3 Mary Lee Waters Haddox   Place: Washington, DC
  - Birth: 27 Jun 1875   Death: 11 Jun 1969   Burial: 14 Jun 1969
  - Mort: Robert Pumphrey   On stone with Horace B. Haddox MD
- Site 4 Horace B. Haddox, MD   Place: Gaithersburg
  - Birth: 10 Jan 1867   Death: 24 Feb 1930   Burial: 27 Feb 1930
  - Mort: E.C. Gartmer   h/o Mary Lee Waters Haddox
- Site 5 Dorothy Haddox Yates   On stone with Edwin Langhorn Yates
  - Birth: 5 May 1903   Death: 23 Jul 1990   Burial: 26 Jul 1990
- Site 6 Edwin Langhorn Yates   h/o Dorothy Haddox Yates
  - Birth: 5 Jan 1903   Death: 14 Apr 1972   Burial: 18 Apr 1972

Lot: 2 Upper   Owner: Anna Waters Thompson
- Site 2 Lucy Waters Lonergan   Mort: R. A. Pumphrey   Place: Washington, DC
  - Birth: 18 Dec 1883   Death: 15 Jan 1950   Burial: 18 Jan 1950
- Site 4 Dr. Joseph Lawn Thompson Jr., MD   h/o Cassie Parker Thompson
  - Birth: 30 Mar 1909   Death: 8 Dec 1994   Burial: 22 May 1995
- Site 4 Anna Waters Thompson   Place: Washington, DC
  - Birth: 12 Feb 1881   Death: 25 May 1960   Burial: 26 May 1960
  - Mort: Robert A. Pumphrey   On stone with Joseph Lawn Thompson

Monocacy Cemetery, Beallsville, Montgomery County, Maryland

Site 5 Joseph Lawn Thompson, MD
    Birth: 16 Oct 1873   Death: 3 Sep 1946
    Mort: W.R. Pumphrey
    Place: Washington, DC
    Burial: 5 Sep 1946
    h/o Anna Waters Thompson

Lot: 3   Owner: Thomas W. & Walter E. Perry
Site 3 Mary Alice Perry
    Birth: 8 Jul 1900   Death: 5 Sep 1990
    w/o Thomas W. Perry
    Burial: 7 Sep 1990
Site 4 Thomas W. Perry
    Birth: 20 Oct 1883   Death: 13 Oct 1962
    Mort: Robert A. Pumphrey
    Place: Washington, DC
    Burial: 16 Oct 1962
    h/o Mary Alice Allnutt Perry
Site 9 Sallie Fontaine Perry
    Birth: 2 Oct 1882   Death: 20 Nov 1931
    Mort: W.R. Pumphrey
    Place: Washington, DC
    Burial: 22 Nov 1931
    TS: [1st] w/o Walter E. Perry
Site 10 Walter E. Perry   Mort: Samuel J. Scotie   Place: Lake Worth, FL
    Birth: 16 Nov 1874   Death: 17 Aug 1957   Burial: 20 Aug 1957
    h/o Sallie Fontaine Perry & Willie Greene Day Perry
Site 11 Willie Greene Day Perry
    Birth: 28 Mar 1897   Death: 14 Dec 1969
    Mort: Robert Pumphrey
    Place: Delray Beach, FL
    Burial: 20 Jan 1970
    TS: [2nd] w/o Walter E. Perry

Lot: 4   Owner: Miscellaneous
Site   Elisha Miles   No marker   Mort: Hilton & Price
    Place: Frederick   Death: 1 Oct 1933   Burial: 2 Oct 1933

Lot: 4 Lower   Owner: William B. White
Site 2 William B. White
    Birth: 1868   Death: 30 Apr 1937
    Mort: W.B. Hilton
    Place: Barnesville
    Burial: 2 May 1937
    h/o Ollie White
Site 3 Ollie White
    Birth: 1866   Death: 6 Oct 1932
    Mort: W.T. Hilton & Sons
    Place: Frederick
    Burial: 8 Oct 1932
    w/o William B. White

Lot: 4 Upper   Owner: George A. Roberts
Site 3 Cleta Alma Dove Roberts
    Birth: 7 Nov 1911   Death: 26 Jun 1976
    On stone with George A. Roberts
    Burial: 1 Jul 1976
Site 4 George A. Roberts
    Birth: 9 Oct 1910   Death: 19 Feb 1977
    h/o Cleta Alma Roberts
    Burial: 22 Feb 1977

Lot: 4A   Owner: William B., Robert W. & Benoni D. Allnutt
Site 3 Robert Wilkerson Allnutt Jr.
    Birth: 26 Nov 1906   Death: 28 Sep 1980
    h/o Elizabeth S. Allnutt
    Burial: 30 Sep 1980
Site 3 Robert Wilkerson Allnutt III
    Birth: 12 Dec 1944   Death: 8 Apr 1990
    Burial: 15 Apr 1990
Site 5 William Baker Allnutt
    Birth: 12 Nov 1898   Death: 10 Feb 1978
    h/o Harriette Sproul Allnutt
    Burial: 13 Feb 1978
Site 6 Harriette Sproul Allnutt
    Birth: 8 Dec 1901   Death: 28 Nov 1976
    w/o William B. Allnutt
    Burial: 1 Dec 1976

Monocacy Cemetery, Beallsville, Montgomery County, Maryland

Lot: 5 Owner: George W. Morrison

Site 1 Alfred Christie Jr.
Birth: 30 Apr 1893
Mort: Tyson Wheeler
Death: 16 Dec 1963
Place: Olney
Burial: 19 Dec 1963

Site 2 Helen M. Christie
Birth: 18 Apr 1894
Death: 7 May 1966
Mort: Ernest C. Gartner

Site 3 Sarah Florence Williams
Place: Silver Spring, MD
No marker
Death: 29 Jun 1968
Mort: Arthur Walters
Burial: 2 Jul 1968

Site 5 Marjorie Ann Christie
Death: 1 Apr 1985
Burial: 5 Apr 1985

Site 8 George W. Morrison
Birth: 28 Dec 1869
Mort: S.H. Hines Co.
Death: 5 Feb 1941
Place: Washington, DC
Burial: 8 Feb 1941

Site 9 Mary McGlue Morrison
Birth: 11 Jun 1870
Mort: S.H. Hines Co.
Death: 6 Aug 1936
Place: Washington, DC
Burial: 10 Aug 1936

Site 10 Esther E. Morrison
Birth: 28 Oct 1897
Mort: S.H. Hines Co.
Death: 4 Aug 1929
Place: Washington, DC
Burial: 6 Aug 1929

Site 11 Esther May Christie
Birth: 16 May 1918
Mort: E.C. Gartner
Death: 8 Nov 1931
Place: Washington, DC
Burial: 10 Nov 1931

Lot: 5A Upper Owner: Leroy Thompson

Site 6 Leroy Thompson
Birth: 30 Dec 1919
Death: 13 Oct 1994
On stone with Dorothy M. Thompson
Burial: 17 Oct 1994

Lot: 6 Owner: M.C. Fink

Site 1 Charles Ernest Fink, Jr.
Birth: 1900
Death: 5 Feb 1974
h/o Sarah W. Fink
Burial: 9 Feb 1974

Site 2 Sarah W. Fink
Birth: 22 Jun 1905
Death: 17 Jul 1981
On stone with Charles Ernest Fink, Jr.
Burial: 20 Jul 1981

Site 4 Doris Jeanette Fink
Birth: 6 Jul 1925
Mort: W.B. Hilton
Death: 11 Jun 1943
Place: Washington, DC
Burial: 12 Jun 1943

Site 5 Walter Lee Fink
Birth: 28 Feb 1904
Mort: Hilton
Death: 9 Sep 1967
Place: Washington Hospital
Burial: 12 Sep 1967

Site 6 Sallie Eloise Fink
Birth: 4 Nov 1906
Death: 25 May 1996
Burial: 29 May 1996

Site 9 Milton Colfax Fink
Birth: 1868
Mort: W.B. Hilton
Death: 14 Sep 1954
Place: Barnesville
Burial: 18 Jun 1954
TS: h/o Lillie B. Fink

Site 10 Lillie B. Fink
Birth: 1871
Mort: W.T. Hilton & Sons
Death: 26 Jan 1927
Place: Frederick
Burial: 29 Jan 1927
TS: w/o Milton Colfax Fink

Site 11 Paul M. Fink
Birth: 1901
Mort: W.R. Zern
Death: 11 Feb 1956
Place: W. Palm Beach, FL
Burial: 15 Feb 1956
TS: h/o Mary Fink

Lot: 6A Lower Owner: John F. McAuliffe

Site 1 Ben F. Vickers
Birth: 30 Aug 1903
Death: 26 Oct 1973
Burial: 30 Oct 1973

Lot: 6A Upper Owner: Mr. & Mrs. Peter Simon
Site 4 Catherine Ann Simon
Birth: 23 Feb 1959   Death: 3 Jan 1969
Mort: Tyson Wheeler
Place: Bethesda, MD
Burial: 6 Jan 1969
d/o Peter Simon

Lot: 7 Owner: Charles B., Charles G., & Richard B. Sellman
Site 3 Charles Byron Sellman
Birth: 22 Jan 1881   Death: 28 Feb 1947
Mort: W.B. Hilton
Place: Dickerson
Burial: 3 Mar 1947
h/o Sarah Griffith Sellman
Site 4 Sarah Griffith Sellman
Birth: 14 Jun 1884   Death: 30 Oct 1963
Mort: Robert A. Pumphrey
Place: Aberdeen, MD
Burial: 2 Nov 1963
w/o Charles Byron Sellman
Site 7 Richard Brooke Sellman
Birth: 12 Feb 1915   Death: 8 Feb 1997
h/o Margaret Burns Sellman
Burial: 15 Feb 1997
Site 8 Margaret Burns Sellman
Birth: 31 May 1917   Death: 9 Oct 1985
w/o Richard B. Sellman
Burial: 11 Oct 1985

Lot: 7A Lower Owner: Mrs. Mary B. Vann
Site 1 Priscilla Tobias
Birth: 26 Aug 1902   Death: 25 Aug 1983   Burial: 30 Aug 1983
Site 1 Priscilla Ann Tobias
Birth: 15 Sep 1928   Death: 2 Oct 1993   Burial: 30 Nov 1993
Site 5 Mary Beall Bridges Vann
Birth: 20 Dec 1904   Death: 20 Mar 1973
TS: w/o Dr. Homer King Vann
Burial: 22 Mar 1973
Site 6 Homer King Vann, MD
Birth: 21 Jan 1902   Death: 12 Jun 1969
Mort: Joseph Gawler
Place: Baltimore, MD
Burial: 14 Jun 1969
h/o Mary Beall Bridges Vann

Lot: 7A Upper Owner: Mrs. P.D. Ford
Site 1 Estella C. Bucknam   Mort: John H. Walters Place: Takoma Park, MD
Birth: 13 Jun 1874   Death: 22 Mar 1969   Burial: 24 Mar 1969
Site 2 Pearl Dean Ford   TS: Father   Place: Washington, DC
Birth: 15 Jul 1895   Death: 2 Apr 1971   Burial: 5 Apr 1971
Mort: Takoma Park Funeral Home   h/o Violet Ford
Site 3 Violet Estella Ford   TS: Mother   On stone with Pearl Dean Ford
Birth: 31 Jul 1905   Death: 27 Oct 1989   Burial: 30 Oct 1989
Site 4 Melanie Joy Poetzman   TS: d/o Robert L. & Margery L. Poetzman
Birth: 28 Jan 1965   Death: 5 Sep 1976   Burial: 8 Sep 1976

Lot: 8 Lower Owner: Charles R. & Zada F. Bodmer
Site 3 Charles Rozier Bodmer   Mort: Hilton   Place: Bethesda
Birth: 15 Nov 1892   Death: 3 Jul 1966   Burial: 6 Jul 1966
h/o Zada Ryman Bodmer   TS: MD PFC 313 AMB Co. 79 Div. WWI SS
Site 4 Zada Florence Bodmer   w/o Charles Rozier Bodmer
Birth: 1901   Death: 17 Jan 1994   Burial: 25 Jan 1994

Lot: 8 Upper Owner: Campbell & Myerly (All on one stone)
Site 2 Fred Munger Campbell   h/o Jessie Bodmer Campbell
Birth: 1899   Death: 27 Apr 1986   Burial: 30 Apr 1986

Monocacy Cemetery, Beallsville, Montgomery County, Maryland 249

Site 3 Jessie Bodmer Campbell   On side with Fred M. Campbell
        Birth: 1897   Death: 12 Apr 1989   Burial: 14 Apr 1989
Site 4 Minnie Louise Bodmer Myerly   On side with Harry Stockton Myerly
        Birth: 1895   Death: 25 May 1996   Burial: 29 May 1996
Site 5 Rev. Harry Stockton Myerly   h/o Minnie Bodmer Myerly
        Birth: 8 Dec 1897   Death: 23 Nov 1988   Burial: 25 Nov 1988

Lot: 8A Owner: W.K. Matthews Family
Site 3 Eleanor Mae Luhn Matthews   w/o Walter Kirts Matthews
        Birth: 30 Mar 1889   Death: 14 Mar 1976   Burial: 17 Mar 1976
Site 4 Walter Kirts Matthews   Place: Frederick, MD
        Birth: 2 Oct 1889   Death: 1 Sep 1969   Burial: 3 Sep 1969
        Mort: Wm. Hilton   h/o Eleanor Mae Luhn Matthews
Site 7 Charles Elmer Orme   h/o Vivian Matthews Orme
        Birth: 6 Mar 1914   Death: 8 Nov 1988   Burial: 11 Nov 1988
Site 12 Earl Wendell Lewis   h/o Doris Matthews Lewis
        Birth: 8 Mar 1928   Death: 10 Oct 1995   Burial: 20 Oct 1995

Lot: 9 Lower Owner: James E. Brooks
Site 4 James Evans Brooks   On stone with Anna Titus Brooks
        Birth: 12 Apr 1902   Death: 16 Aug 1979   Burial: 20 Aug 1979

Lot: 9 Upper Owner: Margaret Turner Keller
Site 4 Margaret Turner Keller   Mort: Robert Pumphrey
        Place: Sykesville, MD Death: 26 Feb 1971   Burial: 1 Mar 1971
        w/o Ira E. Keller   No marker
Site 5 Ira E. Keller   Mort: Robert A.
        Place: Bethesda   Death: 3 Feb 1961   Burial: 10 Feb 1961
        h/o Margaret Turner Keller   No marker
Site 6 Alton Higgins Keller   Mort: Robert A.   Place: Washington, DC
        Birth: 9 Jul 1912   Death: 8 Feb 1959   Burial: 11 Feb 1959

Lot: 9A Lower Owner: William M. & Julia B. Waddell
Site 1 Charles Offutt
        Birth: 15 Aug 1907   Death: 22 Nov 1981   Burial: 25 Nov 1981
Site 1 Elsie L. Offutt   On stone with Charles E. Offutt
        Birth: 11 Apr 1910   Death: 9 Jan 1990   Burial: 12 Jan 1990
Site 2 Julia B. Waddell   w/o Woolwine Waddell
        Birth: 17 Oct 1907   Death: 6 Nov 1994   Burial: 9 Nov 1994
Site 3 W.M. (Woolie) Waddell Birth: 29 Aug 1915   Death: 4 May 1997
Site 5 Elizabeth Nichols Thompson   No marker
        Birth: 25 Feb 1917   Death: 14 Nov 1995   Burial: 20 Nov 1995

Lot: 9A Upper Owner: Mrs. Charles Thompson
Site 3 Hilda M. Nichols
        Birth: 18 Oct 1889   Death: 16 Nov 1975   Burial: 18 Nov 1975
Site 4 Clarence N. Nichols   Mort: Pumphrey   Place: Washington, DC
        Birth: 24 Apr 1888   Death: 5 Sep 1969   Burial: 8 Sep 1969
        h/o Hilda M. Nichols

Site 6 Dr. Charles Waters Thompson
  Birth: 30 Jun 1915   Death: 23 Oct 1995   Burial: 25 Oct 1995
  TS: LCDR US Navy WWII, Physician & Teacher

Lot: 10 Lower   Owner: Miscellaneous
Site 5 Maude Gross Darby   On stone with Thomas Gordon Darby
  Birth: 19 Mar 1904   Death: 8 Jan 1991   Burial: 14 Jan 1991
Site 6 Thomas Gordon Darby, Sr.   h/o Maude G. Darby
  Birth: 26 Oct 1912   Death: 4 Jun 1987   Burial: 8 Jun 1987

Lot: 10 Upper   Owner: Ray C. & June R. Bodmer
Site 2 Debra Kay Bodmer   Mort: Hilton   Place: Ellicott City
  Birth: 26 Oct 1960   Death: 21 Jun 1961   Burial: 24 Jun 1961
  d/o Ray C. & June R. Bodmer

Lot: 10A Lower   Owner: Miscellaneous
Site 5 Annie Eleanor Nicholson Ward   On stone with John Newton Ward
  Birth: 17 Aug 1904   Death: 15 Jan 1988   Burial: 19 Jan 1988
Site 6 John Newton Ward   h/o Annie Eleanor Nicholson Ward
  Birth: 21 Nov 1900   Death: 29 Aug 1977   Burial: 1 Sep 1977

Lot: 10A Upper   Owner: Doris B. & Alfred W. Stoner
Site 2 Alfred W. Stoner   h/o Doris Bodmer Stoner
  Birth: 17 Feb 1903   Death: 2 Nov 1978   Burial: 4 Nov 1978
Site 3 Doris Bodmer Stoner   Place: Prince Geo. Hospital
  Birth: 15 May 1911   Death: 2 Apr 1971   Burial: 7 Apr 1971
  Mort: F. Gasch's & Sons   On stone with Alfred W. Stoner

Lot: 11 Lower   Owner: Norman A. Grant
Site 3 Genevieve K. Grant   Place: Washington, DC
  Birth: 1912   Death: 29 Jul 1963   Burial: 1 Aug 1963
  Mort: Joseph Gawler   w/o Norman A. Grant
Site 4 Norman A. Grant
  Birth: 17 Apr 1915   Death: 19 Jul 1982   Burial: 22 Jul 1982
Site 5 Eileen J. Grant   No marker   w/o Norman A. Grant
                              Death: 5 Sep 1994   Burial: 12 Sep 1994

Lot: 11 Upper   Owner: A. Robertson & Alvin L. Evans
Site 4 Alvin Lee Evans   h/o Wilma E. Evans
  Birth: 16 Jan 1925   Death: 27 Oct 1981   Burial: 30 Oct 1981
Site 6 Atlee R. Robertson
  Birth: 18 Oct 1902   Death: 6 Nov 1973   Burial: 8 Nov 1973

Lot: 11A   Owner: Dorothy J. & Charles W. Elgin
Site 6 Charles William Elgin Sr.   On stone with Dorothy Jones Elgin
  Birth: 18 Sep 1915   Death: 18 Jan 1997   Burial: 21 Jan 1997

Lot: 12 Lower   Owner: Mr. & Mrs. John Ammerman
Site 3 Raymond S. Hallman   h/o Neva B. Hallman
  Birth: 31 Jan 1912   Death: 20 Oct 1973   Burial: 23 Oct 1973

Monocacy Cemetery, Beallsville, Montgomery County, Maryland   251

Site 4 Neva B. Hallman   On stone with Raymond S. Hallman
        Birth: 8 May 1904   Death: 30 Jun 1985   Burial: 3 Jul 1985

Lot: 12A   Owner: C.L. Poole, Eugene Hurd, & C.E. White
Site 3 Maxine E. Ruffner White   TS: Mom   On stone with Charles E. White
        Birth: 24 Dec 1916   Death: 24 Feb 1972   Burial: 26 Feb 1972
Site 4 Charles Ernest White Jr.   TS: Dad   h/o Maxine E. Ruffner White
        Birth: 19 Feb 1913   Death: 31 Oct 1991   Burial: 2 Nov 1991
Site 6 Eugene Hurd Jr.
        Birth: 27 Jun 1937   Death: 3 Jun 1990   Burial: 6 Jun 1990

Lot: 25   Owner: Charles G. & Nellie B. Cooley
Site 3 Dr. Charles Garrett Cooley TS: Veterinarian   h/o Nellie White Cooley
        Birth: 5 Apr 1904   Death: 17 Aug 1979   Burial: 21 Aug 1979
Site 4 Nellie B. White Cooley   TS: w/o Dr. Charles Garret Cooley
        Birth: 8 Dec 1908   Death: 3 Nov 1975   Burial: 5 Nov 1975

Lot: 27 Lower   Owner: Betty Anne Ford
Site 3 Lewis Eugene Ford   TS: Son
        Birth: 27 Jul 1950   Death: 1 Mar 1982   Burial: 4 Mar 1982
Site 5 Betty Ann Ford   No marker   w/o Lewis E. Ford
        Birth: 15 Sep 1926   Death: 29 Nov 1994   Burial: 1 Dec 1994
Site 6 Altus Lacy Ford   TS: Father
        Birth: 23 Jul 1925   Death: 30 Mar 1977

Lot: 27 Upper   Owner: J. Edward & Mary Louise Day
Site 4 James Edward Day   h/o Mary Louise Day, age 82 yrs.
        No marker   Death: 29 Oct 1996   Burial: 10 Nov 1996
Site 5 James Edward Day Jr.
        Birth: 11 Dec 1948   Death: 5 Nov 1975   Burial: 8 Nov 1975
        s/o Edward & Mary Louise Day   TS: ATN 1 US Navy

Lot: 28 Lower   Owner: Mrs. Earl N. Heap, Jr.
Site 4 Olga Terecia Heap   On stone with Earl Nicklin Heap, Jr.
        Birth: 17 Apr 1897   Death: 12 Jul 1981   Burial: 15 Jul 1981
Site 5 Earl Nicklin Heap Jr.   Place: Altoona, PA
        Birth: 18 Feb 1898   Death: 29 Oct 1969   Burial: 1 Nov 1969
        Mort: Francis A. Stevens   h/o Olga Tericia Heap
Site 6 Patricia June Heap Heaton
        Birth: 21 Jun 1928   Death: 6 Feb 1989   Burial: 9 Feb 1989

Lot: 28 Upper   Owner: Irvin N. & Margaret K. Wright
Site 1 Margaret Ireland Kimball   TS: Mother of Margaret K. Wright
        Birth: 10 May 1878   Death: 11 Jun 1974   Burial: 14 Jun 1974
Site 2 Florence Hamilton Irvin Wright   TS: w/o E. Nisbet Wright
        Birth: 15 Jul 1881   Death: 23 Jun 1975   Burial: 26 Jun 1975
Site 3 Margaret K. Wright   w/o Irvin N. Wright
        Birth: 19 Nov 1903   Death: 14 Aug 1979   Burial: 20 Aug 1979
Site 4 Irvin N. Wright   h/o Margaret K. Wright
        Birth: 17 Jun 1903   Death: 27 Dec 1983   Burial: 30 Dec 1983

Monocacy Cemetery, Beallsville, Montgomery County, Maryland

Lot: 29 Lower   Owner: Miscellaneous
- Site 1   Mary Elizabeth Ricketts Johnson   On stone with Jacob M. Johnson
  - Birth: 3 Jun 1909   Death: 25 May 1993   Burial: 28 May 1993
- Site 2   Jacob Middleton Johnson   h/o Mary E. Ricketts Johnson
  - Birth: 23 Feb 1900   Death: 27 Aug 1977   Burial: 30 Aug 1977
- Site 4   John R. Beach   On stone with Virginia Myrtle Beach
  - Birth: 30 Nov 1922   Death: 22 Oct 1977   Burial: 26 Oct 1977
- Site 5   LeRoy Davis   Mort: Hilton
  - Birth: 1931   Death: 14 Jan 1978   Burial: 20 Jan 1978
  - s/o Ray & Effi McDonough Davis, sister of Myrtle Beach
- Site 6   James E. Steiner
  - Birth: 7 Jan 1908   Death: 14 May 1978   Burial: 17 May 1978

Lot: 29 Upper   Owner: Agnes M. & James N. Beach
- Site 1   John C. Beach   Place: Rockville, MD
  - Birth: 4 Mar 1894   Death: 12 Feb 1970   Burial: 16 Feb 1970
  - Mort: Tyson Wheeler   h/o Agnes Mary Beach
- Site 2   Agnes Mary Beach   On stone with John C. Beach
  - Birth: 29 Apr 1906   Death: 29 Nov 1975   Burial: 3 Dec 1975
- Site 3   James Norman Beach Sr.
  - Birth: 8 Sep 1925   Death: 10 Oct 1992   Burial: 14 Oct 1992

Lot: 30 Lower   Owner: Howard L. Cook
- Site 4   Helen Louise Cook   w/o Howard L. Cook
  - Birth: 15 Aug 1906   Death: 22 May 1978   Burial: 26 May 1978
- Site 4   Howard Lee Cook, Sr.   h/o Helen L. Cook
  - Birth: 13 Aug 1905   Death: 3 Jun 1981   Burial: 6 Jun 1981

Lot: 31 Lower   Owner: Miscellaneous
- Site 3   Dorothy Chiswell Walker
  - Birth: 12 Dec 1922   Death: 16 Sep 1990   Burial: 19 Sep 1990
- Site 5   Laura Elizabeth Walker   d/o Barbara & Gary Walker Jr.
  - Birth: 25 May 1980   Death: 6 Jun 1980   Burial: 11 Jun 1980

Lot: 31 Upper   Owner: Miscellaneous
- Site 1   Charles Harold Pearson   On stone with Margaret Louise Pearson Kidd
  - Birth: 21 Jul 1909   Death: 18 Nov 1988   Burial: 22 Nov 1988
- Site 3   Raymond K. Harvey   h/o Laura I. Harvey
  - Birth: 27 Mar 1901   Death: 10 Dec 1980   Burial: 13 Dec 1980
- Site 4   Laura Irene Harvey   On stone with Raymond K. Harvey
  - Birth: 1902   Death: 31 Jul 1991   Burial: 3 Aug 1991

Lot: 32 Lower   Owner: Martin A. & Anna R. Wiseman
- Site 3   Anna Roberson Wiseman   On stone with Martin Andrew Wiseman
  - Birth: 22 Sep 1927   Death: 16 Oct 1993   Burial: 19 Oct 1993
- Site 4   Martin Andrew Wiseman   h/o Anna Roberson Wiseman
  - Birth: 25 Mar 1922   Death: 14 Dec 1988   Burial: 17 Dec 1988

Monocacy Cemetery, Beallsville, Montgomery County, Maryland   253

Lot: 32 Upper   Owner: Leonard H.. & Fannie N. Roberson
Site 2   Ola M. Jarrett
     Birth: 1 Mar 1990   Death: 30 Sep 1991   Burial: 3 Oct 1991

Lot: 33 Lower   Owner: Mr. & Mrs. Irving Dixon
Site 6   Irving Doyle Dixon   TS: M SGT US Army WWII Korea
     Birth: 4 Jul 1922   Death: 21 May 1990   Burial: 26 May 1990
     On stone with Irene F. Dixon

Lot: 33 Upper   Owner: Edna M. Stowers
Site 6   Charles Wade Stowers Sr.
     Birth: 14 Apr 1908   Death: 20 Aug 1979   Burial: 23 Aug 1979
     TS: PVT US Army WWII   On stone with Edna Warfield Stowers

Lot: 34 Lower   Owner: Miscellaneous
Site 1   Basil Bowman   TS: PVT US Army WWII
     Birth: 9 Feb 1917   Death: 11 Apr 1979   Burial: 16 Apr 1979
Site 2   Dock B. Bowman   No marker
     Birth: 31 Oct 1925   Burial: 14 Apr 1989
Site 5   John Hollyday Dawson   h/o Dorothy Wootton Dawson
     Birth: 2 Aug 1905   Death: 3 Oct 1995   Burial: 7 Oct 1995
Site 6   Dorothy Wootton Dawson
     Birth: 25 Jun 1913   Death: 13 May 1993   w/o John H. Dawson

Lot: 34 Upper   Owner: Miscellaneous
Site 3   Walter Jackson Lewis   TS: POP
     Birth: 19 Oct 1919   Death: 16 Apr 1979   Burial: 19 Apr 1979
Site 4   Lena Mae Lewis   TS: MOM   Mother of Donald Lewis
     Birth: 28 Jun 1921   Death: 28 Dec 1986   Burial: 31 Dec 1986
     On stone with Walter Jackson Lewis
Site 6   Raymond Lloyd Grubb Jr.   s/o R. Lloyd & Thelma H. Grubb, DD
     Birth: 21 Oct 1951   Death: 24 Jul 1993   Burial: 27 Jul 1993
     On stone with Nancy L. Grubb

Lot: 35 Lower   Owner: Miscellaneous
Site 1   Mary Elizabeth Weinlein
     Birth: 11 Dec 1922   Death: 4 Jan 1981   Burial: 6 Jan 1981
Site 2   Robert Andrew Weinlein
     Birth: 30 Dec 1954   Death: 25 Jul 1972   Burial: 1 Aug 1972
Site 3   Anthony Gerard Weinlein
     Birth: 1 Jun 1913   Death: 18 Dec 1979   Burial: 21 Dec 1979
Site 6   Larry Mack Bower   s/o John M. & Belva Bower
     Birth: 15 Mar 1955   Death: 11 Feb 1972   Burial: 15 Feb 1972

Lot: 35 Upper   Owner: Miscellaneous
Site 1   Ola Lee Evans   On stone with Joseph Evans
     Birth: 24 Mar 1909   Death: 6 Oct 1977   Burial: 10 Oct 1977
Site 2   Joseph Evans   h/o Ola Lee Evans
     Birth: 12 Jun 1904   Death: 13 Jan 1973   Burial: 15 Jan 1973

Monocacy Cemetery, Beallsville, Montgomery County, Maryland

Site 3 Walter Lawrence Fyffe   No marker
       Birth: 7 Nov 1907   Death: 14 Jul 1995   Burial: 18 Jul 1995
Site 5 Joseph Lee Fyffe
       Birth: 20 Nov 1910   Death: 2 Aug 1995   Burial: 5 Aug 1995

Lot: 36 Lower   Owner: Miscellaneous
Site 7 Clayton Morris
        Birth: 20 Apr 1904   Death: 27 Feb 1979   Burial: 2 Mar 1979
Site 8 Daryl Lynn Bladen   s/o Thomas C. Bladen, Sr.
        Birth: 1960   Death: 13 Aug 1972   Burial: 16 Aug 1972
Site 11 Michael Wayne Ward   Mort: Barber   Age 17 yrs
                                                         Burial: 16 Jun 1992
Site 12 Sabrina Lynn Ward   d/o Gary Lynn Ward
        Birth: 1973   Death: 26 Mar 1973   Burial: 29 Mar 1973

Lot: 36 Upper   Owner: Hazel D. & Irene O. Ward
Site 1 Jesse James Morris
       Birth: 2 Jun 1902   Death: 29 Apr 1990   Burial: 3 May 1990
Site 2 Nettie Ola Morris   Married Jesse James Morris 7 Jun 1927
       Birth: 12 Jan 1910   Death: 22 Nov 1981   Burial: 25 Nov 1981
Site 4 Byron LeRoy Ward   Age 59   On stone with Irene Ola Ward
       Birth: 11 Dec 1930   Death: 13 May 1990   Burial: 17 May 1990

Lot: 37 Lower   Owner: Miscellaneous
Site   William C. Austin   Birth: 21 Dec 1912   Death: 4 May 1997
        On stone with Mildred W. Austin
Site 12 Fred Samuel Evans   On stone with Louise B. Warfield Evans
        Birth: 9 Oct 1913   Death: 23 Apr 1978   Burial: 29 Apr 1978

Lot: 38   Owner: Miscellaneous
Site 1 Berry Thurman Wright III   s/o Berry T. & Jane Francis Wright
       Birth: 9 Jan 1955   Death: 5 Dec 1972   Burial: 8 Dec 1972
Site 2 Jane Frances Wright   w/o Berry Thurman Wright, Jr.
       Birth: 14 Dec 1928   Death: 12 Aug 1987   Burial: 14 Aug 1987
Site 3 Berry Thurman Wright, Jr. Birth: 15 Aug 1924   Death: 23 Jun 1997
Site 5 Charles Richard Hewitt   No marker
                                 Death: 23 Apr 1973   Burial: 25 Apr 1973
Site 6 Charles Guy Tadlock   On stone with Edna F. Tadlock
       Birth: 1912   Death: 14 Nov 1973   Burial: 17 Nov 1973
Site 7 Constance Duplessie Bennett   On stone with John Bonifas Bennet t 2nd
       Birth: 15 Mar 1938   Death: 6 Jun 1973   Burial: 8 Jun 1973
Site 8 Corrine C. Waldhuetter Bennett   w/o Bonifas Bennett I
       Birth: 25 Apr 1906   Death: 27 Nov 1979   Burial: 30 Nov 1979
Site 11 Amos Perkins Booty
        Birth: 22 Mar 1894   Death: 25 Jul 1973   Burial: 28 Jul 1973
        h/o Florence A. Booty   TS: Indiana 2nd Lieut. Marine Corps WWI
Site 12 Florence A. Booty   On stone with Amos Perkins Booty
        Birth: 3 Mar 1900   Death: 8 Jun 1993   Burial: 11 Jun 1993

Monocacy Cemetery, Beallsville, Montgomery County, Maryland

Lot: 39 Lower   Owner: Miscellaneous
Site 2   William Guy Fox
          Birth: 30 Dec 1910   Death: 6 Mar 1975   Burial: 8 Mar 1975
Site 4   Etta Cochran Leith   TS: Mother
          Birth: 4 May 1905   Death: 1 Oct 1983   Burial: 4 Oct 1983

Lot: 39 Upper   Owner: Miscellaneous
Site 2   Frank Ames Tyler, Jr.   On stone with Ruby Gott Tyler
          Birth: 12 Aug 1906   Death: 23 Sep 1973   Burial: 26 Sep 1973
Site 3   Samuel H. Leith   TS: Father   h/o Ruby Ellen Leith
          Birth: 11 Jun 1928   Death: 9 Jul 1993   Burial: 12 Jul 1993
Site 4   Michael Dale Leith   TS: Son   s/o Samuel H. Leith
          Birth: 13 Aug 1961   Death: 15 Oct 1973   Burial: 18 Oct 1973
Site 5   Ruby Ellen Leith   TS: Mother
          Birth: 24 Oct 1927   Death: 12 May 1993   Burial: 14 May 1993
Site 6   Myrtle Pearson   w/o Alfred L. Pearson   No marker
                                  Death: 4 Mar 1976   Burial: 9 Mar 1976

Lot: 40 Lower   Owner: Miscellaneous
Site 2   Rebecca (Betsy) Hartshorn Rice   On stone with Craig Shelby Rice
          Birth: 25 Dec 1929   Death: 16 Dec 1991   Burial: 19 Dec 1991
Site 3   Ellen Straughan Barrick
          Birth: 22 Feb 1900   Death: 13 Apr 1975   Burial: 15 Apr 1975
Site 4   Clarence S. Neel   On stone with Julia L. Neel
          Birth: 10 Jan 1916   Death: 17 Jun 1977   Burial: 30 Jun 1977
Site 5   Nellie M. Jenkins   On stone with Fred A. Jenkins
          Birth: 17 Jan 1916   Death: 16 Aug 1976   Burial: 21 Aug 1976
Site 6   Fred A. Jenkins   h/o Nellie M. Jenkins
          Birth: 22 Feb 1913   Death: 24 Apr 1981   Burial: 24 Apr 1981

Lot: 40 Upper   Owner: Miscellaneous
Site 1   Kathleen Fern Bauman   On stone with Mahlon & Betty J. Bauman
          Birth: 18 Nov 1960   Death: 21 Apr 1974   Burial: 24 Apr 1974
Site 3   Mahlon Clifford Bauman   h/o Betty J. Bauman
          Birth: 4 Apr 1928   Death: 28 Apr 1974   Burial: 1 May 1974
Site 5   Mary Edrie Jenkins   On stone with Garland Thomas Jenkins
          Birth: 26 Dec 1907   Death: 2 Dec 1980   Burial: 5 Dec 1980
Site 6   Garland Thomas Jenkins   h/o Mary E. Jenkins
          Birth: 24 Dec 1910   Death: 9 Oct 1974   Burial: 12 Oct 1974

Lot: 41 Lower   Owner: Miscellaneous
Site 2   Eleanor Crumine Stewart   On stone with Lyman R. Stewart
          Birth: 19 Sep 1925   Death: 30 Apr 1995   Burial: 4 May 1995
Site 3   Lyman Robert Stewart   h/o Eleanor C. Stewart
          Birth: 9 May 1925   Death: 23 Nov 1981   Burial: 28 Nov 1981
Site 4   Sadie M. Powers   Birth: 22 Aug 1935   Death: 18 May 1997
Site 6   Virginia H. Kidd   No marker
                                  Death: 11 Apr 1982   Burial: 15 Apr 1982

Lot: 41 Upper Owner: Miscellaneous
Site 1 Ida Jane Fox Leppo   w/o Joseph Leppo
        Birth: 26 Aug 1964   Death: 2 Apr 1997   Burial: 7 Apr 1997
Site 4 Charles LeRoy Young   On stone with Carol Ann Young
        Birth: 1937   Death: 25 Sep 1976   Burial: 28 Sep 1976
Site 6 Edward Earl Hall   On stone with Madeline G. Hall
        Birth: 13 Dec 1914   Death: 18 May 1975   Burial: 20 May 1975

Lot: 42 Lower Owner: Miscellaneous
Site 1 John Gilman Tighe   On stone with Charlotte S. Tighe
        Birth: 25 Dec 1906   Death: 30 Apr 1996   Burial: 4 May 1996

Lot: 42 Upper Owner: Miscellaneous
Site 5 Helen Elizabeth Jones   On stone with George G. Jones
        Birth: 17 Nov 1916   Death: 23 Jun 1995   Burial: 27 Jun 1995
Site 6 George Gleeves Jones   w/o Helen E. Jones
        Birth: 14 Jan 1911   Death: 19 Mar 1976   Burial: 23 Mar 1976

Lot: 43 Lower Owner: Miscellaneous
Site 1 Emory L. Comer Jr.   No marker
        Birth: 21 Sep 1970   Death: 21 Oct 1983   Burial: 26 Oct 1983
Site 5 Tom Henry Stream   On stone with Margie Tubbe Stream
        Birth: 10 Jul 1920   Death: 17 Jun 1991   Burial: 20 Jun 1991
        TS: CPL US Army WWII

Lot: 43 Upper Owner: Miscellaneous
Site 1 Robert Andrew Stream
        Birth: 24 Jun 1953   Death: 5 Jul 1985   Burial: 10 Jul 1985
Site 2 Floyd Preston Monroe
        Birth: 27 Sep 1932   Death: 7 Oct 1983   Burial: 11 Oct 1983
Site 6 David Franklin Stream, Jr.   h/o Marilyn A. Stream
        Birth: 30 Jun 1943   Death: 1 May 1983   Burial: 5 May 1983

Lot: 44 Owner: Miscellaneous
Site 6 George Randolph Titus   h/o Margaret M. Titus
        Birth: 17 Dec 1902   Death: 26 Dec 1982   Burial: 28 Dec 1982
Site 6 Margaret Merithew Titus   On stone with George Randolph Titus
        Birth: 26 Nov 1906   Death: 10 Dec 1979   Burial: 13 Dec 1979
Site 8 Mary V. Heatherly   Birth: 1893   Death: 28 May 1985

Lot: 45 Lower Owner: Miscellaneous
Site 2 Irene Gertrude Butt   w/o Ernest Lee Butt
        Birth: 16 Jan 1916   Death: 1 Oct 1986   Burial: 4 Oct 1986
Site 3 Doris Marie Ferris   Mort: Hilton   Death: 6 Nov 1996
Site 4 William R. Lawrence
        Birth: 18 Oct 1940   Death: 17 Jan 1987   Burial: 22 Jan 1987

Lot: 46 Lower Owner: Miscellaneous
Site 1 Anna Fawsett Noyes   On stone with Judge Alfred D. Noyes
        Birth: 27 Mar 1901   Death: 20 Jan 1986   Burial: 23 Jan 1986

Site 3 Constance M. Callahan   On stone with Stephen M. Callahan, Jr.
        Birth: 11 May 1920   Death: 9 Jul 1987   Burial: 13 Jul 1987
Site 4 Stephen M. Callahan Jr.
        Birth: 1 Feb 1922   Death: 17 Feb 1997   Burial: 19 Feb 1997

Lot: 46 Upper   Owner: Miscellaneous
Site 1 Mary H. Wright Stock   On stone with Edward Stock
        Birth: 14 Nov 1904   Death: 2 May 1993   Burial: 10 May 1993
Site 2 Edward Lilley Stock, Jr.
        Birth: 8 Jun 1906   Death: 21 Mar 1991   Burial: 25 Mar 1991
Site 5 Sally Ann Stokes
        Birth: 12 Sep 1941   Death: 15 Jan 1990   Burial: 20 Jan 1990

Lot: 47 Lower   Owner: Miscellaneous
Site 1 Billie Gene Parks   s/o Albert Fred & Ona Parks
        Birth: 30 Nov 1953   Death: 21 Sep 1989   Burial: 26 Sep 1989
Site 6 Viola Sutherland
        Birth: 9 Jun 1900   Death: 20 Jun 1989   Burial: 24 Jun 1989

Lot: 47 Upper   Owner: William F. & Winifred A. Brill
Site 1 Amy Maria Griffiths   d/o Dave Griffiths
        Birth: 1 Jan 1987   Death: 26 Feb 1987   Burial: 26 Feb 1987
Site 6 Martin William Brill
        Birth: 20 Jul 1962   Death: 30 Nov 1986   Burial: 3 Dec 1986

Lot: 48 Lower   Owner: Miscellaneous
Site 1 Christopher Millar   s/o Jack W. & Jane B. Millar
        Birth: 8 Jul 1957   Death: 28 Mar 1989   Burial: 1 Apr 1989

Lot: 48 Upper   Owner: Miscellaneous
Site 2 Annie Belle Benson   On stone with James W. Benson, Jr.
        Birth: 25 Dec 1921   Death: 21 Mar 1989   Burial: 25 Mar 1989
Site 3 Marion LeRoy Bagley
        Birth: 22 Jan 1902   Death: 27 Jan 1990   Burial: 18 Oct 1990
Site 4 Dorothy S. Bagley   On stone with Marion LeRoy Bagley
        Birth: 31 May 1901   Death: 15 Feb 1984   Burial: 18 Oct 1990
Site 4 Infant   No marker   Burial: 18 Oct 1990
Site 5 Lauren Christine Antonelli   age 6 yrs.
        Birth: 3 Nov 1987   Death: 16 Jun 1994   Burial: 25 Jun 1994

Lot: 50 Lower   Owner:
Site 1 Paul Thompson Young   No marker
        Birth: 30 Sep 1937   Death: 1 Dec 1992   Burial: 5 Dec 1992

Lot: 50 Upper   Owner: Miscellaneous
Site 1 Eloise Mattie Robbins McGlothlin   m/o Geneie Stokes
        Birth: 23 Apr 1921   Death: 4 Oct 1990   Burial: 7 Oct 1990

Lot: 51 Lower   Owner: William Russell Baker, Jr.
Site 1 William Russell Baker III
    Birth: 23 Dec 1976   Death: 14 Dec 1991   Burial: 17 Dec 1991
Site 4 David Titus
    Birth: 9 May 1917   Death: 19 Mar 1991   Burial: 23 Mar 1991
Site 5 Catherine Davis Everhart   Age 89 yrs
    Birth: 5 Oct 1902   Death: 6 Jun 1992   Burial: 10 Jun 1992

Lot: 51 Upper   Owner:
Site 5 Elizabeth Ann Stuart   On stone with Leonard D. Stream
    Birth: 26 Sep 1936   Death: 6 Oct 1990   Burial: 10 Oct 1990

Row M

Lot: 1   Owner: James H. Littlepage & John C. Livingston
Site 2   Joan Gamble Palmer
         Birth: 26 Apr 1938   Death: 13 Jan 1983   Burial: 18 Mar 1983
         d/o Townley & Mabel Griffith Gamble, w/o David Rulison Palmer
Site 4   James Hemenway Littlepage   On stone with Mabel Griffith Littlepage
         Birth: 3 Dec 1910   Death: 28 May 1989   Burial: 1 Jun 1989
Site 6   John Cope Livingston   On stone with Margaret Griffith Livingston
         Birth: 5 Jul 1908   Death: 13 Dec 1981   Burial: 16 Dec 1981

Lot: 2 Lower   Owner: Miscellaneous
Site 2   Edward Buford Wynne Sr.   On stone with Ella Mae Lester Wynne
         Birth: 25 Oct 1909   Death: 12 Sep 1992   Burial: 16 Sep 1992
Site 4   Hubert Sherman Neal   h/o Ida Wynne Neal
         Birth: 19 Feb 1905   Death: 6 Nov 1990   Burial: 9 Nov 1990
Site 6   John McKimmy Titus   On stone with Mildred Geisbert Titus
         Birth: 9 May 1917   Death: 9 Dec 1972   Burial: 12 Dec 1972

Lot: 2 Upper   Owner: Mrs. Barbara Kephart Crane
Site 1   Clarence Edward Bunge MD
         Birth: 1914   Death: 23 Dec 1975   Burial: 27 Dec 1975
         h/o Frederica M. Bunge, Major USAF 1942-1946
Site 5   Leonard Wheeler Kephart   h/o Frances Kephart
         Birth: 10 Jan 1892   Death: 10 Feb 1988   Burial: 13 Feb 1988
Site 6   Frances Frazer Kephart   Place: Silver Spring, MD
         Birth: 23 Jun 1887   Death: 26 Jun 1971   Burial: 29 Jun 1971
         Mort: Tyson Wheeler   w/o Leonard W. Kephart

Lot: 3 Upper   Owner: Miscellaneous
Site 5   Henry Clyde Hough   On stone with Ruth H. Hough
         Birth: 18 Jun 1913   Death: 11 Aug 1971   Burial: 14 Aug 1971

Lot: 4 Upper   Owner: Jasper F. & Forest Hough
Site 5   Myrtle L. Hough   Birth: 1902   On stone with Jasper F. Hough
Site 6   Jasper F. Hough   h/o Myrtle L. Hough
         Birth: 1899   Death: 17 Oct 1971   Burial: 20 Oct 1971

Lot: 5 Lower   Owner: Miscellaneous
Site 3   Eula L. Wynne Luhn   On stone with Maynard Clark Luhn Sr.
         Birth: 22 Oct 1905   Death: 5 Apr 1994   Burial: 7 Apr 1994
Site 4   Maynard Clark Luhn Sr.   h/o Eula Wynne Luhn
         Birth: 28 Apr 1905   Death: 6 Apr 1978   Burial: 10 Apr 1978
Site 6   James Edgar Grubb   On stone with Ruth Wynne Grubb
         Birth: 1 Jun 1914   Death: 9 Apr 1988   Burial: 12 Apr 1988

Lot: 5 Upper   Owner: Miscellaneous
Site 5   Beulah Brooks Brubaker   On stone with Louis Creglo Brubaker
         Birth: 30 Sep 1900   Death: 13 Nov 1990   Burial: 17 Nov 1990

Monocacy Cemetery, Beallsville, Montgomery County, Maryland

Site 6 Louis Creglo Brubaker h/o Beulah Brooks Brubaker
Birth: 21 Jul 1898 Death: 6 Sep 1979 Burial: 10 Sep 1979

Lot: 6 Low: Mr. & Mrs. J.G. Arrington & Mr. & Mrs. O.S. Munger
Site 1 Ormond Surber Munger h/o Mary L. Munger
Birth: 27 Apr 1912 Death: 10 Apr 1989 Burial: 14 Apr 1989
Site 2 Mary L. Munger On stone with Ormond S. Munger
Birth: 29 Jan 1913 Death: 8 Jul 1977 Burial: 12 Jul 1977
Site 5 J. Guy Arrington No marker
Birth: 14 Jan 1909 Death: 3 Apr 1997 Burial: 7 Apr 1997

Lot: 6 Upper Owner: Miscellaneous
Site 3 Catherine A. Burke DD On stone with Earl E. Burke
Birth: 3 May 1940 Death: 21 Mar 1986 Burial: 24 Mar 1986

Lot: 7 Lower Owner: Beatrice Williams & M. Woodbridge
Site 1 Milo Woodbridge Williams Jr. Place: Bethesda, MD
Birth: 1959 Death: 16 Feb 1970 Burial: 18 Feb 1970
Mort: Wm. Hilton s/o M. Woodbridge & Bea Williams

Lot: 7 Upper Owner: Paris W. Lambert
Site 3 Elsie Pearl Lambert Place: Frederick, MD
Birth: 29 Jul 1902 Death: 9 Jun 1970 Burial: 11 Jun 1970
Mort: Wm. Hilton On stone with Paris Wesley Lambert
Site 4 Paris Wesley Lambert h/o Elsie Pearl Lambert
Birth: 25 Sep 1890 Death: 31 May 1973 Burial: 2 Jun 1973
Site 5 William Wesley Lambert Jr.
Birth: 26 Mar 1954 Death: 14 Sep 1981 Burial: 17 Sep 1981
Site 6 William Wesley Lambert Sr. Age 67 yrs On stone with Mary Jane Lambert
Birth: 10 Mar 1925 Death: 1 Jun 1992 Burial: 4 Jun 1992

Lot: 8 Lower Owner: Miscellaneous
Site 4 Lucy Ellen Lonergan
Birth: 1943 Death: 24 Mar 1978 Burial: 4 Apr 1978
Site 5 Kathryn Soper Crone w/o Charles B. Crone
Birth: 22 Aug 1907 Death: 23 Aug 1980 Burial: 26 Aug 1980
Site 6 Charles B. Crone h/o Kathryn Soper Crone
Birth: 2 Jun 1902 Death: 23 Apr 1975 Burial: 3 May 1975

Lot: 9 Lower Owner: Owen L. & Margaret M. Scott
Site 4 Owen Legrand Scott On stone with Margarete M. Scott
Birth: 1898 Death: 27 Aug 1985 Burial: 4 Sep 1985

Lot: 9 Upper Owner: John E. Oxley, Sr.
Site 1 Annie Branson Oxley Place: Rockville, MD
Birth: 10 Jun 1914 Death: 25 May 1970 Burial: 29 May 1970
Mort: Tyson Wheeler w/o John Edgar Oxley, Sr.
Site 2 John Edgar Oxley Sr. h/o Annie Branison Oxley
Birth: 27 Nov 1899 Death: 18 Oct 19 73 Burial: 22 Oct 1973

Monocacy Cemetery, Beallsville, Montgomery County, Maryland   261

Lot: 10 Upper   Owner: Miscellaneous (All on one stone)
- Site 5 John P. Allan   No marker
         Birth: 1906   Death: 23 Apr 1978   Burial: 29 Apr 1978
- Site 5 Jack C. Wright
         Birth: 1928   Death: 1983   Burial: 7 Mar 1983
- Site 6 Catherine W. Allan   Wife of John P. Allen
         Birth: 30 Sep 1907   Death: 31 Aug 1987   Burial: 4 Sep 1987

Lot: 11 Lower   Owner: Miscellaneous
- Site 5 Olivia Pauline Jewell   On stone with Edgar Guy Jewell
         Birth: 5 May 1902   Burial: 3 Oct 1980
- Site 6 Edgar Guy Jewell
         Birth: 1 Sep 1901   Death: 2 Mar 1984   Burial: 5 Mar 1984

Lot: 12 Lower   Owner: Miscellaneous
- Site 6 Charles W. Johnson IV   s/o Mary Ann B. & Charles W. Johnson
         Birth: 21 Jul 1948   Death: 10 Mar 1977   Burial: 14 Mar 1977

Lot: 12 Upper   Owner: Adams S. Tanner
- Site 3 Gladys B. Tanner
         Birth: 18 May 1933   Death: 4 Oct 1993   Burial: 8 Oct 1993
- Site 4 Harold James Tanner
         Birth: 1 Jun 1910   Death: 17 Dec 1986   Burial: 22 Dec 1986
- Site 5 Eva Bardach Tanner   w/o Adam S. Tanner
         Birth: 12 Oct 1912   Death: 2 Jul 1977   Burial: 6 Jul 1977
- Site 6 Patricia Sara Alise Tanner   d/o Adam S. & Eva B. Tanner
         Birth: 6 Jan 1958   Death: 1 May 1974   Burial: 4 May 1974

Lot: 13 Lower   Owner: Lois & Robert Hastings
- Site 5 Lynn H. Hastings   TS: Place: Chapel Hill, NC
         Birth: 22 Feb 1953   Death: 14 Aug 1971   Burial: 4 Dec 1971
         d/o Lois & Robert Hastings   TS: Born Madison, WI
- Site 6 Robert Hathaway Hastings   TS: Born Antigo, WS, died Washington, DC
         Birth: 7 Jun 1926   Death: 31 Jan 1985   Burial: 17 Jul 1985

Lot: 13 Upper   Owner: Frank H. Weller
- Site 4 Frank Harlow Weller   TS: Maryland LCDR USNR WWII
         Birth: 14 Jun 1913   Death: 27 Feb 1972   Burial: 19 Feb 1972
         On stone with Amelita Alfaro Weller

Lot: 14 Lower   Owner: Miscellaneous
- Site 2 Ardle Patrick O'Hanlon   h/o Patricia O'Hanlon
         Birth: 11 Sep 1909   Death: 22 Apr 1977   Burial: 26 Apr 1977
- Site 3 Eva Kristina Rakusja   w/o Joseph Rakusja
         Birth: 25 Jun 1924   Death: 14 May 1978   Burial: 17 May 1978
- Site 4 D. Bruce Tuxhorn   No marker   Burial: 12 Jul 1978
         Moved from St. Mary's Cemetery, Washington, DC
         h/o Roma O'Hanlon Tuxhorn
- Site 6 Richard T. Willis
         Birth: 5 May 1913   Death: 13 Feb 1977   Burial: 16 Feb 1977

Monocacy Cemetery, Beallsville, Montgomery County, Maryland

Lot: 14 Upper Owner: Leo & Robert Roberson
Site 3 Leo Roberson   h/o Elizabeth Hicks Roberson
        Birth: 1 Jul 1902   Death: 20 Sep 1989   Burial: 22 Sep 1989
Site 4 Elizabeth Hicks Roberson   w/o Leo Roberson
        Birth: 21 Jan 1899   Death: 27 Nov 1984   Burial: 30 Nov 1984
Site 6 William Walker Roberson   s/o Leo & Elizabeth Roberson TS: CTI US Navy
        Birth: 29 Nov 1933   Death: 5 Nov 1975   Burial: 8 Nov 1975

Lot: 15 Lower Owner: Bertha M. Cregger & Frances Lemarr
Site 1 Bertha Mae Cregger   On stone with Floyd W. Cregger, age 82 yrs.
        Birth: 1909   Death: 19 Nov 1992   Burial: 25 Nov 1992
Site 2 Floyd W. Cregger
        Birth: 1905   Death: 19 Dec 1985   Burial: 27 Dec 1985
        h/o Bertha Mae Cregger, s/o Eli & Mae Thompson Cregger
Site 3 Frances I. Cregger Lemar   d/o Floyd & Bertha Cregger, age 48 yrs
        Birth: 21 Dec 1930   Death: 15 Sep 1979   Burial: 18 Sep 1979

Lot: 15 Upper Owner: Irving R. & Esther Young
Site 1 Irving Rodney Young
        Birth: 1 Aug 1909   Death: 13 May 1985   Burial: 16 May 1985
Site 4 Esther I. Carlisle Young
        Birth: 8 May 1908   Death: 9 May 1982   Burial: 12 May 1982
Site 5 Evangeline Welch   No marker
                                Death: 11 Oct 1980   Burial: 13 Oct 1980
Site 6 George C. Cochran   TS: Age 80
        Birth: 1 Feb 1903   Death: 14 Mar 1983   Burial: 17 Mar 1983

Lot: 16 Lower Owner: Miscellaneous
Site 2 Warren Edward Irvin   Age 86 yrs   On stone with Marguerite Irvin
        Birth: 1896   Death: 20 Jan 1983   Burial: 28 Jan 1983
Site 4 Walter R. Benson   No marker   Death: 25 Jan 1993
Site 5 Roger Lee Anderson Jr.
        Birth: 22 Jun 1954   Death: 11 Dec 1981   Burial: 15 Dec 1981
Site 6 John William Klaess   No marker   h/o Mary Frances Klaess
                                Death: 19 Jun 1979   Burial: 21 Jun 1979

Lot: 16 Upper Owner: Miscellaneous
Site 1 James C. Lambert   On stone with Evelyn Cubitt Lambert
        Birth: 2 Oct 1910   Death: 2 Jul 1994   Burial: 6 Jul 1994

Lot: 17 Lower Owner: Miscellaneous
Site 1 Virgie G. Houser Bodmer
        Birth: 5 Nov 1922   Death: 20 Feb 1985   Burial: 23 Feb 1985
        On stone with Charles Wesley Bodmer & Wayne Wesley Bodmer
Site 2 Wayne Wesley Bodmer   s/o Charles Wesley & Virgie G. Bodmer
        Birth: 3 Aug 1963   Death: 31 Aug 1980   Burial: 3 Sep 1980
Site 3 Charles Wesley Bodmer
        Birth: 30 Jul 1919   Death: 22 Apr 1993   Burial: 24 Apr 1993

Monocacy Cemetery, Beallsville, Montgomery County, Maryland   263

Site 4 George Thomas Fling
    Birth: 10 Oct 1910   Death: 16 Jan 1982   Burial: 19 Jan 1982
    h/o Elizabeth L. Fling, s/o Howard & Bertha Simpson Fling
Site 6 Phillip Whisner
    Birth: 17 Apr 1953   Death: 24 Feb 1984   Burial: 26 Feb 1984

Lot: 17 Upper   Owner: Kathleen B., John W. Jr., & Kathleen P. Moore
Site 6 John White Moore   TS: US Army WWII   h/o Kathleen B. Moore
    Birth: 16 Jul 1919   Death: 4 Apr 1975   Burial: 23 Apr 1975

Lot: 18   Owner: Miscellaneous
Site 4 Samuel Arthur Hopkins   TS: "Buddy"
    Birth: 9 Dec 1938   Death: 2 Feb 1980   Burial: 5 Feb 1980
Site 7 Barbara Lee Smith   No marker   w/o Joseph I. Smith
                                   Death: 9 Jul 1994   Burial: 15 Jul 1994
Site 7 Joseph I. Smith Jr.   No marker
                                   Death: 24 Feb 1986   Burial: 8 Mar 1986
Site 8 Louanna Stottlemyer Deadrick   w/o Robert Deadrick
    Birth: 1 Aug 1941   Death: 9 Oct 1994   Burial: 13 Oct 1994

Lot: 19 Lower   Owner: Miscellaneous
Site 1 Dorothy I. Morningstar Hightman   Birth: 9 Mar 1909
Site 4 Beryl F. Vickers   On stone with Kathryn L. Vickers
    Birth: 15 Jun 1909   Death: 14 Aug 1978   Burial: 24 Aug 1978
Site 5 Lorena Mae Vanhoozer   On stone with Joseph Robert Vanhoozier
    Birth: 7 May 1913   Death: 26 May 1995   Burial: 31 May 1995
Site 6 Joseph Robert VanHoozer   h/o Lorena M. VanHoozer
    Birth: 1909   Death: 9 Jul 1978   Burial: 12 Jul 1978

Lot: 20 Lower   Owner: Miscellaneous
Site 5 Mary Jane Jones   w/o Robert N. Jones Jr.
    Birth: 1944   Death: 11 Aug 1979   Burial: 13 Aug 1979

Lot: 20 Upper   Owner: Miscellaneous
Site 6 Rev. Charles Lee Hagy
    Birth: 1 May 1930   Death: 31 Jul 1981   Burial: 3 Aug 1981

Lot: 21 Lower   Owner: Walter C. Heflin, Sr.
Site 4 Mildred C. Fawley Heflin   On stone with Walter C. Heflin, Sr.
    Birth: 6 Jun 1912   Death: 11 Jan 1992   Burial: 13 Jan 1992
Site 5 Walter Calvin Heflin Sr.   h/o Mildred Fawley Heflin
    Birth: 12 May 1910   Death: 24 Jan 1987   Burial: 28 Jan 1987

Lot: 21 Upper   Owner: James A. Baisey
Site 6 Thomas G. Baisey Sr.   h/o Virginia M. Baisey
    Birth: 21 Dec 1907   Death: 31 Aug 1980   Burial: 6 Sep 1980

Lot: 22 Lower   Owner: Miscellaneous
Site 1 William R. Pearson   Age 69 yrs
    Birth: 13 Jan 1918   Death: 10 Oct 1987   Burial: 14 Oct 1987

Site 2 Grace Belle Rinker   On stone with William R. Pearson
        Birth: 29 Dec 1900   Death: 22 Dec 1978   Burial: 27 Dec 1978
Site 5 Elizabeth W. Heflin Shawver   On stone with Charles E. Shawver
        Birth: 7 Nov 1918   Death: 31 May 1978   Burial: 3 Jun 1978

Lot: 22 Upper   Owner: Miscellaneous
Site 4 Charles Robert Jones   h/o Reva Alexander Jones
        Birth: 28 Jan 1918   Death: 5 Jul 1995   Burial: 7 Jul 1995
Site 6 Thomas A. Conlon, Jr.
        Birth: 28 Mar 1920   Death: 1 Apr 1984   Burial: 5 Apr 1984

Lot: 24 Lower   Owner: Miscellaneous
Site 6 Charles P. Savage   TS: "Rick"   s/o Donald S. & Gloria K. Savage
        Birth: 14 Apr 1964   Death: 8 Nov 1981   Burial: 11 Nov 1981

Lot: 25 Upper   Owner: Miscellaneous
Site 1 Maria K. Frances Phillips   Mort: Keeney & Basford
        Birth: 1 Oct 1936   Death: 12 Apr 1997   Burial: 10 Apr 1997
Site 1 Nellie Tommie Pierre
        Birth: 9 Jan 1901   Death: 27 Sep 1982   Burial: 29 Sep 1982
Site 2 Louise Dean Simsar   On stone with Mehmed A. Simsar
        Birth: 14 Feb 1900   Death: 19 Nov 1986   Burial: 21 Nov 1986
Site 3 Mehmed A. Simsar
        Birth: 14 Aug 1902   Death: 11 Apr 1981   Burial: 13 Apr 1981
Site 5 Shirley June Eaton Penrod   On stone with Luther S. & Nora C. Johnson
        Birth: 24 Jan 1936   Death: 3 Sep 1980   Burial: 6 Sep 1980
Site 6 Nora C. Johnson   w/o Luther Johnson
        Birth: 25 Feb 1915   Death: 3 May 1988   Burial: 6 May 1988

Lot: 26 Lower   Owner: Miscellaneous
Site 2 Myrtle Marie Catron Williams   Mother of Mrs. Charles Eader
        Birth: 18 Jun 1909   Death: 24 Apr 1988   Burial: 27 Apr 1988
Site 5 Hager Mills Hurd   w/o Eugene Hurd
        Birth: 27 Aug 1910   Death: 28 Aug 1991   Burial: 30 Aug 1991
Site 6 Eugene Hurd
        Birth: 26 Mar 1907   Death: 2 Jan 1983   Burial: 5 Jan 1983

Lot: 26 Upper   Owner: Miscellaneous
Site 6 Raymond Harvey Baker Sr.   h/o Helen Beach Baker
        Birth: 10 Aug 1925   Death: 20 Nov 1981   Burial: 23 Nov 1981

Lot: 27 Lower   Owner: Miscellaneous
Site 1 John Douglas Burdette
        Birth: 19 Feb 1935   Death: 30 Apr 1972   Burial: 3 May 1972
Site 2 Franklin Henry Magaha   s/o Archie & Virginia Magaha
        Birth: 9 Feb 1949   Death: 25 Mar 1973   Burial: 28 Mar 1973
Site 6 James Samuel Keeney   On stone with Meredith D. Keeney
        Birth: 1 Jul 1931   Death: 30 Oct 1971   Burial: 2 Nov 1971

Lot: 27 Upper   Owner: Miscellaneous
Site 1 Mildred Waters Dean   On stone with Charles E. Dean
        Birth: 17 Feb 1904   Death: 11 Sep 1981   Burial: 17 Sep 1981
Site 2 Charles Earle Dean
        Birth: 23 May 1898   Death: 9 Nov 1993   Burial: 3 Jan 1994
Site 3 Thelma Gilliam Bourne   On stone with Trube Terry Bourne
        Birth: 10 May 1906   Death: 15 Jun 1986   Burial: 18 Jun 1986
Site 4 Trube Terry Bourne   TS: PVT US Army WWI
        Birth: 24 Jul 1896   Death: 22 Nov 1980   Burial: 25 Nov 1980
        h/o Thelma Gilliam Bourne
Site 5 Susie V. McAtee
        Birth: 9 Sep 1892   Death: 12 Dec 1980   Burial: 16 Dec 1980
Site 6 James Arthur Phillips
        Birth: 24 Sep 1910   Death: 15 Sep 1976   Burial: 17 Sep 1976

Lot: 28 Lower   Owner: Miscellaneous
Site 3 Judith Ann Vogel   Age 53 yrs
        Birth: 6 Oct 1939   Death: 14 Dec 1992   Burial: 19 Dec 1992
Site 4 Kathryn Lynne Vogel   TS: "Trini"   d/o Hall & Judith Ann Vogel
        Birth: 10 Nov 1965   Death: 7 Apr 1978   Burial: 12 Apr 1978
Site 5 Marilyn Whittaker Johns   On stone with Brooke Johns II
        Birth: 6 Jan 1928   Death: 19 Dec 1984   Burial: 28 Dec 1984
Site 6 William Brook Johns II
        Birth: 1926   Death: 23 Nov 1974   Burial: 26 Nov 1974

Lot: 28 Upper   Owner: Miscellaneous
Site 2 Jean Frances Kaempfer deCarlo   w/o Joseph Nicholas deCarlo
        Birth: 7 Oct 1949   Death: 27 Jan 1996   Burial: 31 Jan 1996
Site 3 Clarence Parsley   Mort: Barber
        Birth: 25 Aug 1900   Death: 27 May 1982   Burial: 1 Jun 1982
Site 4 Hunter Lindsay Gardner   Mort: Hilton   h/o Mary Ellen Gardner
        Birth: 1919   Death: 9 Mar 1 978   Burial: 13 Mar 1978

Lot: 29 Lower   Owner: Miscellaneous
Site 2 Calvin C. Davis Sr.   No marker   h/o Mildred Davis
        Birth: 1907   Death: 24 Mar 1977   Burial: 28 Mar 1977
Site 3 Charles Eclon Scott   US Marine Corps
        Birth: 26 Jun 1948   Death: 4 Jan 1975   Burial: 7 Jan 1975
Site 6 Ervin Ramseur   On stone with Eleanor V. Ramseur
        Birth: 1 Jul 1924   Death: 21 Dec 1973   Burial: 24 Dec 1973

Lot: 29 Upper   Owner: Miscellaneous
Site 1 Charles Grover Burdette   TS: Maryland PVT US Army WWI
        Birth: 11 Sep 1893   Death: 23 Sep 1973   Burial: 26 Sep 1973
Site 2 John Tyler Ricketts Jr.   TS: Capt US Army   h/o Mildred Frank Ricketts
        Birth: 22 Aug 1924   Death: 28 Oct 1974   Burial: 31 Oct 1974
Site 5 Kelly Orville Williams III   s/o Kelly O. & Karen S. Williams
        Birth: 11 Sep 1973   Death: 8 Apr 1975   Burial: 12 Apr 1975

Monocacy Cemetery, Beallsville, Montgomery County, Maryland

Lot: 30 Lower   Owner: Miscellaneous
Site 3 George Thomas Wood   w/o Diana T. Wood
        Birth: 29 Jul 1898   Death: 25 Jul 1980   Burial: 28 Jul 1980
Site 4 Diana Tennis Wood   w/o George Wood
        Birth: 31 Jan 1900   Death: 30 Jun 1992   Burial: 3 Jul 1992

Lot: 30 Upper   Owner: Miscellaneous
Site 3 Russell Franklin Smith
        Birth: 10 Oct 1937   Death: 17 Jul 1987   Burial: 20 Jul 1987
Site 4 Beulah I. Whipp   On stone with Paul Cole Whipp
        Birth: 26 Sep 1908   Death: 21 Mar 1984   Burial: 26 Mar 1984
Site 5 Paul Cole Whipp
        Birth: 6 Aug 1921   Death: 6 Jul 1996   Burial. 9 Jul 1996
Site 6 James Robert Smith
        Birth: 11 Aug 1939   Death: 23 Apr 1995   Burial: 25 Apr 1995

Lot: 31 Lower   Owner: Miscellaneous
Site 1 William T. Wolfrey   h/o Patricia A. Wolfrey
        Birth: 21 Aug 1925   Death: 30 Dec 1978   Burial: 3 Jan 1980
Site 3 Glenn Edward Barnhouse
        Birth: 1956   Death: 11 Jan 1986   Burial: 16 Jan 1986
Site 3 Rebecca Dawn Gravely   c/o Donald Gravely
        Birth: 10 May 1985   Death: 26 May 1985   Burial: 31 May 1985
Site 3 Samantha Jean Seabolt   Cause: Burned in fire
        Birth: 10 Feb 1984   Death: 11 Jan 1986   Burial: 16 Jan 1986
Site 4 Carroll Clifton Barnhouse Sr.   No marker
        Birth: 19 Aug 1921   Death: 1 Jan 1987   Burial: 6 Jan 1987
Site 4 Rachael Virginia Barnhouse   No marker
        Birth: 14 Aug 1923   Death: 20 Aug 1980   Burial: 23 Aug 1980
Site 6 Alexander Herbert Uhl   h/o Gladys Uhl
        Birth: 11 Jun 1899   Death: 24 Aug 1976   Burial: 29 Aug 1976

Lot: 31 Upper   Owner: Miscellaneous
Site 2 Dorothy A. Hill
        Birth: 26 Feb 1920   Death: 6 Jul 1982   Burial: 8 Jul 1982

Lot: 32 Upper   Owner: Miscellaneous
Site 1 Hilda Marie Pasti   w/o Nicholas Pasti
        Birth: 4 May 1929   Death: 26 Feb 1981   Burial: 3 Mar 1981
Site 2 Nicholas Pasti
        Birth: 24 May 1922   Death: 29 Dec 1995   Burial: 3 Jan 1996
Site 3 Emma Williams   On stone with Bernie Williams
        Birth: 4 Oct 1895   Death: 11 Nov 1981   Burial: 13 Nov 1981
Site 4 Bernard D. Williams   Birth: 1902   Death: 26 Sep 1994
Site 6 Catherine C. Carter
        Birth: 7 Dec 1919   Death: 19 Aug 1981   Burial: 24 Aug 1981

Monocacy Cemetery, Beallsville, Montgomery County, Maryland 267

Lot: 33 Lower Owner: Miscellaneous
Site 1 William M. Jenkins   h/o Glaytha V. Jenkins
        Birth: 6 Aug 1901   Death: 3 Oct 1984   Burial: 6 Oct 1984
Site 3 Margaret Blackwell Mann   On stone with James Harold Mann
        Birth: 1919   Death: 8 Jun 1995   Burial: 13 Jun 1995
Site 4 James Harold Mann   h/o Margaret B. Mann
        Birth: 23 Nov 1913   Death: 26 May 1985   Burial: 28 May 1985
Site 5 Margaret Verna Lewis Phelps   On stone with George H. Phelps
        Birth: 16 Jan 1926   Death: 2 Feb 1986   Burial: 5 Feb 1986
Site 6 George Herbert Phelps   TS: PFC US Army WWII
        Birth: 11 Mar 1921   Death: 18 Jan 1984   Burial: 20 Jan 1984

Lot: 33 Upper Owner: Miscellaneous
Site 4 Walter Lee Evans Jr.
        Birth: 1 Feb 1964   Death: 25 May 1985   Burial: 27 May 1985

Lot: 34 Lower Owner: Miscellaneous
Site 1 Judith Teresa Burress
        Birth: 23 Feb 1956   Death: 28 Aug 1994   Burial: 1 Sep 1994
Site 3 Annie V. Lydard
        Birth: 23 Nov 1908   Death: 19 Dec 1987   Burial: 23 Dec 1987
Site 6 Mitchell Lee Nealon
        Birth: 16 Apr 1947   Death: 17 Jun 1985   Burial: 19 Jun 1985

Lot: 34 Upper Owner: Miscellaneous
Site 4 Dennis Eric Austin   No marker
        Birth: 4 Jan 1923   Death: 4 Oct 1988   Burial: 7 Oct 1988
Site 5 Dorothy Claire Sirk Austin No marker   w/o Dennis E. Austin
        Birth: 6 Oct 1931   Death: 20 Feb 1997   Burial: 24 Feb 1997
Site 6 Lynn Alison Sirk
        Birth: 1 Jul 1961   Death: 21 Jul 1983   Burial: 27 Jul 1983

Lot: 35 Upper Owner: Miscellaneous
Site 6 Joshua Matthew Rinzel   Cause: Stillborn
                               Death: 12 Jul 1985   Burial: 12 Jul 1985

Lot: 36 Lower Owner: Miscellaneous
Site 1 Nelson John Minter
        Birth: 15 Sep 1957   Death: 3 Dec 1993   Burial: 5 Nov 1994
Site 2 Robert W. Taylor   No marker   h/o Judi W. Taylor
        Birth: 4 Oct 1929   Death: 23 Aug 1985   Burial: 27 Aug 1985
Site 3 Ruth M. Vail
        Birth: 1928   Death: 1967   Burial: 22 May 1996
Site 4 Dora Hall Wright   No marker   w/o Clifton W. Wright
        Birth: 21 Apr 1900   Death: 20 Dec 1985   Burial: 23 Dec 1985

Lot: 36 Upper Owner: Miscellaneous
Site 3 Donaline Mae Wallach   TS: Married Edward H. Wallach, Jr. 2 Sep 1948
        Birth: 17 May 1931   Death: 9 Feb 1995   Burial: 13 Feb 1995

Monocacy Cemetery, Beallsville, Montgomery County, Maryland

Site 5 Brandon George Carter   s/o George F. & Sherry A. Carter
       Birth: 11 Oct 1985   Death: 13 Jan 1986   Burial: 16 Jan 1986

Lot: 37 Lower   Owner: Miscellaneous
Site 1 Laura Smythe   w/o John W. Smythe
       Birth: 28 Mar 1923   Death: 30 J an 1989   Burial: 2 Feb 1989
Site 3 Raymond Lee Archer
       Birth: 25 Nov 1945   Death: 22 May 1990   Burial: 24 May 1990
Site 6 Dale O. Hitchcock
       Birth: 8 Jan 1952   Death: 24 Oct 1987   Burial: 27 Oct 1987

Lot: 37 Upper   Owner: Miscellaneous
Site 2 Charles R. Patterson   No marker
       Birth: 10 Aug 1919   Death: 14 Sep 1986   Burial: 18 Sep 1986
Site 3 Robert William E. Woods, Jr.   w/o Martha Woods
       Birth: 15 Jan 1933   Death: 17 Mar 1988   Burial: 19 Mar 1988
Site 6 James Bruce Baker
       Birth: 18 Apr 1938   Death: 16 Jan 1988   Burial: 19 Jan 1988

Lot: 38 Lower   Owner: Miscellaneous
Site 6 Walter K. Atwell   h/o Dorothy A. Atwell
       Birth: 5 Jan 1925   Death: 28 Dec 1993   Burial: 30 Dec 1993

Lot: 38 Upper   Owner: Miscellaneous
Site 1 Nick Karayianis   Age 54 yrs
       Birth: 17 Aug 1931   Death: 25 Feb 1989   Burial: 28 Feb 1989
Site 3 Linda Lou Leith Jerrell   h/o John P. Jerrell, d/o Samuel & Ruby Leith
       Birth: 20 Oct 1947   Death: 9 Dec 1988   Burial: 13 Dec 1988
Site 4 Eppie H. Leith   Age 81 yrs
       Birth: 4 Jun 1905   Death: 19 Jul 1986   Burial: 25 Jul 1986
Site 6 Thomas Lee King
       Birth: 1933   Death: 1986   Burial: 28 Apr 1986

Lot: 39 Lower   Owner: Miscellaneous
Site 6 Charles Thomas Reed, Sr.   h/o Grace V. Reed
       Birth: 9 Oct 1913   Death: 8 Dec 1995   Burial: 12 Dec 1995

Lot: 39 Upper   Owner: Miscellaneous
Site 3 Charles Edward Smith   TS: TEC 5 US Army WWII   h/o Alice F. Smith
       Birth: 23 Jul 1920   Death: 23 Nov 1988   Burial: 26 Nov 1988
Site 4 Charles Edward Smith Jr.   Mort: Hilton
       Birth: 4 Jul 1945   Death: 12 Jul 1993   Burial: 17 Jul 1993
Site 5 Paul Luther Stream
       Birth: 7 Jul 1924   Death: 25 Sep 1988   Burial: 28 Sep 1988
       TS: Married Gladys Marie Stream 29 Dec 1953, TEC 5 US Army WWII
Site 6 Robert G. Pierce
       Birth: 13 May 1963   Death: 27 Jan 1994   Burial: 28 Feb 1994

Lot: 40 Lower Owner: Barbara J., David A. & Douglas Ward
Site 4 Elmer Charles Ward Jr. TS: AMH 3 US Navy Korea
Birth: 10 Apr 1934 Death: 11 Nov 1989 Burial: 14 Nov 1989

Lot: 40 Upper Owner: Miscellaneous
Site 1 Walter D. Sheron
Birth: 1919 Death: 1993 Burial: 19 Feb 1993
Site 2 Mary Ann Sheron On stone with Walter D. Sheron
Birth: 1925 Death: 1990 Burial: 16 Feb 1990
Site 6 William Billek
Birth: 13 Apr 1933 Death: 30 Dec 1988 Burial: 2 Jan 1989

Lot: 41 Lower Owner: Miscellaneous
Site 3 Judith Mary Ford w/o Joseph D. Ford
Birth: 25 Aug 1946 Death: 21 May 1991 Burial: 25 May 1991

Lot: 41 Upper Owner: Miscellaneous
Site 1 Robert Eugene Cole TS: SP 4 US Army
Birth: 7 Apr 1959 Death: 19 Oct 1990 Burial: 25 Oct 1990
Site 2 Hosley J. Gravley TS: US Army WWII
Birth: 2 Jul 1909 Death: 19 Dec 1990 Burial: 22 Dec 1990
Site 3 Clarice Whisman Gravley w/o Hosley Gravley
Birth: 31 May 1915 Death: 4 Apr 1994 Burial: 6 Apr 1994
Site 5 Elizabeth Ann Fowler Age 11 yrs
Birth: 10 Oct 1979 Death: 11 Oct 1990 Burial: 18 Oct 1990

Lot: 42 Lower Owner: Miscellaneous
Site 5 Flora B. Ward On stone with Austin Louis Ward
Birth: 27 Jul 1934 Death: 13 Oct 1994 Burial: 17 Oct 1994
Site 6 Austin Louis Ward Age 77 yrs
Birth: 16 Apr 1916 Death: 7 Jul 1993 Burial: 13 Jul 1993

Lot: 42 Upper Owner: Miscellaneous
Site 1 Susan Marie Kamman-Levol
Birth: 9 Sep 1959 Death: 16 Dec 1993 Burial: 20 Dec 1993
Site 2 Donald Ray Gravley
Birth: 7 Mar 1959 Death: 25 Jan 1992 Burial: 30 Jan 1992
Site 4 Debra Patricia Kamman Fagan TS: Fagan not on stone
Birth: 5 Sep 1961 Death: 6 Jan 1992 Burial: 8 Jan 1992

Potters Field or Free Ground

The following were reported to be buried in "Potters Field" or "Free Ground" These areas are unknown today. It is thought that the burials were made in small available areas between or just outside the lots which had been sold.

Lot:	Owner:	
Site	Mrs. Lew Alison	Burial: 13 Mar 1896
Site	Mrs. Lew Alison	Burial: 18 Mar 1892
Site	Mr. Jame W. Boswell	Burial: 19 Apr 1885
Site	Thos Aernon Forde	Burial: 31 Jan 1907
Site	Infant of J. B. Mellott	Burial: 21 May 1907
Site	Miss Barbra Morningstar	Burial: 2 Jun 1898
Site	Child of Giypie	Burial: 10 Nov 1877
Site	Moses Wood	Burial: 31 May 1891
Site	Mr. James Engles	Burial: 8 Dec 1877
Site	Child of Carlton Huffers	Burial: 9 Jun 1884

The following burials were picked up from the Interment Books. Their placement is unknown. They have possibly been removed, buried in unmarked areas such as above, or are duplications which I have not been able to identify:

Site	James Edward Baker		Mort: Albert J. Baker
	Place: Takoma Park	Death: 12 Sep 1925	Burial: 14 Sep 1925
Site	Chas. E. Burkhart	No marker	Mort: W.T. Hilton & Sons
	Place: Comus	Death: 24 Jun 1917	Burial: 26 Jun 1917
Site	William T. Butcher		Mort: Roy W. Barber
	Place: near Cedar Grove	Death: 27 Dec 1939	Burial: 29 Dec 1939
Site	Infant of Frank Childris	Cause: Stillborn	Mort: W.T. Hilton & Sons
	Place: Poolesville	Death: 8 May 1923	Burial: 8 May 1923
Site	Infant of Margerete Cooley	Mort: W.W. Chambers	
	Place: Washington, DC	Death: 27 Oct 1930	Burial: 29 Oct 1930
Site	Baby boy Cregger		Mort: W.B. Hilton
	Place: Olney	Death: 10 Jan 1946	Burial: 11 Jan 1946
Site	Linda Carroll Cregger		Mort: W.B. Hilton
	Place: Poolesville	Death: 31 Jul 1944	Burial: 31 Jul 1944
Site	Infant of Roy Robert Cregger		Mort: Ray Robert Cregger
	Place: Poolesville	Death: 19 Jul 1950	Burial: 19 Jul 1950
Site	John Crosby		Mort: Willard H. Crosby
	Place: Martinsburg	Death: 11 Aug 1939	Burial: 11 Aug 1939
	Cause: Premature infant		Infant of Willard H. Crosby
Site	Mary Elizabeth Earp		Mort: W.T. Hilton & Sons
	Place: Sellman	Death: 7 Jun 1914	Burial: 9 Jun 1914

Monocacy Cemetery, Beallsville, Montgomery County, Maryland

Site	Priscilla Earp		Mort: W.T. Hilton & Sons
	Place: Barnesville	Death: 7 Aug 1919	Burial: 8 Aug 1919
Site	Mr. John Gandley	No marker	Burial: 25 Jan 1897
Site	Child of John Gandly	No marker	Burial: 30 Nov 1890
Site	Daughter of John Gandley	No marker	Burial: 18 Apr 1899
Site	Miss Olive Gandly	No marker	Burial: 7 Apr 1898
Site	Lewis Marcoe Gravely		Mort: Hilton & Price
	Place: Poolesville	Death: 16 Jan 1935	Burial: 17 Jan 1935
Site	Nathan C. Griffith	No marker	Burial: 20 Feb 1905
Site	Joseph Hall	No marker	Burial: 25 Feb 1891
Site	Catherine Hornbeck	No marker	Mort: W.W. Chambers
	Place: Washington, DC	Death: 25 May 1943	Burial: 28 May 1943
Site	Infant "B" Hornbeck	No marker	Mort: W.W. Chambers
	Place: Georgetown	Death: 21 Aug 1942	Burial: 25 Aug 1942
Site	Daniel M. Howard	No marker	Mort: R.W. Pumphrey Jr.
	Place: Quince Orchard	Death: 23 Jun 1932	Burial: 25 Jun 1932
Site	Eugene M. Keller		Mort: Hilton
	Place: Olney	Death: 23 Dec 1966	Burial: 26 Dec 1966
Site	Harry Eugene Lee		Mort: Hilton & Hall
	Place: Poolesville	Death: 17 Dec 1922	Burial: 18 Dec 1922
Site	Katherine S. Lee		Mort: Hilton & Hall
	Place: Poolesville	Death: 3 Dec 1924	Burial: 3 Dec 1924
Site	Edward Liroy Loring	No marker	Mort: Herman Snyder
	Place: Damascus	Death: 17 Apr 1935	Burial: 18 Apr 1935
Site	Mrs. Mackintosh and 2 children	No marker	Burial: 25 Nov 1877
Site	William Maxey		Mort: W.B. Hilton
	Place: Dickerson	Death: 31 Aug 1944	Burial: 2 Sep 1944
Site	Henry W. Mossburg	No marker	Burial: 27 Oct 1877
Site	Child of Mrs. H. Mossburg	No marker	Burial: 15 Jul 1884
Site	Herbert V. Morningstar		Mort: W.B. Hilton
	Place: Baltimore	Death: 1 Jul 1947	Burial: 5 Jul 1947
Site	Dorothy Mae Norris	No marker	Mort: Warner E.
	Place: Washington, DC	Death: 23 May 1940	Burial: 26 May 1940
Site	Thomas Howard Norris Jr.	No marker	Mort: Warner E.
	Place: Kensington	Death: 25 Dec 1935	Burial: 27 Dec 1935
Site	William Henry Norwood	No marker	Mort: Ernest C. Gartner
	Place: Rockville	Death: 29 Jan 1949	Burial: 2 Jan 1949
Site	Robert S. Orme	No marker	Mort: W.T. Hilton & Sons
	Place: Owings Mills	Death: 31 Oct 1918	Burial: 2 Nov 1918
Site	Mary C. Poole		Mort: W.K. Hunteman
	Place: Washington, DC	Death: 5 Jun 1937	Burial: 9 Jun 1937
Site	Earl Reed		Mort: Hilton & Hall
	Place: Poolesville	Death: 20 May 1936	Burial: 20 May 1936
Site	Chas. Henry Riley		Mort: Hilton & Hall
	Place: Poolesville	Death: 10 Mar 1927	Burial: 11 Mar 1927
Site	Mrs. Rosea Rutter	No marker	Burial: 22 Dec 1903
Site	Mary F. Scheckles		Mort: W.W. Chambers
	Place: Washington, DC	Death: 12 Mar 1941	Burial: 15 Mar 1941

Site	Sarah Seelock		Mort: Hilton & Hall
	Place: Martinsburg	Death: 17 Aug 1925	Burial: 18 Aug 1925
Site	Infant of Henry H. Shawver		Mort: Hilton & Hall
	Place: Martinsburg	Death: 9 Feb 1934	Burial: 10 Feb 1934
Site	Infant Shiflett	No marker	Mort: Warner E.
		Death: 17 Jul 1944	Burial: 18 Jul 1944
	Place: Montgomery Co. Hospital		
Site	Ruth Smith		Mort: Warner E. Pumphrey
	Place: Washington, DC	Death: 23 Feb 1943	Burial: 24 Feb 1943
Site	Son of Mr. Charles Stevens		Burial: 9 Mar 1895
Site	Child of William Stunkel	No marker	Burial: 8 Mar 1904
Site	Mrs. Thompson and child		Burial: 25 Mar 1892
Site	Mr. Carle Thompson		Burial: 9 Oct 1890
Site	Lenard Trail		Burial: 28 Nov 1877
Site	Ruth G. Tydings		Mort: Mr. Roberts
	Place: Washington, DC	Death: 1 Jan 1929	Burial: 3 Jan 1929
Site	Infant Unnamed		Mort: W.T. Hilton & Sons
	Place: Barnesville	Death: 10 Jul 1914	Burial: 11 Jul 1914
Site	Baby boy Weller	No marker	Mort: W.B. Hilton
	Place: Frederick Hospital	Death: 27 Oct 1945	Burial: 29 Oct 1945
Site	Wife of John Willard	Burial: Jan 1878	No day given
Site	Jesse Eugene Wright	No marker	Mort: W.R. Pumphrey
	Place: Potomac	Death: 12 Jun 1934	Burial: 14 Jun 1934

Index

A

Adkins	
Claude S.	186
Rebecca F.	186
Ainsworth	
J. Trent	205
J.T.	95
Judah T.	205
Mary Sellman	95, 205
Ruth Sellman	205
Throop	95
Alison	
Lew	270
Allan	
Catherine W.	261
John P.	261
Allen	
David Wayne	64
Viola Moxley	223
Allison	
Rose Alberta L.	148
Allnutt	
Ada Perry	219
Albert S.	89
Alice Thomas	218
Americus Dawson	218
Anna Chiswell	106
Annie Lee	218
Arthur W.	106
Barbara Ann	27
Benjamin Nourse	219
Benjamin W.	90
Benjamin White	89
Benoni	89, 105
Benoni D.	89, 219, 246
Bettie Ann	27
Bettie Maude Padgett	235
Carrie Williams	152
Charles Edward	218
Dorothy Williams	106
Edna W.	238
Edwin	105
Edwin R.	107
Edwin Ruthvin	152
Effie Miller	218
Eleanor	105, 107
Elizabeth	27
Elizabeth Brown	54
Elizabeth Virginia	27
Ella V. Thomas	220
Elzey D.	106
Emily Dawson	89, 105
Ernest C.	114
Estelle	106
Evelyn Darby	55
Evelyn Souder	218
Franklin Thomas	220
Frederick A.	219
Gladys Bauserman	219
Guy Francis	218
Harriette Sproul	246
Henry White	90
Herbert Thomas	235
Hilda Perry	218
James	105
James Gott	114
James Laurence	220
James N.	27
James Robert	27
James Russell	219
Jane Williams	90
John H.	83
John Hanson	235
Joseph Frank	106
Joseph Kenneth	54
Joseph N.	105, 106
Julia Miller	218
Juliana Virlinder	27
Laurence	105
Lawrence	90, 105
Lawrence A.	220
Lawrence E.	89
Lewis Phillip	218
Lucie Williams	106
Lucille Gott	114
Lucille Johnson	219
Lutie Chiswell	218
M.G.	106
Margaret	106

Margaret E. White	106	Martin	143
Margaret Eleanor	106	Roger Lee	262
Margaret Valeria	220	Rose	54
Mildred Thomas	220	Rosemary S.	217
Minerva Henrietta	27	Virginia Hays	167
N.S.	106	Andrews	
Nathan B.	89	Martha A. Kendall	41
Nathan W.	106	Antonelli	
Nathan White	106	Lauren Christine	257
Nellie (Eleanor)	89	Archer	
Nelva Thomas	219	Raymond Lee	268
Nena Reed	235	Arrington	
Oscar	107	Bessie V.	179
Rachel Ann	89	J. Guy	179, 260
Rachel White	89	John Thomas	179
Reginald Cecil	238	Astlin	
Richard Walter	54	George R.	192, 193
Robert Henry Clay	27	Indiana	37
Robert Wilkerson	218, 246	James Richard	193
Sadie	89	James Walter	193
Sadie Lucile	105	Mary B.	193
Sarah	106	Mary M.	193
Thomas Dawson	218	Richard B.	37
Verlinder	105	Walter W.	37
Walter Doyne	105	Atterton	
Warner Stutler	235	Marie Ann Nicholson	243
William Baker	246	Atwell	
Ammerman		Dorothy A.	268
John	250	Sarah E.	100
Anders		Walter K.	268
Callie Frances	244	Aud	
Dave Joshua	214	Carrie Virginia	18
Willie J.	244	Edgar T.	18
Anderson		Ena M.	18
Alde B.	138	Eva Louise	119
Carl E.	214	Grace Susan	162
Claude	26	Kathleen Louise	119
Daisy Irene	26	Laura T. Pugh	18
David Barber	217	Seneca Veirs	18
Elizabeth E.	26	Susan Ann Veirs	18
Evelyn Hersperger	138	Susan E.	119
Hugh	26	Trujean Handy	119
James H.	216	William E.	162
Jessie I.	26	William Lee	18
John W.	22	William T.	18
Mae S. Whisman	216	William Thomas	18
Marian E.	214	Austin	
Martha Waesche	143	Catharine	1

Dennis Eric	267	Garnett Cawood	21
Dorothy Claire Sirk	267	Ballenger	
William C.	254	Albert	138
Ayers		Carol Hope	157
John Wakeman	181	Ernest B.	138
Julia L.	181	Irving Thompson	158
		Lillie May	138
B		Luther Albert	138
		Nellie Holland	157
Babington		Sarah A.	138
C. Anna	184	Barnes	
Harriet A.	184	Nettie	73
Backman		Barnhouse	
Elizabeth Lucille	165	Carroll Clifton	266
Backus		Dewayne C.	212
Anne Griffith	189	Glenn Edward	266
John A.	189	Rachael Virginia	266
Bagley		Thomas Larry	241
Dorothy S.	257	Wanda Jean	241
Marion LeRoy	257	Barr	
Baisey		Emma Whitman	237
Thomas G.	263	Estelle Marie Jamison	237
Virginia M.	263	Harold Bryan	237
Baker		William Lincoln	237
Charles Russell	40	Barrick	
Edward	167	Ellen Straughan	255
Ellis Lee	241	Bassford	
Ethel Irene	41	Bessie May Wire	20
Harriet A. Hays	167	Gladie	20
Helen Beach	264	Marion	20
Henry Curtis	41	Marion Isaac	20
James Bruce	268	Bastable	
James Edward	270	Alvin B.	69
Katherine Virginia	40	Harriet Griffith	69
Raymond Harvey	264	Baugher	
Rose	242	Michele Rene	187
Sarah E.	13	Nikki C.	187
Viola E.	175	Patricia M.	187
Viola W.	40	Thomas M.	187
Viola Whisman	175	Bauman	
Walter	40	Betty J.	255
William	40	Kathleen Fern	255
William Claude	241, 242	Mahlon Clifford	255
William G.	182	Baxter	
William R.	175	Andrew James	70
William Russell	258	Frances Metzger	70
Ball		Beach	
Ambrey Lewis	20	Agnes Mary	252

Name	Page
James Norman	252
John C.	252
John R.	252
Virginia Myrtle	252
Beacht	
Alice	81
Charles M.	81
Edward	39
Effie B.	81
Mollie	81
Nellie	39
Roy Thomas	39
Beall	
Barthommea	51
Bessie Frances	199
C.R.	186
Caroline Eleanor	141
Carrie T.	199
Catherine	23
Catherine E.	198
Charles R.	216
Charles Wilson	43
Dorothy Gott	141
E. Rudolph	141
Elias	199
Eliza C. West	141
Emma Maxwell	149
Erwin O.	199
Evelyn	215
Frank T.	176
Helen Rutter	43
Henry Brooks	141
Ida	199
James M.	177
James Maurice	177
John Alvin	177
John William	199
Lemuel Larkin	10
Lester Erwin	214
Lucie Frances Rutter	216
Margaret	212
Marion T.	141
Marion W.	43, 177
Mary Elizabeth	10
Melissa Moulden	221
Pearl A. Selena	177
Rebecca Schoole	141
Roger William	243

Name	Page
Rudolph Gott	141
William H.	199
William Rudolph	141
William Thomas	215
Winfield Scott	221
Beck	
Katherine Hughes	180
Marjorie Saxton	181
Nellie Saxton	181
William Christian	180, 181
Beever	
Annie G. Norris	84
Behers	
Walter	39
Beitzel	
George Randall	215
Leora M.	215
Belcher	
Alberta M.	160
Claude Hicks	160
D.L.	22
Donald Lee	22
Dorothy J.	22
H.F.	22
J.W.	22
James Walter	160
M.B.	22
Mattie B.	160
Bellman	
Consuelo N	174
Belt	
Ann Amelia	120
Ashby	1
J.R.	25
John Richard	25
Mary Barbara	25
Mary E.	25
Virginia Lee	25
Bennett	
Catherine E. (Kate)	61
Constance Duplessie	254
Corrine C. Waldhuetter	254
John Bonifras	254
Benson	
A. M.	73
Addie S.	185
Allen M.	70
Annie Belle	257

Bruce	70	Hester Ayers	181
Charles E.	185	John F.	181
Elizabeth	70	Bobb	
Henrietta	70	Robert Alexander	135
Isabella A.	70	Bodmer	
James W.	257	Carrie Melissa Wiles	174
James Wade	212	Catherine Ricketts	173
Jonathan	88	Charles Rozier	248
Lillian P.	61	Charles Wesley	262
Mary E.	70	Debra Kay	250
Mary M.	70	Dorothy Cooley	59
Nellie Holland Ballenger	157	George Jacob	59
Temperance M.	212	Henry LeRoy	173
Thomas P.B.	70	Jacob	174
Thomas R.	70	John Davis	173
Walter R.	262	June R.	250
William B.	200	Lyda	174
William H.	70	Marjorie G.	173
William P.	61	Mary Catherine	174
Betson		Mollie M. Cubitt	173
Clayton	82	Ray C.	250
Donna Marie	6	Roy	173
Edward Arlington	213	Virgie G. Houser	262
H.C.	82	Wayne Wesley	262
Harry C.	6	William Eugene	173
Helen Elizabeth	82	William LeRoy	173
S.W.	82	Zada Florence	248
Sallie E.	6	Bolinger	
William Clayton	213	A. L.	51
Billek		Clayton Lewis	51
William	269	Elsie May	51
Binnix		Emma Jane	51
George W.	242	Ethel	51
Bittinger		Mary	51
Catherine Moxley	223	Warner	51
Black		Wilbur Warner	51
Elizabeth Elgin	198	William. H.	51
Harvey O.	198	Booty	
Bladen		Amos Perkins	254
Daryl Lynn	254	Florence A.	254
Thomas C.	254	Bosley	
Blair		Annie Laura Brown	170
Samuel Joseph	30	George W.	170
Blanchard		Boswell	
Jean Charles Edmond	117	Jame W.	270
Blevins		James Montgomery	162
Robert H.	24	Bouic	
Blood		Ella H.	130

John P.	viii		Braady	
John Peter	130		Margaret Astlin	193
Lelia May	130		Bradshaw	
Susan E.	130		Maurice E.	240
Bouis			Tressie E. Dove	240
Joseph Elwood	3		Brady	
Bourke			Robert Edward	210
Eleanor Chiswell	53		Brewer	
Bourne			Aletha T.	111
Thelma Gilliam	265		Arthur	112
Trube Terry	265		Bettie Williams	153
Bower			Camillus	111
Belva	253		Charles M.	153
John M.	253		Cornellus	111
Larry Mack	253		Edith Fink	78
Bowers			George	111
Barbara J.	229		George W.	111, 153
George Raymond	172		Harry Spencer	78
Bowling			Ida White	111
St. Clair Brooke	188		James Burch	140
William Sinclair	188		Joseph	111
Bowlus			Lawrence Newton	140
Charles H.	3		Martha Plater	112
Bowman			Mary McDonnell	140
Basil	253		Mary R.	111
Benjamin Franklin	21		N.	112
Catherine E.	222		Nicholas	112
Dock B.	253		Ruth Chiswell	140
Elizabeth Jane Darby	145		Ruth E.W. Jones	112
Evelyn T.	145		Stephen Newton	140
Frederick	21, 145		Warnetta	111
Frederick E.	222		William	111, 112
John Darby	145		William G.	111
John H.	21		Brill	
Martha Ellen	21		Helen M.	43
Mary Elizabeth	21		Martin William	257
Rezin	21		William F.	257
Richard	21		Winifred A.	257
Richard H.	145		Brodnax	
Ruth Gue	21		James Henry	48
Ruth R. Darby	21		Minnie Cooley	48
William Arthur	222		Brooks	
William Harrison	222		Anna M.	219
Boxer			Anna M. Titus	249
Ida Walter	73		Estelle White	219
John S.	73		Harold B.	219
Boyce			James E.	219
Thomas W.	235		James Evans	249

Leo Franklin	220	Americus E.	126
Lewis Franklin	220	Catherine	45
Lois	219	Catherine E.	126
Margaret Elizabeth	220	Elizabeth	45
Mary Ann	219	George W.	125
Mary Katherine	220	George William	126
Mary Margaret	41	Joseph	45
Brosius		Julia A.M.	125
Charles T.	181	Lydia	45
Charles Thomas	181	Malista C.	125
Dorothy Gott	114	Michael	45
Ellen Ayers	181	William L.	125
Genevieve T. Darby	181	Bryant	
John William	134	Janice Dunnigan	181
Louise D.	134	William Penn	181
Mildred Lewis	156	Buckey	
William J.	134	Charles Wesley	5
Brown		Maggie J.	4
Andrew Clinton	81	Bucknam	
Annie K.	203	Estella C.	248
Annie M.	81	Bunge	
Clinton	81	Clarence Edward	259
David H.	203	Frederica M.	259
Elizabeth Oxley	146	Burch	
Erma Louise Hubble	238	C.W.	193
Ethel Moore King	237	Carroll A.	230
George David	203	Charles W.	230
H. C.	167	Dora Luellen	193
H. D.	9	Edith M.	230
Hatton Darby	79	Elizabeth C.	230
Herbert	79	Francis Albert	230
J. Herbert	146	Francis E.	viii, 116
James W.	81	George W.	230
John W.	79	Harriet	116
Mary Elizabeth	79	Henry Clay	116
Mary Poole	79	L.W.	193
Mollie Darby	79	Lula W. Astlin	230
Pearl M.	155	Mary R.	116
Richard Haffen	238	Burdette	
Sarah Elizabeth	79	Anna Eliza Smith	227
William Clifton	79	Charles Grover	265
William Curtis	81	George McClellan	227
Browning		Helen Carlisle	104
William W.	211	Helen Mulligan	227
Brubaker		James T.	227
Beulah Brooks	259	John Douglas	264
Louis Creglo	260	John Russell	227
Brunner		Lloyd Wilkens	104

Otis McLelland	227		Charles Spates	146
Susan Campbell	104		Chas M.	viii
Burgner			Cinderella Titus	146
Infant	45		Corrie F.	150
Burke			Elspet Garen	130
Catherine A.	260		Emma Reese	131
Earl E.	260		Frances Thomas Spates	150
Elizabeth Goldsmith	127		George R.	146
Burkhart			George W.	viii, 131
Chas. E.	270		Gorman Lee	151
Burlingame			Harry Lee	146
Della Jones Emerson	170		Hattie Alice	146
Frederick H.	170		Jennie I. Brunner	146
Burress			Joseph Gorman	151
Judith Teresa	267		Kathleen Mable	131
Burroughs			Lucile	146
George	106		Lucille Irene Cox	151
Julia L. Ayers	181		Lula C.	150
Leonard	15		Richard	130
Nettie Lee Jones	15		Richard T.	131
Rebecca	106		Rosa E.	131
S. Eleanor	106		Rosa May Cubitt	239
Burrows			Rosser Eugene	150
Elizabeth Spreadbury	87		Ruth Ann	151
John Thomas	87		Virginia Clark	146
Bussard			Walter Mason	239
Charles Arthur	204		William George	150
Elizabeth W.	203		Butt	
Elnor Frances	172		Charles Upton	216
Elsie Naomi	204		Ernest Lee	256
Enos C.	172		Irene Gertrude	256
John Maurice	204		Kenneth P.	215
John W.	172		M. Estelle	215
Joseph Henry	204		Perry Oliver	242
L.T.	34		Susanna	242
Margaret A.	172		Byrd	
Olga Lou	34		Annie	126
Ophelia L.	204		Clara	126
Robert Lee	203		Elsie May	126
Thelma C.	34		George W.	126
Tracy	19		John B.	126
W.J.	204		Joseph Dyson	190
William W.	172		Lillian Brewer	190
Butcher			Mary Jane	126
William T.	270		Sallie T.	126
Butler			Sallie T. Veirs	126
Charles M.	130		Samuel D.	126
Charles Martin	146, 150		William L.	126

Byrne
  James F. ... 16
  Sarah E. ... 16

C

Cady
  Josephine ... 8
  Mary ... 8
  Sarah Ellen Poole ... 8
  William Appleton ... 8
Calavetinos
  Frances M. ... 177
Callahan
  Constance M. ... 257
  Stephen M. ... 257
Campbell
  Blanche Virginia Cross ... 62
  Fred Munger ... 248
  Jessie Bodmer ... 249
  Nell James Mundy ... 245
  William C. ... 245
Canady
  Carolyn ... 220
Carlin
  Virgie M. ... 180
  William Melvin ... 180
Carlisle
  Anna Virginia ... 81
  Bettie C. Fields ... 176
  Christie A. ... 60
  Frances C. ... 176
  George Richard ... 178
  Grover C. ... 1
  J. Maurice ... 166
  James Maurice ... 176
  James William ... 81
  Lucy Lavina ... 176
  Mary Ann Poole ... 166
  Richard C. ... 176
  Richard Vernon ... 176
  William O. ... 180
Carr
  Arthur B. ... 139
  Nannie Davis ... 139
  Terry Annette ... 243
  William H. ... 243
Carter
  Anna Lucille ... 109
  Brandon George ... 268
  Brenda Lou Selby ... 229
  Burrel ... 109
  Carrie Virginia ... 133
  Catherine C. ... 266
  Claud Augustus ... 212
  David H. ... 109
  Elizabeth Ann ... 109
  Elsbey ... 22
  George F. ... 268
  George Henry ... 109
  Grover C. ... 109
  James A. ... 22
  Jane E. ... 22
  John Jacob ... 109
  Joseph ... 109
  Joseph E. ... 109
  Joseph L. ... 109
  Laura A.G. ... 109
  Lester Franklin ... 243
  Martin Slemp ... 9
  Mary E. ... 109
  Mary Virginia ... 109
  Maude M. ... 133
  Molly ... 109
  Robert ... 109
  Samuel Henry ... 184
  Sherry A. ... 268
  Thomas ... 231
  Thomas H. ... 133
  Virginia M. Whitaker ... 184
Cassedy
  Mable Claire ... 52
  Miller Aiken ... 52
Cassell
  Augusta Rogers ... 210
  Robert N. ... 210
Catalano
  Salvatore Vincent ... 230
Cator
  Carrie W. ... 80
  Margaret S. ... 80
  Richard T. ... 80
  S.H. ... 80
  Samuel H. ... 80
Catron
  Carrie E. Smith ... 209

James A.	209
Raymond Luther	206
Cecil	
Clara L.	156
Luther E.	156
Mary C.	156
Oscar T.	158
Selma G.	158
Chalmers	
Alice C.	42
Chambers	
Annie Laurie	102
D. Clopton	102
Hathaway	102
Laura Ligon	102
Louise Lanier	102
William H.	102
William Lea	102
William Lee	102
Chapman	
Barbara Jean	141
Dorothy Anne Beall	141
Elizabeth Claire	215
Mabel B.	215
Mabel C.	141
Robert H.	141, 215
Childris	
Frank	270
Chisolm	
Isabel C.	41
Julian J.	41
Chiswell	
Byron Walling	225
Caroline Hilleary White	127
Carrie Bodmer	174
Carroll Thomas	148
Edgar B.	85
Edward Fowler	90
Edward J.	viii, 90
Edward Lee	90
Elizabeth Ellen	124
Elizabeth Susan Gott	53
Eloise Wootton	49
Elsie Lee	219
Eugenia G.	53
Evie W.	90
Geo. W.	viii
George William	174
Haddie Smith	85
Hattie Hersperger	140
Helen	90
John A.	53
Joseph T.	121
Joseph Thomas	127
Lawrence	140
Lawrence A.	140
Leah Griffith	124
Linda Young	121
Lulu Helen	124
Maggie M.	127
Margaret White	53
Marjorie Waters	140
Mary Collison	52
Mary Eleanor Jones	91
Mary Elizabeth	92
Maurice H.	140
Maurice Waters	135
Mildred Thornton	49
Naomi North	90
Olivia Marguerite	121
Ruby A.	121
Sallie D.	127
Sarah	69, 91, 93, 124
Sarah P.	124
Stephen N.	93
Thomas Fletchall	91
Thomas Franklin	49
Thomas H.	85
Thomas Hilleary	127
William	69, 91, 124
William Greenbury	124
Christie	
Alfred	247
Carlton Lee	123
Esther May	247
Helen M.	247
Marjorie Ann	247
Christmas	
A. Mabel Mae Norris	93
Chriswell	
George Walter	124
Cissel	
Charles LeRoy	69
Elizabeth	72
Elmo	69
Eugene E.	171

Georgie Newton	69	Clugston		
Julia G.	68	Samuel Nelson	144	
Mary Eleanor	72	Coates		
Pauline Jones	154	Clarence J.	52	
Philip A.	72	Eleanor Elgin	52	
R. Humphrey	68	Cochran		
Rachael S.	72	George C.	262	
William	72	Cole		
William Griffith	154	Annie M.	178	
William Howard	69	Bertha M.	162	
Cissell		Carrie E. Smith Catron	209	
Philip A.	72	Charles Albert	178	
Claggett		Charles Lee	178	
Laura LaVonne	36	Douglas Raymond	206	
Linda Mae	36	Ellen M.	206	
Mae Flood	36	Ezra E.	42	
Minnie Flood	36	James R.	205	
Minnie Mae Flood	64	John Edward	206	
Richard	36	John Morris	42	
Richard G.	36, 64	Joseph R.	205	
Clapperton		Leonard S.	206	
Anita Dora	113	Maggie E. Cooley	162	
Clark		Margaret Ann	162	
Alice L.H.	242	Margaret I.	238	
Blanche Griffith	136	Martha Ann	42	
Emily Darby Brown	79	Mary E.	205	
Henry T.	166	Minnie Pearl Smith	244	
James Brent	242	Myrtle E.	178	
Margaret	182	Norman	41	
Morrison	136	Norman R.	41	
Myrna Livingston Jones	166	Paul M.	244	
Clarke		Richard	42	
Elizabeth	242	Robert Eugene	269	
Clements		Thomas E.	162	
Edna G.	227	William U.	178	
Leona L. Waddell	227	Collier		
Thomas Henry	227	Annie C.	35	
William Joseph	212	Beulah L.	34	
Cline		Carrie M.	83	
Mary Louise Stream	65	Henry L.	34	
Clipper		J.W.	34	
Christine Kohlhoss	221	John R.	35	
Clopton		John W.	34	
David	102	Marcus S.	83	
Clothier		Martha Virginia	22	
Archie Ball	85	Mary F.	34	
Horace Truman	83	Mary Louise	83	
Sarah Pauline Hays	85	Olga Hume	34	

Richard H.	34, 83	Charles L.	118
Ruth L.	35	Charles T.	118
Theresa	83	Claude	79
Thomas Peyton	22	Claude O.	80
William	35	Earl Calvert	203
William F.	34	Eldridge M.	233
Collins		Elgie N.	118
Raymond W.	142	Ella Mossburg	40
Robert L.	142	Eugene	101
Colwell		George Fulton	59
Abbie Mae	73	Gladys Lee	80
Comer		H. Herbert	48
Emory L.	256	Herbert William	233
Compher		Horace	48
Eva May	80	Isabella Virginia	80
Henrietta	40	James	101
Jonas C.	40	John Bernard	202
Miriam E.	40	June	80
Nettie L.	80	Laura J.	80
Ruth Ellen Beall	199	Lillie May	233
Samuel P.	80	Lucy	101
Wilfred Clinton	40	Lucy Elizabeth	203
William J.	40	Magie E.	48
Zachariah M.	199	Margerete	270
Conley		Maria E.	48
John W.	73	Maria E. Belt	48
Conlon		Martha Maria	79
Thomas A.	264	Martin S.	101
Connelly		Mary A.	101
Barbara M.	123	Mast Clark	48
John W.	74	May Etta	118
Margaret E.	74	Mitchell W.	40
Conwell		Mollie D.	48
Seymorus	99	Nathan S.	233
Cook		Nellie B. White	251
Helen Louise	252	Otho B.	203
Howard Lee	252	Robert J.	58, 101
Cooley		Robert T.	58
Alice May	233	Royie G.	233
Ann	101	Sandra L.	203
Annie Willett	58	Sid	101
Barbara A.	118	Sterling T.	118
Betty Columbia Wood	59	Vernon Thomas	233
Beulah Frances	118	William Henry	48
Brown	101	William Smith	80
Calvin	101	Wynona	48
Carol Jean	40	Zachariah G.	79
Charles Garrett	251	Cooper	

Arthur Berkely	226	Eli	262
Elva G.	160	Esther Thelma	211
Frances L.	160	Floyd W.	262
John H.	160	Kenneth Floyd	212
Martha Annie Phelps	226	Linda Carroll	270
Corbin		Mae Thompson	262
Ella J.	220	Ray	211
Corley		Roy Robert	270
Blanch J.	79	Steven Mark	64
R.S.	79	Crissey	
Cornwell		Bertha A.	224
Ada Belle	11	James Beverley	225
James A.	20	Cromwell	
John L.	178	Authur Hays	223
Lafayette A.	11	Cleveland	223
Mary Virginia	178	Grace Olivia	224
Corse		Mary Elizabeth	223
Barbara	213	Pearl B.	223
Barbara Lee	242	Richard	224
Thomas P.	213	Crone	
William	213	Charles B.	260
William C.	242	Kathryn Soper	260
Cosgrave		Crosby	
Ada Viola	238	John	270
Elmer Lee	207	Willard H.	270
Frances C.	207	Cross	
Lawrence Snowden	238	Anastatia	1
Rose Marie	208	Charles Upton	62
William D.	208	Emma Irene	61
Covert		John	1
Mabel Elizabeth	229	Joseph Thomas	1
Newton J.	229	Mary	1
Cowell		Reginald Whalen	61, 62
Frank B.	199	Sarah Elener	1
Crane		Cruit	
Barbara Kephart	259	Alice Maude	53
Cranford		Alice Nora	53
Ida J. Moxley	221	Charlotte C.	53
Joseph Winfield	221	Charlotte E.	53
Creger		Edith Ellen	54
Charles C.	133	Edwin D.	53
Floyd Bascum	133	Katherine W.	183
Lettie Argirtha	133	Luther R.	53
Margaret R. L.	133	Luther Reed	183
Margie A.	133	Russell C.H.	54
Cregger		Thomas D.	53
Baby Boy	211, 270	Cruitt	
Bertha Mae	262	Edwin	183

Virginia	183		William Franklin	45
Cubitt			Wm. F.	viii
Carrie V.	172		Dahn	
Edna Lee Dodd	230		Frank W.	155
Elizabeth Rebecca Luhn	171		Norrine Norris	155
Frank Edward	171		Dailey	
George Washington	171		James F.	153
Isaac Davis	230		Daniel	
James O.	172		Elsie White	184
John Allen	171		Mansfield White	184
John Isaac (Jack)	230		Mary White	184
Mary Christine	171		William Aglionby	184
Millard O.	172		Darby	
Rodney William	172		Albert Allnutt	191
Tina	230		Alice Harrison	191
Cummings			Basil	105
Ann Mildred Jones	92, 117		Benoni Dawson	107
Franklin	92		Bessie Dawson	108
Joseph Franklin	117		Catherine Vaughn	170
Curtis			Charles F.	115
Annie Cooley	118		Charles R.	115
Robert Elmer	118		Clara F.	116
			Cora John	116
D			Debora Tienny	170
			Edward	110
Dade			Edward Spencer	108
Alexandra	96		Elizabeth	170
Alonzo	96		Ellen R.	115
Anna Laura	2		Estelle Allnutt	21
Annie M.	113		Eva W.	115
Catherine H.	2		George	105
Charles Grason	156		George Dawson	107
Edwin Franklin	2		Gertrude E.	35
Frank Bond	156		Gertrude Hyatt	131
Grayson	35		Grace Newton	110
Grayson C.	156		H.D.	170
John H.	2		Harry	35
John Liston	156		Harry Clay	170
Mary Ruth	96		Harry Dunbar	170
Robert T.	2		Helen Pyles	66
Ruth	2		J.W.	35
Sarah E.	2		James W.	35
Serena Elizabeth	96		John E.	115
Thomas	156		John Edwin	131
Thomas Collison	96		John Riggs	66
Townsend	2		John W.	115, 132
Viola	156		Joseph N.	55, 108
Wade Hampton	96		Joseph Newton	108

Julia Allnutt		191	Valeria W.	21
Katie Dyson		170	Verlinda	105
Laura		15	Virginia L.	132
Laura Allnutt		156	William Hendren	115
Lawrence Allnutt		110, 191, 192	William LeRoy	156
Lawrence Jones		116	William W.	15
Lee W.		35	Zachary T.	115
Margaret Allnutt		106	Darne	
Margaret Eleanor		21	Cora Arnelia	39
Mary C.		55, 108	Dorian P.	39
Mary Eleanor		108	Isabel E.	39
Mary Eleanor Chiswell		108	Thomas F.	39
Mary Elizabeth		21	Davidson	
Mary Hays		17	John Edward	243
Mary Jane		115	Davis	
Mary Verlinda		110	Annie Ruth	12
Maude Gross		250	Arundel Thomas	52
Milton George		106	Calvin C.	265
Mollie J.		35	Carolyne Virginia	139
Natalie A.		156	Catherine S.	38
Nellie		35	Charles Horace	140
Nellie Hall		115	Chester H.	12
Nellie Vaughn		115	Clara P.	38
Nettie		116	E.G.	112
Rebecca		105	Effi McDonough	252
Rebecca Dawson		105	Frances Lucille	12
Reginald J.		17	Francis E.	11
Remus R.		116	Frank	139
Richard Edwin		116	Frank Isaac	139
Robert Doyne		108	George Alfred	232
Roger William		110	George F.	232
Ruth Ellen		116	George Vernon	38
Sallie		115	Harriet A. Hays	134
Sallie Anne Chiswell		110	Harriet Jane	154
Samuel C.		115	Harry J.	213
Samuel Porter		115	Horace M.	139
Sarah		21	Isaac	38
Sarah Ann Valinda		107	James L.	112
Sarah Elizabeth		107, 108	James Lynn	112
Sarah Virginia		115	Jane Plater Brewer	112
Susan Augusta		107	Jesse Wilson	185
Susan Elizabeth		110	John J.	12
Thomas		105	John W.	154
Thomas C.		21	John Wallace	134
Thomas Chiswell		21	L. Wilson	38
Thomas Dawson		107	LeRoy	252
Thomas Gordon		250	Lucie Dodson	139
Thomas P.		35	Lula H.	11

Mabel Coatsworth	140	Mary E.	128
Margaret J.	154	Mary Elizabeth	93
Margaret Nolia	232	Mary Margaret	91
Mary Brewer	112	Nicholas Lowe	108
Mary Brosius	134	Rachael White Trundle	129
Mary E.Y.	55	Rebecca	27
Mary Emma	139	Robert	105
Mary Harrison	38	Robert D.	182
Mildred	265	Robert Doyne	27, 93
Mildred Lucille Briggs	12	Robert Thomas	91
Nannie Hamner	112	Sarah	91, 105
Nina R.	26	Sarah Newton	182
Notley Hays	134	Sarah Newton Chiswell	93
Ray	252	Sarah Newton Jones	91
Reginald W.	214	Susan	183
Rufus Hamilton	38	Susan A.	91
Ruth H. Young	185	Susanah H.	182
Sarah Ellen	52	Thomas	93, 182
Solomon	2	Thomas G.	109
Susie	139	Virginia Mays	108
Susie Griffith	139	Virginia O.	128
Thomas Harold	52	William	105
Victorine Smith	38	William Cyrus	105
Davison		William Edward	91
Annie Leah	186	William P.	108
Dawson		William Veirs	108
Adelaide Louisa	91	Day	
Americus	129	Charles William	211
Ann	183	James Edward	251
Benoni	91	Lynne R.	183
Charles E.	108	Mary Elizabeth	211
Cyanne Prince	108	Mary Louise	251
Dorothy Wootton	253	Mary Louise Brown	211
Eleanor	183	Deadrick	
Elizabeth	93, 105	Joseph M.	244
Emma C.	108	Juanita B.	213
Fred A.	93	Louanna Stottlemyer	263
Frederick A.	91	Raymond M.	213
George Washington	93	Robert	263
Henrietta	27	Dean	
James M.	128, 183	Charles Earle	265
James P.	128	Lucille Fox	216
John Hollyday	253	Mildred Waters	265
Joseph Henry	91	Smith P.	216
Joseph N.	93	DeAtley	
Laura A.	91	Helen	6
Louisa V.	128	deBeck	
Mary Doyne	105	Gail Wade	185

Thomas O.	185	Dobson		
deCarlo		James Andrew		2
Jean Frances Kaempfer	265	Dodd		
Derr		Harry H.		230
Hannah R.	12	Ocie Ella		231
Harriet A.	12	Phebe Ella		230
Devilbiss		William H.		230
Caroline	19	Dodson		
I. A.	20	Burgess E.		207
Dickerson		Dollie T.		207
Alonzo	164	Ida		207
C. Milton	163	Luther		231
Charles Milton	163	Robert Edison		207
Christie A.	57	Upton Leon		207
Edith	163	Donn		
Edwin Trundle	163	Frances Cookman		113
Elizabeth Ellen Trundle	163	Nannie Estelle		113
Eugenia T.	164	Dorsett		
George H.	164	Helen Elizabeth Jeffery		238
Jennie R. Bier	163	Telfair Bowie		238
Lillian	163	Dove		
Martha H.	163	John Harvey		241
Mary Margaret	47	Martha Etta		241
Moselle Jarboe	221	Downs		
Myrtle M.	164	Clara N.		88
Nathan C.D.	57	James Robert		88
Nathan Cook	57	Mary Haskell		129
William H.	163	Maurice Allen		244
William Harrison	163, 221	Maurice C.		88
Wm. H.	viii	Maurice W.		88
Dickinson		Sarah F.		88
Carol L.	32	Driver		
Dill		Charles Wilson		236
Catherine M.	161	Myra Munger		236
Elmer B.	161	Dronenburg		
Dillehay		Harry Nicholas		44
Martha Jane Nicholson	175	Mary Poole		44
Dixon		Duff		
Albert Sidney	63	Corinne D.		108
Calvin S.	63	Duffy		
Eberly Thomas	187	Harold Arthur		224
Esther Macie	43	Margaret Estelle		224
Irene F.	253	Dugan		
Irving Doyle	253	Phebe		1
John Paul	63	Dulcan		
Margaret F.	63	James Newman Brown		43
Sidney E.	43	Duley		
Zora Viola	187	Harriet A. Reed		158

Dunnigan	
Arthur Blaine	181
Bess Blanche Leffel	181
Dutrow	
B. Hershey	192
Lulu Belle	192
Duvall	
Malinda Eliza	22
William D.	21
Dyson	
Benjamin F.	97
Benjamin Franklin	148
Catherine Jane	97
Clara Manakee	154
Eddy	97
Elijah V.	97
Joseph	107
Joseph B.P.	97
Lena M.	148
Mary J.	97
Matilda T.	97
Paul	97
Samuel	107
Vernon II.	148
William Jerry	97

E

Eader	
Ella Sears	198
Paul L.	198
Eagle	
Elizabeth	120
William	120
Earl	
Essie R. Stephens	159
George Russell	159
Earp	
Mary Elizabeth	270
Priscilla	271
Eaton	
Ella May	61
James H.	61
Lawrence Campbell	61
Edmonston	
Anne Elizabeth Williams	68
William E.	68
Edward	

Charles E.	231
Edwards	
Winfield Scott	240
Elgin	
Ann Eliza	88
Arthur Carpenter	220
Arthur Gorman	198
Charles Fenton	74
Charles Ogelbie	197
Charles William	15, 250
Cleopatra	74
Clifford Howard	198
Diana Carpenter	198
Dorothy Jones	250
Edward Wootton	74
Ellen Allnutt	220
Emily Blandford	198
Estelle White	78
Fannie C.	197
Fannie Jones	15
Franklyn Estelle	78
Hattie K.	197
Helen Douglas Smith	74
James B.	197
John Edward	198
John Thomas	74
Mary Aldridge	198
Mary Estelle	78
Sarah Taylor	197
William Franklin	78
Elkins	
Catherine	202
George R.	202
Joseph Milton	202
Elliott	
Clara Poole	117
George Thomas	51
Elsdon	
Bruce Harry	148
Mary Reid	209
Robert M.	148
Thomas	209
Elton	
Ellen Reid	153
Reuel W.	153
Embrey	
Helen	182
Emerson	

Benjamin Lee	170		Ida Marie Wright	196
Edward Simpson	169		John A.	196
Etta Bready	170	Ferril		
Georgiana	169		Dale Ray	44
Grover C.	170		Dorothy Edna Clements	44
Lulu Thompson	170	Ferris		
Maurice A.	170		Charles W.	45
Worthington B.	169		Doris Marie	256
Engles			Helen Violette	32
James	270	Fields		
English			Armstead (Army) W.	82
Paul P.	9		C. G.	82
Evans			Charlie	82
Alvin Lee	250		Clayton	82
Fred Samuel	254		Clayton S.	82
Joseph	253		Clayton Spencer	82
Louise B. Warfield	254		Elizabeth Ann	87
Ola Lee	253		Frances W.	82
Walter Lee	267		Gladys Mae	82
Wilma E.	250		Helen M.	82
Everett			Jetson G.	87
Annie Duvall White	17		Mary S.	166
William B.	17		Roger E.	82
Everhart		Fike		
Catherine Davis	258		Denzil Raymond	186
Daniel H.	220		Mary E.	186
William	220	Fillebrown		
			Helen W.	125
F			Julia M.	125
			Thomas C.	125
Fagan		Fink		
Debra Patricia Kamman	269		Charles Ernest	247
Fawcett			Clara Edith	65
Alfred	1		Doris Jeanette	247
Fawley			Lillie B.	247
Ada Catherine	245		Milton Colfax	247
Charles William	245		Paul M.	247
Chasi David	168		Sallie Eloise	247
Eileen B.	245		Sarah W.	247
Harland B.	168		Walter Lee	247
Harry B.	167	Fisher		
Lillian Lee	167		Agnes Lauretta	87
Margaret Anne	167		Albert Boyd	87
Robert Berkley	245		Anita Willard	87
Virgie	168		Anna M.	101
Virgie O.	168		C.A.	101
William B.	168		Carl T.	83
Feeney			Frank S.	65

George Allnutt	158		George Thomas	263
George C.	87		Howard	263
Helen D.	65		James H.	162
Herbert I.	76		Jean A.	162
Herbert Y.	76		Fogle	
Jacob T.	83, 215		Gilbert	244
John G.	77		Marie Edith Leppo	244
Joseph R.	76		Ford	
Laura Willard	87		Altus Lacy	251
Lelia Gertrude	215		Aubrey Thomas	228
Lelia H.	83		Betty Ann	251
Lulu	87		Daniel F.	195
Martin	76, 87		Ellen F.	195
Martin T.	25		Henry	194
Mary	76		Henry W.	194
Mary E.	158		Ida Mae	194
Mary V.	76		James	195
Pricilla Poole	76		John J.	195
Ruth Fega	83		Joseph D.	269
Ruth M.	87		Judith Mary	269
Sarah Agnes	87		Lee N.	228
Thomas S.	158		Lewis Eugene	251
Fisk			Lottie E. Fox	228
Mary Virginia Johnson	177		Mary Elizabeth Fox	228
Richard Carroll	177		Pearl Dean	248
Fitzgerald			Thomas Davis	228
Charles W.	160		Violet Estella	248
Virginia Jones	160		William H.	228
Fitzsimmons			Forde	
Caroline B.	141		Thos Aernon	270
Paul B.	141		Forrest	
Fletchall			Julius Crawford	94
Annette Rose	26		Margaret Ann Norris	93
Arthur	26		Foster	
Arthur Poole	26		Francis	30
Bertha Estelle	26		Virginia Lyddane Darby	30
Genevieve	26		Fowler	
George Walter	54		Charles Grundy	212
Harriet Eleanor	54		Elizabeth Ann	269
John	54		Jennie Marie	212
John T.	26, 54		Fox	
Lulu	26		Charles E.	211, 231
Lulu Hall	26		Charles Edward	231
Mary S.	54		Effie C. Munger	203
William Thomas	54		Emma L.	205
Fling			Emma M.	231
Bertha Simpson	263		George	231
Elizabeth L.	263		John Henry	231

Martha Ellen	231	**G**	
Owen Stanley	231		
Thomas Benton	204	Gallion	
William Guy	255	Albert N.	30
Frazier		Gamble	
Alice Georgeanna H.	186	Mabel Griffith	259
Freeman		Townley	259
Anna Lee Poole	75	Gandley	
Julian D.	64	John	271
Rosalie Jones	64	Gandly	
William Edmund	75	John	271
Fregoing		Olive	271
Myrtle E.	170	Garbers	
Fritz		David Theodore Roosevelt	182
Charles W.	214	W.C.	182
Lana Fisher	214	Gardner	
Frye		Hunter Lindsay	265
Alice Beall	221	Mary Ellen	265
Caroline	221	Garrett	
Herman Leon	180	Addie Florence	81
Howard	221	Harry F.	81
Mary I.	176	Gassaway	
Mason Lewis	176	Mary Elizabeth	46
Nina E.	180	William Augustus	46
Fulton		Gattis	
Jane Pollock	192	Lilly Belle Price	58
Jennie Coleman	171	Gause	
Richard J.	192	Elsie Mae Pearson	229
Robert	192	Geiger	
Ward Alexander	171	Washington	37
Fyffe		Getzendanner	
Agnes Willet	71	Daniel	30
Benjamin Richard	72	Joseph T.	131
Elizabeth	72	Mary Jane	131
Elizabeth Darby	148	Gibson	
Evelyn Darby	148	Florence M.	158
Isaac	72, 148	Peggy Janet	187
John Thomas	72	Robert F.	158
Joseph Lee	254	Giddings	
Martha Cooley	72	Edward Francis	137
Mary E.	71	Virginia Stonestreet	137
Sarah Aldah	72	Gilchrist	
Thomas	72	Eleanor Waters	135
Thomas E.	71	Ralph A.	135
Thomas H.	72	Ralph Alexander	135
Walter B.	148	Gilliam	
Walter Lawrence	254	Ira Howard	211
		L.C.	23

L.G.	23	Richard V.	114
Margaret M.	211	Samuel Roger	97
Giypie		Susan A.	97
Child of	270	Thomas B.	237
Glick		Thomas N.	52
Maurice Allan	230	Thomas Norris	53
Gochenour		William C.	53
Sarah Frances	16	Gough	
Goldsborough		Gertrude	67
James Claud	194	Grant	
Goodwin		Eileen J.	250
Austin M.	232	Genevieve K.	250
Gordon		Martha E.K. Reed	235
Franklin D.	217	Norman A.	250
Susie Mae	217	Gravely	
Gossard		Donald	266
Isaih Franklin	152	Hosley J.	244
Marguerite E. Knott	152	Lewis Marcoe	271
Gott		Mable	244
Alice Poole	76	Rebecca Dawn	266
Ann E.	115	Virginia M.	244
Ann Mary	53	Gravley	
Anna Mary Scholl	52	Clarice Whisman	269
Annie Laurie Covington	114	Donald Ray	269
Annie Warfield	115	Hosley J.	269
Benjamin C.	114	Gray	
Benjamin N.	52	Adeline	154
Cora Norris	93	Augusta	17
Eleanor White	53	Ethel	20
Elizabeth Beall	114	Evelyn White	17
Elizabeth L. Allnutt	114	Florence Jones White	84
Ethel F.	67	G. Robert	6
Ethel Fenwick Wood	67	Gustavus Robert	139
Eugenia	53	Ida Cooley	155
Florence E.	97	Jerome B.	155
James Perry	114	John R.	6
John Forest	67	Joseph	17
John S.	97	Joseph Alexander	17
Lillian Pearl	114	Joseph B.	155
M. Luella	97	Margaret Williams	139
Marguerite Hayden	114	Martha Kelley	155
Mariel Rebecca	114	Mary C.	22
Mary E.	97	Mason Wilbur	84
Nathan E.	115	Richard H.	22
Nellie McDonald	96	Sallie E.	6
Richard	76, 97	Greer	
Richard Brook	97	Margaret Luse	236
Richard T.	52	Virginia N. Dodd	231

Name	Page
Gregg	
Edgar Ernest	21
Evaline Duvall	21
Griffith	
Alice Darby	116
Angelica C.	69
Armistead Hempstone	98
Bettie	69
C. Dade	7
Carolina V. Hempstone	69
Charles Greenberry	69
Charles Howard	136
David Porter	18
Elizabeth Dade	7
Elizabeth Dickerson	57
Elizabeth Perry	136
F.M.	57
Francis M.	57
Francis Moore	57
Greenberry	69
Greenbury	57
Gustava Lamond	136
Harry W.	69
Howard	69, 136
J. Howard	7
Jemima A.	69
Lizzie	7
Lutie	69
Lutie Brewer	136
Nathan C.	271
Prudence	69
Prudence Jones	57
Raymond	69
Sarah Hersberger	98
Sarah Newton	69
Thomas Perry	136
W.T.	7
William	69
William Franklin	116
William Howard	7
William Robert	116
William Thomas	7, 18
Willie	69
Griffiths	
Amy Maria	257
Dave	257
Griggs	
Sallie Cummins	46
Walter Gassaway	46
Walter Porter	46
Grimes	
Bertie Estelle	11
C.T.	54
John R.	11, 12
Lola Wade	54
Lucinda	73
Mary	54
Ruth V. Stream	65
Samuel D.	12
William W.	12
Groff	
Buna E.	210
Morris Claire	210
Grubb	
Bettie Lorene Padgett	191
Carrol Edgar	188
Catherine Chiswell	225
Elizabeth Neer	190
Fannie Eaton	61
Harold Dunbar	191
Harry Daniel	191
James Edgar	259
John Edgar	190
Leah Roberta (Berta)	191
Margaret E.	225
Margaretta C.	190
Mary Ruth Wynne	259
Nancy L.	253
R. Lloyd	253
Raymond Lloyd	253
Sarah E. Ludwig	188
Thelma H.	253
Thomas L.	225
Grunwell	
S. Elizabeth	118
Gue	
Ruth	23
Gumaer	
Elias	23
Sarah Ann	23
Gutherie	
George W.	10
Mary Alice Veatch	10
Guthrie	
Lawrence Rawlin	64
Mary Cornelia Tuthill	64

H

Haddox	
Horace B.	245
Mary Lee Waters	245
Hagan	
Annie Virginia	13
Janet Spates	43
Robert Gordon	43
Hagy	
Charles Lee	263
Hall	
Abigail	29
Annie	28
Beulah White	168
Clarinda Beecher	29
Dora C.	29
E. T.	8
Edward Earl	256
Elizabeth Owens	168
Emily W.	30
Emily Wiliiams Lyddane	30
Ira	30
Ira Montgomery	144
John M.	10
John R.	28
John William	8
Julius	28, 29
L. C. (Quintis)	22
Louisa V.	1
Luther	28
Madeline G.	256
Margaret Dutrow	28
Margaret M. Dutrow	28
Margaret Rebecca	28
Minnie	28
Minnie E.	29
Mortimer Beecher	168
Rebecca	29
Rebecca M.	22
Sallie	28
Sarah C.	28
Solomon	8
Susie Elizabeth	8
Thomas Randolph	29, 168
William T.	8
Haller	
Alice Gertrude Titus	83
Carl Joseph	65
Gladys S.	214
Joseph Z.	83
Robert Lee	214
Sally Shelton	65
Hallman	
Neva B.	251
Raymond S.	250
Halmos	
Elizabeth Ann	65
Eugene F.	65
Halvosa	
Albert C.	120, 121
Margaret Hughes	120
Hamill	
Henry Phelps	163
Sarah E. Corcoran	163
Hamlett	
Lewis Bohannon	44
Margaret Ann	44
Hammann	
Anna Hoyle	223
Reid Leroy	223
Hammett	
Margaret Geiger	179
Nancy E.	178
William F.	179
Hammontree	
Dorcas	7
William W.	7
Handley	
Austin B.	75
Charles F.	74
John P.	74
Sarah P.	74
Hankins	
Louie	67
Louise W.	66
Mary Douglas Poole	67
Hanson	
Harriet Mornigstar	159
Joseph S.	159
Hardcastle	
Edmund L.	29
Sarah R. Hall	29
Harding	
Cosmos M.	144
Hardy	

Mary E. Hayes	155	Julia Anders	214
Harris		Laura F.	60
Abraham Simmons	167	Lucille	60
Alfred John	167	Lucy Viola	208
Charles Abner	167	Mary Case	103
Estelle Mae	167	Mary Jane	79
Harvey Joseph	167	Myra Lorraine	60
Mary E. Taylor	167	Sidney Smith	103
Mildred Moore	234	Thomas Clinton	186
Nettie Irene	167	Viola Woodfield	208
Harrison		Wilson S.	103
Helen Hildebrand	231	Windsor T.	208
Raymond B.	231	Hayes	
Harvey		Minnie Abigail	154
Charles	188	Thomas Preston	155
Laura Irene	252	Hays	
Linda Sue	188	Alice R. Cole	188
Neva	188	Annie R.	167
Raymond K.	252	Benjamin J.	155
Hash		Bettie B.	35
Ella May	212	Bettie Batson	35
Robert Lee	212	Eleanor	18
Hastings		Eleanor Ray	19
Lois	261	Eliza	149
Lynn H.	261	Eliza Medora	149
Robert Hathaway	261	Elizabeth Z.	35
Hauver		Frederick Albert	188
William Eugene	155	Frederick Leonard	18
Havener		Frederick Poole	17, 18
Iva Viola	102	Frederick Sprigg	18, 19
Minnie G.	102	George R.	128
Phillip A.	102	Ida Lee	17, 18
Hawes		Kathryn White	17
Cora	133	Lawrence Dade	17
John William	133	Leonard	18, 19, 149
Hawkins		Leonard Batson	36
A.R.	60	Leonard I.	18
Algie Raymond	61	Mary E. White	19
Annie Elizabeth	60, 103	Mary T.	167
Annie Gertrude	186	May	166
Arlene Comegys	208	Nana P.	35
Charles	60	Otho T.	128
Clara M.	60	Richard Kenton	36
David Hubert	208	Richard P.	viii, 35
Gilmer Richard	208	Richard Poole	35
John R.	186	Robert Lee	35
John T.	60	Robert T.	17
Joseph Charles	61	Samuel Edward	128

Samuel Simmons	167		Kathryn Robertson	202
Sarah A.	128		Warrick W. Stephens	202
Sarah Ida	128		Heil	
Thomas L.	167		Marjorie A.	84
Virginia Lorraine	154		Robert	84
William Notley	167		Hempstone	
William Reginald	17		Ann Elizabeth Poole	122
Hazelwood			Armstead T.	56
Frances Carter	184		Christie D.	56
Fred	184		Flavius Braden	124
Headley			Harriet B.	56
Anna Louise W.	137		Harry D.	56
Bradford Nelson	137		Lutie A. Norris	56
Claire Williams	168		Mary M.	124
Louis Taliaferro	168		Robert Whitney	123
Heap			Samuel Harris	124
Earl Nicklin	251		Snowden Lee	124
Olga Terecia	251		Townley	122
Heatherly			Vernon	122, 123
Mary V.	256		Vernon Stanley	122
Heaton			William	56
Patricia June Heap	251		William A.	56
Hedge			Henderson	
Ivan	203		Carrie	34
Matilda Fox	203		Evelyn Mae	222
Heffner			Howard W.	103
Addie Welling	84		John B.	33
C.D.	71		Maggie	34
Clara Stephen	100		Mollie E.	34
Daniel T.	71		Hendron	
Edward	9		Anne Louise	115
Henry Chandler	99		Henry	
Jacob Henry	99		Annie M.	16
John T.	84, 100		Edwin D.	16
John Thomas	99		Herbert	
Martha J.	100		Mary A.	145
Heflin			Herring	
Carrie Gibson	119		Helen C.	178
Dorothy Lucile	237		Hersberger	
Ethel Payne	119		Aaron B.	98
Goldie Matthews	237		Arthur Cropley	66
Herbert H.	119		Cecilia Dronenberg	66
Herbert Marshall	119		Edna Earle	159
John W.	237		Hester Ann	98
Maggie L.	119		Hesterell	98
Mildred C. Fawley	263		John A.	66
Walter Calvin	263		Julia Eliza	98
Hefner			Marshall	159

Verlinda Jones	66		Mary Ida Trundle	147
Hersburger			Mollie Magaha	100
A. B.	98		Nancy Lee	147
Nell Rebecca	98		Purnell	100
Hershey			Thomas A.	147
Christian R.	14		Thomas T.	147
James Edward	15		William T.	100
Margaret E.	15		Hicks	
Victoria Amelia	14		Eliza Virginia Walker	232
Hersperger			Hattie Susan Walker	233
Anna P.	138		Hubert Nelson	112
Elmer Clayton	138		James Robert	232
Virginia Gatrell	138		Jane Davis	112
Webb Sellman	138		Jennie Lynn Davis	112
Hewitt			Robert K.	232
Charles Richard	254		Saunders Lee	232
Virginia Reeder	240		Higgins	
Hibler			Alice Cross	206
C. Arthur	218		Bertha	11
Susan Allnutt	218		Ellen R.	132
Hickerson			George T.	11
Catherine S.	110		James L.	206
Clara V.	110		Joseph R.	132
Elizabeth Frances	110		Maude Virginia	206
Henry C.	110		Montgomery E.	206
Henry V.	110		Hightman	
J.B.L.	109		Dorothy I. Morningstar	263
Lindsay R.	110		Hildebrand	
Lucy Francis	110		Anna Mae	232
M. C.	109		George Luther	232
Marcie W.	110		Nathan Davis	232
Mary L.	110		Nellie Selby	232
Sophie C.	109		Ruth Davis	232
Virgil M.	110		Ruth Margaret Elizabeth	232
Hickman			Hill	
Allie	100		Dorothy A.	266
Beulah M.	117		Eleanor Medora Hays	188
Blanche	100		Hugh Peter	188
Carolyn R.	117		Hillard	
Della Trundle	147		Carroll E.	70
E.A.	147		Cecilia V.	70
Hazel	100		Edward C.	70
Hazel H.	118		Erma White	5
Ida Marie	147		Gertrude E.V.	5
James Buchanan	20		Hattie	10
John W.	117, 118		Helen E.	10
Lula	100		James W.	5
Margaret A.	100		Jane S.	70

John W.	10	Christine G.	203
Rebecca	56	Daisy Elizabeth Bussard	203
Robert T.	70	Earl L.	208
Thomas	10	Emily A.	130
Thomas Bolden	10	George Otis	209
Hillcary		James B.	130
Thomas	36	James W.	203
Hilleary		John W.	viii, 130
Aldridge G.	55	Richard Waters	130
Clement T.	24	Holmes	
John Thomas	55	Della M.	155
Lelia N.	55	Hominal	
Mary	24	Louise deCostella	213
Hilton		Hood	
Alonnie Brosius	165	Myrtle Burch	230
Claggett C.	165	Wilbur C.	230
Constance Chiswell	140	Hopkins	
Frances R. Snyder	165	Dorothy Butler	239
Henry Mortimer	165	Hollis Edward	239
Mary J.	201	Sallie L.	47
Rufus E.G.	201	Samuel Arthur	263
Sarah Elizabeth	166	Thomas S.	47
W. T.	165	Horine	
William Brosius	140	Bessie E.	134
Hines		Douglas Edwin	134
Soper	24	Grace Umstead	134
Hitchcock		John Philip	134
Dale O.	268	Hornbeck	
Hitt		Catherine	271
Flora Elkins Shry	236	Infant "B"	271
Hobbs		Hoskinson	
George Willard	24	Dorcas A.	94
Margaret Emma	24	John Fletchall	94
Hoffacker		Lula B.	94
Edward M.	242	Mary Dorcas	94
Ginger Bodmer	59	Mary Gertrude	94
Kristin Georgeann	59	Stella G.	94
Larry	59	Thomas	94
Mary I.	242	Walter B.	94
Hogman		William C.	94
Ernest Paul	159	William T.	94
Holcomb		Hottinger	
Clem Lee	241, 242	Agnes Jane Offutt	195
Clemens Riley	242	Virgil	195
Helen Gilliam	241, 242	Hough	
Holland		Forest	259
Annie Mary	208	Henry Clyde	259
C. Ernest	130	Jasper F.	259

Margaret Gertrude Tetlow	186	Huffers	
Margaret Tetlow	80	Carlton	270
Mortimer	80	Huges	
Mortimer B.	186	Catharine	71
Myrtle L.	259	Hughes	
Ruth H.	259	Alice Julia	178
Houser		Benjamin E.	120
Harry C.	34	Catherine S.	120
Mary E.	34	Edgar	120
Howard		Elizabeth E.	120
Brooklin	32	George Edward	121
Daniel F.	32	Joseph Adolphus	71
Daniel M.	271	Louisa Dutrow	121
Eleanor	149	Preston Brooks	120
Elisha	149	William Arthur	178
Eliza Medora Hays	149	Hull	
Frances M.	32	Edward Seabrook	104
Howe		Hunt	
John Stewart	232	Dorothy Juanita	209
Myra Hicks	232	Frances Lucille	209
Hoyle		Joyce Anne	210
Alda Brent	223	Rachael	212
Anna Lee	233	Robert L.	214
Arthur Gloyd	233	Woodrow Wilson	209
Elmer Eugene	223	Hunter	
Franklin Jones	159	Catherine B. White	161
Joseph C.	223	Mattie L.	161
Joseph Henry	160	William Pierce	161
Margaret Bowers	160	Hurd	
Mary A.	223	Arthur	64
Mary Lee	223	Eugene	251, 264
Sadie T.	159	Hager Mills	264
Sara (Sallie) Elizabeth	36	Hurt	
Sarah Trussell	159	Della M.	202
Hubbard		Emma R. Lambert	201
James H.	5	Eugene William	202
Hubble		Flora Mae Whisman	171
Aubra Virginia Thompson	238	George W.	201
Clara	19	John Stephen	201
Donald E.	19	S.H.	201
Donald T.	238	Sallie Bone	201
George Grady	238	Hurtt	
Herman	19	Bessie E. G.	57
Otis Knox	206	Herbert Marple	57
Sophia E.	206	Hyatt	
Huey		Alvin L.	5
Hester Carter	184	Ann W.	5
Samuel Robert	184	Carson	5

Mary E.	6		Mark Pulliam	65
Hyde			Richard W.	65
Emily Wailes	76		Jeffery	
T.W.	76		Bessie O.	238
Thomas W.	76		Jenkins	
			Fred A.	255
I			Garland Thomas	255
			Glaytha V.	267
Iglehart			Mary Edrie	255
Basil R.	115		Nellie M.	255
Ellen Ruth	115		William M.	267
Irvin			Jennings	
Marguerite	262		Charles C.	144
Warren E.	213		Clara C.	144
Warren Edward	262		Joseph E.	144
Irwin			Jerrell	
Ida Ann Brewer	111		John P.	268
Reginald Herbert	111		Linda Lou Leith	268
Isherwood			Jewel	
R. J.	76		Edna Leola	150
Israel			Elizabeth Blanchard	150
Alice Grace	104		Grace Magaha	150
Charles F.	104		Mamie E.	150
Charles Reid	104		Jewell	
Lillian B. Hoyle	104		Edgar Guy	261
			Olivia Pauline	261
J			Samuel Edgar	150
			Johns	
James			Marilyn Whittaker	265
Mary Ellen	193		William Brook	265
Jarboe			Johnson	
Elizabeth Ann	6		Alonzo	164
Ethel M.	206		Baby	229
Raymond H.	206		Blanche McCloud	211
Susie Ella	206		Charles M.	164
Thomas H.	206		Charles W.	261
Thomas L.	206		Effie L.	214
Jarrett			Eugenia Tyson	164
Ola M.	253		George	1, 88
Jarvis			George Haslip	164
Jerry Lee	243		Harry C.	211
Linda Moore	243		Helen	244
Jeffcoat			J. Thomas	1
Errol Wilson	41		Jacob Middleton	252
Jeffers			L.B.	164
Blanche P.	65		Levin B.	164
Donald E.	65		Lule	1
Julia E.	65		Luther	264

Luther Eugene	187	Earl Manokee	154
Marian L.	229	Edgar Hartley	16
Marie	229	Edna Manakee	154
Martha H.	164	Edward	92
Mary Ann B.	261	Edward Wilkerson	92
Mary Elizabeth Ricketts	252	Edwin	48
Mary Elizabeth Roberson	187	Eleanor May	168
Mattie B.	164	Eleanor Woodward	164
Myrtle M.	164	Elizabeth	92
Nora C.	264	Elizabeth Darnell	169
Richard Edwin	230	Elizabeth J.	16
Robert	64	Elizabeth R.	165
Sarah A.	229	Eugene	165
Sarah Ann	25	Eugene Phillips	178
Sarah C.	164	Evie Wales	45
Thomas M.	214	Frances Lavinia	137
William I.	25	Frederick	15, 17, 62
Jones		Frederick A.	17
A. Dawson	129	Frederick Reginald Freemont	48
A. Jackson	72	George D.	168
Achsah D. Waters	164	George Darby	45
Adelia L.	137	George Gleeves	256
Agnes Estelle	75	George Lawrence	45
Airy Ann	94	Harvey T.	31
Alethea A.	31	Hays	75
Alfred Leroy	178	Helen Elizabeth	256
Ann Maria	182	Helen N.	16
Anna Elizabeth	62	Isaac Thomas	101
Anna Virginia Gott	62	James H.	129
Anne Newton Chiswell	93	James W.	31
Ara Lee Hicks	45	John	1, 75, 169
Arthur	101	John A.	92, 154
Arthur L.	15	John Augustus	92
Arthur Lee	67	John Blake	164
Beckie	72	John Frederick	75
Benjamin J.	viii	John J. Isaac	94
Benjamin John	62	John Paul	73
Bettie L.	15	John Rufus	137
Charles C.	165	Joseph James Wilkerson	93
Charles H.	144	Joseph W.	16
Charles Robert	264	Josephine	48
Clara Conley	165	Julia Ada	31
Columbia	94	Katie Barbee	129
Constance Beulah Nicholson	166	Kirtley	129
Daniel	112	L.H.	75
Daniel T.	112	Laura Kathleen	62
David T.	182	Laura Virginia	182
E. Medora	76	Lawrence Beall	166

Lawrence R.	166		Thomas L.	48
Lee Allnutt	45		Walter Gant	73
Leo Lawrence	137		William	92, 94
Leonidas	16		William A.	92
LeRoy Albert	178		William Edward	16
Lillian Elizabeth	166		William T.	31, 164, 187
Linwood Thomas	137		William Thomas	94
Lottie C.	178		Jordan	
Lottie E. White	17		Margaret Estelle	55
Louis John	187		W.W.	55
M.K.	75		Justus	
Mamie	163		Alda	215
Mamie Pyles	92		Betty Jo	187
Margarete A.	154		Mark Steven	215
Marilou	186		Michael B.	215
Martha E.	48			
Mary	112		**K**	
Mary (Mamie) McCubbin	164			
Mary Alice	220		Kamman	
Mary Alta	62		Debra Patricia	269
Mary Ann	182		Kamman -Levol	
Mary Hays	75		Susan Marie	269
Mary Jane	263		Karayianis	
Mary Leona	101		Nick	268
Mary M.	48		Karger	
Mary Poole	75		Frances White	46
Mary Sellman	112		Kauffman	
Mary T.	47		Jesse D.	185
Mary Tomscy	48		Kay	
Maurice R.	137		Thomsey W. Lilly	176
Nannie	164		Keeney	
Nellie Jane Titus	187		James Samuel	264
Nettie Hempstone	17		Meredith D.	264
Nettie L.	15		Keesee	
Poole	48		George Sureace	235
Priscilla John	48		Georgia Gray	235
Reginald Sprigg	75		Lois Jean	235
Reva Alexander	264		Keller	
Richard Edwin	62		Alton Higgins	249
Robert N.	263		Eugene M.	271
Rose M. Darby	92		Ira E.	249
Sallie C.	72		Margaret Turner	249
Samuel Creighton	166		Kendale	
Sarah	47, 92		Joseph Franklin	178
Sarah L.	144		Kendall	
Sarah Poole	48		Ellis	41
Sprigg	48		Laura E.	113
Thomas	47		Kennedy	

Emma I.	184	Kneesi		
Henry	184	Ellen	159	
Kenyon		Knill		
Audrey Virginia	179	Annie Neal	161	
Robert Rowlodge	179	Charles E.	161	
Kephart		Knott		
Frances Frazer	259	Annie Blance Carlin	152	
Leonard Wheeler	259	Hazel Rudolph	172	
Kidd		William D.	152	
Ellis Saunders	241	Kohlenberg		
Joseph Eugene	242	John Charles	215	
Margaret Louise Pearson	252	Kohlenburg		
Mary Effie	41	William Thomas	10	
Virginia H.	255	Kohlhoss		
Walter Steve	241	C. E. Munsey	60	
William Frazier	209	Charles	60	
Kimball		Charles E.	60	
Margaret Ireland	251	Charles Edward	60	
Kimberling		Ellen Jane	60	
Jennie C. Staub	28	Emma Mae Thornton Haller	60	
Kimmerling		Harry	60	
John	28	Minnie (Carrie) S.	60	
King		Winifred Steiner	60	
Luther Roland	237	Koss		
Mary Ann	13	Dorothy Brosius	181	
Mary Magaline Burriss	135	Joseph P.	181	
Thomas Lee	268	Kraft		
Thomas Matthew	135	Alice A. Metzger	70	
Warren	13	J.G.	70	
Kinna		Kremer		
Gladys Irene Morningstar	189	Minnie Irene	101	
Russell J.	189	Kubeck		
Thomas Russell	188	Eleanor	219	
Kinney		Frederick J.	219	
Jane H.	109	Thomas	219	
Kirsch				
Robert	225	**L**		
Kitts				
Bettie Lou	24	Lacey		
Doris Elizabeth	24	John Stinson	85	
Irvin	64	Mary Fisher	85	
Lulu Whisman	24	Ladson		
Vaden	24	Barbara Moore	234	
Klaess		LaGasse		
John William	262	Alfred Henri	180	
Mary Frances	262	Nettie Mae Orme	180	
Klippel		Lamarr		
Shelly Rae	238	Edgar Carl	213	

Lambert		George Franklin	71
Edith Carlin	43	George N.	71
Elsie Pearl	260	George Randolph	71
Evelyn Cubitt	262	George W.	23
Jack T.	43	Margaret	23
James C.	262	Margaret A.D.	71
Jasper Thomas	43	Margarett Avilda	71
Martha A.	224	P. F.	52
Mary Jane	260	Lee	
Paris Wesley	260	Estelle Perry	136
Thomas Benton	224	Gracie E.	1
Viola Virginia	224	Harry Eugene	271
Virginia F.	224	Katherine S.	271
William Wesley	260	Leith	
Lane		David Harrison	243
Jesse Melvin	135	Douglas Ray	212
Lanon		Eppie H.	268
Mrs.	1	Etta Cochran	255
Larman		Jerry Moore	243
Benjamin H.	133	Michael Dale	255
Bessie Violet	133	Ruby	268
Charles	133	Ruby Ellen	255
Charles A.	132	Ruth E.	243
Edward	132	Samuel	268
Elizabeth May	205	Samuel H.	255
Fannie Elizabeth	200	Thomas G.	243
Frank E.	200	Lemar	
George	133	Frances I. Cregger	262
George F.	133	Leon	
Henry Milton	205	Herbert	62
James R.	132	Leopold	
John W.	132	Erna H.	216
Joseph Edgar	200	Max	216
Mary A.	132	Leppo	
Mary Anna George	200	Charles H.	213
William Clifton	200	Ida Jane Fox	256
William Edward	200	Joseph	213, 256
William H.	200	Leslie	
Lawrence		Bernice Elizabeth	88
William R.	256	Leon S.	88
Lawson		Lester	
Alfred S.	212	Charles E.	10
Annie E.	212	Maude M.	10
Lazell		Lewis	
Katherine E. Oxley	147	Alma Dennie	204
Leapley		Anne Ursula	157
Catherine Jennie	71	Donald	253
George Edward	23	Earl Wendell	249

H.W.	156	Margaret Griffith	259
Irene Lindig	204	Lonergan	
John Edward	120	Lucy Ellen	260
Lena Mae	253	Lucy Waters	245
Margaret Darby	157	Long	
Mary Hughes	121	Elizabeth A.	196
Sarah (Sallie) M.	156	George W.	196
Thomas Waring	157	Mary Carpenter	196
Walter Jackson	253	Loos	
William Latane	157	Emily Allnutt	219
William Motzer	156	Loring	
Lillard		Edward Liroy	271
Bessie B.	142	Louden	
Ernest L.	142	George W.	10
James R.	142	Low	
Mary Ellen	142	Henry	32
William E.	142	Lowe	
Lilly		Clara L.	240
Bertha Jackson	176	Louis Richard	178
Homer Johnston	176	Melvin George	240
Kelly J.	176	Richard H.	37
Linde		Loy	
Douglas B.	141	Albert F.	193, 194
Lindig		Catherine Rebecca	193
Adolph	78	Claude Edgar	193
Adolphus	77	Joseph F.	193
Anna	78	Lelia V.	193, 194
Anna L.	77	Luther F.	201
Anna S.	78	Marie V.	193
Estelle	77	Mary C.	193
Frederick J.	77	Mary M.	193
Henry M.	204	Mary V.	193
Sarah Elizabeth Norris	204	Minnie E.	193
Linthicum		Thomas	194
Charles Gorman	119	Lucas	
Ethel Reid	119	Alfred T.	20
John Dutrow	134	Charles	20
Leona May D.	134	Mary	20
Linton		Luhn	
Julia Frances	244	Agnes Virginia Dixon	214
Littlefield		Alice E. McLain	143
George E.	160	Alice Elizabeth	143
Harriet A.	160	Amelia May Reid	237
Littlepage		Annie Elizabeth Sellman	143
James Hemenway	259	Arthur Price	228
Mabel Griffith	259	Charles Andrew	143
Livingston		Charles McLain	143
John Cope	259	Clara Belle	228

Elizabeth (Bessie) Ellen	228	Manzella E.	99
Ena	236	Maria H.	98
Eula L. Wynne	259	Savilla	98
George Christopher	143	Virginia	264
George W.	237	Walter S.	98
Hazel V.	228	Wesley	98
Helen Virginia	236	Magruder	
Lawrence W.	228	Willie	141
Leslie L.	236	Manaia	
Maynard Clark	259	Barbara Repass	83
Randolph	228	George Westley	83
Sarah Catherine McLain	143	Manakee	
Sarah Elizabeth	227	Harry K.	154
Stonestreet W.	214	Manion	
Thomas E.	236	Annie Edna	176
Wilber	170	William Vernon	176
Wilbur	170	Manly	
William Alexander	143	John	13
Lupton		John S.	8
Emma H.	157	Mary	8, 13
Lydard		Mann	
Annie V.	267	Arthur Howard	198
Thomas I.	211	James Harold	267
Lyddane		Margaret Blackwell	267
Charles William	143	Mary Elizabeth Elgin	198
Frances Hoyle	143	Manuel	
Thomas	30	Agnus T.	23
Lynch		Carrie T.	23
Martha L.	235	Harry	23
Raymond Joseph	235	Martin	
		Annie C.	34

M

		Annie E.	194
		James Franklin	11
Macabee		Janet	188
Margaret	1	John R.	188
Mace 9		Joseph A.	194
Eric Turley	9	Joseph Alan	188
Mackintosh		Maitland Rex	34
Mrs.	271	Mason	
MacLeod		Evelyne Brewer	190
M.C.	93	Henry Clay	22
P.H.	93	Lyle Millan	190
Magaha		Matthews	
Archie	264	Annie S.	36
Charles W.	223	Armstead	212
Franklin Henry	264	Charles Maynard	233, 234
John	98	Edward	36
John Wesley	99	Eleanor Mae Luhn	249

Elsie	192	McNeir	
George Edwin	36	Florence	46
Gertrude	37	R.S.	46
Isabell Mariah	234	McRoberts	
J. Edwin	36	Jesse	20
James B.	192	Meem	
Ruby Mundy	233	Harry Cloriviere	103
Walter Kirts	249	Nora Sellman	103
Mattingly		Mejia	
Evelyn Gertrude	103	Paul Franklin	178
William Francis	103	Richard Carlisle	178
Maxey		Mellott	
William	271	Ida Madeline	226
Maxwell		J. B.	270
James Stevenson	149	Jacob B.	226
Maggie Blance	148	Mentzer	
Sarah Frances Beall	148	Harry Lee	243
McAtee		Julia	227
Susie V.	265	Julia Ellen	243
McAuliffe		Merchant	
Grace Morningstar	207	John O.	71
James Stephen	207	Margaret E.	71
John F.	247	Mercier	
McGlothlin		Emily D.	6
Eloise Mattie Robbins	257	Richard G.	6
McGovern		Metzer	
Anna L.	134	Elizabeth Ann	11
Charlotte (Lottie) Wilhelminia	78	George	70
Gerald	78	Metzger	
Lottie Lindig	78	Amanda E. Cashell	9
Lottie M.	134	Bernard	11
McGovern-Pearthree		Charles	70
Frank Gerald	78	Christana M.	71
McGrady		Elizabeth Ann	11
Mary E.	244	Gerhart	11
William Crawford	243	Hannah Virginia	70
McIntosh		Harriet	70
Anne Virginia	80	Harriet Morehead Trail	71
Annie Maria	80	Jacob	71
C.O.	80	John H.	11
McKeever		Nathan Hazel	9
Antionette Darby	131	Nathan T.	70
William Galen	131	Percival	70
McKimmey		Philip	71
Lorraine Roberts	175	Sarah Ellen	11
McLeod		W.W.	70
Joseph Wilkinson	93	William	70, 71
Mary Elizabeth	93	William W.	9

Michael
- Arthur — 24
- Dorothy How — 24

Miles
- Alice May — 88
- Charles Edgar — 88
- Della Mae — 59
- Elisha — 246
- Ellen Frances — 220
- Elvira M. — 59
- Hanson T. — 59
- Henry — 220
- Howard Montgomery — 59
- Hugh — 69
- James Hanson — 59
- James R. — 88
- James U. — 69
- John Jacob — 220
- Jonathan B. — 88
- M. M. — 59
- Margaret T. — 36
- Mary C. — 69
- Mary Catherine — 59
- Mary Katherine — 58
- Sarah A. — 69
- Sarah L. — 88
- Sarah Lucretia Mossburg — 88
- Thomas H. — 58

Milford
- Cleyland — 98
- Cora V. — 97
- Elizabeth (Betty) Byrd — 126
- Jennie — 97
- Mary Ella — 97
- S.B. — 126
- Samuel B. — 98
- Thomas — 98

Millar
- Christopher — 257
- Jack W. — 257
- Jane B. — 257

Millard
- Mary Eloise Hays Gott — 155

Miller
- Alma Mae — 228
- Edith — 232
- Infant — 153
- Isabelle — 153
- Norman Egbert — 153
- William C. — 228

Mills
- Esker — 216
- Oma M. — 216

Milne
- Andrew K. — 73
- Audrey Lee Moler — 16
- Elsie May — 73
- Mary E. — 73

Minter
- Nelson John — 267

Mobley
- Cornelia Carter Stang — 195
- Ernest Dorsey — 195
- Howard S. — 26
- Howard Victor — 27
- Mollie E. — 26

Mockbee
- William Thomas — 13

Molby
- Frank Lewis — 119
- Grace Kelly — 119
- Richard VanDyke — 119

Moler
- Edna D. — 157
- Gertrude B. — 16
- Gertrude Byrnes — 16
- Ronald G. — 157

Money
- Frank J. — 7
- James E. — 7
- James H., Sr. — 7
- Rose Anna — 7

Monroe
- Floyd Preston — 256

Moore
- Alvin — 214, 215
- Alvin Dean — 214
- Edna Donahoe — 86
- Elizabeth Titus — 214
- Elizabeth Virginia White — 96
- James S. — 234
- John White — 263
- John William — 96
- Joseph Collinson — 86
- Kathleen — 263
- Milward F. — 215

Susan Ann	234	Mossburg		
Moran		Agnes B.		28
Katie Lindig	78	Alice L.		36
William J.	78	Annie Mary		27
Morningstar		Carrie May		37
Agnes Honore	161	Charles Henry		117
Algie Thomas	159	Clara Beall Hillard		40
Anna Mary Larman	205	Claude Eugene		27
Annie Mary	192	Edward Clinton		36
Archie M.	192	Esther Compher		40
Arthur Sylvester	159	George		36
Barbra	270	George LeRoy		36
Bessie I.	101	George P.		36
Charles W.	192	Henry W.		271
Clarke	10	Irving E.		37
Della Virginia	101	Jesse K.		27
Edgar J.	207	Lela M.		27
Edgar John	161	Lela Marie		27
Edward A.	101	Lelia Ellinor Poole		117
Elizabeth M.	101	Margaret L.		36
Emma M. J.	101	Mary		36
Fanny Maude	159	Maurice C.		40
Hazel Edgar	207	Maurice Milton		40
Herbert V.	271	Peter K.		36
Marshall C.	205	Phillip		27
Mary	161	Phillip F.		27
Mary Florine	207	Raymond H.		27
Murel J.	101	Reubie G.		37
Susie E.	101	Sarah E.		36
Thomas	159	Thomas Gilbert		40
Morris		William		116
Clayton	254	William E.		37
Jesse James	254	Moulden		
Nettie Ola	254	Elias		viii, 12
Morrison		Grace Magaha Jewel		150
Charles	123	Mary E.		12
Charles V.	123	Mary Lilly		80
Esther E.	247	R. Etna		80
George V.	123	Moxley		
George W.	247	Annie E.		221
James W.	123	David Samuel		221
Mary Frances	123	Emma S.		98
Mary McGlue	247	Evertt Glenwood		221
Sarah A.	123	Frank		222
Morton		George Bunkingham		221
Claude David	187	Mabel M.		221
Frank Edwin	187	Marion E.		98, 223
Lola E.	187	Nannie Estelle		223

Oliver G.	221	Samuel Robert	239
Thomas E.	221	Thompson Gregory	210
Muir		Nevin	
Dorothy Troth	135	David John	179
Wallace	135	James Hoyle	179
Mulligan		Katherine H.	179
Pearl Rebecca	241	Newman	
Susannah	71	Bettie Jones	92
Mumford		Michael Edward	216
Dorothy L.	150	Thomas E.	244
John M.	150	Newton	
Mumma		Thomas N.	210
Minnie Pearl	244	Nicewarner	
Munger		Sean Russell	175
A. Beulah Mae	153	Nichols	
Cora Ellen	153	Charles S.	124
Eliza	153	Clarence N.	249
Georgia Surber	153	Clinton R.	204
John B.	viii, 153	Daisy Louise	123
Marvin Arthur	153	Delma Bridget	204
Mary L.	260	Edward Alton	123
Ormond Surber	260	Florence Ellen	204
Murphy		George Frederick	204
Grace	201	Hilda M.	249
Musser		Jacob	13
Carl R.	209	Joseph Deets	158
John	209	Louise H.	124
Myerly		Nellie Irving	158
Harry Stockton	249	Sarah	13
Minnie Louise Bodmer	249	Nicholson	
		Annie Ellis	216
N		Annie V. Heffner	175
		Arthur Baker	136
Nash		Arthur Purnell	136
Geneva M.	157	Carrie Roberson	225
Neal		Donald Hubert	174
Hubert Sherman	259	Elizabeth Ann	136
Ida Wynne	259	Elizabeth White	85
Nealon		Franklin B.	136
Mitchell Lee	267	George E.	174
Neel		Gladys	174
Archie Clifton	239	J.F.	180
Clarence S.	255	James Brawner	85
Della M. Strowers	239	John L.	175
Herbert O.	239	John Vernon	175
Julia L.	255	Lawrence B.	136
Lewis Wiley	239	Lawrence Baker	136
Mary M.	238	Linwood Burton	136, 225

Name	Page
Martha	175
Mary C.	174
Mary E.	195
Susan Virginia C.	136
Vernon Leroy	175
Wilfred Donald	174
William Douglas	136
William Mardith	216
William Meredith	215
Nicolaisen	
Jane Allnutt	238
Norris	
Ann R. Fyffe	12
Barney	12
Bernard T.	12
C. Larue	33
Charles J.	222
Charles Olin	94
Charles William	12, 222
Clarence L.	117
Clifton Hershey	155
Clinton A.	93
Cora Ellen	222
Dorothy Mae	271
F. M.	93
Hazel Hickman	117
Henry J.	32, 33
Ida M.	32
James C.	32
James Elmer	93
James H.	155
James Henry	155
James Lawson	12
James Marshall	84
James Walter	155
John T.	93
Joni Lynn	222
Josiah	33
Kathleen S.	84
Laura B.	33
Margaret A.	33, 93
Margaret Ann King	93
Marion A.	93
Mary Magdeline	33
Nonie E.	155
Sarah C. Lowe	33
Shirley Ann	222
Shirley Cubitt	222
Thomas A.	33
Thomas Howard	271
Vera DeEtte	222
Warren King	93
Norwood	
B. Edward	231
Bradley	231
Edward	231
Frances Elizabeth	205
Lelia M.	231
Margaretta	231
William Henry	271
Noyes	
Alfred D.	256
Anna Fawsett	256
Nunnally	
Brick	82
Frances W. Fields	82

O

Name	Page
Oaks	
Forest	147
George Lawrence	147
Ochs	
Hazel Wood	104
Karl William	104
Oden	
Frances	146
Lena Ballenger	138
O'Donnell	
Minnie S. Ryman	208
Patrick	208
Offutt	
Charles	249
Elsie L.	249
George Edward	63
Helen W.	63
John B.	63
L.T.	63
Linwood T.	63
Lucy Morrissey	183
Marie Jones	63
Marie Moore	63
Mattie Marie	195
Roger Delano	63
William Ernest	183
O'Hanlon	

Ardle Patrick	261	John Edgar	260
Patricia	261	Louisa V.	124
Orme		Mary A.	124
Allen S.	194	Robert W.	125
Arthur L.	152	Sallie E.	125
Arthur T.	152	Thomas	124
Bertha	194	Thomas Cummings	127
Catheran Eliza	50	Viletter	124
Charles Clinton	179		
Charles Elmer	249	**P**	
Charles Henry Crab	50		
Charles L.	170	Padgett	
Charles M.	135	Algernon J.	57
Daisy D.	179	Arthur	33
Deborah Brook	50	Clara J.	33
Edgar Thomas	51	Della M.	57
George Ervin	152	Dunbar D.	57
Irene V.	135	Edwin Earl	57
Jean Muir	170	Elizabeth	33
Laura E.	152	Elsie	57
Mary A.	152	Fannie	33
Maurice	194	Frank H.	57
Phoebe Anna	50	Isabel	33
Richard I.	50	James	33
Robert S.	271	James Alonzo	57
Vivian Matthews	249	Jane R.	57
William A.	152	John	33
Orms		John E.	33
Amy	1	Mary Frances	57
Osborne		Maymie A.	57
Harry Oscar	86	Thomas E.	33
Louise H.	86	Painter	
Owens		Baby boy	184
Annie	29	Bertha Helen Hildebrand	232
Preacher	29	Clarence	242
Richard	29	Clarence E.	210
Oxley		Elizabeth Daniel	184
Annie Branson	260	Elmer Lee	232
Annie E.	146	Garland Edward	184
C. Gilbert	146	Nellie	242
Catharine A.	146	Nellie Pearl	210
Charles W.	146	Palmer	
Edgar F.	125	David Rulison	259
Edward	124	Joan Gamble	259
Elizabeth C.	125	Pangle	
Emily Byron Williams	127	Frederick Newton	234
Emily J.C.	124	Gracie Pearl	234
John E.	124	Helen Louise	234

Parker			Perill	
Sharon Lee	64		Samuel	202
Theodore C.	64		Perkins	
Parks			Irene	204
Albert Fred	257		Thomas Eldridge	204
Billie Gene	257		Perry	
Ona	257		Jane D.	105
Parrish			Mary Alice	246
Eldon Matron	215		Sallie Fontaine	246
Glenda Fritz	215		Thomas W.	246
Parsley			Walter E.	246
Clarence	265		William Griffith	154
Pasti			Willie Greene Day	246
Hilda Marie	266		Pessou	
Nicholas	266		Carrie Newsom	109
Patterson			Pettitt	
Charles R.	268		Charles F.	43
Patton			Maria Cole	42
Edna Allnutt	235		Phelps	
Paxson			Andrew Wilson	226
Betty Pearson	44		Annie E.	226
Robert L.	44		Archie C.	226
Payne			Edna	226
Ruby Cubitt	171		Estella L.	209
Twin Daughters	172		George Herbert	267
William Wilson	171		Margaret Verna Lewis	267
Pearre			Patricia Ann	209
Marie Sellman	8		Richard Martin	209
Pearson			Phillips	
Alfred	229		Algye Poole	32
Alfred L.	255		Douglas Eugene	242
Alfred Lee	242		Edgar	32
Charles Harold	229, 252		Elsie Fink	65
Ernest H.	229		Ethel C.	32
Eugene H.	228		Hazel H.	32
John A.	228		James	31, 32
Lillian Anne	229		James Arthur	265
Lily Ann	228		James E.	31, 32
Myrtle	242, 255		Jennings Bryan	125
William R.	263		John L.	31
Penn			Lucille	32
Melvin Stanley	58		Maria K. Frances	264
Minnie May Fyffe	148		Mary Brunner	125
Sarah Ethel Price	58		Mary E.	31
Penrod			Matilda	31
Shirley June Eaton	264		Milton W.	32
Perell			Phillip L.	31
Susie F. Sullivan	202		Susie	32

William	31	Benjamin F.	174
Pierce		Benjamin R.	88
Ort	180	Benjamin T.	23
Robert G.	268	Blanche	3
Pierre		C.L.	251
Nellie Tommie	264	Carrie Williams	66
Pifer		Catherine (Katie) V.	76
Betty Lou	188	Charles E.	142, 177
Piles		Charles Edgar	75
Hilleary	46	Charles Edward	241
Matilda	46	Charles Irving	100
Pleasant		Charles J.	88
Basil Brook	50	Charles Wade	177
D.S.	50	Charlie	88
Deborah	50	Christie E.	74
Harriet Newel	50	Claudia K. Ellen Johnson	104
Miflion	50	Cumberland Willson	3
Webb	50	Daisy F.	196
Pleasants		Deborah Jane	156
James S.	23	Edna Mildred Beall	177
Snowden	23	Edward	9
Poe		Effie Allnutt	173
Carrie Norma	58	Eleanor	3
Poetzman		Eleanor Leonard	123
Margery L.	248	Eleanor N. White	63
Melanie Joy	248	Elizabeth D.	149
Robert L.	248	Elsie May	75
Polen		Emma Gertrude Young	241
Fannie A.	61	Emma R.	100
Pollock		Ernest Bollen	196
Cora Lee	192	Eugene H.	173
George Findlay	192	Evelyn Wailes Hyde	76
Grace Amelia	192	F. H.	74
John Emory	192	F.W.	66
Poole		Fannie E.	3
A. Myrtle	89	Florence P.	67
Adaline G.	199	Francis Marion	100
Algermon	13	Frank Leven	75
Algernon	9, 123	Franklin E.	104
Alta Bertha Young	118	Frederick S.	2
Ann W.	8	Georgia Rebecca	76
Anna Elgin	89	Gertrude	47
Anna Mae	100	Grafton Eugene	238
Annie Evelyn	47	Harriet Hempstone	74
Annie Hoskinson	75	Harriet Thomas	74
Avilda	47	Harry L.	207
B.E.	100	Helen	196
Benjamin	8	Howard Eugene	116

Isaac R.	149	Mary Waters	9
J. Sprigg	47	Maynard S.	142
James Alfred	177	Melvin M.	196
James Franklin	75	Mildred	9
James Harvey	88	Nathan Dickerson	47
James Robert	142	Nettie White	63
Jane Clark	76	Oscar K.	200
Jane Elgin	88	Priscilla John	76
John	66, 149, 150	Prissilla W.	149
John Dickerson	66	Prissilla Woodward Sprigg	149
John E.	88	Rachael Virginia	142
John Elgin	89	Rachel A.	142
John Ethan	161	Raymond	100
John Franklin	233	Raymond Benjamin	104
John Frederick Sprigg	3	Raymond Jerome	174
John Hanson	173	Raymond Lee	89
John Sprigg	76	Rebecca	47, 149
John W.	66	Reginald	76
John William	174	Reginald D.	199
Joseph	74	Richard	66
Katherine Riggs	47	Richard K.	63
Katie Dorsey	200	Robert Willson	2, 3
Laura	88	Roger Raymond	118
Laura Ellen Reed	89	Rosa Lee Hopkins	47
Laura Virginia Hays	75	S. Agnes Jones	47
Leonard Hays	123	Sallie	66
Lewis	63	Sally	150
Lewis W.	63	Samuel Dixon	142
Lois Wilson	64	Sarah A.E. Willson	76
Lucretia W.	63	Sarah Agnes	47
Lyttleton Stewart	156	Sarah Agnes Beall	100
M.R.	142	Sarah Ann Fisher	75
Mabel Rebecca	207	Sarah Anna Beall	161
Mamie L.	174	Sarah Dickerson	9
Margaret D.	149	Sarah Gertrude Matthews	233
Margaret Fox	204	Thomas H.	74, 76
Martha	47	Thomas Jefferson	88
Martha Deborah	149	Thomas Sprigg	76
Martha Sprigg	47	Thomas W.	76, 142
Martin LeRoy	241	Virginia Lee	47
Mary (Mame) Wilson	76	W. Walter	89
Mary C.	100, 271	Walter S.	142
Mary Cooley	23	Walter Stone	207
Mary E.	149	William	74
Mary Gertrude	3	William Alfred	241
Mary Margaret	100	William D.	47, 149
Mary McCauley	74	William T.	9
Mary T.D.	2	William Thomas	75, 123

William Trail Hempstone	74
William Vernon	75
William Wallace	47, 66
Willson Clarke	64
Wilson	3
Pope	
Mary Gertrude	72
Porter	
Mary E.	123
Willie E.	123
Potter	
Texanna Elkins	202
Powers	
Sadie M.	255
Virgie Leo	62
Winfield Scott	62
Pratt	
Charles E.	145
Mary (Mamie) Everline	144
Mary Elizabeth White	145
Price	
Algerene Turner	222
Clara L.	58
Clarence	5
Cora	58
Deborah Jane	181
Elias	viii, 58
Gertrude V.	58
Ida M.	5
Jessie Virginia	182
Laurence Hilton	182
Linwood Samuel	241
Mary E.H.	5
Mary Frances	58
Thomas	5
Wilfred	5
William T.	222
Pridgen	
Sallie Sutphin Tolbert	243
Pugh	
David	210
Mary Stewart	210
Pullum	
Glen Allan	216
Pyles	
Ann Elizabeth Williams	128
Anna Laura	16
Annie E.	24
B. Franklin	viii
B.F.	45
Beatrice Howard	129
Benjamin Franklin	46
Catherine Beall	24
Charles Thomas	7
Claggett	79
Edwin	128
Elizabeth Dade	7
Emma Talbott Williams	129
Emma Williams	128
Enon Kenneth	24
Frances Ellen	79
Isaac Jones	9
J.E.	23
James E.	24
John O.	16
John R.	54
Joseph B.	45
Joseph Brunner	128
Lotta V.	78
Lucinda	9
Lucinda R.	9
M. Thomas	viii
Mary Elizabeth Griffith	7
Mary Florence Williams	128
Mary V.	79
Mary V. (Jennie)	54
Michael Thomas	128
Nellie Brewer	128
Nellie Jenkins	7
Percy Lee	79
Richard	54
Richard Grover	78
Richard T.	78
Ruth E.	23, 24
Ruth Olive Roberts	24
Sarah Ellen Brewer	128
Sarah R.	46
Susan	54
Thomas Walter	129
Walter Williams	129
William C.	54
William Darby	15
William Francis	24
William Griffith	7

R

Rakusja	
Eva Kristina	261
Joseph	261
Ramseur	
Eleanor V.	265
Ervin	265
Randall	
Ernest	185
Leslie Jackson	242
Rasin	
Martha Davis	112
Unit	111
Ratliff	
William E.	206
Rawlings	
Medora C.	238
Robert E.	238
Rawlins	
C. Jane	131
Jane R.	132
Joshua H.	131
Laura Lee	131
Margaret C.	131
Thomas	132
Ray	
Lola Annie	191
Reamy	
Elvira M.	141
Reddick	
Addie May Spurrier	19
George W.	19
Reed	
Ada	52
Amanda	51
Anna	224
Annie M. Allnutt	224
Benjamin Franklin	52
Bertie	52
Cecil Layman	180
Charles C.	59, 224
Charles H.	11
Charles Thomas	268
Charlie	52
Clara I.	147
Clifford	180
Clownie E.	234
Dewey Alton	180
Dorothy Beatrice	147
Earl	271
Etta Mallie	158
Etta Prescott	147
Frank Levin	6
Frederick	147
Frederick A.	147, 188
George L.	235
Gertie	147
Grace V.	268
Harriet A.	158
Hattie	180
Helen Louise	147
Helen Smallwood	52
James T.	158
James W.	viii, 11
Jennie L.	11
Julia Etta Phillips	31
Lena L. May	31
Leona Josephine	180
Lewis T.	147
Luella J.	188
Lulu Lucretia	6
Mary Arlene Lowe Griffith	116
Mary Geneva	51
Mattie Ella	147
Pearl Elizabeth Pangle	234
Philip	51
Phillip	51
Richard Randolph	180
Robert O.	158
Russell C.	180
Ruth Elizabeth	59
Ruth N.	6
Sarah Ann	51
Susan Rebecca	52
Thomas I.	59
Thomas J.	31, 158
Upton D.	147
Wayne D.	158
Woodrow W.	147
Zachariah F.	59
Reesch	
Albert D.	205
Betty White	205
Reid	
Alice Irene Young	152

Clifton S.	38	James Augustine	64
Eliza	152	Louise H.	64
Eliza A. White	38	Richey	
Eliza Estelle Young	153	Sarah White	95
Greeta I.	158	Steven Olin	95
Henry Lee	38	Ricketts	
John A.	38	Bertha S. Warfield	229
John Henry	38	Charles E.	229
John T.	118	Grace I.	191
John W.	38	John Tyler	265
Marion M	153	Mary A.	215
Mark	153	Maurice E.	229
Nannie R.	118	Mildred Frank	265
Nina G.	152	Riley	
Rhoda C. Stewart	38	Agnes	83
Robert D.	158	Chas. Henry	271
Roy O'Dell	38	Marion	82
Stephen A.	153	Richard John	210
William Oakley	152	Rinehart	
Remsburg		Henry	130
Clara	171	Rinker	
Daniel Steven	171	Grace Belle	264
Daniel T.	171	Rinzel	
George Brewer	171	Joshua Matthew	267
Samuel Young	171	Rippeon	
William	171	Annie Laurie	239
Reynolds		Floyd Leslie	239
Lois	27	William M.	239
Rhodes		Ritchey	
Clinton Monroe	239	Charles A.	74
Oscar G.	239	Jessie Virginia Elgin	74
William M.	239	Roberson	
Rhoton		Barbara T.	197
Isaac T.	9	Benjamin F.	195
Laura Louise	9	Charles L.	226
Rice		Charles O.	226
Anna Bell Smith	216	David Franklin	195
Annie C.	141, 142	Edith E.	226
John Andrew	216	Edward V.	196
Leona	141	Elizabeth Hicks	262
Margaret A.	141	Ellis L.	197
Rebecca (Betsy) Hartshorn	255	Fannie N.	253
Richard Alonzo	142	Grace E. White	187
Scott	141	Howard Calvin	203
W.S.	141	James Sedrick	196
William O.	142	Kevin Ellsworth	197
Winfield Scott	142	Leo	262
Richardson		Leonard H.	253

Marshall Knill	226	Ropp	
Mary E.	203	Kathleen Moran	78
Mary F.	195	Ross	
Mary Heffner	194	Bertha Sartain Payne	213
Newton Gilbert	187	Leslie Lee	104
Paul	194	Rotruck	
Robert	262	Edythe Orme	170
Rosa May	197	Gerald Marvin	170
Ruth Margaret	197	Rowe	
William Edgar	196, 197	Earl William	64
William Walker	262	Ruble	
Winona	195	A. Bertie	213
Roberts		Claire Elizabeth Painter	242
Barbara Anne	176	Elbert K.	213
Carrie Frances	117	Elbert Kyle	243
Carrie Peters	117	Elvira Rudasill	242
Charles Edward	175	Nora E.	213
Charles William	176	Ralph Walker	242
Clara V.	175	Ruby	
Cleta Alma Dove	246	Martha Virginia	173
George A.	246	Rullmann	
Joseph Edward	117	Ollie D.	237
Maggie M.	175	William	237
Mildred Luhn	176	Rush	
Robertson		Emerson Stone	183
Amy	10	Rachael Gott	183
Annie L.	99	Russell	
Atlee R.	250	Mervale B.	183
Elizabeth Cameron	202	Rutter	
George	99	C.W.	186
John	1	Charles Henry	186
Mary H.	202	Gertrude Downs	186
Robert	202	John W.	186
Rogers		Nellie Beall	186
Emily Hartley	19	Phillip Henry	186
Joy Young	145	Rosea	271
Mary R.	80	Stella Elizabeth	209
Merrill	145	Ryman	
William J.	80	Cora A.	208
Rohman		Homer K.	208
Edna Ann Chisholm	41	Norman W.	208
Rollison			
Audrey Marie	20	**S**	
Charles Edward	20		
Harriet	20	Sauerwein	
John Carter	20	Catherine S.	191
Laura Bell	20	George W.	191
William H.	20	George William	191

Howard C.	191	Pauline Eleanor	210
Lucille F.	191	Scrimeger	
Saunders		John	20
Emily Catherine Wailes White	107	Seabolt	
John	107	Samantha Jean	266
Savage		Sears	
Charles P.	264	Airy V.	198
Donald S.	264	Dorothy P.	197
George D.	173	Edward Charles	197
George F.	157	Faith Virginia	197
Gloria K.	264	Florence Ellen	197
Greta M.	173	Fulton D.	197
Harry R.	172, 173	Ira T.	197
Helen	172	Ira Thomas	197
Joseph M.	157	Lottie V.	197
Kenneth S.	173	Marjorie V.	198
Leonard Michael Upton	172	Sarah Jane	197
LeRoy Edward	173	William Henry	198
Margaret M.	157	William Linwood	198
Martha E.	173	William Thomas	197
Osie Bertha	173	Willie Millard	197
Schaeffer		Seelock	
Edith Clugston	144	Sarah	272
Ellen May	55	Selby	
Frank Gallion	144	Helen Wilson	229
Frank William	144	Sarah Catherine	81
Katie L.	144	Sellman	
Margaret Elizabeth	55	Ada May	9
Sallie Coleman	143	Alonzo	viii, 122
Thomas H.	55	Alvin Gassaway	10
Thomas L.	55	Ann Estelle	8
Thomas Murray	144	Ann Hempstone	8
William A.	144	Ann Priscilla Woodward Poole	112
William Light	144	Benjamin G.	113
Scheckles		Charles	94, 95
Mary F.	271	Charles Byron	248
Schneider		Charles G	248
Eleanor Stout	55	Damaris	113
Norman Lee	55	Damaris Almira	113
Scholl		Edward J.	4
Louis B.	11	Elizabeth L.	8
Schwerin		Ellis T.	4
Laura E.	164	Florence May	8
Scott		Frederick	113
Charles Eclon	265	Frederick Oliver	113
Clifton Harold	210	Gassaway	112, 113
Margarete M.	260	Helen G.	121
Owen Legrand	260	Howard Maynard	94

Hunton Dade	8	Shaw		
Ida Lee	8	Anna R.		165
Isabel E.	4	Shawver		
John P.	viii	Alice L.		233
John Poole	8	Charles Edgar		264
Juletter	113	Charles Stephen		211
Lewis L.	113	Elizabeth W. Heflin		264
Lizzie Gould	121	Henry H.		272
Lucy Veirs	94	Samuel Stephen		211
Margaret Burns	248	Sanders Lee		233
Marion L.	4	Saunders Lee		233
Mary I.	4	Vaennie Elizabeth Leffel		211
Mary Serena	122	Shepherd		
Oliver Gassaway	113	Hilton L.		219
Richard Brooke	248	Minnie Brooks		219
Richard E.	4	Sheppard		
Robert	121, 129	Donnelly		237
Roger B.	95	Hilton Lawson		219
Ruth	129	Sheron		
S. Belle	122	Mary Ann		269
Sarah Ann	122	Walter D.		269
Sarah Griffith	248	Shiflett		
Serena Dade	121	Infant		272
Susan G.	113	Shipley		
Wallace	viii, 121	Frank Sterling		81
William	95, 112	Nora		81
William Arthur	121, 122	Shoemaker		
William M.	129	James William		168
William Oliver	112	Louise M. Fawley		168
Willie	121	W.S.		24
Senat		Shreve		
Mary Ellen Elgin	78	A.B.		42
Sexton		Benjamin F.		42, 177
Richard	215	Claudia Stella H.		100
Seyferth		Daniel Herbert		111
Oswald	99	Earl Thomas		134
Ruth E.	99	Laura		177
Seymour		Margaret Brewer		111
Carolyn Irene Mossburg	37	Mary E.		42
Shannon		Mary Elizabeth Trundle		42
Adam S.	162	Thomas J.		99, 100
Catherine Fry	161	Virginia F.		134
Ethel Grubb	162	Shry		
James Lee	161	Baby Boy		133
Margaret B.	161	Bessie Mae		160
Sharkey		Donald M.		160
Eleanor Allnutt	219	Laura I.		22
Thomas Leo	219	Nelson Fillmore		160

Sydney W.	22	Ruth	272
Shumaker		William F.	10, 213
Carrie	24	Smolley	
Silcott		Donald M.	65
Elizabeth	224	Therese R.	65
Simon		Smoot	
Catherine Ann	248	Brian William	236
Peter	248	Elizabeth Jones	236
Simpson		Harriet Ann	125
Annie Eliza	194	Heidi D.	236
Henry R.	194	Henry G.	125
Margaret	150	Margaret A. White	125
Nathan	150	Robert W.	125
Simsar		William S.	236
Louise Dean	264	William Sothoron	236
Mehmed A.	264	Smythe	
Sirk		John W.	268
Lynn Alison	267	Laura	268
Small		Snyder	
Andrew F.	138	Florence Brooks	240
Smith		Jacob H.	240
Alice F.	268	Robert F.	162
Annie E.	120	Soper	
Barbara Lee	263	Alice Louise Haller	61
Charles Edward	268	Cornelius	84
Cleveland C.	188	Elias R.	84
Elizabeth C.	210	Georgia K.	11
Floyd	242	Henry E.	61
Franklin	210	James M.	10
Franklin Lee	210	Lingan Dow	61
George Washington Hunter	74	Mollie	84
Gordon Murdock	206	Mollie P.	61
Howard M.	44	Oliver	84
Ida L. Kegley	10	Paul Mackley	61
James Preston	213	Spahr	
James Robert	266	Isabel	132
Jennette	211	M. R.	132
John Henry	211	Sparrough	
Joseph F.	120	Benjamin F.	81
Joseph I.	263	Catherine A.	81
Lillian H.	206	Spates	
Martha	211	Ann Boyd	87
Martha Norm	211	Annie Essie	165
Mary E. Rice	74	Clara C.	165
Mildred Poole	89	Clara Elizabeth Karn	165
Robin Ellis	210	Dorothy Ruth	43
Roderick Gordon	215	Franklin Pearce	165
Russell Franklin	266	George Edward	43

George W.	87	Frederick C.	84
Howard Jetson	165	Henrietta	77
Jeanette C.	43	Joseph F.	83
John R.	43	Joseph H.	77
Joseph Roger	165	Martin J.	77
Nellie Elizabeth	165	Oscar Francis	77
Richard Fremont	165	Peter J.	77
Roger William	43	Peter Joseph	77
Thomas P.	87	Robert L.	83
William Outerbridge	165	Rose Mossburg	84
Specht		Walter Hoffman	77
Alice M.	102	Stanton	
Lewis Altha L.	102	Dorothy Meem	102
Lewis Edward	102	Stanley	102
Spencer		Starkey	
Sidney H.	213	Gregory Andrew	189
Viola Clarihe	213	Rebecca Price	181
Spratt		Staub	
Harvey George	233	George A.	28
James Perry	233	Isaac Newton	28
Sarah D.A.	233	Jennie Butler	28
Spreadbury		Mary Ann	28
Henry	87	Newton	28
Spurrier		William E.	28
Ethel Grubb	19	Steele	
Guy H.	19	Clarence Fogleman	224
Howard Wilson	19	Edward Wade	61
John H.	19	Frank E.	42
Martha J.	19	Joyce Ann	42
Willie Brunner	19	Mary A.	42
Staggs		Mary Lambert	224
Erwin Brown	146	Steiner	
Stallings		James E.	252
Eleanor	51	Stephens	
J.S.	56	Cabble Carr	37
John	56	Catharine T.	37
John William	51	Charles E.	3
Lucy	56	Edith Virginia	37
Richard	51	Esther Cooley	159
Richard S.	viii, 51	James A.	37
Robert L.	56	Lola Lee	37
Stang		Mabel C.	37
Anna	77	Mary E. (Mollie)	37
Anna Ollive	77	Mary Lou	159
Annie May	83	Nora Blake Talbott	3
Cornelia Carter	195	Robert Edgar	159
Edward Ludwig	77	Stevens	
Frederick A.	83	Charles	272

James E.	39		Herbert	244
Kathryn Darne	39		Mahala C.	39
Mary E.	23		Martin L.	39
Robert T.	33		Roland K.	244
Rufus W.	23		Rosalie Marie	39
Steward			Viola A.	39
Mary Louise	108		William	39
Willard Gilbert	108		William L.	39
Stewart			Stouffer	
Eleanor Crumine	255		Albert F.	200
Lyman Robert	255		Charles H.	200
Stock			Charles Henry	200
Edward Lilley	257		Georgia A.	200
Mary H. Wright	257		Grace	200
Stokes			Stout	
Geneie	257		Annie Rebekah	55
Sally Ann	257		Bessie M.	145
Stoner			Claudia C.	55
Alfred W.	250		Harry L.	145
Doris Bodmer	250		Mamie F.	55
Stonestreet			Robert E.	145
Gertrude Worthington	137		Robert W.	55
J. Harris	137		Stowers	
Joseph Harris	138		Charles Wade	253
Mae Montgomery	138		Edna M. Warfield	253
Storm			George W.	179
Howard William	191		John W.	179
Katie May	191		Ollie I.	179
Martin L.	191		Strange	
Nellie M.	191		Andrew	71
Story			Andrew Roscoe	71
Edward H.	166		Susan	71
Frank W.	166		Stream	
Henry Wingert	166		David Franklin	256
Lillian	166		Gladys Marie	268
Mary W.	166		Leonard D.	258
Sidonia Francis	166		Margie Tubbe	256
Thomas S.	166		Marilyn A.	256
Stottlemeyer			Paul Luther	268
Harry J.	217		Robert Andrew	256
Louise	217		Tom Henry	256
Mildred V. Poole	217		Stuart	
Stottlemyer			Elizabeth Ann	258
Alice C.	39		Studebaker	
Alice Murphy	39		Rebecca	63
Grayson Edward	216		Stunkel	
Harry	142		William	272
Harry F.	39		Sullivan	

Alexandra W.	202	Nathan T.	68
John M.	202	Rosie Elizabeth	2
Louisa J.	202	Roy Linwood	2
Surber		Sarah	3, 4
Martha Rose Hilleary	153	Sarah F.	4
Sutherland		Sarah P.	68
Viola	257	Talley	
Swain		Alice Nevin	179
Frederick	43	Tanner	
Frederick O.	44	Adams S.	261
Patricia	43	Eva Bardach	261
Patricia Ann	44	Gladys B.	261
Robert L.	43	Harold James	261
Virginia M.	43	Patricia Sara Alise	261
Swank		Tascher	
Jessie Irene H.	201	Evelyn A.	214
M.S.	23	Wendell Russell	214
Roy William	201	Taylor	
W.S.	23	Ann Mary	99
William Samuel	201	Asbury	99
Sweeney		James William	99
Kathryn Leigh Chiswell	85	Joe Early	241
Wayland Whitney	85	John W.	99
		Judi W.	267
T		Leona Madelin Jones	136
		Rhoda	99
Tadlock		Robert W.	267
Charles Guy	254	Sarah Jane	99
Edna F.	254	Sarah R.	99
Talbott		Tedore	
Emma Gertrude	3	Bessie Cole	177
Ernest	2	Dorothy Louise	177
Ernest L.	2	Genevieve	177
Ernest Linwood	2	Joseph	177
Fannie B.	3	Thomas E.	177
Hattie M.	3	Temple	
Henrietta B.	68	Marcus L.	215
Henry	4	Virginia Beall	215
Henry W.	3	Tetlow	
Hilda V.	3	Nina	186
Hilda Virginia	3	Nora R.	186
Jonathan	3, 4	Stanley C.	186
Joseph N.	3	Thierles	
Joseph Nathan	3	Fannie	13
Joseph Nathan, Jr.	3	Thom	
Marion	4	Gertrude Emma	13
Mary J.	2	Thomas	
Nathan J.	4	Albert Melvin	143

Anna Hays Trundle	184	Dorothy Marie	225
Charles P.	184	George Basil	225
Henry	47	George Prentice	225
Katherine Lee	143	Marie Roberson	225
Levin	184	Tobias	
Rosalie Poole	47	Priscilla	248
Thompson		Priscilla Ann	248
Anna Waters	245	Tolbert	
Bowie Frank	209	Jannette Dean	243
Carle	272	Leonard N.	243
Charles Waters	250	Tolle	
Dorothy M.	247	Bettie	71
Elizabeth Nichols	249	Henry C.	71
Fannie O.	235	Trail	
James M.	235	Elizabeth E.	4
Joseph Lawn	245, 246	Hannah Lawrence	4
Katherine Walling	140	Lenard	272
Leroy	247	Nathan L.	4
Marne Stewart	141	Richard F.	4
Mrs. and child	272	Sarah E.	4
Nettie Lee Holland	209	Trout	
Sidney	140	Florence Ann Rhodes	239
Virginia Mae Stonestreet	140	Trundle	
Wayne Eugene	235	Americus Dawson	44
Thurston		Anna Virginia	130
Eleanor White	103	Barbara E.	130
Robert Lamont	103	Barbara Jennings	5
Tighe		Clara Brunner	5
Charlotte S.	256	Clara I.	130
John Gilman	256	Clara Jennings	5
Tillett		Clarisa A.	100
Annabel Lee	62	Daniel T.	42
Isabella Dean	62	David	5
John W.	62	David H.	99
Tipton		David Henry	100
Charles Muzzy	90	Della	125
Elizabeth White	90	Della Brunner	5
Titus		Elizabeth Ellen Chiswell	44
Annie V.	185	Esther B.	42
David	258	Esther Belt	42
Edward W.	188	Gail Dawson	44
George Randolph	256	Helen Kessler	44
James G.	135	Horatio	130
John Franklin	185	James E.	99
John McKimmy	259	James T.	44, 130
Margaret Merithew	256	James Thomas	44
Mildred L. Geisbert	259	John	5
Tobery		John Horatio	5

John R.	5
Lulu Spates	5
Mamie E.	130
Margaret E.	130
Mary E.	130
Norman	5
Perry L.J.	130
Perry Lewis	5
Robertus	130
William B.	5
William Bryan	44
Turner	
Annie L. Aud	18
Helen F.	231
Isabel Irene	172
John William	172
Oliver P.	172
Zelma Catherine	172
Tuxhorn	
D. Bruce	261
Roma O'Hanlon	261
Tydings	
Ruth G.	272
Tyler	
Frank Ames	255
Ruby Gott	237, 255

U

Uhl	
Alexander Herbert	266
Gladys	266
Umstead	
Frances Ella	133
John J.	133
Sallie E. White	133

V

Vail	
Ruth M.	267
Vance	
Janet	64
William Foust	64
VanDerCook	
Helen Butler	151
Wesley M.	151
Vanhoozer	
Joseph Robert	263
Lorena Mae	263
VanHorn	
Sadie	41
Vann	
Homer King	248
Mary Beall Bridges	248
Vaughn	
Bettie I.	115
Veihmeyer	
Susie E.	16
Veirs	
Benjamin Franklin	82
Elijah	viii, 50
Elizabeth A.	68
Emiline	82
Georgia Lee	68
Henry B.	viii, 98
J. Montgomery	68
Jesse	50
L. Dorcas	50
Lavinia C.	50
Lorenzo	82
Maria Louisa	50
Minerva Jane	50
Mollie E.	50
Rose Anna	50
Samuel E.	106
Sophia	50
Turner	82
Valeria Wailes	106
W. Seneca	viii
William Felix	82
William S.	50
William Turner	30
Vickers	
Ben F.	247
Beryl F.	263
Katheryn L.	263
Vinson	
Ann	23
Annie E.	31
Annie Elizabeth	31
B. Frank	31
Eliza W.	31
Elmer P.	31
Frank	31
Harriet	22

John		31	Alice Lakin	84
John T.		22	Charles E.	120
John William		157	George Ernest	84
Louisa M.		31	Henry Theodore	182
Mary		23	Hugh Henry	182
Thomas W.		31	J. Richard	120
William		31	John F.	120
William B.		31	John William	143
William R.		31	Lucy Peyton	182
Violette			M. Elizabeth	120
Arthur		32	Margaret Belt	120
Katie Howard		32	Margaret Elizabeth	120
Vogel			Thomas	120
Hall		265	William H.	120
Judith Ann		265	William L.	143
Kathryn Lynne		265	Wm. H.	viii
			Wainwright	
W			Mable C.	196
			Walker	
Wacker			Barbara	252
John Frederick Herman		183	Charles E.	59
Kitty Morrissey		183	Dorothy Chiswell	252
Waddell			Gary	252
Annie E.		234	Hallie G.	199
Aura Elmeda		236	Laura Elizabeth	252
Dorothy		234	Mable P.	200
Julia B.		249	Mary F.	59
Prentice C.		234	William Hughes	199
Reese A.		236	Wall	
Sarah Anderson		234	Helen Wessel	113
Stewart		234	Lawrence D.	114
Woolwine		249	Lawrence Dade	113
Waddle			Malcolm	113
Sofronia E.		24	Mary C.	113
Wade			Mary Catherine	113
Alice		227	Maze	113
Courtney Anne		151	Nena J.	160
Crawford Francis		151	Robert Dade	114
Emma Frances		151	Virginia B.	113
Frances S.		226	Virginia Blanks	114
Harriet Ann		227	William E.	113
J. Paul		151	William Edwards	114
James Perry		226, 227	William Guy	113
Marcellus Eugene		151	Wallace	
Mary Eliza		227	Virginia Poole	66
Wallace		226	Wallach	
Zourie P.		151	Donaline Mae	267
Waesche			Edward H.	267

Walling		John Newton	250
Byron W.	140	Mary Myrtle Nicholson	175
Emily W.	140	Michael Wayne	254
Walter		Sabrina Lynn	254
Daniel	73	Sarah John Williams	68
Dora	73	Thomas Newton	174
E.	73	Virginia Darby	132
Elizabeth	73	William Harrison	132
G.B.F.	73	Wilson Stewart	68
George B.F.	73	Ware	
George T.	73	Clayton Ellms	179
Harriet L.	73	Elizabeth Elgin Black	198
James	73	Harriet Arrington	179
James P.	73	Warfield	
Jesse	74	Bettie E.	236
L. C.	73	David D.	236
Mary Ann	73	Mabel Poole	123
Maurice	72	Shirley Ann	236
Nettie	73	William G.	236
Stella	72	Waters	
Thomas	73	Allnutt Hess	122
W. T.	73	Alta	122
William T.	73	Bowie Barton	46
Ward		Bowie Jennings	46
Alice Rebecca Nicholson	174	Charles Clark	131
Annie E.	174	Charles H.	122
Annie Eleanor Nicholson	250	Charles Lewis	122
Annie Elener	175	Doris Hammond	200
Arthur Harry	240	Eleanor Allnutt	122
Austin Louis	269	Ella Yates	122
Barbara J.	269	Emily Howard	127
Byron LeRoy	254	Joseph Henry	200
Carson W.	212	Maria Elizabeth Lorain	131
Claudia	13, 99	Martha Dawson	91
David A.	269	Maud Estelle Getzendanner	131
David T.	174	Norma Marie Lilly	176
Dorothy S.	212	Paul Yates	122
Douglas	269	Perry Davis	122
Elmer Charles	175, 269	Samuel Dever	135
Flora B.	269	Thomas	91
Gary Lynn	254	William	11
Hazel A.	240	William A.	131
Hazel D.	254	Watkins	
Infant	192	Elizabeth Jarrels	135
Irene O.	254	Watson	
Irene Ola	254	Freda Bryant	86
J.V.	174	George Hugh	86
John Henry	99	Webber	

Nicole Marie	241
Weber	
Sue Ann	241
Webster	
Annie M.	39
E.	38
George	39
Harvey	39
M. W.	39
Maggie L.	39
Raymond F.	39
Weinlein	
Anthony Gerard	253
Mary Elizabeth	253
Robert Andrew	253
Welch	
Betty	63
Evangeline	262
George	41
Weller	
Amelita Alfaro	261
Baby boy	272
Frank Harlow	261
Geno D.	55
Mary Victoria	161
Parker L.	161
Wells	
Clinton F.	64
Elizabeth	65
Whitfield Wesley	65
West	
Minnie Sellman	122
Wettengel	
Lucy Ann Y.	152
Whalen	
Fannie F.	34
John A.	34
John C.	34
Mary C.	34
William	1
Whipp	
Alice W.	38
Amos	39
Beulah I.	266
Mattie Arbanna	179
Paul Cole	266
Whisman	
Annie Harrison	210

Frank	210
Frank W.	243
Marco M.	185
Perlina E.	185
Rose Anne May	241
Ruth A.	243
Stewart C.	171
Whisner	
Phillip	263
Whitaker	
A. L.	157
Beulah	157
Harriet Elizabeth	157
Hester E. Trundle	157
Theresa	157
White	
A.T.G.	96
Abbie May Specht	205
Albert	77
Alethea Brewer Jones	168
Alice V.	62
Alvin E.	95
Alvin H.	95
Amy R.	95
Ann Veirs	14
Anna Dade	29
Anna F.	127
Annie (Nannie) E.	77
Annie Belt Trundle	25
Annie Oliver Belt	17
Arthur	25, 145
B. Frank	145
B.S.	viii
Benjamin	29, 30, 54, 85
Benjamin Franklin	90
Benjamin Rush	6
Benjamin Stephen	13
Bessie S.	144
Byron Dyson	169
Catherine Boland	85
Charles Ernest	205, 251
Creszensa L.	148
Donald C.	205
Edith B.	96
Edward C.	96
Eleanor Linthicum	86
Elijah	14
Elijah Wootton	85

Elizabeth C.	25	Margaret	92, 127
Ella Clarke Bouic	13	Margaret A.	90
Ella F.	6	Margaret L.	103
Ella R. Whitmore	90	Maria Louise Hillary	14
Emma F.	127	Marshall	29
Eva Goldsborough	194	Mary	14, 30
Evelina Wailes	107	Mary C.	96
Flora Darnell	29	Mary E.	12, 30
Florence May Williams	6	Mary Elizabeth Veirs	14
Florence Pyles	85	Mary Ellen	95
Grace Boteler	96	Mary Ethel Garner	91
Harry B.	96	Mary Lucile	86
Harvey J.	29	Mary Virginia Bowman	103
Harvey Jones	169	Matilda Thompson	169
Helen Catherine	96	Maurice	96
Helen V.	155	Maxine E. Ruffner	251
Henry	95	N. Smith	13
Henry (Harry) B.	96	Nannie Poole	169
Henry Whitmore	90	Nathan Smith	6, 107
Herndon	77	Oliver C.	95
Howard	62	Ollie	246
Huldah A. Piles	77	R.E.	155
Ida D.	29, 127	Rachael Ann	107
Ida Dyson	169	Rachael Chiswell	54
Ingrid Ann	14	Rachel Ann	14
J. Collison	viii, 96	Richard G.	77
J. Furr	14	Richard T., Jr.	12
Jenny Katherine Westesson	14	Richard T., Sr.	12
John Collinson	205	Robert N.	127
John Collison	96	Rosalie Carr	91
John Russell	30	S. Olin	95
Joseph	14	S.N.C.	25
Joseph Collinson	86	Sallie Estella	95
Joseph Collison	96	Samuel C.	viii, 92
Joseph Meade	148	Sarah Aldah	6
Joseph Newton	144	Sarah E.	29, 96
Joseph Roger	14	Sarah Elizabeth	96
Joseph T.	95, 127	Sarah Elizabeth Jones	30
Joseph Thomas	127	Sarah Ellen Nichols	13
Julian N.	144	Sarah Graves	85
Laura A.	127	Stephen	30
Laura R.	95	Stephen N.	14
Laura V.	77	Stephen Newton Chiswell	25
Lawrence Allnutt	17	Thomas	62
Leah Griffith	124	Thomas H.	viii, 95
Leonard D.	84	Thomas Henry	95
Lutie	29	Thomas Oliver	77
Mansfield	90	Washington W.	46

Wellstood	91	Catherine Amelia	72
William B.	246	Charles M.	126
William Lingham	103	Charles McGill	127
William Lingin	103	Colmore W.	72
William Marshall	86	Dorsey Waters	126
William Rodney	96	E.W.	112
Willis	95	Elisha	23
Whittaker		Elizabeth Adell Schaeffer	30
Florence Allnutt	212	Elizabeth Stinson	139
Whorton		Emily Howard	127
Bradford	135	Emma	266
Edna Louise Shreve	134	Florence Ray	23
Wiggins		Frances Poole	169
Joseph St. Clair	128	Frances T.	viii
Mary Emma	128	Francis G.	163
Wilkins		Francis T.	68, 163
Katherine Sue	209	Frank	107
Wilkinson		Frankie Alberta	212
Eileen Davis	38	Georgia Griffith	163
Gilbert Dean	38	Golden Ellsworth	199
Willard		Harry McGill	139
Annie Catherine Cubitt	240	Helen	169
C.F.M.	56	Henry Ralph	139
Charles Victor	240	Hester Chiswell	54
D. Josephus	56	Ida F. Beall	199
Delmah Dutrow	185	James Dawson	129
Dewalt Joseph	56, 185	Jane Plater	23
Earnest Garfield	56	John Edwin	6
Ellis A.	240	John Henry	68
George D.	56	John T.	4, 129
Harry	56	John Thomas	129
Harry L.	185	Julia Elizabeth	129
John	272	Julia May	163
Mary M. Farr	56	Julia Nannette White	17
Maurice	56	Karen S.	265
Sarah Etta	56	Kelly Orville	265
Williams		Kelly Prevo	212
America	72	Mable White	154
Ann M.	4	Mariel H.	72
Ann Perry	169	Mary Chiswell	68
Anna Poole	66	Mary Louise Dawson	163
Annie E. Dawson	129	Mary Shaw Brown	154
Archibelle Arnette	30	Mary V.	30
Arnold Melvin	243	Mary Virginia Schaeffer	30
Arthur	17, 129	Mary Whaling	139
Arthur White	127	Milo Woodbridge	260
Belle	59	Myrtle Marie Catron	264
Bernard D.	266	Nellie White	139

Prudence Jane Waters	127	Reubin C.	216
R. Walter	54	William T.	266
Rebecca Gott	137	Wood	
Richard Mortimer	54	Ada C.	225
Richard Poole	169	Albert Worth	104
Richard Walter	30	Charles W.	30
Robert M.	137	Columbia	30
Roger W.	154	Diana Tennis	266
Roger Walter	154	Ernest	30
Sarah (Sallie) White	68	Ernest P.	225
Sarah Ann E.	72	George Thomas	266
Sarah Florence	247	Hazel M.	41
Sarah Newton Cissell	129	Ida Cole	41
Sarah White	137	Jessie Phillips	104
Stephen	29	Katie	67
Vernon	68	Mary L.G.	31
Walter	66	Moses	270
William Edward	169	R. Vinton	67
William J.	30	Stanford Edward	104
William Jeremiah	30	Virginia Ann	67
William McKendree	137	Worth	30
William White	169	Woodbridge	
Willis		Beatrice Williams	260
Richard T.	261	M.	260
Winder		Woods	
Catherine A. Hall	29	Martha	268
Edward R.	29	Mary Virginia Waddell	240
Wingate		Ollie Virginia	240
Grover C.	209	Robert W. E.	240
Rebecca	209	Robert William E.	268
Winstead		Woodward	
Anna B. Hersberger	98	Charles W.	26
Wise		Clarine Fletchall	26
Anna Genevieve	28	Mary Elizabeth	204
Martin Irenius	28	Wootten	
Wiseman		Edward	viii
Anna Roberson	252	Wootton	
Martin Andrew	252	Albert	49
Wolfe		Alice	49
D.M.	57	Bettie	49
Dora Padgett	58	Bettie Hampton	49
Norman Hyatt	58	Edith	216
Wolfrey		Edith Chiswell	49
Bert B.	135	Edward	49
Hilda May	189	Emma V.	49
Leona F.	135	Henry Edgar	49
Patricia A.	266	Hugh Hampton	49
Philip Lee	189	Josephine Dawson	49

Lola H.	50	Lewis B.	109
Lutie	49	Lola Imogene	201
Mary Sheppe	50	Ralph W.	201
Norman	49, 216		
Norman D.	216	**Y**	
Roland	49		
Tah-Wee-Nah M.	216	Yates	
Turner	49	Adelaide Reed	245
William Turner	50	Dorothy Haddox	245
Works		Edwin Langhorn	245
James William	51	Young	
Wright		Agnes E.	41
Berry Thurman	254	Albert Edward	117
Clifton W.	267	Alfred	241
Dora Hall	267	Alice Irene	152
E. Nisbet	251	Amos S.	15
Florence Hamilton Irvin	251	Annie Mary	15
Frances M.	208	Carol Ann	256
Irvin N.	251	Charles LeRoy	256
Jack C.	261	Courtney Richard	151
Jacob Franklin	225	Drucilla Trundle	171
Jane Frances	254	Edwin M.	45
Jesse Eugene	272	Elle Lee	121
John Robert	196	Emily	111
Laura L.	195	Emma D.	117
Lula Bee	225	Ernest A.	42
Margaret America Ann	196	Ernest Lee	229
Margaret K.	251	Esther I. Carlisle	262
Nettie E.	195	Eugenia T.	55
Owen	195	George Llewellyn	117
Owen F.	195	Harold Alfred	229
Rachel Ella	132	Harriet Oden	145
Rella Grace	225	Henry	45
Robert Silas	208	Henry Cissel	45
Rose Clagett	132	Irene	121
Roy Leslie	226	Irene Mary	14
Rush Lee	132	Irving Rodney	262
Samuel P.	196	Isaac	121
Wynn		Jane Hunton	14
Irene Darby	170	Jessie Lowe	151
Wynne		John	15
Edward Buford	259	John L.	14
Edward Johnson	201	John Mortimer	152
Ella Mae Lester	259	John Rodney	152
Ethel Virginia	201	John William	117
Harriet J.	109	Lavinia Darr	241
Ida Lake	201	Leonard Upton	152
James Wiley	201	Lester S.	118

Llewellyn	117, 152	Stella	152
Louise Bayard	146	Stella M.	117
Lucy Anna	151	Theodore Hazel	118
Ludwick Craven	145	Victoria Hampton	14
Lula May Pearson	229	William (Tom) M.	151
Madeline Louise Roberts	117	William Leroy	41
Margaret Catherine Schaeffer	15	Zora Dove	42
Margaret R.	121	Zourie Petzman	151
Martha Ann Cissel	45		
Mary	171	**Z**	
Mary Bertha	117		
Mary Catherine Schaeffer	15	Zimmerman	
Mary E. Cissel	45	Amanda M. E.	190
Mary Ethel	151	Charles J.	190
Mary Ryan	145	D. Howard	190
Matilda Nesbit	146	Edward J.	190
Minnie Hunton	14	Harriett F.S.	190
Nellie V. Hickman	118	Helen Moore	234
Paul Thompson	257	Margaret A.	190
Rebecca Ardella	45	Maurice H.	190
Richard Thomas	42	Susan B.	190
Robert L.	152	Zittle	
Roy E.	215	Jessie Vernia	174
Samuel C.	55		
Sarah E.	45		

www.ingramcontent.com/pod-product-compliance
Lightning Source LLC
Chambersburg PA
CBHW050333230426
43663CB00010B/1837